The History
of Islam

(Volume One)

First Edition: April 2000

Supervised by :

ABDUL MALIK MUJAHID

DARUSSALAM

Corporate Head Quarter:
P.O. Box: 22743, Riyadh 11416 KSA
Tel:4033962/4043432
Fax: 4021659 Showroom 4614483
E.mail: darussalam@naseej.com.sa

Branches & Agents:
● Jeddah Tel : 6712299 Fax: 6173448
● Al-Khobar: Tel : 8948106
● Pakistan: 50 Lower Mall Lahore
   Tel: 0092-42-724 0024 Fax: 7354072

● Houston, USA Tel: 001-713-722 0419
   Fax: 001-713-722 0431
● 572, Atlantic ave, Brooklyn, Newyork 11217
   Tel: 001-718-625 5925
● Al-Hidaayah Publishing & Distribution
   522 Coventry Road Birmingham B10 OUN
   Tel: 0044-121-753 1889 Fax: 121-753 2422
● Muslim Converts Association of Singapore
   Singapore 424484, Tel: 440 6924, 348 8344
   Fax: 440 6724
● Darul Kitab 6, Nimal Road, Colombo 4,
   Sri Lanka Tel: 0094-1-589 038 Fax:0094-1-699 767
● Bangladesh: 30 Malitola, Bangshal, Dhaka-1100
   Tel : 9557214, Fax : 9559738

The History of Islam

(Volume One)

By
Akbar Shah Najeebabadi

Revised by
Safi-ur-Rahman Mubarakpuri

Edited by
Abdul Rahman Abdullah
Formerly
Raymond J. Manderola
Fordham University, USA
and
Muhammad Tahir Salafi

Darussalam
Int'l Publishers & Distributors
Riyadh, Houston, New York, Lahore, Dhaka

In The Name of Allah, The Most
Beneficent, The Most Merciful

Publishers Note

We are presenting before you the *History of Islam* in three volumes. This book was originally written in the Urdu language in 1922 (1343 AH) by Akbar Shah Khan Najeebabadi. This was the time about 25 years before the partition of Indian Subcontinent into Pakistan and India. For the purpose of brevity, the compiler has presented the authentic events in concise form from the famous histories of Islam written in the Arabic and Persian languages by the great Muslim historians like Tabari, Ibn Athir, Mas'udi, Abul-Fida', Ibn Khaldûn and Suyuti, apart from getting benefited from the authentic books of *Ahadith* for the compilation of the part about the biography of the Prophet Muhammad 鑢. So, this compilation is actually the extract of the works of the famous Muslim historians.

Although Islam, the religion of Allâh, has been sent from the beginning with Adam 鑢, the father of man, but it is recognized as the religion which our Prophet Muhammad 鑢 brought to the mankind. So, this compilation has the mention of our Prophet 鑢 in the start. After that, useful information has been added about history, its beginning and its benefits, and some mention of the best possible ruling system for mankind has been presented which Islam advocates. Then the book takes its course of history from the conditions prevalent in Arabia before Islam, and moves forward to the Prophet's life history, the Rightly-Guided Caliphate and then to the other caliphates and kingdoms after it.

This book was the need of the time to present the true Islamic events and their actual causes before the English readers because other books in English found on the Islamic history have been written by such authors and compilers who did no justice in presenting the true picture of Islamic Era but their prejudice prevented them from doing so.

We hope that the readers will find this compilation of great help in the study of Islamic history. The famous scholar Safi-ur-Rahman Mubarakpuri has revised the Urdu edition before its translation to check the authenticity aspect.

The translation was done by the Translation Department of Darussalam, and every care has been taken to reproduce the events and the names of the persons and places as accurately as possible. We thank all the persons who have cooperated with us to complete this task and produce it before you into a presentable form. May Allâh accept our humble efforts in this regard and send His peace and blessings on our Prophet Muhammad, his Companions and his followers.—*Amin!*

Abdul Malik Mujahid
General Manager
Darussalam

Table of Contents

Publishers Note 5
Foreword 20
   There is no God except Allâh 20
   Muhammad ﷺ is the Messenger of Allâh 21
   Magnificent Deeds of the Muslims 24
   The Nature and Facts about Islamic History 27
Introduction 29
   History 29
   Need of History 30
   Benefits of History 30
      Preservation of Martial Characters through History 31
      History and Family Virtues 31
   Historian 32
   Readers of History 33
   Sources of History 34
   Types of History 34
   Historical Ages 35
   Islamic History 36
   History of Histories 36
   Beginning of History 37

Real Beginning of History 37
History of Sultanate 38
Personality and Democracy 40
Democratic Rule..42
Autocratic Hereditory Rule......................................44
Autocratic Democratic Rule......................................46
Our Starting Point 48
Relation between History and Geography 49

Chapter - 1

The Country of Arabia 51
Situation and Physical Features 52
Climate and Inhabitants 53
Ancient Peoples of Arabia 53
Arab Bâ'idah..54
Arab 'Âribah..55
Arab Musta'ribah 57
Adnan Tribes...61
How Abdul-Muttalib was named 62
Family of Abd Manâf 63
Moral Condition of Arabia 63
Assertions of Dignity 65
Months of Peace..67
Faith and Religion 67
    Idolatry...68
    Sacrifice 69
    Star-Worshipping..69
    Soothsaying...70
    Omens...70
Fighting..70
Illicit Sex..71
Poetry 72
Passion for Hunting 72
Food and Clothes...73
Plunder...73
Conceit 74
Unending Malice 74
Mourning the Dead 74

Superstition and Credulity..75
Killing of Daughters...76
Gambling 77
Arabian Ignorance and Other Countries 77
Persia (Iran) 78
Greece and Rome..79
Depravity of the Christians..81
Egypt 81
India 82
China 83
Conclusion...83
The Choice of Arabia 85

Chapter - 2

Prophet Muhammad ﷺ...87
The Dawn of Guidance...87
The Sacrifice of Abdullah bin Abdul-Muttalib 89
The Father of Muhammad ﷺ 91
The Birth of the Prophet ﷺ 93
Childhood Days 94
Death of Abdul-Muttalib 95
Support of Abu Tâlib...95
First Journey to Syria 96
Harb Al-Fijâr, First Participation in Battle.............................96
Trade 97
Offer of Khadijah ؙ 98
Second Journey to Syria 98
Marriage 99
Titles of *Sâdiq* & *Al-Amin* (Truthful & the Trusty).....................99
Renewal of *Hilf-ul-Fudul*...99
Appointed as Arbitrator by the Quraish 101
Support for the Poor 102
His Love for Zaid bin Hârithah..103
Inclined to Allâh...104
Sunrise 104
Historic Words of Khadijah ؙ 105
Preaching of Islam..106
Proclamation of Truth from Mount of Safa 107

Open endeavor to preach..108
First Educational Institution...109
Antagonism of the Quraish 109
Insulting Behavior to the Prophet ﷺ 110
An Offer of all earthly Desires and a Plain Reply 111
Deputation of the Quraish to Abu Tâlib....................................112
Migration to Abyssinia..113
Quraish's demand from the King of Abyssinia 115
The Beautiful Speech of Ja'far bin Abu Tâlib ﷺ 115
Hamzah ﷺ accepts Islam...116
Umar bin Khattâb's conversion to Islam 117
Social Boycott..120
The Year of Sorrow (The Tenth Year of Prophethood).............122
The Journey to Tâ'if 124
    Obstinate Behavior of the People of Tâ'if 124
    Back to Makkah 125
Marriage with 'Âishah ﷺ, and *Mi'râj* 127
Preaching Islam in Different Places and Tribes 127
Suwaid bin Sâmit 128
Iyâs bin Mu'âdh ﷺ..128
Dimâd Azdi..129
Tufail bin Amr Dausi ﷺ..129
Abu Dhar Ghifâri ﷺ..130
Six Fortunate Souls of Yathrib..131
First Pledge of Aqabah 132
Success of Mus'ab bin Umair ﷺ in Al-Madinah 133
Second Pledge of Aqabah 134
General Permission to migrate to Al-Madinah..........................137
Holding Counsel by the Quraish in Dar An-Nadwah...............138
Making Preparations for the Journey...139
The Sun and the Moon in the Cave of Mount Thaur 141
Migration...143
End of the Journey 145
Entry into Al-Madinah 147
Calendar Year 149
First Year of Migration 149
    First Political Document 152

Beginning of Hypocrisy...153
The Second Year of Migration..154
  The Battle of Badr..156
    Lack of Means...157
    Beginning of War 159
    General Treatment of the Prisoners...163
    The Issue of the Captives 163
  Revengeful Enthusiasm of the Makkan Infidels...........................164
The Third Year of Migration..166
  Hostile Attitude of the Jews..166
  The Jewish Tribe – Banu Qainuqâ'...168
  The Battle of Uhud, 3 AH 169
    Mischief of the Hypocrites..171
    The Battle starts..173
    Martyrdom of Hamzah bin Abdul-Muttalib 174
    A Reversal...174
    Moths at the Lamp of Prophethood 175
    Stability of the Prophet 176
    A View of the Battleground...177
The Fourth Year of Migration..180
  A Breach of Promise and Mischief-making 180
  A Soul-shattering Incident 182
  Faithfulness to the Promise..183
  Mischief of the Jews 183
  Banishment of Banu Nadir..184
  The Expedition of *Dhât-ur-Riqa'* 184
  Expedition to Sawîq 184
The Fifth Year of Migration 186
  Expedition to Banu Al-Mustaliq..187
  Mischief of the Hypocrites 188
  Release of the Captives 189
  Reproving the Jews 189
  Ghazwah Khandaq 190
  Banu Quraizah's Breach of Trust 195
  Incidents during 5 AH 197
The Sixth Year of Migration..198
  Preaching of Islam 199

A Criminal Event...199
The Truce of Hudaibiyah 199
    Position of Hudaibiyah 200
    The Pledge of Ridwân 202
    Deep Love of the Companions for the Messenger ﷺ..............203
    Conditions..204
    Reaction to the Peace Treaty...204
    Unique Victory 205
Consequences of the Truce of Hudaibiyah 205
Return of the Muslims from Abyssinia 207
The Seventh Year of Migration 207
    Conquest of Khaibar 207
    After the Conquest of Khaibar...209
    Invitation Letters to Islam 211
    Arrival In Makkah...212
    Amr bin Al-Âs accepts Islam 213
The Eighth Year of Migration...214
    The Expedition to Mu'tah 214
    Khalid ﷺ - *Saifullâh* 216
    The Expedition to Qudâ'ah (*Dhât-us-Salâsil*) 217
    Conquest of Makkah..218
        Abu Sufyân in Al-Madinah 220
        March to Makkah..221
        Abu Sufyân ﷺ honored 222
        Historic Address of the Prophet ﷺ......................................223
        The Truth came and Falsehood vanquished.........................223
    Battle of Hunain...225
    Siege of Tâ'if 227
    Deep Love of the *Ansâr* for the Messenger ﷺ.......................227
    First Governor of Makkah..229
The Ninth Year of Migration 230
    Expedition to Tabuk...230
        Islamic Army's Departure 232
        At Tabuk..233
    Dirâr Mosque burnt down 234
    The People of Tâ'if accept Islam..235
    First Deputy of the Prophet of Allâh 236

The Tenth Year of Migration 237
  Musailimah Kadhdhâb 238
  Mubâhalah 238
  The Farewell Pilgrimage...239
  The Farewell Address 240
  The Consolation of Ali ﷺ 241
The Eleventh Year of Migration..241
  The Sickness of the Prophet ﷺ...241
    Jihâd in the way of Allâh from the Sick-bed 242
    Illness increases...243
    Asking Abu Bakr ﷺ to lead the Prayers....................................243
  A little before Death 244
  Death 244
  The Condition of Umar ﷺ 245
  Firmness of Abu Bakr ﷺ 245
  Hall of Banu Sâ'idah 246
  The Funeral Prayer and Burial 246
  Noble Features 247
  Children 247
  Character and Features...248
    Various States and Conditions of the Prophet ﷺ 248
    Cheerful and Perfect Manners 249
    Informality 253
    Moderation 254
    Cheerful Disposition 254
    Laudable Traits of Character...254

Chapter - 3

The Rightly-Guided Caliphate...257
  Caliph and Caliphate 257
  Claim to Caliphate...258
  Islamic Caliphate 260
  Objection to the Procedure of electing a Caliph..............................261
  Difference between Caliphate and Temporal Rule..............................262
  Relation of Caliphate with a Nation, Tribe or Family 262
  The Caliphate and Spiritual Guidance as a Profession.....................264
Abu Bakr Siddiq ﷺ 265
  His Name and Genealogy 265

Age of Ignorance..267
Islamic Era 268
Valor 268
Generosity..269
Knowledge and Excellences...270
Beautiful Living 271
Important Events of the Siddiqi Caliphate..272
Hall of Banu Sâ'idah and the Pledge of Caliphate.............................272
Bai'ah (Pledge) 273
Address of Abu Bakr 276
Usâmah's Army marches on..277
    Exhortations to Usâmah 278
    Success achieved by Usâmah 279
Trial of Apostasy 280
    Edict of Abu Bakr Siddiq 282
    Uprooting the Apostates..283
    The Manifesto of Abu Bakr Siddiq 284
Tulaihah Asadi...285
Sajâh and Mâlik bin Nuwairah..286
    Marriage of the Liar prophetess 287
    Assassination of Mâlik bin Nuwairah 287
Musailimah the Liar...289
    Deviation to Nationality 290
    Furious Fight 290
Hatm bin Dubai'ah...292
Laqit bin Mâlik...293
Apostasy in Mahrah...294
Apostasy in Yemen...294
Complete Eradication of Apostasy 296
Rome and Persia 297
Policy of the Muslims...300
The Battle of *Dhât-us-Salâsil* 301
The Battle of Qârin 302
The Battle of Walajah 302
The Battle of Ullais 303
Conquest of Hirah 303
Message of Khâlid 303

Conquest of Anbâr 304
Conquest of Ain-ut-Tamr 304
Upper Iraq 305
Conquest of Dumat-ul-Jandal 305
The Battle of Husaid 306
The Battle of Mudaiyah 306
The Battle of Firâd 307
Khâlid bin Walid ؏ in Syria..308
The Battle of Yarmuk 310
Death of Abu Bakr Siddiq ؏ 312
Last Address of Abu Bakr Siddiq ؏ 313
Impressions of Ali ؏ 315
Governors of the Siddiq Caliphate 317
Wives and Children 317
Umar bin Al-Khattâb ؏ 318
Birth and Pedigree 318
Some Specific Excellences ....318.
Physical Features of Umar ؏ 321
Important Events of the Fâruqi Caliphate 321
Khâlid bin Walid ؏ deposed 323
Banishment of the Najrân Christians 325
Conquest of Damascus 326
The Battle of Fihl 328
Conquest of Baisân 329
Conquest of Saida, Irqah and Beirut 329
Campaigns in Iraq 329
First Deed of Abu Ubaid bin Mas'ud ؏ 329
Conquest of Kaskar 330
The Battle of Baqshia 331
The Last Deed of Abu Ubaid bin Mas'ud ؏ 331
The Battle of Buwaib 333
After the Defeat of Buwaib 334
Umar Fâruq's Readiness to face the Persians 335
Sa'd bin Waqqas in Iraq 337
Rustam's Departure from Madâ'in 338
Islamic diplomatic Mission 339
Speech of Qais bin Zurârah 339

The Battle of Qâdisiyah 343
Conquest of Babylon and Kutha 347
The Fall of Bahurasir 348
Horses across the River 348
The Conquest of Madâ'in 349
The Conquest of Jalula 350
Syrian Engagements 352
The Fall of Hims 352
Fall of Qinnasrin 352
Conquest of Halab and Antâkiyah 352
Fall of Baghrâs, Mar'ash and Hadath 353
Conquest of Qaisâriyah and Ajnâdain 354
Conquest of Jerusalem 354
Umar Fâruq's Journey to Palestine 355
A Peace Document for the Christians 356
Fall of Takrit and Jazirah 357
Return of Iyyâd Tribe 357
Deposition of Khâlid bin Walid ﷺ 358
Basrah and Kufah 360
Conquest of Ahwâz, and Hurmuzân accepts Islam 360
Graceful Treatment of Umar ﷺ 361
The Conquest of Egypt 362
The Battle of Nahâwand 363
General Conquest of Persia 365
Famine and Plague 367
The Conquests of Umar Fâruq ﷺ 368
Martyrdom of Umar Fâruq ﷺ 368
Wives and Children 371
Accomplished Firsts by Umar Fâruq ﷺ 371
Various Conditions and Special Features 372
The Summary of Conquests 375
First Half of the Rightly-Guided Caliphate 377

Chapter - 4

The Second Half of the Rightly-Guided Caliphate 379
Uthmân bin Affân ﷺ 379
Name and pedigree 379
Excellences 379

Physical Appearance...381
Selection for Caliphate...381
First Case in the Court of Uthmân 384
Governors of the Provinces..385
Important Events of Uthmân's Caliphate..385
The Conquest of Alexandria 385
The Conquest of Armenia 386
Events and Changes in Egypt...388
The Conquest of Africa..389
The Conquest of Cyprus and Rhodes...391
Administrative Changes in Persia 392
Revolts of the Persians and the Islamic Conquests...........................393
Hajj of 29 AH...394
Events of 30 AH...395
The Event of Abu Dhar Ghifâri 396
The Ring of the Prophet 397
Fall of Tabaristan 397
Circulation of the Qur'ân..398
Events of 31 AH...398
Yezdgird killed..399
Events of 32 AH...399
Events of 33 AH 400
Abdullah bin Saba 401
Events of 34 AH..404
Edict of Uthmân 408
Objections...409
Events of 35 AH...410
Conspiracy of Abdullah bin Saba...411
Departure of the Caravan of Mischief-Mongers 411
Ali intercedes..413
Abu Ayub Ansari leads the Prayer 414
Martyrdom of Uthmân bin Affân 415
A Summary of Uthmân's Caliphate...418
Features and Characteristics of Uthmân 424
Some Significant Indications...425
Rioter's Rule in Al-Madinah 426
Ali bin Abu Tâlib 427

Name and Pedigree...427

Distinctive Features..427

Excellences...428

Justice and Words..429

Wise Sayings 431

Important Events of Ali's Caliphate...................................433

Bai'ah of Caliphate 433

Second Day of the Caliphate..434

Disobedience of the Rioters...435

Useful Counsel of Mughirah and Ibn Abbas 🙵...............435

Deposition and Installation of Governors........................436

Mu'âwiyah's Support to Truth...437

Deviation of the Followers of Ibn Saba 438

Preparations for the Invasion on Syria 438

Military Action against the Muslims 439

Preparations of the Mother of the Believers in Makkah ...439

Departure from Makkah to Basrah 441

The Governor of Basrah opposes the Plan.......................441

Battle-Array 442

Ali 🙵 marches from Al-Madinah 443

Abdullah bin Saba—the Jew and Hypocrite 444

The Two Muhammads in Kufah 444

Ashtar and Ibn Abbâs 🙵 in Kufah...................................445

Ammar bin Yasir and Hasan bin Ali 🙵 in Kufah.............445

Endeavor for Mediation 446

Consultations for Mischief-Making 448

The Battle of Jamal..449

Peacemaking Efforts of Zubair 🙵 453

Separation of Talhah 🙵 453

One more Mischief of the Saba Sect.................................456

Kufah becomes the Capital 457

Egypt and Muhammad bin Abu Bakr 🙵 458

Amr bin Al-Âs 🙵 was with Mu'âwiyah 🙵 461

Preparations for the fighting in Siffin...............................462

First Stage of the Battle of Siffin 465

Another Peace Effort during Muharram...........................466

The Speech of Ali 🙵..467

One Week of the Battle of Siffin 468
The Last Two Days of the Battle of Siffin..469
The End of the Battle..473
Making out the Documentation and the Return 477
Trouble caused by the Khawârij..478
The Decision of the Arbitrators at Adhruh.....................................480
The Verdict...482
Disruptive Activities of the Khawârij...487
Battle of Naharwân 488
State of Egypt..491
Attempts made to capture Other Provinces 493
Ali's Caliphate confined to Iraq and Iran..494
Abdullah bin Abbas' Departure from Basrah 494
Ali's Martyrdom...495
Dangerous Plan of the Khawârij 495
Ali's Grave traceless..498
Wives and Children 498
A Glance at Ali's Caliphate..499
Hasan ﵁ 505
Physical Features and Pedigree..505
Praiseworthy Traits...505
Mentionable Events during the Caliphate of Hasan ﵁.......................506
Verdict of disbelief against Hasan ﵁ 507
Peace Treaty 509
Prophecy of the Prophet ﷺ...511
Concocted Story of Poisoning..512
A Glance at Hasan's Caliphate...512
Few Sentences about the Guided Caliphate.......................................513
Saeed bin Zaid ﵁ 516

Foreword

There is no God except Allâh

A glance at world history makes it clear beyond doubt that, in every country of the world and in every age, all the Prophets, reformers, guides and founders of religions had belief in one God, and all of them made all-out efforts to convince their people of the existence of one Elevated Creator. Although Adam, Nûh (Noah), Ibrahim (Abraham), Mûsa (Moses) عليه السلام and Muhammad ﷺ lived in ages hundreds and thousands of years far from one another, but their teachings had Oneness of the Creator as the common factor.

Krishnji, Ramchandraji, Gautama Buddha and Guru Nanak happened to be in India; Kaiqbad and Zoroaster in Iran; Confucius in China, Luqmân in Greece; Yûsuf (Joseph) عليه السلام in Egypt; Lût عليه السلام in Syria and Palestine — but Oneness of God lies at the base of the teachings of all.

Almost all men and children, old and young, male and female, Christians and Jews etc., believe in Allâh the Almighty. May be, some people in very small number, refuse to utter the name of God but within their hearts they too feel His Presence. They have to admit that this process of cause and effect goes on created and supervised by some power wise to the extreme. This Wise and Well-Intentioned One is known as Allâh the Almighty.

None but the insane can reject the unanimous belief of the men of intellect and the magnificent creation of Allâh the Almighty.

Muhammad ﷺ is the Messenger of Allâh

The magnificent kingdom of Rome had already been broken into pieces and its semi-brute laws and constitution had become distorted enough to wipe out whatever good points happened to be therein. Persian Empire had become the storehouse of corruption and atrocities; China and Turkistan appeared to be the haven of bloodshed and ferocity; in India, the administrations of Asoka and Kanishka were non-existent: none could even think of the reign of Maharaja Vikarmajeet, nor was there any model of Buddhism nor of Brahmanism.

Those paying respects to Buddha would commit amply shameful acts for the sake of power and worldly comforts or out of weakness in belief. Those reading the rosary of Shri Krishn had no hesitation in making men the most honorable among the created things to prostrate before the vegetables and the stones. If Europe was like a forest with its men as bloodthirsty and ferocious as the beasts, the whole of Arabia had been reduced to the state of animality. In short, nowhere in the world human race appeared sticking to its pure quality of humanness and nobility. In a situation when the entire world had turned dark and dismal, it was the duty of the people of India to ponder over the fourth chapter of Gita where Shri Krishn Maharaj says:

> "O Arjun! Whenever faith falls in jeopardy and faithlessness grows, I provide safety to the virtuous and establish faith by wiping the evils out."

It was the sheer duty of the Persians to come out in search of a guide as per the dictates of Zoroaster. It was for the Jews to wait for the appearance of the light from the peaks of the Faran range and held themselves back from stopper stone becoming the cornerstone. It was the bounden duty of the Christians to make the prayer of Ibrahim (Abraham) and the glad tidings of Jesus, center of their hope. But the global corruption and disruption and all-round darkness had caused human eyes to become so dark and blind that nobody was conscious enough to take himself to be ailing and go ahead for any medicine.

In such an age and in a territory like Arabia, Muhammad ﷺ rose to remove the mischief of polytheism, darkness of idolatry, pollution of corruption and disruption and defilement of vices and shamelessness, and raising the voice of *La ilâha illallâh*, he performed his singular and sacred duty of making men out of men-like people, and men to be men of high morals, and such noble people to be men of God to change darkness into light, righteousness, peace, uprightness and virtue; and carve pure Muslims out of the deviated, idolaters and evil persons.

Nûh ﷺ was forced by the circumstances to do them away with the sword of "My Lord! Leave not one of the disbelievers on the earth!" (71:26) after his relentless efforts of hundreds of years to bring the deviated people of Iraq and Arabia back to the right path. Mûsa ﷺ tried hard to show the Egyptians and the arrogant king the right path but at last, Mûsa (Moses) ﷺ and Children of Israel saw the sight about which the noble Qur'ân then said:

> "...and drowned Pharaoh's people while you were looking (at them, when the sea-water covered them)." (2:50)

It is for this that Maharaja Ramchandraji invaded Lanka and fought with the demons, and Shri Krishn Maharaj persuaded Arjun to fight in the battlefield of Krukshetra, and had to destroy the defying Kurûs at the hands of the Pandûs. In Iran, Zoroaster made the wrestling of Isphandiyar and the Empire of Kiyani the base of his preaching and propagation of his faith.

But ancient scriptures and sociological traditions reaching the erudite scholars are unanimous that all the revered founders of religions and honorable guides in the way of righteousness have no example to show that, in a short span of less than 25 years, the worst country and the ignorant and brute people became the teacher and the most civilized and well-mannered people on the earth. In less than a hundred years, i.e., in 80 years only the followers of the Faith brought by Muhammad ﷺ encompassed an area ranging from Atlantic Ocean to Pacific Ocean, i.e., up to the eastern coast of China, and, to say, the whole of the civilized world. This world of ours cannot present any other example of this miraculous success. And if the teaching of Islam is superior to all other religious codes and doctrines for its supreme qualities, who can then question the status of Muhammad ﷺ, being the best of all mankind, the Seal of the Prophets and the Mercy for the world? And who can muster courage to challenge the Divine claim for the Glorious Qur'ân brought by the Prophet ﷺ to be matchless and irrefutable? As the Qur'ân says:

"Verily, We, it is We Who have sent down the *Dhikr* (the Qur'ân) and surely, We will guard it (from corruption)." (15:9)

History stands as the most effective and valuable source of putting nations on the course of progress and prosperity and saving them from the path of disgrace and degradation. Whenever nations have gone up to great heights, they have achieved inspiration from nothing but history.

The Noble Qur'ân has also told us that the study of history was quite essential for human grace and success in this world and the Hereafter. The events of the past nations remind us that such and such nations bore the brunt of their evil deeds while some others achieved grand success on account of their good deeds. Events of Adam, Nûh, Ibrahim, Mûsa and others and the plights of Pharaoh, Nimrod, Ad, Thamûd etc., have not been mentioned in the Noble Qur'ân for the sake of amusement and entertainment and to bring about sleep, but for producing in us courage to perform good deeds and keep away from misdeeds, and changing our present into bright future.

The Prophets who have happened to be the greatest well-wishers and most affectionate of all for mankind, have always reminded them of their past history to save them from destruction. None among the great leaders and reformers of the world appears to have ignored the past conditions and events in bringing about alertness and consciousness among the unconscious and self-denying people of their times. It is because of this, every sermonizer or speaker has recourse to interesting historical events to encourage and activate their audience. Among the past heroes too, we refer those who are closely related to us nationally and religiously, and they exert more influence on our lives. The study of the lives and deeds of Rustam,

Isphandiyar and Gustap can arouse sense of religious zeal, justice and
equity more for the Iranians and Parsees than the Jains or Indians.
Similarly the stories of Bhim, Arjun, Vikarmajeet and Prithivi Raj
influence the Hindus far more than the Christians.

Today, when they have become aware of the influences and
consequences of the histories of nations and the fact has come to light
that this is the only way of bringing a nation back to life and keep it
alive, we see with our naked eyes that those nations which are bereft
of glorious histories, present concocted stories and fabricated fictions
in the name of their histories studded with sparkling events and
scintillating accounts to fill the minds and hearts of the individuals
and youths of their nations so that they come to believe them.

These shameless efforts of transforming wrong into right go on just
for the sake of convincing their people of their past grandeur without
which no nation could be aroused to compete with others in the race
of achieving excellence in various fields of human life and
development. This is the reason why the nation antagonistic and
hostile to another one tries to distort its history and render its men
ignorant of and careless about their history.

Magnificent Deeds of the Muslims

Among the nations of the world, Muslims are the only nation which is
replete with splendid deeds and marvelous performance. And, above
all, it has such tested and trusted knowledge and information about
the deeds of its elders and heroes which are irrefutable and beyond all
doubts. The Muslims need not be introduced to the Iliad and the
Odyssey of Homer, nor they are in need of Mahabharat and Ramayan,
for they, in their real history, have all kinds of more splendid and
amazing models than those of Iliad and the Odyssey, and Mahabharat
and Ramayan contain.

The Muslims have also nothing to do with the Shahnamah of Firdausi
and tales of the Spartans; for every page of their history can present many
Rustams and the Spartans. The Muslims need not hear the stories of
Nushirwan the Just and Hâtim Tâi; for in their true and authentic history,
countless Hâtim and Nushirwan appear radiating light and luster. The

Muslims also require no Aristotle or Bacon, Ptolemy or Newton; for in the assembly of their ancestors, such philosophers and astronomers are present which is a matter of pride for them.

How pitiable and amazing it is that, at a time, when there is tough competition among the nations of the world to excel one another, the Muslims, despite having the most glorious history, appear to be detached and careless as regards their history. The class which may be said to be more wakeful and vigilant among the Muslims, also quotes in its lectures, speeches, writings, articles, magazines, newspapers and books any eminent person from Europe or Christian world wherever it needs to cite example of high morals or amazing performance, since it is unaware of such personalities among the Muslims.

Who can deny this fact that the educated class among the Muslims quote in their speeches and writings names of Hannibal, Shakespeare, Bacon, Newton etc., more frequently than those of Khâlid bin Walid, Salahuddin Ayubi, Hassân bin Thâbit, Firdausi, Tusi, Ibn Rushd (Averroes) and Bu Ali Sina (Avicenna). The sole reason behind this is that the Muslims are unaware of and careless about their history. And they are so, firstly, because they are much less fond of knowledge in comparison to other nations; secondly, they have least opportunity and leisure for acquiring knowledge; thirdly, Government schools and colleges have almost wiped out Islamic educational institutions in India; fourthly, the class which is generally called the educated class among the Muslims and which is considered to be forerunner of the Indian Muslims, comes out totally from the Government schools and colleges where Islamic history does not form part of the syllabus or if it is there, it is something other than what is known as history of Islam. After obtaining diploma from colleges, the age of acquiring further education is almost passed and one cannot have time left at his disposal for studying Islamic Sciences. In all cases, our Muslim educated class has to depend on the Islamic histories written in English in a distorted form by the rivals and opponents of the Muslims.

Before Islam, no nation of any country would turn towards the art of writing history or compile any authentic history of its elders and ancestors. In order to know how much progress in the art of history writing could have been made before Islam, the scriptures of the Bible and Mahabharat and Ramayan are enough to establish and believe it. The caution, determination and courage the Muslims showed in the preservation and narration of *Ahadith* has no parallel in the inhabited quarter of earth.

The principle of *Hadith* and *Asma'-ur-Rijâl* (branch of knowledge judging merits or otherwise of the narrators of *Hadith*) etc., came to be invented as Sciences by the Muslims for the sake of the service and safeguards of the *Ahadith* of the Prophet 鐄, against all odds. The strong, firm and unshakable principles invented by the Muslims for research and minute study are so matchless that the like of which the world never witnessed in its long years.

The first memorable work of the Muslims in connection with the art of writing history is the arrangement and compilation of the Science of *Hadith*. And in this connection and in the same manner, they penned the accounts of their caliphs, nobles, kings, scholars, philosophers etc. This whole treasure should be taken as Islamic history. The art of writing history by the Muslims was a new and novel thing and an unexpected blessings and essential asset for the world. When other nations consider their books like Bible and Mahabharat as an asset and a matter of pride, a man is left wonder-struck that the Muslims take out and keep aside even Khatib's history from the shelves of authentic books of history.

European historians, these days, appear to be engaged in hairsplitting and the Muslims seem to be awe-stricken with and all-praise for their perfection in this art and they do it with all the sincerity at their command. But, they are ignorant even of the fact that the *Introduction to History* written by Muslim historian, Ibn Khaldûn belonging to an Arab family of Spain living in North Africa, made the entire Europe and the whole world to understand such unique points about the art of writing history that all the efforts of European historians can be safely sacrificed on the historical sense and acumen of Ibn Khaldûn. But the high ambition and height of fondness of the Muslims can be gauged from the fact that even in the assembly of scholars of Islam, the original history written by Ibn Khaldûn fails to attract their sense of importance and glory, except the *Introduction to History*.

The praiseworthy endeavors of thousands of Muslim historians from Ibn Hisham, Ibn Al-Athîr, Tabari, Mas'ûdi etc., to Ahmad bin Khawand Shah and Zia Barni and up to Muhammad Qasim Faristha and Mulla Badâûni, which are still preserved in fat volumes — each one of them is the portrait of the fascinating magnificence and grandeur of the past Muslim era. And each book on Islamic history needs deep study, and lessons derived from it may be of great use to the readers. But, how pitiable it is that not a single Muslim among a hundred appears to be aware of his Islamic history and goes through history books written by Muslims historians, although a large number of Muslims have the ability to read and understand books of history written by Mill, Carlyle, Eliot, Gibbon and others.

Since all the books of Islamic history have been written in the Arabic and Persian languages and even one among a hundred Muslims in India does not know Arabic or Persian to go through these books, it becomes a bounden duty to write Islamic history in the Urdu language. As now, I am presenting this book, other farsighted persons have an opportunity to write Islamic histories in Urdu in the form better than this humble effort.

The Nature of and Facts about Islamic History

Islamic history is a science or art of permanent nature which has in its fold thousands of voluminous books written by highly experienced and esteemed writers. The Muslim historians have generally penned separately histories of a dynasty or country or any one nation or any one ruler or a king or an event of tremendous importance and value. Some of them have compiled biographies simply of scholars of Islam or philosophers of Islam or saints of Islam and their number reaches up to thousands. This magnificent treasure and collection may be safely brought under the title of Islamic history or the art of Islamic history. And this treasure is multiplying with the passage of time.

The number of Islamic countries and kingdoms is also so large that even a book of history of each one of them, if selected, can not be put in a few shelves but in several rooms of a library. To produce an average book of history in the Urdu language is, in fact, to extract essence of books of Islamic history and to summarize the whole thing. It is easier to take a photograph of a very big scenery on a card or to put the photograph of a palatial building into the hole of a bead of rosary, but it is very difficult to produce a gist of the whole history of Islam in a volume containing merely two thousand pages. Hence, I myself cannot convincingly say that I have achieved success in my attempt. I leave it to my readers to decide what place does this book occupy as a book of Islamic history and how could the Muslim *Ummah* (nation) be benefited by it.

As for the events and occurrences, for each and every event, I have tried my level best to judge its veracity in the authentic histories of the period when the event occurred. I have then tried to put the gist of the events in my own words. Wherever any sharp difference of opinion arose among the different historians and I found it difficult to decide about the authenticity thereof, I have translated the opinion of the historian exactly, and also expressed my personal opinion where the situation demanded it. I have written this book as a service to Islam and as a matter of religious duty and expect my recompense only from Allâh the Almighty.

I admit my incapability to undertake such a gigantic task and if I, anyhow, come out with success, it is nothing short of wonders. And anyone who takes the course of constructive and sincere criticism exclusively for the sake of reforms, will be welcomed as a benefactor, while the one who does it out of jealousy and malice is to be consigned to Allâh.

Akbar Shah Khan
Najibabad, India
Muharram-ul-Harâm
1343 AH

Introduction

History

Technically speaking, History is a science which deals with the events and occurrences attached to Prophets, kings, conquerors and eminent personalities and significant events of the ages past. These events give us to know about the way of living, moral values and social learning in the past. Some people have defined History in a manner that humans living together form society and that collection of men gives birth to city, and all the states and conditions undergone by them put together take the shape of historical events, while collecting such events by the latter from the former and leaving them for the posterity as a model for learning lesson and benefiting from, is called History. Some others say that the Arabic word *Târikh* (history) has been constructed by reversing the last constituent of the word *Takhir*, and *Takhir* means to relate the past with the future; for instance, it is to tell that so-and-so religion or rule or battle occurred at such and such period. Thus, it is the only source of knowing what happened in a certain period. In short, much hairsplitting has been done in defining History. But the sum and substance of all the definitions is the same what has been described above. If the gist of the gist is meant, one can say: "The states and conditions and information which are chronologically arranged make History."

Need of History

History produces in our heart and mind blessed fervor by acquainting us with the living conditions of our elders and ancestors. Human nature has a particular kind of thirst and desire which activates man to travel through the countries, to stroll in gardens and roaming the mountains and forests. This demand of human nature keeps children restless to hear stories of cock-sparrow and hen-sparrow, and to the young to hear tales of parrots and starlings.

And this is what urges to carry out the command of Qur'ân: "So ask of those who know if you know not." (16:43) and turns human mind to go through historical books. And keeping this in view, the Creator of natures has put some taste in heavenly Books. What a great nation was Children of Israel that they had claimed: "We are the children of Allâh and His loved ones." (5:18) but the more they were getting unaware of the states and conditions of their elders and ancestors, the more they kept falling into the quagmire of disgrace. Consequently, Allâh the Almighty has addressed them repeatedly with the words "O Children of Israel! Remember..." and reminded them of the conditions of their elders.

Benefits of History

Study of history sends ambition high, draws toward virtues and keeps away from vices. It develops wisdom and insight, sets farsightedness to grow and creates sense of caution and vigilance. It fills the heart with utmost joys by warding off sadness and gloom. Its study produces in man power to stabilize the truth and falsify the untruth and enhances power of decision. It creates patience and firmness and keeps heart and mind studded with freshness and growth.

In short, knowledge of history is a preacher of thousand preachers and the best source of learning lessons. By studying history, a man finds himself constantly in the company of Prophets, kings, conquerors, friends of Allâh, wise men, scholars and men of consummate skill and learning, and benefits from the fountain of their knowledge, wisdom, excellence and virtues. And he can easily save himself from the mistakes committed by great kings, viziers, military commanders and philosophers. No other study can fill human hearts with so much joys without putting any mental pressure or causing boredom as a study of history can do.

Preservation of Martial Characters through History:

The nation, fully aware of its historical background and events of the past, can essentially and successfully preserve its national character and distinction, and can restrain its people from getting demoralized in any field of activity; it rather leads them to the lost pinnacle of perfection.

An individual, who is uninformed of the background of his fathers, may indulge in embezzlement. But one who knows that so-and-so among his fathers achieved name and fame on such and such occasion, keeps his honesty intact caring least for lacs of rupees. A person who is uninformed of his fathers' past, may like to escape from the battlefield. But one who is informed of some occasion when one of his fathers took the field in an adverse situation and fought fearlessly even at the cost of his life, will never flee the battlefield, and the very background of his elder will serve as fetter for him.

Now imagine about the high morals like loyalty, truth, piety, modesty, generosity etc. The way the elders and ancestors lived, can produce the spirit of living in the nations and peace in the world. And, perhaps, because of this reason that our neighboring states who have no glorious history of their own, get their purpose served by changing fictitious tales and false stories into historical accounts thinking least about their disgraceful position in the court of the historians.

History and Family Virtues:

Since history contains virtues of the good and evils of the evildoers, an individual belonging to a mean or low family can give only scant attention to true historical accounts. Noble nations preserve the great and unique deeds of their ancestors in their memory which they follow to keep their nobility intact. Ignoble nations forget even some of the good deeds of their ancestors with the passage of time. To a family or nation whose ancestors have achieved a place of distinction in the sphere of Divine worship, bravery, art and learning, power and grandeur etc., and they have not totally ignored it, they could be activated by producing in them sense of courage, determination, shame and honor. But this device cannot be attempted in case of the mean nations. This is the reason why most often men from the respectable nations, of the honorable lineage, sons of saintly people and the virtuous have especial interest in and fondness for the knowledge of history. None among the atheists and well-known coward had ever been a historian or a leader of the historians.

Historian

The best among the historians is one who is righteous in creed and pure in religious affairs; what he writes should be true as a statement; he is supposed to neither conceal anything nor add anything untrue on his own behalf. Wherever there is chance of stumbling or being victim of misunderstanding, it is permissible to explain and clarify it. It is essential for a historian neither to indulge in sycophancy nor harbor malice against anybody. The style of writing should be simple, intelligible and spontaneous.

Orientation in words and style kills the very purpose of the historiography. This is the reason why histories written in the form of poems are considered below standard with respect to reliability and authenticity. He must be noted for honesty and integrity; he has to be distinguished in speaking truth and acting gracefully; he is to be miles away from nonsense talking, hate and dejection.

The work of compiling, collecting and editing needs very hard labor and determination from a historian, but still, he is not to be very sure of the veracity of events, for sure access to facts behind an event is not guaranteed. Besides having considerable knowledge of astronomy, geology, civics and religions of the world, a historian must be intelligent, discerning and fair-minded along with being a litterateur and a man with perfect command on expression so that he could state his motive easily and effectively. Despite all this, there are some difficulties which appear to be insoluble; for instance, a narrator relates about someone going to a theatre. Now, such a narration gives a number of reasons about his visit and nothing can be said to be essentially true:

1. The person who went to the theatre is fond of songs.
2. He is not fond of hearing songs but is actually a lover of beauty.
3. He is not a lover of beauty but, all of a sudden, he has fallen in love with an actress.
4. He is not a lover of anybody but he was essentially to meet a friend there.
5. He wanted to write an article on theatre and hence he was bound to go there.
6. He had to deliver a lecture against theatre and hence had to observe it closely.
7. He is employed in secret service and his bounden duty led him there.
8. He himself hated theatre but his friends forced him to go there.
9. He was a godly person and a pious man of high degree, but he went to theatre to dissolve the devotion of the people to himself.
10. He had gone there with the sole purpose of picking pockets.

In short, one narrative can give birth to hundreds of deductions. Moreover, any one healthy deduction needs support of many other causes. Those supportive causes also have different possibilities. If the historian is not just and he feels himself attracted to any predetermined deduction, he very easily and carelessly overlooks opposing pleas and collects favorable arguments by searching them everywhere. Thus he seeks to mislead others by getting himself misled.

Readers of History

As compiling or writing a book of history is an uphill task, to study history and derive full benefits from it is equally difficult. Readers of history should consider the study of the past events as source of taking lesson and warning. They are required to save themselves from the mistakes and evildoings which the people of the past had committed and paid for them, and try to practice virtue by being acquainted with the best consequences of the virtues of the virtuous. To decry or abuse anyone who has already departed from this world is not an act of bravery. However, it is not a matter of shame to express love for the dead and gone and to invoke blessings of Allâh for him.

To roam the countries, cities, mountains, forests, show places and bazaars, and to study history books are very similar. The only difference is that the experience a tourist collects through tourism and travels of his whole life, the reader of history can collect more of it by the study of history books for a day or a week. The more a reader of history is victim of uncalled-for fanaticism, the more he will find his study of history barren and unproductive for him.

Sources of History

The sources of history are generally divided in three types:

Solid Evidences: It refers to all written works like books, memoranda, official papers, commands, decisions, documents etc.

Repeated Narratives: It means things that are talk of the town; for instance, stories, poems, proverbs etc.

Archaeological Finds: It contains signs and relics, for instance, ruins of the cities, forts, buildings, plaques of buildings, sculpture, ancient weapons, coins, utensils etc.

But it is however, not easy to exploit all these three kinds of materials to compile a book of history. These all appear to be meager without intellectual power of high degree, labor, courage, urge and insight. Besides national character, particular habits, rites and customs, background and geographical conditions prove helpful to the historian.

Types of History

From different respects history may adopt different forms. Quantitatively speaking, it may be divided into two parts — general and particular. General history makes mention of the people of the whole world; particular kind of history gives knowledge about one particular nation or country or dynastic rule. Qualitatively speaking, it is also of two kinds — narrative and critical.

Narrative history is one where the statement of the narrator is being enlisted on the basis of his personal observation, and the acceptable and satisfactory narratives have been available to the historian; or the historian would have directly observed the occurrence of the event. Such histories are useful most of all because they need not translating conjectural and imaginary matters into real one. Such histories rather bring about reforms in conceptual mistakes and rationalistic faults.

Critical history is one which is based totally on archaeological finds, reported materials and rationalistic frauds, and any statement of the contemporary historian or narrator regarding the event is not available, like the recently compiled histories of ancient Egypt, Iraq, and Iran. However, these histories are also not without utility. But one cannot be sure of real knowledge.

Historical Ages

Some of the historians have divided history in three ages:

1) The Earlier Ages
2) The Middle Ages
3) The Modern Ages

The Earlier Ages contain historical account from the beginning of the world to the Roman rule. The Middle or Medieval Ages comprise the period from the last of Roman rule to the conquest of Constantinople (Istanbul) under Sultan Muhammad Usmani, the second.

From some great events are traced the periods of the occurrences of some other events, for instance, such and such events occurred so many years after the birth of Adam, or so many years before or after the Deluge. Similarly, years are counted from the birth of Jesus Christ or Vikarmajeet, or the emigration of Muhammad ﷺ from Makkah to Al-Madinah or from the enthroning of a certain king. Currently, Christian or Hijrah Era is in vogue most of all.

Islamic History

Among all the nations and religions of the world, from the beginning to the end, Islam alone is such a religion and Muslims alone are a nation which have their history wholly and solely preserved and intact, and no part thereof has ever been doubtful. The Muslims have never from the days of the Prophet ﷺ up to the present day, acted with negligence and carelessness in reducing states and events to writing and preserving them for days to come. The Muslims are, therefore, privileged to take pride in the fact that they can at any time, compile the whole history of Islam with the help of contemporary historians and eyewitnesses. Moreover, they can very safely show the similar statements about events with unbroken chain of different authoritative narrators.

In short, the Muslims are the only nation which has a complete, exhaustive and authentic history of its own, and no nation of the world can share this peculiarity and distinct feature of this nation. Historians of Islam have practiced as much caution as to take down the event and its nature as it were, without their personal opinion whatever so that the readers are influenced not the least with the views of the historian. Thus, the readers are at liberty to make their own decisions and form their own opinions in their own way, without toeing the line of thinking adopted by the historian. The greatness and glory of Islamic history exerts deeper impressions on heart when it is noticed that any time or any part of Islamic history can be safely put to the acid test of reasoning and it will pass off without any impurity, flaw and defect.

History of Histories

Having seen the ruins of Babylon and Nineveh, pillars of Ad and Iram in the desert of Najd, pyramids and mummified idols of Egypt etc., an urge is aroused in man to know about the builders. They have attempted to write about the Babylonian people and have collected immense materials on account of their incomplete critical analysis. However, the lives and works of the founders of pyramids can be penned through the strange letters available.

Zoroastrian scriptures, Dasatirah Safrang, Bible and the present scriptures, Ramayan of Balmiki Mahabharat are such books which may give some right or wrong information. Idioms, phrases, proverbs, stone weapons, iron tools, ornaments of silver, gold and copper etc., idols of stone, preserved dead bodies of Egypt, pillars of Asoka, Caves of Ellora, idols of Sarnath and Sanchi, Throne of Rustam, Wall of China etc., put together make interesting materials which may shed light not only on the whole inhabited quarter of earth as brightly as it is required, but however, they can bring to light some of the areas here and there, howsoever dim the historical rays happen to be. True or false stories of the Indians, old plaques of the Egyptians, ancient traditions of Chinese, ruins of the Iranians, writings of the Greek—particularly the book of Herodotus, Israelite traditions, Arabic morals—these are all vital and elementary parts of history.

Beginning of History

Roman and Greek eras, particularly from the conquests of Alexander, start that part of history which has presented before us the states and conditions of most of the countries of the world that there is far less chances of the chains being snapped in the middle. And it is from here that history is generally considered to take a start. As the study of histories of Greece, Egypt and Iran fills its readers with joys, they are equally enraged against the Indians, for even in that historical age, India seems to be engulfed in darkness. This utter carelessness of the people living here has always made the historians of the world to shed tears of blood that they always cast fictitious stories in the mould of truth and never allowed truth to take its course. As against the green country India, there is another desert country Arabia, which is contrary to India with respect to authenticity, power of memory, preservation of table of genealogy and narration of events exactly as they occurred. And, hence, even the historical assets of those religions of the Age of Ignorance are reckoned as something valuable.

Real Beginning of History

Now, the Noble Qur'ân is sent down. Arabia overcasts the entire world. All the societies appear to be (according to the Qur'ân) "... scattered floating particles of dust." (25:23) before Arab society. History, in fact, starts from here. Apart from magnificent task of arranging and compiling *Ahadith* and *Asma'-ur-Rijâl*, thousands of Muslim historians are there who have worked such wonders in this field that one is filled with amazement. There is no branch of society or human living which has been left unnoticed or untouched by the Muslims. Authenticity of narration is the life and running spirit behind all historical activities. And the Muslims have taken this aspect into consideration in such magnitude that none except the Muslims as a nation may be cited as an example. The Muslims have devoted their supreme abilities in compiling histories even of other nations and countries. It is the Muslim nation alone which has taken the art of writing history to the level of a science, and the name of Ibn Khaldûn, the originator of the principles of history, will keep receiving laurels till the end of this world. From the time the Muslims have been overcast by clouds of decline and ill-luck as a nation, and lost much of their promptitude in their endeavors in this field, their pupils, i.e., the European historians have picked up from there to some extent.

History of Sultanate

The distinctive feature of man as against other animals is that while the animals have been kept within limits and their required provisions are within their reach without endeavor, humans have been given opportunity to get according to their efforts and struggle. This object may also be described in the manner that man is constantly in a state of travel and is being created to go from lower to higher ranks. Among men one makes more travel or reaches greater heights, looks upon others who are lower or lagging behind, but as he is never to attain perfection, he being higher than others, is also inferior to those above him. He by nature is endowed with the sense of devotion and obedience as has been said:

> "And I (Allâh) created not the jinn and mankind except that they should worship Me (Alone)." (51:56)

Thus, the man who is ahead of others is forced by his very nature to obey some power greater than and superior to him. This explains the existence of kingdom and rule. A king or ruler is only lawfully perfect, and not in real terms, for real perfection is found in the one who is absolute and not limited, immortal and not mortal, one and not numerous.

And that One Self-Existent is Allâh the Almighty Who is free from every flaw, defect and evil and is the Possessor of all attributes in their perfection. And thus, He is the real King, real Ruler and real Authority. Since man is obeying by nature, hence, he is to obey and follow others as a part of his very nature. And his real Ruler has prevented him from doing so, as has been said:

"Obey Allâh and obey the Messenger (Muhammad ﷺ), and those of you who are in authority." (4: 59)

Shadow law-enforcing authority or king may be only one who is more perfect than others. Hence, it is the demand of human nature to keep under sway whoever appears lesser in position, status and rank. But since, man against his nature, has also the capability of moving towards his downfall instead of rising up, it is the logical aspect of mental attitude to develop a desire for something he doesn't deserve. This is the reason why constant conflict is a common spectacle in the world of rules and kingdoms. Enforcing authorities may be kept in two different categories — spiritual and physical, or to say Prophethood and Sultanate.

The skills required for materialistic rule have been stated in regard to kingdom of Tâlut (Goliath) and Dâwud (David) ﷺ in these words:

"And their Prophet (Samuel) said to them: 'Indeed Allâh has appointed Tâlut (Saul) as a king over you'." (2:247)

When the people heard of the kingship of Tâlut, they objected to it and got the reply:

"Verily, Allâh has chosen him above you and has increased him abundantly in knowledge and stature." (2:247)

It was further said about Dâwud ﷺ:

"… and Dâwud killed Jâlut, and Allâh gave him the kingdom and *Al-Hikmah* (Prophethood), and taught him of that which He willed." (2:251)

Now, from the study of histories, it comes to light that whoever got an opportunity to become the center of the support of his people and got superiority over others in respect of learning and physical power, he was at once accepted as their ruler and sultan.

Three thousand years ago only physical power, wrestling and bravery added by mental power were considered as essential assets for ruling over others. But when human race gradually developed other qualities, conditions and qualities for kingship were also added. In short, the best and the most valuable person has always been a man to rule. And mischief and trial, conflict and disruption, bloodshed and plunder came to surface only when the undeserving got the throne. And you will find no exception to this rule. Since every man is equal with respect to his nature and rights, hence the acquired qualities and skills alone could lead one to have power and throne, as the Qur'ân says:

"And that man can have nothing but what he does." (53:39)

Every head of the family who becomes the ruler or king is so because of his fine qualities of head and heart. Every village headman is the ruler and king of his village. And this is the model of the rule or government of early ages of humankind which is still existing and we cannot pick holes in this system. Nevertheless, if any flaw or defect is to be found out, it is solely on the basis that any undeserving and incapable person in the family has captured power by foul means, or if the headman of the village, or head of the locality happens to be an undeserving person.

Personality and Democracy

Human face which is, on one hand, the noblest creation of Allâh the Almighty, and the served of the entire universe, has in his nature on the other, to treat any exalted and powerful being as the center and an object of worship, and this demand of human nature leads him to the concept of Oneness of God and to worship one God by rejecting all other false gods. The greatest satanic cunningness and deception was that man put heredity and lineage as precondition for getting throne and forming government. It resulted in undeserving persons not capable of kingship to become kings and look down upon those who really deserved it. This blunder of mankind gave birth to many evils, corruption and disruption and the children of Adam had to bear the brunt thereof.

The Noble Qur'ân after being revealed and Muhammad 🌸 after being commissioned as Prophet, remedied the evil; and this embodiment of the total human qualities, himself led the people of the state and thus put before the world at large best example of the blend of Prophet-hood and temporal rule at a time. He explained to the human kind the duties of a king and his realm of power. After him, his foremost trained and benefited band, i.e., the noble Companions 🌸 elected the best among them to rule over them in line with the teachings of the Prophet 🌸.

Thus, for the first time, broke the satanic spell that heredity could ever play a role in making one a ruler. The choice of Umar Fârooq 🌸 after Abu Bakr Siddiq 🌸 was governed by the same principle. Although Uthmân Ghani 🌸 was also chosen without any consideration of heredity and lineage, but some individuals and sections of the people had some reservation about it, and Uthmân Ghani 🌸 himself did some favor to his relatives and the people of his own tribe. Hence, his period was not without trials and tribulations.

Thus, it may be safely said that as the Prophet Muhammad 🌸 presented his example as a Messenger for 23 consecutive years to redeem humanity, so also from 1 to 10 AH, i.e., for about 10 years, he put before the world glaring example of righteous rule. And as the 23 years of the Prophet 🌸 are worth following for mankind, so the Madnian life of the Prophet 🌸, the caliphate of Abu Bakr Siddiq and the caliphate of Umar Fârooq 🌸 put together and spreading over a span of 23 years, are also worthy of being emulated.

At the end of the Righteous Caliphate, human weakness and satanic swindling once again made hereditary relations necessary for succeeding to the kingdom or rule. And the rule, instead of going to the able and deserving, was unfortunately came to be considered as the right of some particular dynasties. Thus, the unworthy sons of worthy fathers appeared 'gracing' the thrones or seats of power. The people of those period had to undergo untold miseries and sufferings to get rid of such evil and despotic rulers.

At last, their patience being exhausted, they took recourse to the democracy practiced in France and America etc., today; although like hereditary autocratic rules, democracies also cannot prove a source of blessing for mankind. The only type of government corresponding to human nature and a source of peace and blessing for mankind is one whose model came to be seen in the first four centuries of the Hijrah era. And that is, in fact, the system that lies between democracy and autocracy.

Democratic Rule

In a democratic setup, a person is elected by the people for a period of three or five years and he is called either the President of the republic or the Head of the democratic government. But the President of the republic does not enjoy the same powers which is required by an affectionate ruler of mankind. Even in some ordinary matters the President feels helpless and has to work against his will. It means the government has no real center of power, and government affairs are divided in a manner that they go to belong to all the people of the state.

When seen from a distance, this system of government looks pleasant. And since, the people generally find themselves ruling over themselves and feel that the chains of despotism or tyrannical rule are broken, they are happy with the system, but ultimately they are put to great loss as well.

Human sense of nobility lies against unbridled freedom. This is the reason that in France and America etc., where democratic system is working, the spiritualism desired by the religion is going to the dogs. High morals taught by religion cannot grow and flourish in a country where the flood of democracy is surging. Democratic system of government seeks to put man on a path of such an unnatural freedom that he can no longer retain his Divine values. Pure democratic system is, in fact, a very strong movement of atheism and secularism. As nothing grows in a desert, fish can't live out of water, and man cannot keep healthy in a dark place and polluted air, in the same way, religious thoughts, restraints and prayers cannot stay and grow in a democratic system of government.

The fundamental principle of religion is restraint and obedience. And one's following of a true religion keeps intact the true feeling of human nature that every high and respectable being is to be given a high place and shown respects, and since, Allâh the Almighty is the Highest of all, one should bow down before Him saying *Subhâna Rabbiyal-A'la* (Glorified be the Lord, the Most High). Every Messenger, every Prophet and every guide in the world has rightly demanded that all men should obey him and carry out his command. And none can deny that human race has always achieved success simply by following and obeying those Messengers, Prophets, guides and leaders.

It is a fact that human race has reached the stage of progress and development from the lowest level of disgrace and depravity. Thus, the system of government which is injurious to the righteous course and sets humanity free from all decent and reasonable restraints, can never prove healthy and beneficial to mankind. Every father wants his son to obey him and it also behooves the son to do so. Every teacher wants his pupils to obey him and the same is demanded of disciples, followers and soldiers, and they must respond to the call in their own interest. But, under the effect of democracy every son, pupil, disciple, follower and soldier looks upon obedience to his father, teacher, saint, leader and commander as a matter of an unpleasant duty to be performed against one's will. And, by and by, all these things are so dissolved that man finds before him nothing but atheism and secularism which ultimately lead to barbarism.

Democracy is basically against sense of religiosity, and hence the more this sense is injured, the more there is chance for peace to go out of sight. Real peace can be established on earth only through religion, but governments have always eaten humble pie in this field. Inside houses, in forests, deserts and pathways, a man is free from the watchful eyes of the police. It is religion alone and not the government which can hold one back from indulging in evil acts of murder, theft, adultery etc. If all the inhabitants of the earth turn secular, it will become a hell for mankind by freely adopting the course of killing and carnage, theft, adultery, lies, deception, mischief and unmannerly behavior.

In the democracies of Europe and America, we find nothing which could create a sense of envy in us. These are the countries where more irreligiousness is found. In these very countries, human society is more inclined to immodesty, and it is here that breach of promise, disloyalty, self-centeredness, falsehood, deceit etc., have become ingredients of their character. Democratic government can never give birth to any Napoleon, Kaiser, William, Julius Caesar, Temur, Hannibal, Salahuddin, Sulaiman Qanuni, Sher Shah, Alamgir. And, in case one is born, he cannot remain alive, what to speak of the birth of Khâlid bin Walid.

It is, perhaps, the most ugly example of human depravity that we, today, find even Muslims desiring of European and American type of democracy, which is totally against the teachings of Islam and something highly injurious to mankind. Such a shift in Muslim thought is the result of the timidity and lack of courage, and it is reduced to such a state because of ignorance and ignoring the teachings of the Qur'ân and *Hadith*.

Autocratic Hereditary Rule

When a person ascends the throne, his blood relation and natural love demand that his son being inheritor of his property and possessions, should also be his successor as a king. But this is his sheer mistake, for kingship is not his property but a trust entrusted to him by his country and nation. Hence he is not within his rights to put his rule to his disposal and pass it on to anybody at will.

A trust is always consigned to its real master. Hence, it is up to the nation to hand it over to any tested and trusted person most suitable to the job. But it requires utmost courage and very strong resolution to hold the king back from committing breach of trust and confidence. Such dauntless courage can be produced by Islam alone which it has done through the ages and what the Prophet ﷺ had implanted into his Companions.

The Muslims evaded teachings of Islam with the result they lost much of their courage, determination and ambition which Islam had produced in them in the past, and hence, they could not put a check on their rulers. Instead they shut their eyes to the misappropriations of their rulers in every department of life. At last, the ugly practice of forming autocratic hereditary rule which was obliterated during the Righteous Caliphate, was once again brought back to life, and the Muslims as a whole, had to bear the brunt of their agreeing to wrong practice.

Hereditary crown princeship's unreasonable and praise-less practice so often paved the way for most of the unworthy and incapable persons to become rulers of the Muslims — persons who were even lacking in the qualities of getting a seat in the assembly of worthy and civilized men. Certainly there should be only one ruler or caliph or king of the Muslims, but he must be the best among them and they elect him with general agreement or majority opinion. Anybody's birth in the house of a caliph or king doesn't mean that he has necessary abilities to make a worthy ruler.

Had this practice of hereditary rule not been permitted, and the Islamic concept of governance and the ruling system had been as well-guarded as it was during the Righteous Caliphate, the Islamic rule and the Muslims would not have reduced to such a sad plight we see today. But it was the Will of Allâh and hence it came to pass. Had the Muslims opposed it right from the beginning and not slackened their efforts to keep it intact, then although they had to give supreme sacrifices at the outset, but later, none would have mustered courage enough to get his son elected to the throne or declared him his successor. Abu Bakr ﷺ had more than one worthy son to make a good ruler but he found Umar ﷺ best among the Muslims and recommended his name for the next caliph. Abdullâh ﷺ the son of Umar ﷺ was, undoubtedly, worthy of being the caliph after his father, but since, Umar Fârooq ﷺ was essentially bent upon uprooting this evil practice, issued command that Abdullah bin Umar ﷺ should, in no case, be elected caliph.

The greatest folly and blindness of people is that they see with their naked eyes the evils of autocratic rule but still never take the trouble of going deep into the causes of these evils. By opposing autocracy, they start praising democracy. The main cause behind the evils of autocratic rule is that it had made room for heredity and snatched away from the people the right to elect the ruler of their own choice. Thus, it is the demand of reason that first of all the origin of all evils, i.e., the system of hereditary rule be debarred from making entry to the sphere of human activity. They should make it a point not to allow at any cost the son of a ruler to succeed if he is not worthy of becoming one. And he should be elected with consensus or majority opinion even if he deserves the throne or seat of power. What sort of wisdom it is to commit another such mistake to avoid one. It is the timidity and lack of courage on the part of the public that encourage the despotic and unworthy rulers to go unbridled. The obedience shown with a sense of duty is far apart from one which is done out of cowardice. To make it more clear, we can cite the example of Umar ﷺ whose governors would say that they felt Umar's one hand below and another about the jaws and he would tear our jaws apart on slight deviation from the prescribed course. Khâlid bin Walid ﷺ receives the order of Umar Fârooq ﷺ and he very silently obeys it in spite of being a commander of great victories. Umar ﷺ is on the other hand, challenged right on his pulpit and a very common and ordinary person examines his honesty and trusteeship. A woman listens to Umar's speech regarding bridal-money and has the courage to raise objection against a point therein, and the Commander of the Faithful had to admit from his pulpit that even the women of Al-Madinah could inform him of his mistake.

Now, one can easily think of the sort of obedience shown to Umar ﷺ, and compare it with the kind of obedience shown to the last Mogul kings in the courts and in the very country they ruled. Royal orders were not carried out not only in the Punjab, Sindh, Deccan, Bengal and other provinces, but also in Agra, Allahabad and Delhi.

Autocratic Democratic Rule

The type of rule Islam has formed on this earth is known as Autocratic Democratic Rule. The system of rule suggested by Islam lies between pure democracy and pure autocracy. Every Islamic section has its say in the election of caliphate, king or ruler. In the election of the most suitable and most deserving person for the rule or caliphate, all possible fair means should be made use of, and the best person to be elected at all costs. The Muslims need no institution of law or constitution or formation of any modern system of government, for they possess the noble Qur'ân and the *Sunnah* of the Prophet ﷺ.

Thus the task of electing best man for the job is also not difficult for the Muslims. The man who knows the Qur'ân and *Hadith* more and acts more upon them is the most deserving of all to become the ruler of the Muslims. To run the administration according to the teachings of the Qur'ân and *Hadith* and to enforce Divine and Prophetic commands, are the main duties of a Muslim ruler.

The Muslims have every right to challenge their rulers if and when he makes even slight deviation from the path set by Allâh and His Messenger ﷺ. But it is incumbent on each and every Muslim to follow every order of the ruler, if it is not contrary to the dictates of the Qur'ân and the *Sunnah* without even thinking to revolt against the ruler. In case a Muslim ruler shows sign of deviation from the right path, he may be deposed then and there. But if he carries out his duties to his nation with Divine sense and good intentions, his deposition would be the height of idiocy after passing a tenure of three or five years.

The caliph of the Muslims happens to be the servant, watchman, guard and trustee of the Muslims; why should then we remove him from a position wherefrom he is serving the Muslims with all the power at his command just for plunging in the trouble of a new experiment. The Muslims do not want their caliph to enact laws for them nor allow him to pass a luxurious life at the cost of public exchequer. The caliph of the Muslims, under a moderate and reasonable system, collects wealth from the wealthy section in reasonable proportion and spends it on the poor, the needy and the orphan for their welfare. Since, a reasonable tax is collected from the wealthy section to be given to the needy, there is no chance of any conflict arising between the capitalists and the laborers which has, now, taken the whole Europe in its grip.

The caliph of the Muslims is the guard and watchman of the Muslims as well as their teacher, guide, commander, servant and king. In important matters and national affairs, for instance, if an enemy country is to be invaded or peace is to be brought about with the hostile power, or troops to be sent to help any people or for protecting the Muslims, or keeping peace in the country, the caliph has to hold consultations with the Muslims for the Qur'ân had ordained him to do so. But the purpose of consultation is not to force the Muslim ruler to toe their line by holding back his own. The sole purpose of such consultation is that the caliph should listen to favorable and unfavorable opinions about the issue and then form his own opinion in the light of wise counsels. The Qur'ân says:

> "... and consult them in the affairs. Then when you have taken a decision, put your trust in Allâh." (3:159)

The model of the system of government Islam wants to set up, as mentioned above, may be seen in the era of the Righteous Caliphate. After that, the system of rule changed into autocratic hereditary one. However, the bright points of Islamic teachings and morality kept glaring out the rules established by the Muslims, and taken as a whole, the type of rule set up by the Muslims has no parallel in the annals of history. Democratic governments whose example Europe and America are presenting today, can never come at par with the type of rule Islam wants to establish.

Our Starting Point

Muslim historians have generally started their books from Adam ﷺ while others have done it from the creation of the earth and the heaven. But I shall begin my history of Islam from the last Prophet ﷺ of Allâh, for states of things before him were not beyond doubt, and there was also no particular arrangement of writing history in the world before the Prophet ﷺ. Moreover, it is from him that the beginning of Islamic history is thought of, because it is commonly called that he was the founder of Islam and the people of his *Ummah* alone are called the followers of Islam, otherwise Islam has made its presence on earth right from Adam ﷺ, the father of man.

Relation between History and Geography

Geography is very closely and strongly related to history and hence the histories recently written in conformity with the European historians contain geography. Even the biographers of the Prophet ﷺ have also included the geography of Arabia to illustrate some points. But since I mean a complete but a brief history of the Muslims, inclusion of geography means writing the geography of the whole world, for the Muslims and their rule belong to the world at large. But this is most difficult if brevity is to be kept in view.

Moreover, I have taken advantage of the good opinion about the Muslims that they must be knowing the geography of the entire world along with the maps of the countries. However, it is a part of my plan to include in the book the maps of countries and states wherever they are needed. However, this book will not contain accounts of the Age of Ignorance, Arab nations, the Quraish, practices of Ignorance etc., in great detail.

In case of the life history of the Prophet ﷺ, I have largely benefited from *Sihah Sittah* (the six famous collections of the Prophet's traditions made by Imam Bukhâri, Muslim, Tirmidhi, Abu Dâwud, Nasa'i and Ibn Mâjah) and preferred *Ahadith* books to the books of history. I have taken out common materials from the history books *Târikh Tabari, Târikh Al-Kâmil* of Ibn Athir, *Târikh Mas'udi, Târikh Abul-Fida', Târikh Ibn Khaldûn, Târikh Al-Khulafa'* of Suyuti etc., and recorded them in my book. And thus the brief account of the whole history has been recorded in the best possible manner.

I have also taken accounts from the books of contemporary historians about Islamic rules established in various countries after the decline and downfall of the Abbasid caliphate. I have also quoted here and there passages from Christian historians, but I have quoted these passages just for the sake of getting support and using them as witnesses. I have firm conviction that compared to the Muslim historians, Christians are far less in true historical qualities. Hence, we should never turn towards them for getting facts.

Chapter 1

The Country of Arabia

A little mention of Arabia is essential at the outset for the Prophet Muhammad ﷺ was born in the city of Makkah and emigrated to another famous city Al-Madinah, which also became the first Islamic capital of the first Islamic State. Arabian Peninsula is the area which converted to Islam completely during the lifetime of the Prophet ﷺ. This country of Arabia was the first center of the grandeur of Islam. It was in this country and in its language that Revelation was sent and the last heavenly Book was revealed, which is the source of guidance to all the countries and nations of the world till the Day of Judgement. It is from this country of Arabia that the light of Islam spread to everywhere in the world. In the city of Makkah lies the Ancient House, the Ka'bah, towards which Muslims come from all over the world and appear together on the plain of Arafât worshipping and praying to Allâh, praising and glorifying His Name. We find here the wealthy and the poor side by side chanting praises of the Creator of the earth and sky. Arabia dominated the entire world and became for it the torchbearer and lamp of guidance.

Situation and Physical Features

On the map of Asia there can be seen a big rectangular peninsula. This is called the Arabian Peninsula or Arabia, which has the following four boundaries:

The Arabian Peninsula is bounded on the east by the Arabian Gulf and that of Oman; on the south by Arabian Sea or Indian Ocean; on the west by the Red Sea; on the north by Jordan and Iraq.

The total area of the Arabian Peninsula is 1,250,000 square miles of which 450,000 square miles is pure desert and forms part of a completely desolate area. The most famous desert is known as *Ar-Rub' Al-Khâli* (the Empty Quarter) which stretches over an area of 250,000 square miles and extends to the southeast from middle of the Arabia. On the north of this vast desert is Al-Ahsa or Bahrain, and Oman lies on the south and east of *Ar-Rub' Al-Khâli*. In the Arabian Gulf, Dubai, Abu Dhabi and Muscat are most famous cities. On the south of *Ar-Rub' Al-Khâli*, we find Hadramout and Mahra, which are situated on the coast of the Arabian Sea and the Indian Ocean. To the south and west of *Ar-Rub' Al-Khâli*, is San'â' which is the famous city of Yemen, situated on the coast of the Arabian Sea and the Red Sea. At the time of the advent of Islam it was the center for Christians in Arabia. To the west of *Ar-Rub' Al-Khâli*, lie Asir and Najrân, which are on the coast of the Red Sea. To the north of Asir, the Red Sea touches a small territory called Tihâmah, which is considered as a part of Hijâz. On the north of *Ar-Rub' Al-Khâli* is Najd in the shape of a square, on the east of which is Bahrain, to the west is Hijâz and on the north is the desert of Iraq and Syria. The name of the northeastern part of Najd is Yamâmah. Hijâz is situated at the west of Najd and east of the Red Sea, it includes the cities of Makkah and Al-Madinah and the harbors of Jeddah and Yanbu. Between Syria and the Hijâz lies a territory called Khaibar and Hijr. It is another territory bound by Syria, Hijâz and Najd. Inside *Ar-Rub' Al-Khâli* and between Hadramout and Yamâmah is a famous desolate area called Al-Ahqâf, which was once the dwelling place of the people of Âd. A look at the above mentioned places in the map will give an idea of Arabia and its famous territories.

Climate and Inhabitants

In Arabia there is no river worth mentioning. Almost the entire country comprises of burning desert and barren land and the areas lying along the seacoast alone are in a flourishing state with population. Scarcity of water has made human inhabitation almost impossible in the middle areas. All the populated areas lie at the seacoast except Najd, which is situated to the north of *Ar-Rub' Al-Khâli* and in the middle of the country. Najd is actually a plateau, it is mostly desert and the desert range of Najd meets the vast deserts of Syria.

Arabia is dotted with mountains here and there but no mountain is fresh and green. Yemen and Hijâz, situated on the coast of Red Sea, are fresher and greener than the rest of the area. The entire Arabian population is 12.5 million meaning ten people per square mile. [The figures relate to the past, at the time when the book was written.] The sun is very hot there, and sunstroke is so sharp and violent that it is generally considered poisonous. Even the camel, which is purely a desert animal, falls down dead with a stroke of this poisonous and burning wind. The camel is very useful in this country. For hundreds of miles one cannot find a trace of water. The camel is a desert ship. Long journeys are made on its back. Nothing significant grows except dates, and the population generally lives on camel's milk and dates, fish is eaten on the coastal areas. A greater part of the population of this country lives a nomadic life so there are few big flourishing cities. [After the establishment of a single union territory by King Abdul-Aziz bin Âl Saud, and by the current development in Arabian Peninsula, the above mentioned status has been changed.]

The scope of this book doesn't permit more space for writing about the geography of the Arabian Peninsula.

Ancient Peoples of Arabia

Since very early times the progeny of Sâm (Shem), the son of Nûh (Noah) ﷺ, has inhabited Arabia. As regards designating eras, the historians have put the inhabitants of Arabia into three categories namely, *Arab Bâ'idah, Arab Musta'ribah* and *Arab 'Âribah*. Some of them have held both *'Âribah* and *Musta'ribah* as the same and designated them in two categories only *Arab Bâ'idah* and *Arab Bâqiyah*. *Arab Bâ'idah* refers to only those peoples who had inhabited Arabia from the earliest age and they have all perished without leaving any trace behind. *Arab Bâqiyah* means those people who are still found in Arabia. They also form two categories namely, *'Âribah* and *Musta'ribah*. Other historians have designated the Arabs into four categories — *Arab Bâ'idah* or *Arab 'Âribah, Arab Musta'ribah, Arab Tâbi'ah*, and *Arab Musta'jimah*.

Arab Bâ'idah:

Some of the earliest tribes were called Âd, Thamud, Abil, Amâliqah, Tasm, Jadais, Umaim, Jurhum, Hadramout, Hadur and Abd Dakhm etc. These all were the progeny of Laudh bin Sâm (Shem) bin Nûh (Noah). They dominated the whole of the Arabian Peninsula and some of their kings expanded their military conquests up to Egypt. Books of history do not give any account about them and their conditions. Ruins of their buildings, archaeological finds, some pillars of stone, ornaments and sculpture have been found in Najd, Ahqâf and Hadramout, which tell us that they were the strongest civilization of their time with much grandeur and awe. Among these tribes, Âd was the most renowned. These people lived in Ahqâf. Âd bin Aus bin Iram bin Sâm by whose name this tribe became famous, was the first and foremost king of Arabia. He had three sons, named Shaddâd, Shadid and Iram. They ruled one after another.

About the same Shaddâd bin Âd, Allâmah Zamakhshari has written that he built the city of Iram in the desert of Aden but it is now traceless. The Noble Qur'ân has also made mention of Iram but it refers to the Iram tribe, not the city of Iram nor the garden of Iram. The Iram tribe was perhaps, another name for the Âd tribe or perhaps it was a branch of Âd tribe or the Âd tribe was itself a branch of the Iram tribe, Allâh the Almighty says in the Qur'ân:

> "Did you not see how did your Lord treat the Âd of Iram who were of so commanding stature that no creature of such a physical strength was ever born in the cities (of the world)?" (89:6-8)

Mas'udi has written that, before Âd, his father Âs was also a king. A king named Jairun bin Sa'd bin Âd bin Aus of this very dynasty had rampaged Syria and built a house of marble and precious stone, and he had named it Iram. Ibn Asâkir has also mentioned the name of Jairun in his history of Damascus. The Prophet Hud ﷺ was sent to the Âd tribe or the people who were raised from the same people. But his people disobeyed him and were sent to their doom. The Glorious Qur'ân has detailed this event. Âd was followed by Abil, Amâliqah, Thamud, and Abd Dakhm, who ruled the country one after another until Ya'rub bin Qahtân brought about their end and set the beginning of a new era. Prophet Saleh ﷺ was sent to the Thamud tribe or the people of Thamud. Thamud lived in Hijr while Yamamah was the place where Tasm and Jadais lived; Amâliqah lived in Tihâmah and Jurhum in Yemen. As mentioned above, all the tribes of Arabia were the progeny of Sâm, the son of Nûh (Noah) ﷺ, which are shown in the genealogical table.

Arab 'Âribah:

This category of Arabs is the progeny of Qahtân. Prior to Qahtân from Nûh ﷺ none of these ancestors had Arabic as their language. The progeny of Qahtân used Arabic for the first time, which they amalgamated from the *Arab Bâ'idah*. The Qahtân tribes are divided in two types, Yemeniah and Sabâiyah.

Scholars are widely divided over the genealogical issue of Qahtân. Some of them say that he was the son of Aber bin Shâlikh (Shelah) bin Arfakhshand bin Sâm bin Nûh, and the brother of Qane and Yaqtan. Torah doesn't mention it, but Qane and Yaqtan are mentioned therein. According to others, Yaqtan is derived from Qahtân, in other words, what has been called Yaqtan is actually Qahtân. Ibn Hishâm says that Ya'rub bin Qahtân is also called Yemen and the country of Yemen was named after him. Now, if Qahtân belonged to the progeny of Ismail (Ishmael) ﷺ, the whole of Arabia would be descending from Ismail ﷺ for only two persons, Qahtân and Adnân are the remote ancestors of all the tribes of Arabia. But the most confirmed and acceptable understanding is that Qahtân and Yaqtân are the same person and the Qahtân tribe does not precede Banu Ismail.

Genealogy of Banu Sâm

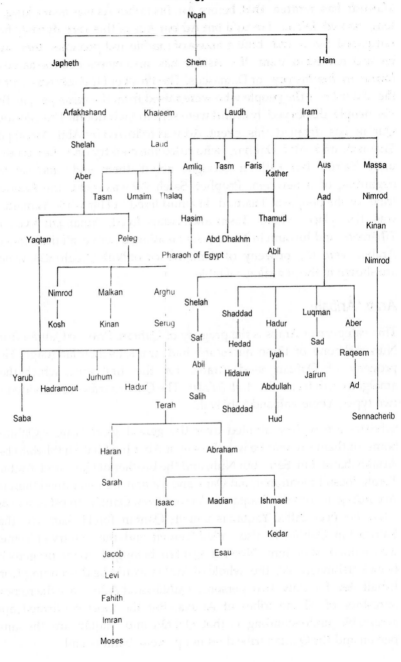

.*Arab 'Âribah* or Qahtân tribes have produced some famous kings who had the whole of Arabia under their control. Ya'rub bin Qahtân did away with all the races and traces of the *Arab Bâ'idah*. A short genealogical table of Banu Qahtân may be seen on the next page.

Yemen is supposed to be origin and the ancient land of the Qahtân tribes. Among them, Himyari and Azdi tribes are most renowned. Azdi tribes ruled over the city of Saba and southern Arabia. They paid special attention to the progress and prosperity of the Yemenite population. Queen Bilqis was from them and she was a contemporary of Sulaiman (Solomon) ﷺ. The *Tâbi'iyah* kings who reigned over Yemen and Hadramout also belonged to them. One of the tribes of Azdi shifted to Al-Madinah, settled and ruled there. Khuzâ'ah turned towards Makkah and defeated the Jurhum tribe who was then in control of the affairs there. Nasr, the son of Azd settled in Tihâmah; and Imrân, a son of Khuzâ'ah settled in Oman, and their children came to be known as Azd Oman, while another one named Ghassân settled in the frontier area of Syria and ruled over the frontier tribes. In Yemen, the rule of Qahtâni sultans extended up to 7 CE. Ghassân bordered on the Roman Empire, while the Qahtâni state of Hirah was near the Persian Empire. At the time of the advent of Islam, the Qahtân tribes were very strong and in a commanding position in the whole of Arabia.

Arab Musta'ribah:

This category of the Arabs refers to Banu Adnân or the progeny of Ismail (Ishmael) ﷺ. They came to Arabia from the outside, therefore they are called *Arab Musta'ribah* or the mixed Arabs. Ibrahim's mother tongue was 'Ajami or Persian. When Ibrahim (Abraham) ﷺ left Ismail (Ishmael) ﷺ in Makkah along with his mother Hâjira (Hagar), they learned Arabic from the Qahtâni tribe Jurhum, which was already settled in Makkah, and later Arabic became the mother tongue of the progeny of Ismail ﷺ. Ismail's mother passed away when he was only 15 years old. After the demise of his mother, Ismail ﷺ made up his mind to leave Makkah and to settle somewhere in Syria. But the people of the Jurhum tribe in unison requested him to change his mind.

Genealogy of Banu Qahtan

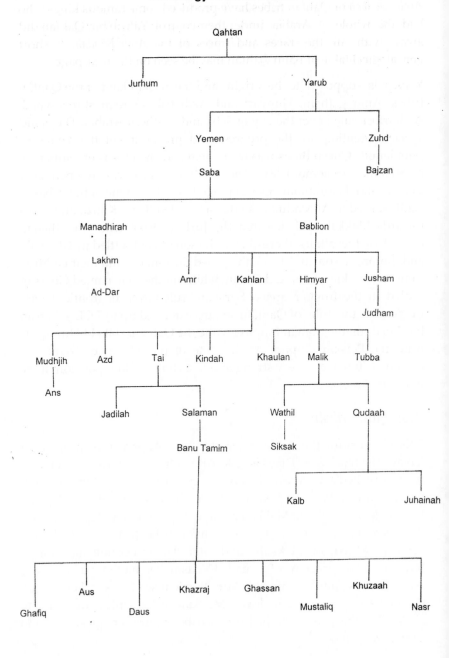

He was then married to Amârah bint Saeed bin Usâmah belonging to Amâliqah family. After a short time, Ibrahim ﷺ came and Ismail divorced his wife according to the instructions of his father, and then married Syedah bint Mudâd bin Amr of the Jurhum tribe. Following these events, both Ibrahim ﷺ and Ismail ﷺ started building the Ka'bah on the old foundations made by Adam ﷺ. Ibrahim ﷺ would lay the bricks while Ismail ﷺ would hand him the kneaded clay and the stones while both of them were supplicating:

"Our Lord! Accept this from us. Verily, you are the All-Hearer, the All-Knower." (2:127)

When the wall of the Ka'bah was raised to such an extent that the work of construction was impeded, Ibrahim ﷺ stood up on a piece of stone to resume his work. This place is called the 'Station of Ibrahim'. When the Ka'bah was near completion, Ibrahim ﷺ asked Ismail ﷺ to bring a special stone to be put at the base as a cornerstone so that place could be distinguished. Ismail ﷺ led by Jibril ﷺ brought *Hajar Aswad* (the Black Stone) from Boqabis mountain and Ibrahim ﷺ put it in the selected spot. This is the same stone that is kissed during the circumambulation (*Tawâf*) of the Ka'bah. After rebuilding the Ka'bah, Ibrahim ﷺ and Ismail ﷺ took their followers to Mina and Arafat, sacrificed their animals and circumambulated the Ka'bah. Ibrahim ﷺ later departed to Syria and continued to visit the Ka'bah every year, performing *Hajj* until the end of his life.

Ismail ﷺ settled in Makkah for the rest of his life. The tribe Banu Jurhum (Jurhum the second) had already settled in Makkah and the Amâliqah tribe settled in the suburbs of Makkah. (This was not the Amâliqah tribe of *Arab Bâ'idah*.) Some people from these tribes believed in Ismail ﷺ while others kept to their old faith. Ismail died, according to the Torah, at the age of 137 years. He was survived by twelve sons whose descendants multiplied so much that the land of Makkah could not contain them, and so they spread all over the Hijâz. The trusteeship of Ka'bah and the leadership of Makkah remained continuously with the descendants of Ismail ﷺ. Among his children was Adnân, the son of Kedar. The progeny of Adnân includes all the renowned tribes of Banu Ismail, and so the *Arab Musta'ribah* of Banu Ismail are called the people of Adnân.

Genealogy of Banu Adnan

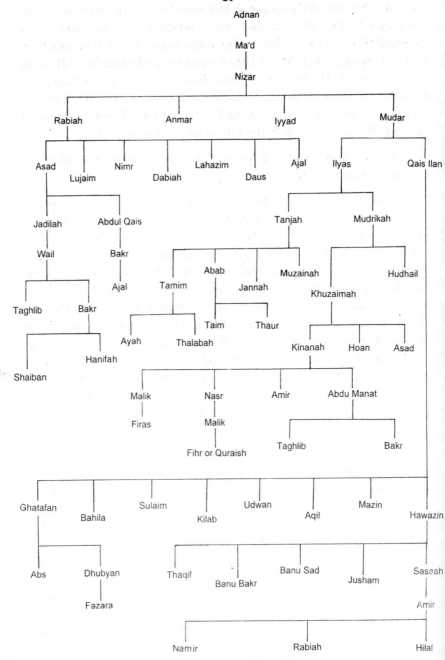

The son of Adnân was called Ma'd and his grandson was called Nizâr. Nizâr had four sons from whom all the Adnân tribes branched out. As a result of this all the Adnân tribes are called Ma'di or Nizâri. The genealogical table of the Adnân tribes is given on the facing page.

Adnân Tribes:

Among the Adnân tribes Iyyâd, Rabi'ah and Mudar achieved fame. To the well-known tribe of Mudar, belonged the Kinânah tribe which had an eminent person named Fihr bin Mâlik who was also called Quraish. The progeny of Quraish gave birth to many tribes, among them Banu Sahm, Banu Makhzum, Banu Jumh, Banu Taim, Banu Adi, Banu Abdud-Dâr, Banu Zuhrah, and Banu Abd Manâf gained much fame. Abd Manâf had four sons namely Abd Shams, Naufal, Abdul-Muttalib and Hâshim. Among the children of Hâshim was born Muhammad ﷺ bin Abdullâh bin Abdul-Muttalib bin Hâshim who is the last Prophet and to whom belongs the entire Muslim *Ummah* (community). The aim of this book is to clarify the state and condition of his *Ummah* (community) alone.

Abd Shams' son was Umayyah whose offspring are called Banu Umayyah. When the Adnân tribes, defeated by Khuzâ'ah left Makkah, they spread over different parts of Arabia. Banu Bakr settled in Bahrain, Banu Hanifah in Yamâmah, Banu Taghlib on the banks ːf Euphrates, Banu Tamim in Algiers, Banu Sulaim in the suburbs of Al-Madinah, Banu Thaqif in Tâ'if, Banu Asad in the west of Kufah and Banu Kinânah in Tihâmah. Only the Quraish tribes from among the Adnân remained living in Makkah and its suburbs and they were in disarray. Qusai bin Kilâb (who was in 5th century Christian Era) united them. By uniting various Quraish tribes, he brought not only Makkah but also the entire Hijâz under his control. Thus, the trusteeship of the House of Ka'bah once again came to the Adnân tribe. Qusai did some repair work on the Ka'bah and constructed for himself a big palace of which a spacious hall was set aside for the people to assemble for consultations and serious discussions. It was named Dâr-un-Nadwah. It also served as the seat of power from where Qusai performed official business. Qusai had also advanced a proposal that during the *Hajj* days the pilgrims should be served food for three days and all the Quraish should make contributions for that. In short, Qusai had achieved both religious and temporal power in Makkah and the Hijâz. Qusai died in 480 CE and his son Abdud-Dâr became his successor.

After the death of Abdud-Dâr, his grandsons and the sons of his brother Abd Manâf fell out with one another. Mediation by the influential people of Makkah brought the situation back to normal by defining each group's responsibilities such as providing water, collection of contributions and taxes, and acting as host to the pilgrims. Abdud-Dâr's grandsons were entrusted with the task of military arrangements providing security for the Ka'bah and looking after Dâr-un-Nadwah. After a short time Abd Manâf's son Abd Shams handed over his right to rule to his younger brother Hâshim. Hâshim was very popular among the Makkans for his trading ability, wealth and generosity. He benefited the Quraish immensely, he persuaded the Quraish to widen the scope of their trading activities, which was very profitable for them.

How Abdul-Muttalib was named:

Hâshim married the daughter of the chieftain of Al-Madinah (Yathrib at that time). She gave birth to a son who was named Shaibah. While the boy was still a child, Hâshim died. His brother Muttalib became the ruler of Makkah. Hâshim's son, Shaibah was raised in Al-Madinah. When Muttalib came to know that Hâshim's son had grown up, he himself went to Al-Madinah to bring his nephew back to Makkah. When Muttalib came to Makkah along with his nephew Shaibah, the Makkans mistook him as the slave of Muttalib. Although Muttalib tried his level best to remove the misunderstanding, it proved an exercise in futility and the name stayed with him and he was thereafter called Abdul-Muttalib. Abdul-Muttalib resembled his father in regard to character, honor and renown. The power and influence of Abdul-Muttalib aroused competition until it became unbearable for Umayyah's son Harb. He challenged Abdul-Muttalib to combat. In accordance with the practices of the time, a judge was appointed who gave his judgment in favor of Abdul-Muttalib. This decision aggravated enmity between Banu Umayyah and Banu Hâshim.

During the time of Abdul-Muttalib, an army from Abyssinia headed by a chieftain called Abrahah, launched an attack on Makkah; but the army, known as the people of the *Fil* (Elephant), was completely destroyed by a natural calamity and heavenly intervention. The genealogical relations of the Quraish tribes are given in the table on the facing page.

Family of Abd Manâf:

Of all the tribes, Abd Manâf was considered, in the whole of Arabia, as the most noble and respectable. After them their sons also excelled all the nobles of Arabia. The real name of Abd Manâf was Mughirah, who was also called Qamar and Syed. Since his brothers were named Abdud-Dâr and Abdul-Uzza, he came to be called Abd Manât and finally Abd Manâf.

Moral Condition of Arabia

Arabia was, as mentioned in previous pages, the cradle of the Sâm (Shem, son of Noah ﷺ) dynasty from the days old. Since very little is known of the *Arab Bâ'idah*, it cannot be definitely said what was the moral condition of the *Arab Bâ'idah* as compared to contemporary nations of the world. However, it may be conjectured that in the earlier times when human population was very sparse in the inhabited quarter of the world, by and large, there would be many similarities concerning their moral standing. Before the progress and development made by Banu Ismail, and after the *Arab Bâ'idah*, traces are found of many realms and kingdoms from the time of the Qahtân Arab's power throughout Arabia. But in no period of their history did any one kingdom enjoy undivided power over the entirety of Arabia. There were provinces with separate rulers, some of them more renowned than others. However, inside the country, independent homeless bands wandered aimlessly with their tents loaded on their camels. Lack of pasture, water and the necessities of life always kept the Arabs wandering and passing their days in hardship and monotony. The lack of the necessities of life caused them to neglect building a society. Their way of life showed no distinct mark or sign of change and reform.

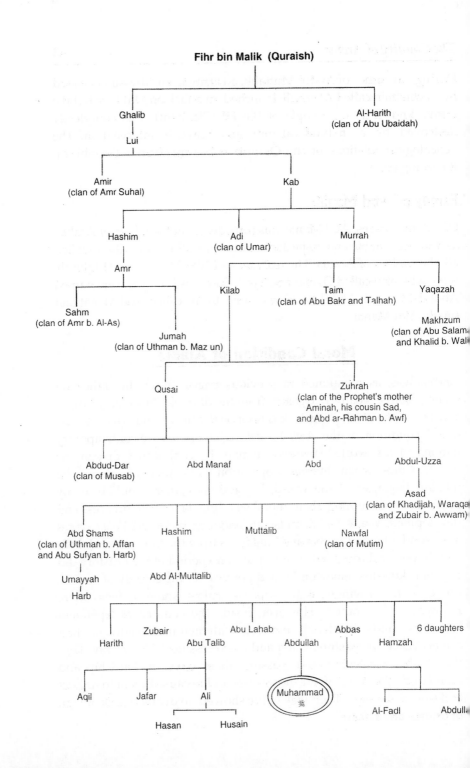

Life consisted of few activities and it had a uniformity of events that gave them a great deal of leisure time. A large number of vast deserts, the absence of production and indigenous things of value and the dearth of populated lands and cities never interested any foreign power to turn towards Arabia with expansionist ideas, nor were there any means or reasons to attract tourists and traders to the peninsula. Thus the people of Arabia were generally unaware of the progress and development of other nations of the world and their society, character and way of living. No foreign nation even exercised its influence on the Arabs.

Assertions of Dignity

Under these circumstances and in such an environment only two traits of character easily developed in the people of Arabia. One, the development of the art of poetry for which they had a great deal of leisure time at their disposal, passing nights in the open desert and they were free of any disciplined stream of thought. Both of these states served as great stimuli. Second, the tremendous effort to survive and the subjection to a life of hardship made them extremely fond of fighting and tests of strength. Constant mutual combat led them naturally to self-praise and a growing discretion for exhibiting a sense of dignity.

Pride and boasting, two typical qualities of man, led to bravery and generosity defining distinct roles which they followed with great interest. Idleness and deep indulgence in poetic composition turned them to lovemaking and drinking. But bravery and boldness had made them hospitable to a high degree and firm in fulfilling their promise as a matter of honor. Gambling, archery, assemblies for the recital of poetic verses, assertions of dignity, and competitions were some of the means of passing their time. In short, Arabia and its climate conditioned the Arab character.

Hud ﷺ and Saleh ﷺ and several other Prophets were sent to the *Arab Bâ'idah*. But the disrespect and disobedience shown to these Prophets resulted in their utter and total destruction. Some Prophets were also sent to another sections of the Arabs, the Qahtân Arabs, but they paid very little attention to their call with the result that they met their doom time and again. Moreover, they could not profit substantially from the teachings of their Prophets on account of their rebellious attitude and undisciplined thinking. Some of the people of Arabia believed in Ibrahim ﷺ and Ismail ﷺ. In the sphere of faith and religion, their genealogical pride and egotism and the glorification of their ancestors led them to hero worship which ultimately paved the way to carving idols in their names to be worshipped. Idol worship led them to superstitions and many other irrational ideas.

When the Qahtân tribes were on the decline and Banu Ismail (the Adnân tribes) had gained ground, the invasion of Makkah by the Khuzâ'ah tribe resulted in the defeat of the Jurhum tribe. The integrity of the Adnân tribes was violated by this defeat and it injured the power and dignity of the emerging Banu Ismail in the Hijâz. It resulted in a fierce rivalry between the Adnân and Qahtân tribes, which gave birth to small clans which were unable to transform themselves into a united rule of significant importance.

The larger domains were not much better than anarchy, no Arabian king and his system of rule over his subjects was as remarkable for law and order as that of the ordinary feudal system used in Persia. This anarchy and unbridled freedom gave rise to untold immorality, misbehavior and disrespectful rudeness which permeated the whole social life of the Arabs and this human depravity continued until the light of Islam rose from the dark horizon of this country.

Most of the Arabs were nomads, and very few had settled permanently in townships and populated areas. The Arabs were very fond of keeping an exact genealogy of their ancestors preserved by memory. They would mention the names and deeds of their forefathers with pride and thus animate zeal and the valor of their people during fighting.

Perhaps it was the impact of the climatic conditions of the country or their fondness for genealogy that caused the Arabs to have a very strong memory. It was something simple for them to keep in memory accurately odes of tribute that were several hundred verses long, after hearing them only once. Their art of poetry and command of language led them to such a state of development that they named all the non-Arabs as '*Ajam* (literally: mute). If an individual of one clan was killed by that of another, the clan belonging to the dead person would not rest until they took revenge. To be at rest without an act of retaliation was a matter of utter shame and disgrace for them. Reverence for the Ka'bah and performing *Hajj* was a sign of power for all the Arabs through all their generations. Helping the helpless and the oppressed and keeping firm against the oppressors were qualities appreciated by one and all. Timidity and miserliness were taken as the greatest defects and the worst flaw of character.

Months of Peace

They fixed one or several months of the year when they considered fighting as unlawful. During this span of peace and order all fighting was suspended. And during those specific days they would visit the Ka'bah and perform the *Hajj*. It was during these days that large commercial fairs were held with poetic recitals and they offered great opportunities for making new trading contacts. Some other traits of the Arabs are also worthy of notice.

Faith and Religion

Before the appearance of Islam, the Arabs were passing through a state where some of their tribes acknowledged neither the Creator nor reward and punishment, while others were convinced of the existence of the Creator but not of reward and punishment and the Day of Judgment. Mostly they worshipped idols and stars; some of them worshipped fire also.

They had transformed the Ka'bah into a center of idolatry and kept 360 idols inside the Ka'bah. Jews had also come from Syria to settle in Al-Madinah (Yathrib at that time) and in its suburbs. They began to arrive there from a short time after the death of Musa ﷺ. Among those Jews, Banu Quraizah, Banu Nadir, and Banu Qanuqâ' were the most renown. Some Christians also settled in the Ghassân and Najrân area and some people of Quzâ'ah tribe had also converted to Christianity.

Idolatry:

Idolatry was openly practiced all over Arabia. Four hundred years before the advent of Muhammad ﷺ in era of King Shâpur of Persia, Amr bin Luhai bin Hârithah bin Imrâ'-ul-Qais bin Tha'labah bin Mazin bin Azd bin Kahlân bin Bablion bin Saba, the King of Hijâz was the first to install the idol named Hubal at the top of the Ka'bah and placed two idols Isâf and Nâilah at the well of Zamzam and persuaded the people to worship them. This Amr bin Luhai had totally rejected the concept of the Day of Judgment.

Yaguth, Ya'uq, Nasr, Wadd and Suwâ' were adopted by different tribes for each of them had its separate idol. Wadd was carved in the shape of man while Nâilah and Suwâ' were in the form of a woman. Yaguth had the shape of a lion, Ya'uq of horse, and Nasr of vulture. Some tribes shared idols, Tasm and Jadais had a common idol. The Kalb tribe worshipped Wadd whose center was Dumat-ul-Jandal. Banu Tamim adored Taim. Suwâ' was worshipped by the Hudhail, Mudhij and the Yemenite tribes worshipped Yaguth. Dhil-Kalâ' worshipped Nasr at Himyar, the Hamdân worshipped Ya'uq, Banu Mughith of Banu Thaqif tribe served as the guards of Lât at Tâ'if, the Quraish and Banu Kinânah worshipped Uzza while Banu Shaibah were the caretakers of Uzza. Manât was adored by the Aus and Khazraj tribes, Jehar by Banu Hawâzin, Awâl by the Bakr and Taghlib, Muharraq by Banu Bakr bin Wâil, Sa'd by Banu Malkân, Sa'eer by Banu Antarah, Amyanas by Banu Khaulân, Raza by Banu Tai, and Dhul-Kaffain by the Daus. Besides the idols mentioned, many idols like Jarish, Shâriq, A'im, Madân, Auf, and Manâf were very famous and every one of them was the deity of one tribe or another. Whenever any congregation of idolaters was organized, and if an Arab was not able to attend it during the fixed days, he would fix a stone called *Duwwâr* and go around it like the Ka'bah to compensate for missing the congregation.

In Arabia, there were other centers of idolatry besides the Ka'bah. Ghatfân had constructed a house similar to the Ka'bah and called it Qalis and they even performed *Hajj* there. Banu Khath'am had also built a house calling it Dhul-Jhalasah to perform *Hajj* there. Dhul-

Ka'bât was the center for worship of the Rabi'ah. There was a tribal temple in Najrân also which was built with three hundred skins and was called the Ka'bah of Najrân. The idolaters of Arabia would visit it as they did with the Ka'bah. Moreover, they had also built a *Haram* (sanctuary) around it where even a murderer or assassin was safe. On the top of the Ka'bah there was another idol called Shams. Pictures of Ibrahim, Ismail, Isa (Jesus) and Maryam (Mary) عليهم السلام were also worshipped in the Ka'bah.

Sacrifice:

The idolaters, when coming to perform *Hajj*, brought camels for sacrificing and offering to their idols. They had a practice to suspend shoes from the necks of the camels and marked them to signify them as sacrificial animals. Nobody would then get in the way of the animals. Moreover, the calves of the camels and sheep and other animals were sacrificed to the idols. Some of the tribes even sacrificed humans to the idols. According to some historians, the idolaters of Arabia believed in the Oneness of God and acknowledged Him as One. They worshipped idols because they believed that they will intercede with Allâh for them. Some of the tribes entertained the belief that the person on whose grave a she-camel was sacrificed, will on the Day of Judgment, rise from his grave mounted on his she-camel. This belief indicates that they believed in Day of Resurrection and some form of Judgment.

Star-Worshipping:

When the Arabs were still in ignorance, worshipping stars was very common. Historians have no substantial proof if Arabia, Egypt, Greece or Persia were the first to institute the worship of stars or if they came to it separately. However, it is hard to imagine that worshipping stars came to Arabia from outside. The sun was worshipped by Himyar tribe, the moon by the Kinânah, Dahrân by Tamim, Jupiter by the Lakhm and Judhâm, Suhail by the Tai, Shera by the Qais and Mercury by the Asad. Most of the tribal idols were named with the names of stars. Stone idols and noted stars were worshipped commonly by different tribes. They often based their important affairs on the rising and setting of certain stars.

It is not surprising that the people passing their days and nights in open fields and deserts had their attention focused on the stars and planets and acknowledging some of them as their deities. From *Sûrat Nuh* of the Qur'ân it comes to light that even during the era of Nuh الـعـليه, Iraqi Arabs worshipped Yaguth, Ya'uq, Wadd, Nasr, and Suwâ', which are all named after stars. It makes it very clear that star worship in Arabia was a very old affair. The moon was worshipped more than any other object.

Soothsaying:

Soothsayers were found in large number in Arabia. A *Kâhin* was one who claimed to have information about the unseen events of the past while, those giving information of the future were called *Arrâf*. Both men and women claimed knowledge of the unseen. Among the soothsayers of Arabia Af'a, Jadhimah, Abrash, Shaq and Satih were well-known. Another kind of soothsayer was known as *Nâzir*, they could tell about the unseen by focusing their eyes on a mirror or on a tray of water. They included casters of pebbles and the pits of fruit. They all belonged to the same category but they were ranked below the soothsayers, while those making amulets were considered the lowest.

Omens:

The Arabs also believed in good and bad omens. They held crows to be very inauspicious and something that causes separation. Since the crow is called *Ghurâb* in Arabic, they called travelling as *Ghurbat*, and the traveler as *Gharib*, as according to them, the influence of a crow causes separation and causes man to suffer the hardships of travelling. And owl was also very unlucky to them for its hooting cries, they believed caused death and destruction. Sneezing also carried an ill omen to them. Some of them were sorcerers and they dealt in sorcery and performed heavy exercises to befriend Satan.

Fighting

Fighting would break out over petty matters and insignificant incidents. Once hostilities began they could linger on for several generations and even centuries. Most of their fighting started without any substantial reason. There were more than one hundred feuds during the Days of Ignorance in Arabia that were famous, for instance, Bu'âth, Kilab, Fatrat, Nakhklah, Qarn, Subân and Hâtib were the names of well-known feuds.

No tribe ever benefited from these feuds; they only suffered destruction and the loss of life and property. They had an old practice of putting to death the women and children of the defeated enemy after taking them prisoner. However, if a person had eaten from their food or had received hospitality from them previously, they were safe from being killed. They would shave the heads of those whom they released.

Most disputes would be settled by a challenge to single combat. They took special care of their horses and weapons. The battle array of armies was not in practice. Anyone achieving perfection in swordmanship, archery, cavalry, or fighting with lances was held in high esteem and his name and reputation would quickly spread far and wide. Some particular tribes gained distinction in the use of some particular weapon. They had special names for weapons, swords, bows and horses, which were famous throughout the land. For instance, the name of the sword of Harth bin Abu Shimr Ghassâni was Khudhum, while the sword of Abdul-Muttalib bin Hâshim was called Atshân and that of Mâlik bin Zubair was Dhun-Nun. These evidences let us know that the people of Arabia had a great zest for fighting and killing. This is the reason behind thousands of names given to horses and swords in Arabic.

Illicit Sex

Arabs in the Age of Ignorance had no custom of observing *Hijâb* (covering of women) and their women would come freely before strange men. The lack of the necessities of life and other time-consuming affairs, an irresponsible sense of freedom, over indulgence in poetic composition, their assertion of pride and superiority, and the hot climate of the country was enough to instigate this tendency. Anyone who never fell in love with a strange woman was disrespected. Some tribes were renowned for their love making. Banu Adhrah's love gained so much celebrity and renown that it became proverbial:

أشق مِن بنى عذرة

That is, so-and-so is a lover greater than Banu Adhrah. Someone asked a bedouin which tribe did he belong to? He replied that he was from a tribe that when they fall in love they pass away. A girl heard it and remarked: "By the Lord of Ka'bah, you are from Banu Adhrah."

Poetry

During the Age of Ignorance in Arabia everyone participated in the art of poetry. Men, women, children, old and young, all were poets of higher or lower degree. They were born with poetry and eloquence. Their poetic exercises generally were impromptu. They needed no thinking or reflecting and never needed to search for topics. They were so proud of their eloquence and command of language that they considered all the non-Arabs as unable to speak. But the Qur'ân shattered the arrogance of their eloquence and rhetoric into pieces and they had to bow down before the glory of the Book of Allâh.

The one whose ode of tribute was acknowledged as the best in a poetic congregation on the occasion of fairs, special functions and *Hajj,* was immediately accepted as the best among them in position and stature. To them poets were equal to brave commanders and kings or even greater than them in status. In fact, it was an easy job for the poets to cause tribes to fight against one another, to make tribes extraordinarily brave, to keep the fighting going or to put an end to it. The best odes of tribute were hung over the walls of the Ka'bah. Thus seven such odes of tribute known as the Seven Golden Odes, which were written by Imra'-ul Qais bin Hijr Kindi, Zuhair bin Abu Salma Muzani, Labid bin Rabi'ah, Amr bin Kulthum and Antarah Absi.

Passion for Hunting

During the Age of Ignorance, the Arabs had a great enthusiasm for hunting and so there are a great number of terms in Arabic for hunting activities. The game which moves from right to left was called *Sâneh,* while the one going from left to right was called *Bâreh.* The game coming from the front was called *Nâteh* and the one from behind was *Qa'eed.* The hunter's ambush was named *Qarrah. Zabiah* was the name given to the ditch dug for hunting a lion. They gave the name *Talabbud* to the state of the hunter when he crawled on his stomach sticking close to the earth, and the state of going out to hunt and coming back without hunting was called *Ikhfâq*. On hunting an animal they ate its meat without any sense of its being permitted or prohibited. Islam brought about the limitation of lawful and unlawful and imposed certain restrictions on hunting.

Food and Clothes

Arabia produces neither silk nor cotton. Some regions produce them in such a meager quantity that is quite insufficient for the needs of the people. Yemen has been noted for its cloth from ancient times. The Arabs generally had very simple clothes to wear. Wearing coarse clothes with leather patches was customary. Some people would make a sheet by joining small leather patches held together by pins, and such a sheet or mantle served the purpose of wrapping and spreading. Garments were also woven from camel and sheep hair, and those pieces of cloth were also used for making tents and for bedding and carpeting. Loose low hanging colorless shirts, waist sheets and turbans or scarves on the head were standard dress. They knew about aloeswood, ambergris, and incense. Their food was also very simple and unceremonious. They could be content with unpalatable food with a bad taste. Meat and flesh happened to be very tasty and valuable things to them. Milk and meat were most common. Cheese, battered barley grain, dates, olive oil, and *Harirah* were their common items. Sieving of flour was not a common practice; they rather baked bread with unsieved flour. They had no proper etiquette of dining. This can be assessed from the dos and don'ts prescribed by the Prophet ﷺ for eating and drinking in *Ahadith* which forbid many kinds of misbehavior like gluttony, shamelessness, unclean habits and nonsensical talk while eating.

Plunder

As mentioned previously, Arabia had two types of people, one settled in cities and settlements and another living a nomadic life, the latter were larger in number. Although the citizens carried some qualities like rights of neighbors, trusteeship and honesty, but the defects of deceit, cheating and conniving in trade and business were plentiful. They were expert in raiding and highway robbery of the nomadic type Almost all were addicted to looting the travelers and snatching away goods by force. On finding someone making a journey alone, they covered and hid the wells which were on the way with grass and other things so that the traveler would die of thirst and they would take his goods. Some of them were proverbially expert in committing theft. These thieves were called *Dhubân-ul-Arab* (wolves of Arabia).

Conceit

Conceit had touched its peak during Arabian Ignorance. Jadhimah Abrash was so haughty that he never appointed any one as an adviser to consult with. He would say that *Farqadain* (the two brilliant stars near the Polestar) were his companions. Many other tribes were well known for these base qualities and none of the tribes were free from this conceit. As a result of this, they never listened to the good counsel and preaching of the Prophets and religious guides for obedience was a trait shameful to them.

Unending Malice

In case they failed to take revenge on their enemy or assassin during his lifetime, they made his sons and grandsons the target of their revenge and they passed their days in discontentment until they took out their vengeance on their enemies. They would take revenge even if the reason behind it had been forgotten. They would be intent to kill someone out of enmity without even telling anyone what was the cause of the hostility.

Mourning the Dead

Upon the death of someone, his relatives would tear at their faces and hair and cry in pain. Women would follow the funeral with their hair untied and head dusted. Like the Hindus in India shaving their head and beard out of sorrow for the dead, in Arabia during the Days of Ignorance, women would shave their heads. Women were also called for lamenting which they did at the top of their voices; after the burial, these women were served food.

Superstition and Credulity

They believed in the existence of jinns, demons and fairies. They also believed that fairies could fall in love with human males, and jinn could form physical contacts with human females. Although they considered jinn as invisible creature, they believed that the union of the material and immaterial could bear babies. The Arabs believed that Jurhum was born as a result of union between a human and an angel. This was their belief also about the Queen Bilqis of Saba (Queen of Sheba). About Umar bin Yarbu they thought that he was born with the union of a human and a fairy.

The she-camel bearing five calves and the fifth being a male, was called *Bahirah* and they left it free by piercing its ears. She was at liberty to go and graze anywhere and nobody objected to it. In case any sheep bore a male, it was offered to the idols; and if it happened to be female, they kept it for themselves. In case of a male and female, they held back from sacrificing them and called them *Wasilah*. The male camel that had fathered ten calves was held in great honor. They neither loaded it nor made it a mount and left it free like a bull. It was called *Hâm*.

They used to keep three arrows before the idols or at the threshold of the temples. They wrote *La* (no) on one arrow and *Na'm* (yes) on another. The third would be blank. In case of any problem they would take out one arrow from the quiver. If the arrow with *La* written on it came out, they dropped the plan of doing what they wanted, and if the arrow showing *Na'm* was picked, they thought themselves permitted to do whatever they had planned. If the blank arrow came out, they continued the exercise until the arrow with either *La* or *Na'm* came out. While setting out on a journey they would tie a knot on a thin branch of a certain type of tree called *Ratm*. On coming back they would notice whether the knot was intact or untied. If they found the knot untied, they believed that their wives must have committed adultery while they were away. At the death of a person, his she-

camel was fastened to his grave with her eyes closed until she died
there or the head of the she-camel was pulled towards her breast and
tied to it, and they would left her until she died. It was done in
accordance with the belief that the dead person, when raised from his
grave, would find the she-camel and have it as his mount. They
believed that if a person went to a settlement and was afraid of an
epidemic there, he would be saved if he cried loudly like an ass
standing at the gate of the settlement. When the number of camels in
one's possession would reach more than one thousand, he would take
out both the eyes of the bull among them to save all the other camels
from calamity. When a camel would develop mange, the healthy one,
instead of the sick, was branded with the belief that the sick one
would restore its health. The famous poet Nâbighah says in his
couplet:

> "You left the stranger and loaded his burden upon me, as they
> leave the camel suffering from mange and brand the healthy
> camel grazing peacefully instead."

Similarly, they would beat the ox if a cow refused to drink water.
They believed that the ox was possessed by a jinn who would stop the
cows from drinking water. They believed that if the killer of someone
went unpunished, a bird named *Hamah* would come out of the skull
of the dead person and would go on crying: "Give me water, give me
water," until the crime was avenged. They believed that some person
had a snake in his stomach and when it was hungry it would tear and
eat away the flesh from the ribs of the person. They had a belief that if
the children of a woman kept dying, they could be saved from dying
if the woman concerned trampled the dead body of a noble and
wealthy person with her feet. They also believed that the jinn feared
rabbits and so they suspended rabbit bones from the neck of their
children to keep them safe from the ill effect of the jinn.

Killing of Daughters

The custom of killing their daughters was rampant among the Banu
Tamim and the Quraish. They took pride in killing their daughters
and it was for them a status symbol. This heartlessness reached such a
height in some tribes that when the daughter became five or six years

old and start uttering sweet words, the stone-hearted father would take her in beautiful garments to a place outside his settlement where he had already dug a deep ditch. He would then make his daughter stand beside the ditch and then push her into the ditch stoning her to death while she called for her father's help. No screaming and crying could melt his heart and he would return after filling the ditch. They took pride in burying their daughters alive. Qais bin Âsim, a man from Banu Tamim, buried his ten daughters alive in this manner. Although no tribe of Arabia was free from this inhuman custom, some tribes did it more than others.

Gambling

The Arabs were very fond of gambling too. They gambled with arrows which had no feathers. They were ten in number, and their names in order were: (1) *Ghadh*, (2)*Tawam*, (3) *Raqib*, (4) *Nâfis*, (5) *Hals*, (6) *Mabal*, (7) *Mualla*, (8) *Fasih*, (9) *Manih* and (10) *Waghd*. Each of them had its own share, for instance, *Ghadh* had one, *Tawâm* had two, and *Raqib* had three, and it kept increasing in this way till *Mualla* had seven shares, while the last three arrows had no share. Ten wealthy persons would buy fat goats and divide them into twenty-eight shares. The arrows would be handed to a designated person who would take out and give each person an arrow one by one, and each person got his share according to his arrow's share. They played such games of chance before Hubal at the Ka'bah. Another form of gambling was that they collected some sand and hid something in it. Then after dividing the sand into two heaps they asked the players to tell in which heap was the hidden object. The one who guessed it correctly was declared the winner and those guessing incorrectly were declared as the losers.

Arabian Ignorance and Other Countries

What has been described in the previous sections refers to the condition of Arabia and its people before the appearance of Islam and the advent of the Prophet ﷺ. What has been stated regarding character, habits, living, religion, and beliefs reflects the conditions from one century before the era of the last Prophet ﷺ and remained unchanged until he was declared a Prophet. The reader can ponder over what kind of environment the Prophet ﷺ was sent to and how depraved were the people when Islam came to them. The following pages will give a picture of the magnificent revolution brought about by the teachings of the Prophet ﷺ and the impact of Islam as a force. This assessment may be correctly made when we cast a glance at the overall situation prevailing in the world and to see how Islam brought about change in the existing situation. It is appropriate at this time after assessing the situation in Arabia to take a look at what condition the world contemporary to that time was experiencing.

Persia (Iran)

Persia was reckoned among the most renowned, ancient and venerable civilizations. During the ancient times the people worshipped the moon, and a large number of religious guides came on the scene one after another to reform the situation. Before the end of this period Zoroaster gave currency to the fire worship. [The religion of Zoroaster was free from fire worship and proclaimed oneness of God but fire worship took over this religion later on.] He offered himself as a true guide and very soon it became the state religion and that of its subjects.

The Persians, possibly surpassed all other countries in terms of progress and development. During the height of its greatness and glory, Persian rule had stretched from Egypt to Mongolia and from the Himalayan range and Persian Gulf to the Altai Mountains. Persian society ruled over the whole of the Asian continent and their culture, civilization and ethical standards were considered worth following in every Asian country. At the time of the appearance of Islam, they had become so low and depraved that they had lost most of their good qualities after falling into the dark quagmire of polytheism. They had given Zoroaster divine attributes and enlisted him among their false deities. The creators of good and evil were worshipped in the name of *Yazdân* (Ahura Mazda—god of goodness) and *Ahriman* (Angra Mainyu—god of evil and darkness). They worshipped fire and light openly and fervently. The worship of the moon, the sun, the stars and the planets was also in vogue. Theft and highway robbery were rampant. Adultery was so much in force that the wicked Mazdak asked for a liaison with the Princess of Kisra (Chosroes) openly in the court and the ruler of Persia did not think it necessary to oppose this most unreasonable and immodest demand. Mutual dissension and bestiality, malice and enmity, cheating and deceit, treating the weak by the strong more disgracefully than even the animals were some of the defects that had sent Persia to the lowest level of depravity and degradation. Persia was bereft of all ethical and human qualities, and the country that was once the center of culture and civilization was groping in the dark. Not only that worship of stars, fire and heroes was their custom, the kings, ministers, commanders and nobles also made the people worship them. The Persian subject rose to freedom from this torment and the darkness was dispelled only when the Muslims marched into the Persian territories and brought it under their control.

Greece and Rome

Another great power and rival of Persia was the Roman Empire. Greek and Roman civilizations were also very ancient and magnificent and their arts and sciences and grandeur and glory had been universally known. No country of the world could surpass Greece in the spheres of medicine, mathematics, astronomy, logic, and philosophy. This country had produced Socrates, Hippocrates, Luqmân, Plato, and Aristotle. It was in this country that a conqueror and king like Alexander was born. The Roman Caesar whose capital was Constantinople, was not only an emperor but considered also a religious guide. But, despite all these material and scientific developments, both Greece and Rome had, during the sixth and seventh centuries, become steeped in such degradation and depravity that the darkness prevailing in Persia was in no way deeper than in Greece and Rome. As every indebted person in Persia would sell himself like a slave, Greece too had several kinds of slaves. One kind of slave could not be sold outside Greece, but all other kinds of slaves were sold in foreign lands like horses, oxen, camels, and goats. Any master had the right to kill his slave as anybody has the right to slaughter his animal. Parents would sell their children and make them slave of others. In Greece and Rome, slaves had no right to marry and there was no legal relation between the slaves and their children.

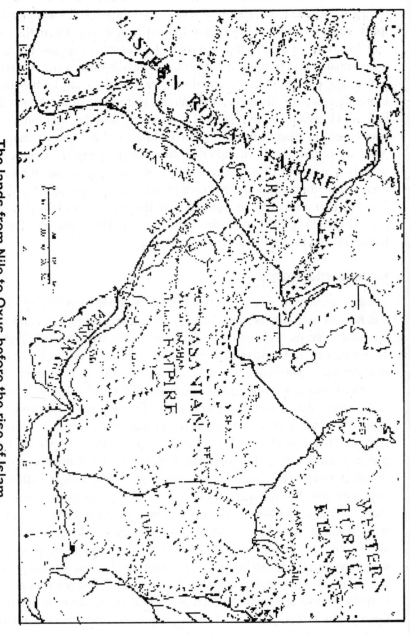

The lands from Nile to Oxus before the rise of Islam

Depravity of the Christians

For the first two hundred years after the birth of Isa (Jesus) ﷺ, there was no trace of a monk among the Christians. But during the sixth century, the number of monks rose to such an extent in Syria, Greece and Rome that anybody desirous of being held in high esteem became a monk. Gradually this custom prevailed among the womenfolk with the result that monasteries became centers of all kinds of shameful acts. Some monks lived in deserts.

Respect of women and parents had no place in their lives. Theft, adultery and cheating were most common. Begging was not a matter of shame which was in fact the logical result of being a monk. The concept of the oneness of God and divine worship was virtually lost. Certificates of deliverance could be had from the monks and religious guides by pleasing them through services. The rich considered it their legal right to have the poor serve them. Kings and commanders treated their subjects like animals and took control of the efforts of their labor and left them very little to live on.

Egypt

To assess the ancient position of Egypt and its social greatness, the mammoth construction of the Sphinx, the Egyptian pyramids and objects and articles recovered from the many excavations in recent times have a lot to tell about the glory and grandeur of ancient Egyptian society. Since Egypt is an agricultural country, it became the target of successive foreign attacks when it had grown weak. Persians, Greeks and Romans invaded it time and again and kept it under their control for long periods. It is a matter of conjecture that the society and civilization of the invaders favorably influenced the Egyptians.

Christianity was followed by a large section of the Egyptians during the reign of Romans. But, before the advent of Islam in Egypt, it was a country immersed in darkness and depravity. Christianity in Egypt was in no better position than pure idolatry. All the defects that had been part of Egyptian idolatry could be found among the Christians. The Romans and the Greeks who were known as ruling nations treated their subjects more disgracefully than even their animals. The defects found among the Greeks and the Romans took their worst forms among the Egyptians. Slavery was rife in the most wretched form. Alluring principles and rules were instituted for committing adultery and pillage. Human killings served as a source of entertainment. Women were encouraged to commit suicide. In short, the darkness prevailing in Egypt was not less than that of anywhere else. Egypt was replete with all the forms of degradation that could be thought of.

India

Great Maharajahs like Asoka, Chandra Gupta and Vikarmajeet had already passed away. Indians were particularly proud of their astronomy, mathematics and philosophy. They also retained the tales of founders of religions like Krishn, Ramchandra and Gautama, and the epics of Mahabharata and Ramayana. But the era we are referring to here is one when Buddhism was declining and making a way for Brahmanism. No province of the country had a magnificent leader. Idolatry was rampant in the entire country. Idol worship was considered as the only means of deliverance both in Buddhism and Brahmanism. In most cases, idols of Brahmans and Buddhas were kept side by side in the same temple and were worshipped with great fervor.

A Chinese traveler writes that no household was free from idols. The immodest and impure ways of Bam-Marga had achieved popularity all over the country. They had also instituted, like the Egyptians, rules and principles for committing adultery, which were essentially made a part of their religious rites. The Rajahs of Sindh set the example of marrying their own sisters. When Rajahs and rulers had reduced themselves to such human degradation, it is not surprising that their subjects followed them in meanness of character. Some books written in that period that are now available as part of the Hindu scriptures and religious books, bring to light the utter degradation of their style of living. Worship of stars, planets, mountains, rivers, trees, animals, snakes, stones and human genitals was rife in India. One can easily infer from this the depth of terrible darkness prevailing in India at that time.

China

The countries mentioned above lie around Arabia and these alone are taken as civilized. Only China may be added to this list. China was worse than all the others. The mixture of Confucianism, Taoism and Buddhism had made a mess of the cultural and moral condition of China. However, peace returned to China only when a band of Muslims settled in China and impressed their neighbors with their high moral examples. Human populations existed in Turkistan, Russia, and Europe too but either they were unknown to the rest of the world or they could hardly be called humans and they possessed no enviable qualities.

Conclusion

From the states and conditions observed above, it can be easily understood that, before or at the time of Muhammad ﷺ being commissioned as Prophet, the entire world had steeped in darkness. A state of ignorance had overtaken the entire inhabited part of the earth in a manner that not even a twinkling light of hope and guidance was visible. Never before had such a state came to pass when civilization, society, morality, knowledge, wisdom, and knowledge of Allâh had perished everywhere at the same time.

The whole inhabited earth had been sent the guidance of Allâh the Almighty, which kept coming to every country, and the sight of light and darkness continued appearing alternately like days and nights until night spread over the whole world. The time was right for the Prophet of Truth to be sent to all the countries of the world. Allâh the Almighty put to an end the teachings brought by the former Prophets. He brought to the surface the dire need for a new guide and leader for every part of the world. Thus the sad plight of the mankind was thirsting for a new guide. Allâh the Almighty chose Arabia to be the place of Prophethood and the birthplace of His Perfect Messenger and Guide. Thus the sun of Prophethood rose from Makkah to dispel darkness from the inhabited parts of the earth and illuminated the whole world with its bright rays.

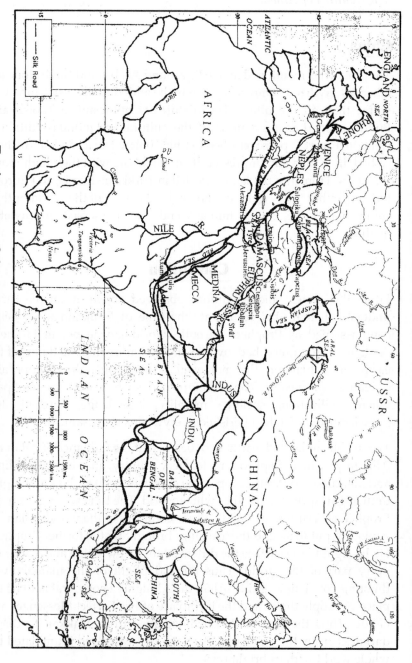

Trade routes of the seventh and eighth centuries CE

This book is inspired by this same rising sun. But, before coming to this point, the answer to the question why Arabia was chosen for the Prophethood of Muhammad ﷺ demands answers. Why was he not sent to any other country?

The Choice of Arabia

The most reasonable and definite answer to this question is that the last Prophet had, after all, to be born in any one particular country and so the question arises in every case. So, the question becomes meaningless.

Another answer to the question is that all the well-known countries had at one time attained progress and development and achieved distinction in the sphere of civilization, society, ethics and science. Moreover, every country had tasted victory and defeat in due course. No language of any other country of the world had achieved such perfection as Arabic, which had surpassed other languages in the power of expression.

If the Prophet ﷺ had been sent to any country other than Arabia, the message of the last Prophet ﷺ would have encountered complications due to the past and the previous history of victories and defeats and possession of or possession by the chosen country. There was also the risk of his message losing its power and grace and a part thereof might have been attributed to ancient traditions of the chosen country. The magnificent task of redressing civilization, character and spiritual values could not have been accomplished and all his endeavors would be lost in the ancient customs and traditions of the country concerned.

Moreover, any complete book of guidance is in need of a language superior to all others in power of expression, and no language was more appropriate than Arabic to bear the heavy spiritual and intellectual burden of Revelation. So, by any logic and reason, the last Prophet ﷺ must have honored Arabia as his birth place.

The people of Arabia neither became subject of any foreign power nor captured and ruled over any other country. Thus, to the Arabs, every nation or every country was alike. When they came out with Islam, all the civilized countries and nations from Spain on the eastern coast of Atlantic Ocean to China on the western coast of Chinese Sea, the entire human population was equally strange to them. Thus, Allâh the Almighty sent his religion through a nation for whom the whole world was equally strange.

Since the Arabian character, civilization and society were far from progress and development, it was obvious that it was this universal religion that made them highly civilized, morally disciplined, and a graceful nation, and the teachers and leaders of the world. The spiritual power of the Prophet ﷺ was so tremendous that every nation in every period during his time and after him benefited from him. Moreover, the Qur'ân is the culmination of all the teachings imparted by all the Prophets and guides.

The above last few sentences may be considered strange to the concrete principles of history writing. Since, this book of history is solely meant for Muslim readership and I, too, am a Muslim by the Grace of Allâh the Almighty, I cannot take back these words, which have naturally come from my pen. Whether I am expelled from the assembly of the historians or not, I shall feel happy if I am left to join the company of the Muslim *Ummah*.

Chapter 2

Prophet Muhammad ﷺ

The Dawn of Guidance

A little before sunrise, a soft light starts appearing from the east. As stated previously, the entire world was engulfed in the darkness of ignorance and disbelief. When the time came for the end of the dark night, the dawn broke to give glad tidings of the rising sun. Arabia which was then the center of darkness and whose deserts were facing the storms and evils of paganism, gradually began to show signs of the sun of Prophethood coming out and a stream of guidance gushing forth.

Nations of Arabia were living the life of moral depravity, ignorance and deviation. But right from the birth of the Prophet ﷺ, Arabian tribes began to show signs of noble sentiments and the dislike of evil. Waraqah bin Naufal bin Asad bin Abdul-Uzza, Uthmân bin Al-Huwairith bin Asad and Zaid bin Amr bin Nafil-the uncle of Umar bin Khattâb, and Ubaidullah bin Jahsh assembled at a place and began to think over their beliefs and actions. At last, each one of them showed disgust at the worship of idols and stones and set out to various places in search of the religion brought by Ibrahim ﷺ. Waraqah bin Naufal accepted Christianity and went through the Torah and the Gospel with rapt attention. Ubaidullah bin Jahsh found himself unshaken in the quest for religion seeking the worship of one God till Islam appeared and he earnestly embraced it. Then he migrated to Abyssinia and became a Christian. Uthmân bin Huwairith joined Caesar of Rome and accepted Christianity. Zaid bin Amr neither accepted Judaism nor Christianity nor continued to tread the path of idolatry. He acknowledged as unlawful the use of blood and dead animals and gave up bloodshed and severing of ties with relatives. On inquiry he would say that he worshipped the Lord of Ibrahim ﷺ, decried idolatry and counseled his people to desist from evil acts. He would often say:

> "O Allâh, had I been aware of the manner of worshipping, I would have worshipped none but You Alone and sought Your Pleasure. But I am unknown to the path of Your Pleasure."

Saying this he would fell down in prostration.

Even the soothsayers and astronomers began to say that a grand Prophet was about to be born in Arabia. Both Jews and Christians populated Arabia. Thus, scholars of both the religions gave the people glad tidings from the Torah and the Gospel of the coming of a great Prophet.

The King of Abyssinia had captured Yemen for a very short period. During the lifetime of Abdul-Muttalib, Yemen was under the rule of the King of Abyssinia. Those days Abrahah Ashram was the governor of Yemen on behalf of the king. He built a temple in Yemen and persuaded the Arabs to perform *Hajj* at the temple of Yemen instead of the Ka'bah. He was not crowned with success in his movement. Moreover, an Arab, in order to put him to disgrace, defecated in the temple. Abrahah grew so furious that he invaded Makkah with the intention of destroying the House of Allâh–the Ka'bah. He also used elephants in his attack, so the people of Makkah called them the people of the Elephant and the year came to be known as the year of the Elephant. When the Quraish came to know of the attack, they were filled with fear, as they were no match for such a large and strong army. They jointly requested their chief, Abdul-Muttalib to go to Abrahah and explore a way to avert the battle. When Abdul-Muttalib presented himself to Abrahah, he was greatly impressed and held him in high esteem. Abdul-Muttalib stated that Abrahah's army had captured two hundred camels, which belonged to him. Thereupon Abrahah remarked that he took him to be a wise person but he obviously was mistaken. He (Abdul-Muttalib) was quite aware that Abrahah had come with the sole purpose of demolishing the House of Allâh–the Ka'bah. But, intentionally ignoring the topic, he only spoke of his camels instead of saving the Ka'bah. Abdul-Muttalib said:

> "I am merely owner of the camels, but this House also has an Owner and He will save it."

The answer enraged Abrahah and he burst out in anger saying he would see if the Lord of the House would save it. His army was destroyed and left like an empty field from which all the corn has been eaten up and only the straw with stalks and stubble was left. The complete rout of Abrahah's forces after the daring reply of Abdul-Muttalib was a very significant event for Arabia which put great fear of Allâh in their hearts.

After that fateful event, the rule of Yemen went out of the hands of the Abyssinian king and Saif bin Dhi Yazin captured the country. Abdul-Muttalib took some nobles of Quraish and went to congratulate Saif on his victory. Saif bin Dhi Yazin gave Abdul-Muttalib glad tidings that the last Prophet would be raised from his (Abdul-Muttalib's) offspring. This prophecy found wide currency and fame. All the members of the delegation thought that the last Prophet would be raised from their progeny. Each of them contacted the soothsayers and monks hoping for good news but returned disappointed.

On the occasion of an important Prophet or Messenger's birth or declaration, the stars in large number would be seen shooting in the sky. Thus close to the birth of last Prophet ﷺ, bright flames appeared in the sky and the scholars of the Scriptures foretold that the time of the birth of the last Prophet ﷺ was near. Thus on Rabi' Al-Awwal 9, in the year of the Elephant corresponding to April 22, 571 CE on Monday, the last Prophet ﷺ was born at dawn before sunrise.

The Sacrifice of Abdullah bin Abdul-Muttalib

The well of Zamzam originated for the sake of Ismail عليه السلام, when he and his mother Hâjira (Hagar) were over taken by thirst, Allâh the

Genealogy of Abdul Muttalib

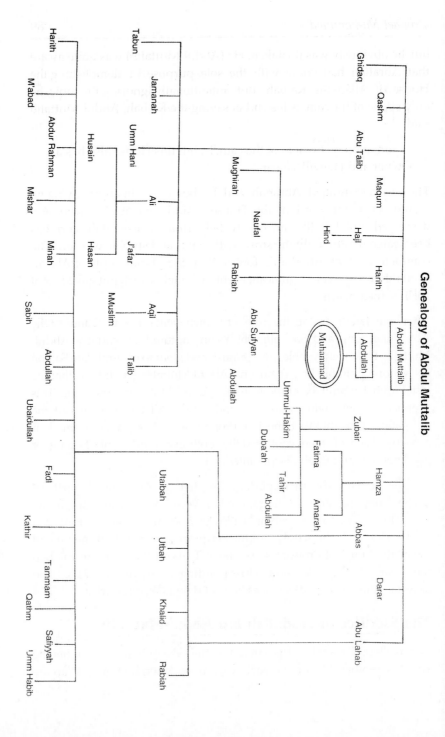

Almighty caused a stream of water to flow in the empty desert. Hâjira contained the flowing water by building a mound around it and it turned into a well. At the time of leaving Makkah, Jurhum tribe covered it with dust and so for a long time it became traceless. When the task of giving water to the pilgrims was entrusted to Abdul-Muttalib, he started searching for it along with his elder son Hârith, but their efforts proved fruitless.

The Father of Muhammad 卐

One day Abdul-Muttalib saw in his dream the location of the well of Zamzam and started digging for it. In that spot two idols Isâf and Nâilah were being kept. The Quraish resented this disturbance and became hostile and ready to fight. Although they were only two, father and son, they dominated the scene and continued digging the well. Realizing his isolation Abdul-Muttalib invoked Allâh the Almighty that in case He gave him ten sons, he would sacrifice one of his sons in the name of God. After a short period the well appeared and he was also blessed with ten sons.

The appearance of the Zamzam well established the prestige of Abdul-Muttalib over the Quraish and all of them acknowledged his leadership and virtues. When his sons had grown, he got ready to fulfil his vow. He went to the Ka'bah along with all his sons and drew lots before Hubal. By chance the arrows of chance chose his youngest son, Abdullah who was very dear to Abdul-Muttalib. Since Abdul-Muttalib was adamant in fulfilling his vow, he left for the altar along with Abdullah.

All his brothers, sisters and chiefs of the Quraish tried hard to hold Abdul-Muttalib back from implementing his plan but he remained unshaken. After much discussion they turned to Sajâ', a famous soothsayer. She pointed out that blood money for their (Abdul-Muttalib's) clan was ten camels. Thus they should put Abdullah on one side and ten camels on the other and then draw the lots.

In the case, that the camels were chosen they would be slaughtered, but if Abdullah is chosen they should add ten more camels and draw again. They should keep adding to the number of the camels until the

Family of Muhammad ﷺ from Mother's Side

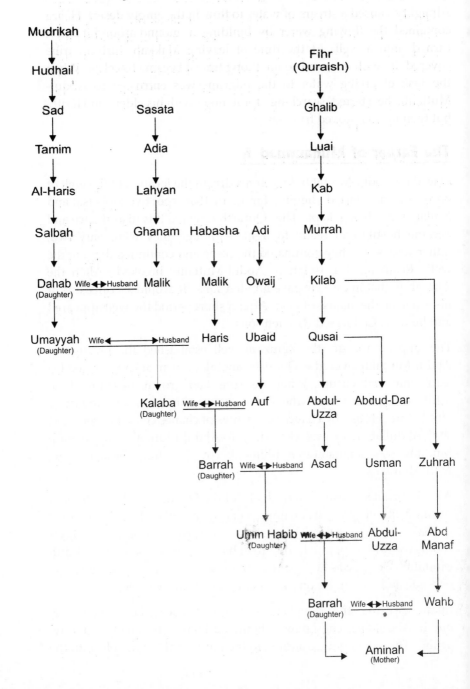

camels were drawn. This exercise went on until the number of camels reached one hundred. Abdul-Muttalib drew the lots twice more for his personal satisfaction but each time it fell upon the camels. Hence one hundred camels were slaughtered and Abdullah was saved. Since that time, the blood money of one killed was fixed at one hundred camels. The table of genealogy of Abdul-Muttalib is given on the facing page.

The Birth of the Prophet ﷺ

Only a few days before the year of Elephant, Abdul-Muttalib married his son, Abdullah to Âminah bint Wahb belonging to a noble family of the Quraish in Yathrib (Al-Madinah). Abdullah was then 24. On the same occasion Abdul-Muttalib himself married Hâlah bint Wuhaib, a relative of Âminah. Hamzah was born from his marriage to Hâlah bint Wuhaib.

A few days after the marriage, Abdul-Muttalib sent Abdullah to Syria along with a trade caravan. On his return, Abdullah fell sick and stayed in Yathrib (Al-Madinah) with his relatives and sent his father news about his illness. Abdul-Muttalib sent his son Hârith to bring Abdullah back to Makkah under his care and protection. But Abdullah died before Hârith reached Al-Madinah and was already buried in the graveyard of his relatives, Banu Najjâr.

Hârith came back to Makkah empty-handed and gave Abdul-Muttalib this soul shattering news. Abdullah had left behind a few camels, goats and a slave-girl, Umm Aiman. Âminah was then pregnant and so the Prophet ﷺ became an orphan while still in the womb of his mother.

He ﷺ was born 52 or 55 days after the event of the year of Elephant. His mother had dreamt an angel telling her that the baby to be born had been named Ahmad. Thus she named him Ahmad, while Abdul-Muttalib named his grandson Muhammad. According to the report of Abul-Fida, when the people asked Abdul-Muttalib as to why he gave his grandson a new name, setting aside all the names current in his family, he replied: "It is because I have a longing that my grandson should be praised and commended by one and all in the world."

Childhood Days

Initially, after his birth, Thuwaibah, the freed slave-girl of Abu Lahab bin Abdul-Muttalib suckled him for seven days. She had suckled Hamzah, the uncle of the Prophet 鐵 also. Thus both Masruh bin Thuwaibah and Hamzah 鐵 were his foster brothers. According to the custom of the Arab nobles, on the eighth day he was entrusted to lady Halimah of the Banu Sa'd clan of the Hawâzin tribe to suckle him and bring him up. The nobles of Arabia would entrust their babies to bedouin women so that they would become healthy and strong in the open and free climate of the desert. Besides it would help develop eloquent speech, because the language of the bedouin was more pure, graceful and eloquent than those living in urban areas.

Halimah Sa'diyah would come to Makkah twice a year to show him to his mother and grandfather. Halimah Sa'diyah suckled him for two years and he remained with her for four years altogether. His mother summoned him to Makkah at the end of four years. When he was six, his mother took him to his relatives in Al-Madinah (Yathrib). On the return journey after a month, she passed away at Abwa. Abdul-Muttalib took upon himself the responsibilities of looking after the boy. According to other narrations, he 鐵 remained with Banu Sa'd for five years. He 鐵 was five years of age and he was out grazing goats along with his foster brother and sisters and other boys of the same age when the event of the opening up of his chest occurred.

According to a narration of *Seerat Ibn Hishâm*, Halimah bint Abu Dhuaib relates this event in these words: "One day both of my children came fearfully to me and said that two cleanly dressed persons seized our Quraishi brother and split open his chest. I went to the spot along with my husband (Hârith bin Abdul-Uzza) and saw that he 鐵 was sitting there with his face turned pale. Upon inquiry he stated that two cleanly dressed persons came to him, laid him down with his face up, took out his heart, and extracted something from it." But Halimah found no trace of any injury or spot of blood. Having thought that the boy was affected by a jinn or something, she brought him to Makkah without loss of time and related the whole event to his mother. But his mother instead of being afraid of what had happened, spoke with all the confidence at her command that her son would achieve a very distinctive place in the world, and would surely remain safe from all calamities. She told that when he was in her womb, she heard many things from the angels and noticed many uncommon happenings. Imam Muslim reports from Anas bin Mâlik 卷 that one day when he 卷 was playing with the boys of Makkah, Jibril (Gabriel) 卷 came to him, split his chest, took out a black drop from it and said: "It was the portion of Satan." Following that he washed his heart in a tray of gold with Zamzam water and then put it in its place.

Death of Abdul-Muttalib

After being brought up for two years under the care and guardianship of Abdul-Muttalib, he 卷 reached eight years of age that Abdul-Muttalib passed away. When Abdul-Muttalib's funeral procession was proceeding, he 卷 joined it with tearful eyes. However, Abdul-Muttalib had entrusted him to his son Abu Tâlib before his death, stressing the utmost care and protection for the boy. Despite having several other sons, Abdul-Muttalib was wise enough to give him to the care of Abu Tâlib because he and Abdullah, the father of the boy, were born of the same mother. The assessment of Abdul-Muttalib came true and the nephew became Abu Tâlib's favorite.

Support of Abu Tâlib

Abu Tâlib took special care of his nephew and held him dearer than his own sons. He made him sleep on his own bed. He 卷 passed his childhood days in a manner quite strange for the Arabian society. Instead of playing with children of his age group, he felt disgusted in their company and preferred to be in solitude. Allâh the Almighty had kept him aloof from every kind of debasement and depravity. A few boys of Quraish forced him to enjoy a marriage celebration where there was dance and music too. But as he reached the spot he was overtaken by sleep and kept sleeping the whole night and got up only when the assembly had dispersed at the end of the celebration. He 卷 was thus saved from the undesirable and forbidden activities of the marriage ceremony.

He ﷺ was, perhaps, seven years old when the Quraish started re-building the Ka'bah which had suffered damage from a flood. During the construction work, he ﷺ joined the party of workers carrying stones and giving them to the masons. He was wearing *Izâr* (waist sheet) which was causing him some trouble doing the work. The nakedness of a boy of seven was not then considered something improper. So, his uncle Abbâs grabbed hold of the waist sheet and pulled it so violently that he ﷺ became naked. He grew shameful to the extent that he fell down unconscious. At last, the people felt the gravity of the situation and put his waist sheet back on and he recovered.

First Journey to Syria

He ﷺ was twelve years old when Abu Tâlib planned to go with a merchant caravan to Syria leaving him behind in Makkah. But he ﷺ was so used to the company of Abu Tâlib that he could not bear separation from his uncle. Abu Tâlib felt moved and agreed to take him to Syria. When the caravan reached Busra, the southeastern part of Syria, a Christian monk named Bahira saw and recognized him as the Last Prophet. He came to Abu Tâlib and let him know that his nephew was set to become a Prophet as he had noticed with him all the signs of Prophethood written in the Torah and the Gospel. He then advised Abu Tâlib to hurry back with his nephew. Abu Tâlib acted upon the advice.

Harb Al-Fijâr, First Participation in Battle

A great fair was regularly held at Ukâz. This fair would organize a number of programs including horse races, wrestling, demonstrations of the art of combat and poetic competitions. All the tribes of Arabia were highly belligerent by nature and drew swords against one another at the smallest incident.

Once, in the course of the fair at Ukâz, the Hawâzin and Quraish tribes challenged each other due to a slight provocation. At the outset some wise and sober people stood in the way and put the matter right. But some mischief-mongers worsened the situation which led to large-scale fighting and killing on both sides. The war was known as

Harb· Al-Fijâr because it took place in the month of Dhul-Qa'dah when fighting was altogether forbidden. This war was based on a series of four wars in which three firsts were small and the fourth war happened to be more fierce than the preceding one as all the tribes of Qais joined the Hawâzin tribe while all the tribes of Kinânah came to the help of the Quraish. Thus this war developed to become a war between the Qais and Kinânah tribes. The fourth and the last war was so terrible that some of the chieftains had their feet chained so they couldn't leave from the field of battle.

The Prophet 🕌 joined this fourth war for the first time armed with weapons. Among Banu Kinânah, every tribe had its separate commander. Thus the commander of Banu Hâshim was Zubair bin Abdul-Muttalib, an uncle of the Prophet 🕌 while Harb bin Umayyah was the commander of all the troops of Banu Kinânah. Muhammad 🕌 was then fifteen or twenty years of age. He was entrusted with the service of picking up the arrows for his uncles. However, he was saved from combat action. At the outset Banu Hawâzin seemed to be dominating, but at last, Banu Kinânah turned the table against the Banu Qais and war ended on peace treaty.

Trade

When the Prophet 🕌 became a young man, he turned towards trade as a vocation. His uncle Abu Tâlib also liked this work for his nephew. Several times he accompanied trade caravans with his merchandise and every time he returned with a substantial profit. The people during these journeys had ample opportunity to observe his qualities of honest dealings and graceful behavior. Besides, all those in Makkah with whom he entered into business terms, became witness to his trusty, truthful, upright and gracious character.

A Companion, Abdullah bin Abul-Hamsa relates: "Before his deputation to the Prophethood, I had entered into a business dealing with the Prophet 🕌. The dealing was not yet concluded when I had to leave for another place in haste. But, before leaving I asked the Prophet 🕌 to wait until I returned to finalize the deal. After taking leave from him I forgot our appointment and when I returned by the same route on the third day, I found the Prophet 🕌 waiting at the same spot. When I drew near the Prophet ﷺ, he said to me only this much: 'You put me through a great deal of trouble. I am still waiting for you here.'" Similarly, when Sâ'ib ؓ embraced Islam, some people spoke highly of him in the presence of the Prophet of Allâh ﷺ. He ﷺ remarked: "I know Sâ'ib more than all of you." Sâ'ib submitted: "May my mother and father be sacrificed for you, once you had been my partner in business and you always made fair dealings."

Offer of Khadijah ؓ

Khadijah ؓ bint Khuwailid, a noble lady of Banu Asad, was a wealthy woman of the Quraish. She was then a widow after marrying two men. Her second husband had left behind much wealth and property. Khadijah ؓ would send her merchandise to Syria, Iraq and Yemen through her workers. When she came to know of the honesty and trustworthiness of the Prophet ﷺ, she sent her nephew Qatimah with her desire that he ﷺ should work for her and go to Syria with her merchandise. He ﷺ after consulting his uncle Abu Tâlib, accepted the proposal. Khadijah ؓ fixed for him a reasonable remuneration. Khadijah's slave Maisarah and a relative of hers named Khuzaimah bin Hakim accompanied him.

Second Journey to Syria

The trade caravan headed by the Prophet ﷺ halted near a monastery in Syria. In the monastery lived a monk named Nastura. When he saw the Prophet ﷺ, he fetched some heavenly book and began to compare his body and face with what was written in the Books about him. Khuzaimah fell in doubt about the monk's intentions and raised an alarm for help. All the Quraish rushed to the spot and the monk ran upstairs. From upstairs he told the people of the caravan that there was nothing to fear, and he was just comparing the Prophet's signs and features with those written in the Books and found in him every sign mentioned. This statement of the monk brought peace of mind to all.

This journey was also crowned with substantial success and profit. It is said that thus he ﷺ headed the trade caravans of Khadijah ؓ to Bahrain, Yemen, and Syria and returned with a profit every time.

Marriage

His honesty, trustworthiness, graceful character, piety, nobility and high quality were no longer a secret from Khadijah 🌸. Although almost every noble and man of means in Makkah had a yearning rooted in his mind to marry her, but she herself, through a woman named Nafisah or Âtikah bint Abdul-Muttalib, sent the Prophet 🌸 her marriage proposal. Abu Tâlib accepted the proposal and delivered the marriage address. All the relatives of the Prophet 🌸 as well as of Khadijah 🌸 participated in the marriage ceremony. At the time of marriage, the Prophet 🌸 was 25 years of age and Khadijah 🌸 was 40. She gave birth to three sons and four daughters.

Titles of *Sâdiq* & *Al-Amin* (Truthful & the Trusty)

Not only in Makkah but also throughout Arabia his virtues, uprightness, honesty and trustworthiness gained such a wide currency that they called him *As-Sâdiq* (the Truthful) or *Al-Amin* (the Trusty) instead of calling him by his name. Mrs. Annie Beasant, the Head of Theosophical Society of India and a noted English lady writes:

> "The exclusive quality of the great Prophet (Muhammad 🌸) which implanted in my heart his greatness and glory is that which led people to call him *Al-Amin* (the honest one). No quality can excel this nor any other thing can be worthy of being followed both by Muslims and non-Muslims. A personality, which is the embodiment of truth, can leave nothing to doubt about. Such a person alone deserves carrying the message of truth."

Renewal of *Hilf-ul-Fudul*

Sometime in the olden days, some selected ones of Arabia had pledged together to help the oppressed and fight against the oppressors. Almost all who had entered the agreement had the word *Fadl* attached to their names and their pledge took the name *Hilf-ul-Fudul*. Although the group was no longer existent in Arabia, the

The Leaders of Quraish Tribes

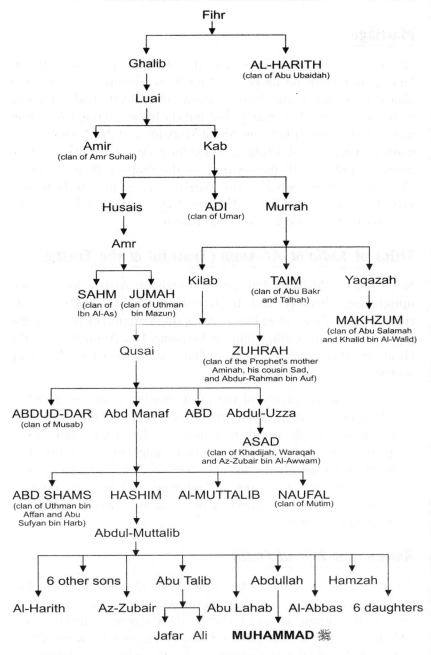

Fihr

Ghalib — AL-HARITH (clan of Abu Ubaidah)

Luai

Amir (clan of Amr Suhail) — Kab

Husais — ADI (clan of Umar) — Murrah

Amr

SAHM (clan of Ibn Al-As) — JUMAH (clan of Uthman bin Mazun) — Kilab — TAIM (clan of Abu Bakr and Talhah) — Yaqazah

MAKHZUM (clan of Abu Salamah and Khalid bin Al-Walid)

Qusai — ZUHRAH (clan of the Prophet's mother Aminah, his cousin Sad, and Abdur-Rahman bin Auf)

ABDUD-DAR (clan of Musab) — Abd Manaf — ABD — Abdul-Uzza

ASAD (clan of Khadijah, Waraqah and Az-Zubair bin Al-Awwam)

ABD SHAMS (clan of Uthman bin Affan and Abu Sufyan bin Harb) — HASHIM — AI-MUTTALIB — NAUFAL (clan of Mutim)

Abdul-Muttalib

6 other sons — Abu Talib — Abdullah — Hamzah

Al-Harith — Az-Zubair — Abu Lahab — Al-Abbas — 6 daughters

Jafar — Ali — MUHAMMAD ﷺ

[The names of the four leaders of clans are given in Capitals.]

people often referred to the name of that organization in their conversations. After the *Harb Al-Fijâr*, Zubair bin Abdul-Muttalib, an uncle of the Prophet 襲 felt the need of reviving the movement. Thus a few people assembled at the house of Abdullah bin Jad'ân and pledged afresh to combat the oppressors and help the oppressed. The Prophet 襲 also joined that pledge.

After a period he 襲 brought to the chieftains and distinguished people around him the idea to rise as one man to redeem the Arab society from evils like oppression, highway robbery, excesses perpetrated on the weak and the poor on the part of the strong and wealthy. His sincere efforts brought fruit and an organization of Banu Hâshim, Banu Al-Muttalib, Banu Asad, Banu Zuhrah and Banu Tamim was set up. Every member had to pledge: (1) We shall wipe out disorder from the country; (2) Safeguard the travelers and wayfarers; (3) Help the poor; and (4) Check the tyrants from doing wrong. The organization served the people gracefully. During his Prophethood he 襲 would say: "If I were invited to have a hand in it even after the advent of Islam, I would have undoubtedly joined again."

Appointed as Arbitrator by the Quraish

The Ka'bah once caught fire due to some carelessness causing deep cracks in its walls. The Quraish agreed to rebuild it but none was ready to demolish it for fear of being overtaken by some calamity. At last, Walid bin Mughirah among the chieftains began it. Other tribes eventually joined the demolition work. About the same time a ship suffered wreckage near the port of Jeddah. The Quraish bought the wooden parts of the broken ship. When the construction work reached up to the point where the *Hajar Aswad* (Black Stone) was to be placed, a serious dispute erupted, for the chieftain of every tribe wanted to place the sacred relic into its place. They were ready to fight and swords were drawn. The impasse continued for five days. At last the Quraish tribes assembled at the Ka'bah and a meeting was immediately convened. Abu Umayyah bin Mughirah brought forward a suggestion that the man first to enter the gate of the Ka'bah would be made umpire in the matter of a dispute. The first man to come in was Allâh's Messenger 鏖. "This is Muhammad," they said as soon as they saw him coming. "He is trustworthy and we all agree to his decision." The fact that every tribe was desirous for and claimed the honor was understandable. However, in their classical destructive manner they were all making pledges to fight unto death by thrusting their fingers into a bowl full of blood according to the custom of the times. It was in this atmosphere that they entrusted to the Prophet 鏖 this major responsibility and honor with all the different factions satisfied and in agreement. This is irrefutable proof of the fact that they all had profound faith in his honesty and justice. He 鏖 first acquainted himself with the matter and then put an end to the dispute quickly so that all the people, old and experienced were left wondering at his sagacity, power of decision and sense of justice. All of them raised their voices in appreciation.

The Prophet 鏖 asked them to bring a piece of cloth. He 鏖 took the Black Stone and put it on the cloth, and asked each tribe to take hold of an end of the cloth and lift it to the required height. When the people lifted the stone in the proper manner, the Prophet 鏖 placed it in its position with his own hands, and the building went on above it. Utbah bin Rabi'ah bin Abd Shams, Aswad bin Muttalib bin Asad bin Abdul-Uzza, Abu Hudhaifah bin Mughirah bin Umar bin Makhzum and Qais bin Adi As-Sahmi were the four persons most deeply involved in the dispute but they, too returned happy and satisfied. Had a war broken out, it would have left all the past wars behind in ferocity and bloodshed. The Prophet 鏖 was only thirty-five years of age when He 鏖 brought an end to the dispute of Black Stone.

Support for the Poor

He 鏖 had excelled all others in Makkah with respect to honor and popularity, and he had no enemy throughout Arabia. His wisdom, uprightness, honesty and trustworthiness were the talk of the country. He was a trader by profession and he was passing his life in easy circumstances after his marriage with Khadijah 鏖. Once famine broke out, Abu Tâlib had to shoulder the responsibility of a big family, and despite being the chieftain of Banu Hâshim, he passed his days in poverty and want. Having seen his plight, the Prophet 鏖 told his uncle, Abbâs bin Abdul-Muttalib about the famine and the difficulties that Abu Tâlib was facing. He further said that it would be better if they each took one of his sons under their care. Abbâs agreed and both of them went to Abu Tâlib and expressed their desire. Abu Tâlib gave his consent for Ali and Ja'far. Thus Ali was taken by the Prophet ﷺ and Ja'far by Abbâs. This happened the same year when the Ka'bah was rebuilt.

His Love for Zaid bin Hârithah

Hakim bin Harâm, the nephew of Khadijah ﷺ had purchased a slave and offered him to his father's sister, Khadijah ﷺ, who gave him to the Prophet ﷺ. It was this slave who was known as Zaid bin Hârithah. He belonged to an Arbian family but was captured during plunder and sold as a slave. When Zaid's father Hârithah and his uncle Ka'b came to know that Zaid lived with a man in Makkah as his slave, both of them went to Makkah and requested the Prophet ﷺ to release Zaid. He ﷺ granted their request at once and said that Zaid was at liberty to accompany them if he so desired.

Zaid was then sent for. He ﷺ asked him, "Do you know these two?" Zaid replied, "Yes! They are my father and uncle." He ﷺ then said, "They have come to take you with them. I give you permission to accompany them." Zaid replied, "I can't part company with you." Thereupon Zaid's father rebuked him and said, "Do you prefer slavery to liberty?" Zaid answered back, "I have noticed in Muhammad ﷺ such things that I can prefer none to him in the whole universe." Having heard this reply of Zaid, the Prophet ﷺ got up, took Zaid with him and entering Ka'bah cried in a loud voice: "O people! Be witness to it that today I set Zaid free and adopt him as my son, this is my heir from today and I am his." This moving sight delighted both the father and uncle of Zaid and they went away leaving their son in the company of the Prophet ﷺ.

From that day the boy came to be called Zaid bin Muhammad instead of Zaid bin Hârithah until Revelation was sent to the Prophet ﷺ after his emigration that an adopted son cannot be a substitute for one's own son. Thus he returned to the name Zaid bin Hârithah. But he enjoyed the love and affection of the Prophet ﷺ in the same measure and it kept increasing with the passage of time. This particular event also tells a lot about the treatment and manners of Muhammad 爨 before being elevated to the lofty position of Prophethood.

Inclined to Allâh

He 爨 was 32 or 33 years of age when he developed in himself a love for solitude and privacy. He so often saw a strange light, which led him to feel a unique joy, although he never saw any figure nor heard any voice. He 爨 naturally abhorred polytheism. Once during a meeting, the pagans served him some food which had already been dedicated to the idols. He 爨 put it aside towards Zaid bin Amr. But he also refused to eat from it and said addressing the pagans: "We do not eat from the food that was offered to idols." This Zaid bin Amr bin Nufail was the uncle of Umar bin Khattâb 爨.

During the hours of privacy and solitude, he 爨 would ponder over the Divine powers and kept praising and glorifying his Lord. The more he 爨 was drawing near the age of forty, the more he felt attracted to privacy. He would very often go to the Cave of Hira, taking with him parched barley meal and water, to pray Allâh in perfect peace and privacy and returned only when the supplies would run short. The Mount of Hira, now known as *Jabal Nur* (Mountain of Light), has a cave. It is situated at a distance of three miles from Makkah towards the north on the way to Mina. The cave has a length of four yards and a breadth of three-quarters of a yard. During those days he had true dreams and had dreams in the night about the happenings of the next day. About seven years passed in the same state, but during the last six months he frequently had true dreams.

Sunrise

Muhammad 爨 was forty years old and now rose the sun of Prophethood. When the power of endurance and shouldering the heavy burden of Revelation had attained full growth by constant prayers, ceaseless exercises and deep reflection in solitude, an angel appeared before him and said addressing him, "Read." The Prophet 爨 answered, "I cannot read." The angel took and pressed him and

then let him go and said again, "Read." The Prophet 變 replied for the
second time, "I cannot read." The angel again pressed him tightly and
then letting him go said, "Read." When the Prophet 變 replied once
again, "I cannot read." He took him and pressed tightly a third time in
the same manner. He then let the Prophet 變 go and said:

> "Read! In the Name of your Lord who has created,
> "Created man from a clot.
> "Read! and your Lord is the Most Generous,
> "Who has taught by the pen,
> "Has taught man that which he knew not." (96:1-5)

Having said this the angel disappeared, but dizzy and frightened, the
Messenger 變 came back home and went to Khadijah 變 and said:
"Wrap me up, wrap me up," Khadijah 變 wrapped him up in a
blanket. When he 變 regained peace of mind after a short while, he
related to Khadijah 變 what had happened to him with the remark, "I
feel my life threatened."

Historic Words of Khadijah 變

Khadijah 變 said in reply:

> "By no means, I swear to Allâh that He would never put you to
> shame. You join the ties of relationship, you speak the truth,
> you bear people's burdens, you help the destitute, you entertain
> guests and you mitigate the pains and grief suffered for the
> sake of truth."

After comforting and encouraging her husband, she took him to her
cousin Waraqah bin Naufal, who had grown old by then. When the
Prophet 變 told him what he had seen and heard, Waraqah cried out,
"There has come unto you the same *Namûs*, who had come unto
Prophet Moses aforetime. Had I been young and living by the time
when your people will cast you out." The Prophet 變 demanded from
Waraqah, "What? will they expel me?" "Yes," replied Waraqah, "for
whenever a Messenger of Allâh came and preached *Tauhid* (Oneness
of Allâh) he was maltreated and put to untold miseries." Afterwards
the Prophet 變 kept visiting the Cave of Hira. But no Revelation came
to him for sometime.

One day he ﷺ was on his way home from the Cave of Hira when he ﷺ sighted the same angel and got frightened. He hurried back home and wrapped himself up in a mantle and lay down. In the meantime he heard a majestic voice saying:

"O you wrapped up in garments! Arise and warn; And magnify your Lord; And purify your garments; And keep away from abomination, polytheism and evils." (74:1-5)

From then on Revelation kept coming after short intervals. One day Jibril (Gabriel), the Trusty took the Prophet ﷺ to the foot of a hill and performed *Wudu'* (ablution) before the Prophet ﷺ and the latter did the same. Afterwards Jibril, the Trusty led the prayer.

Preaching of Islam

He ﷺ embarked upon preaching *Tauhid* (Oneness of Allâh) as he received the Command of Allâh to do so. He started the task of keeping people away from polytheism and inviting to *Tauhid* right from his household, with the result that Khadijah ﷺ was the first to embrace Islam. Ali bin Abu Tâlib ﷺ and Zaid bin Hârithah ﷺ were also converted to Islam the very first day. These all belonged to his household. Abu Bakr bin Abu Quhâfah ﷺ who was the Prophet's friend, accepted Islam the same day. Now, the individuals to become Muslims on the first day were his family members and his best friend. These were the people who knew the Prophet ﷺ well and were aware of his traits and character for a very long time, and no aspect of his life was a secret to them. Now, their embracing of Islam the very first day was an outstanding proof of his truthfulness and uprightness.

At the outset, he kept his teachings and preaching quiet, limiting them to his relatives and close friends. In the earliest period of the preaching of Islam, Abu Bakr ﷺ extended his services most prominently. He had a very wide and large circle of friends and acquaintances under his influence, which brought Uthmân bin Affân, Talhah bin Ubaidullah, Sa'd bin Abu Waqqâs, Abdur Rahmân bin Auf, and Zubair bin Awwâm ﷺ to the fold of Islam. Uthmân bin Maz'un, Qudâmah bin Maz'un, Saeed bin Zaid, Fâtimah—the sister of Umar bin Khattâb and wife of Saeed ﷺ were next to join the caravan of Islam. Another band to enter the circle of Islam constituted individuals like Umair, the brother of Sa'd bin Abu Waqqâs, Abdullah bin Mas'ud, and Ja'far bin Abu Tâlib 🌸. Thus came into being a small group of Muslim men, women, youths, old men and children. The believing men would go beyond Makkah in the mountain pass to pray to Allâh for fear of their lives. Three years passed silently and secretly in preaching Islam, and people renouncing the abominable life of polytheism and idolatry came running to the fold of Islam. But, during this span of three years, every assembly and company of the Quraish was agog with the stir created by Islam. They had nothing to discuss but the new religion.

The Quraish, at the outset, attached no importance to the movement of Islam nor did it look menacing in its early stage. Thus they didn't go beyond poking fun at the believers, jeering at them and hurting them verbally. However, in some cases, mischief-mongers among them inflicted physical troubles on individual Muslims also. Once Sa'd bin Abu Waqqâs 🌸 was performing prayers in a mountain pass along with a few Muslims. All of a sudden a few pagans passed by them and tried to hold the Muslims back from doing so by force. Sa'd bin Abu Waqqâs rose against them and a disbeliever received an injury from his sword. This was the first sword fight in the cause of Allâh the Almighty.

Once the Prophet 🌸 and Ali 🌸 were performing prayers in a mountain pass. By chance, Abu Tâlib arrived at the scene and kept silent watching them. When the prayer was over, he said, "What's this religion that you have adopted?" "This is the Religion of Ibrahim." They said, and added, "you should also accept it." Abu Tâlib replied, "I shall not renounce the religion of my ancestors," and said turning to Ali 🌸,"My son! Never part company with Muhammad. I am sure he will lead you to nothing but good."

Proclamation of Truth from Mount of Safa

Now came the Revelation:

"Therefore proclaim openly that which you are commanded." (15:94)

With this order the Prophet 鷹 ascended the Mount of Safa and gave a call to each and every tribe by name in a raised voice. Having heard this call, the people in a large number gathered in front of him according to the practice of Arabia. Thereafter he 鷹 said addressing them, "O Quraish! If I tell you that your enemy is about to attack you, would you believe me?" They unanimously replied, "Yes." "We have always found you truthful and trustworthy." Having heard this answer, the Prophet 鷹 said to them, "Well, I am a warner to you before a severe chastisement overtakes you." Hearing this they burst into laughter, Abu Lahab exclaimed, "May you perish. Is it for this you have brought us here?" Following this the people dispersed. As Abu Lahab left, *Sûrat Al-Masad* (111) was revealed.

After a few days he 鷹 was ordered:

"And warn your kith and kin." (26:214)

Following this the Prophet 鷹 asked Ali bin Abu Tâlib 鷹 to throw a party and invite his relatives. About forty persons attended it. At the end of the feast the Prophet 鷹 rose to say something but nonsensical utterances of Abu Lahab took away from the Prophet 鷹 an opportunity to warn them of the consequences of their evil doings. After a gap of a few days another feast was arranged and as his relatives finished their meal, the Prophet 鷹 rose to say, "Look! I have come to you with something that none else ever brought for his tribe. Tell me who will lend his support to me in this task?" Hearing this nobody made any response but Abu Tâlib assured him of his support.

Open endeavor to preach

The Prophet 鷹 gave the call to *Tauhid* (Oneness of Allâh) and Islam. During this period his small and weak band of people had to bear the brunt of their new faith. In assemblies and gatherings, in fairs and market places, and by contacting people at their homes, he would teach people the virtues of *Tauhid* (Oneness of Allâh) and forbid them from idolatry. Adultery gambling, lying, embezzlement, theft, and robbery were made taboo. The Quraish were proud people. It was not easy for them to put up with derogatory remarks against their ancestors' faith and practices. They were also very particular about the distinction between slaves and their masters. But Islam believed in the equality of both of them. The Quraish and the Makkans were held in high esteem by all the tribes in Arabia only due to the idols that they would come to Makkah to worship. Islam was, on the other hand, the sworn enemy of idolatry. The chieftains and respectable men of Makkah could not step down from their positions and follow the Prophet 鶯. Most of the tribes were at enmity with Banu Hâshim, so they could not accept a man from a rival tribe to lead them. Thus open preaching ignited the fire of hostility and antagonism all over Arabia which turned into a blaze during the fourth year of the Prophethood.

First Educational Institution

About the same period, the Prophet 鶯 set up the house of Arqam bin Abu Arqam at the bottom of the Mount of Safa as an educational institution. Every new convert would come to this institution to learn the teachings of Islam. Gradually it became a crowded place and the Prophet 鶯 would lead the prayer. This house served as the center of all Islamic activities and the dwelling of the Prophet 鶯 for three years. Those who joined the Islamic movement at this stage are considered to be the Foremost Muslims. The last to embrace Islam in Dar Arqam was Umar bin Khattâb 鶯. His acceptance of Islam proved a turning point in the Islamic movement.

Antagonism of the Quraish

Among the entrants to Islam some were slaves and some of them had no powerful tribes or relatives to defend them. Such weak and powerless people became the easy victims of the disbelievers and suffered physical tortures. Muslims in general were put to ridicule of the most unkind nature so that others would not dare join the new faith. Bilâl 鶯 was the slave of Umayyah bin Khalaf who put him to great torture. He used to bring him out at noontime and throw him on his back on the burning sand, ordering a heavy hot rock to be placed on his chest. At times his both arms were tied behind and he was lashed mercilessly. Sometimes he was kept hungry and handed over to street urchins with a rope tied round his neck and they would pull him through the streets and alleys and to the hills beyond the city. But Bilâl ﷺ would bear all these soul-shattering miseries with *Ahad, Ahad* (One, One) upon his lips. Ammâr ﷺ embraced Islam along with his father Yâsir ﷺ and mother Sumaiyah ﷺ. Abu Jahl tortured them beyond description. The wicked Abu Jahl stuck his spear in Sumaiyah ﷺ and she was honored with martyrdom. Abu Jahl once gave Zanirah ﷺ such a severe beating that she became blind. Hairs stand on end to think of the cruelties committed against the slaves and slave-girls, the weak and the downtrodden. But Islam is such a powerful force that nobody went astray and became an apostate because of these tortures.

Uthmân bin Affân ﷺ was a wealthy man from the Umayyah tribe. On becoming Muslim he was tied with a rope, thrashed severely and put to many other physical troubles. Zubair bin Al-Awwâm's uncle tried to control him by wrapping him in a mat. While reciting the Qur'ân, Abu Dhar Ghifâri ﷺ was so mercilessly beaten that he fell unconscious. He was about to be killed, when Abbâs bin Abdul-Muttalib passed by and asked them to leave him because the Banu Ghifâr tribe inhabited a strategic spot on the route their trade caravans passed through. Abdullah bin Mas'ud ﷺ was also beaten to unconsciousness. Khabbâb bin Aratt ﷺ was once made to lie down on his back on burning embers and a man sat on his chest so that he could not move or change sides, with the result that the flesh and skin of his back and waist were burned off.

Insulting Behavior to the Prophet ﷺ

Once the Prophet ﷺ was saying his prayers at the Ka'bah when Uqbah bin Abu Muait twisted his neck with a piece of cloth until he ﷺ was nearly strangled. On being informed, Abu Bakr ﷺ rushed to the spot and saved the Prophet ﷺ from the mischief, and then said addressing the Quraish: "Would you kill a person simply because he claims that Allâh is his Lord?" Thereupon they left the Prophet ﷺ and grappled with Abu Bakr ﷺ and manhandled him very roughly. Once the Quraish surrounded the Prophet ﷺ on all sides and began to treat him rudely and disrespectfully. Hârith bin Abu Hâlah hurried to the place in order to save him from the clutches of the criminals but the disbelievers martyred him. However, they dared not manhandle the Prophet 🌟. Thorns were spread on the way he had to pass in the night so that his feet were wounded.

Once the Prophet 🌟 was performing prayers in the courtyard of Ka'bah in the presence of the Quraish. Abu Jahl said to the people: "A camel has been slaughtered at such and such place and its intestines are still lying there. One should fetch them and put it on Muhammad." Hearing this, Uqbah bin Abu Muait got up and fetched the intestines and put it on the back of the Prophet 🌟 when he was prostrating. The disbelievers were overtaken by laughter. Although Abdullah bin Mas'ud was present there, he could not muster the courage to do the needful. By chance, Fâtimah 🌸 who was then of tender age, removed the intestines from the back of her father reproaching them in strong words.

They used to throw stones, filth and refuse at his house. Once he 🌟 said, "O Banu Abd Manâf, how well you are at fulfilling the rights of a neighbor." The Prophet 🌟 was sometimes called a poet and at times he was branded as a sorcerer, a soothsayer, or insane. In short, the disbelievers of Makkah left no stone unturned in putting the Prophet 🌟 and his Companions to the utmost physical and mental torture and tried to block his mission. But the Prophet 🌟 was determined to fulfill his sacred mission with unshakable conviction. When the Quraish were perfectly convinced that their opposition to the mission would bear no fruit, they adopted another plan.

An Offer of all earthly Desires and a Plain Reply

The Quraish held consultations over the issue and sent Utbah bin Rabi'ah to the Prophet 🌟 with a proposal. He said very politely, "Muhammad, you are noble and belong to a noble and illustrious family. But you have created a rift in your people. Tell me what do you want? If you want to have wealth, we will collect enough of it that you will be the richest of all of us. If you desire to be a leader, we will make you our chief and are ready to accept your rule. If you want to marry someone, we shall arrange your marriage with the most beautiful lady of the highest and most respectable family and if you are eager for these simultaneously, we can provide you with all this."

When Utbah had finished, the Prophet ﷺ began to recite *Sûrat As-Sajdah* in response to his speech. When he ﷺ came to: "But if they turn away, then say: 'I have warned you of a destructive torment like the torment which overtook Âd and Thamud."(41:13), Utbah turned pale and put his hand on the mouth of the Prophet ﷺ requesting him not to say such things. The Prophet ﷺ then prostrated and raising his head said, "Did you get my reply?" Utbah left the place and came back to the Quraish, and said, "Take my advice and leave this man alone and be neutral in his case. If he brings Arabia under his control then, since he is your brother, his success implies your success; and if he meets his doom, you are happily safe." Hearing this the Quraish said to Utbah, "It appears Muhammad has cast a spell on you." Utbah replied, "You say whatever you like, I have already expressed my opinion."

Deputation of the Quraish to Abu Tâlib

When the efforts of Utbah met with failure, a delegation comprising Utbah, Shebah, Abul-Bukhtari, Aswad, Walid, and Abu Jahl came to Abu Tâlib and complained: "Your nephew doesn't refrain from insulting our idols, make him understand and hold him back from such moves." Abu Tâlib replied to them suitably and protested against their excesses. That day they returned but the very next day they again came to Abu Tâlib after consultations. They made the same suggestions before Abu Tâlib that Utbah had already put forward. They began to say, "O Muhammad, we have sent for you to tell you that none has ever brought so much trouble to the people as you have done. If you, by this new faith of yours, intend to collect money, we can amass it for you that which none could excel. We will make you our chief if you have a longing for rule, we are ready to install you as our king. If you are possessed by a ghost or a jinni of which you have no remedy, we will find a skillful physician and soothsayer for you."

Having heard all this, the Prophet ﷺ recited a few Verses from the Qur'ân in response to what they said, and then said to them, "Allâh the Almighty has sent me as His Messenger to you. I have to convey His Message. In case you accept my teachings, you will be crowned with success in both the worlds; if you reject it, I shall be waiting for the Decision of Allâh the Almighty." In response to this call they said, "Well, if you are the Messenger of God, remove these mountains from Arabia, make the deserts green, bring our forefathers back to life, particularly, Qusai bin Kilâb. If Qusai bin Kilâb, after becoming alive, accepts you as truthful and accepts your Prophethood, we shall also follow suit." The Prophet 🌼 said in reply, "I have not been sent as a Messenger for such things. I have come to convey to you the commands that Allâh the Almighty revealed to me and make you comprehend them fully. I can't do anything out of my own will." After this exchange, the chieftains of the Quraish got up in wrath and left challenging even Abu Tâlib to rise to face them.

After they left, Abu Tâlib said to the Prophet 🌼 with the utmost affection, "My nephew, I have now grown old and it is not within my power to face the onslaught of the Quraish. Put me not in such a trouble, which is beyond my power. It is fitting for you to hold back from reviling the idols." Having heard this, the Prophet 🌼 replied with all the confidence at his command, "Dear uncle! If they put the sun in my right hand and the moon in the left, I shall not forsake it." What Abu Tâlib told him created doubt in the mind of the Prophet 🌼 that he intended to withdraw his support for him. Abu Tâlib commanded the highest respect among the chieftains of Makkah and was the universally accepted chief of the Banu Hâshim tribe. The opponents of the Prophet 🌼 were reluctant to attack him simply because of the presence of Abu Tâlib. Now the disappointing utterances of Abu Tâlib filled the eyes of the Prophet 🌼 with tears. He 🌼 got up and walked away saying, "Uncle! I shall not give up my mission till it is fulfilled or I am undone accomplishing it." When Abu Tâlib heard this, he was moved from within and sent for him and said, "Do keep engaged in your mission; I shall neither withdraw my support nor consign you to your enemies while it is within my power."

Migration to Abyssinia

When all their efforts failed and the mission of preaching *Tauhid* (Oneness of Allâh) remained continuous, they felt the power and strength of it. Thus they reacted violently and stopped the Prophet 🌼

from entering the Ka'bah, and set the louts and riffraff to raise a hue and cry against him and the believers, calling them bad names and making their movements impossible, and they didn't allow them to meet people from outside Makkah. They began to persecute the weak and the poor more intensely. Life became very hard and almost impossible to live.

Witnessing this sad and tragic plight of the believers, the Prophet ﷺ allowed them to leave for Abyssinia (where the Christians ruled). Thus in the month of Rajab, the 5th year of the Prophethood, a band of eleven men and four women left Makkah for Abyssinia. They secretly reached the port of Shu'aibah where there was a ship with its anchor lowered. They boarded the ship and reached Abyssinia. Among those foremost migrants were:

Uthmân bin Affân, his wife Ruqayyah (the daughter of the Prophet ﷺ), Hudhaifah bin Utbah, Uthmân bin Maz'un, Abdullah bin Mas'ud, Abdur-Rahmân bin Auf, Zubair bin Al-Awwâm, Mus'ab bin Umair, Amir bin Rabi'ah and Suhail bin Baida ﷺ.

These people belonged to the renowned and powerful tribes, which makes it clear beyond doubt that not only the weak but also the strong had become the target of their tortures. Finding out about their migration some of the disbelievers set out chasing them but the ship had already departed for Abyssinia. The believers found peace there with the result that other Muslims followed suit.

A few months after the migration, the Muslims came to know that either the entire Quraish population had turned Muslims or made peace with the believers, and Makkah was no longer a risky spot for them. With this good news, a group of Muslims left for Makkah while others waited to make sure about the truth behind the rumor. Those leaving for Makkah found the news baseless when they arrived at a short distance from Makkah. Thus some of them made a retreat while others entered Makkah under the protection of some influential Makkans. Those who went back to Makkah came into contact with the believers and left again for Abyssinia along with other Muslims. This is known as the Second Migration to Abyssinia, which increased the number of the Muslims there to nearly one hundred.

Quraish's demand from the King of Abyssinia

When the disbelievers noticed that the Makkans after being converted to Islam were leaving for Abyssinia and living there in peace, they feared that their power organized outside of Makkah could, one day, pose a great danger to the Makkans. They dispatched a delegation of two respectable persons Amr bin Al-Âs and Abdullah bin Rabi'ah to Negus, the King of Abyssinia. The Makkans had trade relations with Abyssinia for some time. The delegation was sent with costly gifts for the king and his courtiers. After being permitted into the court, they first presented their gifts and then requested the king to hand over some of their slaves who had come to his country after joining a new faith which was against the faith of their ancestors. The king promised to look into their demands only after investigating the matter. The king then sent for the Muslims to come to his court and inquired about their new faith. On behalf of the Muslims, Ja'far bin Abu Tâlib 🌺 moved forward to explain to Negus the truth about the new faith in a remarkable speech delivered before the king and his courtiers.

The Beautiful Speech of Ja'far bin Abu Tâlib 🌺

"O King, we were people plunged in ignorance. We worshipped idols, we ate dead animals, and we committed abominations. We broke natural ties, we ill-treated our neighbors and our strong devoured the weak. We lived like this until Allâh the Almighty raised among us a Prophet of whose noble birth and lineage, truthfulness, honesty and purity we all were aware. He invited us to acknowledge the Oneness of Allâh and to worship Him. He enjoined us to speak the truth, to redeem our pledges, to be kind and considerate to our relatives and neighbors. He forbade us every vice, bloodshed, shamelessness, lies and deceit. He asked us not to encroach upon the belongings of our orphans and not to vilify chaste women. He ordered us to offer prayers. We acknowledged the Messenger 🌺 and believed in him. Because of this our people were estranged and they persecuted us.

"So when they tortured us and tormented us under their tyranny, we fled to your country. We have come here, O King, to your country seeking your protection and we do hope that we shall not be dealt with unjustly."

Negus listened patiently to Ja'far bin Abu Tâlib ⟨⟩. Then he asked him if he had something brought by his Prophet ⟨⟩ from God. Thereupon Ja'far ⟨⟩ recited the opening Verses of *Sûrat Maryam*. Tears started rolling down from the eyes of Negus and his courtiers. The recitation being over, Negus remarked, "This and the Torah of Musa ⟨⟩ are radiations from the same Heavenly Light." Then the envoys of the Quraish flung their last attempt and said, "O King, they are opponents of Jesus too." By this they wanted the Christian king to grow angry at the Muslim migrants. Directly came the reply from Ja'far bin Abu Tâlib ⟨⟩, "Not at all; the fact is rather: He is slave of Allâh and His Messenger." Negus said: "This belief is correct to the core and the Gospel also means the same."

Negus sent the envoys of the Quraish back empty-handed and refused point-blank to give the Muslims up to them. Along with this he returned their gifts thus rubbing salt in their wounds. This event occurred during the sixth year of the Prophethood. With the ignoble defeat of the Quraish's mission, their ill treatment of the Muslims simply was aggravated.

Hamzah ⟨⟩ accepts Islam

The Quraish were going mad with enmity against the Muslims. Once Abu Jahl happened to pass by the Prophet ⟨⟩ near the mount of Safa. He insulted the Prophet ⟨⟩ and heaped all manners of indignities upon him but the Prophet ⟨⟩ did not answer him back. Then he hit him with a stone, which caused bleeding. The Prophet ⟨⟩ came back home silently. Abu Jahl came back too and sat among his friends beside the Ka'bah. Hamzah bin Abdul-Muttalib was the uncle of the Prophet ⟨⟩. He loved the Prophet ⟨⟩ very much but was still a disbeliever. He was in the practice of going to the wilderness every morning with his bow and arrows and passing the whole day in hunting and would return only in the evening and go home only after circumambulating the Ka'bah. That fateful day when Hamzah was on his way back home from the chase, he came across the slave-woman of Abdullah bin Jad'ân who told him about Abu Jahl's abusing and hitting the Prophet ﷺ with a stone and the latter's returning home in perfect silence.

Hamzah besides being the uncle, was also the foster brother of the Prophet ﷺ. This relation of blood and milk sent his temper out of control. He went straight to the Ka'bah, circumambulated it first and then turned back to where Abu Jahl was sitting with his friends. Hamzah was essentially a warrior, the bravest and the most courageous amongst the Quraish. Going straight to Abu Jahl, Hamzah proceeded to strike a bow upon his head causing him to bleed saying, "Would you dare to insult and abuse him if I followed his religion and say what he says?" Abu Jahl's friends got enraged and rose in his support but Abu Jahl pacified them all saying it was he who had crossed the limits. If Hamzah had not taken revenge on me for his nephew, he would have been counted among those bereft of a sense of honor. Abu Jahl was worried that Hamzah might come to the fold of Islam in a fit of anger and antagonism.

When Hamzah returned to the Prophet ﷺ with the news of his taking revenge of him, he remarked: "O uncle, this is not pleasing to me, I would really be pleased if you come into the fold of Islam." Having heard this, Hamzah embraced Islam then and there. The conversion of Amir Hamzah ﷺ to Islam invigorated the weak band of believers. This event occurred during the sixth year of the Prophethood. The Quraish now had to be cautious in dealing with the Prophet ﷺ and his Companions.

Umar bin Khattâb's conversion to Islam

Umar bin Khattâb's acceptance of Islam plunged the Quraish into immense grief and their hostility took a serious turn. Umar bin Khattâb was, like Hamzah bin Abdul-Muttalib ﷺ, a well-known wrestler and one of the most famous brave men of Arabia. He played a prominent role in targeting the Muslims because of their new faith. He took hold of a Muslim and kept on thrashing him till he himself became exhausted and resumed the beating after having to take a rest. He tried his level best to bring the Muslims back to the old faith but miserably failed in this endeavor. Being frustrated to the core he, one day announced in a assembly of the disbelievers his plan to do away with Muhammad 壻, the cause of the discord in Arabia.

Having heard about this heinous plan, Abu Jahl encouraged him by offering one hundred camels and one thousand *Uqiyah* (about 125 kilograms) of silver if the task was accomplished. In this state he came out with unsheathed sword in his hand in search of Muhammad 壻. "Where are you going in this manner?" Sa'd bin Abu Waqqâs asked Umar. "I am going to assassinate Muhammad today so that the calamity that has overtaken the Makkans is not experienced anymore." "Do you not fear the retaliation of Banu Hâshim?" Sa'd bin Abu Waqqâs ♦ pleaded with Umar bin Khattâb. "So far as there is a sword in my hand I fear none." Umar bin Khattâb retorted and added, "As you appear to be a staunch supporter of Muhammad, let me kill you first." Sa'd bin Abu Waqqâs ♦ replied, "Take care of your own household first before killing Muhammad and me, for your sister has already embraced Islam."

Hearing this sarcastic reply, Umar turned mad with rage and proceeded straight towards the house of his sister. His turning towards the house of his sister was, in fact, his turning to Islam. Khabbâb bin Al-Aratt ♦ was then giving Fâtimah 壻, the sister of Umar bin Khattâb and Saeed bin Zaid ♦, her husband, lessons in the Qur'ân.

Having heard the footsteps, Khabbâb ♦ hid somewhere in the house along with the written pages of the Qur'ân. "What were you all reading?" Umar inquired in a fit of anger and grappled with his brother-in-law beating him mercilessly. When his sister intervened to save her husband, Umar hit her too making her bleed. Thereupon she mustered courage enough to throw a challenge to Umar saying "Umar; We have become Muslims and have been obeying Muhammad 壻, so do whatever you want."

On this courageous reply, Umar looked towards the bleeding face of his sister and his heart was moved at the pathetic sight, with the result that his furious storm subsided to a great extent. Umar then asked his sister to show him what they were reading. Since Umar was talking sense, his sister dared to ask him to take a bath first before touching the Scripture. Umar took a bath and then went through the Words of Allâh only to admit with fervor:

"What sweet words these are, I am feeling the impression on my heart."

Having heard this, Khabbâb 鐉 came out from his hiding and said, "Congratulations, O Umar! The prayer of Muhammad 鐉 has been accepted, for I have heard the Prophet 鐉 invoking Allâh: 'O Allâh! Convert to Islam either Umar bin Khattâb or Abu Jahl bin Hishâm.'" Then Khabbâb 鐉 read out the first *Ruku'* of *Sûrat Tâ-Hâ*. Umar upon hearing the Verses of the Qur'ân, started weeping emotionally. Following this, Umar demanded from Khabbâb 鐉 to take him to the Prophet 鐉. Umar still had the unsheathed sword in his hand but his purpose was changed.

Umar knocked at the door of the house of Arqam. Since he had an unsheathed sword in his hand, the Companions were reluctant to open the door. But the Prophet 鐉 asked them to throw the door open. Hamzah 鐉 encouraged them saying, "Let him in. If he has good intentions it is better, otherwise he will be beheaded with his own sword."

As Umar stepped in, the Prophet 鐉 moved forward and said seizing his cloak rather violently: "Will you not leave your path?" Umar answered: "O Messenger of Allâh! I have come to embrace Islam." As the Prophet 鐉 heard this, he raised the cry of *Allâhu Akbar*, and his Companions joined him so loudly that it resounded through the hills of Makkah.

Islam was immensely strengthened with Hamzah and Umar 鐉 marching to the path of Islam one after another. After converting to Islam, Umar bin Khattâb 鐉 proceeded straight to the house of Abu Jahl and knocked at his door. He came out and fervently greeted Umar bin Khattâb 鐉 and said, "What for have you come?" Umar 鐉 replied, "By the grace of Allâh, I have embraced Islam and I now believe in Muhammad 鐉 as the Messenger of Allâh." Hearing this Abu Jahl shut his door in rage and went in. Umar 鐉 also came back. He meant by it to break this news to the greatest enemy of Islam.

Umar bin Khattâb ﷺ soon after believing in Allâh and His
Messenger, suggested to the Prophet ﷺ: "We need not pray to Allâh
secretly in houses, we should do it publicly at the Ka'bah." Umar bin
Khattâb ﷺ fought back anyone who stood against it. Now the
Muslims made it a practice to perform their prayers at the Ka'bah and
Islam made its presence felt open and above board. This event took
place at the end of the last month of the sixth year of Prophethood.
Umar bin Khattâb ﷺ was then 33 years of age. With his conversion to
Islam the number of Muslims in Makkah reached 40.

Social Boycott

Umar's coming to the fold of Islam plunged the Makkan disbelievers
into profound grief. The believers began to perform their prayers
openly at the Ka'bah, while a substantial number of the converts had
been in peace in Abyssinia. The Quraish were rendered helpless and
they had no way within their power to ward off the lurking menace.
Now they went into fresh consultations and discussed ways and
means to combat the challenge.

They came up with a plan to see Abu Tâlib and ask him to hand over
his nephew to them. In case of his refusal they decided to impose a
complete social and material boycott on Banu Hâshim and Banu
Abdul-Muttalib, who were lending their unrelenting support to the
new faith. They reached an agreement that they would sever all
relations with these two tribes and none among them would meet the
Muslims, talk with them and establish marital relations with any of
them. Moreover, they decided to see that no food reached them from
any quarter. They also agreed that the boycott would be kept in force
until they handed over Muhammad ﷺ to them.

They put their agreement in writing with the initials of all the
notables of the Quraish and hung it on the Ka'bah, this gave added
impact to the agreement. Abu Tâlib, along with the Banu Hâshim and
Banu Abdul-Muttalib, deserted their homes and went into the hills of
Makkah to stay there. All the Muslims followed them to the pass
called Shi'b Abu Tâlib. Abu Lahab was the only man of Banu Hâshim
who sided with the disbelievers. The food that Banu Hâshim brought
with them ran short and they had to live in a state of near starvation.

Three years elapsed with untold sufferings forced upon the Muslims. The inhuman persecution endured by them was awe-inspiring. These besieged people would come out during the days of *Hajj* and would buy food and other things they needed. The Prophet 🌸 would also come out in the months of peace and in this atmosphere would preach Islam among the people from outside Makkah. But the Quraish followed him everywhere holding people back from listening to him and branding him as insane and a sorcerer.

The three-year exile of the Muslims to Shi'b Abu Tâlib proves beyond doubt that the sense of honor of the tribes and considerations for race and lineage had substantial value and importance. It was this fact that forced even the disbelieving section of Banu Hâshim to extend their unflinching support to the Prophet 🌸. This miserable period of exile spanning over three years also proved a blessing in disguise. They all became very close to the Prophet 🌸 even the disbelieving group had a real chance of observing the life and activities, conduct and character of one who had nothing but the message of truth, love and righteousness. They watched him directly and came into direct contact with his Divine mission. Three years of inhuman treatment meted out to Banu Hâshim stirred some Quraish individuals from within.

The Quraish of Makkah could easily assess the pathetic situation when the babies of Banu Hâshim were heard crying in front of their starving parents due to lack of food. Zuhair bin Abu Umayyah bin Mughirah was the first to assess the gravity of the sufferings because Abu Tâlib happened to be his maternal uncle. Zuhair drew first the attention of Mut'im bin Adi bin Naufal bin Abdu Manâf on the grounds of relationship to the miseries borne by Banu Hâshim and persuaded him to break the agreement. He then brought Abul-Bukhtari bin Hishâm and Zam'ah bin Al-Aswad round to his plan. A number of persons rose in favor of abrogating the agreement in view of their close relations with Banu Hâshim.

In the meantime, the Prophet 🌸 conveyed to Abu Tâlib that he was informed by Allâh the Almighty that the document bearing the agreement had been eaten by the termites except the word "Allâh" where ever it was mentioned. Hearing this, Abu Tâlib came out of the pass and informed the Quraish that Muhammad 🌸 had told him such and such. He then asked them to see the document and in case it was destroyed, the boycott should also be called off. The disbelievers were dismayed when they found that termites had already eaten up the document except the spots that mentioned the Name of Allâh. They were all deeply bewildered and announced the end of boycott then and there.

Banu Hâshim and all the Muslims came out from Shi'b Abu Tâlib after three years and began to live in their deserted houses. They had lived in Shi'b Abu Tâlib a life of acute depravation which forced them at times to eat the leaves of trees. If they found a dry skin, they would roast and eat it. Hakim bin Hizâm would, sometimes, secretly send by his slave some food to his father's sister Khadijah 🌺. Once it came to the notice of Abu Jahl, he snatched it from the slave and tightened his vigil on them.

The Year of Sorrow

When the Prophet 🌺 emerged from Shi'b Abu Tâlib, the tenth year of Prophethood had started. Instead of showing politeness, the Quraish appeared to be more atrocious. Moreover, some events also took place in this year that it came to be called the Year of Sorrow among the Muslims. During the month of Rajab, Abu Talib fell seriously ill and died at the age of eighty. The death of Abu Talib was encouraging to the hostile Makkans. Abu Talib was the only person who was held in esteem and awe by one and all and with his death, the strength and honor of Banu Hâshim eroded to a great extent. It was a golden opportunity for the mischievous Quraish to create trouble and commit atrocities more openly and fearlessly.

The same year Abu Bakr 🌺 also decided to migrate for the cruelties of the Quraish had taken a turn beyond endurance. He had reached Bark Al-Ghimâd when he came across Ibn Daghinah, the chieftain of the Qârah tribe. On being asked about his departure Abu Bakr 🌺 told him that he had been tortured by his people to such an extent that he was forced to leave Makkah to settle somewhere else so that he could pray to Allâh peacefully. Ibn Daghinah said, "You are a man that neither yourself nor the people should let you go from Makkah. You better come back and worship your Lord in Makkah." Thus Abu Bakr

鑾 returned to Makkah. Ibn Daghinah assembled the notables of the Quraish and put them to utter shame for driving out a man with such high qualities. Abu Bakr 鑾 built in his courtyard a platform for performing prayer where he began to recite the Qur'ân and offer prayers. His loud recitation would leave its impression on the hearts and minds of the women and children of neighborhood. Obviously, the Quraish could not remain silent over this lurking danger. Ibn Daghinah forbade him but Abu Bakr 鑾 boldly answered back, "I abandon your protection now and go to the shelter of Allâh the Almighty instead of giving up the recitation of the Qur'ân."

Two months after the demise of Abu Tâlib, Khadijah 鑾 the wife of the Prophet 鑾 also passed away in the tenth year of his Prophethood. The Prophet 鑾 loved her very much. She was his companion through all his troubles and suffering. She was the first to believe in him. She always encouraged him and consoled him to keep patience. Abu Tâlib and Khadijah 鑾 were such staunch supports that their constant encouragement kept the Prophet 鑾 moving forward with his mission. Their final departure made him sad. He was plunged into frustration also because the atrocities of the disbelievers had taken a turn for the worse.

Once he 鑾 was passing through a place where some scoundrels threw mud on his head with the result that his hair, body and garments were polluted. He came back home in the same pitiable plight. His daughter, Fâtimah Zuhrah 鑾 washed him weeping bitterly. Thereupon the Prophet 鑾 consoled her saying, "Weep not my daughter! Allâh the Almighty will Himself protect your father."

Once the Prophet 鑾 went to the Ka'bah where the polytheists were sitting, Abu Jahl passed a sarcastic remark, "O Abd Manâf, look your Prophet has come." Utbah bin Rabi'ah quipped, "Who are we to reject if one claims to be a Prophet or an angel?" The Prophet 鑾 turned to Utbah and said, "You never lent support to the cause of Allâh and His Messenger and remained insolently persistent in your stand." While addressing Abu Jahl he 鑾 remarked, "The time is drawing near when you will laugh less and weep more." Then he told all the pagans, "The time is nearing when you will enter into the faith you are rejecting now."

The Journey to Tâ'if

The stubbornness of Quraish continued to increase. During the very period of Shi'b Abu Tâlib, the Prophet ﷺ had started preaching Islam among the people arriving in Makkah from outside during the *Hajj* season. But these efforts did not bear fruit. He decided to call the people of Tâ'if to Islam. Tâ'if is at a distance of 60 miles from Makkah and was as a big city as Makkah. It was inhabited by Banu Thaqif who worshipped Lât. In Tâ'if there was a temple of Lât, which was the center of attraction for the whole of the city. In the month of Shawwâl, the 10th year of Prophethood, one month after the death of Khadijah 🌸, the Prophet ﷺ took Zaid bin Hârithah and left for Tâ'if on foot.

In route to Tâ'if he first contacted the Banu Bakr tribe. When they too behaved like the Makkans, he went to the Qahtân people but they were also similar to the Quraish. At last he ﷺ reached Tâ'if and made his first contacts with men of status. Among the chieftains of Tâ'if, Abd Yâlil bin Amr bin Umair and his two brothers, Mas'ud and Habib were the most influential. The Prophet ﷺ met all three and invited them to Islam. They were very haughty. One of them retorted: "Had God made you His Prophet you would not have been walking about like this." Another one quipped: "Did God find none to send as Prophet other than you?"

"And they said: why is not this Qur'ân sent down to some great man of the two towns." (43:31)

The third one pleaded: "I don't like to have a talk with you, for if you are true to your word in being the Messenger of God, it is risky to reject it; if you are lying about God, you are not fit to be talked with."

Obstinate Behavior of the People of Tâ'if:

When the Prophet ﷺ met with failure in the case of Abd Yâlil and his brothers, he ﷺ asked them to keep what came to pass between them a secret. He then left to contact others but Abd Yâlil and his brothers stirred up their slaves and some rabble of the town to harass the Prophet ﷺ. The riffraff of Tâ'if followed the Prophet ﷺ, abusing, screaming, and throwing stones at him until he left Tâ'if but they kept following him. When the shower of stones hit his shins, they bleed profusely. At a distance of three miles from Tâ'if, there was an orchard of Utbah bin Rabi'ah, a wealthy man of Makkah. The Prophet 🌼 took refuge in it. Sitting under the shade of a wall he invoked Allâh the Almighty saying, "O Allâh! You are the Protector and Caretaker of the weak and the helpless and I seek Your help alone."

Utbah bin Rabi'ah was present in his orchard at that time. Arabian nobility and the sense of hospitality pressed him to send through his slave Addâs a bunch of grapes on a plate. The slave was a Christian from Nainua (Nineveh). The Prophet 🌼 ate from the grapes and invited Addâs to accept Islam. He was impressed and kissed the Prophet's hands. Utbah was watching all this. When Addâs returned, Utbah said to him, "Accept not what he says, for his religion was better than that of his (Prophet's)." The Prophet 🌼 took a rest in the orchard for a while and then left. From there he arrived at Nakhlah and passed his night in a date grove. Some of the leaders of the jinn heard him recite the Qur'ân and believed in him.

Back to Makkah:

On his return, the Prophet 🌼 came up to the mount of Hira and sent his message to the chieftains of the Quraish but none showed his readiness to give him refuge. When his message came to Mut'im bin Adi, inspite of being a polytheist, he got up overwhelmed with the sense of national honor and came to the mount of Hira. He took the Prophet 🌼 with him and they went to Makkah. The sons of Mut'im stood in front of the Ka'bah with unsheathed swords. In this way the Prophet 🌼 went around the Ka'bah. Thereafter, Mut'im and his sons accompanied him to his house under the shadow of their swords. "What's your relation with Muhammad?" the Quraish asked Mut'im. He replied, "I have no relation with Muhammad. I am simply his supporter, and nobody can dare look at him with evil eyes while he enjoys my support." Such staunch support from Mut'im silenced the Quraish. As per one narrative, an angel came to the Prophet 🌼 in Tâ'if and said, "If you order me I would join together the two hills between which Tâ'if is located." But he 🌼 replied, "No, if they fail to accept Islam, their progeny will do it."

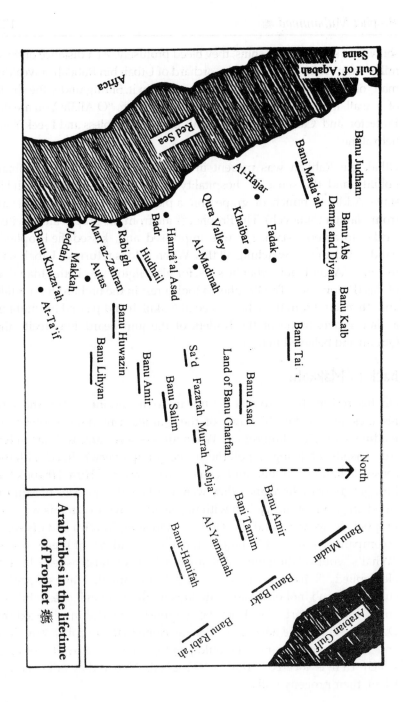

Arab tribes in the lifetime of Prophet ﷺ

Marriage with 'Âishah 變, and *Mi'râj*

The same year in Shawwal, the 10th year of Prophethood, the Prophet 變 married Saudah bint Zam'ah 變 and Âishah bint Abu Bakr 變, and he was also honored with the *Mi'râj* (the Night Journey and his Ascension to the heavens). Scholars are in disagreement regarding the year of the Ascension and some of them are of the opinion that it took place more than once. But this is not the place to discuss the issue in great detail.

Preaching Islam in Different Places and Tribes

Being fed up with the Makkans, the Prophet 變 undertook a journey to Tâ'if but they proved worse than the Makkans. The Makkans ill treatment of the Muslims was multiplying day by day. But he 變 did not lose his courage or determination. Back from Tâ'if he resumed his duty of preaching to the tribes which stayed around Makkah during the *Hajj* days.

He contacted Banu Kindah and Banu Abdullah tribes at their dwellings. To Banu Abdullah he said, "O Banu Abdullah! Your father was Abdullah (literally the slave of Allâh)! You too should become the slaves of Allâh". He 變 also went to the settlement of Banu Hanifah tribe but they meted out treatment worst than ever.

He 變 continued preaching Islam among the caravans from outside Makkah during the *Hajj* season. But Abu Lahab was very keen on interrupting the preaching mission and calling the people not to pay heed to what the Prophet 變 would say. He 變 invited Banu Âmir, Banu Shaibân, Banu Kalb, Banu Muhârib, Fazârah, Ghassân, Sulaim, Abs, Hârith, Adhrah, Dhuhl, and Murrah tribes to accept Islam.

On contacting Banu Âmir, a man named Firâs said, "In case we accept Islam and you attain power, will you then appoint me your successor after you?" The Prophet 變 replied, "This is within the Power of Allâh the Almighty Alone that He choose somebody to succeed me." Hearing this he said, "Wonderful! At present we lay down our lives for your mission, and upon your big victories others plunge in to enjoy the fruits of power! Go away, I want nothing to do with you."

Suwaid bin Sâmit

During the 11th year of Prophethood, from the tribe of Aus, a man named Suwaid bin Sâmit from Al-Madinah came across the Prophet ﷺ and the latter invited him to accept Islam. He said, "You perhaps, have something which I too have with me." The Prophet ﷺ said, "What do you possess at all?" He replied, "The Wisdom of Luqmân." He ﷺ said, "Let me know it." He recited some verses and the Prophet ﷺ appreciated it as a good saying, "But I have the Glorious Qur'ân, which is far better in virtue and excellence and it is perfect in light and guidance." He then recited a few Verses from the Qur'ân. He readily admitted that it was certainly the epitome of light and guidance. As per some narratives, he embraced Islam while others deny it. However, he held himself back from opposing the Prophet ﷺ from that day on. He went back to Al-Madinah and was killed in a battle fought between the Aus and the Khazraj tribes.

Iyâs bin Mu'âdh ﷺ

During these days Anas bin Râfi', accompanied by some persons of his tribe Banu Abdul-Ashhal, came to Makkah to strike an agreement with the Quraish against the Khazraj. As the Prophet ﷺ came to know of his arrival, he quickly went to him before he was able to meet the chieftains of the Quraish to tell him about the issue in view. He ﷺ at once said to them, "I have something with me that is very beneficial for you all; I can let you know it if you so desire." They said in one voice, "Very well, tell us what it is all about." Thereupon he ﷺ said, "I have been sent as the Messenger of Allâh for the guidance of the people. I forbid one and all to practice polytheism and ask you to worship Allâh Alone. Allâh has sent down His Book to me." Following this he taught them a few basic tenets of Islam and read out some Verses from the Glorious Qur'ân. Iyâs bin Mu'âdh, a young fellow in the delegation of Anas bin Râfi' listened to the Prophet ﷺ and his recitation from the Qur'ân with rapt attention, and impatiently said, "O my people! This is far better than that for which you have come from Al-Madinah." Anas bin Râfi', the leader of the delegation rebuked Iyâs bin Mu'âdh and said, "We have not come here for this." Iyâs kept quiet, and the Prophet ﷺ left

the place silently. The delegation from Al-Madinah also met with utter
failure and no agreement with the Quraish could be finalized. A few days
after reaching Al-Madinah, Iyâs bin Mu'âdh passed away declaring his
faith in Islam.

Dimâd Azdi

Dimâd Azdi was a noted sorcerer and citizen of Yemen. Once he came
to Makkah and came to know from Quraish that Muhammad ﷺ was
possessed by jinn. He claimed that he would cure him through his
incantation. Then he came to the Prophet ﷺ and said, "I want to recite
my incantation for you." Thereupon he ﷺ said, "Take from me first
and you will recite afterwards." Then he ﷺ recited the following:

> "Verily all praise is for Allâh, we praise Him and we seek His help.
> Whomsoever Allâh guides, none can misguide; and whomsoever
> Allâh misguides, none can guide. I bear witness that none has the
> right to be worshipped except Allâh Alone, having no partner; and
> I bear witness that Muhammad is his slave and His Messenger.
> Then after,..."

He ﷺ had uttered this much that Dimâd lost control over himself and
exclaimed, "Repeat these words." He made the Prophet ﷺ repeat these
words several times before he said, "I have heard from soothsayers,
sorcerers and poets their words but such words of such a comprehensive
and exhaustive nature I have never come across." Saying this he
entreated the Prophet ﷺ, "Please stretch out your hand, I embrace Islam
right now."

Tufail bin Amr Dausi ﷺ

The Daus tribe belonged to Yemen and its chief Tufail bin Amr was
reckoned among the richest men of Yemen. Besides being an
intellectual he was also a great poet. The same year, the 11th year of
Prophethood, he came to Makkah. The chieftains of Makkah came out
to greet him and brought him into Makkah with high honors. The
Quraish were, however, anxious about his possible meeting with the
Prophet ﷺ and his being charmed by the latter. Thus, with the entry
of Tufail to the town, they told him that there was a sorcerer in the

town who had brought calamities to the people and separated father from son, son from father, brother from brother and husband from wife. So, he must be careful against any word of his coming to his (Tufail's) ears.

One early morning, Tufail reached the Ka'bah with his ears stuffed with cotton. The Prophet ﷺ was then offering the *Fajr* (Dawn) prayer. The way of offering the prayer charmed Tufail and he gradually drew nearer. He happened to hear something from the Prophet's recitation of the Qur'ân. Tufail relates: "I thought, I am also a poet and a wise person and nothing in a speech can elude me. If it is good, I shall accept it; if bad, I shall reject it. With this thought I threw out the pieces of cotton from my ears." Tufail then followed the Prophet ﷺ up to his dwelling and asked him to let him know what he kept saying. The Prophet ﷺ read out some Verses from the Qur'ân and Tufail embraced Islam then and there. He then entreated the Prophet: "Invoke Allâh to favor my whole tribe with Islam through me." Tufail ﷺ came home and embarked on his mission of inviting his people to accept Islam. He also requested the Prophet ﷺ to accompany him and escape the torture of the Makkans. The Prophet ﷺ replied, "I shall migrate on the Order of Allâh the Almighty and to the place enjoined by Him."

Abu Dhar Ghifâri ﷺ

Abu Dhar Ghifâri belonged to Banu Ghifâr and lived in the suburbs of Al-Madinah. News about the Messenger ﷺ reached Al-Madinah through Suwaid bin Sâmit and Iyâs bin Mu'âdh, and when Abu Dhar Ghifâri overheard it he sent his brother Unais, who was also a poet, to find out the facts. Unais met the Prophet ﷺ and reported to Abu Dhar Ghifâri in Al-Madinah that he came across such a person who taught to follow the good and shun the evil. Abu Dhar was not satisfied with this much. So, he left Al-Madinah for Makkah on foot and embraced Islam after presenting himself to the Prophet ﷺ. From there he went straight to the Ka'bah and recited the word of *Tauhid* and some Verses of the Qur'ân at the top of his voice, with the result that he was surrounded by the Quraish on all sides and beaten to unconsciousness. They were about to kill him when Abbâs, who was

still a disbeliever, passed by. He revealed that the victim was a man
from the Ghifâr tribe where they brought dates for trading. Hearing
this they left him. The next day, Abu Dhar ﷺ raised again the word
of *Tauhid* loudly and was again beaten mercilessly. Later on he
returned back to Al-Madinah.

Six Fortunate Souls of Yathrib

It was the last month of the 11th year of Prophethood and the bloody
battle between Aus and Khazraj had come to an end after taking a heavy
toll of noted chiefs from both sides. Caravans from outside had begun
to come into Makkah to perform the *Hajj* rites, and the Prophet ﷺ had
started contacting people and preaching Islam among them at their
places. Abu Jahl and Abu Lahab followed the Prophet ﷺ forbidding
people to give their ears to what he had to say. He, in order to be safe
from their mischief, would come out in the darkness of night to
contact the caravans staying at a distance of several miles from the
Ka'bah.

Once, at a distance of few miles from Makkah, he heard some people
talking during night at Aqabah. He came close and saw that they
were six in all who had come from Yathrib to perform the *Hajj* and
that they were all from Khazraj. The Prophet ﷺ preached Islam and
read out a few Verses from the Qur'ân. They listened with rapt
attention; they looked at each other and embraced Islam on the spot.

The entire population of Yathrib was divided between the Jews and
the idolaters. The Aus and the Khazraj were the two well-known and
mighty tribes of the idolaters and they continually heard from the Jews
about the rising of a grand Prophet in the immediate future, and also
about his dominance over all others. Since they had already heard
about it, they lost no time in accepting Islam.

Those six persons were Abu Umâmah As'ad bin Zurârah (who was
from Banu Najjâr and a relative of the Prophet ﷺ, and was the first to
embrace Islam), Auf bin Hârith, Râfi' bin Mâlik, Qutbah bin Âmir,
Jâbir bin Abdullah, Uqbah bin Âmir bin Nâbi ﷺ. The Prophet ﷺ gave
Râfi bin Mâlik ﷺ in written form the portion from the Qur'ân already
revealed. The small band of believers left for Al-Madinah with the

sincere promise to preach Islam among their people. They set to translate their promise into action immediately after reaching Al-Madinah and Al-Madinah heard the echo of Islam everywhere.

First Pledge of Aqabah

The 12th year of Prophethood had set in. The Quraish were still adamant in their hostility. This whole year passed in a mixed state of hope and fear for the Prophet ﷺ as he did not know about the missionary activities of the six persons who had gone back to Al-Madinah with the promise of preaching Islam among their people. At last, the Prophet ﷺ went to the same place of Aqabah during the next *Hajj* season in search of those persons who had taken the pledge to preach Islam in Al-Madinah the previous year.

All of a sudden, he noticed them along with some new faces belonging both to the Aus and the Khazraj. Those twelve persons were: Abu Umâmah, Auf bin Hârith bin Rifâ'ah, Râfi bin Mâlik bin Al-Ajlân, Qutbah bin Âmir bin Hadbah and Uqbah bin Âmir ﷺ. These five persons belonged to the group, which had accepted Islam the previous year. The other seven persons were: Mu'âdh bin Hârith– the brother of Auf bin Hârith, Dhakwân bin Abd Qais bin Khâlid, Khâlid bin Mukhallad bin Âmir bin Zuraiq, Ubâdah bin Sâmit bin Qais (from Junaib tribe), Abbâs bin Ubâdah bin Nadlah ﷺ. These ten persons were from the Khazraj tribe, Abul-Haitham bin At-Taihân ﷺ (from Banu Abdul-Ashhal) and Uwaim bin Sâ'idah ﷺ, the last two were from the Aus tribe.

These twelve persons pledged their allegiance to Islam at the hand of the Prophet ﷺ. While departing they requested the Prophet ﷺ to dispatch along with them a preacher, and Mus'ab bin Umair ﷺ was made in charge of the mission. He arrived at Al-Madinah and stayed at the house of As'ad bin Zurârah ﷺ and made it his preaching center. During the first pledge of Aqabah, the Prophet ﷺ had asked them to confess the following:

1) We shall worship one God associating none with Him.

2) We shall not go near stealing and adultery.

3) We shall not kill our daughters.

4) We shall vilify none.

5) We shall not backbite

6) We shall obey the Prophet 鑿 in every thing good.

Success of Mus'ab bin Umair ♦ in Al-Madinah

Mus'ab bin Umair ♦ devoted his all-out efforts to preaching Islam in Al-Madinah. By the Grace of Allâh, tribe after tribe in Al-Madinah came into the fold of Islam. From the branches of the Aus in Al-Madinah, Banu Abdul-Ashhal and Banu Zafar clans were very renowned and strong. Sa'd bin Mu'âdh was, besides being the chieftain of Banu Abdul-Ashhal, the commander of all the clans. Usaid bin Hudhair was the chieftain of Banu Zafar clan. His father was the commander of all the clans in the battle of Bu'âth and was killed in the same battle. As'ad bin Zurârah ♦ in whose house Mus'ab bin Umair ♦ was staying was the cousin of Sa'd bin Mu'âdh.Once Mus'ab bin Umair ♦ was sitting by the well of Banu Abdul-Ashhal and was in conversation with As'ad bin Zurârah ♦. Sa'd bin Mu'âdh did not like their preaching of Islam in his locality. Sa'd called Usaid bin Hudhair and asked him to tell them in strong words not to come into their locality from then on. Usaid moved towards them with his sword and reproached both As'ad and Mus'ab 鑿. "There is no harm if you please sit down and listen to what I say; you are at liberty to decide after that." Usaid sat down saying, "Very well." Mus'ab then expounded Islam to him and recited the Qur'ân. Usaid kept listening silently. When Mus'ab bin Umair finished, Usaid bin Hudhair said, "I accept Islam." Usaid ♦ then said, "There is one man that if he becomes a Muslim, there would be none to oppose you." I'll send him to you at once. "Thus Usaid ♦ came back to Sa'd bin Mu'âdh who was waiting for Usaid ♦. "What did you say to them?" Sa'd inquired. Usaid ♦ said, "They have promised not to do anything against your will. But a new incident took place there. A few young men of Banu Hârithah came in and they wanted to kill As'ad bin Zurârah." Hearing this Sa'd bin Mu'âdh stood up with his sword and reached the spot. He saw both As'ad and Mus'ab 鑿 sitting there peacefully. Sa'd fell in doubt about his being sent to them under false pretenses. With this thought entering his mind he began to abuse them and told As'ad 🕮 that he had considerations for relations otherwise he could not have dared come to the locality to preach Islam. Mus'ab 🕮 said, "Please sit down and accept what I say or reject it outright."Sa'd laid down his sword and sat before them. Mus'ab 🕮 told him what he had already stated before to Usaid 🕮 and Sa'd too embraced Islam then and there. On return he assembled the people of his clan and said, "What's your opinion about me?" They said as one man, "You are our chief and your opinion has always been worth practicing." Thereupon Sa'd 🕮 said, "I have nothing to do with you unless you all accept Islam." Having heard this, the entire Banu Abdul-Ashhal accepted Islam.

Thus Islam kept spreading among other tribes and clans of Al-Madinah. It was the 13th year of Prophethood. On one hand, Mus'ab bin Umair 🕮 was achieving successes one after another and the tortures of Quraish were crossing all limits on the other. In Dhul-Hijjah, in the 13th year of Prophethood, Mus'ab bin Umair 🕮 set out to Makkah with a caravan of 72 men and 2 women of Al-Madinah. They were sent with the twin purpose of seeing the Prophet 🕮 and to invite him to come to Al-Madinah.

Second Pledge of Aqabah

The Prophet 🕮 had already been informed of the arrival of this caravan. He came out in the night, took his uncle Abbâs bin Abdul-Muttalib with him and reached the mountain pass of Aqabah. The caravan of believers from Al-Madinah was waiting for him. The caravan also had comprised some disbelievers with it as well. The polytheists from Al-Madinah were unaware of that fateful meeting and they were sleeping in their dwellings. When the people of Al-Madinah expressed their desire to take the Prophet 🕮 to Al-Madinah, Abbâs rose to say:

"O the people of Al-Madinah: Muhammad 🕮 is at present under the protection of his family. Since you want to take him with you, keep in mind, you are alone responsible for his safety and security. But his protection is not easy. Take him with you if you are ready for a series of bloody fights, otherwise abandon such a yearning right now."

Bara' bin Ma'rur ﷺ rose to answer and said, "Abbâs! we listened to what you said. Now we want the Prophet ﷺ also to say something." Thereupon he ﷺ recited some Verses of the Qur'ân and then brought home the rights of Allâh and His slaves and the responsibilities to be thrust upon them on taking him to Al-Madinah. Having heard the speech of the Prophet ﷺ, Bara' bin Ma'rur ﷺ said, "We are prepared for all eventualities." Following this, Abul-Haitham bin Taihân ﷺ said, "You please promise that you will not come back leaving us in Al-Madinah." The Prophet ﷺ said, " I shall live and die with you." At this, Abdullah bin Rawâhah ﷺ said, " O Prophet of Allah! What shall we get in return?" The Prophet ﷺ replied, "Heaven and the pleasure of Allâh!" Abdullah ﷺ said, "Now the bargain is settled. There will be no going back on both sides." In the wake of this, all of them took the oath of allegiance and Bara' bin Ma'rur ﷺ was first. This is called the Second Pledge of Aqabah. After the agreement was finalized, As'ad bin Zurârah ﷺ said addressing everyone, "O people! Bear in mind this mutual agreement implies that we are prepared to face the entire world." All of them said, "Yes, we know very well that we will have to confront the entire world." At the end, the Prophet ﷺ chose twelve persons from among them and appointed them his proclaimers with the duty of preaching Islam. The twelve are listed below:

(1) As'ad bin Zurârah, (2) Usaid bin Hudair, (3) Abul-Haitham bin Al-Taihân, (4) Bara' bin Ma'rur, (5) Abdullah bin Rawâhah, (6) Ubâdah bin Sâmit, (7) Sa'd bin Rabi', (8) Sa'd bin Ubâdah, (9) Râfi' bin Mâlik, (10) Abdullah bin Amr, (11) Sa'd bin Kaithamah, and (12) Mundhir bin Amr ﷺ.

Among these twelve chieftains, nine belonged to the Khazraj tribe and three to the Aus. Addressing them, the Prophet ﷺ said, "Like the partisans of Jesus ﷺ, I assign you the responsibilities of educating your people and I hold responsibility for you all." At the time the pledge of Aqabah was taking its final form, a satan from the top of the mountain cried loudly: "O Makkans! Behold, Muhammad and his party are holding consultations against you." He and his party of believers paid no heed to this call. When everything was finalized, the Prophet ﷺ left the issue of migrating to Al-Madinah to the permission from Allâh the Almighty. Thereafter, they left the place in ones and twos so that secrecy could be maintained. The Prophet ﷺ and Abbâs bin Abdul-Muttalib came to Makkah but the very next morning the Quraish were informed of the meeting that took place the night before. They hurried to the residence of the people from Al-Madinah and said, "Did Muhammad visit you last night?" The non-Muslims or idolaters among them were themselves unaware of such an assembly that was held the previous night.

Abdullah bin Ubai bin Salul was one of them who later on became the head of the hypocrites, he retorted, "How can it be that the people of Al-Madinah finalized any deal without my knowledge?" Thus the doubt in the mind of the Quraish was dispelled and they left. The same moment the people from Al-Madinah started preparations for their return journey and left for their destination. The Quraish came to know of the event later through some other sources and they came out again armed with their weapons. But, by then, the caravan had already traveled a long distance.

Sa'd bin Ubâdah and Mundhir bin Amr ﵁ were left behind for certain reasons. Mundhir ﵁ fled away but Sa'd bin Ubâdah ﵁ was captured by the Quraish and they took him to Makkah beating him mercilessly. Sa'd bin Ubâdah ﵁ relates, "When the Quraish were thrashing me relentlessly, a red and white complexioned man appeared coming towards me and I thought he was the man among the whole lot to treat me gracefully. But he slapped me violently dispelling my hope of any good from those people. Meanwhile, another person came on the scene and said, 'Are you acquainted with anyone from the Quraish?' I replied, 'I know Jubair bin Mut'im and Hârith bin Umayyah, the grandsons of Abd Manâf.' He said, 'Why don't you call them by their names?' Telling me this much he left to contact those two persons and said to them, 'A man from Khazraj tribe is being beaten and he is calling you for help.' They said, 'What's his name?' He said, 'Sa'd bin Ubâdah.' They said, 'We are obliged to him, for we go to him with business and stay under his protection.' Thus both of them came and got me out of their clutches. Soon after being set free, I left for Al-Madinah (Yathrib)." A long time before the Prophet ﷺ was told by Allâh the Almighty that he would have to emigrate. He was shown in a dream where he was destined to go. He had dreamt that it was a land of date palm trees. The dream led him to think it might be Yamâmah, for it too had a large number of date trees.

General Permission to migrate to Al-Madinah

After the second pledge of Aqabah, the persecution of the Quraish knew no bounds. Their hostility can be gauged from the following single event. When the Prophet 🌸, at the height of the atrocities, gave the Muslims general permission to migrate from Makkah to Al-Madinah in order to save their lives, they set out towards Al-Madinah deserting their houses and leaving their relatives, the Quraish could not put up with this provocative development. They began to put up obstructions of many kinds in the way of the migrating Muslims so that they could not live in peace and worship one God in Al-Madinah.

Umm Salamah 🌸 relates: "When Abu Salamah had made up his mind to set out to Al-Madinah he saddled his camel and mounted me on it with my son Salamah. Then taking hold of the camel's halter, he went ahead. When some of the men belonging to our clan saw him, they came near us saying, 'It is all right so far as you are concerned, but how can we allow our daughter to go with you.' Meanwhile the clansmen of Abu Salamah came in and said, 'If she does not go, we will not let our son go with her.' Thus Banu Abdul-Asad took my child away." And Banu Mughirah returned with Umm Salamah 🌸, with the result that Abu Salamah 🌸 was left alone for Al-Madinah. Umm Salamah 🌸 was separated from her husband and son, while Abu Salamah 🌸 received the recompense for migrating without his wife and son.

When Suhaib 🌸 tried to leave for Al-Madinah, the disbelieving Quraish said to him, "You came to us as a destitute beggar and have grown rich among us, and now you want to go away safely with your life and wealth." So they snatched all his possessions and allowed him to leave for Al-Madinah. When Hishâm bin Âs 🌸 decided to migrate, the disbelievers caught and put him in captivity and tortured him. Aiyâsh 🌸 migrated to Al-Madinah but Abu Jahl followed him and deceitfully brought him back to Makkah and made him a captive.

In short, despite these impediments, the believers kept migrating to Al-Madinah one or two at a time. All these migrants were the guests of the Muslims in Al-Madinah. Migrating Muslims were called the *Muhâjirin* and their helpers in Al-Madinah were known as the *Ansâr*. The 14th year of Prophethood had started. Muhammad ﷺ, Abu Bakr Siddiq ﷺ and Ali bin Abu Tâlib ﷺ and their wives and children were yet to migrate, along with some others who were weak and old people. Besides these few, all the Muslims had already migrated to Al-Madinah and their houses were lying vacant. The Prophet ﷺ had not made up his mind, for he was awaiting permission from Allâh the Almighty. He also held back Abu Bakr Siddiq ﷺ to accompany him to Al-Madinah. Ali bin Abu Tâlib ﷺ was also delaying his migration waiting for permission from the Prophet ﷺ.

Holding Counsel by the Quraish in Dar An-Nadwah

When the Quraish noticed that, one by one, all the Muslims slipped out of their hands and they had gone to Al-Madinah in substantial numbers, the Makkans felt it posed a danger to them and they grew anxious about the future. Since the Prophet ﷺ was now living almost alone, after the departure of his Companions, the Quraish targeted the very existence of the preacher of Islam. They were now in a haste to implement their plan, for with the departure of the Prophet ﷺ, the matter would get out of their control. They were all thinking in the same direction until every tribe of Makkah was occupied with the same common thought of putting the Prophet ﷺ to death. Thus, at the end of the month of Safar, the 14th year of Prophethood, the chiefs of all the tribes except Banu Hâshim assembled in Dar An-Nadwah to deliberate upon the issue. The chieftains of the Quraish who took part in the deliberation were:

Abu Jahl bin Hishâm (from Banu Makhzum), Nabih and Munabbeh–sons of Hajjâj (from Banu Sahm tribe), Umayyah bin Khalaf (from Banu Jumh), Abul-Baukhtari bin Hishâm, Zam'ah bin Aswad and Hakim bin Hizâm (from Banu Asad tribe), Nadr bin Hârith (from Banu Abdud-Dâr tribe), Utbah and Shaibah–sons of Rabi'ah, Abu Sufyân bin Harb (from Banu Umayyah tribe), Tuaimah bin Adi, Jubair bin Mut'im, Hârith bin Âmir (from Banu Naufal tribe). Besides these famous names, there were many other chieftains. One of the participants was a very old and experienced devil from the Najd and was the president of the session. There was no disagreement among the participants over the fact that Muhammad 🌸 was the source and center of all their problems . But they had a disagreement over how he should be dealt with.

One of them suggested: "Let him be put in fetters so that he dies of hunger and thirst." Thereupon the Sheikh of the Najd interrupted and said, "This is not a good proposal for his relatives and followers will try to seek his freedom which may result in violence and heavy bloodshed." Another person proposed: "Let him be driven out from Makkah with no permission for his re-entry." This suggestion was also contradicted by the Sheikh of the Najd. Many other suggestions were put forward and were rejected by him.

Lastly, Abu Jahl proposed: "Let a swordsman from each tribe be chosen, and all of them should surround Muhammad 🌸 on all sides and strike at him simultaneously so that his blood will be divided among all the tribes and clans. Moreover, Banu Hâshim will not be able to face the collective force of the entire Quraish tribes. Ultimately they will become content with the blood money, which may be collected easily from the tribes involved in the action." This proposal of Abu Jahl was highly appreciated by the Sheikh of the Najd and the resolution was unanimously passed. The consultations were going on in Dar An-Nadwah and at the same time Allâh the Almighty informed the Prophet 🌸 with all that was taking place. Moreover, permission for his migration was also granted.

Making Preparations for the Journey

With the order for migration, the Prophet 🌸 called at the house of Abu Bakr ⚜ at noon when the burning sun had forced the people indoors. Since it was an unusual time to visit, Abu Bakr ⚜ speculated that migration must have been ordered. First of all he 🌸 inquired if there was any strange person in the house. When he was informed that there was no one in the house except Abu Bakr ⚜ and his daughters, Asma' and Âishah 🌸, he disclosed that migration to Al-Madinah had been ordered.

"Who will accompany you on the journey?" Abu Bakr ⚭ asked. The Prophet ﷺ said, "You will accompany me." Having heard this, tears of joy trickled down from the eyes of Abu Bakr ⚭ and he said, "O Prophet of Allâh! I have already bought two she-camels for this purpose and have made them strong and stout, and I offer you one." The Prophet ﷺ said, "I will purchase it." Thus he paid for it and Abu Bakr ⚭ had to accept it. And from that moment, preparations for migration started. Asma' bint Abu Bakr ⚭ made them provisions of parched barley and some other food, Âishah ⚭ was at that time still of a very tender age. After telling Abu Bakr ⚭ of the plan, the Prophet ﷺ went back home.

The polytheists had made their nefarious plan to assassinate the Prophet ﷺ on the following night. They surrounded his house from that evening. Their heinous plan was to make a surprise attack on the Prophet ﷺ when he comes out to offer his dawn prayers. The Prophet ﷺ had asked Ali bin Abu Tâlib ⚭ to lie in his bed and to wrap himself in his mantle. He also gave Ali ⚭ the valuables that his pagan neighbors had left with him in trust, and instructed Ali ⚭ to give them back to their rightful owners the next morning. He also asked Ali ⚭ to migrate after settling these matters. After completing this, the Prophet ﷺ came out of his house in the dark hours of the night reciting the first nine Verses of *Surat Yâsin*. He threw a handful of dust at them, with the result that they did not see him.

> "And (remember) when disbelievers plotted against you to imprison you or to kill you or to get out you; they were plotting and Allâh too was planing; and Allâh is the Best of the planners." (8:30)

Abu Bakr ⚭ paid Abdullah bin Uraiqit a reasonable sum to deliver both the she-camels at an appointed time and place to be told to him later, although he was a disbeliever, he was trustworthy.

The Prophet ﷺ came out of his house and went straight to Abu Bakr ⚭. They set out right away, and took a low-lying trail to a distance of four miles outside of Makkah. They arrived at the cave of Mount Thaur and hid themselves in it. Ali bin Abu Tâlib ⚭ kept sleeping soundly and peacefully in the bed of the Prophet ﷺ while the disbelievers of Makkah continued their siege around the house the whole night. They were feeling satisfied thinking that Ali ﷺ was the Prophet ﷺ. When Ali ﷺ got up for the *Fajr* (dawn) prayer the disbelievers asked him, "Where's Muhammad?" Ali ﷺ retorted, "How can I know, for I was asleep the whole night. You should know his whereabouts since you have been on guard." The disbelievers held Ali ﷺ and beat him in a state of ferocity and then released him after sometime. Ali ﷺ then gave back the trusts to their rightful owners.

It is worth noticing here that although the disbelievers were thirsting for the life of the Prophet ﷺ, they trusted his honesty and integrity so much so that they left their precious valuables, gold, silver, and jewelry in trust with him. He ﷺ was very particular about it and that is why he left Ali ﷺ, someone he knew he could depend on, to return the trusts to his bloodthirsty enemies.

Leaving Ali ﷺ, the disbelievers called at the house of Abu Bakr ﷺ and knocked at the door. Asma' bint Abu Bakr ﷺ came out. Abu Jahl said, "O girl! Where is your father?" She said flatly, "I know nothing about him." Hearing this the wicked man slapped her so violently that her earrings fell down on the ground. After this, the furious disbelievers mounted a search for the Prophet ﷺ but it was in vain. Now, in a state of frustration, they announced a reward of one hundred camels for anyone who could catch and bring back Muhammad ﷺ dead or alive. The greed for such a substantial reward incited a number of persons to search the area but their efforts met with total failure.

The Sun and the Moon in the Cave of Mount Thaur

When the two arrived at the cave in Mount Thaur Abu Bakr ﷺ requested the Prophet ﷺ to wait until he searched and cleaned up the cave. So he went in, searched it and stuffed the holes with the pieces of cloth torn from his garment and then came out to escort the Prophet ﷺ in. They remained hidden in the cave for three days and nights. Some chieftains and notables from the Quraish reached the mouth of the cave tracking their footprints. Since there was no trace beyond this, some of them suggested that either Muhammad ﷺ was hidden somewhere there or might be inside the cave or had flown to heaven from the same spot. Someone said, "No human has entered this dark cave, it is in an undisturbed state for a long time." Another person noticed, "There is a spider's web across the mouth of the cave and anybody going in would have broken it." The third one pointed to a pigeon flying around and the eggs, which it was hatching. So, all of them grew confident that no human had entered the cave.

These disbelievers had come so close to the entrance that both the Prophet 襤 and Abu Bakr 襤 saw their feet and heard the voices of these bloodthirsty warriors of the Quraish. In such a critical moment Abu Bakr 襤 said, "The disbelievers have at last arrived." The Prophet 襤 very confidently said, "Grieve not, Allâh is with us," and then added, "What do you think of those two with whom the third is Allâh?" The unfortunate disbelievers went back dismayed and disappointed.

Abu Bakr 襤 had already told his son Abdullah bin Abu Bakr 襤 to keep him informed of the daily activities of the disbelievers of Makkah at night. Similarly, he had instructed his slave, Âmir bin Fuhairah to graze his herd of goats anywhere but bring them to the cave of Thaur at night. Asma' bint Abu Bakr 襤 was assigned the duty of bringing meals to the Prophet 襤 and Abu Bakr 襤 in the night with the utmost care. The brother and sister, Abdullah and Asma' 襤, returned after performing their duties, Âmir bin Fuhairah also did his job and his return in the late hours of the night by the way of Mount Thaur hid the tracks made by the others. When the fervor of the disbelievers subsided, Abdullah bin Uraiqit was told to bring the she-camels to the foot of Mount Thaur fulfilling his agreement. It was a credit to the Arabian sense of honor and national character that Abdullah bin Uraiqit who, although not a Muslim, kept the matter secret. He brought the two she-camels and his own camel near the foot of Mount Thaur on a moonlit night of Rabi' Al-Awwal, while Asma' 襤 turned up with parched barley and meal.

Muhammad 襤 and Abu Bakr 襤 came out of the cave of Thaur. He mounted a she-camel named Al-Qaswa, while Abu Bakr 襤 and his slave Âmir bin Fuhairah got on the other she-camel. Abdullah bin Uraiqit serving as a guide, mounted his own camel. This small caravan of four secretly moved forward through routes away from the main road. An event worth mentioning took place when the caravan was about to set out. The bag of food brought by Asma' 🕌, was without a string. When the bag was to be suspended from the camel's saddle, there was no string to serve this purpose. Asma' 🕌 made no delay in tearing her waistband in two tying one half around her waist and with the other half, she tied the bag. This ready solution put forward by Asma' 🕌 won for her praise from the Prophet 🕌 who also named her "The Lady with the String." She was later known by this title. Another interesting event that took place was that Abu Bakr 🕌 took with him all his cash which, amounted to five or six thousand dirhams. His father, Quhâfah who was blind and still a disbeliever, came in and told his grand daughters that Abu Bakr 🕌 went away with all the riches of the house. Asma' 🕌 replied, "Grandfather, he has left enough money for us." Then she wrapped up a large number of pebbles in a piece of cloth and put it at the place where the money was always kept. She then caught the hand of her grandfather and took him to that spot. After touching it he was satisfied about the presence of money. Then he said   to his granddaughters, "The departure of Abu Bakr now is no long a matter of sorrow."

Migration

Before mounting Al-Qaswa, the Prophet 🕌 looked at Makkah and said overwhelmed with grief: "O Makkah! You are to me dearest of all the cities. But your citizens allowed me not to reside here." Following this Abu Bakr 🕌 said, "They have banished their Prophet and they are now bound to be ruined." About the same time this *Ayah* (Verse) was revealed:

> "Permission to fight is given to those who are fought against because they have been wronged; and surely, Allâh is Able to give them victory." (22:39)

It is worth considering how and under what rigorous circumstances they embraced Islam and remained firm and stuck to the truth in the face of opposition from all quarters and at the cost of soul-shattering torture and persecution. Could anyone dare imply that they had come to the fold of Islam under threats or out of greed? No, not at all! Now, after the revelation of this Verse begins the era when the believers were permitted to face and fight those who obstructed the path of Islam. It is interesting to watch how people in large numbers accepted Islam under these trying situation that lay ahead.

This small caravan set out in the early part of the night. The next day, on Rabi' Al-Awwal 1, the 14th year of Prophethood, they arrived at the tent of Umm Ma'bad in the afternoon. That old woman belonged to the Khuzâ'ah tribe. She used to serve travelers water and drinks. The Prophet 鑶 halted there, took milk and then resumed his journey after a short rest. They had moved a little ahead when Surâqah bin Mâlik appeared on the scene pursuing the Prophet 鑶.

Surâqah bin Mâlik bin Ju'shum was a famous warrior. He was once sitting in his dwelling place along with his companions when, in the early morning, a man came and revealed that he had witnessed three riders on camel moving in such and such direction. He presumed that they must be Muhammad 鑶 and his companions. Surâqah made a sign to silence him and said that he knew very well who those travelers were, and that they were such and such persons who had left on a journey last night. By this ploy Surâqah meant to chase and catch the Prophet 鑶 to get the reward of the one hundred camels and he wanted no one else to share in it. He came home in a hurry, sent his horse and weapons outside the dwelling and then he himself reached the spot where his horse was evading others' eyes. He hurried after the fugitives tracking their footprints. He let his horse go at a canter until the fugitives came into the full view. But his horse stumbled abruptly and he was thrown off. He remounted his horse but it again stumbled and he was thrown off. But he continued his chase until his horse stumbled for the third time, and he was thrown off again.

Such a queer misfortune sent fear through his body and he felt sure that his attempt would have to be given up. Then admitting his failure, he called out to the Prophet 鑶 to halt and listen to him. He 鑶 stopped his movement. Surâqah drew near and said, "I had come to take you back to Makkah as a prisoner. But I now seek your pardon. Please write for me a warrant of security besides forgiving me for my evil intentions. I promise to take back with me all those coming in this direction who have the same purpose as I did." Thus, with the order of the Prophet 🕌, either Abu Bakr 🤲 or Âmir bin Fuhairah wrote the warrant sitting on the camel's back and threw it towards him. He turned back with the warrant and took back all others assuring them that the Prophet 🕌 was long gone and traceless. Surâqah embraced Islam after the conquest of Makkah and the warrant of security was a source of safety for him.

From the cave of Thaur and the low-lying land of Makkah, Abdullah bin Uraiqit took the Prophet 🕌 to the coastal area. Passing across the main track to the other side of Usfân. He continued his journey up to Qudaid through the valley of Amaj and then cutting across the main road he came down into the field of Kharâr Laqaf, Mudlijah and Majâj crossing the territory of Dhul-Ghadwin and passing through the grove of Dhu Salam they crossed Al-Ababid and Al-Arj. In the valley of Al-Arj, a camel of the caravan became exhausted. A man of Aslam clan brought a camel from Aus bin Hajar, who also gave a slave to accompany the Prophet 🕌. From there the caravan, after crossing Thaniyatul-Âir, reached the valley of Reem, and from there to Quba' at noon.

After Surâqah bin Mâlik retreated, the caravan had marched a little ahead when Zubair bin Awwâm 🤲 came across them on his way back to Makkah at the head of his trade caravan. He gave gifts of garments to the Prophet 🕌 with his fervent desire to join the Prophet 🕌 in Al-Madinah after reaching Makkah. During this journey, people at various places recognized Abu Bakr 🤲, for they had so often seen him leading trade caravans. However, they were not familiar with the Prophet 🕌 and so, they asked Abu Bakr 🤲 about the person going ahead of him. He replied, "This is my leader and the guide."

End of the Journey

After an eight-day journey, the Prophet 🕌 arrived at Quba' on Rabia al-Awwal 8, the 14th year of Prophethood (corresponding September 23, 622 CE) at noon. Quba' lies at a distance of a few miles from Al-Madinah and was generally taken as the locality of Al-Madinah. It was largely inhabited by Banu Amr bin Auf who had already been enlightened by Islam. A few days before the departure of the Prophet 🕌 from Makkah, the news of his arrival in Al-Madinah was in the air.

The *Ansâr* of Al-Madinah would come out of their dwellings early in the morning and kept waiting till noon everyday. Thus when the Prophet ﷺ arrived at Quba' at noon, they had already gone back after waiting for some time.

A certain Jew who was watching the crowds of Muslims awaiting someone by coming out of their settlement knew that Muhammad ﷺ was about to come from Makkah. This Jew was then, by chance, upstairs when he witnessed the small caravan moving into Quba'. Guessing it to be the caravan of the Prophet ﷺ ,he cried at the top of his voice: "O the people of Arabia, O those taking rest at noon, there has come your object of love." Having heard this call, the people rushed out of their dwellings and waves of exultation gripped the whole atmosphere of Quba'. He ﷺ was emerging from an orchard of dates. Bearing in mind that the people might fall into confusion regarding the identification of the Prophet ﷺ, Abu Bakr ﷺ drew himself back and shaded the Prophet ﷺ with his mantle, thus making a clear distinction between the master and the servant.

The Prophet ﷺ was now entering Quba' and the little girls of the *Ansâr* were reciting in great fervor and boundless joy:

"On the hillside whence caravans are given a send-off,
The full moon comes up in the day.
All the while Allâh is praised.
We had better return our thanks
The noble one, O you sent to us,
You have brought binding commands."

The Prophet ﷺ entered Quba' on Monday and stayed there until Friday. The Prophet ﷺ stayed in the house of Kulthum bin Hadm while Abu Bakr ﷺ stayed with Habib bin Asâf ﷺ. He ﷺ would hold his assemblies in the house of Sa'd bin Khaithamah ﷺ and the people visited him at that same place. During this short stay in Quba', he ﷺ laid the foundation of a mosque which is the first mosque ever built after the advent of Islam. On Friday, the 12th Rabi' Al-Awwal, he left Quba' and made his entry into Al-Madinah. He ﷺ was still in Quba' when Ali bin Abu Tâlib ﷺ came and joined him. Ali ﷺ had made this long and arduous journey on foot. While the Prophet ﷺ was staying in Quba', Ali ﷺ who had been busy returning the deposits of the people to their rightful owners was blessed with the honor of joining the Prophet ﷺ. He had left Makkah the very day the Prophet ﷺ left the cave of Thaur. But Ali ﷺ, a traveler by himself, made his movement during the night and kept himself hidden in the day. The Prophet ﷺ came avoiding the busy thoroughfares and reached Quba' in eight days, while Ali ﷺ undertook the journey by the well-known routes but was made late by three or four days because of being on foot.

Entry into Al-Madinah

Taking leave of the people of Quba' and Banu Amr bin Auf on Friday, the Prophet ﷺ moved forward to make his stay in Al-Madinah. Every household of each locality expressed its strong desire that the Prophet ﷺ would stay with them. He was in the locality of Banu Sâlim bin Auf when the time for the Friday (*Jumu'ah*) prayer drew near. The Prophet ﷺ led the prayer at the same place in a field with about a hundred men behind him. This was the first Friday prayer of the Prophet ﷺ in Al-Madinah and the first time the Friday sermon (*Khutbah*) was ever delivered. Later on, a mosque was built at that place.

After offering the Friday prayer, the Prophet ﷺ mounted his she-camel. Banu Sâlim bin Auf approached him and took hold of his she-camel's halter with the request that he stay with them. The people of other clans and localities also came in groups and made the same request. This led to a clash of words, which ended when the Prophet ﷺ said to one and all: "Let her go her way. She is guided by Allâh. I shall stop where the animal sits down." The *Ansâr* and *Muhâjirîn* followed the she-camel on all sides. He set the halter loose and free and the she-camel moved ahead slowly. All eyes were focused on the animal and they were eagerly waiting for it to kneel down.

When she entered the locality of Banu Biyâdah, Ziyâd bin Labid and Urwah bin Amr, the chieftains of the tribe wanted to take hold of the halter but the Prophet ﷺ forbade them saying: "Leave her for she has already been commanded." Then the she-camel stepped into the locality of Banu Sâ'idah and Sa'd bin Ubâdah and Mundhir bin Amr, the chieftains of Banu Sâ'idah made the same attempt but received the

same words from the Prophet 鸞. After this, she reached the locality of
Banu Al-Hârith bin Al-Khazraj, and Sa'd bin Ar-Rabi', Khârijah bin Zaid
and Abdullah bin Rawahah stepped forward to stop her but received
the same reply. From there the she-camel made an entry into the
locality of Banu Adi bin An-Najjâr. Since Abdul-Muttalib's mother
Salma bint Amr belonged to this clan, they made their claim for the
Prophet 鸞 to stop there. Thus Salit bin Qais and Asirah bin Abu
Khârija, the chieftains of Banu Adi took hold of the halter but he 鸞
asked them to leave it for the animal had prior instructions for herself.
At last the she-camel arrived at the locality of Banu Mâlik bin An-
Najjâr and knelt down in a deserted and fallow land for a while and
then got up and advanced a little only to turn back and be seated on
the same spot again. This time she shook herself and then lay down
on her neck wagging her tail.

Close to this unpopulated land was the house of Abu Ayub Khâlid
bin Zaid Ansâri 鸞. He rushed to the spot with his face beaming with
joy and took the belongings of the Prophet 鸞 to his house. Thus he 鸞
made his stay in his house. The deserted land was the property of two
orphan boys Sahl and Suhail. The piece of land had a few date trees,
graves of the polytheists and a resting spot for the herds of cattle.
"Who is the owner of this land?" The Prophet 鸞 inquired. Mu'âdh bin
Afra' submitted, "This piece of land belongs to two orphan boys
related to me and they are nourished by me; I shall make them agree,
you may take it for building a mosque." But the Prophet 鸞 asserted,
"I want to buy it, and will not take it without paying the price." Abu
Bakr 鸞 made the payment at once. And with the order of the Prophet
鸞 the date trees were cut, the graves leveled, and the construction
work of the mosque was started then and there. The Prophet 鸞 joined
the builders. The walls of the mosque were constructed with stone
and kneaded clay, the roof with the wood of the date palm and date
leaves. Until the construction of a separate house for himself, the
Prophet 鸞 remained staying with Abu Ayub Ansâri 鸞 in his house
as his guest. This is the same Abu Ayub Ansâri 鸞 whose grave lies in
Constantinople where he was honored later with martyrdom during
the siege of Constantinople in the caliphate of Mu'âwiyah in 48 AH.

Prophet 🕌 stayed in the house of Abu Ayub Ansâri 📿 for six months and a few days. The mosque built during the time of the Prophet 🕌 saw no change before the caliphate of Umar 📿. During his caliphate, it underwent an expansion for the first time. Uthmân bin Affân 📿 strengthened it. During the time of Walid bin Abdul-Mâlik, it saw more expansion with the inclusion of the dwellings of the noble wives of the Prophet 🕌. Mâmun Rashid Abbâsi adorned the mosque beautifully. The Prophet 🕌 was in the house of Abu Ayub Ansâri 📿 when he sent Zaid bin Hârithah and Abu Râfi 📿 to bring Fâtimah, Umm Kulthum, Saudah bint Zam'ah, Usâmah bin Zaid and his mother, Umm Aiman 📿. Abdullah bin Abu Bakr 📿 also, along with his relatives, accompanied them. Talhah bin Ubaidullah 📿 also joined the caravan. After the arrival of these people, the Prophet 🕌 shifted to his newly built house.

Calendar Year

Until now the year of Prophethood was being used to keep account of the time. It is notable that the name and the order of the lunar months are the same as was the custom in Arabia from before. Thus the first year of Prophethood elapsed just in a few months. This is the reason why the entry of the Prophet 🕌 into Al-Madinah is being reported in the month of Rabi' Al-Awwal, the 14th year of the Prophethood, while his Prophethood was actually spread over a span of $12^1/_2$ years. Similarly, the Hijrah Calendar starts from the Prophet's emigration to Al-Madinah. Since he 🕌 had come to Al-Madinah on Rabi' Al-Awwal 12, the first Hijrah year began from Muharram; Thus the Prophet 🕌 stayed in the house of Abu Ayub Ansâri 📿 until the 2nd Hijrah year.

First Year of Migration

Among the events of the first year of migration, the construction of the Prophet's Mosque and his house, and the arrival of the rest of the believers to Al-Madinah has already been mentioned. The death of Abu Umâmah As'ad bin Zurârah 📿 is worthy of mention here. Abu Umâmah 📿 was not suffering from any disease. All of sudden he fell ill and passed away. When this sad news was given the Prophet 🕌, he remarked, "The polytheists have got an opportunity to say, 'what

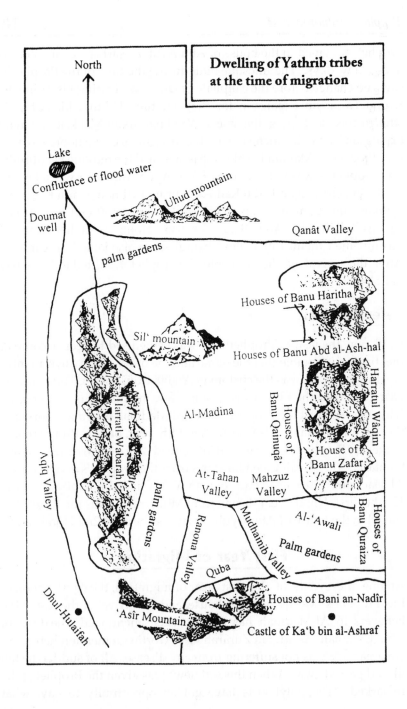

Dwelling of Yathrib tribes at the time of migration

kind of Prophet is he that one of his Companions becomes the target of sudden death'." After his death, the people of Banu Najjâr presented themselves to the Prophet 🕌 and submitted, "Abu Umâmah was our chief. Please choose for us another chief in his place." The Prophet 🕌 replied, "You Banu Najjâr are all my maternal uncles, so I belong to you. Thus I am myself your chief." Hearing this, Banu Najjâr's joy knew no bounds. Moreover, this device warded off the possibility of other candidates for chief clashing over this matter. The courage and determination of the clan increased.

The first objective of the Prophet 🕌 was to achieve law and order and good mutual relations among the people. He 🕌 felt right away that the *Muhâjirin* had come from Makkah and so they must not become a source of constant mental stress for the people of Al-Madinah. But he was equally conscious of the stark reality that the *Muhâjirin* had migrated from Makkah sacrificing everything for their faith, their homes, motherland, relatives, wealth, property, family and clan. They should be treated in a manner that they were not overtaken by a deep sense of loss, dejection and frustration. Thus the Prophet 🕌 convened a meeting of the *Muhâjirin* and the *Ansâr* and told them about the virtues of Islamic brotherhood. He then established bonds of brotherhood between the *Muhâjirin* and the *Ansâr*, putting them together in an atmosphere of mutual welfare. Each *Ansâr* took a *Muhâjir* as his brother.

Abu Bakr's brother in faith was Khârijah bin Zubair Ansâri and Umar bin Khattâb entered the bond of brotherhood with Utbân bin Mâlik Ansâri, Abu Ubaidah bin Al-Jarrah with Sa'd bin Mu'âdh Ansâri, Abdur-Rahmân bin Auf with Sa'd bin Ar-Rabi', Zubair bin Al-Awwâm with Salâmah bin Salâmah, Uthmân bin Affân with Thâbit bin Al-Mundhir Ansâri. Similarly, Talhah bin Ubaidullah and Ka'b bin Mâlik, Mus'ab bin Umair and Abu Ayub Ansâri, Ammâr bin Yâsir and Hudhaifah bin Al-Yamân 🕌 mutually consolidated their bonds of brotherhood.

The *Ansâr* remained faithful to this arrangement with so much caution and sincerity that human history is unable to give any other similar example. The *Ansâr* treated their *Muhâjir* brothers like their own and entrusted to them their wealth and property in abundance. Some of the *Ansâr* went to such an extent that they wanted to divorce one of their two wives and to give one to their brother in faith to marry. But the *Muhâjirin* also disliked being a burden on their *Ansâri* brothers and undertook a life of sweat and toil to shoulder their own burden.

First Political Document

One event worth mentioning after the migration was a pact that the Prophet ﷺ had drawn up for the inhabitants of Al-Madinah, including the Jews and the polytheists. Included in it were a number of terms and conditions. The main condition being that, in case of an attack on Al-Madinah launched by outsiders, the people of Al-Madinah as a whole would raise arms together against the enemies. Another condition being that the Jews of Al-Madinah would not provide refuge to the Quraish of Makkah or their allies. None of the citizens of Al-Madinah would put any hurdle in the way of anyone else's religion, life or property. If two people of Al-Madinah had a falling-out on an issue and were not able to find any solution to it by themselves, they would have to abide by the decision made by the Prophet ﷺ concerning it. The burden of the war expenditures would be shared equally by all the people of Al-Madinah. The Muslims of Al-Madinah would be considered as friends of the Jews, so also they (the Jews) would have to treat as friend those tribes and clans who were in alliance with the Muslims. All kinds of fighting and bloodshed would be treated as prohibited in the territory of Al-Madinah. All the people of Al-Madinah were to be considered bound to help the oppressed. This pact was signed by all the tribes of Al-Madinah.

After the agreement was finalized, the Prophet ﷺ made an all-out effort to bring the clans around Al-Madinah into the fold of this pact so that all kinds of disruptions, disorder and bloodshed were curbed once and for all. The Prophet ﷺ was so eager to widen the scope of this pact that he made a special journey to Banu Damrah bin Bakr bin Abd Manâf to bring them around to this recently signed pact. He ﷺ won over their chief, Amr bin Makhshi to the idea and he put his initials on the document. He also got the people of Mount Buwât and of Dhul-Ushairah in Yanbu and Banu Mudlij to accept the peace treaty. The purpose of the Prophet ﷺ behind this peace pact was to create an atmosphere of peace and order so that the people could be at peace and be able to reflect on the message of Islam in an air of safety and security. These peace efforts were yet to bring fruit when clandestine activities in Al-Madinah and onslaughts from outside plunged Al-Madinah into disorder once again.

Beginning of Hypocrisy

There happened to be in Al-Madinah a man of great wisdom, experience and astuteness and he wielded influence both on the Aus and the Khazraj. A short time before, both of the tribes had the bloody battle of Bu'âth, in this battle they lost much of their power and strength and Abdullah bin Ubai bin Salul was shrewd enough to take advantage of their weaknesses. His clever tricks achieved for him immense popularity among both tribes. While the people were making up their minds about installing Abdullah bin Ubai as the chief or king of Al-Madinah, Islam started to take hold in Al-Madinah. They had planned to celebrate the occasion of Abdullah's ascension to leadership on a very high level and even a crown had already been made for him. With the advent of Islam in Al-Madinah, the atmosphere changed beyond recognition.

After the arrival of the Prophet ﷺ in Al-Madinah, the Muslims became its mightiest power. Furthermore, the peace pact made all the people of Al-Madinah recognize the strength and supremacy of Islam and they all signed it signifying their acceptance of the superiority of the Muslims. The grand dreams of Abdullah bin Ubai were shattered into pieces. Since he was shrewd before anything else, he never highlighted his grievances but he harbored malice against the Prophet ﷺ from the day he appeared in Al-Madinah. The idolaters among the Aus and the Khazraj tribes were still under the influence of Abdullah bin Ubai. When the Quraish of Makkah found out that the Prophet ﷺ and his Companions were enjoying a peaceful life after arriving in Al-Madinah, and the circle of Islam was expanding by leaps and bounds, they felt terribly disturbed. Shooting their first arrow at Islam in Al-Madinah they wrote a letter to Abdullah bin Ubai and the polytheists of Al-Madinah. They warned them against providing refuge to the fugitives and asked them to expel them (the Muslims) from their territory, failing this they should be ready to face an onslaught on Al-Madinah ending in the killing of their young and the capturing of their women.

In the wake of receiving this message from the Quraish of Makkah, Abdullah bin Ubai assembled all the polytheists and kindled flames of fighting in their hearts. At the opportune moment, the Prophet ﷺ was informed of the development and he hurried to the gathering of the people and said to them: "The Quraish of Makkah have attempted to deceive you and you will suffer heavy losses if you become victims of their allurement. It is better for you to reject their warning flatly and keep to your agreement finalized between you and us. In case the Quraish make an assault against the people of Al-Madinah, it will be easier to fight them if we are united. But if you fight the Muslims, you are bound to kill your own sons and close relatives with your own swords and bring upon yourselves complete destruction. Having heard the wise counsel of the Prophet ﷺ, the entire gathering followed his point and dispersed at once. They deserted Abdullah bin Ubai and he was left alone looking pathetic.

The same year, the Muslims began to use the *Adhân* to call the people to perform prayer in congregation. It was also the year when Abdullah bin Salâm ﷺ, a great scholar of the Jews, accepted Islam. Salmân the Persian also embraced Islam after accepting Christianity and had gone through the scriptures of the Jews and the Christians who were awaiting the advent of the last Prophet. The payment of *Zakât* was also made obligatory in this year.

The Second Year of Migration

The Quraish appeared defeated in the wake of the Prophet's departure to Al-Madinah unharmed. The acute sense of shameful defeat had filled them with a maddening pain which could be cured only by taking a satisfactory revenge. The simple goal before the Makkan polytheists was to cause death and destruction to the Prophet ﷺ and his Muslim followers. This wild rage had taken them by storm. Putting aside their petty differences and discord, they had risen to the occasion as one individual with the single purpose of punishing the followers of Islam. There lay a distance of 300 miles between Makkah and Al-Madinah. Special care and preparations were needed for the Makkans to invade Al-Madinah along with winning the sympathies of the tribes living on the way and forming alliances with the forces hostile to Islam.

The Prophet 🌸 was, on the other hand, wise enough to foresee the lurking menace and he had to play his role as a reliable chief and an experienced and skilful commander. Permission for defensive fighting had already been received. Thus the time for removing the obstructions in the way of Islam had arrived. The Muslim population in Al-Madinah was, in no way, more than three or four hundred. But, in spite of lacking numbers and weapons, the evil designs and mischief of the disbelievers was more than enough to kindle in their hearts determination and ignite their Arabian sense of honor and bravery. They repeatedly placed before the Prophet 🌸 their deep desire to raise arms against the enemies of Islam and sought his permission to fight.

When the love of Islam went deep into the hearts of the believers and they appeared mentally prepared to fight the forces inimical to Islam, permission from Allâh the Almighty came for curbing the evildoers. However, the series of events taking place provide ample proof that the Messenger of Islam preferred peace to war and forgiveness to revenge. A chieftain of Makkah, Kurz bin Jâbir came from Makkah along with a band of people, and raided some grazing cattle near Al-Madinah and made off with a large number of camels belonging to the believers. When the Muslims got the news, they chased the criminals but they escaped. However, it was a serious warning for the people of Al-Madinah that their enemies could rob them of their goods and property at a distance of about three hundred miles from their houses. Besides, the disbelievers were constantly in correspondence with Abdullah bin Ubai and the Jews of Al-Madinah conspiring against the Muslim interests.

During Sha'bân of this year, the *Qiblah* (direction of prayer) was changed for the Muslims to Makkah and the fasting of Ramadân was made obligatory before the end of Sha'bân. At the beginning of the month of Ramadân, news came to Al-Madinah that a Makkan caravan was coming from Syria which would pass by Al-Madinah. In order to instill fear in the disbelievers and also to reply to Kurz bin Jâbir's attack, the Prophet 鵜 asked a party of the *Muhâjirin* and *Ansâr* to intercept the caravan so that the Makkans would know that to worsen the relations with the people of Al-Madinah might prove injurious to their trading activities with Syria. This party was sent with the sole purpose of frightening them and not for fighting.

The Makkan trade caravan became informed of the movement of the Muslim party. Abu Sufyân, the head of the caravan, led it off the main routes. He also hired Damdam bin Amr Ghifâri to hurry to Makkah with the information that the caravan was facing danger from the Muslims, and they should rush to help it and save their goods. In the wake of this news, Abu Jahl marched forward with great enthusiasm from Makkah at the head of a large army consisting of seven hundred camels and three hundred horses. The entire army was armed to the teeth and the reciters of martial songs also accompanied the army. Abbâs bin Abdul-Muttalib, Utbah bin Rabi'ah, Umayyah bin Khalf, Nadar bin Hârith, Abu Jahl bin Hishâm and others, a total of thirteen men in all were assigned the duty of serving food to the army. The Muslim party sent to terrorize the trade caravan came back to Al-Madinah.

The Battle of Badr

Abu Sufyân sent word to Abu Jahl that he had arrived at Makkah and that he should also come back. But Abu Jahl turned down the suggestion. Abu Jahl had, in truth, not come out with the army simply to provide safety but also to avenge the killing of Amr bin Hadrami at the hands of a Muslim party dispatched by the Prophet 鵜 to Nakhlah to probe some incident.

The Quraish had already started preparations to retaliate. They were about to invade Al-Madinah when Damdam bin Amr reached Makkah to seek their help. Abu Jahl was marching towards Al-Madinah. The Prophet 鵜 became aware of the movement of the Quraish army and all the notable chieftains like Abu Jahl, Utbah, Shaibah, Walid, Hanzalah, Ubaidah, Âsi, Harth, Tuaimah, Zam'ah, Aqil, Abul-Bakhtari, Mas'ud, Munabbih, Nabih, Naufal, Sâ'ib, and Rifâ'ah accompanying the Makkan troops.

The Prophet 鑾 summoned his followers and asked for their advice regarding the current development and said to the Companions: "Makkah has sent you its darlings. What do you think about facing them?" First of all Abu Bakr 鑾 and then Umar bin Khattâb 鑾 and Miqdâd 鑾 uttered words of valor and determination. The last one said: "O Prophet of Allâh, we will not say as the Children of Israel said to Moses: 'Go you and your Lord and fight, we will sit here'." The Prophet 鑾 asked again for their advice. By this he really wanted to know the reaction of the *Ansâr* for all the three who had pledged their support and loyalty belonged to the *Muhâjirin*. When the Prophet 鑾 put the same question again, the *Ansâr* now realized that the question was meant for them.

Their original pledge with him implied their defending him in Al-Madinah and did not put them under any obligation to take part in a military expedition outside their territory. Sa'd bin Mu'âdh 鑾 immediately got up to say in reply: "O Prophet of Allâh, it seems as if you are speaking to us and you want to have our answer." "Yes," the Prophet 鑾 said. Sa'd 鑾 then said, "We have believed in you and have full faith in your being Allâh's Messenger. How can it be possible that Allâh's Messenger would go out to fight the disbelievers and we remain sitting in our houses? These disbelievers are, after all, men like us. How can we fear them? If you command us to plunge into the sea, we will do so."

Lack of Means:

Satisfied with the staunch support and determination of the Companions, the Prophet 鑾 resolved to march out. The total number of the combatants did not exceed 310 or 312 or 313. When they were finally examined outside the city, some minor children were found accompanying the troops who were not fit to take part in battle yet. Thus the Prophet 鑾 asked them to go back. Some of them persistently entreated to be enlisted and of those some were granted permission to accompany the army. It was in no way a well-equipped force. This Islamic army had only two horses under the charge of Zubair bin Awwâm and Miqdâd 鑾 and seventy camels to be mounted by three or four persons at a time. Many others accompanied on foot. On

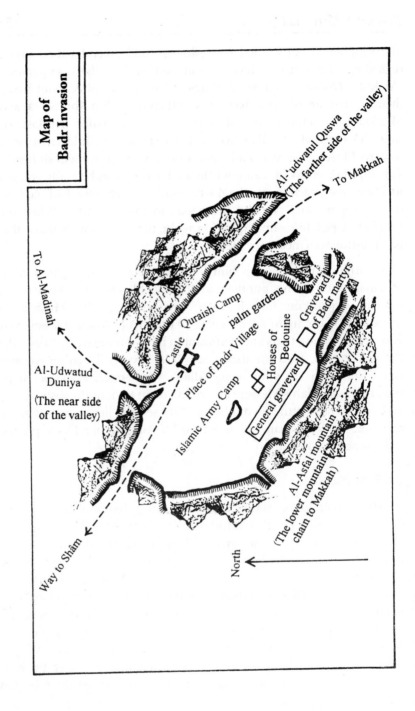

Map of
Badr Invasion

Al-'udwatul Quswa
(The farther side of the valley)

To Makkah

To Al-Madinah

Castle

Quraish Camp

palm gardens

Graveyard of Badr martyrs

Place of Badr Village

Houses of Bedouine

Al-Udwatud Duniya
(The near side of the valley)

Islamic Army Camp

General graveyard

Al-Asfal mountain
(The lower mountain chain to Makkah)

Way to Shām

North

reaching Badr, the Islamic army noticed that the enemy force had already captured the raised piece of land and pitched their tents on it. The Muslims had to take the low-lying sandy spot. However, the wells of Badr were under the control of the Muslim force. The Prophet ﷺ issued orders that any of the disbelievers coming for water must not be stopped. A hut of palm branches was erected for the Prophet ﷺ on an elevation overlooking the battlefield. He prayed and invoked the help and blessings of Allâh.

The number of the Companions were one-third of the Makkans, and their weapons were less than one-hundredth of what the Quraish army had. Their army consisted of young and strong men, and all wearing armor. The Muslims were, on the other hand, starving, weak, sick and old. Most of them didn't even possess simple weapons. Some of them had swords but no bows and arrows, while others possessed spears but no swords. When the Muslims encamped, the disbelievers sent Umair bin Wahb Jumahi as a spy to find out the number of Muslim soldiers. Umair reported that they were not more than 310, having a total cavalry of only two. The height of the disbelievers arrogance may be gauged from the statement of Utbah bin Rabi'ah who scornfully remarked, "Let us go back without a fight," meaning the disgracefully low number of the Muslims was no match for the large and well-equipped army of the Makkans. But Abu Jahl vehemently opposed the proposal expressing his firm determination to exterminate them no matter how few they were.

Beginning of War:

At last, on Ramadân 17, 2 AH, when the two armies came face to face, the Prophet ﷺ returned to his small hut and beseeched Allâh for Divine help. He entreated the Lord:

> "O Allâh! If you were to exterminate this small group of Muslims, you will be worshipped on earth no more."

He then offered two *Rak'ah* of prayer. Following this, he dozed a little and then came out fresh and smiling from his hut and said with utmost confidence:

> "The enemy force is defeated. They took to their heels."

The Prophet 鷺 had already issued an order not to initiate the fighting. There were approximately eighty Muslims from the *Muhâjirin* and the rest belonged to the *Ansâr*. Among the *Ansâr*, sixty-one were from the Aus and one hundred and seventy from Khazraj. The ranks on both sides were set in order. The Prophet 鷺 was setting the ranks with an arrow in his hand.

In the meantime, in accordance with the Arabian fashion, Utbah and Shaibah–sons of Rabi'ah and Walid bin Utbah stepped forward, and in response to their call, three of the *Ansâr*, Auf and Mu'awwidh–the sons of Afra' and Abdullah bin Rawâhah came forward to give them battle. Utbah asked, "Who are you?" "We are the *Ansâr*," they answered. "We need not fight with you," Utbah said in a tone filled with arrogance. He then called out: "O Muhammad; send our peers, men of our own tribe." The Prophet 鷺 said, "Go ahead, O Hamzah bin Abdul-Muttalib to give battle to Utbah, Ubaidah bin Al-Hârith to fight with Shaibah–the brother of Utbah, and Ali bin Abu Tâlib to engage Walid–the son of Utbah." With the order, all the three Companions rose from their spots and came face to face with their respective rivals. Utbah wanted to know their names although he knew them very well. Then hearing their names he said, "Yes, we will fight with you." The confrontation began. Hamzah and Ali 鷺 put the father and the son Utbah and Walid to the sword. Ubaidah 鷺 and Shaibah both received injuries in the encounter. Ali bin Abu Tâlib and Hamzah 鷺, did away with the enemy of Islam and brought Ubaidah 鷺 to the Prophet 鷺.

Now the disbelivers launched a full-scale attack and the Muslim troops also moved forward to face their enemies. Both sides showed great valor. As the day of Badr drew towards its close, the defeated disbelievers fled the battlefield leaving behind seventy men slain and seventy as prisoners. When the fighting started, the Prophet 鷺 came out to have a full view of the situation. He pointed out to the Muslims that Banu Hâshim did not join the enemy force out of their own will and desire, it was due only to compulsion and so they deserved special concessions. So Abbâs bin Abdul-Muttalib must not be killed, and Abul-Bakhtari also deserves forgiveness. Abu Hudhaifah 鷺 said, "How can it be that I kill my brother and leave Abbâs bin Abdul-

Muttalib, I will not let him go if Abbâs fights with me." Later on Hudhaifah ﷺ was deeply repentant for his words and expressed great regret.

Mujadhdhir bin Ziyâd ﷺ happened to face Abul-Bakhtari and said to him, "I have been ordered not to fight with you, so keep away." But Abul-Bakhtari made an attempt to save a friend of his and was killed. Umayyah bin Khalaf and his son Ali bin Umayyah were in great distress to save their lives. During the days of Ignorance Abdur-Rahmân bin Auf ﷺ and Umayyah were close friends, so he gave him protection. But the moment Bilâl ﷺ noticed him, he called some *Ansâr* and they together fell on Umayyah and his son and did away with them despite Abdur-Rahmân's efforts to save them. Umair bin Al-Hamâm ﷺ came to the Prophet ﷺ eating dates and asked, "Shall I go to Paradise at once if I am killed fighting the disbelievers?" He said, "Yes." He threw away the dates in his hand and ran to the battlefield and fought with the enemy until he was honored with martyrdom.

When the battle was in full swing, the Prophet ﷺ picked a handful of dust and threw it towards the disbelievers after reciting something over it. It resulted in the enemy fighters fleeing for their lives. Mu'âdh bin Amr ﷺ, a young *Ansâr* came across Abu Jahl who was armor clad. Mu'âdh bin Amr ﷺ struck at his uncovered leg with his sword so forcefully that it was cut off from the shin. When Ikrimah bin Abu Jahl found his father fatally injured, he fell upon Mu'âdh bin Amr ﷺ and struck him with his sword so violently that his left arm was nearly separated from the shoulder but he kept fighting the whole day with the hanging arm. But when it gave him more trouble, he put the hanging part under his foot and pulled apart by a violent force. At the same moment Mu'awwidh bin Afra' ﷺ, another young man from the *Ansâr* drew near Abu Jahl and put him to the sword.

When the disbelievers fled the battlefield and the believers were victorious in this historic event, Allâh's Messenger ﷺ asked for a search of the dead body of Abu Jahl. Abdullah bin Mas'ud ﷺ searched through the dead bodies and found Abu Jahl lying half-dead. Abdullah bin Mas'ud ﷺ got on his chest and said, 'Behold, O enemy of Allâh, what a disgrace you have been put to by Allâh." Abu Jahl said, "What's the outcome of battle?" Abdullah bin Mas'ud ﷺ replied, "It ended in victory for the believers and defeat for the disbelievers." When he was about to cut his head off he said, "Cut off my head from near the shoulders so that it looks bigger than the heads of all others and it is seen as the head of a chief." Abdullah bin Mas'ud ﷺ chopped his head off and laid it down at the feet of the Prophet ﷺ. Having noticed it, Allâh's Messenger ﷺ thanked Allâh. This battle martyred fourteen believers, six from the *Muhâjirin* and eight from the *Ansâr*. The battle being over, Allâh's Messenger ﷺ buried the believers and ordered that the dead among the infidels should be thrown into a pit or well and let them be covered with dust.

The disbelievers were so frightened when they fled the field that they even lost track of their Commander, Abu Jahl and left him behind fatally injured and dying. Harth bin Zam'ah, Abu Qais bin Al-Fâkihah, Ali bin Umayyah and Âs bin Utbah were young men and had deep sympathy with the Prophet ﷺ in Makkah; or they had secretly accepted Islam. After the migration of the Prophet ﷺ and his Companions, they were flayed and decried by their clansmen and relatives and pressed to return to their former faith. So they openly disobeyed Allâh's Messenger ﷺ and joined the battle against Islam. They were all killed in the battle along with all the notable chieftains from the Quraish. The soul-shattering news of the disbelievers' ignominious defeat in the battlefield of Badr left the Makkans struck with grief.

The Prophet ﷺ entrusted the booty to Abdullah bin Ka'b ﷺ who belonged to Banu Najjâr, and sent Abdullah bin Rawâhah and Zaid bin Hârithah ﷺ with the glad tidings of victory to the upper and lower settlements of Al-Madinah. Usâmah bin Zaid ﷺ who was left in Al-Madinah as the deputy of the Prophet ﷺ, remarks, "The glad tidings of the victory were received by us at a time when we were burying Ruqayyah ﷺ, the daughter of the Prophet ﷺ and the wife of Uthmân bin Affân ﷺ. The news of victory had arrived in Al-Madinah on 18 Ramadân."

Being free from his engagement in the battlefield of Badr, the Prophet ﷺ proceeded to Al-Madinah. On reaching Safra', he with the Command of Allâh the Almighty, distributed the booty equally among the Muslims, and ordered Nadr bin Al-Hârith bin Kildah (from Banu Abdud-Dâr) to be beheaded. Similarly, arriving at Irq-uz-Zabyah, he issued the same order for Uqbah bin Abu Mu'ait bin Abu Amr bin Linah. These two among the prisoners of the battle of Badr were hard-core and ruthless enemies of the Prophet 鑫 and Islam and equal to Abu Jahl in enmity. Thereafter the Prophet 鑫, along with his Companions, speedily left for Al-Madinah leaving the prisoners and their guards behind who joined them in Al-Madinah the next day.

General Treatment of the Prisoners:

When the captives reached Al-Madinah, the Prophet 鑫 said distributing them among the Companions, "Treat them generously." Among them was Abu Aziz bin Umair who was the standard-bearer of the disbelievers' army and also the full brother of Mus'ab bin Umair 鑫. Abu Aziz relates, "When I was being brought to Al-Madinah, I was in the custody of a group of the *Ansâr*. Whenever they sat down to dine, they gave bread to me and they began to eat dates. Being ashamed, I tried to return it but whenever I gave the bread to any of them, he gave it back to me." On reaching Al-Madinah, Abu Aziz was lodged with Abu Yusr Ansâri 鑫. Mus'ab bin Umair 鑫 said to Abu Yusr Ansâri 鑫, "Treat him roughly, for his mother is a wealthy woman." Abu Aziz said, "Brother, is it for you to give this counsel?" "You are not my brother," replied Umair 鑫, "instead he is my brother who is tying up your hands." The mother of Abu Aziz sent four thousand dirhams for his release.

The defeat suffered by the polytheists plunged Makkah into gloom. There was not a house in the city, which did not go into mourning. The Makkans stood aghast and agitated. However, the suppressed Muslims of Makkah breathed a sigh of relief and felt elated. Abu Lahab, who could not join the army at Badr, was so terribly shocked that he died after a week.

The Issue of the Captives:

Concerning the captives, Allâh's Messenger 鑫 sought the advice of the Companions. Umar bin Khattâb 鑫 submitted, "In my opinion everyone of us should kill his own relatives to establish beyond doubt

that, in Islam, love of faith is far greater than love for relations." Abu
Bakr ﷺ said, "Let all the captives be released in return for reasonable
ransoms so that the amount be invested in developing weaponry.
Besides, some of them may embrace Islam in future." The Prophet ﷺ
liked the proposal of Abu Bakr ﷺ. Some of the prisoners were
released without ransom. The Makkans sent from one thousand to
four thousand dirhams to pay for the release of their relatives. The
captives who knew reading and writing but were unable to pay
ransom were allowed freedom after teaching ten children to read and
write.

Zainab ﷺ, the daughter of the Prophet ﷺ, sent her necklace as a
ransom for the release of Abul-Âs, her husband, who was also among
the captives. Allâh's Messenger ﷺ noticed the necklace and said to his
Companions, "If you think it fit, send the necklace back to Zainab, for
it was a gift from her mother Khadijah." The Companions were
pleased to accept it and released Abul-Âs at once. Abul-Âs then
hurried back to Makkah and sent Zainab ﷺ to Al-Madinah at once.
He accepted Islam six years [not six but three or four years] after this
event.

Revengeful Enthusiasm of the Makkan Infidels

In the wake of ignominious defeat at Badr, the Makkans held
themselves back from mourning loudly, for to them, it would be
honoring the victorious Muslims. Safwân bin Umayyah, whose father
Umayyah and son Ali were both killed at Badr, persuaded Umair bin
Wahb to go to Al-Madinah and assassinate Muhammad ﷺ.

Umair arrived at Al-Madinah with a poisonous sword. Umar bin
Khattâb ﷺ was in doubt and catching hold of him by the handle of
his sword, took him to the Prophet ﷺ. Allâh's Messenger ﷺ said to
him, "What are you here for?" "I have come to seek the release of my
son who is among the captives of Badr, do mercy on me and get him
released." The Prophet ﷺ said, "Why don't you speak the truth that
Safwân has sent you to assassinate me?"

Afterwards he related the entire conversation held between Safwân
and Umair. Umair declared without loss of time, "I accept Islam and

bear witness that you are truly the Messenger of Allâh, for our secret dealings were known to none except Safwân and me."

On the day of Badr, Allâh the Almighty helped the Muslims with His angels. The participation of angels in the battle was described by the polytheists on their return to Makkah and by those viewing the battle from a distance. They stated, "On the day of Badr, all of a sudden, we witnessed a piece of cloud passing over our heads towards the battle spot. The piece of cloud was producing the neighing sound of horses. We also heard someone say, "Hurry! Go ahead." This voice struck such terror in us that a cousin of mine fell down dead out of fear.

The battle of Badr being over, the Prophet 🌸 came back to Al-Madinah on Ramadân 22. This very year, during the last days of the current month, *Sadaqah Fitr* was made obligatory and the *Eid* prayers and the sacrifice of an animal (camel, cow or sheep) were also enjoined on the believers. The same year he married his next daughter Umm Kulthum 🌸 to Uthmân bin Affân 🌸 who came to be called Dhun-Nurain (the holder of two lights), and also gave the hand of his youngest daughter Fâtimah 🌸 to Ali bin Abu Tâlib 🌸.

The flames of revenge were burning very strongly in the hearts of the defeated disbelievers of Makkah. Two months after the battle of Badr Abu Sufyân proceeded from Makkah at the head of a cavalry of two hundred men to give battle to the Muslims. When he drew near Al-Madinah the Prophet 🌸 was informed and came out with a band of Muslim combatants. But Abu Sufyân had already left after setting the some date orchards on fire and killing Saeed bin Amr Ansâri and his friend who were engaged in agricultural activities.

When Abu Sufyân heard of Muslims' arrival, the whole party took to their heels. They were in so much of a hurry that, in order to lighten their load, they threw away bags of food on the way. The Muslim troops gave them a very hot chase up to Kadr and found the food lying all over. Having abandoned the chase the Prophet 🌸 came back to Al-Madinah and the event came to be known as the expedition of Suwaiq. The type of food they abandoned is called *Suwaiq* in Arabic.

The Third Year of Migration

It has already been mentioned that Abdullah bin Ubai bin Salul was to be installed as the king of Al-Madinah. But his plan failed as a result of the Prophet's arrival in Al-Madinah. Because of this he fostered enmity against the Prophet ﷺ and his Companions. However, he was wise enough to keep his hateful feelings and hostile attitude a secret. Nevertheless he entered into heinous conspiracies with the Makkans against the Muslims. He tried hard to make the polytheists rise against the believers but was utterly defeated in his purpose. He grew so awe-stricken in the wake of the victory at Badr that he apparently accepted Islam but in truth he remained hostile to the Muslims. He also advised all the non-Muslims to follow in his footsteps and he himself played the role of their leader. The group of men his secret planning gave birth to, are called the *Munâfiqin* (hypocrites). Some Jews too joined his party and tried to benefit from the discord.

Hostile Attitude of the Jews

The dominant position of the Muslims and the speedy spread of Islam was most undesirable to the Jews. Their hostility had far exceeded the enmity of Abdullah bin Ubai. They had their three strongest tribes on the outskirts of Al-Madinah with their separate fortifications. They were Banu Qainuqâ', Banu Nadir and Banu Quraizah. The agreement that the Prophet ﷺ had finalized immediately after his arrival in Al-Madinah, had brought all the Jewish tribes into its fold. The Quraish kept hatching plots with the Jews as they had been doing with Abdullah bin Ubai.

Since the Jews were antagonistic to the progress made by Islam, they had grown sympathetic to the Quraish and their efforts to curb the expansion of Islam. The Jews were enraged and disgruntled when they heard from Zaid bin Hârithah ﷺ the news of the Muslim victory at Badr. And Ka'b bin Ashraf violently reacted to this good news and remarked, "Woe to you! the Makkans are kings and the nobles of Arabia. If Prophet Muhammad has won victory over them, one will not be able to enjoy living on this earth."

When the news of the polytheist defeat was properly verified, Ka'b bin Ashraf left Al-Madinah and went to Makkah where he wrote elegies for the slain and began to sing them throughout Makkah. After igniting the fire of revenge among the Makkan disbelievers, he came back to Al-Madinah and left no stone unturned in flaying and decrying and mocking the Muslims.

The Jewish tribes were wealthy and practiced usury of the most destructive nature. The Aus and the Khazraj tribes of Al-Madinah were indebted to them and financially under their control. The Jews were also proud of their wealth and cunning, and therefore, looked at others as if they were foolish and ignorant. The honorable victory of the Muslims at Badr embarrassed them. They formed new alliances with Abdullah bin Ubai and his hypocrite followers in Al-Madinah, and the Quraish in Makkah. Foul words and abusive language were devices they used to soothe their mental agony. They also drew a dangerous plan to first ask the disbelievers to profess Islam without actually believing in it and then renounce it saying that they accepted Islam but found that it was not a sound religion. They wanted their abandoning of Islam to cause the other Muslims to turn back from their new faith leaving behind disorder and disruption.

Now the Prophet 🌙 and his Companions came across this very ugly situation. Allâh's Messenger 🌙 would visit the Jewish communities and go to their meetings and congregations to try to bring them around to the truth and to put matters right. He said to them, "You are fully aware of the fact that I am the true Messenger of Allâh and you were yourself awaiting the advent of a Messenger from Allâh the Almighty. It was your duty to testify to my Prophethood first before all others, and you should have looked into your heavenly Books in order to find the prophecies regarding me. But you are advancing on the path of rejection and opposition; do fear the wrath of Allâh otherwise you may suffer the same ignoble death and destruction that came to men like Abu Jahl, Utbah and the others at Badr." In response to these noble and wise words, they would lash out at Allâh's Messenger 🌙 saying: "The Quraish of Makkah were unaware of the strategies of battle. We shall teach you a lesson if and when you will face us, do not compare us with the Quraish of Makkah."

The Jewish Tribe—Banu Qainuqâ'

The Prophet ﷺ put up with the highly rude treatment meted out to him with exemplary patience and forbearance. Although these unprincipled and haughty Jews had broken their covenant, Allâh's Messenger ﷺ did not like to punish them. He preferred wise counseling and patience to their shocking rudeness and disrespectful behavior. Finally, their extreme ill-treatment and evil doing led them to the brink of disaster and their doom.

Once a fair was being held in the settlements of Banu Qainuqâ'. A woman from the *Ansâr* went there to sell milk. Following this, she went to a goldsmith's shop to buy an ornament. The Jewish goldsmith molested her. An *Ansâri* raised his voice in support of the woman in trouble. Jews from far and near assembled in no time and fell upon the Muslim which resulted in his martyrdom after he had also put a Jew to death. Other Muslims also reached the trouble spot but suffered attacks from armed Jews. The Prophet ﷺ received information in Al-Madinah. He reached there accompanied by the Companions but found the Jews armed and ready to fight. Fighting took place and seven hundred warriors of Banu Qainuqâ' including three hundred armored men took refuge in their fort. Abdullah bin Salâm ؓ belonged to Banu Qainuqâ'. The Muslims laid siege to the fort, which continued for about a fortnight with the result they captured the fort along with everybody inside.

In accordance with the Arabian practice, the prisoners of war would be mercilessly put to death. The Makkans were amazed to see that among the captives of Badr, only two were killed as a result of their unbounded mischief and crimes. All others were left alive. Again, when seven hundred people were captured, they were expecting death. But Abdullah bin Ubai bin Salul, the head of the hypocrites and apparently a Muslim, interceded with the Prophet ﷺ for the safety of their lives. The Prophet ﷺ was a little hesitant about making the decision. At last Abdullah bin Ubai's repeated efforts materialized and safety was granted to all the prisoners. Thus Abdullah bin Ubai succeeded in his attempt to consolidate his friendly relation with the Jews.

Ka'b bin Ashraf has been referred to above. He grew bold enough to use the names of Muslim women in his love poems. The Muslims were much aggrieved with this state of affairs. Patience on the part of the Muslims emboldened the Jews to hatch a conspiracy for assassinating the Prophet ﷺ with the result he took care while going out at night. When the mischief of Ka'b bin Ashraf crossed all limits, Muhammad bin Maslamah ﷺ, a Companion took permission to kill him. He then took a few friends with him and went to Ka'b bin Ashraf's house and killed him. In the wake of the murder of Ka'b bin Ashraf, another Jew, Salâm bin Abul-Huqaiq took up the gauntlet and exceeded his mischief. Since Ka'b bin Ashraf was killed by Banu Aus, Banu Khazraj took upon themselves the responsibility of doing away with his evil successor. Eight youngsters from Banu Khazraj took the route to Khaibar, killed Salâm bin Abul-Huqaiq there and escaped safe and sound.

The Battle of Uhud, 3 AH

The contemptible defeat of the Makkans had infuriated them to the extreme, while the Jews and the hypocrites of Al-Madinah were making all-out efforts to light the fires of revenge. Furthermore, Hindah the wife of Abu Sufyân, whose father and brother were killed at Badr, was doing all she could to create a sense of shame at the ignominious defeat and loss of pride and prestige besides the loss of precious lives. Abu Sufyân who had achieved the status of undisputed chief after the large-scale massacre of the Quraish chieftains, started upon massive preparations to avenge the defeat.

The trade caravan which had returned from Syria prior to the battle of Badr, brought a huge profit of fifty thousand *Mithqâl* (*Mithqâl* is a kind of weight equaling 4.3 gm approx.) of gold and one thousand camels. But the goods, instead of being distributed among the shareholders, it was decided, were to be utilized for providing weapons and armor to the army that was burning with the rage of revenge. Poets were sent to other tribes of Arabia and they played their role in activating people to rise up to help the Makkans against the followers of Islam. As a result, all of Banu Kinânah and the people of Tihâmah came to their help besides other allies of the Quraish. *Ahbâsh* (the Abyssinians residing near

Makkah) were also enlisted for the purpose. Singers of military songs and the women were exciting the polytheist troops to strong action and were also to be brought to the front lines. The whole year was devoted to large-scale military preparations and they were aided and abetted by the Jews and the hypocrites at all levels.

A heavily armed troop of three thousand warriors proceeded to Al-Madinah at the beginning of the month of Shawwâl. Wives and daughters of the slain chieftains also accompanied the army to see with their own eyes the spectacle of the killers being killed. Poets were also fanning the fire of maddening anger and instigating the soldiers to storm into the settlement of the believers with new vigor. Hindah, the daughter of Utbah was the leader of the women's section as her husband Abu Sufyân was at the head of the Makkan army.

Jubair bin Mut'im had an Abyssinian slave named Wahshi who was skilled in the art of throwing lances and seldom missed his target. Jubair bin Mut'im promised to set him free if he killed Hamzah ﷺ, while Hindah struck a deal with the same person that if he did away with Hamzah ﷺ, she would give all of her jewelry to him.

The polytheist army reached near Al-Madinah. Being informed, the Prophet ﷺ summoned the Companions and asked them to give their advice about the fresh menace. Abdullah bin Ubai (the leader of the hypocrites), considered to be among the Muslims, was also present. The Prophet ﷺ was in favor of facing the enemy within the bounds of Al-Madinah. It was also because he had recently dreamt that a little portion of the edge of his sword had dropped and he inferred from this that an open encounter with the enemy might cause some loss. He had also dreamt that he had put his hand in armor. By armor he meant Al-Madinah. Abdullah bin Ubai also supported the view of fighting the enemy inside Al-Madinah and he felt he might have some advantage by this. However, the majority of the Companions favored the idea of facing the enemy outside of Al-Madinah. Although the old ones preferred to fight from inside Al-Madinah, the young ones differed and showed a burning desire to go out.

The 14th of Sha'bân was Friday. The consultations being over, the Prophet ﷺ led the Friday prayer and then came out of his house clad in armor and armed with his weapons. Now it flashed into their minds that they had differed from his opinion and might, therefore, be overtaken by some calamity. They submitted, "You are at liberty to change your opinion into action and we are ready to follow suit." But the Prophet 🕌 kept to the majority opinion as he had no specific Revelation to follow. Moreover, he liked to satisfy the fervent desire of those who were restless enough to prove their mettle in the battlefield as they weren't able to display their valor in the battle of Badr.

Thus, leaving behind Umm Maktum 🕌 in Al-Madinah, the Prophet 🕌 moved onward at the head of one thousand soldiers.

Mischief of the Hypocrites:

In the morning, he reached near Uhud mountain, Abdullah bin Ubai, the wicked hypocrite, broke away with his three hundred followers pretending that since his opinion of fighting inside Al-Madinah was not accepted, he and his men would not take part in the battle. Now the Muslim army consisted of merely seven hundred fighters. The Prophet 🕌 had also returned the boys of young age before. Soon they arrived at the foot of Mount Uhud. The Makkan army had already pitched its tents there. The Prophet 🕌 encamped keeping Mount Uhud to their back. The next day, on Sha'bân 15, 3 AH, the battle broke out.

Before the battle, the Prophet 🕌 had put 50 archers under Abdullah bin Jubair 🕌 at a mountainside and ordered them strictly to stay there until further order, without leaving the place whatever may be the condition. They were to obstruct the enemy if it comes on the Muslims from the rear.

The Prophet 🕌 then drew up his troops for battle, he appointed Zubair bin Al-Awwâm 🕌 as the commander of the right wing and Mundhir bin Amr 🕌 was given the left wing of the army. Hamzah 🕌 was put in as the advance guard, Mus'ab bin Umair 🕌 was chosen as the standard-bearer of Islam and Abu Dujânah 🕌 was fortunate enough to receive the Prophet's sword. Out of excessive joy he marched on giving an air of vanity. Thereupon the Prophet 🕌

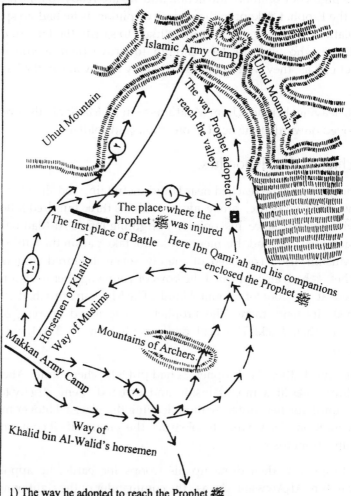

Map of Uhud invasion

Islamic Army Camp

Uhud Mountain

Uhud Mountain

The way Prophet adopted to reach the valley

The place where the Prophet ﷺ was injured

The first place of Battle

Here Ibn Qami'ah and his companions enclosed the Prophet ﷺ

Horsemen of Khalid

Way of Muslims

Mountains of Archers

Makkan Army Camp

Way of Khalid bin Al-Walid's horsemen

1) The way he adopted to reach the Prophet ﷺ
2) The way of the defeated ones ran to the foot of Uhud mountain after retrogression.
3) The way of the defeated ones adopted towards Al-Madinah after retrogression.

remarked: "Such gestures are disliked by Allâh, but it is permissible while facing the enemy on the battlefield."

The Quraish, on the other hand, set their ranks in order and put Khâlid bin Walid (still a disbeliever) as the commander of the right wing of their force with one hundred cavalry soldiers under his command. Ikrimah bin Abu Jahl (still a non-Muslim) was the commander or the left wing with an equal number of soldiers to lead. Banu Abdud-Dâr had been the standard-bearers of the Quraish army since the long past.

In order to get them excited, Abu Sufyân told them rudely that their performance in the battle of Badr brought them misfortune. They should keep it and fulfill its right otherwise it would be handed over to someone else. Banu Abdud-Dâr persistently kept the standard with them and promised to fight gallantly. The commander of the Quraish's archers was Abdullah bin Rabi'ah. The enemy force consisted of three thousand soldiers against seven hundred men in the Muslim camp.

The Battle starts:

In the beginning of the battle, Abu Âmir came forward. He was a monk (belonging to the Aus of Al-Madinah) held in regard by his people. He had settled in Makkah after the arrival of the Muslims in Al-Madinah, and also accompanied the Makkan army to Uhud. He had claimed in Makkah that he would certainly call the Aus to his side right on the battleground. Thus he gave the call but was ruthlessly rebuked by the believing Aus and he was rejected. Following this, each side launched an attack against the other.

Hamzah bin Abdul-Muttalib and Abu Dujânah 爨 fought with such matchless gallantry that the disbelievers lost courage. Abu Dujânah 爨 fought with the Prophet's sword killing everybody that came up against him, and advanced deep into the enemy's ranks. Hindah bint Utbah, the wife of Abu Sufyân was within the range of his sword at that moment she screamed and Abu Dujânah 爨 held his sword back for he did not like that the Prophet's sword be stained with the blood of a woman, so she was saved.

Martyrdom of Hamzah bin Abdul-Muttalib ﷺ:

Hamzah ﷺ sprang into action with matchless valor and killed Talhah, the standard-bearer of the polytheists. He then went deep into the ranks killing and creating chaos and disorder. Wahshi, the Abyssinian slave, noticed him from a distance and then hid behind some rocks. While making a quick forward movement, Hamzah ﷺ came within the range of Wahshi and he flung his lance at him which pierced him from one side to the other.

Hanzalah ﷺ approached Abu Sufyân by breaking the cordon around him with his dashing charge but Shaddâd bin Aswad Laithi killed him before he could attack Abu Sufyân. Nadr bin Anas and Sa'd bin Ar-Rabi' ﷺ proved their mettle before being honored with martyrdom. Twelve standard-bearers of the Quraish army were killed one by one at the hands of Muslim fighters. The Quraish standard remained lying on the ground after the killing of Sawâb, their last standard-bearer, and none had the courage to pick it up after him. The massive Makkan army was routed and after a gradual retreat, they fled the field accompanied by their women who had taken a position to encourage their soldiers to fight fiercely and fearlessly.

A Reversal:

The defeat of the polytheists and the victory of the Muslims left none in doubt of the outcome of the fierce battle. The fleeing of the polytheists and their standard lying on the ground for a long period created in the Muslim archer's hearts a zest and fervor to chase the escaping enemy. They did this in spite of their commander, Abdullah bin Jubair ﷺ trying to stop them from doing so until the Prophet ﷺ signaled them to join the attack. Khâlid bin Walid knew the importance of that mountain pass and he therefore, lost no time in storming into the open passage left by the Muslim archers. No one was there to stop the forward movement of the Makkan cavalry. Abdullah bin Jubair ﷺ was martyred on the spot. This sudden attack of the polytheists created a temporary confusion in the Muslim ranks and they stopped chasing the Makkan army.

The chaotic condition of the Muslim ranks emboldened Ikrimah bin Abu Jahl and Abu Sufyân to stop fleeing and they gathered their soldiers together to launch another attack on the Muslims while they were in a state of turmoil. Their sudden onslaught only added to the trouble and losses in Muslim ranks.

The Muslims were surrounded by a large numbers of polytheist fighters on different fronts. Mus'ab bin Umair 🌺 was standing by the Prophet 🌺 with the standard of Islam in his hand. Ibn Qami'ah Laithi, a noted fighter among the disbelievers made a violent attack and put Mus'ab bin Umair 🌺 to martyrdom. Since Mus'ab 🌺 resembled the Prophet 🌺, he thought that Muhammad 🌺 was martyred. Ibn Qami'ah mounted a raised place and claimed that he had killed Muhammad 🌺. This news sent a wave of great joy through the ranks of the polytheists and in a fit of rejoicing they indulged in jumping and dancing and felt very elated and encouraged. The Muslims were on the other hand, left shocked and stunned. Meanwhile Ka'b bin Mâlik 🌺 saw him and exclaimed loudly, "Muslims! Be happy, for the Prophet 🌺 is alive and perfectly safe and sound."

Following this, the Prophet 🌺 called in a loud voice, "O slaves of Allâh, come to me for I am the Messenger of Allâh." The Muslims rushed to him from far and near fighting and killing the disbelievers. The disbelievers also concentrated on the area where the Prophet 🌺 was surrounded by his Companions. Allâh's Messenger 🌺 was now the main target of the attack. Abdullah bin Shihâb Zuhri struck the Prophet 🌺 and injured his face, while Ibn Qami'ah hit his head so violently that two rings from the metal chain strap of the helmet put on by the Prophet 🌺 were driven into his cheek. Abu Ubaidah bin Al-Jarrah 🌺 pulled out the rings one by one and two of his teeth were pulled out doing this.

Moths at the Lamp of Prophethood:

Some of the devoted Companions circled around the Prophet 🌺. Abu Dujânah 🌺 leaned over the Prophet 🌺 to shield him from arrows until many were stuck in his back. Sa'd bin Abu Waqqâs, Abu Talhah, Zubair, and Abdur-Rahmân bin Auf 🌺 stood like rocks to guard him against the mounting onslaught of the enemy soldiers. Talhah 🌺

used his hand as a shield to stop the sword attacks until it became motionless. Ziyâd bin Sakan Ansâri ﷺ and five of his companions were martyred protecting the Prophet ﷺ, Amârah bin Ziyâd ﷺ met the same fate. Umm Amârah ﷺ whose real name was Nusaibah bint Ka'b, went following the Muslim troops just to see the spectacle of the battle. But when the situation turned against the Muslims, she rushed to be by the side of the Prophet ﷺ in those difficult and delicate moments. When Ibn Qami'ah attacked the Prophet ﷺ, she rushed forward like a flash of lightning and launched several attacks on the enemy of Islam with a sword. But he remained safe because he was wearing a double coat of mail. But his counter attack inflicted a deep injury on her arm near the shoulder.

Stability of the Prophet ﷺ:

During the moments when the fighting was going strong, some wretched and callous person hurled a piece of stone at the Prophet ﷺ from a distance which injured his lip and smashed his lower tooth and he fell on his side into a ditch. Ali bin Abu Tâlib ﷺ caught hold of his hand and Abu Bakr and Talhah ﷺ lent their support in helping him out of the pit. When a small band of the Companions assembled near the Prophet ﷺ the enemy attack slowed down. The Companions, emboldened by the presence of the Prophet ﷺ, smashed their ranks and pushed them back. Now, he went on the nearby mountain along with a party of his Companions to give a fresh call to battle from a raised point. Abu Sufyân also tried to climb the mountain but his efforts were fruitless. When he made an attempt to get on a place higher than that of the Muslims, Umar bin Khattâb ﷺ was ordered to fight Abu Sufyân and his band to push them back and he did it well with the support of his fellows.

Now the Muslim troops began to gather. The scattered Muslims got on the higher ground to be at the service of the Prophet ﷺ, and the disbelievers could not gather the courage to launch a fresh attack. However, a hard-core enemy, Ubai bin Khalaf who had planned from before to assassinate the Prophet ﷺ, made a bold charge at him. When the latter noticed him moving towards him on horseback, he said, "Let him come." He was about to make an attack when the Prophet ﷺ took a lance from his Companion, Hârith bin Samma 鷐 and thrust it in the neck of Ubai bin Khalaf, he scuttled off bewildered and embarrassed. He succumbed to his injury on his way back to Makkah.

Abu Sufyân said in a loud voice: "Is Muhammad among you?"·"Don't make any reply," the Prophet 鷐 said to his Companions. "Is Abu Bakr among you?" he said again and got no reply. "Is Umar bin Khattâb among you?" he said and the reply was only silence. Then he said "It seems all of them have been killed." Now Umar bin Khattâb 鷐 broke his silence in exasperation and answered back: "O enemy of Allâh! All are alive and you will meet your doom." Amazed to hear this he uttered with an air of vanity: "Glory be to Hubal!" The Prophet 鷐 asked Umar bin Khattâb 鷐 to say in reply: "Allâh is the Highest and Most Great!" Having heard from Umar bin Khattâb 鷐, Abu Sufyân said: "We have the idol Uzza, while you have none." The Prophet 鷐 again directed Umar 鷐 to say in reply: "Allâh is our Lord but yours is none." Thereafter Abu Sufyân said: "This battle equalized the score of Badr." Umar 鷐 replied on the instruction of the Prophet 鷐: "No, there is no equality at all, for those killed on our side have gone to Paradise and those on your side are lying in Hell." He then called out, "We shall meet again at Badr next year." The Prophet 鷐 asked Umar 鷐 to reply: "Yes, it is an appointment between us."

Abu Sufyân then departed. The Prophet 鷐 sent Ali bin Abu Tâlib 鷐 after him to witness the manner they adopted in making their departure. If they put saddles on their camels and left their horses free they meant to depart to Makkah; if they got on their horses and did not saddle their camels they had a plan to attack Al-Madinah once again. And in view of their imminent attack, the Muslims should take the initiative in launching an attack. Ali 鷐 went behind but returned in a short while with the news that the Makkans had left their horses free.

A View of the Battleground:

The Prophet 鷐 then descended from the mountain peacefully and the task of burying the martyrs started. Sixty-five *Ansâr* and four *Muhâjirin* in all were honored with martyrdom. The dead bodies of several martyrs were torn to pieces. Hindah bint Utbah, the wife of Abu Sufyân mutilated the body of Hamzah 鷐. She cut off his nose and ears and made a slit in his chest, took out the liver and chewed it but could not swallow it. Safiyyah 🌸, the mother of Zubair bin Al-Awwâm 🌸 was the full sister of Hamzah 🌸. When she came forward to see her brother, the Prophet 🌸 asked her son to send her back so that she might not see her brother's dead body which had been mutilated. On being forbidden, she replied, "Why? I know that my brother has been mutilated. I have not come here for lamentation. I shall rather keep patience and seek forgiveness for him." Having heard this, the Prophet 🌸 gave her permission. She witnessed the body and pieces of liver of her brother lying on the ground. She exercised full-restraint and recited:

"We belong to Allâh and truly we shall return to Him." (2:156)

And sought for him forgiveness of Allâh and came back silently. For Mus'ab bin Umair 🌸, the standard-bearer of Islam, only a piece of coarse cloth could be found as a shroud for his burial. The cloth was so small that when his head was covered, his feet appeared and when his feet were covered, his head was exposed. At last, his head was covered and some reeds were put over his feet.

All other martyrs were buried in pairs in one grave without being given a bath. On the return from the battlefield to Al-Madinah, they came across Hamnah bint Jahsh 🌸, the wife of Mus'ab bin Umair 🌸. She was told about the martyrdom of her maternal uncle, Hamzah 🌸 and she recited, "*Inna lillâhi wa inna ilaihi râji'un.*" (2:156) She was then informed of the martyrdom of her brother, Abdullah bin Jahsh, she recited, "*Inna lillâhi...*" and at last, she was given the news of the martyrdom of her husband, Mus'ab bin Umair 🌸 and she burst into tears. Hearing this the Prophet 🌸 remarked: "A woman loves her husband most of all."

A woman from the *Ansâr*, whose father, brother and husband were honored with martyrdom, came out desperately when there was rumor in the air that the Prophet 🌸 has been martyred. From Al-Madinah in route to Uhud when someone said to her, "Your father has been martyred," she asked, "Tell me, is the Prophet 🌸 safe?" She was moving ahead when someone said, "Your brother has been martyred," but she said, "Tell me about the Prophet 🌸." Then someone said to her, "Your husband has been martyred." But she put the same question, "Is the Prophet 襟 safe?" In the meantime the Prophet 襟 was at a little distance from her and someone pointed out to her that he was coming. Having seen his noble face, the woman uttered, "All sufferings are insignificant if you are safe and sound."

On Abdullah bin Ubai's deserting the Muslim troops and on their number being reduced, some of the Companions submitted to the Prophet 襟 to seek help from the Jews but he rejected the proposal. The Jews kept waiting the outcome of the battle in their safe dwellings. Mukhairiq, a person among the Jews told his people that they must lend support to Prophet Muhammad 襟. "We can't fight for this is Saturday," they replied. "This is the fighting between the Prophet and the disbelievers, so Saturday can't stand in the way." He took his sword and pronounced that in case he was killed, all of his property should be given to Muhammad 襟 and none should go against him. He joined the battle and was killed.

When the Prophet 襟 came to know of this, he remarked, "He was the best of the Jews." A hypocrite named Hârith bin Suwaid accompanied the Muslims to the battlefield. When the battle broke out, he killed two Muslims Mujazziz bin Ziyâd and Qais bin Zaid 襟 and fled to Makkah. He returned to Al-Madinah after a couple of days and was killed by Uthmân bin Affân 襟.

In this battle, the Muslim camp found the hypocrites in their true form and color. The next day, Sunday the 16th of Shawwâl, 3 AH, the Prophet 襟 issued orders that only those who were present at the battle of Uhud would accompany him in pursuit of the disbelievers. So every Muslim, who had fought at Uhud the day before, followed the Prophet 襟 on his way out of Al-Madinah in spite of their fatigue and their wounds. The Prophet 襟 camped with his followers at Hamra' Al-Asad, about 8 miles from Al-Madinah where he remained for three days.

At Rawha', it came across the polytheists minds that they had not won a victory. They said, "What will we say when we meet the people without any Muslim captives and without booty? Moreover, we are returning to Makkah in a state that our noted chieftains like

Walid bin Âsi, Abu Umayyah bin Hudhaifah, Hishâm bin Abu Hudhaifah, Ubai bin Khalaf, Abdullah bin Humaid Asadi, Talhah bin Abu Talhah, Abu Saeed bin Abu Talhah and a few others, who were the famous chiefs of Quraish, have been killed." Pressed hard under the demand of his men, Abu Sufyân showed his inclination to attack Al-Madinah once again.

In this situation Ma'bad bin Abu Ma'bad passed through Rawha' and informed Abu Sufyân that Muhammad 襚 had already came out of Al-Madinah with his army and they were already at Hamra' Al-Asad. Perhaps they will meet you very soon. With this news, great panic and confusion gripped the polytheists and they fled straight to Makkah for fear of their lives. Informed of the polytheists' scuttling off to Makkah in a state of embarrassment, the Prophet 襚 returned to Al-Madinah.

This expedition is known as the expedition of Hamra' Al-Asad. This event sent tremendous terror into the hearts of the disbelievers and Al-Madinah was safe from another attack by this army. It is a grave mistake to think that the Muslims were defeated in the battle of Uhud. During the first phase of the battle, the disbelievers were routed but the mistake of the archers led them to stage a comeback. But after some casualties, the Muslim troops dominated the battle scene once again and the polytheists fled from the battlefield.

The Fourth Year of Migration

A Breach of Promise and Mischief-making

On Muharram 1, 4 AH, the Prophet 襚 was informed that a large number of mischief-mongers of Banu Asad had assembled in Qatan under the leadership of Talhah bin Khuwailid and Salamah bin Khuwailid with the evil intent of launching an attack on Muslims. The Prophet 襚 dispatched a detachment of 150 Muslim soldiers headed by Abu Salamah Makhzumi 襚 to punish them. But the enemies fled before Abu Salamah 襚 reached Qatan. The Muslim soldiers returned with some cattle of the culprits.

There is a place called Uranah near Arafât where Sufyân bin Khâlid Hudhali, a hard-core disbeliever was reported to be collecting people to attack Al-Madinah. When this news came pouring in, the Prophet ﷺ dispatched a detachment headed by Abdullah bin Unais. He made it to the destination undetected and managed to cut off the head of the leader and escape unhurt. After a long and arduous journey of eighteen days, he returned to Al-Madinah on Muharram 23, 4 AH, and laid the head at the feet of the Prophet ﷺ.

In Safar, 4 AH, by way of treachery, the Quraish of Makkah sent seven persons from the Adal and Qârah clans to the Prophet ﷺ saying that their people have decided to enter the fold of Islam so some persons should be sent to them to teach Islam. In response to the request, he sent ten teachers (six according to Ibn Khaldûn) headed by Marthad bin Abu Marthad Ghanawi ﷺ or Âsim bin Thâbit bin Abu Aflah ﷺ.

When this party reached Raji', a water spot, they unfolded their treachery and called in two hundred persons. When the Muslim party saw itself surrounded, they moved to the top of a hill and began to fight in self-defense. When the Muslim party could not be captured, the disbelievers played a trick but they could seize only two while the rest laid down their lives fighting fiercely.

Those two captured were Khubaib bin Adi and Zaid bin Dathina ﷺ who were taken to Makkah. These two were kept hungry and thirsty for a couple of days in the house of Hârith bin Âmir. One day a little child of Hârith, while playing with a knife, drew near Khubaib ﷺ. He had the child seated on his thigh and put the knife aside. This horrible sight made the mother cry in distress. Khubaib ﷺ pacified the woman saying that he would never kill her child.

After a few days Safwân bin Umayyah purchased Zaid ﷺ to avenge the killing of his father. The Makkans assembled to enjoy the spectacle of Zaid's murder. From among the spectators, Abu Sufyân stepped forward and said: "You are going to be killed in a state of hunger and thirst. Would you like to be with your family members while Muhammad is killed instead of you?" Zaid ﷺ retorted "By Allâh, I would never like to be among my family members while even a thorn pricks my Prophet ﷺ." Thereupon Abu Sufyân remarked: "Nobody ever had friends like those of Muhammad." Zaid was then put to martyrdom. Khubaib ﷺ was taken by Hujair bin Abu Ihâb.

Khubaib ﷺ was then brought for execution. He asked if he could offer two *Rak'ah* of prayer. Having performed the prayer in complete repose he said to them, "Were it not that you would think I have delayed out of fear of death, I would have prolonged the prayer." The executioners then sent him to his fate.

A Soul-shattering Incident

Soon after, in Safar, 4 AH, Abu Bara' Âmir bin Mâlik bin Ja'far bin Kilâb bin Rabi'ah bin Âmir bin Sa'sa'ah called on the Prophet ﷺ. He invited him to accept Islam. But he neither confessed Islam nor abhorred it. However, he said, "I have some concern about my people. So let some of your people accompany me to the Najd to give my people the rudimentary teachings of Islam "But I am apprehensive of the people of Najd," the Prophet ﷺ said. "You care not about the Muslims. I shall take them under my protection," Abu Bara' said.

The Prophet ﷺ sent Mundhir bin Amr Sâ'idi at the head of seventy Companions in all. When they arrived at a well Bir Ma'unah, lying between Banu Âmir and Banu Sulaim, a letter from the Prophet ﷺ came to Âmir bin At-Tufail through Harâm bin Milhân ﷺ. This Âmir bin At-Tufail was the nephew of Abu Bara' Âmir bin Mâlik. He put Harâm bin Milhân to death without reading the letter. Then he incited the people to kill the Muslims. Banu Âmir refused but Banu Sulaim's clans Ri'l, Dhakwân and Usayyah carried out his wish. However, Abu Bara' Âmir bin Mâlik felt aggrieved that the incident took place in spite of the protection provided by him. He succumbed to his grief and died after a fortnight. Âmir bin At-Tufail took Amr bin Umayyah Damri ﷺ with him as a captive. He was then set free after his beard was shaved on behalf of his mother who had vowed to free a slave.

He hurried to Al-Madinah and reported the event to the Prophet ﷺ. While in the way he killed two men taking mistakenly as enemies. In a state of profound distress, the Prophet 🕮 invoked the curse of Allâh on the assassins, and Âmir bin At-Tufail died of plague.

Faithfulness to the Promise

The two people killed by Amr bin Umayyah Damri on his way back to Al-Madinah, were under the protection of Muslims so their blood money had to be paid. The Prophet 🕮 himself went to hold consultations with Banu Nadir concerning the blood money as they had an agreement with the Muslims in this regard. The Prophet 🕮 went to the settlement along with Abu Bakr, Umar and Ali 🕮.

Banu Nadir apparently showed their interest in giving their share of blood money. They seated the Prophet 🕮 in the shade of the wall of their fortification and left the place pretending to collect people for the discussion. While away from the Prophet 🕮, they conspired to kill the Prophet 🕮 by pushing a huge stone down on his head from the top of the fortification.

Mischief of the Jews

With this plan in view, Amr bin Jahsh bin Ka'b got on the top of the citadel, but Allâh the Almighty informed His Prophet 🕮 of the plot through Revelation, with the result that he got up at once and came back to Al-Madinah accompanied by his Companions. When the Jews tried to call the Prophet 🕮 back, he rejected the offer point-blank saying, "You hatched a plan to kill me in such and such way, so you cannot be trusted any more." The Jews didn't even deny it nor did they show any sense of shame.

Having arrived in Al-Madinah, the Prophet 🕮 wrote the Jews to finalize another agreement but they refused it. He again wrote them to either sign the agreement or leave the territory. But they agreed to nothing and got ready to fight the Muslims. The Prophet 🕮 invaded their territory and the Jews retreated inside their fortress. The Prophet 🕮 laid siege around the fortification, which continued for a fortnight. Abdullah bin Ubai and the hypocrites of Al-Madinah assured the Jews of their unflinching support if they either fight or accept an exile.

Banishment of Banu Nadir

However, the Jews conveyed to the Prophet ﷺ through Abdullah bin Ubai that they were ready to accept banishment provided they were granted safety of life. The Prophet ﷺ finally ordered them to put on their camels as much goods and belongings as they could, except the weapons, and leave the territory. They demolished their dwellings and broke even their earthen vessels and jars before taking leave. One section went to Khaibar and another one went to Syria and settled there. The rest of the goods and property were distributed among the *Muhâjirin*, except for Abu Dujânah and Sahl bin Hanif 웃, who were from the *Ansâr*, and received a share from the booty as they were extremely poor. Yâmin bin Umair and Saeed bin Wahb from the Jews accepted Islam, so their property remained intact. This expedition is known as the Expedition of Banu Nadir, it took place in Rabi' Al-Awwal, 4 AH. This was exactly six months after the battle of Uhud. *Sûrat Al-Hashr* (59) was sent down during this expedition.

The Expedition of *Dhât-ur-Riqa'*

During this period, news came constantly pouring in about Banu Muhârib and Banu Tha'labah of Ghatfân tribe that they were making large-scale preparations to wage a war against the Muslims. The Prophet ﷺ proceeded to meet the enemy at the head of four hundred Companions, appointing Uthmân bin Affân ؓ the administrator of Al-Madinah. They had collected in an oasis and took to their heels on receiving the news of the arrival of the Muslim troops. No fighting took place. This expedition marched in Jumâda Al-Ula, 4 AH. It was named *Dhât-ur-Riqa'* because the feet of the Muslim army were injured due to making a long and arduous journey through rocky lands and they had to wrap up their feet with rags.

Expedition to Sawîq

While departing from Uhud, Abu Sufyân had fixed the next year to meet again on the battlefield of Badr and the Prophet ﷺ had accepted the challenge. The hypocrites of Al-Madinah sent Nu'aim bin Mas'ud to Makkah to remind the Quraish of their challenge to the Muslims of Al-Madinah. Makkah was then in the grip of a famine. Abu Sufyân told Nu'aim that while he (Abu Sufyân) was making preparations for the battle, he should go back to Al-Madinah and report the massive preparations and readiness of the Makkans for the ensuing fight and so fill the hearts of the Muslims with terror. This was done in hope that they would hold back from coming out of Al-Madinah and in that way the battle would be deferred for a year. He made an offer of twenty camels in case the job assigned to him was accomplished.

Nu'aim came to Al-Madinah to do his deceitful job and began to tell of the massive battle preparations of the Quraish. The Muslims came to the Prophet ﷺ very concerned. Umar bin Khattâb ﷺ called on the Prophet ﷺ and submitted, "Why are the Muslims so disturbed with the news from Makkah when you are a true Prophet of Allâh?" Thereupon the Prophet ﷺ said, "I will go to the battlefield of Badr in accordance with my promise even if there is not a single person to accompany me." Following this he made preparations to give battle to the disbelievers and set out towards Badr. An army of one thousand five hundred soldiers proceeded under his command.

Abdullah bin Rawâhah ﷺ was appointed the administrator of Al-Madinah and Ali bin Abu Tâlib ﷺ was made the standard-bearer of Islam. Although Abu Sufyân wanted to avoid the battle, the coming out of the Muslim troops from Al-Madinah forced him to proceed to the battlefield and he came with an army of two thousand soldiers. They were not carry anything but parched barley as provisions. The Makkans called it the Expedition of *As-Sawiq*.

Abu Sufyân had managed fifty horsemen to accompany his army. When the Makkan army reached Usfân, they found out that the Islamic troops numbered one thousand five hundred soldiers under a strong and solid command. They lost courage for they had already tasted defeat at the hands of armies much less in strength during the battles of Badr and Uhud. The disbelievers retreated with the excuse that they thought it unreasonable to do battle during a drought. When the Makkan army returned from Usfân, the women of Makkah tauntingly remarked: "Have you gone to eat *Sawiq*? Had you proceeded with an intent of fighting, why did you come back at all?"

The Prophet 鏤 waited for eight days at Badr but on the eighth day, Ma'bad bin Abu Ma'bad Khuzâ'i gave him news that Abu Sufyân returned from Usfân to Makkah. After receiving this information, the Prophet 鏤 returned to Al-Madinah. This event took place at the end of Rajab, 4 AH. Although the Muslims didn't get any booty, they did take full advantage of the fair, which was held at Badr during those days. The Prophet 鏤 came back to Al-Madinah in Sha'bân, Husain bin Ali bin Abu Tâlib 鏤 was born the same year and wine was declared as prohibited. Other events of the year were: the deaths of Abdullah bin Uthmân bin Affân 鏤, the maternal grandson of the Prophet 鏤, Zainab bint Khuzaimah and Fâtimah bint Usaid, the mother of Ali bin Abu Tâlib. Moreover, the Prophet 鏤 married Umm Salamah 鏤 after the death of her husband, Abu Salmah Makhzumi.

The Fifth Year of Migration

On return from the second expedition to Badr the Prophet 鏤 remained in Al-Madinah for a period of six or seven months and nothing significant took place during this span. In the beginning of Rabi' Al-Awwal, 5 AH, the Prophet 鏤 got the news that Ukaidir, the Christian ruler of Dumat-ul-Jandal, had collected a massive army to invade Al-Madinah and they also used to plunder the trade caravans on the way to Syria. Since this new enemy could prove itself formidable and the hypocrites, the Jews and other Arabian tribes around Al-Madinah could aggravate the trouble for the Muslims, the Prophet 鏤 thought it fit to stop the menace quickly. Appointing Sibâ' bin Arfatah Ghifâri 鏤 the administrator of Al-Madinah, he 鏤 set out with an army of one thousand soldiers. Dumat-ul-Jandal lay at a distance of five stages from Damascus and ten stages from Al-Madinah. A man from Banu Adhrah was taken to show the way. During this journey they would move during the night and rest during the day. When Dumat-ul-Jandal remained at a distance of one night's journey, the guide said, "The meadow of the enemy is at hand. It is better to seize their cattle." The Prophet 鏤 permitted this action. Informed of the arrival of the Muslim army, Ukaidir, the ruler of Dumat-ul-Jandal fled in a state of great terror. The Prophet 鏤 halted there for a few days and dispatched detachments to the surrounding areas but no one came to face them.

Expedition to Banu Al-Mustaliq

On return from Dumat-ul-Jandal, the Prophet ﷺ took to his mission of teaching and training the Companions peacefully and single-mindedly. But, during Sha'bân, 5 AH, news came that the chief of Banu Al-Mustaliq, Hârith bin Abu Dirâr was making preparations for waging war on Al-Madinah and was also contacting other tribes to be a party to his plan. The Prophet ﷺ sent Buraidah bin Husaib Aslami ﷺ on the mission of collecting information about their real intention. He came back with the news that Hârith bin Abu Dirâr was bent upon overthrowing Islam and the Muslims and he had brought many tribes to his side.

The Prophet ﷺ ordered the Muslims to rise to the occasion without loss of time. Appointing Zaid bin Hârithah ﷺ as the administrator of Al-Madinah, he moved forward at the head of an army consisting of thirty horses, ten of the *Muhâjirin* and twenty of the *Ansâr*. The *Muhâjirin* and *Ansâr* were given separate standards, the standard of the *Ansâr* was given to Sa'd bin Ubâdah ﷺ and that of the *Muhâjirin* was handed over to Abu Bakr ﷺ, while Umar bin Khattâb ﷺ was appointed commander of the advance guard. Since Abdullah bin Ubai had witnessed the Muslims victorious in the past, he along with his group of the hypocrites joined the Muslim army with a great desire for the booty.

Since these hypocrites called themselves Muslims, they enjoyed all the Islamic rights of a Muslim, and so, they could not be debarred from taking part in the battles. This was the first occasion when the hypocrites joined the Muslim camp for fighting. Hârith bin Abu Dirâr had sent a spy who was caught by the Muslim troops and brought before the Prophet ﷺ. When being a spy was proved beyond doubt and he also rejected the offer of coming to the fold of Islam, then according to the Arabian practice he was put to death. When Hârith got the news of the killing of his spy, he felt worried and embarrassed.

At last Umar bin Khattâb ﷺ was ordered to go ahead and invite them to accept Islam, and he did the job adequately. But their response was rude and harsh. Following this, both the sides fell upon each other. The standard bearer of the disbelievers was killed by Abu Qatâdah 🙵 and with his fall, the disbelievers ran off. Among the captives was Juwairiyah, the daughter of the commander of the army, besides booty was taken in a very large quantity. Muraisi', where the battle took place, was at a distance of nine stages from Al-Madinah.

Mischief of the Hypocrites:

On the return journey, the hypocrites made an attempt to create bad blood between the *Muhâjirin* and the *Ansâr*. Abdullah bin Ubai highlighted the issue of the *Muhâjirin* and the *Ansâr*. He went to the extent that he pronounced: "When we return to Al-Madinah, those who are worthy and noble, will drive out the unworthy wretches."

One more event that should be mentioned took place during this journey. 'Aishah bint Abu Bakr 🙵 was also present on this journey. The army made a halt at one stage when resuming the journey. Her litter was set on the camel without her because, at the time, she was away answering the call of nature. The man who set the litter thought that 'Aishah 🙵 was inside it. She was delayed because a pearl necklace she wore was entangled in a bush and the pearls were scattered. Since the necklace belonged to her sister, she was more particular about collecting them. In the meantime the army moved off. When she returned she found nobody there. She grew very anxious.

Meanwhile, Safwân bin Mu'attal 🙵 emerged slowly from behind. He was assigned the duty of looking after all the gear and as a rear guard. Now when he came on the scene he was dumb-founded to see the Mother of the believers. He at once got down from his camel, and seated 'Aishah 🙵 on it and moved ahead holding its halter. He caught up with the Muslim army on the way. When they came to know of this incident, they expressed immense sorrow over it. But the wicked hypocrites had a golden opportunity to capitalize on the incident and created a storm in the Muslim camp.

Filled with tremendous despair, 'Aishah 🙵 went to live with her father in such a state of gloom that the believers as a whole were thoroughly convinced of her innocence and piety. Approximately one month after this incident, Revelation came down vindicating her completely. Thus 'Aishah 🌸 was strongly and firmly declared as 'truthful'.

The ever expanding mischief of Abdullah bin Ubai and particularly the latest incident became intolerable for the believers, and one Companion requested the Prophet 🌸 to do away with the scourge. But the Prophet 🌸 declined saying: "Since Abdullah bin Ubai outwardly proclaims himself a Muslim, killing him will encourage some people to say that Muhammad has now started killing his friends." When his son, Abdullah bin Abdullah bin Ubai came to know that his father had proved himself worthy of being killed, he called on the Prophet 🌸. He said, "Let the task of killing my father, Abdullah bin Ubai be assigned to me so that I, by beheading him, will establish beyond a doubt that Islam is more valuable than a father." "No, I don't want to kill Abdullah bin Ubai," the Prophet 🌸 emphatically said. However, Abdullah 🌸 stopped his father Abdullah bin Ubai at the entrance to Al-Madinah declaring, "You are a hypocrite and I will not allow you to enter Al-Madinah." When the Prophet 🌸 came to know of this, he issued an order to let Abdullah in.

Release of the Captives:

Juwairiyah, the daughter of Hârith, the chief of Banu Al-Mustaliq was given to Thâbit bin Qais 🌸. In the meantime Hârith himself came to Al-Madinah to seek the release of his daughter. He 🌸 himself paid the ransom and set her free. But Juwairiyah refused to accompany her father and showed her eagerness to be at the service of the Prophet 🌸 instead. Thus he took her hand in marriage with the ready consent of her father. In the wake of this marriage, the Companions set all the prisoners of Banu Al-Mustaliq free saying that those entering into relation with the Prophet 🌸 could not be kept as captives. The spoils of war were also given back to them. Thus enmity with a tribe was changed into love simply because of this marriage.

Reproving the Jews:

It is a fact that the Banu Nadir had aggravated their mischievous activities right from the day they had been banished from Al-Madinah. It was only because of their nefarious plans that the polytheists and the Jewish tribes of Arabia rose against the believers. The matter took such a turn that all Arabian tribes even the Christian forces at the Syrian frontiers began to look upon the Muslims as a danger to their peace and solidarity. As a result of all this, the Prophet ﷺ had grown very cautious regarding their hostile activities and 'never failed to dispatch detachments wherever danger seemed lurking.

Ghazwah Khandaq

Hua'i bin Akhtab was the biggest habitual troublemaker among Banu Nadir who had settled in Khaibar along with the larger section of the Jews who were banished from Al-Madinah. Hua'i bin Akhtab, Salâm bin Abul-Huqaiq, Salâm bin Mishkam and Kinânah bin Ar-Rubaiyi' were the prominent chieftains of Banu Nadir. They along with Hud bin Qais and Abu Umârah, the chieftains of Banu Wâ'il, went to Makkah and started raising funds for another battle and the Quraish made lavish contributions to it. After collecting huge amounts of wealth and exciting the people to the extreme, they went the Ghatfân clans and played the same role there. Banu Kinânah also jumped on the bandwagon. Finally they made contacts with Banu Quraizah of Al-Madinah who were still bound to help the Muslims according to the pact signed by both the parties. Banu Sulaim, Fazârah, Ashja', Banu Sa'd and Banu Murrah, and the chieftains of the Quraish, Banu Nadir and Ghatfân that were not less than fifty in number, all went to the Ka'bah and vowed to fight against the Muslims as long as they lived.

They maintained great caution and tight security in view of their past experiences, so the Prophet ﷺ did not receive any news about this greatest conspiracy hatched against Islam until it was too late for the Muslims to do anything.

According to their plan, Abu Sufyân set out from Makkah at the head of four thousand soldiers collected from the allied tribes. At Marr-az-Zahrân the troops of Banu Sulaim also joined the Makkan army; other of their allies kept on joining on the way. Hua'i bin Akhtab was the chief of Banu Nadir, and the chief of the Ghatfân tribes was Uyainah bin Hisn, while Abu Sufyân was the commander in chief of the allied forces.

Coming close to Al-Madinah, the total number of the allied forces came at least to ten thousand or twenty-four thousand according to some narratives. It consisted of four thousand five hundred camels and three hundred horses.

When the Prophet 綦 received news of their nefarious design to invade Al-Madinah, he called a meeting to decide on how to face an enemy with far superior numbers and weaponry. They all agreed to fight a defensive war. Salmân Fârisi (the Persian) 綦 is reported to have said, "When we feared a charge by the cavalry, we used to dig trenches to keep the invaders at bay." The Prophet 綦 agreed to his suggestion and decided to have a trench dug in the open ground lying to the north of Al-Madinah.

The city was exposed only on that side and was well-protected to the west, south and east by large plantations of date palms, volcanic rocky plains and granite hills presenting considerable obstacles to the progress of a mounted enemy. This was, in fact, the fort of the Muslim troops. In the middle, the Prophet 綦 pitched his camp. The trench was dug five yards wide and five yards deep. Groups of ten persons were each assigned the task of digging a part of the trench after equal division of the whole area. The Prophet 綦 was performing the same work along with his loving Companions.

A large rock was causing great difficulty in digging the trench for it could not be broken by the pick. When the Prophet 綦 was informed, he dropped down into the trench and gave such a blow with the pick that the rock was split and a glowing light came out of it. He 綦 said, *"Allâhu Akbar* (Allâh is the Most Great), the keys of Syria have been given to me." With the second blow of the pick, the Prophet 綦 split another portion of rock and said, "Allâh is the Most Great, the keys of Persia have been given to me." On the third attempt the remaining portion of the rock was broken to pieces. The Prophet 綦 then said, "Allâh is the Most Great, I have been given the keys of Yemen." He then added, "Jibril the trustworthy has given me glad tidings that all these countries will be under the possession of my *Ummah*."

At a time when the Muslims were making a desperate effort to save their lives against an army of twenty-four thousand strong and when

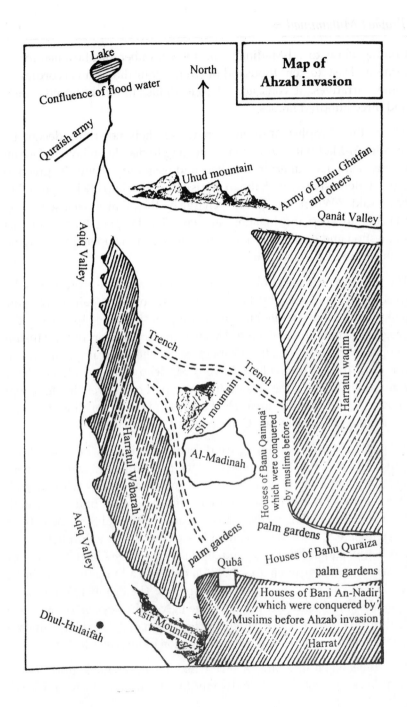

Map of Ahzab invasion

all of Arabia seemed to be thirsty for their blood, glad tidings of the conquest of Persia, Rome and Yemen were given to the Muslims. No one but Allâh the Almighty Alone could do such a thing.

Meanwhile news came to the Prophet ﷺ that even Ka'b bin Usaid, the chieftain of Banu Quraizah had joined hands with the invaders and Hua'i bin Akhtab had made a friendly entry into the citadel of Banu Quraizah to rouse them against the Muslims. The Prophet ﷺ sent Sa'd bin Mu'âdh and Sa'd bin Ubâdah to Banu Quraizah to bring them back to their senses but in vain. In reply to the polite and sensible approach, they very harshly replied that they knew of no Muhammad nor did they have any commitment with him.

When the enemy troops drew near, they exclaimed in amazement at the sight of the trench for it was a new experience for the Arabians. They laid siege of Al-Madinah. It was the most tremendous show of military power and strength on the part of the polytheists. The Muslims had managed to send their women and children to a nearby citadel. A sudden attack by the Jews, who happened to be within the bounds of Al-Madinah, was looming large over the Muslims of Al-Madinah. The hypocrites could prove even more injurious as they were always mixing with them.

Many times the disbelievers tried to cross the trench but failed. They inspected ˙the trench and, at last, found out a spot where it was narrowest and their horses jumped over the moat and carried their riders into the territory of Al-Madinah. One of these was the well-known warrior, Amr bin Abd Wadd who was considered a match for two thousand horsemen. Ali bin Abu Tâlib ﷺ cut off his head with a sweeping slash of his scimitar. The rest who had stormed the trench with him darted back on their horses. Then the actual fight started and both sides got engaged in an exchange of arrows, which would continue from morning till evening. This siege lingered on for about a month, which was very difficult and troublesome. The enemy camp was getting reinforcements from outside supporters but the Muslims were deprived of any such help.

Once a Companion complained to the Prophet ﷺ of being exhausted by hunger, and showed him his stomach on which he had tied a slab of stone to keep himself straight and active. The Prophet ﷺ then showed him his own belly on which he had tied two slabs of rock.

Since they were constantly under the fear of being sniped at by the enemy, the Muslims used to keep guard the whole night under the open sky besides being engaged in facing the enemy the whole day. Mus'ab bin Qushair, a hypocrite, tauntingly remarked: "Though the Prophet is giving Syria, Iran and Yemen to his Companions, I see in fact that they are now unable to even live in Al-Madinah. Some of them used to say, "They cannot even go out to answer the call of nature but see the dream of conquering the empires of Caesar and Chosroes.

The Muslims were in a state of a long-drawn-out siege. They were facing the scorching sun in the day, hunger, the lurking danger of an enemy charge any time, and the nefarious activities of Banu Quraizah and the hypocrites of Al-Madinah.

Mounting pressure of enemy power and strength on one hand, and the lack of men and material on their side, the Muslims were so determined and dauntless that whenever they were asked to accept peace at the cost of their honor, they rejected the offer totally. Even in such a period of distress and desperation, noble and fortunate souls were coming into the fold of Islam.

Suddenly one day Nu'aim bin Mas'ud belonging to the Ghatfân tribe, came to the Prophet ﷺ breaking away from the enemy camp and embraced Islam. He then said that he had a mission to sow the seed of discord between Banu Quraizah and the Makkan army. Thus, he first went off to Banu Quraizah and then to Abu Sufyân and talked in a way that both of them grew doubtful of each other. As a result of this, Banu Quraizah held back from lending any concrete and meaningful support to the Quraish. Both the parties gave their ear and attention to what Nu'aim ﷺ said to them, for his acceptance of Islam was still a secret. When the siege had lasted over 27 days, a violent windstorm uprooted the tents of the polytheists and overthrew their cooking pots.

"We sent a hard gale and such an army they could not witness." (33:9)

Their fires were put out in their camps and the polytheists took it as an ill omen. The polytheists were so much overpowered by fear and frustration that they scuttled off in the darkness of night.

Allâh the Almighty Himself sent to His Prophet 繁 the news that the bewildered polytheists had fled. Thereupon the Prophet 繁 sent Hudhaifah bin Al-Yamân 繁 to bring the news, he gave the glad tidings that the enemy departed leaving no trace behind. The Prophet 繁 remarked, "The Quraish shall not come at you after this year." The Muslims returned to Al-Madinah overwhelmed with joy. This event took place in Dhul-Qa'dah, 5 AH. Ibn Umm Maktum 繁 was appointed the administrator of Al-Madinah in the absence of the Muslims. On returning to Al-Madinah, the Prophet 繁 halted there only for a short while and said after offering *Zuhr* prayer that the *'Asr* prayer would be performed in the locality of Banu Quraizah. So, the Muslims proceeded on to Banu Quraizah before laying their arms aside.

Banu Quraizah's Breach of Trust

Sa'd bin Mu'âdh 繁 who had been sent to Banu Quraizah during the Battle of Trench to bring them back to their senses, was treated rudely by them. He was hurt by an arrow during the battle of Trench. Due to his wound he did not join the expedition to Banu Quraizah. The Prophet 繁 handed over the standard to Ali bin Abu Tâlib 繁 and sent him ahead as the advance guard. Hua'i bin Akhtab was present in the fort of Banu Quraizah and was engaged in rousing them against the Muslims. The Muslims besieged the fort of Banu Quraizah and the siege continued for 25 days.

The chief of Banu Quraizah was Ka'b bin Asad. When he saw that his people were unequal to face the charge of the Muslim troops, he assembled them all at one place. He said, "There can be no doubt about Muhammad being the Prophet of Allâh, for our heavenly Book carries clear and unequivocal prophecies about him and whose advent we have been waiting for. It appears fitting that we believe in him and thus safeguard our lives and our property." But the Banu Quraizah opposed this proposal tooth and nail. Ka'b bin Asad put forward another suggestion then and said, "Kill your women and children first and then go out of the fort and give a fierce battle. If victory is won, women and children can be had again, and if defeated and killed, it will be a death of honor." Banu Quraizah rejected this offer too. Ka'b bin Asad presented a third alternative and said, "Snipe at the Muslims on the night of Sabbath when we are not permitted to launch any invasion or carry out killing activities, the Muslims will be careless on this night and thus incur heavy losses." But they refused to agree to this proposal also for they did not like to violate the sanctity of Sabbath.

Meanwhile, three persons from Banu Quraizah named Tha'labah bin Saeed, Asad bin Ubaid and Usaid bin Saeed, confessed Islam. A man named Amr bin Sa'd said, "I admit that my people have committed a breach of trust and I cannot become a party to it." Saying this he left the fort.

At last one morning, they sent a message to the Prophet ﷺ that they would like to surrender on condition that Sa'd bin Mu'âdh ﷺ was allowed to suggest the punishment for them. He ﷺ accepted the proposal. After Banu Quraizah consigned themselves to the Muslims, the Muslim *Ansâr* of Banu Aus called on the Prophet ﷺ and submitted: "On the eve of the battles between the Aus and the Khazraj, Banu Quraizah would side with the Aus. You have set Banu Qainuqâ' free in accordance with the will of the Khazraj. It is our turn now, please appoint from us a judge to decide the fate of Banu Quraizah." The Prophet ﷺ said, "I have already appointed Sa'd bin Mu'âdh, the chief of the Aus to deliver his judgment about Banu Quraizah, while Banu Quraizah has also suggested his name for the role." Hearing this the Aus expressed utmost joy.

At the same moment they left for the Prophet's Mosque where Sa'd bin Mu'âdh ﷺ was undergoing treatment for his injuries. They brought him to the Muslim troops. On the way they kept pressing Sa'd bin Mu'âdh ﷺ to make concession for Banu Quraizah. However, he told one and all that he would do nothing but justice. When Sa'd bin Mu'âdh ﷺ approached, the Prophet ﷺ asked the *Ansâr* to get up and pay regards to their chief. When he was told that the Prophet ﷺ had entrusted to him the matt ᷻ of Banu Quraizah, his old allies, Sa'd ﷺ turned to his people an l said, "Tell me by an oath to Allâh that you will accept my judgment with pleasure and without any objection to it." All of them expressed their total agreement. Sa'd bin Mu'âdh 🕮 put the same question to the Prophet 🕮 and the *Muhâjirin*, and they all agreed to abide by his judgment. Now Sa'd bin Mu'âdh 🕮 delivered his judgment: "I enjoin that all the men of Banu Quraizah be put to death and their wives and children be treated like prisoners of war while their wealth and properties be divided among the Muslims." Following this judgment Banu Quraizah were ordered to come out of the fort and they were all brought to Al-Madinah in custody. At last, following the judgment, their men were killed and their dwellings were given to the Muslims.

Incidents during 5 AH

In Dhul-Hijjah, 5 AH, Abu Ubaidah bin Al-Jarrâh 🕮 proceeded to see coast area at the head of three hundred Companions under the order of the Prophet 🕮 to make an inquiry into the affairs of the Juhainah tribe, for distressing information was pouring in about them. Abu Ubaidah bin Al-Jarrâh 🕮 and his commandos had to bear untold miseries due to a shortage of food and drink. They had to survive on two or three dates a day. While they were along the shore, a huge fish was thrown up on the beach, which fed them for many days.

About Banu Kilâb it was reported that they were determined to raid and plunder Al-Madinah. In the same month of Dhul-Hijjah, 5 AH, Muhammad bin Maslamah 🕮 set out with a party of thirty Muslims. Banu Kilâb moved forward to take on the Muslims but tasted a sweeping defeat and took to their heels leaving behind ten dead and fifty camels and three thousand goats as booty.

Similarly, Ukâshah bin Mihsan 🕮 was sent to Makkah to look into the state of affairs, while a small party was dispatched to Najd, which returned to Al-Madinah with Thumâmah bin Uthâl as a captive, who embraced Islam wholeheartedly. He then went back to his territory, Yamâmah, and prevented the caravans from carrying food grains to Makkah. The people of Makkah were so hard pressed by the ban imposed by Thumâmah 🕮 that they wrote to the Prophet 🕮 requesting him to get the ban lifted. The Prophet 🕮 asked Thumâmah 🕮 to allow the supplies of food grains to reach Makkah.

The Sixth Year of Migration

It has already been mentioned among the events occurring in 5 AH that on the occasion of the Prophet's return from the expedition to Dumat-ul-Jandal, Uyainah bin Hisn had requested him to allow grazing of his camels in the meadows of Al-Madinah. He was allowed the opportunity for one year. But that thankless fellow paid back by raiding the pasture of the Prophet's camels, killed a man from Banu Ghifâr and carried away his wife along with the camels of the Prophet 鑑.

Salamah bin Amr bin Akwa'鑑 was the first to know of this incident. He raised the alarm, collected a small band and gave them hot chase. Salamah's loud voice made the Prophet 鑑 also to go behind the culprits. Shortly after his departure, Miqdâd bin Al-Aswad, Abbâd bin Bishr, Sa'd bin Zaid, Ukâshah bin Mihsan, Muhriz bin Fadâlah Asadi, and Abu Qatâdah 鑑 followed suit and joined the Prophet 鑑. He appointed Sa'd bin Zaid 鑑 the head of the party and sent him ahead and he himself halted at the stream of Dhu Qirad.

Salamah bin Amr 鑑 caught the miscreants. The pursuers were strengthened by reinforcements, and both the parties set themselves against one another. The Muslims captured their camels besides regaining their own camels. They returned to the Prophet 鑑 at Dhu Qirad. The Prophet 鑑 slaughtered a camel from among the captured ones, and left for Al-Madinah after a night's halt.

In the same year, news reached the Prophet 鑑 that Banu Bakr had entered into a conspiracy with the Jews of Khaibar to invade Al-Madinah. The Prophet 鑑 sent Ali bin Abu Tâlib 鑑 at the head of two hundred soldiers to deal with Banu Bakr.

On the way, the Muslim army captured a spy of Banu Bakr who disclosed the concentration points of the enemy troops on a promise of his safety. He was set free as promised. Ali bin Abu Tâlib 鑑 made a sudden dashing charge against the enemies and they took to their heels after a fierce encounter. The Muslims collected five hundred camels and two thousand goats as booty.

Preaching of Islam

In Sha'bân, 6 AH, the Prophet 鑑 sent Abdur-Rahman bin Auf 鑑 to the surrounding areas of Dumat-ul-Jandal to preach Islam to the people of those areas who were still disbelievers. One of their chieftains, Asbagh bin Umar Kalbi was a Christian. With the efforts of Abdur-Rahman bin Auf 鑑, Asbagh accepted Islam and the majority of the tribe followed suit. Some other chieftains, who declined to accept Islam, got ready to pay the *Jizyah* (a tax levied on non-Muslims to compensate their not taking part in armed defense of the Muslim community). Tamâdar, the daughter of Asbagh was married to Abdur-Rahman bin Auf 鑑 and she gave birth to Abu Salamah who rose to be among the greatest Islamic legal experts.

A Criminal Event

A few persons from Ukl and Urainah tribes who seemingly confessed Islam, expressed their desire to settle in Al-Madinah. But, after a few days, they complained of the unfavorable climate of Al-Madinah and became sick. The Prophet 鑑 sent them to the north of Uhud where his own camels were grazing. When they became strong and stout, they mercilessly killed Yasâr, who was taking care of the camels, and made off with the camels. When this tragic news reached Al-Madinah, the Prophet 鑑 sent Kurz bin Jâbir Al-Fihri behind them with twenty horsemen and they caught the culprits on the way and they were returned to Al-Madinah and put to death there.

The Truce of Hudaibiyah

Although the religion of Ibrahim (Abraham) 鑑 was part of the culture all over Arabia, the people had become immersed in polytheism and idol-worship, they all still held the Ka'bah in high esteem and performed the *Hajj* most regularly. They also stopped fighting during the days of *Hajj*. In the month of Shawwâl, 6 AH, the Prophet 鑑 had a dream that he was entering the Ka'bah along with his Companions. The Muslims had a great desire to visit Ka'bah and the dream deepened this urge. The Prophet 鑑 decided to visit the Ka'bah to perform *Umrah* (the lesser pilgrimage) and he left Al-Madinah for Makkah in Dhul-Qa'dah, 6 AH, with one thousand four hundred Companions and seventy sacrificial camels. They were all in *Ihrâm*. Coming as pilgrims symbolized their peaceful intentions and the Makkans also had no right to prevent the Muslims from visiting the Ka'bah.

Having arrived at Dhul-Hulaifah, the Prophet 襲 sent as a precaution a man from the Khuzâ'ah tribe to check the situation. He came back and informed the Prophet 襲 that the Quraish had collected a large number of people to stop the Muslims from reaching the Ka'bah. The Prophet 襲 consulted the Companions. Abu Bakr 鑾 said, "We have come here for performing *Umrah* and not for fighting. But, if someone stands between the House of Allâh and us, then we must fight against them." Having heard this, the Prophet 襲 ordered the Muslims to proceed on. The Quraish had already sent Khâlid bin Walid with a squad of cavaliers to Kura' Al-Ghamim to stop the movements of the Muslims towards the Ka'bah. The Prophet 襲 took a route towards the right evading the main route and all of a sudden, they passed western side of Khâlid bin Walid. Now he, frightened to the extreme, galloped off on his horse to Makkah to update them of the imminent danger at hand. The Prophet 襲, on the other hand, reached the hilly range below which starts the surrounding areas of the city of Makkah. His dromedary sat down there. The people around remarked: "The dromedary has played foul." Thereupon the Prophet 襲 retorted, "The dromedary has not played foul, but she is prevented by the One Who has prevented elephants to enter the city."

Position of Hudaibiyah:

The Prophet 襲 did not think it proper to launch an attack on Makkah and the House of Allâh for those were the areas where fighting was prohibited by Allâh. He 襲 then chided the dromedary and it got up and moved on. The Prophet 襲 halted at the well of Hudaibiyah. The well was deficient in water which ran short in no time. When the people were on the brink of facing trouble, the Prophet 襲 took out an arrow from his quiver and gave it to Bara' bin Âzib 鑾 to drop it in the well. With the dropping of the arrow, water in the well flowed in such a great quantity that the Muslim army no longer had a scarcity.

When the Prophet 繼 got set at Hudaibiyah, Budail bin Warqa' Khuzâ'i came with a number of men and asked the purpose behind the arrival of the Muslims. He 繼 said, "Don't you see the rows of sacrificial camels ahead of the caravan and notice us in *Ihrâm*?" Hearing this he went away and said to the Quraish, "You are unnecessarily raising an alarm about Muhammad. He has come here with the sole intention of visiting the House of Allâh, not for fighting with you." The mischievous among the Quraish said, "We will not allow them to come here even as pilgrims." But the wiser section began to think in silence.

Then they sent Hulais bin Alqamah Kinâni, the chief of *Ahâbish* tribes (tribes around Makkah) as their envoy. But he returned only after witnessing the sacrificial camels without even approaching the Prophet 繼 and said to the Quraish, "The Muslims have come here not for fighting but to perform *Umrah*, and none has the right to prevent them from doing this." Hearing this the Quraish remarked, "You wild man, you know nothing, we shall never allow the Muslims to enter Makkah, otherwise we will be disgraced." Hulais fell in anger and said, "If you keep the Muslims away from performing *Umrah*, we will fight against you with all our men." In response to these activities, the Prophet 繼 sent Khirâsh bin Umayyah Khuzâ'i with the message that they had come not for fighting but to perform *Umrah* and to sacrifice their animals. The Quraish slaughtered the camel of Khirâsh and attempted to kill him as well. But Hulais and his men saved him and returned him safely. Following this a group of headstrong youngsters came out of Makkah with a plan to launch a sudden attack on the Muslims. They were all caught but were released later on by the order of the Prophet 繼.

He 繼 then wanted to send Umar Fâruq 繼 to the Makkans. Thereupon Umar 繼 submitted, "I have no objection in going there but none of my tribe Banu Adi bin Ka'b is in Makkah to take me under their protection. My visit may land me in trouble, Uthmân bin Affân is a better person to do the job, for a large number of powerful and influential people of his tribe Banu Umayyah are still in Makkah." This suggestion was appreciated by the Prophet 繼 and he sent Uthmân bin Affân 繼 to Abu Sufyân as his envoy. He came across Abân bin Saeed bin Al-Âs as he entered Makkah, Abân took him under his protection without loss of time and took him to Abu Sufyân and the other chieftains of the Quraish. Having heard from Uthmân 🙵 the message of Prophet 🙵 they said, "We give you permission to go around Ka'bah." Thereupon Uthmân 🙵 said, "I can't circumambulate alone without the Prophet 🙵." Hearing this the Quraish grew angry and held him back in Makkah.

The Pledge of Ridwân:

When the return of Uthmân 🙵 was delayed, a rumor spread among the Muslims that he was martyred. Hearing this the Prophet 🙵 said with determination, "We shall not leave this place without avenging the murder of Uthmân." Thus he 🙵 sat down under a tree and took oath from all his Companions on sacrificing their lives for this cause. The Noble Qur'ân says referring to this event:

> "When the believers took the oath at your hand (O Messenger) Allâh the Almighty grew happy with them." (48:18)

But Uthmân 🙵 came back from Makkah after a short while. Although the sober and saner section of the Quraish disliked fighting, the majority opinion persisted in favor of fighting and killing. But finding the Muslims ready to do battle, their belligerent attitude also softened. Thus the Makkans sent Urwah bin Mas'ud, the chief of Banu Thaqif to the Prophet 🙵. He came and said, "O Muhammad! All the clans of the Quraish are determined to give you battle. The people who are now lending you their support, will scurry off leaving you alone for they are unable to stand the onslaught of the Quraish."

Abu Bakr 🙵 answered him back so violently that he kept silent. The Prophet 🙵 said to Urwah, "We have not come here with the intention of fighting but with a desire to perform *Umrah*. But, if the Makkans are bent upon fighting, I shall fight with them to fulfill the duties of my Prophethood till my head is separated from body or Allâh the Almighty Himself decides the matter. If the Makkans so desire, I am ready to finalize a truce with them provided they let us do our preaching work, or accept Islam to do away with the fighting for ever."

Deep Love of the Companions for the Messenger 鑾:

During his conversation with the Prophet 鑾, Urwah was again and again stretching his hand up to the beard of the Prophet 鑾. Mughirah bin Shu'bah 鑾 became displeased at this gesture and by hitting his hand with the handle of his sword, asked him to behave. When he went back to the Quraish he said, "O people of Quraish! I have been to the magnificent royal courts of Rome and Persia, but nowhere did I witness any ruler so dear to his people as Muhammad is to his followers. His Companions have such a deep love and high regard for him that when he performs ablution, they struggle to get the water he has used and don't even let it fall on the ground. If he speaks, everybody listens to him with rapt attention, nobody even dares to look straight into his eyes. They can't leave Muhammad at any cost. Accept what Muhammad has explained to you, and strike a peace deal with him." Following this the Quraish sent Suhail bin Amr with the power of attorney to make a compromise only on the condition that Muhammad 鑾 gives his consent to return back this year with his men only to come next year to perform *Umrah*. As soon as the Prophet 鑾 saw Suhail coming, he said, "The matter has now become easy since they have sent this man, it seems they want peace." Suhail put the terms of the treaty and the Prophet 鑾 accepted them as a whole. He 鑾 then summoned Ali 鑾 and asked him to prepare a draft of the agreement. Ali 鑾 wrote *Bismillâhir-Rahmânir-Rahim* (In the Name of Allâh, the Most Gracious, the Most Merciful) at the head of the document. Objecting to it Suhail said, "We do not recognize *Rahmân* (the Most Gracious), but write *Bismika Allâhumma* (In Your Name, O Allâh), as the custom goes." The Prophet 鑾 said, "Well, let it be." When Ali 鑾 wrote the name of the Prophet, 'Muhammad, the Messenger of Allâh', Suhail again protested and said, "Had we witnessed that you were the Messenger of Allâh, we would not have turned you away from the House of Allâh nor fought with you. You should write 'Muhammad bin Abdullah'." "I am Allâh's Messenger even if you disbelieve in me," replied the Prophet 鑾 and asked Ali 鑾 to rub out what he had written. "By Allâh, I cannot do it," replied Ali 鑾. The Prophet 鑾 asked Ali 鑾 to point out the place to be rubbed out. Ali 鑾 pointed it out to the Prophet 鑾 who expunged it.

Conditions:

The following were the conditions of the Treaty:

1. The Muslims will perform *Umrah* next year instead of this year. While entering Makkah they will carry no arms except their swords, and that too being sheathed. Moreover, they will not stay in Makkah for more than three days.

2. The Treaty will remain valid for a period of ten years. And nobody from any side would lift their hand against the other for the duration.

3. Every tribe or clan of Arabia will enjoy the right to enter into agreement with any party of its choice; but the allies will have to observe the terms and conditions of the Treaty in letter and spirit.

4. If anyone from the Quraish comes over to the Prophet ﷺ without obtaining the permission of his guardian, he will be returned to his guardian, but if anyone of those with the Prophet ﷺ escaped to the Quraish, they are not bound to be returned to him.

Reaction to the Peace Treaty:

The fourth condition of the Treaty was terribly displeasing to the Companions. The Treaty was still being written when Abu Jandal ؓ, the son of Suhail himself, who was put in chains and mercilessly tortured for professing Islam, came to the Prophet ﷺ from his captivity. He showed fresh injuries on his person and expressed his profound desire to be taken to Al-Madinah. Suhail cried in excitement, "Abu Jandal should be handed over to me as per the Treaty." The Prophet ﷺ tried to drive the point home to Suhail but he would not agree. At last, Suhail took Abu Jandal ؓ back to Makkah beating him severely.

Umar ؓ witnessed the pitiable sight and lost control over himself. He then appeared before the Prophet ﷺ and said, "O Messenger of Allâh! Are you not a true Prophet?" "Certainly! I am a true Prophet," the Prophet ﷺ replied. "Are we not believers?" "Certainly! You are believers," the Prophet ﷺ said in reply. "Are they not polytheists?"

Umar ؓ submitted again. "Certainly! They are polytheists," the Prophet ﷺ said. "Why are we then accepting such ignominious terms?" Umar ؓ inquired. The Prophet ﷺ said, "I am the Messenger of Allâh and therefore, cannot oppose the Command of Allâh, nor can I commit any breach of trust. He (Allâh) will never put me to disgrace." Hearing this Umar's anger subsided and he repented very deeply for his being so bold with the Prophet ﷺ and kept on seeking forgiveness of Allâh and setting slaves free to atone for his behavior.

Unique Victory:

Having concluded the Treaty, the Prophet ﷺ and the Muslims sacrificed the animals at Hudaibiyah, put off their *Ihrâm* and shaved their heads. After this Treaty, the Khuzâ'ah tribe formed an alliance with the Prophet ﷺ and the Banu Bakr tribe formed an alliance with the Quraish of Makkah. The Khuzâ'ah and Banu Bakr were at odds with one another for quite a long time. Since each of them, formed an alliance with one party or another, they had to be at peace with each other according to one of the conditions of the Treaty. When the Prophet ﷺ was returning from Hudaibiyah to Al-Madinah, *Sûrat Al-Fath* (The Victory) was revealed on the way. Now what the Companions took as a setback was, in fact, a unique victory. Very soon the Companions saw with their naked eyes that the seemingly weak terms from the Muslim point of view proved very strong and useful. The greatest victory for the Muslims was the condition of peace which the Muslims secured through this Treaty, which paved the way for the spread of Islam so quickly that could not have been possible in a state of fighting and disorder. Islam means peace and it has so often gone to war to establish peace. Battles in Islam have always been fought for winning peace. Thus in only two years after the Truce of Hudaibiyah, enjoying a state of peace, the number of believers doubled.

Consequences of the Truce of Hudaibiyah

The fourth condition of the Treaty was as an irritant of the highest degree. This condition was repulsive to the Muslims, however, the Quraish eventually requested the Prophet ﷺ to cancel this condition

which seemingly was in their favor. The following events will explain
what caused this surprising change. A few days after the return of the
Muslims to Al-Madinah, Abu Basir, who had already confessed Islam
in Makkah, broke away and took shelter in Al-Madinah. The Quraish
sent two of their men to bring Abu Basir ﷺ back to Makkah
according to the recently signed Treaty. The Prophet ﷺ sent him back.
At Dhul-Hulaifah, he, according to a plan, said to one of his guards,
"Your sword appears to be of the highest quality." Hearing this,
another guard unsheathed the sword of his fellow and began to
admire it. Abu Basir ﷺ said, "Let me see the sword." He gave it to
Abu Basir ﷺ without the least care.

Abu Basir ﷺ struck him with the sword so hard that his head came
off and fell down. The other guard took to his heels towards Al-
Madinah and entered into the Prophet's Mosque frightened, and
narrated the incident to the Prophet ﷺ. He was still reporting the
event when Abu Basir ﷺ came in following him with the unsheathed
sword. When he was sure he wouldn't get any protection in Al-
Madinah, Abu Basir ﷺ said to the Prophet ﷺ: "You have already
fulfilled your duty by handing me over to the polytheists, but Allâh
the Almighty caused me to restore my liberty. I will now go away
because you will, in fulfillment of your agreement, give me to the
polytheists again." Saying this he left the place. The man from the
Quraish returned to Makkah and related the incident to them.

Abu Basir ﷺ fled to the seacoast and settled at Eis. When Abu Jandal
bin Suhail ﷺ came to know of this, he also escaped from Makkah and
joined Abu Basir ﷺ. Now, whoever embraced Islam in Makkah fled
from there to join the band of Abu Basir ﷺ. The band grew so strong
that it began to intercept the trade caravans of Makkah. Things got so
bad that the Quraish wrote to the Prophet ﷺ to abrogate the fourth
condition of the Treaty, and they would no longer demand the return of
those who escaped and went to him in future.

The Prophet ﷺ accepted the request of the Quraish and sent a
message to Abu Basir ﷺ to come to Al-Madinah along with his band
of men. This order reached Abu Basir ﷺ at a time when he was
seriously ill and confined to bed. However, he called Abu Jandal ﷺ
and instructed him to carry out the command without loss of time.

Abu Basir then passed away and Abu Jandal left for Al-Madinah accompanied by his fellows. This is how the despised fourth condition of the Treaty was mutually canceled.

Return of the Muslims from Abyssinia

On return from Hudaibiyah, the Prophet sent Amr bin Umayyah Damri with a letter addressed to Negus, the King of Abyssinia, to bring Ja'far bin Abu Tâlib and all other Muslim migrants back to Al-Madinah. Through this dispatch, the Prophet had also invited Negus to accept Islam, which he did at once. He bade farewell to the Muslims with many valuable gifts. From Hudaibiyah, the Prophet reached Al-Madinah in Dhul-Hijjah and stayed in Al-Madinah till Muharram, 7 AH. Towards the end of 6 AH, the Prophet introduced among the Muslims the practice of racing camels and horses. It is said that Aishah's mother died the same year and Abu Hurairah embraced Islam.

The Seventh Year of Migration

Conquest of Khaibar

After the Truce of Hudaibiyah, the Prophet obtained peace with the Makkan polytheists. However, news came to Al-Madinah that there was a plan to launch an attack on Al-Madinah. Being uprooted from Al-Madinah, Banu Nadir and Banu Qainuqa' were staying in Khaibar and the flames of revenge were burning in their hearts, and very soon the Jews of the region were incited to rise up against the Muslims. Khaibar became the center of hostility against the Muslims. They started large-scale military preparations against the believers. They drew Banu Ghatfân to their side by promising them half of the produce of Al-Madinah.

The Jews had the support of the hypocrites of Al-Madinah and even though they were far away from Al-Madinah, they knew of every move the Muslims were making. Informed of their military preparations, the Prophet marched towards Khaibar in Muharram, 7 AH, at the head of one thousand five hundred Companions leaving

Saba' bin Arfatah 🌸 in Al-Madinah as Administrator. He 🌸 chose Raji', a region lying between Khaibar and Banu Ghatfân, to serve as his military camp, with the result Banu Ghatfân who kept fearing a Muslim attack at any time, could not dare go to help the Jews of Khaibar.

In Khaibar, there were three settlements in which the Jews had a cluster of six big forts. They had among them fighters like Marhab and Yâsir who were wrestlers of repute. They stepped forward and made a challenge for a duel. Muhammad bin Maslamah and Zubair bin Awwâm 🌸 accepted the challenge. After a fierce fight, Maslamah 🌸 killed Marhab and Zubair bin Awwâm 🌸 slew Yâsir. As per some narratives, Ali 🌸 was the man who had killed Marhab.

Finding it almost impossible to face the Muslims in the open, the Jews stayed in their forts. The Muslim army launched an attack on the fort called Nâ'im which belonged to Marhab and captured it. The next fort to be captured was Sa'b bin Mu'âdh. Then attack was made on the second settlement of Khaibar. Its forts were also captured. Now came the Qamus, fort of Abu Huqaiq in the third settlement, it also fell. Safiyyah bint Hua'i was brought to Al-Madinah as a captive and the Prophet 🌸 married her after setting her free.

Watih and Salâlim were the two remaining forts that came under siege by the Muslim troops, which continued for ten days. They obtained peace and safety from the Muslims on giving half of the produce from their lands and gardens.

During the battle of Khaibar, fifteen Muslims were honored with martyrdom, four from the *Muhâjirin* and eleven from the *Ansâr*, while 39 Jews were killed. Zainab bint Al-Harth, the wife of a Jewish chieftain, Salâm bin Mishkam served the Prophet 🌸 a poisonous roasted goat. As he took a piece of it, he spat saying that the bones were giving information about the poison. Bishr bin Al-Bara' 🌸 who was sharing the meal, had taken a piece of meat and swallowed it which led to his immediate death. Zainab was called and she confessed her crime. She was handed over to the relatives of Bishr 🌸 but they held back from killing her as she had already accepted Islam. According to another narrative, she did not embrace Islam and was killed in retaliation. Preparations to set out for Al-Madinah were still on when some migrants of Abyssinia appeared before the Prophet ﷺ along with the valuable gifts and a letter from Negus, the King of Abyssinia. Their caravan included Ja'far bin Abu Tâlib, his wife, Asma' bint Umais, his sons Abdullah, Aun, and Muhammad, Khâlid bin Saeed bin Al-Âs bin Umayyah, his wife, Aminah bint Khalaf, and his son, Saeed ﷺ. While Umm Khâlid, Amr bin Saeed, Abu Musa Ash'ari, Jahm bin Qais, Harth bin Khâlid, Muhinah bin Ghidâr, Ma'mar bin Abdullah, Abu Hâtib bin Amr, Malik bin Rabi'ah bin Qais and Amr bin Umayyah Damri ﷺ were those who had gone to bring them back. Some of them went to Al-Madinah and the rest arrived in Khaibar.

On the way back in the eastern side from Khaibar, there lay the flourishing town of Fidak. The Jews of Fidak sent a message to the Prophet ﷺ to take away everything in lieu of their lives. The request was accepted. Since Fidak came under possession without a fight, the property was given to state control as the sole property of Allâh and His Messenger. When the Muslim army passed by Wâdi-ul-Qura, the Jews of the area began to shoot arrows at the Muslims. They were also besieged and they earned peace and safety at the cost of half of their produce. The people of Taima also obtained peace like those of Wâdi-ul-Qura.

After the Conquest of Khaibar

On way back from Khaibar, one morning the Prophet ﷺ and the entire Muslim army slept past sunrise. It was the Prophet ﷺ who got up first and roused the others from their sleep. At a little distance from there, he ﷺ and his Companions offered the *Fajr* prayer. Thus he ﷺ showed the Companions the offering of the prayer when rising late from the sleep.

The Jews were very wealthy and the lands of Khaibar under their possession were also very fertile. After the conquest of Khaibar, the booty and agricultural lands distributed among the Muslims removed their poverty and hardship. Now the *Muhâjirin* became owners of property and became free from the need for help and support of the *Ansâr*. From the lands of Khaibar, the Prophet ﷺ received the property of Fidak, which served the purpose of caring for the many visiting delegations and his other guests, while the land from Banu Nadir sustained his relatives, the orphans and the poor.

A very wealthy man from Makkah, Hajjâj bin Ilât Sulami, left Makkah telling everyone that he was going on a journey but he actually went to the Prophet 鑅 and he became a Muslim in his presence and joined the Prophet 鑅 during the expedition of Khaibar. He said, "The Makkans are still unaware of my conversion to Islam. With your permission, may I go to Makkah and bring my wealth, which is in the possession of my wife and collect the money I have given as loans to the Makkans?" The Prophet 鑅 granted him permission. When Hajjâj 鑅 went to Makkah, he found that the Makkans desperately wanted to know about the outcome of the Muslims action in Khaibar. Hajjâj 鑅 used this event to deceive the disbelievers. He told them nothing about the consequences of the battle of Khaibar and utilized their support in collecting his loans, they considered it a support for a fellow enemy of the Muslims. He then set out from Makkah with his entire wealth after collecting the whole amount that was outstanding, he only informed Abbâs bin Abdul-Muttalib about his accepting Islam and the conquest of Khaibar by the Muslims. The Makkans were angry and depressed at the success of the Muslim military action in Khaibar and Hajjâj's escape from Makkah with such a vast amount of wealth.

On his return from Khaibar, the Prophet 鑅 sent detachments to all those tribes who were still making efforts to inflict harm on the Muslims. The purpose behind sending those detachments was to send terror into their hearts so that any conspiracy would be prevented before it was put into action. Abu Bakr 鑅 along with Salamah bin Akwa' 鑅 and others were sent to the Fazârah tribe, while Umar 鑅 was dispatched to the Hawâzin at the head of thirty horsemen. Abdullah bin Rawâhah 鑅 was sent to arrest Bishr bin Zarâm, the Jew who used to incite the Jews of Khaibar against the Muslims. Bashir bin Sa'd Ansâri 鑅 set out at the head of thirty horsemen to punish Banu Murrah, while Usâmah bin Zaid 鑅 went to the clan Huraqah (Banu Humais) of Juhainah tribe. Ghâlib bin Abdullah Laithi 鑅 was sent to Banu Al-Mulawwih, and Abu Hadrad Aslami 鑅 was sent to Rifâ'ah bin Qais, the chief of the Jusham bin Mu'âwiyah clan. Abu Qatâdah and Muhallim bin Jaththâmah 鑅 were sent to Idam.

All these military detachments came back with success. Usâmah bin Zaid ﷺ lifted his sword to kill a person who immediately pronounced *La ilâha illallâh* (there is no God to be worshipped except Allâh), despite this, Usâmah ﷺ put him to death. When the matter was later reported to the Prophet ﷺ, he asked Usâmah ﷺ to explain his action. He submitted that he had killed him because he had pronounced the *Shahâdah* just to save his life. "Did you split his heart to see if he had pronounced the *Shahâdah* out of hypocrisy?" The Prophet ﷺ angrily expressed himself. Usâmah ﷺ expressed his utmost regret over his behavior and promised not to repeat it again.

In the same way, Abu Qatâdah and Muhallim bin Jaththâmah ﷺ were once going somewhere when they came across Âmir bin Adbat, a man from Ashja' clan who was making a journey with his goods. When Âmir bin Adbat noticed the Muslim detachment, he said *"As-Salamu Alaikum"* in the Islamic manner. But the Muslims doubted his sincerity and Muhallim bin Jaththâmah ﷺ put him to death. When the expedition returned, the incident was reported to the Prophet ﷺ, he expressed his displeasure and said to Muhallim ﷺ, "Why did you kill him in a state of his being a believer in Allâh?" Then he ﷺ gave the relatives of Âmir, fifty camels as compensation and they agreed to free Muhallim ﷺ from retaliation.

Invitation Letters to Islam

In this same year, the Prophet ﷺ sent letters to the kings of the Arabs and non-Arabs. His letter to Negus, the King of Abyssinia has already been mentioned. Negus accepted Islam gracefully. Then the Prophet ﷺ sent Dihyah bin Khalifah Al-Kalbi ﷺ to Heraclius, the king of Rome; Hâtib bin Abu Balta'ah ﷺ to Muqauqis, the king of Egypt and Alexandria; Ala bin Al-Hadrami ﷺ to Mundhir bin Sâwa, the king of Bahrain.

Amr bin Al-Âs ﷺ was sent to the king of Oman; Salit bin Âmiri ﷺ was sent to Haudhah bin Ali, the king of Yamâmah; Shuja' bin Wahb ﷺ to Hârith bin Shimr Ghassâni, the king of Damascus, and also to Jabalah bin Aiham. Muhâjir bin Abu Umayyah Makhzumi ﷺ was sent to Hârith bin Abd Kulâl Himyari, the king of Yemen; and Abdullah bin Hudhaifah Sahmi ﷺ to Chosroes, the king of Persia.

Heraclius, the king of Rome did not embrace Islam fearing the opposition of the Christians and the loss of the throne, but he paid respect to the letter of the Prophet 鬱 and his messenger. The King of Egypt held the letter and the envoy of the Prophet 鬱 in high esteem. In reply he wrote a very courteous letter to the Prophet 鬱 and sent garments, a donkey and two slave-girls to him. Mundhir bin Sâwa also showed respect to his letter and the envoy. The king of Oman embraced Islam when he received his letter. However, Chosroes, the King of Persia, tore the letter into pieces and behaved rudely with Abdullah bin Hudhaifah 鬱. Informed of this, the Prophet 鬱 remarked, "Even so shall Allâh shatter his kingdom to pieces." And it happened exactly as he said.

Arrival In Makkah

The Prophet 鬱 in the early part of Dhul-Qa'dah, 7 AH, asked only those Companions who had taken part in the Treaty of Hudaibiyah to make preparations for the journey to Makkah. Two thousand Companions in all, left for Makkah. Abu Dhar Ghifâri 鬱 was appointed the Administrator of Al-Madinah. According to the Treaty, they took off all their weapons except their swords and entered Makkah.

Reaching the Ka'bah, the Prophet 鬱 asked the pilgrims to lay bare their right shoulder and wrap a part of the *Ihrâm* passing it from below the armpit, and then go around the House of Allâh in a running manner. He did this so that their readiness, determination, strength and diligence would come in to full view of the onlooking Makkan polytheists. A large number of polytheists had shifted to mountain passes and plains to avoid the sight of the believers performing *Umrah*, which would be distressful for them.

After accomplishing the rites of *Umrah*, the Prophet 鬱 married Maimunah 鬱, the sister of Umm Fadl and the wife of Abbâs bin Abdul-Muttalib. The fourth day, Suhail bin Amr and Huwaitib bin Abdul-Uzza came to the Prophet 鬱 and asked him to vacate Makkah as per the Treaty. He said, "Don't worry, I am ready to leave Makkah. But you are quite aware that I have just married a woman here and the bride has not yet been sent to me. If you allow me, I will have a marriage party and invite all the Makkans to a feast before leaving the city. I think you will lose nothing if it is done." Suhail said, "We need no feast or your party, and you should go from here observing the terms of the Treaty." So, the Prophet 🌸 proclaimed their departure then and there. The Prophet 🌸, along with his Companions, came out of the *Haram* (sacred) area and halted at Sarif valley, Maimunah bint Hârith 🌸 joined the Prophet 🌸 there.

On the eve of leaving Makkah, Umârah, the daughter of Hamzah 🌸, who was still a young child, came running and crying to go to Al-Madinah. Ali 🌸 lifted the child and put her on his saddle. Now Ja'far bin Abu Tâlib and Zaid bin Hârithah also rose to make a claim saying, "Since she is my cousin and my wife is her mother's sister, she must be given under my care." The Prophet 🌸 patiently heard all the claims and then entrusted the child to Ja'far saying, "The mother's sister is like the mother, so she should be brought up under the loving care of Ja'far's household." Ali and Zaid 🌸 abided by this decision.

Amr bin Al-Âs accepts Islam

A few days after the arrival of the Prophet 🌸 to Al-Madinah, Amr bin Al-Âs embraced Islam and decided to migrate from Makkah. It has already been discussed how he was sent to the Court of Negus, the king of Abyssinia to bring back the Muslims who had migrated to that country and how his efforts failed leaving him ashamed and disgraced. In spite of all that, the truth of Islam deeply impressed his mind and his old beliefs were getting eroded bit by bit. And a time came when he could not hold himself back. Khâlid bin Walid was his close friend. On the occasion of Hudaibiyah, he (Khâlid) had an opportunity to hear the Prophet 🌸 reciting the Qur'ân in *Isha* prayer at Usfân and he found his heart melting and growing in love for Islam. Amr bin Al-Âs opened his heart to Khâlid bin Walid, and the latter one rose without any reluctance to accompany him. The two friends acquainted Uthmân bin Talhah, their third friend with their intention. He also lost no time in joining the two. These three chieftains of Makkah set out for Al-Madinah, they appeared before the Prophet 🌸 and embraced Islam immediately. Their conversion to Islam gave a tremendous boost to the Muslims. When Khâlid bin Walid and Amr bin Al-Âs 🕮 came to know that embracing Islam brings forgiveness for all past sins, their joy knew no bounds.

The Eighth Year of Migration

Arabia was now apparently out of any grave danger. The act of accepting Islam posed no danger to life and property. Negative internal forces of all types had exhausted their spirit of opposition and their strength fighting Islam. Islam had itself become the greatest power within the bounds of Arabia. However, the Quraish of Makkah, who once wielded matchless honor and distinction, were still active in their opposition to Islam and in practicing unbelief and polytheism.

The hypocrites of Al-Madinah, the Jews of Khaibar and the polytheists of Makkah were the three forces who had left no stone unturned to set Arabia against the Muslims, but their efforts ended in failure. Now they turned towards Persia and Rome and started inciting them against the believers. However, the Prophet 🕮 was not unaware of their conspiratorial aims. The communications sent by the Prophet 🕮 to the various monarchs had left a salutary effect on most of them. But, a few whose minds were permeated with poisonous propaganda showed rudeness to the call of the Prophet 🕮 and set themselves against Islam. It was a very delicate situation for the Muslims, because in case of a foreign invasion, the Arab forces antagonistic to Islam might rise against the believers.

The Expedition to Mu'tah

Among the letters written by the Prophet 🕮 to the different monarchs, one was addressed to the ruler of Busra and was sent through Hârith bin Umair Azdi 🕮. On the way to Busra, Hârith 🕮 had just reached Mu'tah lying on the border of Syria, when Shurahbil bin Amr Ghassâni, a deputy of the Byzantine Emperor held him. When he came to know that the captive was the envoy of the Prophet 🕮 and was carrying a letter from him, he lost his temper and killed him. This tragic news sent the Muslims into a state of outrage. The Prophet 🕮 lost no time in sending an expedition of three thousand soldiers under the command of Zaid bin Hâritha ﷺ. He instructed them that if Zaid ﷺ were killed then Ja'far bin Abu Tâlib ﷺ should take the command. If Ja'far ﷺ were also slain then the command would pass on to Abdullah bin Rawâhah ﷺ, and in case of his falling the Muslims were at liberty to choose anyone as their commander. The Prophet 襄 escorted the army for a distance and then returned to Al-Madinah.

Zaid bin Hârithah ﷺ led his force to Ma'ân where he found out that Shurahbil bin Amr, the ruler of Mu'tah was present at Balqâ' with a hundred thousand Roman troops. This news sent a wave of anxiety into the hearts of the Muslim troops, which were halted at Ma'ân holding consultations about dealing with the new developments. The deliberation were going on when Abdullah bin Rawâhah ﷺ gave a call at the top of his voice:

"Men, you have come out in quest of martyrdom. We do not fight the enemy on the strength of our numbers, or our power; we fight them with the religion we have been honored with by Allâh. Thus advance towards Mu'tah and the army of Heraclius. Keep your right and left wings in order. Come on, we shall be winners both ways; either we win or we gain martyrdom."

In response to Abdullah bin Rawâhah's inspiring speech, Zaid bin Hârithah ﷺ got up with lance in one hand and the standard in the other. And with him rose the entire Muslim army filled with a new spirit and enthusiasm. The Muslim troops moved ahead from Ma'ân and chose a vast field in Mu'tah to give battle. Both the armies stood face to face, three thousand Muslims against one hundred thousand enemy soldiers armed to the teeth. The Muslim army had with them Khâlid bin Walid ﷺ for the first time and he had his first opportunity to test his sword on behalf of Islam. Moreover, it was the first battle between the Muslims and the Christians, Zaid bin Hârithah ﷺ was moving ahead of all with the standard of Islam firmly in his hand. The right wing was led by Qutbah bin Qatâdah Udhri ﷺ, while the left wing was under the charge of Abâyah bin Mâlik Ansâri ﷺ.

Zaid bin Hârithah ﷺ descended on the army and died fighting bravely with innumerable wounds on his body. The standard was now taken in hand by Ja'far ﷺ who led the fight. When the battle became confined, he jumped off his charger and hamstrung its forelegs and fought until he lost his right hand. He took the standard in his left hand but when it was also cut off, he kept the standard flying with the support of his neck. At last, he fell dead on the battlefield. The standard was then held aloft by Abdullah bin Rawâhah ﷺ. He too dismounted from his horse and pressed onwards. He also was granted martyrdom after killing a number of enemy soldiers. After his exit from the battle scene the Muslims were subdued by a sense of anxiety. But Thâbit bin Aqram ﷺ sprang forward and gave a call by lifting the standard: "O Muslims! Unite to choose a man to lead you." The Muslim troops raised their voice: "We agree on your leadership." Thereupon Thâbit bin Aqram ﷺ said, "I am not fit for the job; choose Khâlid bin Walid as your leader." "We agree on Khâlid bin Walid," the people confirmed in one voice.

Hearing this Khâlid bin Walid ﷺ swung into action and took the standard from the hand of Thâbit bin Aqram ﷺ. Now the Muslim troops rallied round him with new zeal. Khâlid ﷺ infused in their hearts a new spirit of do or die. And along with this he launched such successive attacks on all sides that the enemy soldiers were left unnerved. Not only did Khâlid bin Walid ﷺ fight gallantly, he also led his army to show its mettle in the battlefield. He displayed his genius as a military commander and kept the entire military in full control with extraordinary skill. He moved ahead and drew back the right and the left wings according to the demand of the battle. Despite superiority of numbers, the enemy troops did not prove a match for the Muslim army of far less numbers and weaponry. Khâlid bin Walid ﷺ looked like a flash of lightning throughout the battlefield. The whole day he led his three thousand men against the large army of one hundred thousand. By the evening the Romans escaped leaving behind booty and corpses.

Khâlid ﷺ — *Saifullâh*

His instinct for leadership and military skill was acclaimed by everyone and he has received the title of the "Sword of Allâh" from Allâh and His Messenger ﷺ. The same day that the fighters in the cause of Islam were engaged in giving battle, hundreds of miles away, the Prophet 繁 ascended the pulpit to tell the Muslims: "The Muslim troops took on the enemy. Zaid gained martyrdom and Allâh forgave him then Ja'far took the standard in his hand and was surrounded by the enemies, with the result that he was honored with martyrdom, and Allâh forgave him too. Following this, Abdullah bin Rawâhah 繁 took the standard of Islam in his hand and fell down martyred. They were all lifted to Paradise. After these three, Khâlid bin Walid, the sword among the swords of Allâh took the standard in his hand and set the matter right."

From that day on, Khâlid bin Walid 繁 came to be called *Saifullâh* (the Sword of Allâh). As the sad news broke out, the household of Ja'far 繁 was subdued with grief. The Prophet 繁 sent a meal to Ja'far's house. When Khâlid bin Walid 繁 reached near Al-Madinah along with his troops, the Prophet 繁 came out of Al-Madinah to greet them and gave Khâlid 繁 the glad tidings of the title of 'the Sword of Allâh'. One of the Companions saw in a dream Ja'far 繁 flying in Paradise with two wings. From that day he was called Ja'far Tayyâr —'Ja'far, the flier'. As per one narrative, the Prophet 繁 once said, "Allâh the Almighty has conferred two wings on Ja'far with which he keeps flying in heaven." The battle of Mu'tah was fought in Jumâda Al-Ula, 8 AH.

The Expedition to Qudâ'ah (*Dhât-us-Salâsil*)

About a month after the battle of Mu'tah came the news that the people of Qudâ'ah had collected an army near the Syrian border to invade Al-Madinah. The Prophet 繁 at once dispatched a detachment consisting of three hundred *Muhâjirin* and *Ansâr* under the command of Amr bin Al-Âs 繁. On reaching near the enemy, it came to be known that the number of the enemy soldiers was far more than was expected. A courier was immediately sent to Al-Madinah. The Prophet 繁 sent Abu Ubaidah bin Al-Jarrâh 繁 at the head of reinforcements. The enemy army could not stand the joint onslaught and scattered in fear and confusion. The raiding party returned safe and sound. Shortly after this came the news that the Juhainah tribe, along the seacoast, at a distance of five stages from Al-Madinah had collected men and arms to raid Al-Madinah. The Prophet ﷺ immediately sent Abu Ubaidah bin Al-Jarrâh ؓ at the head of three hundred *Muhâjirin* and *Ansâr*, but the expedition came back without engaging the enemy because they were so terrified at the sight of the Muslim detachment that they fled.

Conquest of Makkah

A surprising incident occurred in Sha'bân, 8 AH. Banu Khuzâ'ah and Banu Bakr had halted their long standing feud and made peace after entering into alliances respectively with the Messenger of Allâh ﷺ and the Quraish as part of the Treaty of Hudaibiyah. According to the Treaty they could not attack one another for a period of ten years. But Banu Bakr developed an evil scheme against Banu Khuzâ'ah and they planned to take revenge on their rivals. The Quraish of Makkah should have held Banu Bakr back from implementing their plan against Banu Khuzâ'ah making them uphold the Treaty. Instead of preventing them, the Quraish, totally at variance with their obligation to the Treaty, came out in the open lending full and active support to Banu Bakr with men and material. They broke their covenant to the extent that Safwân bin Umayyah, Ikrimah bin Abu Jahl, and Suhail bin Amr joined the fighting along with Banu Bakr.

The combined attack of Banu Bakr and the Quraish inflicted on Banu Khuzâ'ah a heavy loss of 20 or 30 men. Being caught by a surprise attack at night while they were asleep, they found no where to take refuge except at the House of Allâh, the Ka'bah, and even some of them were killed there (this was also a breach of trust as the Ka'bah was a sanctuary for all). That fateful night when the massacre of Banu Khuzâ'ah took place and the terms of the Peace Treaty were thrown to the wind, a few persons of Banu Khuzâ'ah in Makkah cried for help from the Prophet ﷺ. At that same moment the Messenger of Allâh was in the house of Maimunah ؓ in Al-Madinah and was performing *Wudu* (ablution). He heard what they said in Makkah and replied: "*Labbaik! Labbaik!* (I am at your service)." Maimunah ؓ said, "Whom were you talking to when you said *Labbaik?*" The Prophet ﷺ replied, "At this moment the complaint of Banu Khuzâ'ah was being brought to me and I responded to it." Amazingly, they also heard in Makkah at the same time the consoling voice of the Prophet ﷺ. The next morning the Messenger of Allâh ﷺ said to Aishah 㸒, "Last night, Banu Bakr and the Quraish have jointly massacred some of the Banu Khuzâ'ah." Aishah 㸒 said, "By this did the Quraish violate the Treaty in your opinion?" The Prophet of Allâh ﷺ confidently said, "They have certainly breached the trust, and very soon, Allâh the Almighty will issue His Command concerning it."

A Few days after the incident Budail bin Warqâ' and Amr bin Sâlim came to Al-Madinah and put their complaint before the Prophet ﷺ. Amr bin Sâlim told his tale of woe in a poem filled with gloom and grief at their being brutally attacked and killed. Some of the verses are as follows:

"The Quraish have committed a breach of trust against you, and they have broken the firm treaty signed with you.

They have plundered us like hay, and they believe that we have nobody to help us.

They are mean and deficient in number, and they attacked us at Watir when we were lying asleep."

The Prophet of Allâh ﷺ consoled them saying, "You will be helped." At the time of their departure from Al-Madinah the Messenger of Allâh ﷺ remarked: "Abu Sufyân has set out from Makkah to seek an extension in the duration of Peace Treaty and get it consolidated, but his mission will end in failure."

When the Makkans found time to think over the consequences of their misconduct, they were struck by fear. They sent Abu Sufyân to renew the Peace Treaty. The Messenger of Allâh ﷺ ordered the Muslims, on the other hand, to make preparations for the ensuing battle and to keep it a top secret. On the way back to Makkah, Budail bin Warqâ' and his group came across Abu Sufyân who was heading for Al-Madinah. "Where have you been?" asked Abu Sufyân. "I was only up in this valley," Budail replied. Abu Sufyân was under the impression that the Prophet ﷺ was unaware of the attack against Banu Khuzâ'ah that had just occurred. He was determined to get the Peace Treaty renewed as soon as possible.

Abu Sufyân in Al-Madinah:

Abu Sufyân came to Al-Madinah and made several attempts to contact the Prophet of Allâh 鴻, Abu Bakr Siddiq, Umar and Ali 鴻, but none of them paid attention to him. During this exercise in futility Ali 鴻, in order to make him look foolish, said to him, "You are the chief of Banu Kinânah, so you can go to the Prophet's Mosque and announce that you extend the terms of the Treaty and confirm it." He did accordingly and left in hurry. When he went back to Makkah and related what had happened, they laughed at him saying, "Ali has made a fool of you." Only then did Abu Sufyân become conscious of his stupidity. Immediately after the departure of Abu Sufyân, the Prophet 鴻 asked the Companions to march on Makkah. In spite of the massive size of the military preparations, the Companions did not know the target of attack. It was simply because the Messenger of Allâh 鴻 wanted the Makkans to be caught unaware.

However, a Companion of the Prophet 鴻, Hâtib bin Abu Balta'ah 鴻 informed the Quraish of the impending Muslim attack, in a letter sent through a woman. Allâh the Almighty informed this to His Messenger 鴻 through inspiration. He sent Ali and Zubair bin Awwâm 鴻 immediately after the woman with the description of her features. They caught her after a hard chase, he searched her belongings but the letter remained hidden. However, Ali 鴻 was quite sure about the letter because he knew the Prophet 鴻 did not say anything that wasn't absolutely true. When Ali 鴻 threatened her with dire consequences, she drew out the letter from her hair and handed it over to them. The letter was from Hâtib bin Abu Balta'ah 鴻 to the Quraish. The letter along with the woman was brought to the Messenger of Allâh 鴻. Hâtib 鴻 was sent for and was asked for an explanation. He said, "Since my relatives were still in Makkah and in danger, I liked to oblige the Makkans by informing them about the ensuing Muslim attack so that my relatives would remain safe from them." Having heard this, Umar 鴻 lost his temper and said, "O Messenger of Allâh! Allow me to cut his head off." The Prophet 鴻 observed, "O Umar, Hâtib has committed a mistake which is pardonable." And so Hâtib 鴻 was forgiven.

March to Makkah:

On Ramadân 11, 8 AH, the Prophet 襲 set out from Al-Madinah at the head of a ten-thousand-man army of the Companions. The failure of Abu Sufyân's mission had disheartened the Quraish and they were in the dark about the plans of the believers. The Prophet's march to Makkah was very swift. They came across his uncle Abbâs bin Abdul-Muttalib 襲 on the way who, along with his wife and children, was moving to Al-Madinah after they had embraced Islam. The Messenger of Allâh 襲 took Abbâs 襲 to Makkah and sent his relatives to Al-Madinah. Marching quickly, the Muslim army reached Marr-az-Zahrân at a distance of 8 miles from Makkah. The Makkans were still unaware of the presence of Muslim troops even though they were so close to Makkah. They encamped at that place. The Makkans came to know of the Muslim force only from the shepherds who went back in the night. Informed of this, Abu Sufyân came out to look into the matter. The Prophet 襲 had already deputed Umar 襲 at the head of a patrol party to ward off a night attack.

Abbâs bin Abdul-Muttalib 襲 was anxious about the safety of his people and wanted them to accept Islam and be safe. He came out mounted on Duldul, the mule of the Prophet 襲, in the night and moved towards Makkah. As per the order of the Messenger of Allâh 襲 the entire Muslim army had, in separate groups of one thousand each, lit their campfires.

When Abu Sufyân witnessed the blazing campfires spread over a vast area, he was shocked and stunned to the core to think how such a large army had been collected.

Abbâs 襲 recognized the voice of Abu Sufyân even in the dark night and sounded back that the army belonged to the Prophet 襲 and was ready to invade Makkah the next morning. Abu Sufyân was left more confounded at this disheartening news. He, in a state of utmost bewilderment, drew near Abbâs 襲 to seek his counsel at this juncture. Abbâs 襲 said to him, "Ride on the back of this mule and I will bring you to the Prophet 襲 for he alone can give you protection." Abu Sufyân got on the mule without a moment's delay. Umar Fâruq recognized Abu Sufyân and wanted to kill him at once. But Abbâs ﷺ spurred the mule and quickly went into the camp of the Prophet ﷺ, Umar ﷺ came chasing him and said, "O Prophet of Allâh! Command me to kill this disbeliever, for he has come under our control without any condition." Abbâs ﷺ said, "I have already given him protection." But Umar ﷺ sought permission once again. Abbâs ﷺ replied to him with a pinch of taunt, "Umar'! You would not have insisted on his being killed had he belonged to your family." Thereupon Umar ﷺ said, "Abbas! I felt more happy on your accepting Islam than I would have been, had my father done so because I found the Prophet ﷺ eager for your becoming a Muslim." After this exchange between the two, the Prophet of Allâh ﷺ enjoined, "Well, Abu Sufyân is given respite for a night." Following this he asked Abbâs ﷺ to keep Abu Sufyân in his own camp. And next morning Abu Sufyân appeared before the Prophet ﷺ and confessed Islam.

Abu Sufyân ﷺ honored

Abbâs ﷺ appeared before the Prophet of Allâh ﷺ and submitted, "Abu Sufyân is a person who loves honor, so would you please give him some special honor." At this he said, "He who enters the Sacred Mosque will be safe, he who enters the house of Abu Sufyân will be safe, he who shuts his doors upon himself will be safe and he who goes unarmed will be safe." Abu Sufyân ﷺ felt elated.

The army on the move surged like an ocean. Different tribes had passed by with their tribal colors. Abu Sufyân ﷺ ascended a raised spot to witness the spectacle of the Muslim troops on the march and hurried back to Makkah ahead of all to announce: "He who enters the Sacred Mosque or my house will be safe." The Prophet of Allâh ﷺ wanted to avoid bloodshed at all costs. His exit from Makkah in a state of helplessness and then his victorious and glorious return must have been on his mind. This day he made a triumphant entry into Makkah with his head lowered giving thanks to Allâh the Almighty. He then circumambulated the Ka'bah seven times mounted on his animal and then cleared the Ka'bah of idols. He then took the keys of the Ka'bah from Uthmân bin Talhah, and entered the Ka'bah and prayed to Allâh the Exalted. Following this the Prophet of Allâh ﷺ

stood at the door of the Ka'bah, holding its frame, while the Quraish arranged themselves in front of him in the courtyard filled with fear and shame.

Historic Address of the Prophet ﷺ:

The Prophet ﷺ said addressing them: "There is no God but Allâh Alone. He has made good His Promise and help to His slave. He has alone overthrown all the Confederates. Lo'! All the rites, privileges and claims to retaliation and blood compensation are beneath my feet except the custody of the Ka'bah and the giving water to the pilgrims. Even cutting down a green tree is not valid within the sanctuary. O you people of the Quraish, Allâh has abolished the haughtiness of paganism and the pride of lineage. Man comes from Adam and Adam came from dust. Allâh the Almighty says: 'O mankind! We have created you from a male and a female, and have made you nations and tribes that you may know one another. Verily! the noblest of you, with Allâh is the best in conduct.' (49:13) O Quraish, what do you think I am about to do with you?" "We hope for the best," they replied, "you are a noble brother, son of a noble brother." The Prophet of Allâh ﷺ said in reply, "I say to you what Yusuf (Prophet Joseph) said to his brothers: 'Have no fear this day, go your way for you are all free'."

The address being over, the Prophet ﷺ went up to Mount Safa and sat down to take the oath of allegiance to Allâh and His Messenger from the people. After finishing with men, he deputed Umar ﷺ to take *Bai'ah* from the women, and he kept seeking forgiveness of Allâh for them. Safwân bin Umayyah fled to Yemen for fear of life. Umair bin Wahb from his tribe sought safety for him and he was granted immunity. Safwân was the man who had resisted the entry of the Muslims into Makkah and fled from Makkah after the conquest; so did Ikrimah bin Abu Jahl, and he too was granted safety. Both of them had the pleasure of coming to the fold of Islam after the battle of Hunain.

The Truth came and Falsehood vanquished:

Destruction of idols installed in the Ka'bah meant the destruction of the idols all over Arabia. Likewise, the entry of the Quraish into Islam implied the whole Arabia coming to the fold of Islam, for all eyes were fixed on the Quraish of Makkah to see whether they accepted Islam or not.

A large number of the Quraish were converted to Islam after the conquest of Makkah. However, many of them still remained immovable and unyielding. But none of them were compelled to accept Islam. The sole aim before the Muslims was to do away with disruptions, bring perfect peace and confer on them complete religious freedom. With peace prevailing and freedom of religious practice granted, the idol worshipers got a full opportunity to study, observe and watch Islam in operation. It resulted in their quick conversion to Islam in large numbers.

After the conquest of Makkah, the Prophet ﷺ announced throughout the land that nobody becoming a Muslim was allowed to keep an idol in his house. Following this he sent a few parties to destroy idols installed in the area around Makkah. He sent Khâlid bin Walid ﷺ at the head of thirty soldiers to break Uzza, the idol of Banu Kinânah and to pull down its temple. Khâlid bin Walid ﷺ went and broke Uzza to pieces and razed its temple to the ground. Amr bin Al-Âs ﷺ was sent to destroy Suwa', the idol of Banu Hudhail. When Amr bin Al-Âs ﷺ reached the spot, the priest said, "How will you be able to overpower it?" Amr ﷺ said, "Just watch." Saying this he entered the temple and broke the idol to pieces. Seeing this, the priest renounced idolatry and embraced Islam on the spot. Sa'd bin Zaid Ashhali ﷺ was sent to Qadid to destroy Manât. The priests were sure the Muslims would fail in their task but they saw with their own eyes the believers break the idols and pull the temple down. All idols and temples were destroyed.

The first priority being completed, the Prophet ﷺ resumed his mission of preaching Islam through Muslim missionaries and sent them near and far. Khâlid bin Walid ﷺ was sent to Banu Jadhimah with the order to avoid a fight. But the situation demanded it and a few from Banu Jadhimah were killed. When Khâlid bin Walid ﷺ returned to Makkah with the booty, the Prophet ﷺ expressed regret and sent back the booty along with blood money through Ali ﷺ.

Battle of Hunain

The resounding victory of the Muslims over the Quraish and the ever-increasing conversions to Islam frightened the enemies of Islam out of their senses. Those tribes who were not allies of the Muslims were disturbed and worried. The Hawâzin and the Thaqif were the two tribes who were most hostile to Islam and they also were old arch-rivals of the Quraish. Living between Tâ'if and Makkah, they expected to become the next target of attack by the Muslims. The Hawâzin Chief, Mâlik bin Auf brought around him all the tribes of Banu Hawâzin and Banu Thaqif to fight against the Muslims. Several other tribes like Nasr, Jusham and Sa'd also joined hands with the Hawâzin. Their troops concentrated at Autâs. On receiving this information, the Prophet 🌸 sent Abdullah bin Abu Hadrad Aslami 🌸 as a spy. He came back with the news that the enemy had already completed its military preparations and they were ready to fight.

The Prophet 🌸 ordered quick preparations and led an army of twelve thousands comprising ten thousand men from the *Muhâjirin* and the *Ansâr* and two thousand new entrants to Islam from Makkah. The Muslim army reached Hunain on Shawwâl 10, 8 AH. The enemy had already taken its position in the depressions and hollows and the craters of the valley. As the Muslim army started descending into the valley in the half light of morning, the enemy suddenly rose from their place of ambush and started to attack with full force.

Since the Muslims were caught unaware by the celebrated archers of Hawâzin, they could not withstand the sudden onslaught of the enemy and their flanks fell back. The two thousand Makkans were the first to flee in terror no one paying attention to the other. The Prophet 🌸 was then on the right side of the valley along with Abu Bakr, Umar Fâruq, Ali, Abbâs, Fadl bin Abbâs, and Abu Sufyân bin Al-Hârith 🌸. The Prophet 🌸 had all the while stood firm in his place, riding his white mule without any fear or nervousness. Abbâs bin Abdul-Muttalib 🌸 was holding the bridle of his mule, while the Prophet of Allâh 🌸 was calling aloud: "Verily, I am the Prophet without falsehood; I am son of Abdul-Muttalib."

When the Prophet ﷺ saw his men in confusion, he said, "O Abbâs, call the Muslims to this side." The Muslims recognized his voice and rushed towards the Prophet ﷺ. However, not more than about a hundred men could rally around the Prophet ﷺ for the rest were barred by the intervening enemy and resumed fighting from where they had been.

Calling out *Allâhu Akbar* (Allâh is the Most Great), the Prophet ﷺ advanced with his mule and launched such a fierce attack that the enemy plunged into disorder and confusion and fled from the scene. Now the Muslim troops gathered and bore down upon the army, which resulted in a smashing defeat of the enemies of Islam. At the outset, when the Muslims were suffering reverses, a rude fellow from Makkah who had joined the Muslim army but was still not strong in faith, let out his antipathy to Islam saying, "The spell of their sorcery has ended today." Another person of the same category remarked. "Their flight will not stop before they get to the sea." A man named Shaibah stepped forward towards the Prophet ﷺ with the evil intention of taking revenge on him but fell down unconscious.

The Hawâzin paid a heavy toll in the battle before escaping in terror. Banu Thaqif then attempted to fill the gap but in vain. They could not resist the advancing flood of Muslim troops and fled from the battle field after suffering terrible loss of life. Notable chieftains of the enemy were killed but their commander-in-chief, Mâlik bin Auf escaped unhurt and took refuge in Tâ'if. A part of the fugitives gathered in Autâs while another fled to Nakhlah for their lives. The Prophet ﷺ sent military detachments chasing them and fighting took place at both locations again, they could not withstand the heavy onslaught of the Muslims and gave in.

The Muslims returned victorious with booty and captives. When the captives and spoils of Hunain were brought to the Prophet ﷺ, he ordered them to be taken to Ji'rânah and appointed Mas'ud bin Amr Ghifâri ﷺ to be in charge. The spoils of this battle, known as the Battle of Hunain, went up to six thousand captives, twenty-four thousand camels, more than forty thousand sheep and goats, and four thousand *Uqiyyah* (a measure of weight) of silver.

Siege of Tâ'if

The fortress of Mâlik bin Auf was located in route from the valley of Hunain to Tâ'if and the Prophet 鐵 demolished it along with the fortress of Atam. He found the people of Tâ'if wanting to give battle and so they were besieged. The siege dragged on for twenty days. During this period people from the surrounding areas began accepting Islam. During the battle of Hunain only four Muslims were martyred while during the siege of Tâ'if the number of Muslim martyrs reached twelve. The Prophet 鐵, at last, raised the siege and returned to Ji'rânah with his men and distributed the spoils.

A deputation of the Hawâzin came there and called on the Prophet of Allâh 鐵 and sought forgiveness for the sake of Halimah Sa'diyah. He asked them to come at the time of *Zuhr* prayer when all the Muslims would congregate for the prayer. When they did as told, the Prophet 鐵 gave his reply, "Whatever was apportioned to me and the Banu Abdul-Muttalib is yours." Thereupon the *Muhâjirin* and the *Ansâr* said, "Whatever share has been given to us is passed on to the Prophet 鐵." Saying this, they set all the captives of Hawâzin free. Thus, in a very short duration, about six thousand prisoners were released. Among the captives was also Shimâ' bint Halimah Sa'diyah, the foster-sister of the Prophet 鐵. When she was produced before the Prophet 鐵, she said, "O Prophet of Allâh, I am your foster-sister." The Prophet 鐵 asked for proof, and she replied, "The bite you gave me on my leg. The mark is still there." The Prophet 鐵 accepted the proof and stretched out his robe for her to sit on and treated her courteously. He gave her the choice of living with him in affection and honor or going back to her people. She chose to go back to her tribe. And the Prophet 鐵 gave her a bondsman, a slave girl and a considerable quantity of wealth and goods.

Deep Love of the *Ansâr* for the Messenger 鐵

When the Prophet 鐵 began to distribute the spoils at Ji'rânah, he gave a large portion to the Quraish whose faith in Islam, he wanted to strengthen. Since most of the Makkans were from the Quraish, and they were relatives and fellow-countrymen of the Prophet 鈴, some of the young men among the *Ansâr* aired their grievances at the meager gifts given to them and the large portion given to the Prophet's relatives and compatriots.

The Prophet 鈴 also got wind of what was going on among the younger section of the *Ansâr*. The Prophet of Allâh 鈴 ordered the *Ansâr* to assemble in an enclosure. He then said addressing them, "Did you say such and such?" The *Ansâr* submitted in reply: "Our young men have said so no doubt, but none of the discerning, respectable and mature persons has ever thought it nor has such a thought ever entered our minds."

Having heard this, the Prophet of Allâh 鈴 said: "O the *Ansâr*, did I not come to you when you were astray, and Allâh guided you through me?" The *Ansâr* replied, "Yes, indeed, Allâh and His Prophet are most kind and generous." The Prophet 鈴 again asked them, "You were divided and He softened your hearts and you united through me?" They again submitted, "Yes, indeed, you did us this great favor." The Prophet 鈴 asked once again, "You were poor and Allâh made you rich through me?" The *Ansâr* admitted, "Yes, indeed, Allâh and His Messenger did this great favor for us." The Prophet 鈴 again asked them, "O *Ansâr*, why don't you speak to me?" He then added, "I would have acknowledged it if you had replied: 'You came discredited and we believed you; you came deserted and we helped you; you were a fugitive and we gave you shelter; you were poor and we comforted you.' O *Ansâr*, are you not satisfied that these men should take away camels and goats while you go back with the Prophet of Allâh?"

The *Ansâr* wept bitterly until tears ran down their beards. The Prophet of Allâh 鈴 further said, "Had migration not been destined, I would have been one of the *Ansâr* myself. If all the people go one way, and the *Ansâr* take another, I would take the way of the *Ansâr*. O Allâh! Have mercy on the *Ansâr* and their children and their children." We can not even conceive of the joys, the *Ansâr* felt at this time. The Prophet of Allâh 鈴 let them understand that these people were new entrants to Islam and they were given more so they would be reconciled to Islam, not by way of any special favor.

First Governor of Makkah

On the way back from Ji'rânah, the Prophet of Allâh ﷺ entered Makkah to perform *Umrah*. Before leaving, he installed as Governor of Makkah, a young man of a little more than twenty years. Also he left Mu'âdh bin Jabal ﷺ as an instructor of the Qur'ân and Islamic injunctions. The young governor named Attâb bin Usaid was given the significant post for his profound fondness of religious knowledge. A dirham per day was fixed for him so that he would not depend on anyone else for his needs. He was the first man in Islam to perform *Hajj* as a ruler.

That year the Muslims and non-Muslims performed *Hajj* according to their own tenets and none got in the way of other. However, they performed their duties so close to one another that the polytheists found ample opportunity to observe the good deeds and moral excellence of the Muslims.

It is worth mentioning here that Urwah bin Mas'ud, a chieftain of Tâ'if was outside when Tâ'if was raided by Muslim troops in 8 AH. Urwah now followed the Prophet ﷺ when he was on his way to Al-Madinah and confessed Islam at his hand before his entry into Al-Madinah. Urwah ﷺ then sought permission of the Prophet ﷺ to preach Islam among his people. He ﷺ said, "Your people take pride in that they could not be defeated by the Muslim army. When you preach Islam to them, you might be killed." Urwah ﷺ submitted, "My people love me very much and I hope they will listen to me." Thus the Prophet ﷺ acceded to his request. Following this, he went to Tâ'if, ascended a raised place and began to call the people to accept Islam. The people of Tâ'if surrounded him on all sides and showered arrows on him, which led to his martyrdom. On being asked about the retaliation, Urwah ﷺ said to his relatives: "By the Grace of Allâh, I have been honored with martyrdom. Now my sole desire is that I am buried beside those Companions of the Prophet ﷺ who were martyred and buried during the Muslim siege of Tâ'if." It was in this year that the Prophet's son Ibrâhim was born to Maria Qibtiyah (Coptic). Also in this year his daughter Zainab ﷺ passed away. The same year, a wooden pulpit was made for the Prophet ﷺ, and he wrote a letter to Mundhir bin Sâwa. Mundhir bin Sâwa ﷺ had already embraced Islam in response to an earlier letter sent to him, according to which he began to charge the *Jizyah* (protection tax) from the Jews and Magians of his territory.

The Ninth Year of Migration

Following the Prophet's return to Al-Madinah after the conquest of Makkah and Hunain, the pagans of Arabia started coming into the fold of Islam. At the outset of 9 AH, people from the far off regions of Arabia began to send their representatives to the Prophet of Allâh ﷺ to announce their declaration of Islam. That is why, 9 AH came to be called the Year of Deputations. From the temporal standpoint too, the Prophet ﷺ had become the ruler of Arabia. The believers had *Zakât* made obligatory on them, while the disbelievers had to pay a nominal amount as *Jizyah* (protection tax). In order to collect the *Zakât*, tax collectors were sent to various tribes. At times the tax collectors suffered resistance and even were martyred, while on other occasions they punished the wrong doers. At last, a regular system of *Zakât* was established.

Expedition to Tabuk

The Ghassanide King collected a big army to avenge his ignominious defeat at Mu'tah. He then sought help from Heraclius of Rome, who was pleased to send an army forty thousand strong to his help and decided to march with the large army. The monk named Abu Âmir, referred to before, went to the Byzantine monarch, Caesar with the sole purpose of inducing him to invade Al-Madinah. Abu Âmir was also regularly but secretly in correspondence with the hypocrites of Al-Madinah, who had already started construction work of a mosque named Dirâr Mosque. News of such serious matters kept pouring into Al-Madinah for some time. Military movements of this magnitude could not be ignored. The Prophet of Allâh ﷺ gave a call to the believers in general to come and join hands to take on the massive army of Heraclius. The Muslims from all areas of the country rushed to Al-Madinah in response to th call.

The Prophet of Allâh 繼 generally kept the military preparations and movements a secret to keep the hypocrites and the enemy in the dark. But, since such large-scale preparations were not possible secretly and silently, the Prophet 繼 announced that the preparations were to give battle to the Roman army. It was the year of a bumper crop and the time of reaping the harvest was upon them and some of the people felt a little unwilling to leave and lose the crop.

Heraclius and his ministers had brought the hypocrites to their side as a part of their military campaign. The hypocrites were constantly in league with the Jews of Al-Madinah and were holding regular consultations against the Muslims. A band of twelve hypocrites built their own separate mosque as a center for carrying out their hostile activities and anti-Islamic propaganda, and for creating a rift among the Muslims. When they saw the Muslims engaged in preparing for the impending battle, they started passing discouraging remarks along with mentioning the hardships of such a long and arduous journey. What they wanted was the Caesar to invade Al-Madinah and to frustrate all the efforts of the Muslims to stop this Christian movement towards Al-Madinah.

The Prophet 繼 had, on the other hand, ordered all the Companions to join the expedition. Since coming face to face with the massive Christian army meant large-scale preparations from the Muslim camp which needed provisions, mounts, and weapons in large quantities and numbers. The Prophet 繼 had, therefore, made an appeal to the Muslim masses to lavishly contribute to the war fund.

The Muslims had also showed an astonishing response to the appeal. Uthmân bin Affân 繼 was about to dispatch his trade caravan to Syria, but contributed the whole of it to the Muslim campaign. Abu Bakr Siddiq 繼 contributed all goods and chattels of his household, entrusting his wife and children to Allâh the Almighty, while Umar Fâruq 繼 divided everything in his house in two and gave one half to the fund being raised by the Prophet of Allâh 繼.

The poor among the Muslims who lived on their sweat and labor contributed their wages to the Muslim war preparations. The hypocrites didn't give any contributions. An army of thirty thousand strong collected in Al-Madinah. The Muslim army could hardly prepared footwear because the Prophet ﷺ said to them that footwear raises foot soldiers to the category of cavalry.

Islamic Army's Departure:

The Messenger of Allâh ﷺ set out for Tabuk with an army of 30,000 men from Al-Madinah. The campaign was undertaken in the month of Rajab, 9 AH. They had hardly covered a distance of one hour and reached Dhi Awân when the hypocrites submitted, "We have built a mosque. Please offer prayer therein to bless it." The Prophet ﷺ replied, "Presently, I am busy making preparations for the journey; I shall see to it on my return." Departing from Al-Madinah, he ordered the army to pitch the camp at Thaniya-tul-Wada and he put Muhammad bin Maslamah Ansâri ﷺ in charge of Al-Madinah.

The chief of the hypocrites, Abdullah bin Ubai also left Al-Madinah with his band of people and camped at the low-lying area of the Thaniya-tul-Wada. He apparently wanted to show that he also accompanied the Muslim troops, but in fact, he broke away from the Muslims and came back to Al-Madinah with his men. However, a few of them went along to work as spies for the forces hostile to Islam. The Prophet ﷺ had left behind Ali ﷺ to look after his family.

The hypocrites used this as an opportunity to spread false rumors about Ali ﷺ. They implied that the Prophet ﷺ gave little importance to Ali ﷺ and, therefore, left him alone in Al-Madinah. When his patience ran out, he hurried from Al-Madinah and joining the Prophet ﷺ at Al-Jurf asked, "The hypocrites are saying such and such about me and so I have come to you." The Prophet of Allâh ﷺ said, "They are liars. I have left you behind to look after my household; so go back." In order to sooth his feelings the Prophet ﷺ further said, "You are to me as Hârun was to Musa, except that there will be no Prophet after me." Ali ﷺ returned to Al-Madinah pacified and satisfied.

When the Muslim army arrived at Al-Hijr (presently Al-Qura Valley), the destroyed territory of Thamud, the Prophet ﷺ exhorted, "Pass on swiftly seeking forgiveness of Allâh even without drinking a drop of water from its wells." When the Muslim troops had to pass a night at

Al-Hijr the Prophet ﷺ told them that no one was to go alone out of the camp. When passing through the ruins of the deserted territory, he covered his face with his mantle and drove his mount fast. He also instructed his Companions to hurry up seeking the forgiveness of Allâh the Almighty while passing through the settlements of the tyrants and sinners lest they be overtaken by what they (the Thamud) had suffered.

At Tabuk:

When the Muslim expedition arrived at the stream of Tabuk near the Syrian border, Heraclius recognized him as a true Prophet and withdrew out of fear. The Christian troops and the Ghassanide king also left their positions and cleared out of the area of the Muslim force. Tabuk lay at a distance of fourteen or fifteen stages from Al-Madinah where the Prophet ﷺ stayed for about twenty days. During this period, Yuhannah bin Ru'bah, the ruler of Ailah appeared before the Prophet ﷺ to offer his obedience to him, his request was accepted in return for *Jizyah* (tax) which he paid on the spot. The people of Jarbâ' also followed suit and earned peace on the same conditions, and the same came to pass with the people of Adhruh.

Dumat-ul-Jandal was located near Tabuk whose ruler Ukaidir bin Abdul-Malik was a Christian and belonged to Banu Kindah tribe. He refused to obey the Prophet ﷺ and showed arrogance. He sent Khâlid bin Walid ﷺ at the head of a detachment saying, "You will see Ukaidir hunting a white antelope." When Khâlid ﷺ came near to his palace after a night's journey, he saw an amazing event.

It was a hot summer moonlit night, Ukaidir was enjoying his rest with his wife on top of his palace. All of a sudden a white antelope came out from the adjacent forest and started rubbing its horns against the gate of his palace. His wife drew her husband's attention to this. Ukaidir, along with his brother Hassân, chased the animal on horseback. He had covered a short distance when Khâlid's detachment surrounded them. Ukaidir was captured alive while his brother was killed in the encounter. His beautiful silken garment was sent ahead through a courier and Ukaidir himself was brought by Khâlid bin Walid ﷺ. The Prophet ﷺ spared the life of Ukaidir who showed his obedience and

promised to pay the *Jizyah*. After returning to his palace, he sent to the
Prophet ﷺ two thousand camels, eight hundred horses, four hundred
pieces of armor and four hundred lances and was granted a peace
treaty.

Dirâr Mosque burnt down

When the rulers of the Syrian frontier were totally subdued, the
Prophet ﷺ and his Companions decided to go back to Al-Madinah. At
a distance of one hour from Al-Madinah, the Prophet ﷺ sent Mâlik
bin Dukhshum Sâlimi and Ma'n bin Adi Ajli ﷺ to burn down and
demolish the mosque built by the hypocrites, the Prophet of Allâh ﷺ
was instructed to do so from the Verse: "And as for those who put up
a mosque by way of harm…" (9:107)

The Prophet ﷺ and his Companions came back to Al-Madinah in
Ramadân, 9 AH. [According to the occurrence of events, his return to
Al-Madinah seems in the month of Rajab.]

Ka'b bin Mâlik, Murârah bin Rabi' and Hilâl bin Umayyah ﷺ were
the three Companions who did not join the Muslim expedition to
Tabuk on account of their indecision. On the return of the Prophet of
Allâh ﷺ all three appeared before him and confessed their faults. The
Prophet ﷺ forbade everyone to speak to them. For fifty days they kept
seeking the forgiveness of Allâh, then Allâh granted them a pardon.
Before they were pardoned, no one including their family members
would even respond to their salutations.

They felt forsaken and abandoned and the whole world seemed to
have closed on them. When the King of Ghassan came to know of this
ordeal, he sent a courier to Ka'b bin Mâlik ﷺ with a letter in which he
had written: "You are a man of wealth and honor and Muhammad
has ill-treated you to the extreme. You better come to me. I shall hold
you in the highest honor and grant you very good treatment." Having
gone through this letter, Ka'b ﷺ threw it into an oven.

When the repentance of Ka'b bin Mâlik ﷺ was accepted, the Prophet
ﷺ and the Companions congratulated him and he gave away all his
wealth and property in the way of Allâh.

The People of Tâ'if accept Islam

When the people of Tâ'if heard the news of the Muslim's successes in Tabuk they were totally sure that they were no match for the Muslim force. Urwah bin Mas'ud 🕌 had been martyred in Tâ'if, but his son Abul-Mulaih along with a few others came to Al-Madinah and embraced Islam. On the Prophet's return from Tabuk, Abd Yâlil bin Amr came to Al-Madinah at the head of a deputation of the people of Tâ'if. He allowed them to camp in a corner of the Prophet's Mosque. Abd Yâlil and his fellows accepted Islam and took an oath of allegiance at the hand of the Prophet 🕌 on behalf of their people. The Prophet 🕌 sent Uthmân bin Abu Al-Âs 🕌 there as their ruler, and Mughirah bin Shu'bah 🕌 to demolish their temple of idol Lât. From the treasures of the temple, the blood money of Urwah bin Mas'ud 🕌 was paid and the rest was distributed among the Muslims.

The deputations started arriving after the Prophet's return to Al-Madinah. They would come to accept Islam and then return to their people along with some Companions to teach them Islam. He would give gifts and rewards at the time of their departure. Meanwhile Ali 🕌 was sent to the Tai' tribe at the head of a detachment, which stormed the region and Adi bin Hâtim, the ruler of the Tai' ran away. However, Hâtim's daughter was brought as a captive.

She requested the Prophet 🕌 to favor her. He set her free but asked her to stay until a noble man was available to take her to her region. In a few days the people of Syria came to the Prophet 🕌 and he sent her with them along with some clothes and provisions.

When the girl reached her brother Adi bin Hâtim, he asked his sister: "What kind of man is the Prophet?" She replied, "He is a man to meet with; he is very noble and polite and a great benefactor." Adi got right up and left for Al-Madinah as a representative of his people. The Prophet 🕌 gave him respect, took him to his home from the Prophet's Mosque and seated him on his bed. On the way home a woman stopped him (the Prophet 🕌) and he stayed with her until she finished talking. Such a kind and noble gesture affected Adi. Following this the Prophet 🕌 gave him some good counsel. At the end, Adi bin

Hâtim stretched out his hand, took the oath of allegiance, became a Muslim and returned to his people.

First Deputy of the Prophet of Allâh

After returning from Tabuk the arrival of deputations kept the Prophet 鑿 so busy that he could not spare himself to lead the *Hajj* caravan to Makkah. He delegated Abu Bakr 鑿 to perform the job. Abu Bakr 鑿 departed at the head of three hundred *Hajj* pilgrims along with twenty camels from the Prophet 鑿 and five of his own to be sacrificed during *Hajj*. Soon after the departure of the *Hajj* caravan under Abu Bakr 鑿, forty Verses of *Sûrat At-Taubah* were revealed. These Verses delineated some essential injunctions like banning the polytheists' entry into the zone of the Sacred Mosque from the next year, banning the naked circumambulation of the House of Allâh, and the fulfilling of the covenant made with the Prophet 鑿. These injunctions were supposed to be announced on the occasion of the *Hajj*.

The Prophet 鑿 immediately sent Ali 鑿 riding on his (the Prophet's) dromedary with the instructions that these Verses be read out to the audience on the Day of Sacrifice after the *Hajj* was completed. Ali 鑿 traveled quickly and caught up with the caravan of Abu Bakr 鑿 at Dhul-Hulaifah. Abu Bakr 鑿 asked him whether he had come as the commander or the commanded. "I have come as the commanded and you will remain the commander. I have been entrusted with the duty of reading out these Verses." On reaching Makkah, Abu Bakr 鑿 oversaw the Muslims perform the rites of *Hajj* while Ali 鑿 read out the Verses of *Sûrat At-Taubah*.

The same year the Prophet's daughter Umm Kulthum 鑿 passed away, *Hajj* was declared as obligatory and was performed under the guidance of a Muslim leader and Abu Bakr 鑿 gave them instructions on the rites of *Hajj*. The polytheists were given a duration of only four months to vacate the sacred zone otherwise Allâh and His Messenger 鑿 would bear no responsibility whatsoever concerning them. Hearing this announcement even those in Makkah who had remained polytheists accepted Islam. Abdullah bin Ubai died the same year.

The Tenth Year of Migration

From Muharram 10 AH up to the end of the year, deputations kept arriving and Arab tribes continued joining the caravan of Islam. In Rabi' Al-Âkhir, Khâlid bin Walid ﷺ was sent to Najrân and its surrounding areas accompanied by four hundred Companions with instructions to call the people thrice to accept Islam and avoid fighting. They were pleased to embrace Islam when Khâlid bin Walid ﷺ reached there. Banu Al-Hârith bin Ka'b was one of the tribes who was converted to Islam. The Prophet ﷺ called Khâlid ﷺ and the Companions back while Amr bin Hazm ﷺ was sent to those areas as an instructor of Islam.

In Ramadân 10 AH, a deputation from Ghassan tribe came, which consisted of three members. They accepted Islam with all pleasure and returned to their people, but they refused to come into the fold of Islam.

In Shawwâl 10 AH, a seven-member deputation from Banu Salâmân came headed by its chief Habib bin Amr, and returned after accepting Islam. One day Habib bin Amr ﷺ asked the Prophet ﷺ, "Which is the most excellent deed in Islam?" He replied, "It is to offer prayer on time."

During the same period came the deputation of ten members from Azd and accepted Islam, by their preaching the whole tribe converted to Islam. For the same reason a fight broke out between Azd and Jursh tribes. Before the fight, Jursh people had sent their two men to Al-Madinah to enquire about the Prophet ﷺ. When these men approached the Prophet ﷺ, he said to them, "The Jursh and the Azd engaged themselves in fighting against one another and the Jursh were defeated." It had happened the same day. When both went back and related the event, the entire Jursh tribe accepted Islam. The same year, Ali ﷺ was sent to Yemen to teach them *Tauhid* and forbid polytheism. With his efforts, Hamdân, the well known tribe of Yemen, embraced Islam entirely. During this year the deputation from Murâd tribe came after breaking away from Muluk Kindah and accepted Islam. The deputation of Banu Abdul-Qais also came headed by Jârud bin Amr and they all converted to Islam from Christianity. They went back and brought their whole tribe to Islam.

Musailamah Kadhdhâb

In the same year the deputation of Banu Hanifah came from Yamâmah which included Musailamah bin Hubaib Kadhdhâb (liar), Jurjân bin Ghanam, Talq bin Ali and Salmân bin Hanzalah. They stayed for a fortnight and learned the Qur'ân from Ubai bin Ka'b During this period, other persons used to be in the company of the Prophet ﷺ, but Musailamah was away most of the time, with the permission of the Prophet ﷺ, under the pretext of looking after the belongings of the group. Among the deputations which came during this year were those of Banu Kindah, Banu Kinânah and Hadramout and accepted Islam. In the same year, Wâ'il bin Hujr appeared before the Prophet ﷺ and embraced Islam. Expressing his joy over this, the Prophet ﷺ asked Mu'âwiyah bin Abu Sufyân ﷺ to make him his guest. On the way to his home Mu'âwiyah ﷺ was on foot and Wâ'il bin Hujr was on his mount. Mu'âwiyah ﷺ asked Wâ'il for his footwear because his feet were burning from the heat. "I shall not give them for I have already worn them," Wâ'il replied rather rudely. "Well, let me ride behind you," Mu'âwiyah ﷺ proposed as an alternative. "You can't ride the mount of a king," Wâ'il replied with an air of arrogance. "But my feet are burning," Mu'âwiyah ﷺ spoke rather painfully. "It is enough for you to walk in the shadow of my camel," Wâ'il retorted. This is the same Wâ'il that when he approached Mu'âwiyah ﷺ during his caliphate, he showed him so much respect.

Mubâhalah

This means mutual condemnation and the asking of God's punishment to come down on the one who is false. The same year a Christian deputation came from Najrân along with their chief Abdul-Masih and bishop Abu Hârithah, they were 60 people with 24 from the distinguished families. They entered the Prophet's Mosque and started bitter arguments. Meanwhile, the earlier Verses of *Sûrat Âl-Imrân* and the Verse regarding *Mubâhalah* were sent down. When the Prophet ﷺ asked them to accept Islam, they showed rudeness. The Prophet ﷺ said, "Isa (Jesus) was raised out of clay by Allâh like

Adam." "No, Jesus was the son of Allâh," they contended. The Prophet 🌸 said, "If you are true in your claim then come along to a field with me and my relatives, and both the parties shall sit separately and say: 'May the torment of Allâh descend on the one who is a liar'." Hearing this they kept silent. The next morning the Prophet 🌸 took Ali, Fâtimah, Hasan and Husain 🌸 with him and said to the Christians, "When I invoke Allâh to send down His torment on the one who is telling a lie, you say, 'May it be so'." The straight forwardness of the Prophet 🌸 frightened them so much that they declared: "We don't want to enter into *Mubâhalah*." "Accept Islam if you don't want *Mubâhalah*, and become one with all the other Muslims," the Prophet 🌸 said firmly. "We don't accept this offer either," they replied. "Be ready then to either pay the (*Jizyah*) tax or measure your swords with us. "We shall pay the tax," they said. The Prophet 🌸 later said, "Had they accepted the *Mubâhalah*, they would have been destroyed up to their hairs and nails." When going back, they wished to have an escort sent with them. The Prophet 🌸 sent Abu Ubaidha bin Al-Jarrâh 🌸 with them and, after a short time, all the Christians became Muslims.

All the Yemenite tribes and their ruler Badhân had already turned to Islam. The Prophet 🌸 had allowed his rule to continue intact, but he died that year. Following this, he installed Shahr bin Badhân, Âmir bin Shahr Hamdâni, Abu Musa Ash'ari, Ali bin Umayyah, and Mu'âdh bin Jabal 🌸 as rulers of different parts of Yemen. Also, Ali 🌸 was sent at the head of a few Companions with the instructions that arms must not be raised against any unless it was done by others first. He was sent with the sole purpose of collecting *Zakât* and charitable donations.

The Farewell Pilgrimage

These events were followed by the month of Dhul-Qa'dah, 10 AH, when the Prophet of Allâh 🌸 set out on the journey to the House of Allâh to perform *Hajj*. A large number of Companions accompanied him with a hundred sacrificial camels. This caravan from Al-Madinah entered Makkah on Sunday, Dhul-Hijjah 4. Ali 🌸 joined the caravan from Yemen and performed *Hajj* with the Prophet 🌸.

The Farewell Address

On this occasion the Prophet ﷺ taught his Companions the rites of *Hajj* and delivered an address at Arafât. He said after praising and glorifying Allâh: "O people! Behold I am not sure of meeting you here next year or after that. O people! Your blood and your property are inviolable like the sacredness of this day in this month in this city of yours. Do no wrong to others lest you are wronged. The Devil has lost hope of ever being worshipped by those who pray. However, he will be followed in lesser matters. Therefore, you should shun his company. O people! You have rights on your womenfolk and they on you. Be good to them. Behold! Whoever holds anything in trust should return it to the person who has entrusted him with it. I leave among you two things, one the Book of Allâh and the second is the *Sunnah* of His Messenger. You will not go astray while you hold to the Book and the *Sunnah*. You will be asked if I have conveyed the Message of Allâh and fulfilled the mission?" "We testify that you have conveyed the Message of Allâh," the Companions replied with one voice. The Prophet ﷺ said, "O Allâh! Be Witness."

The Prophet ﷺ spoke addressing his Companions in words and manner, which are used when bidding farewell or saying good-bye. This is why this *Hajj* is called the Farewell *Hajj* (*Hajjat-ul-Wada'*). More than one hundred thousand Muslims performed their *Hajj* that year under the guidance of the Prophet of Allâh ﷺ. That day he also said: "These are the best words ever spoken by any of the Prophets: 'There is no true God except Allâh Alone, Who has no partner to Him, all praise is due for Him, He has power on every thing'." On the day of Arafât, the Prophet of Allâh ﷺ was still in Makkah when the following Verse was revealed:

> "This day, I have perfected your religion for you, completed my favor upon you, and have chosen for you Islam as your religion." (5:3)

Most of the Companions appeared jubilant at the revelation of the above Verse, for they thought that their religion was perfected and completed. But a few among them, like Abu Bakr ﷺ, who had deeper insight and wisdom, grew sad for the Verse indicated their separation from the Prophet ﷺ, because the existence of the Prophethood would no longer be required after the perfection of the religion.

The Consolation of Ali ؓ

During the *Hajj* some of the fellows of Ali ؓ who had been with him to Yemen complained to the Prophet ﷺ about Ali ؓ. Some of the misunderstandings of the people of Yemen had given rise to these misgivings. Addressing the Companions at Ghadir Khum, the Prophet of Allâh ﷺ said admiring Ali, "The one who is my friend is the friend of Ali and the one who is an enemy of Ali is my enemy." Following the address Umar ؓ congratulated Ali ؓ saying, "From this day on you are a very special friend of mine." The Prophet ﷺ then came back to Al-Madinah and his son Ibrahim ؓ passed away.

The Eleventh Year of Migration

The Sickness of the Prophet ﷺ

In Muharram 11 AH, the Prophet ﷺ developed a temperature which kept getting higher. When the news of his illness spread, the evildoers had an opportunity to start their treacherous activities. Musailamah, Tulaihah bin Khuwailid, Aswad and Sajâh bint Hârith all claimed they were prophets. They thought that they would also achieve success due to their claims like the Prophet of Allâh ﷺ did. But Allâh the Almighty put the seal on the Prophethood of Muhammad ﷺ and demonstrated it once again by driving each one of them to an ignominious failure and defeat for their heinous claim. Musailamah the liar gained notoriety in Yamâmah and Aswad bin Ka'b Ansi in Yemen.

One day the Prophet ﷺ came out while sick with a bandage tied around his head because of a headache. Addressing the Companions he said, "Last night I saw in a dream that I had two bracelets of gold on my wrists and I threw them away out of dislike. I interpreted this dream to mean that the two bracelets stand for the men of Yamâmah and Yemen (Musailamah the liar, and Aswad the liar)." Aswad the liar

was killed by a person named Firoz during the lifetime of the Prophet
of Allâh 鏊, while Musailamah the liar was killed by Wahshi, the killer
of Hamzah 鏺 during the caliphate of Abu Bakr Siddiq 鏺. Wahshi
used to say: "I have killed the best man while I was in a state of
disbelief and the worst man after I became a believer in Islam."

Jihâd in the way of Allâh from the Sick-bed:

When the Prophet 鏊 felt a little relief on Safar 26, 11 AH, he ordered
to make hasty preparations to take on the Romans because of
menacing news from the borders of Syria and Palestine. The next day
he appointed Usâmah bin Zaid bin Hârithah 鏺 as the commander of
the Muslim detachment and said to him, "Hurry up to the land of
your father and go quickly so that they won't have time to find out
about your movements. You will be, Allâh willing, crowned with
success."

Marching on the Romans was necessary because due to the events of
Yamâmah and Yemen and the Christian conspiracies against Islam, it
had once again encouraged the Romans to turn against Arabia. The
departure of the Muslim troops was so necessary and so significant
that in spite of the severity of his illness, the Prophet 鏊 got up to fix
the standard of Usâmah 鏺 with his own hands and let them go
ahead. He had ordered all the distinguished Companions to join the
detachment. Thus Abu Bakr, Abbâs, Umar, Uthmân and Ali 鏺 were
all going under the command of Usâmah 鏺. However, Ali and Abbâs
鏺 were held back in Al-Madinah to attend to the Prophet 鏊 during
his illness. Usâmah 鏺 took his detachment out of Al-Madinah and
made camp at Jurf about 5 km from the city. Abu Bakr and Umar 鏺
would come to the Prophet 鏊 from there with the permission of the
army commander Usâmah 鏺 and then go back.

In the meantime the Prophet's condition grew worse while Usâmah
鏺 and his troops anxiously awaited the news about him. The Prophet
鏊 also gave his approval to their holding up at Jurf. However, some
people expressed their misgivings at the commandership of Usâmah
鏺 because his father had once been a slave. When the Prophet 鏊
heard about the disapproval, he summoned the people and said,
"Why there is an objection against his appointment as commander

when his father had already been the commander of previous Muslim detachments?" He further added, "Zaid is among the foremost Muslims and commands a place of distinction in Islam." Those raising the objection subsided, showed their repentance and accepted Usâmah ﷺ as the commander of the Muslim detachment.

Illness increases:

The illness went on increasing day by day. The Prophet ﷺ sought permission from his wives to stay in the room of Âishah ﷺ, which they readily acceded to. He entered the apartment of Âishah ﷺ and then came out to say, "I tell you to fear Allâh. May Allâh guide you all, I leave Him with you and entrust you to Him. I am a warner against Hell and a giver of glad tidings of *Jannah* (Paradise). *Jannah* is for those who seek not oppression in the earth, nor corruption. The next life is for those who ward off evil. Never give yourselves to arrogance and vainglory." After a pause the Prophet ﷺ said, "My family members should wash my body," and added, "leave the spot for a while after putting my body beside the grave so that angels may perform their funeral prayers in groups one after another. The males of my family should come first to perform their funeral prayers followed by their women." The Prophet of Allâh ﷺ lay bed-ridden for three successive days.

Asking Abu Bakr ﷺ to lead the Prayers:

The Prophet ﷺ deputed Abu Bakr ﷺ to lead the Muslims in prayers in the Prophet's Mosque. Âishah ﷺ submitted, "My father is not able to serve in this capacity for he is too tender-hearted to do this. Please ask Umar to do the job." He said, "No, Abu Bakr will do it." Abu Bakr ﷺ was leading the prayer when the Prophet ﷺ felt a bit better and came into the mosque. As soon as Abu Bakr ﷺ came to know of the Prophet's arrival, he tried to get back, but the Prophet ﷺ motioned for him not to leave his place. Thus the Prophet ﷺ led the prayer sitting while Abu Bakr ﷺ was standing in the prayer. The *Sahihain* (*Sahih Bukhari* and *Sahih Muslim*) report that one day, during his illness, the Prophet of Allâh ﷺ asked for a pen and paper. Since he was then undergoing the intensity of his illness, Umar ﷺ intervened to say that he must not be put to any trouble for the Qur'ân is enough for us all as he has already said. But some of the Companions were in favor of letting him dictate. The Prophet ﷺ disliked the clamor of voices and asked the people to leave. At the time he was suffering from a violent headache and this was the reason why Umar ﷺ had suggested not to trouble him in any way. When his pain had subsided a little, he called the people in and said, "Make it a practice to keep the visiting deputations happy with gifts and rewards. Drive the polytheists out of the Arabian Peninsula and send the army of Usâmah ﷺ. Show kindness to the *Ansâr* and forgive their mistakes and consider none superior to Abu Bakr ﷺ in your assemblies." Following this he fell unconscious again due to the pain.

A little before Death

Ali, Abbâs, Fadl bin Abbâs, Abu Bakr, and Umar ﷺ remained at the service of the Prophet ﷺ most of the time during his fatal illness. The Prophet of Allâh ﷺ disliked anything to be left with him at the time of his final departure. He, therefore, asked Âishah ﷺ to give away in charity five or six dinars remaining with her. He extorted Ali ﷺ to take care of the prayers and relatives. Abu Bakr ﷺ led thirteen prayers in all during the Prophet's illness. On Monday, Rabi' Al-Awwal 12, 11 AH, he came out with a bandage tied around his head when Abu Bakr ﷺ was leading the dawn prayer. Following this he went back home and lay down with his head in the lap of Âishah ﷺ. Abu Bakr ﷺ also left for home happy and satisfied. Just at that moment Abdur Rahmân bin Abu Bakr ﷺ entered the room with a green toothstick (*Siwâk*—a natural toothbrush) in his hand. The Prophet ﷺ looked at it in a way that she thought he wanted it. She then took the toothstick from her brother, chewed it a little to make it soft and pliable, and then she gave it to him. He rubbed his teeth with it, and then leaving it, he put his head against Âishah's breast and stretched out his legs.

Death

A cup of water was kept near him. He dipped his hand in it and wiped his face with it, saying, "O Allâh, help me in the pangs of death." Âishah had been keeping her eyes fixed on his face when his eyes became glazed saying, "With the Highest Companionship in *Jannah* (Paradise)." Thus the Prophet passed away from this mortal world. The news of the Prophet's death fell like a thunderbolt on his Companions and they all were stunned.

The Condition of Umar

Umar was so terribly shocked that he temporarily lost his senses. He got up with his sword drawn and said at the top of his voice: "Some of the hypocrites have developed a notion that the Messenger of Allâh has passed away. But, in fact, he has not died. He has rather gone to his Lord as Moses had done. He shall come back and cut their hands and legs." Umar had gotten so emotional that nobody had the courage to ask him to sheathe his sword. After a short while Abu Bakr arrived and went straight into the room. He took the head of the Prophet in his hands, watched it and said, "May my mother and father be sacrificed for you, verily you have tasted the death which Allâh the Almighty had decreed for you, and never will you face any other death hereafter." He then came out saying *Inna lillâhi wa inna ilaihi raji'un* (to Allâh do we belong and to Him do we return) on his lips.

Firmness of Abu Bakr

Abu Bakr asked Umar to keep quiet but he paid no heed. He then stood at a short distance from him to address the people who now left Umar to cluster round Abu Bakr. He praised Allâh and then said: "O men, if anyone of you worships Muhammad, let him know that Muhammad is dead. But if anyone of you worships Allâh, then Allâh is alive and He does not die." Then continuing his speech he recited the Qur'ânic Verse:

> "Muhammad is no more than a Messenger, and indeed Messengers (the like of whom) have passed away before him. Will it be that, when he dies or is slain, you will turn back on your heels? He who turns back does no hurt to Allâh and Allâh will reward the thankful." (3:144)

All those who were present on that occasion felt pacified and their state of shock and bewilderment subsided quickly. Umar 🖎 says: "At first I paid no heed to the call of Abu Bakr. But when he recited the Verse, it seemed as if it had just been revealed. I was taken aback and fell down as if I had no legs. I felt as if I had just then come to know of the Prophet's death."

Hall of Banu Sâ'idah

Deliberations upon the new developments were going on when the news came that the *Ansâr* had collected in the hall of Banu Sâ'idah and were about to take the oath of allegiance at the hand of Sa'd bin Ubâdah 🖎. Some of them disputed the idea of choosing two leaders, one from the Quraish and another one from the *Ansâr*. Abu Bakr and Umar 🖎 accompanied by a group of *Muhâjirin* got up without losing a moment and proceeded towards the trouble spot to put the matter right. However, Ali, Abbâs, Usâmah, and Fadl bin Abbâs 🖎 the near relatives of the Prophet 🖎 were left behind to look after the burial affairs in conformity with the instructions of the Prophet 🖎 himself. Ali 🖎 washed his body while Abbâs 🖎 and his two sons helped moving him from one side to the other, while Usâmah 🖎 was pouring water over the body.

The Funeral Prayer and Burial

The task of washing the body being over, the Companions were divided over the place of burial. Abu Bakr 🖎 then said, "I have heard from the Messenger of Allâh 🖎 that every Prophet is being buried on the spot where he has breathed his last." The Prophet's bedding was accordingly removed from the place and a grave was dug for him at the same spot. The grave being completed, the people came to perform the funeral prayer in groups one after another. The women came in after the men and after them the children, all of whom prayed over him. Nobody acted as an *Imâm* for the funeral prayers of the Prophet 🖎.

On receiving the sad news of the Prophet's illness and then of his final departure, Usâmah bin Zaid 🖎 and his men moved back to Al-Madinah and the military standard was placed upright at the door of the Prophet's room. The funeral prayer was performed in the room of Âishah 鱗, where his burial was to take place. Obviously, it was impossible for the men, women and children of the entire city to perform the prayer together. Moreover, the prayer was not to be led by an *Imâm*. Thus it was natural that all took some time in performing the prayers in separate small batches in the small room. The Prophet 鱗 passed away on Monday and was buried the next day, on Tuesday.

Noble Features

The Prophet 鱗 was neither very tall nor short in stature. Among the people he appeared to rise higher than the others. His complexion was white and reddish, head large, beard full and thick, hair black and slightly curly and thick, sometimes touching his ear lobes and sometimes reaching down to his shoulders. His eyes round, wide, black, attractive, with red lines in the white parts and slanting thick brows parted in the middle. A vein protruded between the two eyebrows, which became more prominent in anger. His cheeks were even, soft and full. His teeth white and bright like pearls, and he would never burst into laughter he would simply smile. He was of a smiling countenance, soft-spoken, eloquent, and a man of all-round human qualities. The Seal of Prophethood was between the two shoulders. He used to do his work with his own hands

Children

Apart from Ibrâhim 鱗, who was born to Maria Qibtiyah (Copt) 鱗, all his children were born to his first wife Khadijah 鱗. First of all she gave birth to his son Qâsim 鱗 who died in Makkah at the age of four years. It is after his name that the Prophet 鱗 came to be called Abul-Qâsim (father of Qâsim). Thereafter for the Prophet 鱗 she had Zainab 鱗 followed by Abdullâh 鱗 who was surnamed as *Taiyib* (pure) and *Tâhir* (clean). She then gave birth to Ruqaiyah 鱗, Umm Kulthum 鱗 and Fâtimah 鱗 in order. While all his sons died in infancy, all his daughters grew up to be married. But none except the youngest daughter Fâtimah 鱗 was blessed with progeny. She bore four children to Ali bin Abu Tâlib, Hasan, Husain, Zainab and Umm Kulthum 鱗.

Character and Features

Various States and Conditions of the Prophet ﷺ:

The Prophet ﷺ had become an orphan in the womb of his mother and he began his life in hardships and difficulties. But when he departed from this mortal world, he had the whole of Arabia under his authority and none of the states of Arabia was beyond his control. But his simplicity, purity and uprightness served as a guiding light throughout his life.

Bukhari reports Âishah ﷺ to have said, "The Prophet ﷺ never preferred himself to anyone in worldly affairs. He would do his household chores as you all do. He would milk the sheep and repair his shoes. When the construction work of the Prophet's Mosque was being done, the Prophet ﷺ also participated in the work like a common laborer carrying bricks for the mosque. He was one of the workers digging the trench, breaking stones and carrying clay in preparation for the Battle of the Confederates (also known as the Battle of the Trench). His common diet was barley bread of unsieved flour. But even the barley was sometimes not available for days at a time. Sometimes no fire was lighted in the hearth of his houses, and members of the Prophet's household had to live on dates and water. He never openly disliked any food nor criticized it. He would eat from whatever was served to him and held himself back when he wasn't hungry or when the food was disagreeable to him."

When Âishah ﷺ was asked about his bedding she related, "It was made of coarse animal skin filled with date-bark." When the same question was repeated to Hafsah ﷺ, she said, "It was just a piece of sackcloth. One night I folded it in four parts to make it more comfortable for the Prophet ﷺ. The next morning he asked as to what I had spread as the bedding. I told him that it was the same piece of sackcloth, but I had folded it in four parts to give him more comfort. The Prophet ﷺ asked me to make it as it was because it held him back from performing the night prayer."

The Prophet's coat of mail had been pawned with a Jew in return for 30 dirhams but he didn't have enough money to get it back from him.

The Messenger of Allâh 🌺 departed from the world and the coat of mail was still with the Jew. He left his weapons, a mule and a coat of mail as inheritance but with the instructions that these things were to be given in charity.

Are they not blind who accuse him of lifting his sword against his own people for (Allâh forbid) personal gain, sensual desire, for power, wealth or for fulfilling a lust for territorial gain?

Anas 🌺 says, "I came to the Prophet 🌺 when I was only 8 years old and served the Prophet of Allâh 🌺 for 10 years. During such a long time he never uttered a painful word nor blamed me for doing anything wrong."

Abu Hurairah 🌺 relates that once the people said to him, "Please invoke on the polytheists, the curse of Allâh." He replied, "I have not been sent to invoke the curse of Allâh; I have rather been sent by Allâh as mercy for mankind."

Âishah 🌺 says, "His taste and temperament had nothing to do with nonsensical things." He would lift children in his lap to play with them, go to far off places to fulfill the needs of the sick. He would be the first to salute others and never pulled his hand back after a handshake before the other did. He would call his Companions with their surnames out of respect and addressed them with suitable and likeable names. He would never cut in while anybody was talking. However, he would forbid anyone from talking nonsense or he would get up to stop it.

Cheerful and Perfect Manners:

Abdullah bin Hârith 🌺 says, "I have never seen a person more cheerful than the Messenger of Allâh 🌺." As per his saying, "The strong man is not one who knocks another down but the one who controls himself when his anger reaches its peak."

Anas 🌺 said, "He was the bravest of all. Once the people of Al-Madinah found themselves in an unknown terror thinking it an invasion from the enemy. The people followed the commotion. But the panic-stricken people found to their utmost wonder that the Prophet 🌺

was already returning from the center of the trouble riding bareback on a horse. He came across them on the way and pacified the people saying, "Don't worry; there is nothing to fear."

Barâ' bin Âzib ⁂ states, "The people fled the field on the day of Hunain, while the Prophet ﷺ was going forward reciting the martial lines: 'I am surely the Prophet, I am son of Abdul-Muttalib.' None was more valiant and courageous than he on that day. We took refuge behind him from forceful attacks. The one who could bear the charge of the enemy being beside the Prophet ﷺ on the battlefield was considered the bravest among us."

Anas ⁂ relates, "Once I was walking with the Prophet ﷺ who was wearing a cloak with a coarse fringe, a bedouin met him and violently tugged his cloak. I saw that the man's tugging had left a mark on the neck and shoulder of Allâh's Prophet ﷺ. When the Prophet ﷺ turned towards him, the nomad said, "O Muhammad, give me two camels loaded with what Allâh has given you, for it neither belongs to you nor your father." The Prophet ﷺ kept silent out of his grace and politeness despite such rude and bitter words. Then speaking rather softly, he said to the nomad, "Should you be treated as you have treated me?" "No," the nomad said emphatically. "Why not?" The Prophet ﷺ asked. "It is because you don't believe in tit for tat," he very confidently replied. The Prophet ﷺ smiled at his plain talking and then ordered to load one of his camels with barley and another with dates."

Once Zaid bin Sa'nah, a Jew came to the Prophet ﷺ and demanded payment of the money owed by the Prophet ﷺ and addressed him rudely, saying, "You son of Abdul-Muttalib are late." Although the Prophet ﷺ kept smiling at his rudeness, Umar ⁂ rebuked and reproached him. Thereupon the Prophet ﷺ said to Umar ⁂, "This man was entitled to better treatment from you. You ought to have advised me to repay the loan promptly and asked him to make his demand politely." At the same time he asked Umar ⁂ to pay the loan and give Zaid twenty *Sa'* (60 kilograms) extra so as to compensate him for his threatening attitude towards Zaid. The gracious and obliging behavior of Allâh's Prophet ﷺ caused Zaid to embrace Islam then and there.

Anas relates, "I accompanied the Prophet to Abu Saif, the smith whose wife would suckle his son, Ibrâhim , who was then on the brink of death. This sad plight brought tears to the eyes of the Prophet . Thereupon Abdur-Rahmân bin Auf said, "Do you also show impatience, O Prophet of Allâh?" The Prophet replied, "O Ibn Auf, these are the tears of mercy and affection, not of impatience and thanklessness. The heart saddens and the eyes shed tears, but we must not say anything that goes against the Will of Allâh."

Abu Khudri relates, "Once some people from the *Ansâr* asked for something from the Prophet and he gave them. He gave all he had, when they repeated their demands, the Prophet remarked, 'I never lay aside whatever comes to me. Verily, Allâh the Almighty saves those from the disgrace of asking for something who beg Allâh for it; Allâh makes rich those who long for it; Allâh makes them patient who keep patience; and none has ever been given a better gift from Allâh than patience'."

Abu Hurairah states, "The Prophet has said more than once: 'If I had gold equal to Mount Uhud, I would feel happy only when I had distributed all of it before the end of three days. I keep nothing with me save what is necessary for the repayment of a loan'."

The Prophet would rise to help the needy even when he had nothing to give. In such a situation he helped by borrowing from others, even when he already had loans of the same nature, otherwise he never borrowed anything from anybody for his own personal needs.

Jâbir bin Abdullah relates, "I accompanied the Prophet on an expedition. My camel lagged behind because of exhaustion. After a short while the Prophet passed by and asked, 'How are you Jâbir?' I told him, 'My camel is exhausted.' He hit my camel and it sped up. Then we moved ahead talking with each other. During this exchange he asked me, 'Will you sell the camel.' I replied in the affirmative. Thus he bought it from me and moved ahead. I reached the destination late in the day. I tied it to the door of the mosque. 'Leave it there and come in to perform two *Rak'ah* of prayer,' the Prophet said to me. The prayer being over, he asked Bilâl to make payment for the camel. When I moved a little with the amount, he called me back. I was afraid if the camel was to be returned. But on my return he said, 'Take the camel with you along with its price, which has already been paid to you'."

Once the Prophet 鑿 was passing through a grove along with a person. He cut two toothsticks one straight and another bent. He took the bent one and gave the straight one to his companion. Although he insisted on him (the Prophet 鑿) to take the straight one, the Prophet 鑿 refused saying that everyone will on the Day of Judgment be asked about his etiquette with the company he has passed sometime with.

Ibn Abbâs 鑿 relates that once some dispute arose between a hypocrite Muslim named Bishr and a Jew. Both of them came to the Prophet 鑿 for a verdict. After hearing both of them and looking into the matter, he gave his verdict in favor of the Jew. When they came out, Bishr said, "The verdict is not fair; let us go to Umar." Both of them went to him. The Jew stated before Umar 鑿: "Both of us have gone to the Prophet and he gave his verdict in my favor, but this man (Bishr) didn't accept it and has now brought me to you to seek and accept that of yours." Umar 鑿 verified the statement of the Jew with Bishr who said, "This is a fact that we had gone to the Prophet for his verdict in the dispute but now I seek to prefer your verdict to that of his." Umar 鑿 said, "Just wait, and I will give my verdict right away." He went into his house and came out with his sword and cut off the head of the hypocrite Bishr, and remarked, "Anyone who rejects the decision of Allâh and His Messenger 鑿 after claiming himself a Muslim, I decide his matter in this manner." Following this his hypocrite fellows raised much hue and cry against this action but Allâh the Almighty lent support to this decision of Umar 鑿 through His Revelation, and it is said that from that day he came to be called 'Fâruq'.

After the conquest of Makkah, Fâtimah bint Al-Aswad of Banu Makhzum was apprehended on the charge of theft. The Prophet 鑿 ordered to cut off the right hand of the culprit after her crime was proved. The notables among the Quraish felt this was disgraceful. They wanted to save her from punishment by virtue of intercession, but none of them had the courage to go before the Prophet 鑿 with this purpose in view. At last they approached Usâmah bin Zaid 繼 to intercede with the Prophet 繼 on the issue. When he brought the matter to the notice of Prophet 繼, his expression completely altered. He said, 'Usâmah! Do you speak to me about the limits set by Allâh?" He got up then and addressed the people saying, "The people before you were destroyed because they used to overlook when a highborn or a man of substance among them committed a theft, but when the poor or the weak did the same, they chastised him as ordained by the law. I swear by Him Who holds my life, if Fâtimah bint Muhammad had committed this theft, I would have amputated her hand."

Informality:

Once the Prophet 繼 said: "Keep away from praising me beyond a limit like the Christians who crossed all limits in adoring Isa bin Maryam. I am one of the slaves of Allâh, so call me Abdullah (the slave of Allâh)."

Once the Prophet 繼 came out and all the Companions got up to pay their respect to him. Thereupon he said, "Do away with the practice of standing up to adore anyone like the *Ajami* people (non-Arabs)."

He would keep very close to his Companions and took his seat wherever he found a place. He took part in the work done by the servants and made them sit beside him.

He has said that one who endeavors to do the needful for the hungry and the poor, attains the status of one who fights in the way of Allâh, and one who prays the whole night and observes fast the whole year.

A certain person called on the Prophet 繼 and asked, "O Prophet of Allâh, what is the way to *Jannah* (Paradise)?" He said, "Truth. It is because when a person is truthful, he adopts virtue, which leads to the light of Faith, and Faith leads him to *Jannah* (Paradise)." On another occasion he said, "Keep truthful even if your truth leads you to face death and destruction, for undoubtedly it is where salvation rests."

Once, on the way to Badr from Makkah, Akhnas bin Shuraiq said to Abu Jahl, "O Abul-Hakam, I ask you one thing, and none is here except we two; tell me truthfully whether Muhammad is truthful or a liar." Abu Jahl replied, "By God, Muhammad always speaks the truth and he never uttered anything untrue."

Abu Saeed Khudri ﷺ is reported to have said, "The Prophet ﷺ was more modest than a graceful and veiled virgin. We read from his face the sign of his displeasure. When he disliked anything, he would indicate it indirectly so that the person was not shamed. However, he made no concessions in matters of the Word of Allâh and the upholding of the Truth."

Moderation:

Âishah ﷺ related that when the Prophet ﷺ said anything of anyone, he never mentioned the person by name. He would rather say, "What type of person are those who do such things." Most of the time he kept silent and never talked unnecessarily; his speech was always clear and lucid, neither so long as to contain loose substance nor so short as to exclude some essential points. His movement was moderate, neither so slow as to become undesirable to others in his company nor so fast to cause exhaustion. In short, he practiced moderation in every aspect of life.

Cheerful Disposition:

He radiated cheerfulness. Once he promised to give someone a camel. When that person asked for it, he ﷺ said, "I can give you the calf of a she camel." "What shall I do with the calf?" the person said with a touch of disappointment. Thereupon he ﷺ said, "If a camel is not the calf of a she-camel, whose calf is it?" But the Prophet ﷺ never uttered a word of untruth even during casual talk.

Laudable Traits of Character:

When the Prophet ﷺ was in the company of his Companions, he was so close to them that a newcomer wouldn't recognize him distinctly and would ask for the Prophet ﷺ to be pointed out to him. He did not like to eat anything that might cause a bad smell to emit from his mouth. He wore clothes with patches; he liked simple but clean garments. He used a toothstick several times a day. The people sitting beside him never complained of his body, clothes or mouth emitting a bad smell. He sought forgiveness between parties where it could be helpful in bringing about reforms, but in case of crimes demanding punishment, he never held himself back, because refraining from chastising the criminals was to him tantamount to aiding and abetting in promoting crimes.

Charities from Muslims were not limited to the Muslims, he extended it to the Christians, Jews and polytheists too. He put up with exemplary ease whatever calamities befell him but he became restless to find anybody else in trouble. He applied all sources and resources in accomplishing any job but left the outcome to Allâh the Almighty, and he was least afraid of the result going against his hope. He showed humility but not meanness; he was awesome but not rude and rash; he practiced generosity but not extravagance; whoever came before him, all of a sudden felt awe-stricken but when seated beside him, began to love him. He asked to keep away from epidemics, forbade quacks to treat patients and disliked the use of prohibited things as medicine. Whenever he had two ways to do a thing, he used the easier one. He served the prisoners of war like his guests. He took part in manly sports and exercises like archery, shooting, and horse racing along with his Companions.

Chapter 3

The Rightly-Guided Caliphate

Caliph and Caliphate

Caliph means successor and caliphate means the succession of rule, and in historian's terminology, caliph approximates the words king, monarch or ruler. It is not at all necessary that before dealing with the events of Abu Bakr's caliphate after the Prophet 攀, a historian should devote his time and space in discussing the word caliph or caliphate. But since the succession of Prophet 攀 has taken the form of an ethical issue between two sections, the task of a historian has become rather difficult. Moreover, it has also become incumbent on the historians to put forward their own point of view and belief concerning the caliphate before embarking upon the topic of the Rightly-Guided Caliphate.

Wherever the word *Khalifah* (caliph) appears in the Qur'ân, it is immediately followed by the word *Al-Ard* (earth). Moreover it is proved beyond doubt from the Verse:

"I am going to place generation after generation on earth." (2:30)

Allâh the Almighty has appointed Adam and the children of Adam, as His caliph on earth. It is also abundantly clear that the children of Adam are the most eminent of all created beings and their being rulers on earth is beyond doubt. The caliphate of men on earth is certainly a Divine caliphate and man is the caliph of Allâh. Allâh the Exalted is far above any creature including the most eminent of the created beings that becomes His vice-regent on earth. So, man can be nothing more than the apparent ruler of the earth and makes all other creatures obey His rule. It is clear now that in Verse 2:30. The word caliph stands for 'generation after generation' or 'ruler' and for nothing else. The Qur'ân says at another place:

"He it is Who has made you successors on the earth, and He has raised you in ranks, some above others." (6:165)

Here caliphate stands for something specific, your people have been made ruler, and all other people are to be ruled by you. Here also the word 'caliph' makes its appearance, which gives the meaning of nothing but a 'ruler'. Again, it has been mentioned in another Verse:

"O Dâwud! Verily, we have placed you as a successor on earth." (38:26)

Here also, the rule or empire of a person, Dâwud ﷺ, finds mention and the word caliph signifies a king, monarch or ruler. About the same rule of Dâwud ﷺ, it has been said at another place:

"We made his kingdom strong." (38:20)

Regarding the Muslims and particularly about the Companions it has been said:

"Allâh has promised those among you who believe and do righteous good deeds that He will certainly grant them succession in the earth as He granted it to those before them." (24:55)

It means: As We have installed others as rulers in the past, so also those among the followers of the Prophet ﷺ, who believed and performed good deeds, will be conferred upon the rule on earth.

Claim to Caliphate

From the Qur'ân it becomes clear beyond doubt that rule or caliphate on earth is from Allâh and He Alone can take it back.

It is said:

"O Allâh! Possessor of the kingdom, You give the kingdom to whom You will, and You take the kingdom from whom You will." (3:26)

Now it is to be seen as to who really deserves the caliphate or rule, and what are the distinctive signs of those who are given caliphate. According to the Qur'ân, it is knowledge on which the rule over mankind is based.

"And He taught Adam all the names (of everything)." (2:31)

While the angels considered the traits of corruption and disruption against a righteous caliphate, and the mention and glorification of Allâh the Almighty to be the consideration for making one deserve the caliphate. We have seen clearly that human beings established their rule over other creatures due to their power of knowledge only. Had man not been adorned and strengthened with deep and wide knowledge, even a gust of wind, a wave of water, a leaf of some tree or a particle of dust could have rendered him helpless. It is by virtue of his knowledge that even a lion, an elephant, river, mountain, wind, fire, and lightening are at his service and are ready to obey him and comfort him like his servants. The Qur'ân informs us when there were objections to the kingship of Tâlut (Saul), Allâh the Almighty answered the detractors through His Prophet:

"Verily Allâh has chosen him above you and has increased him abundantly in knowledge and stature. And Allâh grants His kingdom to whom He wills." (2:247)

Having conferred rule and caliphate on Dâwud ﷺ, Allâh the Almighty commanded

"So judge you between men in truth and follow not your desire." (38:26)

In another Verse, He said:

"And indeed We destroyed generations before you when they did wrong, while their Messengers came to them with clear proofs, but they were not such as to believe! That do We requite the people who are sinners. Then We made you successors after them, generations after generations in the land that We might see how you would work." (10:13,14)

Hundreds of Verses from the Qur'ân may be produced to establish that caliph stands for 'ruler' and caliphate for 'rule'. And in order to rule establishing knowledge, justice, reform, power and welfare of mankind are some of the prerequisite conditions, which have always been required from a king or ruler without which he cannot keep his rule intact. All these good qualities can only be obtained through the teachings of the Prophets and the Messengers of Allâh. However, it is also necessary that a Prophet has to be a ruler in order to set the example. Had mere prayers and glorification of Allâh the Almighty been enough, only Prophets or angels would have ruled the world. In short, the caliphate is another name for the rule which Allâh the Almighty confers on those He wants. However, when a ruling nation indulges in corruption and wrongdoing, Allâh the Almighty takes it away from them.

Islamic Caliphate

All the progress made by mankind so far along with all his academic and moral virtues are the outcome of the teachings of the Prophets. Prophets have sometimes came as teachers, for instance, like Isa عليه السلام (Jesus Christ), and at times as monarchs like Dâwud (David) عليه السلام. The religious codes brought by monarch-Prophets are more perfect and magnificent than those of the teacher-Prophets. The teacher-Prophets set examples for every member of their *Ummah* (community) while the monarch-Prophets not only set examples but have the power to enforce codes and make the people follow them. When the teacher-Prophet departs from the world after finishing his task, none can succeed him in matters of Prophethood, for the Prophet receives Revelation from Allâh the Almighty to convey to his people.

Now as a matter of general principle, the successor of a Prophet must be a Prophet. But since a Prophet departs from the world only after completing the task assigned to him, he needs no successor after him. This is why no teacher-Prophet has ever had a successor. However, as far as a monarch-Prophet is concerned, nobody can succeed him as a Prophet but his rule may be succeed by anybody as a successor. Since the successor would have been brought up under the shadow of the Prophet's teachings, he is supposed to be the most suitable person to do the job. Since Muhammad ﷺ was the perfect and the last Prophet and had been sent with the complete guidelines, he was, therefore, a ruling-Prophet and his rule is the best and most perfect example for rulers and leaders to the Day of Judgment.

He was essentially supposed to have a successor or caliph after him, and there actually have been many who have succeeded him in temporal affairs. In addition, there were those among them who were brought up in the mould of the Prophet ﷺ and had the stamp of Prophetic character and adopted the pattern of his Prophetic rule. Their rule came to be called the Rightly-Guided Caliphate. But the farther they happened to be from the days of Prophetic rule, their caliphate showed a difference from that of the primary example.

Objection to the Procedure of electing a Caliph

After the time of the Prophet ﷺ, some people among the Muslims raised doubts of a ridiculous nature regarding the procedure adopted for electing a caliph. But, in truth, all such charges are false and fabricated for the choice of a ruler or caliph rests wholly and solely with Allâh the Almighty. He Alone gives it to someone and takes it away from others. He never left this job to any human.

The Qur'ân delineates the task of a caliph and its dos and don'ts. It gives detailed guidance about the prayer, fasting, *Hajj*, *Zakât*, the rights of Allâh and His servants but doesn't mention the succession of the Prophet. This is because He gives it to the one He chooses for the job and makes arrangements for this. Allâh the Almighty Alone knows who deserves the job. The one who succeeded the first caliph was the one whom Allâh chose for the job. If any other person is brought forward as the most deserving for the post, in fact, it is to say that Allâh the Almighty failed to bring a man of His choice for the post. It means He (Allâh forbid) was defeated in His Plan.

Thus to raise a dispute in this matter is tantamount to objecting to the choice of the Almighty. Thus, the detractors of Abu Bakr's caliphate are like those who object to the decision of a judge in a court of law, the judge cannot alter his judgment because of their deprecation. Now if anybody disapproves of the caliphate of a person, in fact, he stands against the Judgment of Allâh the Exalted and Most High.

Difference between Caliphate and Temporal Rule

The above discussion may create misunderstanding that if the caliphate is simply like temporal rule then any king may be called a caliph and caliphate has nothing to do with religion. But, let it be known that in Islam the caliph is strictly one who patterns his rule according to the rule established by the Prophet of Allâh ﷺ and only such a ruler may be included among the successors of the Messengers.

The first and foremost duty of the successor of the Prophet ﷺ as a ruler is to establish a rule according to the Divine code and enforce it. Such a ruler alone can serve humanity in the best possible way observing the laws and tenets of Islam.

Thus to say that the caliphate has nothing to do with Islam is something nonsensical. A despotic ruler can never bring peace and welfare to mankind. The rule established by the righteous caliphs was based on the example set by the Prophet ﷺ himself. And before or after that no rule was similar to that which was set up by the Prophet ﷺ. This rule was called the Rightly-Guided Caliphate. Ever since that system of governance, Islamic rule has been continuing but the set up has kept changing with the passage of time.

Relation of Caliphate with a Nation, Tribe or Family

The Qur'ân clearly and unequivocally says:

"O people: We created you of a single man and woman and made of you separate families and tribes to know each distinctively from others. To Allâh the most honorable is the one who is most God-fearing; Allâh is All-Knowing and Aware." (49:13)

Islam has tried to carve out one nation by doing away with family pride, national superiority and vanity.

"The believers are nothir else than brothers." (49:10)

He has made one brotherhood of all brotherhoods and one nation of all nations and gave its name as Muslim or *Momin* (believers). Families and nations of the entire world may be divided in two categories following the teachings of Islam; believers or Muslims and disbelievers or polytheists. After making entry into the realm of *Tauhid* (Oneness of Allâh), all such differences of nations and tribes are a mere source of recognizing clearly one from another. Thus the pious and righteous alone deserve honor and power whichever nation or tribe they belong to.

In each case, piety and faith lie at the base. For wielding power, Allâh the Almighty has put knowledge, health, physical strength, piety, justice and reform as prerequisite conditions but no particular nation or tribe finds a place in such a list. Islam made a high-ranking man of the Quraish to become the victim of the youngsters of Al-Madinah, and made Bilâl ﷺ, the Abyssinian slave, superior to the nobles of Arabia. Usâmah bin Zaid ﷺ became the commander of an army with both Abu Bakr and Umar ﷺ under his command. Islam made the king and the slave stand side by side with the same rank.

Islam made the Prophet ﷺ to declare that if Fatimah ﷺ, his own daughter committed theft, her hand would be amputated like any other person committing the same crime. Islam made the Prophet of Allâh ﷺ to announce: "O people! If an ordinary Abyssinian slave is made your ruler or caliph, you must obey him." It was Islam, which made Umar ﷺ to say in the last moments of his life, "Had Sâlim, the slave of Abu Hudhaifah been alive, I would have appointed him my successor." In short, Islam broke to pieces the idols of family and hereditary arrogance. It was a unique, exclusive and spectacular service that Islam rendered to the world of humanity. Islam has a right to take pride in that no other religion or set of laws was ever able to cause the idol of hereditary arrogance to shake even a little, while Islam pulled it down.

How strange that even the Muslims following the tenets of Islam are found saying that the Prophet ﷺ had made caliphate the special privilege of the Quraish tribes or Banu Hâshim or Ali ﷺ or his progeny and deprived all others of this right. Had it been so, the Qur'ân would have expounded it in unequivocal terms and the

Prophet of Allâh ﷺ would have defined it in clear words. If a particular section claims that Allâh the Almighty had sent down any orders regarding the rule or caliphate which were cleverly concealed by the usurpers of the caliphate, then, Allâh's Claim of preserving the Qur'ân would be rendered 'false' as He has said:

"Verily, We it is Who have sent down the Qur'ân and surely, We will guard it (from corruption)." (15:9)

Moreover, His Messenger ﷺ would have failed in his duty of conveying the Message of Allâh fully and adequately, although he declared before a huge congregation of one hundred thousand people that he had completed the task of his preaching and asked the people to testify to it. Furthermore, he counseled his people concerning very small details from his deathbed but told them nothing about his successor.

It is because he knew very well that the act of choosing a ruler or caliph rested exclusively with Allâh and He did not entrust this duty to the Prophet ﷺ. However, inspiration from Allâh the Almighty had already let him know who was going to succeed him as caliph. Therefore, he asked Abu Bakr ؓ to lead the Muslims in prayers during his illness. He had also counseled the *Muhâjirin* to take care of the *Ansâr* for he, perhaps, knew that the caliphate was to be entrusted to the *Muhâjirin*. From the knowledge gained from Allâh, he had already disclosed that *Imâm* will come from the Quraish. But all these were among his prophecies, not his orders. The Quraish were chosen for shouldering the heavy but very delicate burden of the caliphate because they had a very profound knowledge of the workings of Islam and they were ahead of all in observing piety. However, the caliphate or rule is not particular to any certain race, tribe or family. It is the reward of Allâh for the deserving. When a ruling class or family loses its integrity and capability, Allâh the Almighty brings someone else to replace it. And this is the demand of justice.

The Caliphate and Spiritual Guidance as a Profession

Some people are of the opinion that the caliphate referred to in *Sûrat An-Nur* deals with the system of spiritual guidance as a profession. To me it is an utterly wrong belief. Although a spiritual guide rules over his disciples, he has no power to enforce the Islamic code and Divine order. The Qur'ân has left nothing to guesswork by referring in clear terms to the caliphates of Adam and Dâwud. We are ordained to follow the Qur'ân in all walks of life.

Abu Bakr Siddiq ﷺ

His Name and Genealogy:

His family lineage is Abdullah bin Abu Quhâfah bin Âmir bin Amr bin Ka'b bin Sa'd bin Tamim bin Murrah bin Ka'b bin Luai bin Ghâlib bin Fihr bin Mâlik bin Nadr bin Kinânah. Murrah serves as the meeting ground for the lineage of the Prophet ﷺ and Abu Bakr ﷺ, and both of them have a distance of 6 generations.

His mother was Salma bint Sakhr bin Ka'b bin Sa'd. She was the cousin of Abu Quhâfah and was widely known as Umm-ul-Khair. The name of his father, Abu Quhâfah was Uthmân. Abu Bakr ﷺ was called Abd Ka'bah in the Days of Ignorance. The Prophet ﷺ named him Abdullah, and his name was Atiq also. However, Jalâluddin Suyuti writes in his book *Târikh Al-Khulafa*: "The majority of *Ulama'* (religious scholars) is of the opinion that Atiq was his surname, not his name." To some, he was called Atiq because of his being handsome and graceful while others argue that since his genealogy was spotless, he was known as Atiq.

There is a complete consensus among the true followers of Islam that his surname was *Siddiq*, for he testified to the Prophethood without any hesitation and fear and took it upon himself to follow the truth. When the event of *Mi'râj* (Ascension) occurred, he showed his unshakable firmness and conviction to lend his support to it and did it in the face of all opposition. He was younger than the Prophet ﷺ by two years and two months. He was born and brought up in Makkah. He would go on journeys with trade caravans. He migrated to Al-Madinah along with the Prophet ﷺ and embraced death in the same city.

Relationship of Muhammad ﷺ with the Four Caliphs

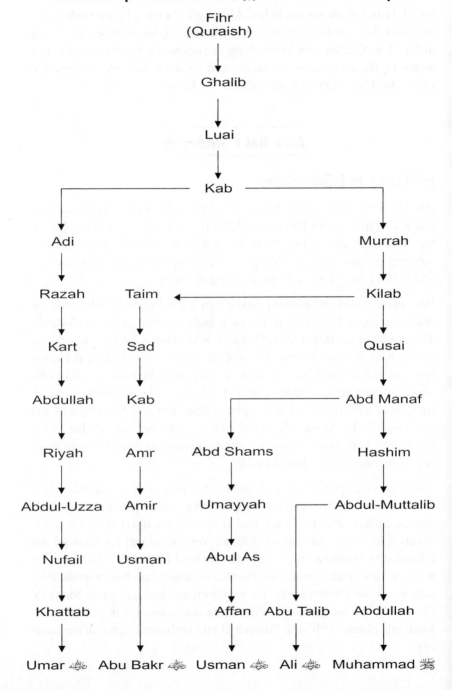

Fihr
(Quraish)

Ghalib

Luai

Kab

Adi

Murrah

Razah

Taim

Kilab

Kart

Sad

Qusai

Abdullah

Kab

Abd Manaf

Riyah

Amr

Abd Shams

Hashim

Abdul-Uzza

Amir

Umayyah

Abdul-Muttalib

Nufail

Usman

Abul As

Khattab

Affan

Abu Talib

Abdullah

Umar ﷺ   Abu Bakr ﷺ   Usman ﷺ   Ali ﷺ   Muhammad ﷺ

Age of Ignorance:

During the Age of Ignorance, the power and nobility of the Quraish were shared by ten clans: (1) Hâshim, (2) Umayyah, (3) Naufal, (4) Abdud-Dâr, (5) Asad (6) Taim, (7) Makhzum, (8) Adi, (9) Jumh and (10) Sahm. These clans were entrusted with different jobs to do. Banu Hâshim had it as their right to provide water to the pilgrims. Banu Naufal had the right to give provisions to those who happened to be in need of it. Banu Abdud-Dâr had the key of the Ka'bah along with guarding it. Banu Asad had to give counsel and maintain Dar An-Nadwah (the House of Assembly). Banu Taim decided about blood money and penalties. Banu Adi had intertribal ambassadorship responsibilities, Banu Jumh had the arrows of omen and Banu Sahm managed offerings to idols.

Abu Bakr ﷺ would give his judgment about blood money and penalties on behalf of Banu Taim and the entire Quraish had to abide by his decision. Besides, Abu Bakr ﷺ was the chief of his clan and wielded deep influence as a man of substance. Among the Quraish, he commanded distinction for his wide responsibilities and for entertaining guests on a large scale. They took his counsel in their important affairs and he was regarded highly for his prudence, patience and firmness. He was well-versed in the art of genealogy. He naturally kept away from evil and depravity. When asked if he had ever drunk wine, he curtly replied, "Allâh forbid, never!" "Why not?" the person asked. "I hated that my body would emit foul smells and happen the loss of good manners." When the matter was stated in the presence of the Prophet ﷺ, he said twice, "Abu Bakr is true."

Abu Bakr Siddiq ﷺ was the embodiment of good and was spotless, just and righteous. It is because of this that when the Prophet ﷺ invited him to accept Islam, he embraced it without delay and promised to lend all help and total support, which he fulfilled in the face of all opposition and extreme hardship and misery. The Prophet ﷺ once said, "The sun never rose over anyone better than Abu Bakr except the Prophets." Since he attributed such great respect, many including Uthmân bin Affân, Talhah bin Ubaidullah and Sa'd bin Abu Waqqâs ﷺ accepted Islam under his direct influence.

Islamic Era:

Abu   Bakr Siddiq ﷺ was the first to believe in the Prophet ﷺ and was
the first to perform prayers led by the Prophet ﷺ. Somebody asked
Maimun bin Mehrân, "Who is better in your opinion, Abu Bakr or
Ali?" He became   angry and very indignantly uttered, "I never knew
that I would remain alive until the day these two would be compared
with each other. They were, in fact, like the head of Islam. Abu Bakr
was the first to accept Islam among the adults, Ali among the boys
and Khadijah among the women."

The religious scholars are unanimous that Abu Bakr ﷺ never left the
company of the Prophet ﷺ without his permission. He migrated for
the sake of his love for Allâh and His Messenger ﷺ leaving his wife
and children alone and stayed with the Prophet ﷺ in the cave and
accompanied him in every battle. In the battle of Badr, the Prophet ﷺ
said about Abu Bakr and Ali ﷺ, "One has Jibril (Gabriel) and another
Mikâ'il (Michael) with them." In the battle of Badr, his son Abdur-
Rahmân bin Abu Bakr had joined the polytheist army. Once after
accepting Islam, he said to his father, "Several times on the day of
Badr you came within the range of my arrows but I held my hand
back." Thereupon Abu Bakr ﷺ replied, "If I had to face you, I would
have made you the target of my arrow."

Valor:

Once Ali ﷺ put the question, "Who is the most valiant person to
you?" "You are the most valiant," they replied with one voice. "I
always take on my equals; this is not bravery," Ali ﷺ replied and
said again, "Tell me the name of the most valiant person." "We don't
know," all of them replied. "Abu Bakr is the most valiant," Ali ﷺ
replied and added, "On the day of Badr we had erected a hut for the
Messenger of Allâh ﷺ. We then asked each other as to who will
accompany the Prophet ﷺ to save him from the onslaught of the
polytheists. By Allâh none of us had the courage to offer his services.
But Abu Bakr stood alone drawing his sword and allowed no one to
draw near the Prophet ﷺ, and whoever attempted an attack on the
Prophet ﷺ, came under the charge of Abu Bakr. The polytheists of

Makkah once surrounded the Prophet ﷺ saying, 'It is you alone who says God is One. No one else has ever said so.' They were dragging him when Abu Bakr stepped forward and set about beating and moving them and saying, 'Woe to you, you want to kill a person who simply says: my God is One'." Saying this, Ali ﷺ burst into tears and further said, "Tell me whether the believing men of Âl-Firaun (family of Pharaoh) are better or Abu Bakr?" When the people made no answer, he himself said, "Why don't you reply? By Allâh, a moment of Abu Bakr is far better than a thousand moments of those people, for they kept their Faith concealed and Abu Bakr brought his Faith to the fore."

Generosity:

He was the most generous among the Companions of the Prophet ﷺ. It was about him that the following Verses were sent down:

> "The pious will be far removed from it (Hell). He who spends his wealth for increase in self-purification." (92:17, 18)

The Prophet of Allâh ﷺ said, "The wealth of Abu Bakr proved more useful to me than the wealth of anybody else." Having heard this, Abu Bakr ﷺ burst into tears and said, "What is the worth of my wealth, it is all because of you."

As per one *Hadith*, the Prophet ﷺ spent from the wealth of Abu Bakr Siddiq ﷺ as he did from his own. The day Abu Bakr ﷺ accepted Islam, he possessed forty thousand dirhams, and he spent this all on the Prophet ﷺ.

One day Umar ﷺ said referring to the expedition of Tabuk, "When the Prophet ﷺ urged upon his Companions to donate to the war fund, I resolved to surpass Abu Bakr in the matter of contribution and I gave away half of my wealth and property in the way of Allâh. The Prophet ﷺ inquired of me, 'What have you left for the children?' I submitted 'The remaining half.' In the meantime, Abu Bakr came in with his entire wealth and property and the Prophet ﷺ put to him the same question. He replied, 'Allâh and His Messenger are enough for the children.' Having seen and heard this, I said to myself that I would never be able to surpass Abu Bakr in anything."

Abu Hurairah ﷺ relates that the Prophet ﷺ once said, "I have done a good turn in return for everyone's favor but the obligation of Abu Bakr still rests on my shoulders and Allâh the Almighty will, on the Day of Judgment, compensate for it. The wealth and property of none benefited me so much as did that of Abu Bakr."

Knowledge and Excellences:

Among the Companions, he was the most learned and wise. Whenever some difference of opinion arose among the Companions, the issue was put before Abu Bakr Siddiq ﷺ. His ruling was considered as final. He had knowledge of the Qur'ân more than all others, and so the Prophet ﷺ asked him to lead the Muslims in prayers. He also had perfect knowledge of the *Sunnah* and the Companions turned to him for his opinion.

His memory was also very strong and he happened to be very sagacious. He enjoyed the sacred company of the Prophet ﷺ right from the beginning of his Prophethood until his final departure. During his caliphate whenever an issue came up, he turned to the Qur'ân for the solution. If he failed to find it in the Qur'ân, he gave his verdict according to the sayings and doings of the Prophet ﷺ. If any such saying or doing was not known, he would ask the Companions if anyone of them knew any *Hadith* concerning the issue. If nothing was known about the issue in question, he called a meeting of the illustrious Companions and took a decision according to the opinion of the majority.

Abu Bakr ﷺ was the greatest genealogist of the Quraish and one of the greatest in the whole of Arabia. Even Jubair bin Mut'im ﷺ, one of the most noted genealogists of Arabia, learned it from Abu Bakr ﷺ. He was also an eminent interpreter of dreams and he interpreted dreams even during the lifetime of the Prophet ﷺ. He was also the most eloquent speaker among the Companions of the Prophet ﷺ. Scholars are agreed that Abu Bakr and Ali ﷺ were the most eloquent.

Ali ﷺ has said more than once that Abu Bakr ﷺ was the most excellent among the Companions of the Prophet ﷺ. Ali ﷺ once said, "I shall beat the person who holds me superior to Abu Bakr and

Umar." Ali 🕮 relates that the Prophet 🕮 said, "May Allâh show mercy to Abu Bakr, he gave his daughter to me in marriage, escorted me to Al-Madinah and gave Bilâl freedom from slavery. May Allâh show mercy to Umar for he speaks the truth no matter how bitter it might be; may Allâh show mercy to Uthmân for even angels observe modesty before him; may Allâh show mercy to Ali and keep truth along with him wherever he may be."

Imam Shâfi'i says, "Siddiq was unanimously chosen as caliph for a better man was not available on earth." Mu'âwiyah bin Qurrah 🕮 opines: "The Companions never expressed any doubt regarding the caliphate of Abu Bakr and they always addressed him as the caliph of the Messenger of Allâh 🕮, and the Companions can never reach a consensus on a misdeed."

Beautiful Living:

Ata' bin Sâ'ib 🕮 states: "The day after the oath of allegiance (*Bai'ah*), Abu Bakr 🕮 was seen going to the market with two sheets. 'Where are you going?' Umar 🕮 inquired of him. 'To the market,' he replied. 'You should leave this business for you have now become the Leader of the believers,' Umar 🕮 argued. 'From where will my wife and children and myself eat?' Abu Bakr 🕮 asked. 'Leave it to Abu Ubaidah 🕮,' Umar 🕮 said. Following this, both of them called on Abu Ubaidah 🕮. Abu Bakr 🕮 said to him, 'Collect from the *Muhâjirin* a maintenance allowance for me and my wife and children. Everything should be very ordinary. Garments for summer and winter will be needed and they are to be returned when worn out before the demand for new ones are made'."

Abu Bakr bin Hafs 🕮 states that Abu Bakr 🕮 said to Âishah 🕮 before his death, "I was only benefited from the service done to the Muslims by eating and wearing whatever rough and coarse clothes were available. I have nothing of the public funds with me except a slave, a dromedary and an old sheet. Send all of these to Umar when I am no more."

Hasan bin Ali 🕮 relates that on the eve of his death, Abu Bakr 🕮 said to Âishah Siddiqah 🕮, "After my death you will send to Umar

this she-camel whose milk we drank, this big bowl I ate from and
these sheets. I had taken these articles from the *Bait-ul-Mâl* (public
funds) in my capacity as the caliph." When these things reached Umar
🙵 he remarked, "May Allâh show mercy on Abu Bakr, how terribly
he suffered for us." Abu Bakr 🙵 never kept wealth and goods
deposited with the *Bait-ul-Mâl*. He spent on the Muslims whatever
came to the public treasury. At times he purchased horses and
weapons to be given in the way of Allâh and sometimes he bought
clothes for the poor and the bedouins. When Umar 🙵, along with
some Companions, examined the *Bait-ul-Mâl* after Abu Bakr's death,
it was empty. The little girls of the locality would come to him with
their goat to be milked and he would do it for them. Abu Bakr Siddiq
🙵 used to sit among people in a manner that nobody could recognize
who was the caliph.

Important Events of the Siddiqi Caliphate

Hall of Banu Sâ'idah and the Pledge of Caliphate

When Abu Bakr Siddiq 🙵 came to know of the congregation of the
Ansâr in the Hall of Banu Sâ'idah to choose an *Amir* (Chief) from the
Ansâr, he hurried to the spot accompanied by Umar 🙵. It was a
crucial moment in Islamic history. A little delay or neglect might have
disrupted the unity between the *Muhâjirin* and the *Ansâr* causing the
Muslims immense harm. But since Allâh the Almighty had decided
otherwise, He infused in Abu Bakr 🙵 the courage and determination
necessary to face the troubled situation and by his wisdom the
situation was resolved. The Prophet of Allâh 🙰 had unified the
Muslims in a manner that the idols of tribal and national arrogance
and discrimination had been broken to pieces. Abu Bakr 🙵 saved the
situation and stopped the trouble in its beginning.

Although the number of the *Muhâjirin* in Al-Madinah was less than
the *Ansâr*, the *Ansâr* were divided in two large sections, the Aus and
the Khazraj, who had been rivals from the pre-Islamic days. Thus the
Muslims of Al-Madinah could possibly be divided along their old
tribal lines into three large sections, the third being the *Muhâjirin* or
the people of Quraish.

Bai'ah (Pledge)

Shortly after the demise of the Prophet ﷺ, all the *Muhâjirin* assembled in the Prophet's Mosque because the majority of the *Muhâjirin* lived in the vicinity of the Mosque while the *Ansâr* were much less in number. Another Muslim gathering in Saqifah Banu Sâ'idah consisted of the *Ansâr* and a *Muhâjir* or two. With Islam still in its beginning, its growth, the hostile endeavors of its opponents, turbulence and turmoil created by battles and expeditions, the extermination of polytheism and the Muslims bowing their will before the Islamic codes made it tremendously important for the Muslims as a whole to choose for themselves an *Amir* without any delay.

The loving sentiments of Umar ؓ gave the people no opportunity to think over the issue of the caliphate. Had Abu Bakr ؓ not hurried to the spot on hearing the terrible news of the Prophet's demise, nobody can say how long the people in the Prophet's Mosque would have been in the grip of that distressing situation. The congregation held at the sitting place of Sa'd bin Ubâdah ؓ was different. They were comparatively peaceful and were seriously deliberating the issue of choosing a successor of the Prophet ﷺ in temporal affairs. This congregation belonged to the *Ansâr* and was held at the place of Sa'd bin Ubâdah ؓ who was the chief of the Khazraj. This section of the *Ansâr* were superior to the Aus in number and wealth, it was only natural that the majority of them would be in favor of the Khazraj chief.

Although the *Muhâjirin* numbered less in Al-Madinah, they were so influential and in command of the affairs that an *Ansâri* got up to say how could the *Muhâjirin* be forced to accept a caliph from the *Ansâr*. Another *Ansâri* rose to suggest that a caliph from *Muhâjirin* and another from the *Ansâr* was the best and the most reasonable solution. "But it will be a show of weakness on our part," Sa'd bin Ubâdah ؓ said objecting to the dual system. In response to this plea, an *Ansâr* rose to say, "In case they reject our caliph, we shall drive them out from Al-Madinah at the point of our swords." However, the few *Muhâjirin* in the assembly protested against this attitude and this led to a dispute and disorder of a serious nature and a fight between the *Muhâjirin* and the *Ansâr* seemed possible.

When the situation took this ugly turn, Mughirah bin Shu'bah ﷺ left the trouble spot and came to the Prophet's Mosque to relate what was going on in Saqifah Banu Sâ'idah. The situation on this side was that Abu Bakr ﷺ had just finished his speech and was now engaged in making arrangements for the burial. But on hearing this awful news he left everything to go to the *Ansâr* and bring the situation under control.

He took with him Umar and Abu Ubaidah ﷺ and left Ali ﷺ and others to make arrangements for the burial of the Prophet ﷺ. In a situation packed with confusion, disorder, anger and emotion only a man like Abu Bakr ﷺ could do what was necessary. When Umar ﷺ made an attempt to say something, Abu Bakr ﷺ put a check on him for he knew that an emotionally charged Umar ﷺ could mishandle the already deteriorating situation.

Abu Bakr ﷺ himself rose to speak and said in a tone filled with confidence and firmness, "The first among the chiefs will be from the *Muhâjirin,* and the *Ansâr* will be their advisors." Thereupon Hubâb bin Al-Mundhir ﷺ said, "It seems reasonable that there should be one *Amir* (chief) from us and another from you." Umar ﷺ replied, "You remember very well that the Prophet ﷺ had exhorted the *Muhâjirin* to take care of the *Ansâr* and did not ask the *Ansâr* to make concessions to the *Muhâjirin.* This will of the Prophet ﷺ goes in favor of the *Muhâjirin* to be at the helm of affairs."

Hubâb bin Al-Mundhir ﷺ tried to answer back but Abu Ubaidah ﷺ pacified both of them. Meanwhile Bashir bin An-Numân bin Ka'b Ansâri ﷺ got up and expressed his feeling, "The Prophet ﷺ most certainly belonged to the Quraish tribe so the people of the Quraish alone deserve the caliphate. We, no doubt, lent our help and support to Islam, but our efforts were meant solely for seeking the Pleasure of Allâh, and we don't want its compensation in this world nor do we want to pick a quarrel with he *Muhâjirin.*"

Following this, Hubâb bin Al-Mundhir ﷺ said, "You have showed utmost timidity and undid our position as a whole." Bashir ﷺ replied, "I have not showed any timidity and I have preferred not to bicker over the caliphate with the people who really deserve it. Have you not heard O Hubâb that the Prophet of Allâh ﷺ had said, 'Imams will come from the Quraish.'?" These utterances of Bashir ﷺ received support from some other *Ansâr* too. Hubâb bin Al-Mundhir ﷺ also kept silent and changed his opinion. In this way the religious and spiritual considerations prevailed over the material and temporal ones.

Now the entire congregation plunged in deep silence and the growing conflict between the *Muhâjirin* and the *Ansâr* over the issue of the caliphate disappeared. In this state of perfect peace, Abu Bakr Siddiq ﷺ said, "Umar and Abu Ubaydah are here, choose anyone of them." Umar ﷺ said, "No, Abu Bakr is the most excellent among the *Muhâjirin*. He has been the Companion of the Prophet ﷺ in the cave; the Prophet ﷺ asked him to officiate in leading the Muslims in prayers, and prayer is the most superior of all other Articles of Faith. Therefore, none is entitled to assume the duties of the caliphate in the presence of Abu Bakr." Saying this Umar ﷺ stretched his hand first of all to take *Bai'ah* (oath of allegiance) at the hand of Abu Bakr Siddiq ﷺ followed by Abu Ubaidah and Bashir bin Sa'd Ansâri ﷺ. After that the people on all sides of Abu Bakr ﷺ came to take *Bai'ah*. As the news spread, all the believers rushed to pledge their allegiance to the caliph.

Sa'd bin Ubâdah ﷺ from the *Ansâr* and those from the *Muhâjirin* who were engaged in making arrangements for the burial, did not take the *Bai'ah* in Saqifah Banu Sâ'idah. However, Sa'd ﷺ took the *Bai'ah* with Abu Bakr ﷺ later the same day. Ali, Zubair and Talhah ﷺ didn't take *Bai'ah* for 40 days or according to some narratives for six months with the complaint that they were not included in the consultations that were held at Saqifah Banu Sâ'idah concerning the *Bai'ah*.

One day Ali ﷺ came to Abu Bakr ﷺ and said, "I don't refuse to admit that your virtues entitle you to the caliphate. My sole complaint is that we are the close relatives of the Prophet ﷺ, why did you then take *Bai'ah* at Saqifah Banu Sâ'idah without consulting us. Had you called us there, we would have taken *Bai'ah* at your hand ahead of everyone." Abu Bakr ﷺ said in reply, "To treat the relatives of the Prophet ﷺ well is dearer and more desirable to me than to do so for my own relatives. I went to Saqifah Banu Sâ'idah not for the taking of

Bai'ah but for putting an end to the dispute arising between the *Muhâjirin* and the *Ansâr*, which had caused a difficult situation. I did not seek their support, they rather took their oath of allegiance to me on their own and demonstrated their complete unanimity in this matter. Had I delayed the matter, it would have posed a greater danger to the unity, integrity and solidarity of Islam. How could I send for you when there was no time." Ali 🌸 listened to what Abu Bakr Siddiq 🌸 said with rapt attention and withdrew his complaint gracefully. The next day he pronounced his allegiance to Abu Bakr 🌸 before a large congregation in the Prophet's Mosque.

Address of Abu Bakr 🌸

After the meeting at Saqifah Banu Sâ'idah and being absolved from his duty of the burial of the Prophet 🌺, Abu Bakr 🌸 took the oath of allegiance from the general population and then rose to deliver his address. After praising and glorifying Allâh, he said to the people:

> "I have been chosen as your chief although I am better than none of you. Thus, if I do good work it is incumbent on you to extend your help and support to me; if I go wrong it is your duty to put me on the right path. Truth and righteousness are a trust and untruth is a breach of trust. The weak among you are strong to me unless I give them full justice, and the strong among you are weak to me unless I receive what is due from them. Abandon not *Jihâd*, when the people hold back from *Jihâd*, they are put to disgrace. Obey me while I keep obeying Allâh and His Messenger 🌺; renounce me when I disobey Allâh and His Messenger 🌺, for obedience to me is not incumbent on you then."

That was the day when thirty-three thousand Companions pledged their allegiance to Abu Bakr 🌸. The dispute between the *Muhâjirin* and the *Ansâr* was solved leaving no hard feelings behind. It was because the Companions of the Prophet 🌺 had thoroughly learned to prefer Faith to temporal affairs and due to this quality no other segment of humanity ever attained the level of development that the Companions of the Prophet 🌺 had gracefully reached.

Usâmah's Army marches on

The people of Yemen and Najd had come into the fold of Islam just a few months before the death of the Prophet 鬱 and Islam had not yet entered their hearts perfectly bringing about the complete transformation of their thoughts and actions. This resulted in men like Aswad and Musailamah raising their heads to claim prophethood and leading a section of new Muslims astray in each territory. The final departure of the Messenger of Allâh 鬱 came as a golden opportunity for them to cash in on the prevailing shock and feeling of disappointment among the Muslims at large.

Every age produces some mischiefmongers of an evil nature and they try to take advantage of these type of situations. Thus some people and tribes having an extreme lust for power and fame, raised their heads and set about devising ways and means to capture power and bring the Muslims under their direct influence. As a result of the winds of apostasy and hypocrisy blowing here and there, the pure and sincere Muslims felt shocked and deeply disturbed. Had they not been brought up by the Prophet 鬱 and his sacred company to instill courage, determination and firmness, the binding force of Islam would have been miserably disintegrated.

Almost every where in the Arabian continent except Al-Madinah, Makkah and Tâ'if, the flames of apostasy were fiercely raging threatening to burn down the citadel of Islam. Still more disturbing were the reports that forces inimical to Islam had once again mustered courage to invade Al-Madinah, and preparations were on to implement their long standing and wicked plans. The Prophet 鬱 had already dispatched an expedition headed by Usâmah bin Zaid 鬱 to take on the Romans in Syria, which had halted its movement due to the serious illness of the Prophet 鬱.

Now when Abu Bakr 鬱 wanted to send the same expedition after the death of the Prophet 鬱, the Companions put forward their suggestion to the Caliph that in the wake of the clouds of apostasy gathering on all sides, the expedition should be held back for sometime. It shows the fathomless depth of courage, grit, determination and power of

Faith wielded by Abu Bakr Siddiq 🙠 when he answered them, "If I was convinced that a beast would tear me apart after the dispatch of the army, I would not hold back at any cost what the Prophet 🙟 had ordered to go ahead."

In response to the call of the Caliph, the Companions already enlisted collected in the military camp outside Al-Madinah. Although they joined the army of Usâmah 🙠 a section still had some reservations about it for two reasons. One, Usâmah 🙠 was the son of a slave and he was only 17 years old, and therefore, too young and inexperienced to lead an army of distinguished Companions. Before moving ahead Usâmah sent Umar 🙠 as a soldier of his army to Al-Madinah with the message that the eminent Companions should be called back as the headquarters of Islam was under the threat of an enemy attack. The *Ansâr* also sent a message to the Caliph through Umar 🙠 that an elderly person of noble stock be appointed as the commander of the Muslim troops. Responding to the message of Usâmah 🙠, the Caliph said, "Had the departure of Muslim troops rendered the city of Al-Madinah vacant and I would be left alone to be taken away by beasts of prey, the march of the army would not be put off." As to the message of the *Ansâr*, Abu Bakr 🙠 said "They still carry the impression of arrogance and snobbery in their hearts." Following this he got up and left on foot for the military camp outside Al-Madinah to personally see off Usâmah 🙠 and his army. Usâmah 🙠 moved ahead and Abu Bakr 🙠 walked along with the mount of the commander talking and discussing matters of importance. Usâmah 🙠 said to the Caliph, "Either you mount the animal or allow me to get down to accompany you on foot." The Caliph replied, "I shall not ride nor do you need to get down. What harm shall I be inflicted with if I accompany you over some distance in the way of Allâh." This act of Abu Bakr 🙠 was the practical answer to the *Ansâr* who had some misgivings regarding the command of Usâmah 🙠.

Exhortations to Usâmah 🙠:

Walking along with the mount of Usâmah 🙠, the Chief of the believers instructed Usâmah 🙠 about a ten-point doctrine, which he should follow strictly during the battle and they are as follows:

1) Do not approach embezzlement. (2) Do not tell a lie. (3) Do not commit a breach of trust. (4) Do not kill children, women or the aged. (5) Do not cut down trees with fruit. (6) Slaughter not camels, cows or goats for any purpose other than eating. (7) Call to Islam the people you find. (8) Pay due respect to anyone you meet. (9) Start eating in the Name of Allâh when the meal is served to you. (10) Fight not with those among the Jews and the Christians who have taken refuge in their places of worship. And finally, neither add to what the Messenger of Allâh ﷺ has ordered you to do nor subtract from it. Fight the disbelievers with the Name of Allâh and in His way.

Abu Bakr Siddiq رضي الله عنه went along with Usâmah رضي الله عنه up to Jurf and then came back. Before taking leave, he said to Usâmah رضي الله عنه, "If you grant permission I want Umar to be in Al-Madinah to assist and give me advice." Usâmah رضي الله عنه promptly permitted Umar رضي الله عنه to return back to Al-Madinah.

It is significant and exemplary that the Caliph took permission from the military commander to keep Umar رضي الله عنه with him although he was totally within his rights to order this on his own.

Success achieved by Usâmah رضي الله عنه:

Usâmah رضي الله عنه reached the valleys of Jardon and Balqa' and defeated the Roman army. He returned after forty days with an immense amount of spoils of war and prisoners. Even as the departure of the Muslim army was in an atmosphere charged with disorder, disruption and misdirected emotion, and to invade and punish the formidable Romans looked unreasonable and risky to the extreme, the fruits of this adventure were justly wholesome and sweet. It sent terror into the hearts of the apostates and the opponents of Islam and convinced them to the core that the absence of the Prophet ﷺ did not diminish the Muslim's invincible determination and courage and love for Islam. As a result, the claimants of prophethood like Tulaihah Asadi and Musailamah the liar could not muster enough courage to step forth from their own territories. Those who had refused to pay *Zakât* meekly surrendered to the will of Islam. Moreover, the substantial quantity of spoils of war played a significant role in strengthening the Islamic army and improving the economic condition of the believers.

Trial of Apostasy

To assume that the death of the Prophet ﷺ sent Arabia except Al-Madinah, Makkah and Tâ'if into the fold of apostasy is not the truth. They had not shifted from *Tauhid* to *Shirk* (polytheism) all of a sudden and took to idol worship. The fact is that even the false claimants to prophethood were not against *Salât* (prayer). They were, however, particularly against the payment of *Zakât* for it went against their sense of freedom and dignity, and these new Muslims were ahead of others in rejecting what they claimed as an 'undignified' demand of Islam. Since they could be easily aroused against this most important pillar of Islam, men like Musailamah and Tulaihah used it as a tool to fulfil their evil plans.

In short, the issue before the Muslims was not polytheism and idol worship; what was threatening and injurious was the question of unity and solidarity of the system Islam had established at the cost of many sacrifices. The rejection of the demand of *Zakât* was even more dangerous to the cause of Islam than the battles fought by the Muslims against the external forces inimical to Islam. The Chief of the believers, Abu Bakr ﷺ held an emergency meeting of the Companions on this explosive issue. But they put forward their opinion against fighting with the rejecters of *Zakât*, just as they were not in favor of Usâmah ﷺ leading an army against the Romans. But on this occasion too, the inimitable courage and determination of Abu Bakr ﷺ prevailed over all kinds of anxieties and misgivings. He announced with indomitable spirit and firmness that he would go and fight against any tribe who refused to pay even one animal or one rope that was due.

In the meantime the deputations of the apostates came to Al-Madinah and said, "We perform prayer but we want an exemption from *Zakât*." But this hard-hitting reply made them silently go back to their respective places. In the wake of the hard line adopted by Abu Bakr Siddiq ﷺ, they rose as one man against the Islamic State. The prevailing confusion and threat to the unity and integrity of Islam needed a leader of outstanding courage and determination. Abu Bakr ﷺ was fit to face this disorderly situation and the unruly people who were making preparations to invade Al-Madinah, in the absence of Muslim troops, who were fighting the Romans far away from their center.

However, even in the face of such a trying situation, the Caliph of Islam was not ready to give any concession concerning his decision and would not compromise with the forces seeking to break the basic tenets of Islam. He was in full control of the situation both internally and externally. He kept himself in close contact with the Muslim forces fighting in the far off lands and issued the necessary orders to the collectors of *Zakât*. He encouraged the people of Al-Madinah to keep firm and unified and he made the preparations necessary to deal with the opportunistic alliances of those who had vested interests.

He asked the fighters among the people of Al-Madinah to keep alert and be on guard in front of the Prophet's Mosque, while Ali, Zubair, Talhah and Abdullah bin Mas'ud ﷺ were sent on patrol duty around Al-Madinah. Information reached the headquarters that the people of Abs, Dhubyân, Banu Kinânah and Banu Asad tribes had collected to attack the Muslims. Their march towards Al-Madinah was checked by the patrols, which also sent news to Al-Madinah about the enemy movement. Abu Bakr Siddiq ﷺ himself went to repulse the enemy attack up to Dhu Khushub. However, when Abu Bakr Siddiq ﷺ went again for an encounter, they used drums and other instruments that caused the camels of the Muslims to get scared and they fled back to Al-Madinah. Abu Bakr Siddiq ﷺ organized them and made a fierce charge on the enemy and routed them completely killing many of them after a fight of five or six hours.

Abu Bakr Siddiq ﷺ sent the spoils of war to Al-Madinah under the charge of Nu'mân bin Muqrin ﷺ and a small party, and himself went to Dhul-Qassah in hot pursuit of the enemy. Meanwhile the enemy invaded some tribes in the back area and martyred many Muslims there. When Abu Bakr ﷺ came to know of the incident on his return, he vowed to kill as many apostates equal to the number of Muslims who were martyred at their hands. He was on the verge of leaving Al-Madinah when Usâmah ﷺ entered Al-Madinah with booty in large quantity. Because the detachment was terribly exhausted, he left it in Al-Madinah to take rest and guard it against any fresh attack. And he himself left Al-Madinah at the head of a small detachment and went up to Dhu Khushub and Dhul-Qassah raiding their centers and routing who ever faced them. After finishing his task, he stayed at Abraq for a couple of days before his departure to Al-Madinah.

Edict of Abu Bakr Siddiq ﷺ:

Immediately after his return to Al-Madinah, Abu Bakr ﷺ penned an edict and sent copies to the apostate tribes through his messengers to be read out in public gatherings. The contents of the edict were as follows:

> From Abu Bakr, the Caliph of the Messenger of Allâh ﷺ, to each and every person whether he has accepted Islam or not. Let it be known to one and all that Allâh the Almighty sent Muhammad ﷺ as a true Prophet who sought to give glad tidings and to warn and to call to Allâh by His Order, he is the illuminated lamp of guidance. Allâh the Almighty guides one to the right path who accepts the invitation of Islam, but anyone who rejects it is made to show obedience through struggle and fighting. The Prophet of Allâh ﷺ made his final departure after accomplishing his task of calling people towards Islam and the straight path of Allâh. And Allâh the Almighty has already acquainted all with this in the Qur'ân:
>
> "Verily, you will die and they will also die." (39:30)
>
> "And We granted not to any human being immortality before you, the : you die, would they live forever?" (21:34)
>
> "Muhammad is no more than a Messenger and indeed Messengers have passed away before him. Thus, if he is dead or killed, will you turn back? If anyone turns back, he will do no harm to Allâh the Almighty. Allâh the Almighty will give good reward to those who give thanks." (3:144)
>
> Thus, one who worshipped Muhammad ﷺ then Muhammad ﷺ is now dead and gone, but one who worshipped Allâh Alone then Allâh is living and He has not died; He is neither overpowered by sleep nor touched by drowsiness. He looks

after His Own Orders and will at anytime take revenge on His enemies. I exhort you all to fear Allâh, to share what the Prophet ﷺ brought in the form of light and guidance from Allâh, to follow the guidance of Allâh and to hold firmly to the rope of the religion of Allâh. Anyone who is not guided by Allâh the Almighty, goes astray; he is helpless and alone who is deprived of the support of Allâh. No deed of a man is acceptable in this world and the Hereafter while he rejects Islam. I have come to know that some of you have turned to follow Satan and acts of ignorance forsaking Allah the Almighty. Allâh the Almighty says that Satan is your sworn enemy, so be hostile to Satan, for he seeks to make his followers dwellers of Hell-fire. I have decided to send the detachment made up of the *Muhâjirin* and the *Ansâr* to you, they follow virtue. I have instructed them not to fight anybody without calling them to Islam and to lend support to those who accept Islam, to keep from evil and reject not the good, and to fight those who reject Islam. It is good for the one who accepts Islam. I have ordered my emissary to read out this message at a large gathering. When a Muslim detachment draws near and its caller calls the *Adhân*, you too respond to it by calling the *Adhân*, this symbolizes your acceptance of Islam and thus spares your life. If you fail to call the *Adhân*, you will invite the Muslims to attack.

Uprooting the Apostates:

As a follow-up action, after the dispatch of emissaries with the circulars, Abu Bakr ﷺ made eleven banners. Each to be given to eleven heads who were chosen to lead separate detachments with the instructions that they should take some men from Makkah, Tâ'if and other places, and leave the rest to look after the home front. The first of the flags was handed over to Khâlid bin Walid ﷺ with the order to launch his first attack at Tulaihah bin Khuwailid Asadi and to make Mâlik bin Nuwairah his next target at Butah. Another standard was given to Ikrimah bin Abu Jahl to make an attack on Musailamah the liar at Yamâmah. Shurahbil bin Hasanah ﷺ was given the third banner to first assist Ikrimah ﷺ and then go to Hadramout to invade

Banu Kindah and Banu Qudâ'ah. The fourth one was entrusted to Khâlid bin Saeed bin Al-Âs 🙵 to go to Syria and put down uprisings with a firm hand. Fifth standard was given to Amr bin Al-Âs 🙵 for Banu Qudâ'ah. Hudhaifah bin Mihsan 🙵 was sent to the people of Oman, and Arfajah bin Harthamah 🙵 to Mahrah with the seventh one. The eighth one was given to Tarqah bin Hâjib 🙵 to go to Banu Sulaim and Banu Hawâzin. Suwaid bin Muqarrin 🙵 was ordered to go to Yemen (Tihâmah) with the ninth one. Ala' bin Hadrami 🙵 with the tenth standard was sent to Bahrain. Muhâjir bin Abu Umayyah was sent to San'â' with the eleventh. All these heads were given a circular with the same content, which is given here:

The Manifesto of Abu Bakr Siddiq 🙵:

This is a covenant from Abu Bakr, the Caliph of the Messenger of Allâh 🕌, which is handed over to so-and-so, the head of the detachment on the eve of his departure to fight the apostates. From the commander of the detachment I have obtained his undertaking to fear Allâh the Almighty in all affairs of life inwardly and outwardly. I have ordered him to make them see reason before falling on the apostates and to stop fighting if and when they accept Islam and then make them learn their rights and duties and their rights be given and the duties due on them be taken without showing concessions whatsoever. Whoever keeps any other kind of belief after the confessing of Islam is left to Allâh to be accountable to Him. But those who will carry the matter to the point of fighting by rejecting Islam outright, if overpowered or defeated by the believers, their spoils are to be distributed among the Muslims after taking out the fifth part therefrom. I have also issued orders to the commanders to stop their troops from creating disturbances and taking hasty actions resulting in chaos and havoc and from admitting strangers to their detachment without their knowing perfectly their identity. I have also written them to treat the Muslims politely and show mercy to the people while camping at and decamping a place.

All these detachments left Al-Madinah in the month of Jumâda Al-Ukhra 11 AH, for the territories assigned to them.

Tulaihah Asadi

Tulaihah was a soothsayer who entered Islam but claimed for himself prophethood during the last days of the Messenger of Allâh ﷺ. Some tribes of Children of Israel joined his party. Dirâr bin Al-Azwar ﷺ was sent to punish him but the task was not completed because he hurried back to Al-Madinah on hearing the sad news of the demise of the Prophet ﷺ. During that period, Tulaihah Asadi had an opportunity to rebuild his position. The people of Ghatfân and Hawâzin tribes who had already been routed by Abu Bakr ﷺ collected themselves once again to join the bandwagon of Tulaihah's party. He pitched his camp at Buzâkhah, the well-known stream of Najd, and the people of Ghatfân, Hawâzin, Banu Asad, Banu Âmir and Banu Tai gathered around him to make it a massive force.

Khâlid bin Walid ﷺ launched an attack on Tulaihah's troops at Buzâkhah, which was fighting under the command of Tulaihah's brother Khayyâl. Tulaihah himself was sitting farther from his troops in a mantle pretending to be waiting for a 'revelation'. The battle became intense.

When the apostates' troops began to suffer reverses, Uyainah bin Hisn came to Tulaihah and asked him if any revelation was sent down to him. "Not yet," Tulaihah replied. After a while he came again, repeated the same question, and received the same reply. Now the Muslim detachment was clearly dominating the battle scene and the apostates were getting routed. When Uyainah came to Tulaihah and put the same question to him for the third time, he replied rather cunningly, "Jibril has come to me to say that things will happen according to what is in store for us." Uyainah got enraged at this artful reply and exclaimed, "O people! Tulaihah is a liar, so I am leaving now." Having heard this, the apostates took to their heels leaving behind a great number of dead and many were captured. A large number of people returned to Islam on the spot.

Tulaihah, along with his wife fled on horseback and took refuge with the Qudâ'ah tribe. When all the other tribes, including his own, came back to the fold of Islam, Tulaihah also confessed Islam and came to

Al-Madinah during the caliphate of Umar ⚙. Uyainah was brought before Khâlid bin Walid ⚙ as a captive and was sent to Al-Madinah. Here he accepted Islam in state of humiliation but afterward he made himself sincere to it.

The fugitives from the army of Tulaihah, made up of the Ghatfân, Sulaim and Hawâzin tribes, collected at Hawâb and chose Salma bint Mâlik bin Hudhaifah bin Badr bin Zafar as their chief. Following this they made large-scale preparations against the Muslims. Informed of this, Khâlid bin Walid ⚙ moved to meet the lurking threat. Salma was herself heading the army. Khâlid bin Walid ⚙ attacked the enemy which resulted in fierce fighting between the two forces. About one hundred apostates were killed safeguarding her dromedary. At last she fell down from the injured she-camel and was instantly killed. Her followers immediately disappeared from the battleground.

About the same time a chieftain of Banu Sulaim, Al-Fajâh bin Abd Yâlil called on Abu Bakr Siddiq ⚙ and said to him, "I am a Muslim. Please help me with weapons so that I can go and fight against the apostates." Abu Bakr ⚙ granted his request. When he left Al-Madinah, he pronounced his apostasy and sniped at the sections of Banu Hawâzin and Banu Sulaim who had confessed Islam. After being informed of this treachery, Abu Bakr ⚙ sent Abdullah bin Qais ⚙ with a small party who caught the culprit, who was trying to escape, and brought him to Al-Madinah where he was killed.

Sajâh and Mâlik bin Nuwairah

Banu Tamim inhabited a few settlements where, during the lifetime of the Prophet ﷺ, Mâlik bin Nuwairah, Waki' bin Mâlik, Safwân bin Safwân, Qais bin Âsim were working as collectors of *Zakât* and other charities. Now as the news of the Prophet's demise spread, Qais bin Âsim turned apostate while Mâlik bin Nuwairah expressed his joy. However, Safwân bin Safwân ⚙ remained firm as a Muslim.

In the meantime Sajâh bint Al-Hârith bin Suwaid of the Taghlib tribe declared her prophethood. Hudhail bin Imrân–the chief of Banu Taghlib, Uqbah bin Hilâl–the chief of Banu Namir and Salil bin Qais–the chief of Banu Shaibân accepted her claim. She was able to collect about four thousand soldiers around her and she moved ahead to invade Al-Madinah. She came to know that Khâlid bin Walid 🌺 was also on the move from the opposite direction. This news was quite disturbing for her. Moreover Sajâh and Musailamah were afraid of each other, as both of them had claimed prophethood. Their anxiety multiplied when they came to know that both Ikrimah and Shurahbil 🌺 had reached Yamâmah with Muslim detachments. Thus both of them were practicing caution.

At last, Musailamah wrote a letter to Sajâh to find out her intentions. She wrote back, "I wanted to invade Al-Madinah. Since both of us are prophets, let us launch a joint attack." Musailamah very haughtily replied, "While the Prophet Muhammad was alive, I had surrendered half of my country in his favor; after him I am the sole ruler of the country. However, since you too claim prophethood, I shall confer half of my prophethood on you. It is better that you come to me alone leaving your troops behind so that we can sit together in consultations concerning the division of the prophethood and the invasion of Al-Madinah."

Marriage of the Liar-prophetess:

Immediately after receiving the message of Musailamah she left to meet him. He welcomed her in a camp specially erected in front of his fortress. They held secret talks, which resulted in Sajâh accepting his prophethood and giving herself to him in marriage. She stayed with Musailamah for three days and then came back to her camp. The army asked about the bride price. She sent this request back to Musailamah and he exempted them from the dawn and night prayers as her bride price. As she moved ahead she came across the Muslim army led by Khâlid bin Walid 🌺. The soldiers of Sajâh became so terrified that they fled to far off places leaving Sajâh alone and she could barely save herself. She joined her tribe and passed the rest of her life in obscurity.

Assassination of Mâlik bin Nuwairah:

It has already been mentioned that Mâlik bin Nuwairah expressed joy over the death of the Prophet 🌺. He had also made peace with Sajâh but had later on severed his relation with her. When he was captured and brought before Khâlid bin Walid ◉, the Muslims argued that the people of the settlement of Mâlik bin Nuwairah had responded with *Adhân* and so he should not be killed. Others discounted this point since the *Adhân* was not called as a response and he should be killed as per the order of the caliph of the Prophet of Allâh ◉. The investigation of Khâlid bin Walid ◉ could not bring the matter to light. But during his talk with Khâlid ◉ he referred to the Prophet ◉ more than once as: "Your chief has said such and such." Being enraged at such a manner of address, Khâlid ◉ said, "Was he not your chief?" But Mâlik bin Nuwairah did not make a satisfactory reply.

According to Tabari, Dirâr bin Al-Azwar ◉, who was then standing near by with his sword in hand, cut the head of Mâlik off after taking a sign from Khâlid ◉. Such are the things that happen on the battlefield. But historians mention it for other reasons. Abu Qatâdah ◉ was also in the detachment of Khâlid bin Walid ◉ and was in support of the section which argued that *Adhân* was called in the settlement of Mâlik bin Nuwairah. Because of this he grew angry at the killing of Mâlik and returned to Al-Madinah without taking permission from Khâlid bin Walid ◉, the commander of the Muslim detachment. He lodged a complaint with the Caliph that Khâlid bin Walid kills the Muslims without valid reasons. Umar ◉ and others advised the Caliph to first depose Khâlid ◉ and then take retaliatory action against him. It was easy to accuse him of killing a Muslim because he (Khâlid ◉) had later married the wife of Mâlik bin Nuwairah.

After a patient hearing of all the details, Abu Bakr ◉ found Abu Qatâdah ◉ guilty of disobeying his commander and leaving the detachment without his permission. He was then ordered to go back and join Khâlid ◉ and carry out his orders and he did so accordingly. Abu Bakr ◉ then informed Umar ◉ and the others that Khâlid ◉ had merely committed a mistake in judgment. According to the principles of war and the military system, Khâlid–the Sword among the Swords of Allâh, could neither be brought to pay *Qisâs* (retaliation) nor deposed. Abu Bakr Siddiq ◉ then paid the blood money from the public treasury.

Musailamah the Liar

Banu Hanifah was one of the tribes, which appeared in the form of a deputation before the Prophet ﷺ after the conquest of Makkah. Musailamah bin Hubaib belonged to this same tribe. On his return to Yamâmah from Al-Madinah, he heard about the illness of the Prophet ﷺ and declared his prophethood. He also sent a letter to the Prophet ﷺ saying, "Since prophethood is being shared by both of us, each one is entitled to possess half of the country." The Prophet ﷺ wrote back: "In the Name of Allâh, the Most Gracious, the Most Merciful. From Muhammad, the Messenger of Allâh to Musailamah the liar. Peace be upon whom who follows the guidance. After that, the earth is Allâh's. He gives it as a heritage to whom He wills of His slaves and the end is for the pious."

Following this letter, the Prophet ﷺ sent Rajjâl bin Anfuh, a respectable man of Banu Hanifah to bring Musailamah back to the path of guidance.

Rajjâl reached Yamâmah and then lent support to Musailamah instead, and became his follower. His notorious mission gained wide popularity. At last, Ikrimah bin Abu Jahl ﷺ was sent to punish him and then Shurhabil bin Hasanah ﷺ was dispatched with reinforcements. Ikrimah ﷺ invaded Musailamah's army before the arrival of the reinforcements and was defeated. Having heard this news, Abu Bakr ﷺ sent word to Ikrimah ﷺ not to return to Al-Madinah but to join Hudhaifah and Arfajah ﷺ and fight with the people of Mahrah and Oman under their command. Having finished that campaign he had to leave for Yemen and Hadramout along with his detachment to join Muhâjir bin Abu Umayyah ﷺ. He wrote to Shurhabil bin Hasanah ﷺ to go towards the territories of Khâlid bin Walid ﷺ; and leave for Qudâ'ah and fight along with the people under the command of Amr bin Al-Âs ﷺ and punish the apostates there. In the meantime, Khâlid bin Walid ﷺ came back to Al-Madinah. Abu Bakr ﷺ instead of calling him to account, sent him to punish Musailamah the liar at the head of a detachment including both the *Muhâjirin* and the *Ansâr*, which actually was a sign of respect to him.

Deviation to Nationality:

Musailamah had with him forty thousand warriors of the Rabi'ah tribe. Some of them knew him as a liar but their misdirected sense of national pride led them to wish him success. They would openly say, "Musailamah is a liar while Muhammad is truthful. However, to all of us, the liar-prophet of Rabi'ah is dearer than the truthful Prophet of Banu Mudar." After sending Khâlid bin Walid ﷺ, the Caliph Abu Bakr Siddiq ﷺ dispatched a few more columns to strengthen the army of Khâlid ﷺ who joined him on the way. Now the strength of the Muslim army under the command of Khâlid ﷺ rose to thirteen thousand. When he was at a distance of one day from the city of Yamâmah, he sent a small column as an advance guard.

The same day Musailamah had dispatched Mujjâ'ah bin Murârah at the head of sixty men to snipe at Banu Tamim. Thus this party came across the advance guard of the Muslim army. In the encounter, all the apostates were killed and their head Mujjâ'ah was brought before Khâlid ﷺ. When Khâlid ﷺ reached Yamâmah, Musailamah came out of the city and encamped in a fortified garden at the gate of the city.

Furious Fight:

The forty thousand strong army of Musailamah the liar attacked the Muslim troops not exceeding thirteen thousand in number. A very furious and dreadful fight broke out. The Muslim fighters sustained the fierce attack of the enemy with exemplary patience and firmness. Soon after they collected themselves at the center and fell on the enemy like hungry tigers and routed them thoroughly. The apostates fled the field but collected at the gate of the garden and showed some courage and firmness. At this stage Thâbit bin Qais ﷺ, the standard bearer of the Muslim army was honored with martyrdom. Zaid bin Khattâb ﷺ lifted the standard and the Muslims showed such valor and virility that the enemy had to retreat behind the walls of the garden but the Muslims broke into it.

Now the people asked Musailamah, "When will the promise of victory be fulfilled that your god has given to you?" He replied, "This is not the time to talk all this; everyone is now required to fight for the safety of his wife and children." When his garden too turned into the battleground, Musailamah got on his horse and began to call his people to give battle. However, when he witnessed that the situation was under the full control of the Muslims, he got down and moved secretly towards the exit. Wahshi (the one who assassinated Hamzah ﷺ) happened to be at the gate of the garden aiming at Musailamah, he threw his lance so forcefully that it cut through his double coat of mail and cut across his belly. Panic and terror overtook the enemy and in a short while there was none left to be seen on the battlefield other than the Muslims. This battle took a heavy toll on the enemy force leaving seventeen thousand dead while one thousand from the Muslim side were honored with martyrdom. Among them were a large number of *Huffâz* (those who had committed the entire Qur'ân to memory).

The rest of Banu Hanifah fled the battlefield fleeing for their lives leaving their women and children behind. Since a great number of Muslims had sustained injuries, Khâlid bin Walid ﷺ decided to conquer the city of Yamâmah the next day. Mujjâ'ah bin Murârah, the captive took advantage of this decision. He misled Khâlid ﷺ by saying that the greater number of men of his tribe were still alive and they were well-equipped and formidable enough to win by the power of the sword. He then asked Khâlid ﷺ that if he was freed, he could go to persuade them not to give battle. Thus both the city and its citizens would come under their control without blood and toil. Khâlid ﷺ accepted his proposal and freed him.

Mujjâ'ah went into the city and asked the women to get on the ramparts with their weapons. He then came back and said to Khâlid ﷺ, "My people are not ready to make peace merely in return for their safety." When Khâlid ﷺ looked towards the city, he found that the ramparts showed nothing but swords and spears, which verified the statement of Mujjâ'ah. Keeping an eye on his injured soldiers and the expectation of a long drawn out battle, Khâlid ﷺ thought it reasonable to make peace with the enemy. Thus he offered to leave for them half of their wealth and possessions, half of the planted gardens and half of the captives of Banu Hanifah. Mujjâ'ah went to the city once again and came back with the report: "They are not ready to accept this offer, you can win peace by taking from them one-fourth of their possessions." Khâlid ﷺ agreed to the proposal and the peace treaty was written down.

Following this, Khâlid ﷺ went inside the city. He, to his utmost amazement, found there none but women and children. "Why did you play a trick on me?" Khâlid ﷺ asked Mujjâ'ah. "My people were virtually on the brink of death and destruction, so it was my duty to pull them out of this situation, please excuse me," Mujjâ'ah replied. Khâlid ﷺ kept silent not thinking in the least about breaking the agreement. A short while after Musailamah bin Waqsh, an emissary of Abu Bakr ﷺ gave Khâlid ﷺ a letter from the Caliph directing him to kill their men and make their women and children captives in case the battle was won. But the peace treaty was signed before the arrival of the emissary, so the order from Al-Madinah could not be implemented. This event is a memorable example of how particular the Muslims were about keeping their promises and upholding their treaties.

Khâlid bin Walid ﷺ sent a deputation of Banu Hanifah to Abu Bakr ﷺ with a letter. He had mentioned in it the details about the recent victory and Banu Hanifah's re-entry to Islam. Abu Bakr ﷺ held them in high esteem and bade farewell to them in the same spirit. The battle of Yamâmah took place in Dhul-Hijjah 11 AH.

Hatm bin Dubai'ah

It has already been mentioned that Abu Bakr Siddiq ﷺ had sent Ala' bin Al-Hadrami ﷺ to Bahrain at the head of a detachment. Banu Abdul-Qais and Banu Bakr bin Wâ'il along with their branches inhabited Bahrain. It has also been stated that Jârud bin Al-Mualla ﷺ had once represented Abdul-Qais tribe to the Prophet ﷺ. The people of Abdul-Qais tribe renounced Islam when they heard of the death of the Prophet ﷺ with the idea that had he been a Prophet, he would not have died. Jârud bin Al-Mualla ﷺ assembled his people and put the question to them, "Had there been other Prophets before Muhammad ﷺ?" "Yes, there had been many," they admitted with one voice. "Had they not passed away after passing their lives like common people?" he put another question. "They all passed away after passing their days of life," they admitted. ' The Prophet ﷺ also completed his span of life and then passed away exactly in the same manner," he said and called in a loud voice: "I testify that there is no God but Allâh and Muhammad in His slave and Messenger." The hearts of the people of Abdul-Qais tribe were moved so deeply that they all expressed deep sorrow for their wrongdoing and returned to the fold of Islam.

Though Abdul-Qais tribe was saved through the timely efforts of Jârud bin Al-Mualla 🙵, but Banu Bakr bin Wâ'il tribe took to apostasy and made Hatm their chief. He marched ahead with a large number of men from Banu Bakr and camped between Qatif and Hijr. He then sent a small party to Abdul-Qais tribe to make them apostates and to come back. However, Abdul-Qais flatly refused to turn apostate. Hatm then sent Ma'rur bin Suwaid with a group to either make them apostate or fight with them. In the meantime Ala' bin Al-Hadrami 🙵 arrived in Bahrain with his detachment. He sent word to Jârud bin Al-Mualla 🙵 to launch an attack on Hatm in the company of Banu Abdul-Qais.

With the spread of this news, Muslims from the surrounding areas collected around Ala' bin Al-Hadrami 🙵 while the apostates gathered round Hatm. Ala' bin Al-Hadrami 🙵 moved ahead with his army and camped near the military camp of Hatm. Hatm had dug trenches around his camp. The fight between the two started but none of them was crowned with victory even after a long period of one month. However, Ala' bin al-Hadrami 🙵 lost his patience and launched such a furious attack across the enemy trenches that the enemy force was filled with wild terror, and with the killing of Hatm at the hands of Qais bin Asim, the entire enemy front was completely routed. Gradually all the apostates turned back to Islam.

Laqit bin Mâlik

It has been mentioned above that Abu Bakr Siddiq 🙵 had sent Hudhaifah bin Mihsan 🙵 to Oman and Arfajah bin Harthamah 🙵 to the people of Mahrah with the order that they should keep together. On hearing the news of the death of the Prophet 𝕤, Laqit declared his prophethood in Oman. The people of Oman and Mahrah turned apostate and forced out of their territory the collectors of charity appointed by the Prophet 𝕤. Abu Bakr 🙵 had sent a message to

Hudhaifah bin Mihsan Himyari ﷺ to first go to Oman and then leave for Mahrah after finishing his task. He had also directed Ikrimah ﷺ to join Hudhaifah and Arfajah ﷺ in Oman. Thus all the three commanders of the Muslim detachments stayed together in Oman. On being informed, Laqit collected his fighters and moved ahead to face the Muslim army. Ikrimah bin Abu Jahl was the head of the advance guard while Hudhaifah had the command of the right wing and Arfajah the left one and in the middle of the army were the rich and influential persons of Oman who had been firm on Islam.

Fighting broke out at the time of the dawn prayer. The Islamic army was fighting from the low-lying areas while the enemy force was giving battle from the high ground. At the outset the Muslim troops suffered reverses but the proverbial patience and firmness of the believers turned the tables and forced the enemy to retreat. They turned and ran away leaving behind a thousand dead, four thousand as captive and a large quantity of booty. The Muslim army returned to Al-Madinah victoriously. Ikrimah ﷺ left for Mahrah and after a short period of time, the entire Oman returned firmly to Islam.

Apostasy in Mahrah

Mahrah had some people from Oman and some others from Abdul-Qais, Azd and Banu Sa'd tribes that inhabited this territory. But they were divided in two factions after turning apostate, each faction fighting with the other. In this situation Ikrimah ﷺ arrived in Mahrah and one of the factions accepted Islam. The next one, whose head was Musabbih, rejected the offer and remained adamant in his attitude. Thereupon Ikrimah ﷺ attacked the apostates giving them a crushing defeat and killing their chief. This victory led a large number of people from all the tribes to join the forces of Islam.

Apostasy in Yemen

Aswad Ansi, referred to before, had claimed prophethood for himself and created disturbances all over Yemen. But he met his doom during the lifetime of the Prophet ﷺ. Although Islam had been gaining ground after the cloud of apostasy cleared, the death of the Prophet ﷺ

let it stage a comeback. They were now getting strong under the leadership of two chiefs, Qais bin Makshuh and Amr bin Ma'dikarib. The Muslims were small in numbers and were brutally tortured by the Yemenite apostates, with the result they had left the area. Abu Bakr Siddiq ﷺ had sent Muhâjir bin Abu Umayyah ﷺ with a detachment to pass through Makkah and Tâ'if and then to go to Najrân taking Muslim fighters from these cities. Qais and Amr had already received the news of Muhâjir's arrival. Amr bin Ma'dikarib was a well known wrestler whose swordsmanship had won him admiration throughout the country.

Muhâjir ﷺ saw himself and his army surrounded by a swarm of enemy forces and this infused in them a sense of courage, fervor and determination, and they attacked the enemy with full force and vigor. The chieftains, Qais and Amr were caught after a thorough defeat of the enemy troops. Qais and Amr were sent to Al-Madinah and both of them admitted their wrongs and returned to Islam.

Muhâjir bin Umayyah ﷺ reached San'a' and cleared the entire territory of apostates. It was there that Ikrimah bin Abu Jahl met him. From there both the commanders made a joint march to punish Banu Kindah who were busy making large-scale preparations against the Muslims under the command of Ash'ath bin Qais and their strength was increasing day by day. Informed of this, Muhâjir bin Abu Umayyah ﷺ took a fast squad of horsemen from his army and hurried towards Ash'ath leaving his army under the command of Ikrimah ﷺ. He attacked the enemy force so suddenly and violently that they fled in terror. Ash'ath made a quick escape and took refuge in a fort where he was joined by other apostates. Muhâjir bin Abu Umayyah ﷺ besieged the fort. In the meantime he was joined by Ikrimah ﷺ.

The severity of the siege and the blockade of reinforcements forced him to lay down his arms. He then appealed to the Muslim commander to spare the lives of only nine persons including his wife and children. But Ash'ath forgot to include his own name. Thus all, exclusive of those nine persons were held captive. Ash'ath was also among the captives. They were presented before Abu Bakr ﷺ, Ash'ath expressed regret for his past deeds and accepted Islam on the spot. Abu Bakr Siddiq ﷺ set free all the captives including Ash'ath issuing them strong warnings not to repeat their past actions.

Complete Eradication of Apostasy

Abu Bakr Siddiq ﷺ was able to put down all the uprisings of apostasy in less than one year. Now the entire Arab Peninsula was free from the filth of polytheism and apostasy. Not a tinge of malaise of this nature was to be traced anywhere within the bounds of Arabian continent. Only a few months before, the sky of Islam looked cloudy everywhere except Al-Madinah, Makkah and Tâ'if, and swords and spears, lances and arrows seemed to be flying everywhere. However, in this very short period the situation turned around completely.

It was unflinching courage and unyielding determination that faced the hostile storm and stress on all fronts and came out victorious in all events. Even the legendary grit and valor of Rustam and Isphandiyar could not come face to face with the hundredth part of what was shown by Abu Bakr Siddiq ﷺ. And the reason is that the qualities of head and heart displayed by the Caliph of the Prophet ﷺ were the direct result of his upbringing under the blessed shadow of the Messenger of Allâh ﷺ.

The army of Siddiq ﷺ had no doubt, matchless men of lasting courage like Khâlid, Ikrimah, Shurhabil, and Hudhaifah ﷺ, but it was the dauntless courage of Abu Bakr ﷺ, which kept control over the state of affairs, organized the campaigns and dispatched the detachments to far off lands. He never allowed fear, anxiety or timidity to enter the hearts of the true believers. His strategies of war had no parallel and Muslim commanders were leading their detachments and Muslim troops were fighting only according to the plans chalked out by the Caliph of the Prophet ﷺ.

At first consideration it appears that the eleven detachments sent to various places were instrumental in wiping out apostasy from the face of Arabia, but in fact, it was simply the clever devices and the expert opinion of Abu Bakr ﷺ alone that swept away all the rubbish lying in the path of Islam. And this gigantic task was accomplished within a very short span of a few months. In the discouraging and frustrating situation that he was facing, none else was there to show such a magnificent farsightedness as he demonstrated. He neither agreed to hold back the expedition of Usâmah bin Zaid ◈ planned by the Prophet ◈ himself during his last days nor did he pay heed to Umar's outbursts nor did he delay the collection of *Zakât* from the apostates. Who could then be the true successor of the Prophet ◈ in his temporal affairs?

Rome and Persia

There were two fabulously magnificent and large empires existing at the time of the advent of the Prophet ◈, the Roman and the Persian. The world was then ruled by these two civilizations. Arabia was steeped in dismal darkness where the last Prophet ◈ was raised. It was through Islam that a new power and a new civilization emerged and engulfed the glittering civilizations of both Rome and Persia and left its mark as the only important power.

There was a time when the Persian Empire had in its fold the Mediterranean Sea, the Black Sea, the Persian Gulf, the Indus River, Kashmir, Tibet, Mount Altai and the Caspian Sea. Alexander the Great of Greece tore this large and grand empire to pieces. But Persian culture and civilization were still going strong. About four hundred years before the advent of the Prophet ◈, Ardsher Babkân laid the foundation of the Sassanid dynasty and brought under its control the Persian Gulf, the Euphrates, the Caspian Sea, the Indus, Oxus and the whole continent of Asia.

The center of Roman power was Rome, the city of Italy, which was ruled over by Julius Caesar and his heir Augustus. Egypt, Asia Minor and the whole of Europe formed part of the Roman Empire. It was later divided into two parts. While Rome remained the capital of the western part, the eastern part made Constantinople its capital. The king of Constantinople was also called Caesar and he ruled over Egypt, Abyssinia, Palestine, Syria, Asia Minor and the Balkans. The Eastern Roman Rule was far ahead of Western Rome in grandeur and power. The two parts had no natural border between them and so they were occasionally at war with one another.

At the time of the birth of the Prophet ﷺ, Nushirwan Sassani was the emperor of Persia and his grandson Chosroes (Khosrau) was the ruler when Muhammad ﷺ was honored with Prophethood. Rebellion broke out against Caesar Publius, his nobles and the subjects dethroned and killed him. Heraclius, the son of the governor of African territories was enthroned in Constantinople as the Caesar. In the meantime the Persians and the Romans rose up against each other and the war between the two dragged on for six or seven years. During the eighth year of Prophethood, the Persians conquered Syria and took away the Cross when they captured Bait-ul-Maqdis (Jerusalem).

The polytheists of Makkah expressed wild jubilation at the victory of the Persians, for the Persians were polytheists while the Romans were people of the Book. The Muslims naturally had sympathy for the Romans, so it was sad news for them. Allâh the Almighty revealed the Verses of _Sûrat Ar-Rum_ and let them know that although Rome had been defeated at that time, but in a few years they would gain victory to the rejoicing of the Muslims and so it happened. Heraclius rose from the position of defeat and frustration and after preparing for six or seven years with indomitable courage and determination, took his revenge on the Persians on the battlefield of Syria.

The Romans defeated the Persians on one hand, and about the same time, the Makkan disbelievers tasted a crushing defeat at the hands of the Muslims on the other. Thus the prophecy of the Qur'ân came true word for word. And with this, started a new spate of battles between the two rivals, which came to an end only in 7 AH, when they at last made peace after large-scale bloodshed and destruction. After winning peace, both of them set out on the way to progress and prosperity. It was the same year that the Prophet ﷺ sent invitation letters to a number of monarchs.

Chosroes of Persia received the letter from the Prophet ﷺ at Madâ'in and he tore it up with disdain, while Heraclius of the Roman Empire showed due respect to it. Not only did Chosroes show disrespect to the letter of the Prophet ﷺ but he sent word to his governor Bâdhân in Yemen to round up the Arabian Prophet and send him to Madâ'in. Bâdhân sent two persons to Al-Madinah who appeared before the

Prophet ﷺ and informed him of the royal order. The Prophet ﷺ said, "Chosroes, whom you treat as your god, has been killed by his son last night." When both of them went back to Bâdhân they came to know that Chosroes was killed by his son, Sherweh.

The assassination of Chosroes took place the same night the Prophet ﷺ referred to as the night when Bâdhân, the governor of Yemen embraced Islam. With his acceptance of Islam, the religion of Allâh spread rapidly in the whole country. The Prophet ﷺ approved Bâdhân as the governor of Yemen. Sherweh was too deeply preoccupied with his internal problems to turn towards the Muslims and Arabia. After many turns of events, Purân, the daughter of Chosroes Pervez and the sister of Sherweh took the throne but could rule the country only for one year. The Prophet ﷺ passed away during her time. After many successors, Yazdgurd was on the throne of Persia when it fell to the Muslims. In short, the lofty palace of the Persian Empire kept decaying day by day from the time the letter of the Prophet ﷺ was torn up with disrespect.

The Persians, being polytheists, were most arrogant and haughty. They looked down upon the Arabs and particularly the Muslims, since the news of their strength and patience was a source of constant mental trouble for them, they wanted to uproot them completely. But Allâh the Almighty had entangled them so deeply in family feuds that they had no chance to look towards Arabia.

The Jews and hypocrites who were turned out of Al-Madinah, constantly sent messages to the Persians and the Romans to attack Muslims in Al-Madinah. Since the Heraclius' court was free from such plotting and counter-plotting, he was in a position to implement the conspiratorial suggestions of the hypocrites and the Jews of Al-Madinah.

The time when the Prophet ﷺ had sent his letter to Heraclius, he had also dispatched letters to Busra and Damascus. But both the rulers ill-treated the emissaries of the Prophet ﷺ. Shurahbil, the sub ruler of Busra had gone to the extent that he put the emissary to death. In the battle of Mu'tah, Heraclius was on the side of Shurahbil Ghassâni. Following this, the Romans invaded Arabia and the Prophet ﷺ went to Tabuk along with his army. But the Romans evaded the battle.

The news of the Prophet's death stirred the atmosphere throughout Arabia and this sad news brought both the Romans and Persians to heave a sigh of relief. Since Arabia had risen on the map of the world for the first time as a country wielding, unity, courage, power and influence, the Romans and the Persians could not but watch it with a shade of care and anxiety. The tempest of apostasy added fuel to the flames, with the result the Romans and the Persians began to collect their forces in Syria and Iraq respectively. It was the height of wisdom, prudence, military acumen and the courage of conviction of Abu Bakr ﷺ, which guided him to first eradicate apostasy and then galvanize the whole country into fighting back the forces hostile to Islam. It was due to the sterling qualities of the illustrious personality of Abu Bakr Siddiq ﷺ, the first Caliph of the Prophet of Allâh ﷺ, that he guided the destiny of Islam with unparalleled determination, firmness, conviction and trust in such crucial moments, which had brought soul-stirring challenges to the very existence of Islam, immediately after the final departure of the Prophet of Allâh ﷺ.

Policy of the Muslims

Abu Bakr Siddiq ﷺ was well aware of the designs of the Persians when he approved the departure of Usâmah's detachment. At a time when Al-Madinah itself was under great pressure, he adopted a policy of buying time before opening a war front against the major powers until the threat of apostasy was put down. He, therefore, sent a small column to Iraq under Muthanna bin Hârithah ﷺ not to start a pitched battle but to function as a raiding party meant just to terrorize the men in power so that the Persians dared not attack Arabia. He had in mind the same purpose when he had dispatched Usâmah ﷺ against the Romans.

When the situation in Najd and Yamâmah came under control, Siddiq ﷺ addressed a letter to Iyâd bin Ghanam ﷺ in Najd to take with him those Muslims who were still beyond the reach of apostasy, and launch an attack on the upper parts of Iraq. Following this, he wrote another letter to Khâlid bin Walid ﷺ in Yamâmah to turn towards the lower parts of Iraq. Both the Muslim commanders met at Uballah according to the instructions of the Caliph.

The Battle of *Dhât-us-Salâsil*

When Khâlid bin Walid 🙵 took stock of his entire army at Aballah, he found that he had not more than eighteen thousand fighters. His fresh target was Hafir, the Persian province of Iraq, and Hurmuz was its governor who was well known throughout Arabia for his valor and military skill. He was a terror for India also for he so often led assaults on the Indian coast with his war fleet.

Khâlid bin Walid 🙵 first addressed a letter inviting him to Islam. But Hurmuz responded with leading a large and strong army against the Muslim commander. With his instinctive military acumen, Khâlid 🙵 divided his army into three parts. He then handed over the command of one part to Adi bin Hâtim 🙵, another part he entrusted to Qa'qâ' bin Amr 🙵 and the third one he kept with himself. All the three wings marched ahead to meet at Hafir with the difference of a one-day-journey and pitched their camps facing the Persian army.

First of all, Khâlid bin Walid 🙵 himself came out and threw a challenge to Hurmuz for a duel. He responded to the call and stepped forward. Both the commanders got down from their horses. Khâlid 🙵 was the first to strike. Hurmuz made a hasty retreat and parried the stroke, then he struck Khâlid with agility. Khâlid 🙵 got up quickly, rushed forward and snatched away his sword by twisting his wrist. Now Hurmuz clasped his body which led to wrestling between the two. Khâlid 🙵 lifted him high by his waist with lightening speed and then threw him on the ground so forcefully that he failed to move. Khâlid 🙵 then got on his chest, cut his head off and threw it away.

When a squad of the Persian army witnessed its commander being overpowered, it moved ahead to help him but Qa'qâ' bin Amr 🙵 stood like a rock. Following this, troops from both sides fell on one another and a fierce battle broke out in no time. But the Persians could not withstand the heavy Muslim onslaught and fled in panic and terror.

Hurmuz was such an exalted governor and commander among his people that he wore a crown on his head. This costly crown came to Khâlid 🙵 and it was valued at one hundred thousand dinars. A section of the Persian army had chained themselves with the determination of winning or dying. But they had to break their chains and flee leaving thousands of men dead and injured. This battle is known as *Dhat-us-Salâsil* because of these chains.

Khâlid ﷺ asked Muthanna bin Hârithah ﷺ to give chase to the fleeing Persian fighters. The Muslim forces laid siege round the citadel of Hisn-ul-Marah and conquered it putting the ruler to death. His wife accepted Islam and desired to be married to Muthanna ﷺ.

The Battle of Qârin

In response to Hurmuz's call for help, a large troop of reinforcements was immediately sent by the Persian ruler. The frustrating news of Hurmuz's death and his fleeing soldiers greeted it on the way. The fresh fighters of the reinforcements encouraged them to have a fresh encounter with the Muslim troops. They encamped at a canal and the Muslim fighters marched on to meet them. During the ferocious fight, all the three generals, Qârin, Qibâd and Anushjân, were killed leaving behind thirty thousand fighters dead and a large number of the runaway soldiers drowned in the canal.

As a follow-up action after the conquest of the province, Khâlid ﷺ made the inhabitants pay the *Jizyah* (tax) and appointed a Muslim governor to run the administration according to Islamic law.

The Battle of Walajah

After Qârin and the other generals were killed, the Persian ruler sent a well-known horseman Andarzagar to lead the Persian army which set out from Madâ'in and arrived at Walajah. At the back of Walajah was dispatched another general, Bahman Jadwaih from Madâ'in, at the head of another very strong army.

However, Khâlid bin Walid ﷺ marched with his troops and launched an attack on the Persian army which was routed after a fierce battle. Their general also died of thirst right on the battlefield. However, Bahman Jadwaih reached Ullais and the Persian fugitives joined his army. Many Christian Arabs also extended their unconditional support to them.

The Battle of Ullais

Informed of the presence of a large army at Ullais, Khâlid bin Walid
 himself marched ahead and launched his attack. Khâlid first
called a man for a duel. Mâlik bin Qais was sent from the Persian
camp and Khâlid killed him. Now an all-out battle started, which
resulted in seventy thousand enemy fighters being killed at the hands
of the Muslims.

Conquest of Hirah

From Ullais, Khâlid bin Walid marched to Hirah and besieged it.
When the siege drew long and the citizens were tired of it, the chief of
Hirah, Amr bin Abdul-Masih along with others appeared before the
Muslim commander. The Persian general and army had already fled
in panic with the news of the demise of Chosroes Ardsher. Abdul-
Masih won peace in return for two hundred thousand dirhams as
tribute. After the conquest, Khâlid bin Walid sent Dirâr bin Al-
Azwar, Dirâr bin Al-Khattâb, Qa'qâ' bin Amr, Muthanna bin
Hârithah and Uyainah bin Ash-Shamâs at the head of small
columns to make the surrounding tribes and settlers accept either the
Jizyah (tax) or Islam. Thus the entire territory up to the Tigris fell to
Khâlid bin Walid .

Message of Khâlid

From Hirah, Khâlid sent letters to the important personalities and
circulars to the feudal lords who were wise enough to obey the truth
and follow the good. In the letter addressed to the influential persons
of Persia he wrote:

"All praise is due to Allâh Who created chaos in your system
and slackened your hypocrisy and broke your unity. Had we
not invaded this country, it would have been disastrous for
you. Now it is better for you to obey us and we shall leave your
territory and go somewhere else. If you refuse to obey us, you
will come across such people who love death as you love your
life."

Another general circular carried the following:

> "Glorified is Allâh the Almighty Who humbled your pride, broke your alliance to pieces and razed your grandeur to the ground. Hence do accept Islam and you will be safe or seek our protection to become *Dhimmi* and pay the *Jizyah*, otherwise, I have brought to you a people who keep death as dear as you love drinking."

These letters and circulars brought unity among them and they achieved success in choosing their king unanimously to face the Arabian invasions.

Conquest of Anbâr

The Persians collected a big force in Anbâr and appointed Sherzâd, the ruler of Sâbât as its commander. Khâlid ﷺ marched from Hirah to Anbâr. Sherzâd had erected a high mound of clay outside the ramparts of their fort to consolidate his position. When Khâlid ﷺ surrounded Anbâr, the besieged soldiers showered arrows on the Muslim army with the result that the eyes of about one thousand Muslim fighters were injured. But the lion-hearted commander of the Muslim forces was not to be intimidated through such tactics and devices. He outsmarted his enemy by slaughtering the weak and exhausted camels and piling them up to reach the ramparts and then beat the enemy thoroughly. Although the Persians showed courage and gallantry, they had to surrender before the Muslims who outwitted them in every department of warfare. When Sherzâd witnessed that Muslim victory was around the corner, he sent his men to Khâlid ﷺ on peace mission. He replied that he could allow Sherzâd to leave the city peacefully along with a few comrades with provisions for not more than three days. Sherzâd left the city and Khâlid ﷺ entered it victoriously. He then put Zabrqân bin Badr in charge of Anbâr and marched to Ain-ut-Tamr.

Conquest of Ain-ut-Tamr

Uqbah bin Uqbah heard of the advancement of Muslim troops and contacted the Persian Commander Mehrân bin Bahrâm to say that only Arabs knew the war tactics of the Arabs, so they (Uqbah's men) should be allowed to confront the Muslim forces. Mehrân was happy enough to give his consent to this proposal. Uqbah was too excited to come out first and challenge for a duel. Khâlid ﷺ stepped forward and captured him alive, with the result his men fled in terror and were also taken captive. Mehrân bin Bahrâm grew so awe-stricken that he fled his fort, which later fell to the Muslim army.

Upper Iraq

Khâlid bin Walid ﷺ finished his task in a comparatively short period but Iyâd bin Ghanam ﷺ dispatched about the same time, was still engaged on his mission. His target of attack was a large territory forming part of Iraq, Iran and Syria and so his combats affected Persia and Heraclius equally. The time when Khâlid ﷺ conquered Ain-ut-Tamr, Iyâd engaged the rulers of Dumat-ul-Jandal after winning victories over the polytheists and Christian tribes. Dumat-ul-Jandal had two rulers, Ukaidir bin Mâlik and Judi bin Rabi'ah, who had collected all the Christians of the surrounding areas against the Muslims. In this distressing situation, Iyâd ﷺ addressed a letter to Khâlid ﷺ, who was then at Ain-ut-Tamr, to come to his help against the huge army of the enemy.

Conquest of Dumat-ul-Jandal

Khâlid bin Walid ﷺ appointed Qa'qâ' bin Amr ﷺ his deputy in Hirah and proceeded to Dumat-ul-Jandal without loss of a moment. The burning news of Khâlid's arrival was so terrifying that Ukaidir counseled Judi to make peace with the Muslims but he and other Christian chiefs rejected the proposal outright. At last Ukaidir broke his relations with them and left alone for some unknown place. A small column of the Muslims intercepted him on the way and he died fighting. Khâlid ﷺ launched his attack from another side and challenged the enemy commander for a duel. Judi stepped forward and was captured by Khâlid bin Walid ﷺ in no time, with the result his men fled the battleground. Simultaneously, Iyâd bin Ghanam ﷺ also prevailed over his Christian opponents and made them flee for their lives.

The Battle of Husaid

When the Persians noticed that Khâlid bin Walid ﷺ was away from Hirah, they made an all-out effort to take back the province and turn out the Muslim administrators from the territory. The Arabian tribes also lent their support to avenge the killing of their chief, Uqbah bin Uqbah. Two well-known Persian generals Zarmahr and Rozbah marched at the head of a huge army. Qa'qâ' bin Amr ﷺ, the deputy of Khâlid ﷺ in Hirah, also divided his force in two parts, under Abu Laila ﷺ and himself and challenged the enemy at Husaid.

After a heavy fight, both the generals and more than half of their army fell to the Muslim assault. The rest of their men fled to Khanâfis where their commander Bahbudhân was lying with a large army. When Abu Laila ﷺ reached Khanâfis in pursuit of the fugitives, Bahbudhân fled to Mudaiyah where Hudhail bin Imrân along with other Arabian chiefs were awaiting the opportunity to engage the Muslims in a battle. In the meantime, Khâlid bin Walid ﷺ finished his task in Dumat-ul-Jandal and hurried back to Hirah.

The Battle of Mudaiyah

Khâlid ﷺ took over the command of the entire Muslim army and divided it in three parts to attack from three different sides. Qa'qâ', Abu Laila and Khâlid ﷺ himself attacked from three sides as already decided upon. Hudhail fled for his life but the other generals along with a large number of men were put to death. Among the persons killed were Abdul-Uzza bin Abu Ruhm and Labid bin Jarir who sided with the opponents of Islam under compulsion in spite of being Muslims.

When Abu Bakr ﷺ came to know of this, he paid blood money to their relatives and ordered to treat their children well. Umar ﷺ was already angry with Khâlid ﷺ on account of Mâlik bin Nuwairah's assassination, and this incident added fuel to the flames. However, Abu Bakr ﷺ did not seek any explanation from Khâlid bin Walid ﷺ and exonerated him with the remark: "Anyone who accompanies the polytheists will meet with the same calamity."

The Battle of Firâd

Firâd was the meeting-ground of Persia, Syria and Arabia, and was adjacent to Dumat-ul-Jandal. It was the place where Banu Taghlib, Banu Namir and Banu Iyyâd had already collected and the Roman army was camping nearby to back them. Now the series of battles fought with the Persian forces in the lower areas of Iraq had reached the Roman camp.

Khâlid bin Walid ⌖ arrived at Firâd to give battle. The Roman army was across the river Euphrates and sent a message to the Muslim commander to either cross the river or let them cross it. Khâlid ⌖ asked them to cross the river and they did. Now both the forces were facing each other on the same side of the river. The Muslim army was extremely exhausted on account of the continuous travelling and fighting while the Romans were fresh and about eight or ten-fold more in number. However, the battle broke out and went on the whole day. At last the Romans fled the field tasting their worst defeat and leaving behind one hundred thousand dead. After finishing this job, Khâlid ⌖ sent his army back to Hirah and he himself left secretly for Makkah to perform *Hajj* in the company of only a few persons.

After the *Hajj*, Khâlid ⌖ hurried back to Hirah. But the news of his journey to Makkah could not be kept secret and it gradually reached the ears of Abu Bakr Siddiq ⌖. He, however, asked Khâlid ⌖ not to repeat it in future and expressed his displeasure over this act of carelessness.

Khâlid bin Walid ⌖ stayed in Hirah up to Rabi' Al-Awwal 13 AH, which he had entered in Muharram 12 AH. During this period he faced his enemies at every step and fought scores of fierce battles against formidable armies outnumbering Islamic forces in every battle but beating them thoroughly in each one and never tasting defeat in any battle. The Roman and Persian powers used to be shuddered from within at the mention of Khâlid bin Walid's name.

Human history can not perhaps, give any other example of so many successive victories in so short a period with so little resources. But Khâlid ⌖ did it. He deserves all of the blessings of Allâh that we can seek for him and for his matchless military acumen, dauntless courage, unflinching determination and daring operations.

However, we can not ignore the spirit behind all his deeds of wonder and the spirit is that of his selection, training and guidance in Siddiqi style and manner. Muslim columns and troops wherever they fought and whatever lines of operation they adopted were as per the instructions given from Al-Madinah, the headquarters of Islam. In all situations and circumstances, the Caliph of the Prophet 寒 kept himself acquainted with the details of the movements of the Muslim forces and never made any delay in sending the instructions best-suited to the situation.

Khâlid bin Walid 씁 in Syria

The military operations of Khâlid not only uprooted the apostasy from Arabia but also took away from the Persians the courage to invade Al-Madinah as part of their strategy. Now the first and the most important issue that demanded their immediate attention was the Syrian front under the Romans and the Ghassanids. Shurahbil bin Amr, the Ghassani king had martyred the emissary of the Prophet 寒, which led to the battle of Mu'tah. Besides, the joint forces of the Romans and the Gassanids were ready to invade Al-Madinah and the Prophet 寒 himself went up to Tabuk to ward off their evil intentions. Again, the news of huge military preparations at the Syrian borders led the Prophet 寒 to send an army under the command of Usâmah bin Zaid 씁. Even in the thick of military actions against the apostates the Caliph could not afford to ignore the Syrian threat and sent Khâlid 씁 to deal with the Syrians.

Khâlid bin Walid 씁 left the headquarters with a small column but he took within him, according to the Caliph's instructions, Muslim fighters from the regions and territories that were on his way. Despite this, Khâlid 씁 was instructed to avoid direct encounter with the Christian army. Internal problems of Arabia and the issue of apostasy topped his list.

When Heraclius came to know of the presence of the Muslim army within the bounds of Syria, he incited the surrounding tribes and the notables of the area against the Muslims. At last Heraclius made Mâhân, a well-known Roman general, go ahead with a huge army. As a result of the encounter, the troops under Mâhân tasted ignominious defeat besides leaving a large quantity of booty. Informed of this defeat, Heraclius himself proceeded from Constantinople, came to Syria and collected a huge army to avenge the defeat.

Khâlid sent a detailed account of the state of affairs to the Caliph. The day the letter was received in Al-Madinah, was the day when Ikrimah bin Abu Jahl returned to Al-Madinah after his arduous campaigns. At this time, tribes and clans from all over Arabia were pouring into the headquarters with the sole purpose of laying down their lives in the way of Allâh.

Siddiq ﷺ sent Ikrimah ﷺ to assist Khâlid ﷺ in his campaign. Close on his heels was dispatched Amr bin Al-Âs ﷺ with a detachment to help Khâlid bin Walid ﷺ by targeting the Romans in route to Palestine. As a follow-up action, the Caliph sent a detachment of tribes from various parts of Arabia under the command of Yazid bin Abu Sufyân with instructions to invade Damascus.

One more detachment headed by Abu Ubaidah bin Al-Jarrah ﷺ was dispatched to attack Hims. He sent yet another detachment headed by Shurahbil bin Hasanah ﷺ, after he returned to Al-Madinah from his campaign in Iraq, to launch an attack from the side of Jordan. These four strong detachments went to attack Syria from four sides. This campaign took place in Muharram 13 AH.

When all the four detachments crossed into Syria, and Heraclius came to know that the Muslim force has divided itself in four groups to attack four positions, he also made four groups of his army to be commanded by four generals. He sent his full brother, Tadhâraq at the head of 90 thousand armed men to face Amr bin Al-Âs ﷺ in Palestine. Jurjah bin Budhiyah was given 40 thousand soldiers to combat Yazid bin Abu Sufyân in Damascus. General Râqis was dispatched with an army of 50 thousand men to fight with Shurahbil bin Hasanah ﷺ in Jordan and Rafiqa bin Nasturas was asked to take on Ubaidah bin Al-Jarrah ﷺ in Hims with 60 thousand men under his command.

Thus, he collected two hundred and 40 thousand troops strong to go to war against the Muslims, who were altogether 30 thousand in number. It makes it clear what kind of major preparations, Heraclius had undertaken to rout the Muslim forces. Although Heraclius was wise enough to avoid the battle, his courtiers, nobles and chiefs were adamant in their ambition to invade Arabia.

Although the Muslim generals were making separate movements, each of them was bound by the Caliph's order to keep close contact and be aware of one another's state of affairs. When the Muslim commanders entered Syrian territory, they found to their amazement that for each Muslim detachment the enemy had eight times more forces. They took stock of the situation and informed Abu Bakr Siddiq 🙙 of what they were facing at the time and took a decision to jointly face the enemy. As the four Muslim generals assembled at Yarmuk, they received orders from the Caliph to face the enemy jointly.

Moreover, the Caliph sent orders to Khâlid 🙙 to rush to the spot of danger with half of the troops and put Muthanna bin Hârithah 🙙 in Hirah with the other half. He was also commanded to take charge of the joint command as the supreme commander. With the receipt of these orders from headquarters, Khâlid bin Walid 🙙, the Sword of Allâh, hurried to Syria with a contingent of ten thousand soldiers leaving an equal number in Hirah.

Following the Muslim strategy, Heraclius also ordered his commanders to form a united front. His full brother Tadhâraq headed the huge army of Heraclius. Besides, he dispatched a well-known general, Mâhân with a large detachment to strengthen the army arranged against the Muslim forces.

The Battle of Yarmuk

Khâlid 🙙 examined the situation like a seasoned commander. One night he sensed the enemy would attack the next morning, and that night he divided his army of about 40 to 46 thousand into small squads headed by separate commanders of high caliber, keeping a small but selected squad for his own company. He then instructed the head of every squad about the strategy to be followed.

The Romans proceeded with the attack with a contingent of 40 thousand soldiers, which was immediately repulsed. Next came the noted Roman general Jurjah bin Budhiyah with his column and expressed his desire to talk to Khâlid bin Walid ﷺ. When Khâlid ﷺ moved near to him, he wished to know about Islam, which the Muslim commander did adequately. He embraced Islam on the spot and moved along with Khâlid ﷺ to become a part of the Muslim army. He then fought against the Romans gallantly and then fell martyred.

Both the armies were locked together in a fierce fight. Although the Muslim army was deficient in number, it was more than a match for the Romans in courage and vitality. Their fervor was so high that even women plunged into the battlefield to prove their mettle as fighters for Islam. Abu Sufyân ﷺ was encouraging the Muslim soldiers with his martial songs. Mean while Ikrimah ﷺ cried out: "Who are they to promise me about death?" Dirâr bin Azwar ﷺ and other four hundred men pledged their allegiance at the time on either being martyred or victorious on the battlefield. Following this, the entire party fell on the Roman army like hungry tigers. Miqdâd ﷺ was reciting aloud Verses of *Sûrat Al-Anfâl* to produce in them the spirit of martyrdom.

The brave sons of Islam Khâlid bin Walid, Abu Ubaidah bin Jarrâh, Shurahbil bin Hasanah, Yazid bin Abu Sufyân, Ikrimah bin Abu Jahl, Qa'qâ' bin Amr, Abu Sufyân, Abud-Darda, Amr bin Âs, Hârith bin Dirâr and Jurjah bin Budhiyah ﷺ performed such deeds of valor that have never been witnessed before. From morning to evening swords and daggers, arrows and spears remained in action. *Zuhr* (noon) and *Asr* (afternoon) prayers were performed only symbolically while the fighting was going on. The day drew to an end but not the battle. Exhausted with the day-long operations and frustrated with failure after failure, the Romans lost heart and began to retreat till they had the mountain at their back, while the Muslims kept advancing and pushing them back till they started to flee. The pursuing Muslim troops forced them into the river, many were drowned, and others fell to their death. In this way, one hundred and thirty thousand soldiers were killed. The rest fled for their lives.

The morning sun rose with the message of Muslim victory and the Roman soldiers were nowhere to be seen. Tadhâraq, the Roman commander and full brother of Heraclius was killed along with a few other generals. Three thousand Muslims were honored with martyrdom. Among the martyrs the names of Jurjah bin Budhiyah, Ikrimah bin Abu Jahl, Amr bin Ikrimah, Salamah bin Hishâm, Amr bin Saeed, Abân bin Saeed, Hishâm bin Al-Âs, Habbâr bin Sufyân and Tufail bin Amr 🙵 were of those well known.

The battle of Yarmuk is stated to have been fought in Rabi' Al-Awwal or Rabi' Al-Âkhir 13 AH. However, this does not appear to be correct. The battle of Yarmuk must have taken place by the end of Jumada Al-Ukhra. The Muslim troops had conquered Busra before the Roman army reached Yarmuk. Moreover, the news of the conquest of Yarmuk had not reached Al-Madinah until after the death of Abu Bakr Siddiq 🙵. It is impossible that the news of the Muslim victory in Yarmuk would have taken two or two-and-a-half months to reach Al-Madinah.

Death of Abu Bakr Siddiq 🙵

The battle of Yarmuk in Syria had left Heraclius bewildered for he could not reason the crushing defeat of several hundred thousand armored Roman troops at the hands of a handful of Muslims. Dejected and embarrassed, he left Hims and proceeded to some unknown place. However, before his departure, he laid stress on strengthening the forts of Damascus and Hims. Damascus had come under the siege of the Muslim army and the entire land of Syria was about to be captured by them. Now, instead of looking towards Arabia, they were anticipating their own death and destruction. The green and fertile land of Iraq had already come to the Muslim fold. Islamic rule was now engaged in expanding Arabian territory by pushing the Persians and Romans back.

At the beginning of Jumada Al-Ukhra 13 AH, Abu Bakr 🙵 caught a fever and its intensity continued unabated for a fortnight. When he grew sure of his last hours drawing near, he sent for Abdur-Rahmân bin Auf 🙵 and held consultation with him regarding the caliphate and said, "What's your opinion about Umar?" He replied, "He is very

strict and severe in his treatment and behavior." Thereupon Abu Bakr
صلى said, "His strictness was simply due to my softness. I have myself
examined that Umar was inclined to adopt a hard-line in matters I
happened to be polite about, but he always turned soft when he
found me strict. I think the caliphate will make him soft and moderate
in his opinion and approach." Following this, he called Uthmân bin
Affân صلى and put the same question to him. He said in reply, "Umar's
internal self is better than his external one; he is superior to us all."

When Ali صلى was consulted, he made almost the same answer. Then
came Talhah صلى and when Abu Bakr صلى said to him, "I would like to
appoint Umar as the caliph of the Muslims." He said, "What answer
will you give to Allâh the Almighty about what you have done to the
people you ruled over?" In response to this he said, "I shall answer
Allâh the Almighty that I have appointed the best of Your creatures as
caliph for Your creatures." Having heard this, Talhah صلى kept silent.
Abu Bakr صلى asked Uthmân صلى to put down his will, which is given
below.

> "This is the pledge which I, the caliph of the Messenger of
> Allâh ﷺ have made at a time when his last hour in this world is
> at hand and the first hour of the Hereafter is approaching fast.
> In such a state, even a disbeliever comes to believe and a
> transgressor too attains conviction. I have appointed Umar bin
> Al-Khattâb to be your caliph, and I have never fallen short of
> your expectation in doing good for you all. Thus, if Umar takes
> to justice and endurance, it is quite within my knowledge; if he
> commits anything wrong, I am unaware of the unseen. What I
> have decided upon is nothing but good. Everybody has to face
> the consequences of his deeds."

> "Those who have wronged will come to know by what
> overturning they will be overturned." (26:227)

Last Address of Abu Bakr Siddiq صلى

When the piece of writing was completed, Abu Bakr Siddiq صلى asked
it to be read out to the people. Following this he came out in spite of
his precarious health condition and said addressing this audience:

"I have not appointed any relative of mine as caliph, and I have not installed Umar as caliph on my own. I have rather done it only after holding consultations with men of sound judgment. Are you then agreed to his being your caliph?" Hearing this they said, "We all agree with your choice and opinion." Following this he said, "You should then carry out Umar's orders and obey him."

All the people declared their allegiance. Abu Bakr 🙼 then said addressing Umar 🙼 in the presence of the audience:

"O Umar! I have made you my deputy for the Companions of the Messenger of Allâh 🙼; keep fearing Allâh from within and without. O Umar! There are some rights of Allâh the Almighty related to night, which he does not accede to in the day; similarly, some are the rights related to day, which He does not accede to in the night. Allâh the Almighty does not accept *Nawâfil* (supererogatory prayers) unless *Fard* (obligatory prayers) are performed. O Umar! Those alone get salvation on the Day of Judgment, whose record of deeds will be weighty, while the deficient in virtuous deeds will suffer. O Umar! The ways to success and salvation are found by following the Noble Qur'ân and what is right. O Umar! Don't you know that the Verses relating to inducement and awe, warning and glad tidings are revealed in the Noble Qur'ân simultaneously so that a believer keeps fearing Allâh the Almighty and seeking His forgiveness. O Umar! Whenever you find in the Noble Qur'ân mention of men of Hell, pray to Allâh not to make you one of them; whenever you find mention of men of Paradise, pray to Allâh to make you one of them. O Umar! When you will follow these counsels of mine you will find me sitting beside you."

This piece of writing and will making were all done by Monday, 22 Jumada Al-Ukhra, 13 AH, and between the night of Jumada Al-Ukhra 22nd and 23rd, after sunset he breathed his last and was buried before the *Ishâ* (night prayer) or at any time of the night.

His caliphate spanned over two-and-a-half years. Attâb bin Usaid 🙼, the governor of Makkah died the same day in Makkah.

The day Abu Bakr ﷺ wrote his will and informed the Muslims that the end of his life was near, Muthanna bin Hârithah ﷺ returned to Al-Madinah from Hirah (Iraq). When Khâlid ﷺ proceeded from Hirah to Syria along with half of the army leaving Muthanna ﷺ there with the other half, the Persian general, Bihman Jâdhwaih thought that it would be easy for them to drive out the Muslims from Hirah. Thus, he set out with a strong army. Muthanna bin Hârithah ﷺ marched from Hirah to Babylon and repulsed his attack, chased them up to Madâ'in and then came back to Hirah.

In the wake of this ignominious and devastating defeat, the Persian generals, ministers, nobles and chiefs buried their old differences and rose together to avenge their defeat. A wave of fervor and courage rose across the entire country. All the Persian tribes and chiefs of the nation rose up to uproot the Muslims. Such a large-scale military preparation worried Muthanna ﷺ who hurried to Al-Madinah to acquaint the Caliph with the impending threat leaving Hirah in the charge of Bashir bin Khasâsiah ﷺ.

Muthanna ﷺ reached Al-Madinah only a few hours before the final departure of the Caliph. However, the Caliph heard him with rapt attention and instructed Umar ﷺ to do the needful. When Umar ﷺ went out, Abu Bakr ﷺ said:

"O Allâh'! I have chosen Umar as caliph after me for the welfare of the Muslims as a whole and to remove all sorts of dangers from their path. You know very well the feelings of all hearts. After holding consultations with the Muslims, I have selected the best among the Muslims to take care of them and look after their peace and welfare. Make the guardians of Your slaves trustworthy and firm for their lives, their safety is in Your Hand. Make Umar a good caliph and his people be a benefit for him."

Impressions of Ali ﷺ

As the soul-shattering news of Abu Bakr's death spread in Al-Madinah, the whole city plunged into deep grief and untold woes and turmoil. The dismal day of the Prophet's final departure cast its tragic

reflection once again. When Ali ﷺ heard this sad news he burst into
tears, came to his house weeping and uttered at his door the following
words immersed in deep sorrow and profound pain:

"O Abu Bakr! May Allâh show mercy to you. By Allâh you
believed first of all in the entire *Ummah* and made your belief
the base of your behavior and manners. You were the man
excellent in trust and conviction, the most generous and the
greatest caretaker of the Prophet ﷺ. You were the greatest
supporter of Islam and well-wisher of all creatures. In manners,
virtues and guidance you were close to the Prophet ﷺ most of
all. May Allâh confer on you the best reward on behalf of Islam
and the Muslims. You affirmed the Prophet ﷺ when others
denied him; you showed sympathy when others were
ungenerous to him; you rose to help the Messenger of Allâh ﷺ
when others held themselves back from help and support.
Allâh entitled you as *Siddiq* (the Truthful) in His Book:

'And he who brought the truth and believed there in.' (39:33)

You stood like a rock in support of Islam and drove away the
disbelievers. Neither your argument was ever misdirected nor
your insight weakened; your soul never showed timidity. You
were firm like a mountain; strong winds failed to uproot or stir
you. About you the Prophet ﷺ had said: 'Weak in body, strong
in Faith, humble, exalted by Allâh, venerable on earth and
worthy among the believers.' Nobody could show greed in
your presence nor could give free expression to his desires; the
weak happened to be strong to you and the strong weak till the
right of the weak was given to him and the strong was forced to
give what was due."

When Umar ﷺ heard this news he expressed his deep feelings in the
following words:

"O Caliph of the Messenger of Allâh ﷺ, you put your people to
great hardship with your departure. It is hard enough to be on
a par with even your dust. How can I vie with you? "

Governors of the Siddiqi Caliphate

The Trustee of the believers, Abu Ubaidah bin Al-Jarrâh 🌸 was in charge as public exchequer, Umar 🌸 looked after the Department of Justice and Uthmân and Ali 🌸 were entrusted with the administrative work and correspondences. In the absence of one, the next would take over the responsibility. Attâb bin Usaid 🌸 was the governor of Makkah who passed away the day Abu Bakr 🌸 breathed his last. The governor of Tâ'if was Uthmân bin Abul-Âs 🌸. San'â' was governed by Muhâjir bin Umayyah 🌸 and Hadramout by Ziyâd bin Labid 🌸. Khaulân province was governed by Ya'la bin Umayyah 🌸, Yemen by Abu Musa Ash'ari 🌸, Janad by Mu'âdh bin Jabal 🌸, Bahrain by Ala' bin Hadrami 🌸, Dumat-ul-Jandal by Iyâd bin Ghanam 🌸 and Iraq by Muthanna bin Hârithah 🌸. Abu Ubaidah bin Al-Jarrâh 🌸 was later sent to Syria as the commander of the Muslim forces, while Yazid bin Abu Sufyân, Amr bin Al-Âs, Shurahbil bin Hasanah 🌸 were already engaged in Syria as commanders of various Muslim detachments. Khâlid bin Walid 🌸 was the commander-in-chief of the Muslim army during the Siddiqi Caliphate.

Wives and Children

Abu Bakr's first wife was Qutailah bint Abdul-Uzza who gave birth to Abdullah bin Abu Bakr 🌸 followed by Asma' bint Abu Bakr 🌸, the mother of Abdullah bin Zubair 🌸. From Umm Rumân 🌸, the second wife, were born Abdur-Rahmân bin Abu Bakr and Âishah Siddiqah 🌸. When Abu Bakr 🌸 was converted to, Islam his first wife refused to follow suit and was immediately divorced. The second wife, Umm Rumân 🌸 accepted Islam. After being converted to Islam, Abu Bakr married Asma'a bint Umais 🌸, the widow of Ja'far bin Abu Tâlib 🌸, who gave birth to Muhammad bin Abu Bakr 🌸 and then he married Habibah bint Khârijah Ansâriyah 🌸 who belonged to the Khazraj. From her was born to him a daughter named Umm Kulthum after his death.

Umar bin Al-Khattâb ☙

Birth and Pedigree:

He was among the nobles of the Quraish. During the Days of
Ignorance, diplomatic missions were attached to his family. In the
event of the Quraish being at war with any tribe, his family's leaders
would be sent on peacekeeping missions. They also took the lead
when there was occasion to highlight greatness and superiority of the
Quraish over others. His family lineage is as follows: Umar bin
Khattâb bin Nufail bin Abdul-Uzza bin Riyâh bin Abdullah bin Qurat
bin Razâh bin Adi bin Ka'b bin Luai. Ka'b had two sons, Adi and
Murrah. Murrah was among the ancestors of the Prophet ﷺ. Some
eight generations back the ancestry of the Prophet ﷺ and Umar ☙
becomes common. Umar's filial appellation was Abu Hafs while the
Prophet ﷺ gave him the title of 'Fâruq'. He was born 40 years before
the migration of the Prophet ﷺ. He passed his childhood days in
grazing camels. After attaining youth, according to Arabian tradition,
he was instructed in genealogy, swordsmanship, horsemanship and
wrestling. He adopted trade as his profession before and after
converting to Islam.

Some Specific Excellences:

Before being converted to Islam Umar Fâruq ☙ used to enter into
wrestling matches in the arena of Ukaz where a grand annual fair was
held so that the followers of different arts might gather from all parts
of Arabia and display their respective abilities. This justifies the
inference that Umar had attained perfection in the art of wrestling.
His claim to equestrian skill is also well established. Umar ☙ used to
literally jump on to his horse's back and his seat was so firm that he
appeared to be a part of the horse he rode. At the time of the advent of
the Prophet ﷺ, as per *Futuh-ul-Buldân*, there were only seventeen
persons in the whole clan of Quraish who could read and write, and
Umar ☙, the son of Khattâb, was one of them. He joined the ranks of
Islam after forty men and eleven women who were remaining in
Makkah after the migration to Abyssinia. According to other

narratives, he came to the fold of Islam after thirty-nine men and twenty-three women or forty-five men and eleven women. He was one of the earliest believers and among the blessed ten. He was also the father-in-law of the Prophet ﷺ. He is counted among the scholars and pious Companions. He has narrated 539 *Ahadith* in all which have been reproduced by Uthmân, Ali, Talhah, Sa'd, Ibn Mas'ud, Abu Dhar, Abdullah bin Umar, Abdullah bin Abbâs, Abdullah bin Zubair, Anas, Abu Hurairah, Amr bin Âs, Abu Musa Ash'ari, Barâ' bin Âzib, Abu Saeed Khudri ﷺ and others.

Ibn Abbâs ﷺ relates that the day Umar Fâruq ﷺ accepted Islam, the polytheists said, "Today the Muslims have settled their score with us." The same day the following Verse was revealed:

"O Prophet! Allâh is sufficient for you and for the believers who follow you." (8:64)

Ibn Mas'ud ﷺ is reported to have said: "The day Umar accepted Islam, it continued to grow in honor. It was, in fact, a conquest for Islam, and his *Hijrah* (migration) was a real victory, and his leadership was a blessing. We did not have courage enough to perform our *Salât* (prayers) at the Holy Ka'bah until after Umar accepted Islam. He made the disbelievers the target of so much pressure, encounters and fightings that they, at last, yielded in allowing us to offer our prayers at the Ka'bah." Hudhaifah ﷺ is reported to have said: "When Umar accepted the Faith, Islam rose like a fortunate person making progress at every step, and it continued retreating with his martyrdom and its fortune was on the decline."

Ibn Sa'd and Suhaib bin Sinân Rumi ﷺ reported: "Islam came to the fore when Umar accepted Faith and we became able to sit around the Ka'bah, and pay them in the same coin." Ibn Asâkir reports Ali ﷺ to have said: "Everyone migrated secretly, but, when Umar decided to migrate, he took an unsheathed sword in one hand and arrows in another and put his bow across his shoulders, and went to the Ka'bah. He went around it seven times followed by two *Rakât* of *Salât* (units of prayer) at the Station of Ibrahim. He then came to the circle of the chiefs of the Quraish and said throwing a challenge at them, 'May you be disgraced! Whoever likes to see his mother without a son and wife without a husband, should face me.' But none of them moved from their place."

Imam Nawawi reported: Umar ﷺ accompanied the Prophet ﷺ in every battle and kept firm on the day of Uhud. The Prophet ﷺ once said, "I had a dream that a woman was performing *Wudu'* (ablution) in Paradise sitting beside a palace. I inquired whose palace this was. I was told that it belonged to Umar." Then turning towards Umar ﷺ he said, "The same moment your sense of honor came to my mind and I went away from there." Hearing this, Umar ﷺ burst into tears and submitted, "Shall I show my sense of honor to you?" The Prophet ﷺ once said, "I dreamt that I took milk and its freshness reached up to my nails. I then gave the rest to Umar." "What is the interpretation of this dream, O Prophet of Allâh?" they asked. "Milk here means Knowledge," the Prophet ﷺ explained. The Prophet ﷺ said, "Once I had a dream that people were brought before me in their shirts, some wearing them up to their chests, and some of them longer than this but Umar's shirt was dragging." "What's meant by the shirt?" they asked. "Religion," he explained.

On one occasion the Prophet ﷺ said to Umar ﷺ: "By Allâh, Satan will never tread the way you pass through." The Prophet ﷺ once said: "Had there been a Prophet after me, he would have been Umar." He once said: "Umar is the lamp of the heavenly people." On one occasion the Prophet ﷺ remarked: "The door to things useless and futile will remain closed while Umar lives among you." He ﷺ once said: "Every angel of the heaven pays respects to Umar and every devil on earth fears him." *Ahadith* from Abu Saeed Khudri ﷺ let us know that the Prophet ﷺ said: "Each one of the Prophets had a *Muhaddith*, if there could be a *Muhaddith* in my *Ummah*, he is Umar." On being asked about the *Muhaddith*, he said: "One from whose tongue angels speak."

On one occasion Abu Bakr ﷺ said: "None is dearer to me than Umar." Ali ﷺ is reported to have once remarked: "While mentioning pious people, never forget Umar." Ibn Umar ﷺ is reported to have said: "After the Prophet ﷺ, we found Umar to be the most intelligent." Ibn Mas'ud ﷺ said: "If knowledge of the entire world is put on one scale, and that of Umar on the other to be weighed, Umar's will have the heavier weight." Hudhaifah 🕸 says: "Knowledge of the whole world lies in the lap of Umar." He further said: "None has dared to receive as much censure in the way of Allâh as Umar did." Ali 🕸 once saw Umar 🕸 wrapped in a piece of cloth and remarked: "None is dearer to me than the one who is now wrapped in a cloth." On being asked, Ali 🕸 remarked: "Umar is full of firm resolve, consciousness and courage." Ibn Mas'ud 🕸 is reported to have said: "Umar's excellence is established by four things: firstly, he counseled the killing of the captives of the battle of Badr which was followed by the Verse: 'Were it not a previous ordainment from Allâh, a severe torment would have touched you for what you took.' (8:68) Secondly, he asked the Mothers of the believers to observe *Hijâb* and then the Verse concerning *Hijâb* was revealed and the Prophet 🕸 said to Umar: 'Revelation is caused in my house and you were already inspired.' Thirdly, the Prophet's praying to Allâh for strengthening Islam by causing Umar to accept Islam; fourthly, he pledged allegiance to Abu Bakr before anyone did." Mujâhid said: "We would so often mention that the devils remained in confinement during the caliphate of Umar and got freedom after his death." Abu Usâmah 🕸 said: "Do you know who were Abu Bakr and Umar? They were like mother and father for Islam." Ja'far Sâdiq 🕸 said: "I am rather disgusted with him who remembers not Abu Bakr and Umar gracefully."

Physical Features of Umar 🕸:

He was fair-complexioned inclined to redness. He was so tall that he appeared to be riding while walking on foot. His cheeks were deficient in flesh; beard was thick, moustache noticeable and baldness in the frontal part of the head. Ibn Asâkir relates: "Umar was tall and solid with color inclined to redness, cheeks pressed, moustache noticeable with a red halo. His mother was the sister of Abu Jahl and hence Umar 🕸 called him maternal uncle."

Important Events of the Fâruqi Caliphate

The Muslims at large took *Bai'ah* (oath of allegiance) at the hand of Umar 🕸 in Al-Madinah on Tuesday, 23rd of Jumada Al-Ukhra, 13 AH. Abu Bakr 🕸 had issued the following instructions to Umar 🕸

after the arrival of Muthanna ﵁ on 22nd of Jumada Al-Ukhra, 13 AH, and hearing from him the account of affairs:

> "I am sure to pass away today. Thus, you will dispatch Muthanna for fighting tomorrow before the end of the day. No suffering whatsoever should hold you back from carrying out the religious tasks and the Commands of Allâh the Almighty. You have seen what I did after the death of the Prophet ﷺ even though it was the greatest calamity for us. When the Syrians are conquered, make it a point to send back the Iraqis to Iraq for they know their own business very well and they are at ease only in Iraq."

The above words make it amply clear that from the day the Prophet ﷺ made his final departure to the day of his own last journey, every moment of his life was devoted to Divine duties. He made no will concerning his wives and children.

After accepting the oath of allegiance for his caliphate, Umar ﵁ aroused in the people the fervor for taking part in *Jihâd*, but they made no response and this state of indecision continued for three days. Abu Ubaid bin Mas'ud Thaqafi ﵁ offered his name for Iraq on the fourth day. He was then followed by Sa'd bin Ubaid Ansâri ﵁, then by Sulait bin Qais ﵁ and many others. Thus was formed a large detachment for Iraq. Umar ﵁ appointed Abu Ubaid bin Mas'ud ﵁ as commander for he was the first to show his readiness. He accompanied Muthanna ﵁ to Iraq. The three-day silence of the people over joining the Iraqi detachment led the historians to think that the people were unmoved because they were unhappy over the dismissal of Khâlid bin Walid ﵁ by Umar ﵁ when he took charge of the caliphate.

However, this is a wrong and baseless notion. Nobody opposed the step taken by Umar ﵁. Moreover, no historian has ever mentioned the unhappiness of the people and how this unhappiness was resolved. This is rather derogatory to the high status and pious position that the Companions of the Prophet ﷺ enjoyed. It is a fact that almost every one of them was always inclined to fight in the way of Allâh. However, each of them was waiting for the other to take upon himself the responsibility of the campaign. The reason given by these historians does not hold true and is illogical because the people were encouraged to join the campaign and their initial lack of response occurred before Khâlid bin Walid ﷺ was deposed as commander.

Khâlid bin Walid ﷺ deposed

Abu Bakr Siddiq ﷺ had sent Khâlid bin Walid ﷺ to Syria as the supreme commander of the Muslim army. He was a warrior of the very highest caliber and matchless as a commander. Khâlid ﷺ was also the commander-in-chief in Iraq at the same time. His amazing valor and military acumen had left the Persian Court and Sassanid Empire shocked and bewildered. The Roman Empire also needed the same treatment, therefore, Abu Bakr ﷺ had sent him to the Syrian front as the commander-in-chief of the Muslim army, and his decision proved to be right. He gave them such a crushing defeat on the battlefield of Yarmuk that the Roman Empire's back was broken. Now the time had come for a decisive battle between the two forces and so the Muslim army was urgently in need of a commander not only well-versed in the art of warfare but also a statesman of wide experience and broad vision.

Umar Fâruq ﷺ did not disapprove of Khâlid's martial abilities. However, he considered him a little careless and was, therefore, apprehensive that his lack of caution could possibly cause the Muslims a set back. Abu Bakr Siddiq ﷺ also shared the anxiety of Umar Fâruq ﷺ. However, he, considered Khâlid ﷺ as the most suitable for the initial campaigns in Syria and Iraq. To him as a whole, his strong points were more than the weak ones. But, since, this purpose had already been achieved, his continuation as the supreme commander was no longer necessary. Umar Fâruq ﷺ used to say: "May Allâh the Almighty show mercy to Abu Bakr, he sheltered the command of Khâlid bin Walid, for he instructed me during his last hours about the commanders fighting along with Khâlid in Iraq but uttered not a word about Khâlid."

It is then clear that the steps taken by Umar ﷺ were not against the will of Abu Bakr ﷺ. Besides, the very first act of Umar ﷺ could not have negated the policy of the Caliph whom he held in the highest esteem after the Prophet ﷺ. Historians generally miss the point that Abu Bakr Siddiq ؓ had taken permission from Usâmah ؓ to keep Umar Fâruq ؓ with him solely to seek his advice in state affairs, and this enviable position Umar ؓ enjoined till the last breath of the departed Caliph.

But those who happen to have a superficial look over the matter, attach wrong meaning to it. Umar ؓ objected to some of Khâlid's careless acts and decisions no doubt, but his disapproval never made him cross the limits of *Shari'ah* (Divine codes). The man who gave free expression to his will that everyone among the captives of the battle of Badr be killed by his own relative could not be accused of nourishing a personal grudge against anybody. This is a calumny of the worst nature against the tower of righteousness that Umar ؓ was.

By deposing Khâlid bin Walid ؓ, Umar Fâruq ؓ has set a shining example of preferring Faith to this material world of ours. Khâlid ؓ accepted the orders of his deposition without question and continued to serve the new commander. Whenever the question of devaluing one's own self-importance for the sake of Divine service will be raised, we have the name of Khâlid bin Walid ؓ to present. This exemplary supreme sacrifice of Khâlid bin Walid ؓ, the Sword of Allâh, far exceeds his amazing and soul-stirring deeds of valor and military genius in the battlefield where he was always victorious and never tasted defeat in his entire career as a warrior. Both his martial deeds and sense of Divinity and loyalty to the Chief of the believers are deeds of Khâlid bin Walid ؓ that we can all be proud of.

Some historians have argued a very delicate point that Khâlid bin Walid ؓ was deposed because Umar ؓ wanted to infuse in the mind of the believers that victories were achieved because of Allâh's help, and not through any commander however valiant and seasoned he might be. This viewpoint also lends support to the replacement of Muthanna bin Hârithah ؓ by Abu Ubaid bin Mas'ud ؓ. The Muslim *Ummah* is sure to achieve its past glory in the world even today if such examples of unity, integrity, loyalty and sacrifice are followed.

Among the foremost military services of Umar Fâruq ﷺ after assuming the caliphate was the deposition of Khâlid bin Walid ﷺ as the supreme commander of the Muslim army in Syria and his replacement by Abu Ubaidah bin Al-Jarrâh ﷺ. The order was immediately obeyed. However, after handing over the charge of commander-in-chief of the Syrian army to Abu Ubaidah ﷺ, under him Khâlid bin Walid ﷺ displayed gallantry and military skill of such a high degree that historians are still wanting in words to describe them. He not only fought more efficiently and relentlessly under the command of Abu Ubaidah ﷺ, he also gave him valuable and expert advice whenever needed. History has no other example to offer in the annals of military service to compare with what Khâlid bin Walid ﷺ did as the deposed commander of the same army. It only happened simply because of a high sense of duty to Allâh, a deep love for His religion and a profound attachment to His slaves.

The next job the Caliph did was the installation of Abu Ubaid bin Mas'ud ﷺ as the commander-in-chief of the entire Muslim army in Iraq. The third order of the Chief of the believers came in the form of dispatching Ya'la bin Umayyah ﷺ to Yemen to fulfil the last will of the Prophet ﷺ to drive out every Jew and Christian from the soil of Arabia. It was not accomplished during the caliphate of Abu Bakr ﷺ owing to the uprisings and attacks that needed immediate attention.

Banishment of the Najrân Christians

Umar Fâruq ﷺ asked Ya'la bin Umayyah ﷺ to go to Yemen and tell the Christians of Najrân to leave the country and that they would be provided with land that was more fertile plus other facilities in Syria.

Some narrow-minded persons hold this banishment of the Christians as an unjust step. However, these people ignore the evil designs and conspiratorial activities of the Jews of Al-Madinah injurious to the Muslim cause. They overlook how they incited the Romans to invade Al-Madinah. The Christians of Najrân were playing the same role against the Muslims in that area. Since the Prophet ﷺ was well-aware of the usurious and anti-Islamic activities of the Jews and the Christians of Al-Madinah and Najrân, he wanted them to be driven off Arabian soil lest their evil habits made inroads into the Muslim society. The agreement signed by the Prophet 鷺 and the Najrân Christians included as one of the conditions that they would give up the practice of usury but they failed to implement it. Thus, they deserved such an extreme step by involving themselves in collaboration with the Romans on one hand and hatching conspiracies against the Muslims on the other. We so often come across in history books, newspapers and magazines how people have been or are now being exiled by the civilized nations forcing them to leave hearth and home, wealth and property, they are even indulged in the mass killings also on a very large scale. In comparison to these exiles and brutal killings, the exile of the Christians of Najrân was very humane.

Conquest of Damascus

After a major defeat at the hands of the Muslim troops in the battle of Yarmuk, the Roman soldiers took to their heels and stopped only at Fihl. Heraclius shocked and disappointed issued fresh orders for the Roman soldiers to assemble again. Damascus was refortified and large reinforcements from Palestine and Hims were arranged. Nastas bin Nasturas was appointed the commander-in-chief of the Syrian forces. Mâhân, the governor of Damascus was already there.

The Muslim army was still in Yarmuk. Abu Ubaidah bin Jarrâh 鷺 dispatched the Iraqi detachment accompanied by Khâlid bin Walid 鷺 to Iraq under the command of Hâshim bin Utbah 鷺 as per the orders of the Caliph. He sent a contingent towards Fihl and the rest of the army was divided into a number of divisions. A column was sent under the command of Dhul-Kala'鷺 to obstruct the movement of the Roman reinforcements from Hims to Damascus, and another column was sent to stop them marching from Palestine to Damascus. Abu Ubaidah 鷺 himself proceeded to Damascus at the head of the remaining troops. He conquered Ghutah before reaching Damascus and then laid a siege around the city in the last of Rajab 13 AH. Although the city contained a large garrison, the Romans could not muster enough courage to face the Muslims in the open. They had to take refuge in their strong fortifications and use defensive means of war. Abu Ubaidah bin Al-Jarrâh 鷺 camped at Al-Jâbiah gate while Khâlid bin Walid 鷺 and Am bin Al-Âs 鷺 moved towards Tuma gate, and Shurahbil bin Hasanah ﷺ and Yazid bin Abu Sufyân ﷺ appeared respectively at Farâwis, and Saghir and Kisân gates. Thus, Damascus was besieged on all sides. At times the besieged Romans hurled stones through catapults and shot arrows at the Muslim soldiers, which were countered effectively and without delay. The siege dragged on for about six months. The reinforcements dispatched by Heraclius to Damascus were effectively intercepted by Dhul-Kala'ﷺ. At last, the people of Damascus lost hope of Heraclius' help and their zeal for battle began to dissolve. Abu Ubaidah ﷺ on being informed of their distress and despair, issued orders to all the commanders to launch a full-scale attack the next morning.

When the besieged Romans came to know of the next step of the Muslim army, a deputation appeared before Khâlid bin Walid ﷺ at Tuma gate and sought peace, which the Muslim commander immediately granted and entered the city without any fight. The peace document written by Khâlid bin Walid ﷺ is given below:

"Khâlid bin Walid has made concessions for the people of Damascus that they will be granted peace on the entry of the Islamic army into Damascus and their lives, properties and churches would remain safe and intact. Moreover, neither fortifications of the city nor the houses will be demolished nor any member of the Islamic force will be allowed to reside in any house. The Muslims and their Caliph will practice nothing but good to the people of Damascus while they keep paying the *Jiziyah* (tax)."

About the same time that Khâlid bin Walid ﷺ entered the city with the peace agreement, other commanders and their men forced into the city through ladders and by breaking the gates open. Khâlid ﷺ and Ubaidah ﷺ came across each other in the middle of the city. Abu Ubaidah ﷺ claimed that he had conquered the city with his sword while Khâlid ﷺ argued that he had seized it through the process of peace.

Some narratives lend support to the view that even if the peace agreement was signed at the request of Mâhân, the governor of Damascus, he also wanted to see the might of the Muslim forces. If the

Muslim assault met with failure, their defensive efforts would continue not caring the least for the peace document with Khâlid bin Walid ﷺ, but if the Muslim campaign was crowned with success and they made their entry by force, these documents would come to their rescue. When the two commanders met in the middle of the city, the question that came up was whether the city was peacefully seized or conquered by force. Some people argued the point that since Khâlid ﷺ was simply a commander, he had no right to write a peace document when the commander-in-chief was there to take a final decision. However, Abu Ubaidah bin Jarrâh ﷺ rejected this point by saying that if peace or shelter was provided even by an ordinary member of the army, it applied to everyone. He declared peace to prevail in the entire city according to the peace document of Khâlid ﷺ and every point therein was handled with due care. The citizens of Damascus enjoyed perfect peace. Yazid bin Abu Sufyân ﷺ was appointed as the governor of Damascus who not only brought peace to the city but let the Roman soldiers go at will.

The Battle of Fihl

Providing Yazid bin Abu Sufyân ﷺ with a strong contingent, Abu Ubaidah proceeded from Damascus to Fihl where Saqlar bin Mikhraq, the noted general of Heraclius was lying with a few hundred thousand soldiers. Before leaving Damascus, Abu Ubaidah ﷺ had given the advance-guard to Khâlid bin Walid ﷺ, the middle to Shurahbil bin Hasanah ﷺ, the right wing to Amr bin Âs ﷺ and lead the left wing himself, while Dirâr bin Azwar ﷺ was given charge of the cavalry and Iyâd bin Ghanam ﷺ that of the infantry. Every commander camped at the place of his own choice.

The Romans attacked the middle portion of the Muslim army in night. Shurahbil bin Hasanah ﷺ came out in full force and fervor. The din and bustle of military movements made the Muslim commanders rush to the scene of fighting with their troops. The fierce and hot battle continued day and night for a couple of days. At last, the Romans fled the field leaving eighty thousand men including the Roman general Saqlar dead, and a large quantity of booty. After Fihl, the Muslim army marched to Baisân.

Conquest of Baisân

Here also they anticipated a fierce fight. The Muslim army laid siege to the city and the fort. In the meantime Abu Ubaidah ﷺ was informed that a Roman general had marched at the head of a huge army to restore Damascus. Abu Ubaidah ﷺ dispatched a squad of horsemen headed by Khâlid bin Walid ﷺ. Yazid bin Abu Sufyân ﷺ, the governor of Damascus had moved forward to take on the Romans when the detachment led by Khâlid bin Walid ﷺ attacked from the rear, with the result that not a single Roman soldier was able to save his life. At last, the people of Baisân made an offer of peace, which was immediately granted by the Muslim general and a governor was installed there. Abu Ubaidah ﷺ then sent Abul-A'war As-Sulami at the head of a division to Tabariyah where the Muslim forces won victory without fight.

Conquest of Saida, Irqah and Beirut

Soon after exercising full control over Damascus, Yazid bin Abu Sufyân sent his brother, Mu'âwiyah bin Abu Sufyân to Irqah at the head of a squadron who conquered Irqah without facing any resistance. Yazid then turned to Saida, Habil and Beirut, and these territories easily yielded to the Muslim attack. Thus, Damascus and the entire territory of Jordan came under the control of the Muslims.

Campaigns in Iraq

The smashing victory in Yarmuk led the Muslim army to conquer all of Syria. Now, they were looking forward to conquer Hims, the seat of Heraclius.

First Deed of Abu Ubaid bin Mas'ud ﷺ

As mentioned above, in the very first week after assuming the caliphate, Umar ﷺ dispatched Muthanna bin Hârithah, Sa'd bin Ubaid, Sulait bin Qais and Abu Ubaid bin Mas'ud to Iraq. Even though Abu Ubaid bin Mas'ud ﷺ, the commander-in-chief of the Iraqi forces, left Al-Madinah along with Muthanna bin Hârithah ﷺ, he stopped to take with him men from the Arab tribes along the way and made brief halts at different places, he reached Iraq one month after Muthanna ﷺ. On reaching Hirah, Muthanna bin Hârithah ﷺ saw with anxiety that the Persians had roused all the Iraqi chiefs against the Muslims and Rustam, the governor of Khurâsan, had taken his position in Madâ'in after making massive military preparations. With the arrival of Muthanna ﷺ, Rustam sent a large army to combat him. Rustam sent another huge army to Kaskar headed by Narsi, a very brave and experienced general of the royal family. The third strong army he entrusted to Jâbân and sent it towards the Euphrates, they pitched their camp at Namâriq. Muthanna bin Hârithah ﷺ on the other hand came out from Hirah and camped at Khaffân.

Meanwhile Abu Ubaid bin Mas'ud ﷺ arrived and took charge of the entire Muslim army. He left Muthanna ﷺ at Khaffân entrusting him with the command of the Muslim cavalry and he launched a massive attack on Jâbân at Namâriq and tore apart their ranks, with the result, the Persians fled the battlefield. Jâbân was captured by a Muslim soldier, Matar bin Fiddah, who did not recognize him as Jâbân, the Persian general. Taking advantage of this, Jâbân offered him two valuable slaves in return for his freedom. He was freed but another Muslim soldier caught him for he knew he was Jâbân, the Persian general. He was produced before Abu Ubaid bin Mas'ud ﷺ with the report that he, the Persian general, had obtained safety by fraudulent means. Abu Ubaid ﷺ probed the matter and found to his satisfaction that the Persian general was given peace and safety by a Muslim soldier. Thus, Abu Ubaid ﷺ released Jâbân who joined his people at Kaskar.

Conquest of Kaskar

Narsi was already encamped at Kaskar with thirty thousand soldiers. Now Jâbân and his defeated army also joined him. Informed of the crushing defeat of Jâbân, Rustam dispatched from Madâ'in a huge army headed by a noted general, Jâlinus.

Abu Ubaid bin Mas'ud Thaqafi ﷺ engaged Narsi in battle before the arrival of reinforcements from Madâ'in. Two subordinate generals of the royal family had been entrusted with the right and left flanks and the main body of the army. In the Muslim army, the center was under the command of Abu Ubaid ﷺ while the right wing was headed by Sa'd bin Ubaid ﷺ, the left wing by Sulait bin Qais ﷺ and the advance guard by Muthanna ﷺ. The battle soon became fierce. When Muthanna ﷺ found the battle dragging on, he severed his column from the army and launched a sudden attack from the rear on the Persian army after making a circle of about eight miles. Narsi was caught unaware. However, he turned a contingent towards the back. But a massive attack from Sa'd bin Ubaid ﷺ created chaos in the enemy ranks. Both Sa'd bin Ubaid and Abu Ubaid ﷺ went deep into the heart of the Persian troops and had Narsi within their range. In view of the situation the other Muslim fighters also plunged deep into the enemy ranks with the cry of *Allâhu Akbar* (Allâh is the Most Great).

The Persians could not withstand the assault and gave up fighting particularly when they found Narsi retreating. Muthanna ﷺ chased the fugitives and the rest of the Muslim army took a large number of the enemy as captives and captured their camps and bazaars. After finishing this arduous task, Abu Ubaid ﷺ sent Muthanna, Âsim and Sulait ﷺ to clear the surrounding areas of the Persian troops, and they did their job adequately and appreciably.

The Battle of Bâqshia

Narsi was defeated before Jâlinus could join the Persian army. The news of the smashing defeat led him to stop his movement at Bâqshia. Abu Ubaid ﷺ marched en route to Saqâtiyah and Kaskar and attacked Jâlinus at Bâqshia who fled the area and stopped only in Madâ'in.

The Last Deed of Abu Ubaid bin Mas'ud ﷺ

When Jâlinus reached Madâ'in as a retreating leader, the seat of power stirred from within. Rustam, the prime minister of the Persian Empire, gave a call in the court packed with renowned generals and valiant soldiers, "Who can stop the marching steps of the Arabian army and avenge the successive defeats of the Persians?" "None other than Bihman Jâdhwaih can perform this feat," they all cried with one voice. Rustam agreed and entrusted Bihman Jâdhwaih with a well-equipped huge army along with three hundred combat elephants and a large quantity of provisions. He was also handed the Kavyâni Banner, which the Persians believed made any army carrying it invincible. Also, Jâlinus was chosen to lead the reinforcements with the warning that if he fled again, his head would be struck off. Bihman Jâdhwaih marched on with added confidence and determination and he increased his already strong army with men and materials from the tribes they came across on the way to their destination. He pitched his camp at Quss-un-Nâtif near the bank of the Euphrates.

Informed of this massive Persian military movement, Abu Ubaid bin Mas'ud ﷺ also proceeded from Kaskar and camped at Marwahah on the other bank of the Euphrates. The deep running water of the river kept the two armies apart and silent for a couple of days. At last, a bridge was constructed over the Euphrates with the common consent of the rivals. On completion of the bridge, Bihman Jâdhwaih sent words to his counterpart to choose between fighting from this side of the river or that. Although some Muslim officers were against the Muslim army crossing the bridge, Abu Ubaid ﷺ led his army across the bridge to the Persian side and drew the battle line. Bihman Jâdhwaih put the elephants ahead of his army with archers sitting on them. Horses on the Muslim side had never seen elephants before and they began to flee in terror at the sight of the huge animals. With this scenario of the battle, Abu Ubaid ﷺ asked his men to fight on foot. When the elephants began to trample the Islamic ranks under their feet, Abu Ubaid ﷺ called out to strike their swords at the trunks and he was himself the first to do this. He cut off the trunks of several elephants and inflicted deep injuries on their feet with the result the riders fell down and were killed.

Enthused with the matchless bravery of their commanders and commanding officers, the Muslim soldiers made heroic assaults on the elephants. During these fateful moments, Abu Ubaid bin Mas'ud ﷺ came under the attack of a combat elephant. He fell upon the elephant and struck its trunk off with one stroke of his sword. Despite this the belligerent animal knocked him down and put his foot on him crushing his chest. Following his martyrdom, his brother Hakam stepped forward and held the standard of Islam. An elephant too, killed him. Thus, six more men from Banu Thaqif who held the flag one by one fell down martyred. The eighth one to hold the standard was Muthanna bin Hârithah ﷺ. He took the standard in his hand and encouraged his men with firmness but they appeared disheartened at the loss of seven precious lives to the elephant attacks. Abdullah bin Marthad Thaqafi rushed ahead and broke some planks of the bridge to stop the Muslim soldiers from running away. He then called out his men to fight and be honored with martyrdom like their brethren. Muthanna ﷺ collected his scattered men and stood firmly against the enemy. Abu Mihjan Thaqafi and some other officers stood by him. The bridge was repaired and the Muslim soldiers were asked to cross the bridge to safety while Muthanna ﷺ and the others stopped the enemy from moving ahead. This battle took a toll of six thousand Muslim combatants including valiant fighters like Sulait bin Qais, Uqbah and Abdullah–sons of Qibti bin Qais, Abbâd bin Qais, Qais bin As-Sakan, and Abu Umayyah Fazâri ﷺ. The Persians also lost about the same number of men. The runaway Muslim soldiers remained ashamed and repentant for a long time. This battle took place in Sha'bân 13 AH.

The Battle of Buwaib

When Umar Fâruq ﷺ came to know of the martyrdom of Abu Ubaid ﷺ and the heavy losses incurred by the Muslims, he grew exasperated and with all his energy and resources he commenced preparations for a fresh campaign against the Persians. He dispatched heralds and emissaries to all the tribes and roused them to fight for Islam. Several tribes poured in Al-Madinah and were dispatched to Iraq to lend their help to Muthanna ﷺ who had already launched a recruiting drive, which resulted in a large army.

When the Persians were informed of these preparations, Rustam sent a huge army under the command of Mehrân Hamadâni. The reason for Mehrân's nomination to the command was that he was brought up in Arabia and could, therefore, realize the power and strength of the

Arabs and appreciate the magnitude of the task before him. Informed
of the Persian movements, Muthanna bin Hârithah ﷺ marched with
his army and encamped at Buwaib, along the Euphrates. Mehrân,
marching from the capital, advanced straight upon Buwaib and
pitched his camp on the other side of the Euphrates. He then sent
word to Muthanna ﷺ to either come to his side or let him come to his
(Muthanna's) own side. In the light of the bitter experience of the past,
Muthanna ﷺ invited him to his side. Mehrân crossed the river with
his entire army and combat elephants. He then arranged his forces in
the manner that he put his infantry in the front followed by the
elephants with archers sitting on them and both right and left flanks
were occupied by cavalry divisions.

The Islamic army was also ready to fight. The Persians initiated the
attack, which was answered by the Muslims. The battle grew intense
and both sides displayed bravery. However, the Muslims were
crowned with victory. When Muthanna bin Hârithah ﷺ noticed the
Persians running away, he rushed forward and broke the bridge, with
the result that a large number of the enemy soldiers were either killed
or drowned. Mehrân Hamadâni was also killed on the battlefield. As
per Ibn Khaldun's account, about one hundred thousand Persian
fighters succumbed to death, while only one hundred from the
Muslim side were honored with martyrdom. The Persian fugitives
were given chase up to Sâbât. Now the entire territory from Sawâd to
Tigris came under the Muslim forces. The battle took place in
Ramadân 13 AH.

After the Defeat of Buwaib

Because of the killing of Mehrân and the large-scale destruction, there
arose a tremendous clamor in the imperial court as well as throughout
the entire Persian territory. The ratio of one hundred thousand
Persians lost to one hundred Muslims was really unbelievable and
shocking to the extreme. The result was a terrible terror and fear of
the Muslims came into the Persians' hearts. Although the real power
and administration lay in the hands of Rustam, the Persian throne had
a woman of the royal family to rule the destiny of its subjects. Now in
the wake of the smashing and ignominious defeat, all lips were

moving to say that they had tasted this defeat because a woman was on the Persian throne. Thus the woman was immediately dethroned and Yezdgird, a youth was installed on the throne. Rustam and Firoz were the pillars of the state, but a violent friction raged between them. Now both of them were persuaded to shake hands in the interest of the Persian Empire. Other chiefs and nobles also buried their differences and girded up their lions to serve their country even in the face of death. The coronation of Yezdgird also infused a new life into those who were disheartened because of the adverse state of affairs in every field. The provinces and cities under the possession of Muslim officers began to show signs of unrest and rebellion. The Persian camps were packed with soldiers and the Persian forts and military outposts were fortified and strengthened. Many other regions under the Muslim control broke into revolt and rose in support of the Persians.

Umar Fâruq's Readiness to face the Persians

Umar Fâruq 🙵 came to know of these fresh developments in the month of Dhul-Qa'dah in Al-Madinah. He issued prompt orders for Muthanna 🙵 together with all the troops to fall back towards the frontiers of Arabia. He summoned the tribes of Rabi'ah and Mudar that were scattered throughout Iraq, and strengthened his forces and vacated the threatened areas to gather close to the frontiers of Arabia. He also issued orders to the governors to collect and send warriors to fight in the way of Allâh. As the season for the pilgrimage had arrived, Umar 🙵 set off to Makkah.

On returning from the *Hajj*, he found Arab tribes pouring in Al-Madinah from all sides. The suburbs of Al-Madinah were now teeming with groups of warriors. He entrusted the divisional command of the vanguard to Talhah 🙵 and that of the right wing to Zubair 🙵, while Abdur-Rahmân bin Auf 🙵 was appointed to the command of the left wing of the army. When the army was drawn up, he put Ali 🙵 in charge of the caliphate, left Al-Madinah, and advanced towards Persia. At Sirâr, the first halt was ordered.

The fact that the *Amir-ul-Mu'minin* (Chief of the believers) himself was leading the army, filled them with unbounded confidence and enthusiasm. However, Uthmân bin Affân 🙵 called on the Caliph and said that it was not expedient that the Chief of the believers should go personally into the battlefield. Following this advice, Umar convened a general council of war at Sirâr and invited the opinion of everyone present. All unanimously exclaimed that the expedition could not terminate successfully unless the Chief of the believers led it himself.

Thereupon Abdur-Rahman bin Auf said, "I disapprove of such a suggestion. The Caliph's presence on the battlefield is too risky. In the case, a commander is killed in action, the Caliph can do the needful and keep the situation under complete control; but if Allâh forbid, the Caliph himself is eliminated, it would be extremely difficult to manage the affairs. Ali was also called from Al-Madinah to take part in this crucial deliberation. He and the elite of the Companions lent support to the opinion of Abdur-Rahman bin Auf.

Umar Fâruq got up and made a stirring speech and it ended up by addressing the people thus: "I had a mind to follow your counsel, but the elite of the Companions do not agree to this view. Now who else will do the job?" Following this decision, another problem raised its head. Who will then play the crucial role of commander of the Muslim army at this juncture? When Ali was proposed to shoulder the responsibility, but he refused to it, Abu Ubaidah and Khâlid bin Walid were busy with the expedition in Syria. The people were still in an uncertain frame of mind arguing about this question when Abdur-Rahmân bin Auf stood up and said: "I have found the man and there could not be a better one." Saying this he named Sa'd bin Abu Waqqâs. The entire council agreed including Umar. He was exalted among the Companions of the Prophet and was his maternal uncle. Sa'd bin Abu Waqqâs was then working among the Hawâzins as a collector of *Zakât*. A letter calling him back was immediately dispatched. He came to the Caliph of Islam after a few days. Until then the Muslim army stayed at Sirâr.

After issuing the necessary instructions and asking him to keep the headquarters aware of all the events and movements big or small, Umar dispatched the army under his able command. He set forth from Al-Madinah at the head of a detachment made up of four thousand troops and halted at Tha'labah after making eighteen marches. Directly after the departure of Sa'd's men, Umar Fâruq ﷺ sent a detachment of two thousand Yemeni soldiers and two thousand Najdi soldiers to reinforce the main force. Muthanna ﷺ was awaiting the arrival of Sa'd ﷺ at the village of Dhiqâr, where he was encamped with eight thousand men. It was Muthanna's intention to join Sa'd ﷺ and to advance towards the Euphrates, but the wounds which he had received in the battle of Jasr grew from bad to worse and he finally succumbed to them.

Sa'd bin Waqqâs ﷺ in Iraq

Marching from Tha'labah, Sa'd ﷺ pitched his camp at Sirâf. On route from Tha'labah to Sirâf, three thousand warriors of Banu Asad joined Sa'd's army under the order of the Caliph of Islam. At Sirâf, he was strengthened by two thousand fighters under Ash'ath bin Qais.

At the same place, Mu'anna bin Hârithah Shaibâni ﷺ, the brother of Muthanna ﷺ met Sa'd ﷺ and communicated to him the advice bequeathed by his departed brother regarding the enemy forces and their art of warfare. The eight thousand troops of Muthanna ﷺ joined Sa'd ﷺ there. The troops were counted in round figures to be between twenty and thirty thousand rank and file. The army included three hundred Companions, who were present during the pledge of Ridwân, while seventy of them had taken part in the battle of Badr.

Sa'd ﷺ was still at Sirâf when he received a fresh order from the Caliph directing him to proceed towards Qâdisiyah. The order further enjoined upon him to arrange himself in such a manner as to have the plains of Persia in front and the hills of Arabia in the rear. In this way, he might advance as far as he chose in case of victory and take refuge by retreating to the hills in case of defeat.

Sa'd bin Abu Waqqâs ﷺ decamped as ordered by the Caliph and nominated Zubair bin Abdullah bin Qatâdah as the officer of the vanguard. Abdullah bin Al-Mu'tasim was given the right flank, Shurahbil bin As-Samt Kindi the left, Âsim bin Umar At-Tamimi the rearguard; Salmân Fârisi was the supply officer, Abdur-Rahmân bin Rabi'ah Al-Bâhili the judge and treasurer, Hilâl Hijri the translator, Ziyâd bin Abu Sufyân the scribe or secretary.

From Sirâf, Sa'd 🙵 headed towards Qâdisiyah and arrived at Udhaib. Here the Persians kept their arsenal and military stores which the advancing army confiscated. On reaching Qâdisiyah, they had to wait for the Persian army for about two months. During this long stay, they would raid the surrounding Persian areas whenever they ran short of provisions and other necessities.

Rustam's Departure from Madâ'in

News began to pour into the Persian capital that the Arabian army was encamped in Qâdisiyah and they had ravaged the surrounding areas of the Euphrates. The people of Qâdisiyah and its suburbs stormed the court with complaints against the raids of the Muslim troops. They also threatened that if the needful were not done, they would be forced to obey them.

Rustam was wise enough to advise evasion instead of an open encounter. But the mounting pressure on Yezdgird, the Emperor of Persia, forced him to call Rustam, his war minister, to take action and go to Qâdisiyah personally to bring an end to the longstanding problem created by the Arabian force. Rustam was in favor of dispatching a number of detachments one after another to keep the Arabian forces too engaged to do anything anywhere else. However, Yezdgird disapproved of the plan outright with the result Rustam came under pressure to leave Madâ'in. He marched up to Sâbât where he was joined by forces from almost every part of the country in such great numbers that, in a short time, the total number of the Persian army rose to one hundred and fifty thousand. It was not only a well-equipped army but was showing a maddening rage and fervor against the Islamic forces.

Sa'd bin Abu Waqqâs 🙵 informed the Caliph of the new developments and enemy movements. Umar Fâruq 🙵 wrote back not to fear the least from the magnitude of the enemy forces and keep faith in Allâh the Almighty alone and seek His help and succor in the present position. The Caliph also asked the Commander of the Muslim army to dispatch a diplomatic mission to Yezdgird before engaging the Persians in battle with the object of inviting them to the Islamic faith. If the Emperor rejected the call, he would bear the brunt of his refusal. In pursuance of the instructions from the Caliph, Sa'd bin Abu Waqqâs ﷺ selected celebrated personages from the army who were renowned in Arabia for their sagacity, eloquence, imposing appearance, valor and ambition, and sent them from Qâdisiyah to Madâ'in.

Islamic Diplomatic Mission

The diplomatic mission included men of towering stature like Nu'mân bin Muqarrin, Qais bin Zurârah, Asha'th bin Qais, Furât bin Haiyân, Âsim bin Amr, Amr bin Ma'dikarib, Mughirah bin Shu'bah, Mu'anna bin Hârithah, Utârid bin Hâjib, Busr bin Abu Ruhm, Hanzalah bin Ar-Rabi' and Adi bin Suhail ﷺ. The ambassadors rode straight to Madâ'in at full gallop leaving behind the troops of Rustam. Informed of the arrival of the ambassadors of Islam, Yezdgird arranged his court in great pomp and splendor. When these Islamic ambassadors, the sons of the desert, entered the court in simple soldier-like style, the entire court was filled with wonder at the sight. After a preliminary question and answer session, Yezdgird asked with an air of self-conceit, "How did you dare face us? And how did you forget that your people are considered as foolish and disgraceful? Have you also forgotten that when you showed a sign of rising up, our governors and junior commissioned officers were ordered to put you right, and they did it." Having heard these words dipped in arrogance, Nu'mân bin Muqarrin ﷺ rose to answer with all the confidence at his command. He said in plain words, "We are determined to eradicate idol-worship and polytheism from the face of the earth and present Islam before one and all, for it is through Islam alone that man can attain peace and success. If anyone refuses to accept Islam, it is better for him to entrust himself to the Muslims for peace and safety and pay the *Jizyah*. In case he refuses to accept both, Islam or paying of the *Jizyah*, the matter is decided by the sword."

Speech of Qais bin Zurârah

This speech enraged Yezdgird but he spoke with self-control: "You people are simply brutes and much less in number. So you will never be able to cover any part of our land. However, I can do you this much as a favor that I will give you food to eat and clothes to wear and appoint for you an officer to treat you politely."

Hearing this Qais bin Zurârah stepped forward and said: "These personages before you are the very essence of Arabian society in virtue of the various gifts of head and heart with which they are endowed. Our noble chieftains and notables of Arabia are overtaken by shame when making a reply to such rubbish. However, I seek to reply to what you said right now and these companions of mine will verify it. Listen! The wretched condition of the Arabs and Arabia you have just described is far better than what we were existing in. But Allâh the Almighty bestowed His utmost favor on us when He sent His Prophet to guide us and to lead us to the right path and put the enemies of the truth and righteousness to disgrace and defeat and promised us victories on earth. Now it is better for you to either accept Islam or agree to pay us the *Jizyah* or you will have to cross swords with us."

Having heard this speech, Yezdgird lost his temper and said, "Had it been legitimate to kill ambassadors, I would have put to death all of you." He then ordered his servants to bring a basketful of earth and place it on the leader's head and he should be turned out from Madâ'in in the same state. He then added, "Rustam will shortly go to bury you all in the trenches of Qâdisiyah." Meanwhile the basket of earth was brought in. Âsim moved forward, put the basket on his shoulder saying, "I am chief of the ambassadors." He then immediately galloped off to Sa'd bin Abu Waqqâs ﷺ and said to him: "Accept my congratulations, for the enemy has voluntarily surrendered the earth of his territory to us." Sa'd ﷺ expressed his happiness over such an interpretation.

Followed by the return of the ambassadors, fresh orders came to Rustam from the imperial court of Persia at Sâbât along with reinforcing parties. A greater part of a sixty-thousand-man army was under the command of Rustam. The vanguard was headed by Jâlinus which consisted of forty thousand men; rearguard had twenty thousand soldiers; the right wing commanded by Hurmuzân had thirty thousand men while the left one under the command of Mehrân bin Bahrâm Râzi also had thirty thousand troops. Thus, the total number of Persian soldiers went up to one hundred and eighty thousand. Rustam had in his direct charge one hundred combat elephants while there were seventy-five elephants on the right flank, seventy-five on the left, twenty in the vanguard and thirty in the rearguard. Armed with war equipment and weapons on such a massive scale, Rustam marched from Sâbât and camped at Kutha. Now the distance between the Persian and the Muslim armies was much closer. Small raiding squads would come out from both sides to pounce on the other's provisions and other things of necessity.

Rustam preferred procrastination. He, therefore, spent about six months in covering the distance between Madâ'in and Qâdisiyah. At last, he was compelled to advance and face the Muslims. Pressing injunctions urging him to attack the Muslim forthwith rocked his command center. Contrary to the demand of the Persian Empire, Rustam wanted to achieve success without an encounter. Now in order to put off action still further, Rustam sent words to the Muslim Commander, Sa'd bin Abu Waqqâs ﷺ to depute one of his trusted men with whom the matter might be discussed.

Sa'd ﷺ sent Rib'i bin Âmir ﷺ. Rustam adorned his court with unwanted splendor and pomp to prepare for the audience with the Muslim ambassador. The entire court was carpeted with cloth of gold, the pillows were of rich silk, while a gem bedecked throne was placed in the center. Rib'i ﷺ came right up to the richly carpeted floor and dismounting from his horse, attached the reins to a pillow. He them moved on supported by a spear piercing into the carpet and cutting it and making holes in it with its point and sat beside Rustam. The courtiers made an attempt to pull him down from the throne and disarm him. Thereupon Rib'i ﷺ thundered, "I have come on invitation and not of my own. Our religion strictly forbids anybody sitting like God and the rest standing before him with their hands folded." Now Rustam intervened and asked them not to do anything against the will of the envoy.

However, on second thought Rib'i ﷺ dismounted from the throne, slit a portion of the carpet with his dagger and sat on the earth and said addressing Rustam, "We are not at all in need of your carpet. The earth spread by Allâh the Almighty is enough for us." Rustam then asked Rib'i ﷺ through the interpreter, "What is your object in waging war against us?" Rib'i ﷺ replied, "We intend to bring the slaves of Allâh the Almighty to the expanse of the next world from the narrowness of this world and promote justice and Islam in place of atrocities and false religions. Anyone who adopts justice and Islam will find us non-interfering in regard to his wealth, property and country. But we shall fight with whoever stands in our way until we go either to Paradise or attain victory. If you seek to pay the *Jizyah*, we shall accept it and will cease to go against you and you will find us standing by you if and when you need us for the safety of your life and property." Having heard this Rustam inquired, "Are you the chief of the Muslims?" Rib'i ﷺ replied, "No, I am an ordinary soldier. But each one of us, even the most ordinary can speak on behalf of the most powerful person, and every person has full power in every matter."

The utterances of Rib'i ﷺ left Rustam and his courtiers dumbfounded. Rustam then said, "The scabbard of your sword is quite rotten." Rib'i ﷺ drew his sword out of the sheathe and said, "But it has been tempered very recently." Rustam again said, the blade of your spear is very small. How can it be of any use in battles?" Rib'i ﷺ replied, "This blade pierces deep into the chest of the enemy and goes across it. Have you not seen that a spark is enough to burn down an entire city?" After this brief war of words, Rustam said, "Well, I shall ponder over your utterances and hold consultation with my men of sound judgment." Rib'i ﷺ got up and rode to Sa'd bin Abu Waqqâs ﷺ.

Next day, Rustam sent a fresh message to Sa'd ﷺ requesting him to send an emissary to him. Sa'd ﷺ sent Hudhaifah bin Mihsan ﷺ. He also entered the court riding his horse giving an air of the same stubbornness, which Rib'i ﷺ had displayed previously. He drew close to the throne on horseback. Rustam said, "What's the reason that you have been sent today instead of the one who had come to me last time?" Hudhaifah ﷺ replied, 'Our Commander does justice to one and all and gives everyone an opportunity to do everything. It was his turn yesterday and it is my turn today." Rustam then asked him, "How much respite could you give me?" Hudhaifah ﷺ said, "For three days only from this day." Rustam kept silent, and Hudhaifah ﷺ rode back straight to Muslim camp. The stubbornness and presence of mind of Hudhaifah ﷺ left Rustam and his courtiers astonished.

Next day again Rustam requested an envoy from the Muslim camp and Mughirah bin Shu'bah ﷺ was sent to play his role. Rustam tried both temptation and terror but Mughirah ﷺ remained unmoved and paid him in the same coin. Helpless and embarrassed, Rustam said in a fit of anger, "I shall never enter into any peace agreement with you and I will kill all of you." Mughirah ﷺ got up and left peacefully for his camp.

The Battle of Qâdisiyah

Close on the departure of Mughirah ﷺ, Rustam ordered preparations for a decisive battle. A canal separated the armies. Rustam ordered a bridge to be constructed over the canal, and it was completed within a short period. Rustam then sent word to his counterpart as to who should cross the bridge. Sa'd ﷺ invited him to cross. Thus, the large and strong Persian army moved across the bridge and battle lines were drawn up. Amr bin Ma'dikarib, Âsim bin Amr, and Rib'i bin Âmir ﷺ moved through the Muslim army rousing the soldiers for *Jihâd*, poets went singing martial songs and the reciters of the Qur'ân recited *Sûrat Al-Anfâl*. Sa'd ﷺ could not lead his army into the battlefield for he was then suffering from boils and also sciatica, so he was unable to move or ride a horse. Khâlid bin Urfutah was, therefore, asked to command the Muslim soldiers.

Hurmuz, a well-known Persian prince and wrestler came out first. Ghâlib bin Abdullah Asadi accepted the challenge for a duel and advanced to meet him. Hurmuz was held in no time and brought to Sa'd ﷺ. Another eminent horseman from the Persian ranks threw a challenge which was duly accepted by Âsim ﷺ. However, a stroke or two scared him off. But Âsim ﷺ gave him chase and caught his horse by its tail and dragged Hurmuz back from under the nose of the Persian vanguard. The valor of Âsim ﷺ maddened with anger another noted Persian wrestler who moved forward with a silver mace in his hand. Amr bin Ma'dikarib ﷺ advanced to meet his challenge, apprehended him at once and put him on his side.

Now protests from the Persian warriors compelled Rustam to launch an all-out assault on the Muslim troops, and by way of a war strategy, combat elephants were set off to attack the Muslim ranks. Bujailah tribe obstructed them at the cost of heavy casualties. Sa'd ﷺ who was watching the battle scene very minutely, reinforced the Bujailah with Banu Asad who showed utmost manliness in the assigned duty. But when they also showed signs of reverses, the warriors of Banu Kindah took the field and made such a heavy charge that the Persians were forced to show their back. In view of constant retreat and repulses, Rustam ordered a joint attack. Sa'd ﷺ cried *Takbir* (*Allâhu Akbar* - Allâh is the Most Great) at the top of his voice and the entire Muslim army joining the *Takbir* of Sa'd ﷺ, charged the Persian troops. It looked as if two oceans or mountains collided against each other. When the rival forces were mixed up, the Persian elephants began to cause heavy casualties on the Muslim side. Sa'd ﷺ immediately ordered the archers to shoot arrows at the elephants and their riders. Âsim ﷺ charged at the elephants with his lance followed by others who commenced inflicting deep wounds on the elephants' trunks with their spears and swords. With the result that the elephants retreated leaving the Muslim swordsmen to display their mettle. After an all day long battle, night intervened to stop it until the next day.

Early the next morning after the *Fajr* (dawn) prayer, Sa'd ﷺ buried the martyred in the eastern part of Qâdisiyah. The engagement had left a toll of five hundred men martyred on Muslim side. After sunrise, the armies arrayed themselves against each other once again. Fighting had not yet started when Muslim reinforcements from Syria headed by Hâshim bin Utbah were reported to be approaching. With one thousand fighters, the officer of the vanguard Qa'qâ' bin Amr ﷺ gave the news to Sa'd ﷺ and took the field with his permission. He first challenged for a duel and Bihman Jâdhwaih came forward but was killed by Qa'qâ' ﷺ. After a number of Persian strongmen were killed, Rustam ordered an all-out attack.

Heavy fighting took place. Informed of the prevailing situation, Hâshim bin Utbah, the reinforcements' commander, divided his six thousand strong detachment into small segments and each of them entered into the battlefield with the cry of *Allâhu Akbar* (Allâh is the

Most Great) at short intervals. This new development sent terror into the hearts of the Persian troops. However, their combat elephants were a menace to the Muslims even on this day. At last the Muslim soldiers devised a new plan. They put on their camels long coverings so that they looked like elephants, with the result that the Persians' horses were scared off by the fearful sight inflicting on Persian army even heavier losses. Qa'qâ' 🙵 killed many renowned Persian officers and well-known horsemen. The daylong battle left one thousand martyred on the Muslim side and ten thousand dead on the enemy's side.

The third day, Sa'd 🙵 buried the martyrs just after performing *Fajr* (dawn) prayer and delivered the wounded to the accompanying women to be bandaged and nursed. Then the battle line was drawn between the two forces. The Persians put their elephants at the head. However, Qa'qâ' 🙵 and Âsim 🙵 launched together such a fierce assault on the leading white elephant that it fell dead. When another elephant was targeted, it fled for its life and all the other elephants followed suit creating havoc and causing tremendous loses to the Persian side.

The two forces separated in the evening only for a short while after fighting all day long. And the battle, which began again after sunset, continued until the next morning. Neither Sa'd 🙵 nor Rustam could perceive the battle conditions due to the darkness and loud battle cries. Sa'd 🙵, the commander of the Muslim army, kept praying through the whole night. Sometime after midnight in the din of battle, he heard Qa'qâ' 🙵 yell: "Gather together to attack the main body and catch Rustam." This auspicious voice not only brought satisfaction to Sa'd 🙵 but infused new courage and determination in the Muslim troops.

Extremely exhausted after a daylong battle, all the tribes rose as one man to charge forcefully at the enemy. When the horsemen of Qa'qâ' 🙵 reached near Rustam, he got down from his throne and began to fight. However, on being wounded he took to his heels. But Hilâl bin Ullafah chased him and hit him so powerfully with his spear that his hip was broken and he fell down in a nearby canal. Hilâl dismounted from his horse at once, pulled him out by his legs and put him to death. Following this Hilâl called out at the top of his voice standing on Rustam's throne: "By Allâh, I have killed Rustam." Having heard this announcement, the Muslim troops cried *Allâhu Akbar* (Allâh is the Most Great) and the Persian soldiers were left shocked and astonished. They fled the battlefield. Out of thirty thousand Persian cavaliers only thirty saved their lives. About six thousand Muslims were honored with martyrdom. Sa'd 🙵 gave all the belonging of Rustam to Hilâl bin Ullafah. Qa'qâ' 🙵 and Shurahbil 🙵 were asked by Sa'd 🙵 to chase the Persian fugitives but Zuhrah bin Hawiyah had already done this job and killed Jâlinus who was collecting the runaway Persian soldiers, and seized his belongings. Sa'd 🙵 had some reservations about handing over the belongings of Jâlinus to Zuhrah but Umar Fâruq 🙵 ordered to give them all to Zuhrah and appreciated his services. Immediately after the peace of victory prevailed, Sa'd 🙵 collected the spoils of war and wrote a letter to Umar Fâruq 🙵, the Caliph of Islam, giving him glad tidings of the Muslim victory. A speeding courier was sent to Al-Madinah with the letter.

Ever since the commencement of the campaign of Qâdisiyah, Umar 🙵 used to go out of Al-Madinah at daybreak and await the messenger from the war zone. One day, according to his habit, he went out of the city and saw a camel rider speeding from the opposite direction. Umar 🙵 eagerly advanced and asked him where he was coming from? He said that he was coming from Qâdisiyah with good news. Allâh the Almighty has crowned the Muslims with a clear victory. The Caliph began to make inquires from him. He was running by the side of the camel and plied its rider with questions. The camel rider on entering the precincts of the city found that every man whom they passed addressed his companion on foot as '*Amir-ul-Mu'minin*'. He trembled with fear and said, "My leader, why did you not tell me your name so that I may not have been unwittingly guilty of this misunderstanding?" Umar 🙵 reassured him observing: "Do not be uneasy. There is no harm done. Go on with your news." So he walked by the side of the camel rider on the way to his house. Then convening a large conference of the people of Al-Madinah he told them the joyful tidings and made an eloquent and stirring speech which ended thus:

"O Muslims, I am not a king that it should be my desire to make you my slaves. I am myself a slave of Allâh, though the responsibilities of the caliphate have been made to be heavy upon my head. I should deem myself fortunate if I served you in a manner that secured your sound and tranquil sleep in your homes, but I would be a miserable wretch if it were my desire to make you wait constantly upon me and mount a guard at my doors. It is my object to instruct you not only by words, but by my deeds also."

Conquest of Babylon and Kutha

After their flight from Qâdisiyah, the Persians quartered themselves at Babylon. A number of renowned generals set themselves to making preparations for giving battle again. Fugitives of the battle of Qâdisiyah were also collected and encouraged to avenge their defeat. Sa'd ﷺ stayed in Qâdisiyah for about two months after the Muslim victory. On receiving fresh orders from the Caliph, he marched to Madâ'in leaving his family in Qâdisiyah. Before his departure he dispatched Zuhrah bin Hawiyah at the head of the vanguard who marched on killing, removing and enslaving his enemies until he reached Babylon. Sa'd ﷺ also joined him there with his troops. With the news of the arrival of Sa'd ﷺ, the Persian generals left Babylon and moved to Madâ'in, Ahwâz and Nihâwand destroying the bridges on the way and making the Tigris and its canals impossible to cross. When Sa'd ﷺ heard of the flight of the Persians, he sent Zuhrah at their back and moved behind him at the head of a big army.

When Zuhrah arrived at Kutha, Shahryâr opposed him and came personally onto the battlefield, he challenged the bravest of the Arabs to meet him in single combat. Zuhrah said, "I had intended to fight with you, but in view of your bragging and vaunting, a slave will confront you and he will put down your arrogance." Thus saying he motioned Nâ'il bin Ju'shum A'raj, a slave of the Tamim clan, who pressed his charger forward. Shahryâr had the proportions and strength of a giant. Seeing in Nâ'il a weak and puny adversary, he flung away his lance and grasping him by the throat, pulled him off his horse, hurled him to the ground and then sat upon his chest. Now, as chance would have it, Shahryâr's thumb went into Nâ'il's mouth who bit it so severely that Shahryâr was beside himself with pain. Nâ'il taking advantage of the opportunity sprang up lightly and sitting on the breast of his adversary, plunged his dagger deep into the body of Shahryâr ripping his stomach open. With the sight of the killing of Shahryâr, the Persian troops took to their heels. Shahryâr was clad in brilliant robes and armed with excellent weapons. Nâ'il stripped him off all and placed them before Sa'd 餐. In order to teach his followers a lesson, Sa'd 餐 ordered Nâ'il to put on the dress and armor of the slain warrior. In pursuance of this command, Nâ'il arrayed in the gaudy effects and splendid accouterment of Shahryâr, came before the public assembly and as the people saw him, the vivid spectacle of the ironies of the world and the fickleness of fortunes passed before their eyes.

The Fall of Bahurasir

Kutha was the historical place where Nimrod is said to have imprisoned Abraham (Ibrahim 餐). The dungeon was still preserved as a relic. Sa'd 餐 paid a visit to this sanctuary. At some distance from Kutha was Bahurasir, a city in close proximity to the capital. A very strong squad of the imperial guard and a huge garrison were kept in Bahurasir to guard the seat of power. The Tigris alone intervened between Bahurasir and Madâ'in. Sa'd 餐 advanced and laid siege to Bahurasir. At last, the people of the city came out to face the Muslims but it resulted in their death and destruction. Yezdgird took to flight along with his treasure upon the fall of Bahurasir, his flight marked that the Muslims were still not totally out of danger.

Horses across the River

Sa'd 餐 was now in a rush to capture Madâ'in. However, the Tigris lay in the way. The fleeing Persians had demolished and broken all the bridges. When Sa'd 餐 arrived at the bank of the Tigris, he found neither bridge nor boats. The next day Sa'd 餐 mounted on his horse and said after getting his troops ready, "Who among you is brave enough to promise to save me from an enemy onslaught while I cross the river?" Âsim bin Amr 餐 came forward and offered his services.

He sat on raised ground at the bank of Tigris with a squadron of six hundred archers. Sa'd ﷺ recited:

> "We seek the Help of Allâh, entrust on Him, Allâh is enough for us and what an Excellent Supporter He is. There is no might and strength but with Allâh Who is High and Great."

He then charged right into the surging water of the Tigris. Others also followed suit and rushed their horses into the river. The river was deep and fast moving but the turbulent conditions could not affect the resolute and undaunted spirits of the Muslim army. The waves slammed furiously against the sides of the horses, but the horsemen steered their course coolly and in perfect order. When the cavalry was half way cross the river, the Persian archers began to shoot arrows at the Muslim troops but in vain. The Muslim fighters crossed the river by force and put the opposing force to death.

The Conquest of Madâ'in

With the news of the crossing of the river by the Muslims, Yezdgird took flight from Madâ'in. The Muslim troops began to enter the city from different directions. Sa'd ﷺ stepped in the White Palace (royal palace) reciting the Verses:

> "How many of gardens and springs do they left. And green crops and goodly places. And comforts of life wherein they used to take delight! Thus! And we made other people inherit them." (44:25-28)

He offered eight *Rakât* (units) of *Salât-ul-Fath* (victory prayer). In the palace of Kisra (Chosroes), a pulpit was set up in place of the royal throne and the Friday prayer was performed there. This was the first Friday prayer that was performed in the Persian capital. Nothing of the paintings, portraits and images were destroyed. The commander of the Muslim army ordered that the treasures and curiosities of the royal palaces should be brought and accumulated in one place. There were vast riches including thousands of rare and priceless heirlooms handed down and preserved from the Kayâni dynasty until the time of Nushirwân. They included the coats of mail and swords of the monarchs of the Empires of China, the Emperor of Rome, Dâhir Shah of India, Bahrâm Gour, Nu'mân bin Mundhir, Siyawash. The poniards, swords, coats of mail and the helmets of Kisra, Hurmuz and Firoz were also preserved in the royal museum. The Persians were proud of their antique possessions. Sa'd ﷺ permitted Qa'qâ' ﷺ to choose for himself one of the swords. He was pleased to pick the sword of Heraclius, the Roman monarch. Sa'd ﷺ gave him also the coat of mail of Bahrâm Gour.

Sa'd ﷺ dispatched to the seat of the caliphate all the priceless possessions and curiosities of the conquered palaces of Persia. The most wonderful and exquisitely magnificent of all was a carpet which the Persians called *Bahâr* (Spring). After the season of ethereal mildness was over, this carpet was used for the feast of wine. The carpet was provided with all the effects of spring, which art and wealth could allow to be imitated. In the center was a bucolic landscape bordered on all sides with ornamental avenues around which trees and plants of various descriptions were laden with buds and flowers and fruits. Everything was worked in gold, silver and precious stones. The ground work was of gold, the greenery of emerald, the borders of topaz, the trees of gold and silver, the leaves of silk and the fruits were gems. Umar Fâruq ﷺ distributed the booty among the troops. With regard to the celebrated carpet, the public opinion was that it should not be distributed but preserved. Ali ﷺ persistently held aloof from this opinion and at his instance this carpet also was distributed among the people in cut up pieces. The piece Ali ﷺ shared was not so fine, however, he sold it for thirty thousand dinars.

The Conquest of Jalula

When Madâ'in fell to the Muslims, Yezdgird fled to Hulwân. Kharzâd bin Farkhzâd, brother of Rustam Farkhzâd, who was the commander-in-chief, displayed great skill in gathering a large army. He had a moat built around the city and the fort. *Gokhru* (the many-pointed thorns of murex) were scattered along the roadsides and pathways. These military preparations were so massive that the Muslim camp easily became aware of it. Sa'd ﷺ on receiving the news, wrote to Umar ﷺ who replied that Hâshim bin Utbah should be sent on this expedition at the head of twelve thousand troops. The command of the vanguard, the right wing, the left wing, and the rearguard should be entrusted to Qa'qâ', Ma'shar bin Mâlik, Amr bin Mâlik and Amr bin Murrah respectively.

Hâshim, marching from Madâ'in, reached Jalula on the fourth day and laid siege of the city. The siege continued for several months. Occasionally the Persians would make a sudden attack on the besiegers. In this manner many engagements were contested in which the Persians invariably met with reverses. However, the city was stocked with supplies and provisions of all sorts and their forces numbered hundreds of thousands, they did not lose heart. One day they rushed out recklessly but their forces were smashed leaving about one hundred thousand troops dead and spoils worth thirty million.

When Yezdgird learned the news of the disaster of Jalula, he left Hulwân for Rey, placing Khusru Shanum, an officer of renown, in charge of Hulwân with a few squadrons of cavalry. Qa'qâ' ۰۰۰ was dispatched to Hulwân at the head of some troops. A short but fierce struggle ensued in which Khusru Shanum was routed.

While communicating the joyful tidings of the victory, Sa'd ۰۰۰ dispatched a fifth portion of the booty to Al-Madinah. Ziyâd ۰۰۰, the messenger, described the battle with an eloquence which did him immense credit. Umar ۰۰۰ asked him to recount the events in the same eloquent style before a public assembly. A public assembly was accordingly convened and Ziyâd ۰۰۰ narrated the incidents of the battle with a command of language and an eloquence that portrayed the fray in its minutest detail. Afterwards Ziyâd ۰۰۰ brought forth the spoils, which were stored in the courtyard of the mosque.

In the morning the mantle, which covered the goods was drawn aside, heaps of precious stones were revealed. Tears ran down the face of Umar ۰۰۰ as the sight met his gaze. Abdur-Rahmân bin Auf ۰۰۰ said to him, "Why do you weep instead of giving thanks?" Umar Fâruq ۰۰۰ replied, "Where riches appear, envy and jealousy are bound to follow in their wake."

In response to Sa'd's seeking the Caliph's permission to march towards Persia, he ordered him to take a rest for some days as the Muslim soldiers were exhausted and needed it.

Syrian Engagements

The Fall of Hims

Abu Ubaidah bin Al-Jarrâh ﷺ marched to Hims and halted at Dhul-Kala'. Hims is one of the important districts of Syria. In ancient times it was greatly noted because of a temple dedicated to the sun. People would come from distant places on pilgrimage to this temple, and its devotees prided themselves on this fact. After the fall of Damascus and Jordan, three important cities remained to be conquered, which would mean the subjugation of the whole of Syria. They were Hims, Antâkiyah (Antioch) and Jerusalem. When the Muslim army camped at Dhul-Kala', Heraclius sent General Taudhar to engage them in the battle. Another General Shams was also ordered to join the attack. However, both of them were completely routed and Abu Ubaidah ﷺ killed Shams.

When the fleeing soldiers reached Hims, Heraclius left for Ar-Ruha. Abu Ubaidah ﷺ marched on and besieged Hims. And, in spite of the best efforts of Heraclius, the people of Hims remained without any outside help. At last they yielded followed by Hamah, Al-Lâdhiqiyah and Salamyah.

Fall of Qinnasrin

Following the conquest of Salamyah, Khâlid bin Walid ﷺ, with the permission of Abu Ubaidah ﷺ, marched to Qinnasrin where Minâs, only second to Heraclius in position, faced Khâlid ﷺ but tasted defeat after a fierce encounter. He took refuge in a citadel but Khâlid ﷺ captured it after laying siege to it. Umar Fâruq ﷺ grew happy and added to his power and authority.

Conquest of Halab and Antâkiyah

After finishing his task in Qinnasrin, Abu Ubaidah ﷺ marched to Halab (Aleppo) where he came to know that the people of Qinnasrin had risen in revolt. He at once dispatched a squadron to the spot of the disturbance. When they were brought under siege, they expressed their loyalty once again and saved themselves by paying a heavy penalty. Abu Ubaidah 🕮 halted near Halab and sent in advance Iyâd bin Ghanam, the commanding officer of the vanguard. He marched to Halab and laid a siege around the city, which surrendered to the Muslims.

After Halab, Abu Ubaidah's next target was Antâkiyah (Antioch), which was the Asian capital of Heraclius. It was a fortified city with a number of royal palaces. Thus the fleeing and fugitive Christians took refuge in this city. When the Muslim troops arrived at Antâkiyah, the Christians came out to face the Muslims and were completely routed and fled back to the city. When they came under siege, they earned peace in return for paying the *Jizyah*.

News then came to the Muslim camp that Christian troops were gathering in Mu'arrah Masrin, a place near Halab. Abu Ubaidah 🕮 marched to punish the antagonists and the result was a bloody fight between the two forces which resulted in their earning peace like the people of Halab. Antâkiyah was reported to have again risen in revolt but Iyâd bin Ghanam and Habib bin Maslamah were already there to crush it by force.

The repeated uprisings of the Christians in different regions were putting the Muslim troops to great hardships. Abu Ubaidah 🕮 brought the situation to the knowledge of Umar Fâruq 🕮. He ordered Muslim squadrons to be deputed to all the trouble spots at the cost of *Bait-ul-Mâl* (public exchequer). After the fall of Antâkiyah, dozens of surrounding villages and towns came on their own to the fold of the Muslim forces.

Fall of Baghrâs, Mar'ash and Hadath

After winning decisive victories throughout Syria and deputing Muslim commanding officers and administrators to all the cities under Muslims possession, Abu Ubaidah 🕮 turned towards Palestine. A Muslim detachment under the command of Maisarah bin Masruq was dispatched to Baghrâs, a town in the neighborhood of Antâkiyah bordering on the frontier of Asia Minor. Many of the Arab Christians such as the Ghassâns, the Tanukh and the Iyyâds were preparing at this place to accompany the Romans to the Emperor Heraclius. Maisarah bin Masruq attacked them and a fierce conflict took place. Abu Ubaidah ﷺ dispatched reinforcements under Mâlik bin Ashtar Nakh'i. With the arrival of fresh troops, the Christians fled in terror. Khâlid bin Walid ﷺ led a column against Mar'ash which capitulated on the condition that the Christians should evacuate the city. In the same way Habib bin Maslamah marched to Hadath (old name of Ararat Mountain) and conquered it.

Conquest of Qaisâriyah and Ajnâdain

In course of time when Muslim troops were winning victories in Antâkiyah and its suburbs, Yazid bin Abu Sufyân, the governor of Damascus sent his brother, Mu'âwiyah bin Abu Sufyân towards Qaisâriyah (Caesarea or Kayseri) as per the Caliph's order. After a heavy toll of eighty thousand Christians, the city fell to the Muslims.

Heraclius now ordered Artabun, a noted general, to gather troops in Ajnâdain. Artabun kept a huge army under his direct command and two other detachments in Ramlah and Jerusalem. Well-equipped and huge in number, the opponents of Islam were awaiting the arrival of the Muslim force. Amr bin Al-Âs ﷺ marched to Ajnâdain to face Artabun while he dispatched Alqamah bin Hakim Firâsi and Masrur bin Al-Akki to Jerusalem and Abu Ayub Al-Mâliki to Ramlah with the permission of Abu Ubaidah ﷺ. A fierce battle was fought in Ajnâdain. It was a conflict similar to Yarmuk. Artabun could not muster courage to face Amr bin Al-Âs ﷺ and fled to Jerusalem and the city fell to the Muslim forces.

Conquest of Jerusalem

After the flight of Artabun to Jerusalem, Amr bin Al-Âs ﷺ conquered Ghazzah (Gaza), Sabastiyah, Nâbulus (Nablus), Ludd, Amawâs, Bait Jibrin, and Yâfa (Yafo). He then proceeded to Jerusalem and tightened the siege. About the same time, Abu Ubaidah ﷺ had proceeded to Palestine. The news of his arrival disheartened the besieged Christians who were defending themselves until then. They were left with no alternative but to make peace negotiations. All of them knew about the readiness of the

Muslims to accept a peace proposal and their easy terms. However, the Christians of Jerusalem put a novel condition on finalizing the peace agreement. They wanted the Caliph of Islam to reach Jerusalem to write down the peace document. Even though the fall of the city was only a matter of time, Abu Ubaidah ﷺ was in favor of avoiding further death and destruction, so he preferred peace to war. He wrote a letter to the Caliph delineating the whole account of events with the request that his arrival in Jerusalem could win for them the city without shedding a drop of blood.

Umar Fâruq ﷺ convened a meeting of all the distinguished Companions and consulted them. Uthmân ﷺ declared that the Christians had been struck with terror and lost heart and that if the Caliph were to reject their request, they would be still more humiliated, and consider that the Muslims regarded them with utter contempt, they would lay down their arms unconditionally. Ali ﷺ, however, dissented from this view and gave the contrary opinion. Umar ﷺ shared the same opinion.

Umar Fâruq's Journey to Palestine

On this historic mission to Jerusalem, a bag full of parched barley meal, a camel, a slave, and a wooden cup were all the belongings of Umar Fâruq ﷺ, the Chief of the Muslims, when he left Al-Madinah, the headquarters of Islam. Leaving Uthmân ﷺ in charge of Al-Madinah, he set out on the journey noted for its strain and stress.

It was a novel scenario of Islamic equality and human dignity that the journey undertaken had at times the Caliph on the camel and the slave walking along holding the halter of the camel and vice versa. It was the journey of a magnificent and powerful Islamic ruler whose cavalry had already trampled down palaces and crowns and thrones under the hooves of its horses. It was Rajab 16 AH, when Madâ'in and Antâkiyah (Antioch) had been conquered.

The commanders of the Muslim forces at Damascus and Jerusalem were already informed about the movement of the Caliph of Islam. Thus Yazid bin Abu Sufyân, Abu Ubaidah bin Al-Jarrâh and Khâlid bin Walid ﷺ received the Caliph of Islam with exemplary honor. But when

Umar ﷺ saw them arrayed in brilliant dresses and imposing appearance, he flew into a fit of rage at the sight of them that he remarked: "Within the short span of two years have you fallen into Persian habits?" But when the officers explained that they had their weapons beneath the silken tunics and they had not lost their Arabian character, the Caliph gained peace of heart.

A Peace Document for the Christians

The Chief of believers sojourned for a long while at Jâbiah where some of the nobles of the city proceeded to see him and the treaty was drawn up there which is as follows:

"This is the peace document, which the Chief of the Muslims has written for the people of Iylia'. Peace is given to one and all in Iylia', peace of life and property, and peace to their church, cross, sick, healthy and to the followers of all religions. Nobody is allowed to reside in their churches nor will they be demolished nor are their boundaries to be damaged nor their cross to be desecrated nor their religion to be defiled. Moreover, Jews will not be allowed to live with them in Iylia'. The people of Iylia' are duty-bound to pay the *Jizyah* and turn out the Greeks and Romans. And those among the Greeks and Romans who will leave the city, their life and property will be provided perfect safety until they reach a place of safety. If a Roman prefers to live in Iylia', he is bound to give the *Jizyah* like the rest of the citizens; if an Iylian intends to go with the Romans, he will enjoy complete peace until he reaches a protected place. Whatever this treaty contains is to be fulfilled by Allâh, the Caliphs of Islam and the entire Muslim community provided the Iylians pay the *Jizyah*."

The elite of the Companions like Khâlid bin Walid, Amr bin Al-Âs, Abdur-Rahmân bin Auf and Mu'âwiyah ﷺ subscribed to it. The people of Jerusalem paid the *Jizyah* on the spot and opened the doors of the city. The people of Ramlah also followed suit. Umar Fâruq ﷺ entered Bait-ul-Maqdis (the Dome of the Rock) barefooted. First of all he went to the Mosque of Al-Aqsa and approaching the Arch of David he recited the Verse from the Qur'ân which speaks of the

Prophet David (Dâwud ﷺ) as bowing down to Allâh the Almighty and then he prostrated himself in humble obeisance. He then visited the church of the Christians and walked around the building for sometime.

Fall of Takrit and Jazirah

Takrit was under a junior Persian commissioned officer. When he heard of the fall of Madâ'in, he drew the attention of the Romans to the incident. The Romans also joined the cause easily because they were also against the Muslim forces. Other Christian Arab tribes such as Iyyâd, Taghlib and Namir also followed suit. On the instruction of Umar Fâruq ﷺ, Sa'd bin Abu Waqqâs ﷺ deputed Abdullah bin Al Mu'tam to head the expedition. Abdullah marched on Takrit at the head of five thousand troops and invaded the city. After a bloody battle, the joint Roman and Persian forces were beaten. Most of the Arabian clans embraced Islam.

The province of Jazirah fell between the frontiers of Syria and Iraq and was at times annexed by both the Empires. Successive campaigns and victories of the Muslim forces sent terror into the hearts of the people of Jazirah. They wrote to Heraclius to send a force to guard the eastern cities against the ensuing Muslim attack and they promised to jointly rise to lend their help and support to Heraclius' troops. Heraclius, thinking it to be a sign from the God, dispatched his troops to the eastern cities of Syria. Assessing the crucial situation, Umar Fâruq ﷺ instructed Sa'd ﷺ to keep a check on the forward movement of the people of Jazirah and wrote Abu Ubaidah ﷺ to obstruct the march of Heraclius' detachment towards Hims and Qinnasrin. Both the commanders did their job appreciably well and Iyâd bin Ghanam ﷺ captured the province of Jazirah after small skirmishes. This event took place in 17 AH.

Return of Iyyâd Tribe

When Jazirah fell to the Muslims the Iyyâd tribe, which confessed Christianity, shifted to Heraclius' territory in self-exile and settled there. Informed of the event, Umar Fâruq ﷺ wrote to Heraclius:

"I have been informed that a tribe from among the Arabian tribes has left our country to settle in your cities. If you refuse to turn them out from your country, we shall send to you all the Christians inhabiting our territory."

Immediately after the receipt of this warning from the Caliph of Islam, Heraclius issued orders to banish the people of the Iyyâd tribe numbering four thousand in all. They went back to Syria and Jazirah and settled there. Umar Fâruq ﷺ appointed Habib bin Maslamah and Walid bin Uqbah administrators of Iraq-Ajam and Iraq-Arab respectively. On the return of the Arabs, he wrote Walid bin Uqbah not to force Islam on them and accept the *Jizyah* from them if they so desired. Granting no choice but Islam is a practice, which should be adopted only in case of the Arab Peninsula and Yemen. However the principle applies to the progeny of Muslim parents and they cannot be converted to Christianity by force. Moreover, none should be held back from coming to the fold of Islam.

Walid bin Uqbah made no delay in implementing the orders of Umar Fâruq ﷺ. A few days after, the Iyyâd sent a deputation to Al-Madinah with the request that no amount should be collected from them in the name of *Jizyah*. Umar Fâruq ﷺ issued orders to collect from them double the amount in the name of *Sadqah* (charity) in place of *Jizyah* (tax), which the Iyyâd accepted happily. After some days, the tribe lodged a complaint against Walid bin Uqbah. The Caliph took prompt action and appointed Furât bin Haiyân and Hind bin Amr Al-Jamali to do the job and deposed Walid bin Uqbah without delay.

Deposition of Khâlid bin Walid ﷺ

People are generally mistaken about the event of the deposition of Khâlid bin Walid ﷺ. They subscribe to the misconception that Umar Fâruq ﷺ had deposed Khâlid bin Walid ﷺ soon with his installation as the Caliph of Islam. The fact is that Umar ﷺ did not deposed him during the earlier period of his Caliphate, he had only curtailed his position by reducing him to a deputy commander from commander-in-chief of the Muslim army. Now he had to first consult and receive permission from Abu Ubaidah bin Al-Jarrâh ﷺ before any action, so his leading of Muslim forces through dangerous adventures came to an end.

The incident of Khâlid's deposition occurred in the last months of 17 AH. Umar Fâruq ﷺ used to keep himself informed of the activities of every commander, general, officer and governor. Even though every governor or commander had to inform the Caliph with the account of matters and affairs of all kinds, he also had correspondents in every city and military wing who wrote to him about events and incidents that would take place in their areas of activity.

Thus a correspondent of the Caliph once informed him that on his return to Syria after the fall of Jazirah, Khâlid bin Walid ﷺ had brought with him immense riches and property and granted ten thousand dirhams to Ash'ath bin Qais, a poet, in return for writing an ode for him. Umar ﷺ addressed a letter to Abu Ubaidah bin Al-Jarrâh ﷺ instructing him: "Ask Khâlid in the presence of an audience whether he has made the present in question out of his own purse or from the public treasury. In case he has given it from his own purse, it is a sheer extravagance; and if he has given it from the public treasury, he has committed an offence of criminal breach of trust; and in either case he deserves to be deposed. Let his neck be tied with his own turban. But, if he admits his fault then he is to be forgiven."

Accordingly, he was called before a public gathering. The Caliph's messenger inquired of him, "Wherefrom did you make this present?" Khâlid bin Walid ﷺ kept silent and held back from confessing his fault. Thus the messenger found himself under compulsion to remove his turban and tie his neck with it. On asking again, Khâlid ﷺ revealed that he had given the reward to Ash'ath from his own possessions, not from the public treasury. Hearing this the messenger untied his neck and reported the matter to the Caliph who called Khâlid ﷺ to Al-Madinah for an explanation.

Khâlid bin Walid ﷺ said to the Caliph: "Umar! By Allâh, you are not doing justice to me." Umar ﷺ said to him, "Wherefrom have you collected so much wealth and how did you give away such a substantial amount to a poet for a reward?" Khâlid ﷺ said, "I had given it from my share of booty." Khâlid ﷺ further said, "Well, I will deposit with the public treasury any amount I have exceeding sixty thousand." Thus, after checking the whole account, twenty thousand dirhams exceeded the stipulated amount, which was immediately deposited with the public treasury and the matter was cleared up in good faith from both sides. It was a weakness with Khâlid bin Walid ﷺ that he spent lavishly without submitting the accounts to the financial authorities. Hence, it was purely and totally in the interest of fair and exemplary administration that some curb was put on Khâlid bin Walid's way of dealing with public finance. And the step taken by the Caliph was just a warning and nothing else.

Basrah and Kufah

From the reports of the military commanders and the soldiers returning from Iraq, Umar Fâruq ﷺ gathered that the climate of Iraq did not suit them. He issued orders that cantonments for the Arabian forces should be set up at places where they could enjoy climate similar to that of Arabia so that the Arabian soldiers could, after finishing their job, take rest therein.

One cantonment was set up near the Tigris with thatched roofs. While going on a campaign, they would set the thatch on fire and repaired it again on their return. Umar Fâruq ﷺ constructed some houses in Basrah in 17 AH, and approved a new cantonment for Kufah. With the construction of houses, both these places began to be rapidly populated because of the healthy climate of these regions. And within a short period, both the cities came to be known as the centers of Muslim power.

Conquest of Ahwâz, and Hurmuzân accepts Islam

Running away from the battle of Qâdisiyah, the well-known Persian commander, Hurmuzân took refuge in Khuzestân, the capital of Ahwâz province and devoted himself wholeheartedly to collecting soldiers by capturing the surrounding cities. Muslim forces emerged from the cantonments of Kufah and Basrah and charged at Ahwâz which fell to them. Hurmuzân earned peace from the Muslims in return for paying the *Jizyah*. After a few days, Hurmuzân rose in revolt against the Muslims but was again beaten thoroughly. He again sought peace for *Jizyah* and it was granted. Meanwhile news came that Yezdgird, the Persian monarch, was collecting a huge army to attack the Muslims.

On receiving this disturbing news, Umar Fâruq ﷺ immediately wrote Sa'd bin Abu Waqqâs ﷺ to deploy Islamic squadrons at all the avenues of access. As a precautionary measure, a squadron was also sent to take care of the activities of Hurmuzân. Since he was counting on Yezdgird, he rose against the Muslim force with a big army and the result was a complete rout. Hurmuzân fled to Tustar and devoted himself again to making preparations for battling with the Muslims. When Umar Fâruq ﷺ heard of this, he sent Abu Musa Ash'ari ﷺ as the Commander of the army stationed at Basrah.

Abu Musa ﷺ advanced towards Tustar and after a number of encounters, Hurmuzân took shelter in his fort for a defensive battle. However, he was greeted by an ignominious defeat and the city fell to the Muslims. The fort was about to fall when Hurmuzân sent a petition to Abu Musa ﷺ mentioning that he was ready to surrender on the sole condition that he be dispatched to Umar Fâruq ﷺ and let him decide about him (Hurmuzân). His petition was granted and he was sent to Al-Madinah in the company of Anas bin Mâlik and Ahnaf bin Qais ﷺ. Reaching the area bordering Al-Madinah, he put on costly and glamorous garments and his glittering crown.

Umar Fâruq ﷺ thanked Allâh when he noticed such a general as a captive. The Caliph then said to him, "You have backed out of your promise more than once, what punishment do you deserve then? And what do you want to say in self-defense?" Hurmuzân said, "I am afraid you will slay me before hearing my excuse." The Caliph said, "Fear not, your excuse will be definitely heard." Hurmuzân then asked for some drinking water. He then took the cup of water in his hand and said, "I am afraid you will kill me while I am drinking this water." Umar Fâruq ﷺ said, "Fear not in the least, you will be put to no harm unless you have drunk this cup of water." Hearing this Hurmuzân kept the cup back and said, "I won't drink, and you cannot kill me as per your promise."

Graceful Treatment of Umar ﷺ:

Hearing this, Umar Fâruq ﷺ angrily said, "You tell a lie, I have not given you peace." Thereupon Anas bin Mâlik ﷺ intervened and said, "O Chief of the believers, he tells the truth. You have just promised him that he will not be harmed until he has drunk the cup of water and given his account." Hearing this Umar Fâruq 🌸 was left wonder-struck and said addressing Hurmuzân, "You have deceived me but I will not do the same. It is better for you to convert to Islam."

Hurmuzân accepted Islam at once. Umar Fâruq 🌸 grew very happy. He gave Hurmuzân a place in Al-Madinah to live in and sanctioned for him an annual grant of two thousand dinars. He was also consulted during the campaigns of Persia.

Umar Fâruq 🌸 then said to Anas bin Mâlik and Ahnaf bin Qais 🌸, "You people perhaps fail to treat your *Dhimmi* (non-Muslim citizens of an Islamic state) well. And the result is their uprisings time and again." They submitted, "O Chief of the believers, we make it a point to treat them extremely well and hold them in high regard. However, they rise against us again and again because you have held us back from going ahead. Yezdgird, the Persian Emperor is there in his cities and while he is safe and sound, the Persians will never sit back and abandon their fighting." The Caliph agreed and issued immediate orders for the Muslim forces to march ahead.

The Conquest of Egypt

During Umar Fâruq's stay in Jerusalem, Amr bin Al-Âs 🌸 had obtained his consent for launching an attack on Egypt. Amr 🌸 marched to Egypt at the head of four thousand troops. The Caliph of Islam put before Muqauqis, the king of Egypt, three conditions: Islam or *Jizyah* or battle, in his dispatch from Al-Madinah. The Roman general Artabun along with his entire army was in Egypt at that time. First Artabun moved forward and then fled the battlefield after experiencing a decisive defeat.

Afterwards the Muslim army advanced further and laid siege around Ainu Shams and from there dispatched two squadrons to besiege Farama and Alexandria (Iskandariyah). Both the cities fell to the Muslim troops. Amr bin Âs 🌸 then sent Zubair bin Al-Awwâm 🌸 to Fustât as a commander, he conquered the fortified citadel after a heavy encounter. Amr bin Al-Âs 🌸 attacked Alexandria, which fell after a siege of three months.

The Battle of Nahâwand

After the conquest of Madâ'in and Jalula, Yezdgird shifted to Rey and then to Isfahân. When Ahwâz fell to the Muslims, he fled to Marw in Khurasân located in eastern Persia. He built a fire temple there and was satisfied that the Arabs would not make any advancement. He became full of rage after Ahwâz was destroyed, and Hurmuzân was captured and taken to Al-Madinah. He again started huge military preparations for beating the Muslims and wrote letters to the notables from the surrounding areas putting them to shame over the successive Muslim victories.

These efforts of Yezdgird bore fruit and Tabaristân, Jurjân, Khurasân, Isfahân, Hamadân, and Sindh rose against the Muslims in great fervor. Fighters from various regions rushed to join Yezdgird. He put Firoz or Mardân Shah as a commander of a one-hundred-and-fifty-thousand-man army and dispatched it to Nahâwand. On receiving this news, Umar Fâruq ﷺ decided to lead the army himself. However, Ali, Uthmân and Talhah ﷺ differed with his decision and the Caliph honored their opinion.

He then nominated Nu'mân bin Muqarrin ﷺ as commander and instructed him to go and halt at a stream near Kufah. At that time Sa'd bin Abu Waqqâs ﷺ was in Al-Madinah at the invitation of the Caliph. The Caliph wrote to Abdullah bin Abdullah bin Utbân, the deputy of Sa'd ﷺ to dispatch forces from Kufah under the command of Nu'mân bin Muqarrin ﷺ. The order was immediately implemented. The Caliph also instructed the Muslim troops stationed in Ahwâz to blockade Persia and Isfahân so that the people of Nahâwand could not get any help from Persia.

When troops from other corners gathered together Nu'mân bin Muqarrin ﷺ put his brother Nu'aim bin Muqarrin at the vanguard, gave the right flank to Hudhaifah bin Yamân ﷺ, left flank to Suwaid bin Muqarrin, the infantry to Qa'qâ' and rearguard to Mujâshi' bin Mas'ud. The total number of Muslim troops reached thirty thousand. The army marched from Kufah and halted at a place nine miles from its destination. The Persian army also came out on the field.

The battle started on Wednesday and continued until Thursday but without any decision. On Friday, the Persians moved back to the city and fortified areas. Since they had strewn *Gokhru* (iron-thorns) around the entire city obstructing the movement of the Muslim army towards the ramparts of the city, while the Persians could charge at the Muslim troops at anytime. In the wake of the new developments, Nu'mân summoned the commanders to his camp and sought their opinion about dealing with the situation. Tulaihah bin Khuwailid gave his opinion that the Muslim army, alert and ready, should make a retreat about six to seven miles from the city. And as a next step, Qa'qâ' be asked to charge at them with a column. The suggestion was unanimously agreed upon.

When the Persians noticed a small force before them, they became overjoyed and came out to attack it in full force. The Muslim column, according to plan, kept gradually moving back, while the Persians continued their pressure on the Muslims and moved ahead. They were now at a long distance from their trenches and defensive devices and were caught unaware by the large and fresh Muslim army lying in wait for their arrival. Nu'mân bin Muqarrin ﷺ along with others launched a fierce attack on the Persians with the loud cry of *Allâhu Akbar* (Allâh is the Most Great). The enemy force was thoroughly outwitted, they fled the field leaving a large number of soldiers dead and injured.

During the rage and fury of the killing of the Persians, Nu'mân bin Muqarrin ﷺ fell down from his horse badly exhausted and injured and was martyred. His brother Nu'mân bin Muqarrin appeared on the scene and put on his dress and took the standard of Nu'mân and the Muslim army remained unaware until the end of the battle about the martyrdom of their commander. The fleeing Persian soldiers were entrapped by the *Gokhru* spread by themselves, which took a toll in thousands. The Persian commander and other commanding officers escaped to Hamadân, but Nu'mân and Qa'qâ' conquered Hamadân too. Hudhaifah bin Yamân ﷺ was then appointed commander of the Muslim army, and in that capacity he distributed the spoils of war in Nahâwand and put out the fire temple. Its high priest waited upon Hudhaifah ﷺ and offered to put him in possession of priceless treasures if his own life and property were spared. Hudhaifah ﷺ was very willing to accede to this proposal, the priest accordingly brought and placed before him precious stones of the rarest value from the royal teasure kept with himfor emergencies. Hudhaifah ﷺ distributed the spoils of war among the troops and dispatched one-fifth, together with the precious stones to the Caliph.

For a couple of days the Caliph had received no news from the seat of war and was worried. However, he grew overjoyed at the arrival of the messenger, Sâ'ib bin Al-Aqra' with the tidings of the victory and one-fifth of the booty together with the precious stones. Umar Fâruq ﷺ deposited the precious stones with the public treasury and sent Sâ'ib back. Sâ'ib had hardly stepped in Kufah when a messenger of the Caliph came chasing him and brought him back to Al-Madinah. Umar Fâruq ﷺ revealed, "I had a dream that the angels were threatening me with torment of Fire for depositing the gems and jewels in the public treasury. So I will never preserve them in the public treasury. Take these with you and distribute among the troops their price after selling them all." When Sâ'ib sold those jewels to Amr bin Huraith Makhzumi in Kufah, they fetched two hundred thousand dirhams which were distributed among the Muslim troops. Umar Fâruq's murderer, Abu Lulu was a citizen of Nahâwand and was captured in the same battle.

General Conquest of Persia

The fall of Nahâwand was followed by that of Hamadân but the latter rose in revolt after only a few days. Being fed up with the continual revolts of the Persian regions, Umar Fâruq ﷺ later ordered a general attack.

Isfahân forms the first link in a chain of conquests. Nu'aim bin Muqarrin conquered Rey and Azerbaijân after a bloody battle. Suwaid bin Muqarrin, the brother of Nu'aim bin Muqarrin won Qumis. Isphandiyar, the brother of Rustam, was held by Utbah and released on the promise of paying the *Jizyah*. He then conquered Jurjân and then the entire province of Tabaristân fell to the Muslims. Bukair then conquered Armenia. Baida and Khazar were conquered by Abdur-Rahmân bin Rabi'ah.

Âsim bin Umar ﷺ conquered the province of Seistân and Suhail bin Adi took Kirmân. Hakam bin Amr Taghlabi ﷺ won victory in Makrân, (Baluchistân) and after a severely contested conflict Râsal, the king of Makrân was defeated. Hakam bin Amr's dispatch to the Caliph communicating the news of the victory also was accompanied by a few elephants, which were captured in the spoils. Umar Fâruq ﷺ inquired from Sahâr Abdi ﷺ, the messenger, about the particulars of Makrân and then issued an order instructing Hakam bin Amr ﷺ to stop his forward advances.

It has already been mentioned that Yezdgird was stationed in Khurasân and a full-scale battle was anticipated, Umar Fâruq ﷺ enforced Ahnaf bin Qais ﷺ by several squadrons headed by seasoned and brave commanders. When these fresh reinforcements joined Ahnaf ﷺ, he made Balkh the target of a severe attack. Yezdgird tasted ruinous defeat and fled to Turkistân. Ahnaf ﷺ captured all of Khurasân and made Marwarod the seat of power. Umar Fâruq ﷺ praised Ahnaf ﷺ for his high spirits and deeds of valor but as to his seeking permission for further advancement, the Caliph wrote back, "Would that a river of fire intervened between us and Khurasân." He meant that expansionist policy was not a good thing. So, he instructed Ahnaf ﷺ to stop where he was and advance no further.

When Yezdgird reached Farghâna, Khâqân, the Emperor of China held him in high esteem and accompanied Yezdgird towards Khurasân at the head of a huge army. Khâqân invaded Marwarod, while Yezdgird charged at Marw-Shahjahân. Khâqân was defeated in his conflict with Ahnaf bin Qais ﷺ and he fled back to Farghâna after losing some of his renowned men in the fray. With the flight of Khâqân, Yezdgird raised the siege of Marw-Shahjahân and despairing of victory, he gathered all his treasure and resolved to proceed to Turkistân. Noticing that luck was not in favor of Yezdgird, his courtiers turned against him and despoiled him of all his vast riches. Shorn of his entire splendor, Yezdgird fled to Khâqân and lived at Farghâna, the Khâqân's capital. When Umar Fâruq ﷺ heard of the victory, he assembled all the citizens of Al-Madinah to the Prophet's Mosque and gave them the glad tidings in a powerful oration, the gist of which is given below:

"The empire of the Magians has become extinct this day and from now on they will not possess a span of land to injure the Muslims in any way. Allâh the Almighty has made you master of the Magians, their country, their riches and their properties in order to test your deeds and actions. Muslims do keep in mind not to admit any change in your way of life otherwise, Allâh the Almighty will take the sovereign power from you and give it to others."

A few days after this, the sad event of the martyrdom of Umar Fâruq 🙽 took place in Al-Madinah.

Famine and Plague

During the last days of 17 AH, plague broke out in Iraq, Syria and Egypt and became intense in the early days of 18 AH. Along with this, famine also overtook the Arabian territory. Scarcity of food made life miserable. Umar Fâruq 🙽 rose to the occasion with might and main and showed amazing and exemplary readiness, courage and skill in handling the situation. He immediately issued a volley of letters to the governors to rush food grains to the people of Al-Madinah. In response to this order, Amr bin Al-Âs 🙽 dispatched from Egypt twenty ships laden with food grains, and Umar Fâruq 🙽 himself proceeded to the port to take the delivery and preserve the goods in a protected warehouse. He then prepared a list of the needy and distributed among them food grain according to their need. He vowed not to use butter and milk while the people were under the stress of famine.

Hearing the news of plague spreading in Syria, Umar Fâruq 🙽 himself came out and proceeded towards the Islamic army there. He had been at Sargh when Abu Ubaidah bin Al-Jarrâh 🙽 and other commanders and military officers received him with honor. Some of the Companions requested him not to move any further. Abdur-Rahmân bin Auf 🙽 said that he had heard the Prophet 🙼 to have said, "Go not to the place where an epidemic has broken out, and retreat not from the place already in the grip of an epidemic." Hearing this *Hadith*, Umar Fâruq 🙽 came back to Al-Madinah, instructing the authorities to handle the situation with utmost care and caution. Thus they sprang into action and took all the precautionary measures at their command. Abu Ubaidah ﷺ was then stationed in a low-lying area but as per the order of Umar ﷺ, carried his army to Jâbiah, which had a healthier climate.

However, Abu Ubaidah ﷺ fell victim to the plague at Jâbiah and appointed Mu'âdh bin Jabal ﷺ commander in his place, and succumbed to the disease. Mu'âdh bin Jabal ﷺ also did not live long and the fatal disease took a toll of Mu'âdh ﷺ, and his son was cut down in the prime of his life. Mu'âdh appointed Amr bin Al-Âs ﷺ his successor before his final departure. Amr bin Al-Âs ﷺ climbed a high mountain along with his soldiers and encamped in small groups. After sometime the rage of the epidemic receded. However, this epidemic took a heavy toll of life and some of the distinguished personages of Islam were removed from the scene. As a result of this, the flood of victories came to a sudden halt.

The same year, 18 AH, the Caliph appointed Shuraih bin Hârith Kindi and Ka'b bin Suwr Azdi judges (*Qâdi*) of Kufah and Basrah respectively. Umar Fâruq ﷺ built houses and dug wells between Makkah and Al-Madinah for the welfare of the public, he extended the courtyard of the Ka'bah by purchasing adjoining houses.

The Conquests of Umar Fâruq ﷺ

The conquests cited above include Persia, Iraq, Jazirah, Khurasân, Baluchistân, Syria, Palestine, Egypt, and Armenia. And the conquests, which were made during the decade long Fâruqi Caliphate were not ordinary. The provinces carved by Umar Fâruq ﷺ himself in 22 AH, were Makkah, Al-Madinah, Syria, Jazirah, Basrah, Kufah, Egypt, Palestine, Khurasân, Azerbaijân and Persia. Some of them were equal to two provinces in area with two centers of power and separate governors and their administrations.

Martyrdom of Umar Fâruq ﷺ

There was a Persian origin Christian slave named Firoz in Al-Madinah whose patronymic (literally 'father of' and then usually 'the name of the first born son') was Abu Lulu. One day he came across Umar ﷺ in the marketplace and complained that his master

Mughirah bin Shu'bah had imposed upon him a very heavy tax and begged the Caliph to prevail upon his master to reduce the same. Umar ♦ asked him the amount of the tax. He replied that it was two dirhams per day. The Caliph then asked him his trade. "I work as a carpenter, a painter and an ironsmith," he replied. The Caliph said, "The amount is not that much considering these lucrative vocations." This decision did not suit Firoz and he grew displeased. Umar Fâruq ♦ then said to him that he had heard that he (Firoz) could make windmills, and would he make one for him. "Very well, I shall make for you such a mill whose sound will be heard by the west and the east."

The next day when the people assembled in the mosque to perform the morning prayer, Firoz came into the mosque armed with a poisonous dagger. As the ranks of the congregation were put straight and in order, and Umar ♦ came up and took his position at the head of the ranks to lead the prayer, Firoz suddenly rushed from the first rank and struck Umar ♦ six consecutive blows, one of which fell below his navel. Umar ♦ instantly caught hold of Abdur-Rahmân bin Auf ♦, and ordered him to take his place and he, unable to stand the wounds, fell down unconscious on the floor. Abdur-Rahmân bin Auf ♦ led the prayer while Umar ♦ lay stabbed and mangled.

Abu Lulu wounded other persons also besides putting Kulaib bin Al-Bukair ♦ to martyrdom. At last he was arrested but committed suicide simultaneously. After performing the *Fajr* prayer, they carried Umar ♦ home. "Who is my assassin?" were the first words, which escaped Umar's lips after regaining consciousness. "Abu Lulu," replied the people. "Praised be to Allâh that I am not killed by a man who called himself a Muslim or performed even a single prostration before Allâh," Umar ♦ said with a sense of satisfaction.

A physician was sent for, who administered to him a date cordial and milk. Both these, however, gushed forth from the wounds whereupon the people realized that he would not survive. They accordingly asked him to nominate his successor as Abu Bakr ♦ had done. He sent for Abdur-Rahmân bin Auf, Sa'd bin Abu Waqqâs, Zubair bin Awwâm, Talhah, Ali, and Uthmân bin Affân ♦. Talhah ♦ was somewhere outside Al-Madinah. Umar Fâruq ♦ said addressing those five persons: "Keep wáiting for Talhah for three days: If he returns within this period, he is included in the panel otherwise you should choose your caliph from among yourselves." Thereafter he called his son, Abdullah bin Umar 🕮 and said, "If they are divided in their choice for the caliph, you should side with the majority and if the two groups show equal number, you join the group which has Abdur-Rahmân bin Auf on its side."

He then called Abu Talhah Ansâri and Miqdâd bin Aswad 🕮 and ordered them to be at the door while the panel was in session and let nobody in until the deliberations were over. Following this he said addressing the panel members, "I leave my will for the person who is chosen to the post of the caliph that he should take particular care of the rights of the *Ansâr*, for they are those who lent their support to the Prophet 🕮, let the *Muhâjirin* stay in their houses. The *Ansâr* happen to be your benefactors and so they deserve your obligation. You should mostly overlook their faults and ignore their mistakes. Anybody being elected as caliph, should pay attention to the *Muhâjirin* too, for they are the root of Islam. Fulfill the responsibilities regarding the *Dhimmi* and any promise made to the *Dhimmi* must be honored, their enemies should be kept away and they should never be asked to do anything beyond their power."

Having done with public affairs, Umar 🕮 turned attention towards his private concerns. He asked his son Abdullah 🕮 to go to Aishah 🕮 and tell her that he begged permission from her to be buried by the side of the Prophet 🕮. Abdullah 🕮 accordingly waited upon Aishah 🕮 whom he found weeping. He conveyed to her the greetings and the message of Umar 🕮. She said, "I had a mind to reserve this place for myself but today I will accord Umar precedence over myself." Abdullah 🕮 now hastened back to his father who eagerly inquired: "What news bring you to me, O my son?" "That which will give you satisfaction," rejoined Abdullah 🕮. "It was the greatest wish of my life," said Umar 🕮, the Caliph of Islam and Chief of the believers.

He was wounded on Wednesday, Dhul-Hijjah 27, 23 AH, and died and was buried on Muharram 1, 24 AH. His tenure as caliph was ten and a half years. Suhaib 🕮 led his funeral prayer. Ali, Zubair, Uthmân Abdur-Rahmân bin Auf and Abdullah bin Umar 🕮 lowered his body into the grave and performed the burial service.

Wives and Children

The first wife he married in his state of Ignorance was Zainab, daughter of Maz'un bin Habib bin Wahb bin Hudâfah bin Jumh who gave birth to Abdullah, Abdur-Rahmân (elder) and Hafsah. Zainab ﷺ embraced Islam in Makkah and died in the same city. She was the sister of Uthmân bin Maz'un ﷺ who was one of the earliest Muslims and was the fourteenth to embrace Islam.

His second wife, Mulaikah, daughter of Jarwal Khuzâ'i, was also married in the state of Ignorance, who gave birth to Ubaidullah. Since she refused to accept Islam, she was divorced in 6 AH. His third wife was Qaribah, daughter of Abu Umayyah Makhzumi who was also married in the state of Ignorance and was divorced in 6 AH, after the conclusion of the Truce of Hudaibiah because of her rejection of Islam. His fourth marriage was solemnized with Umm Hakim, the daughter of Al-Hârith bin Hishâm Makhzumi who gave him Fatimah and his fifth wife was Jamilah, the daughter of Âsim bin Thâbit bin Abu Aflah Ausi Ansâri to whom Âsim was born, but she too was divorced for certain reasons.

His sixth marriage was performed with Umm Kulthum ﷺ, the daughter of Ali ﷺ who gave birth to Ruqayyah and Zaid. Among the children of Umar Fâruq ﷺ, Hafsah and Abdullah were much renowned. Hafsah ﷺ was married to the Prophet ﷺ and Abdullah bin Umar ﷺ accompanied the Prophet ﷺ in all the battles. Umar ﷺ also had other wives, namely Âtikah, the daughter of Zaid bin Amr bin Nufail. Âtikah was the cousin of Umar ﷺ. Fukaihah Yamenia is also reckoned among the wives of Umar ﷺ. Some people have written that she was his slave-girl who gave birth to Abdur-Rahmân (the middle one).

Accomplished Firsts by Umar Fâruq ﷺ

Umar Fâruq ﷺ invented and enforced many things in the sphere of financial, political, administrative and social spheres, which are known as accomplishments first instituted by him. Some of them are mentioned below:

He set up a formal *Bait-ul-Mâl* or public treasury and introduced the Hijri calendar, he adopted the appellation of *Amir-ul-Mo'minin* (Chief of the believers), he established a regular department for the military and a separate department for financial affairs and fixed the salaries for men in voluntary services. He also introduced the practice of measuring the land and keeping its record, adopted a census system, he had canals dug and populated cities like Kufah, Basrah, Jizah, Fustât (Cairo) and delineated provinces out of the occupied territories.

He was first to allow rival country's traders to come to Muslim territories for the purpose of business. He was also the first to make use of the whip for corporal punishment and set up a prison and police department. He introduced a system of collecting direct information concerning states and conditions of the masses, he established a secret intelligence service, he had wells bored, built houses and fixed a daily allowance for the destitute among the Christians and the Jews. Moreover, it was from his original planning to make arrangements for congregational *Tarâwih* prayers, he levied *Zakât* on horses for trading purposes and started four *Takbir* for the funeral prayer.

Various Conditions and Special Features

Umar Fâruq ﷺ lived on simple and coarse food. Messengers from outside Al-Madinah stayed with the Caliph and dined with him as his guest. They felt uneasy for they were not in the habit of living on such simple foods. His dress was also simple to the extreme. He would most often wear clothes with a number of patches. At times he had leather patches on his cotton shirts. On one occasion he remained in his home, while the people waited for him outside. On his coming out they understood that he had no clothes to wear. He had washed the one outfit he possessed and until it dried, he could not come out.

After *Hijrah* (migration), he lived in a village two to three miles away from Al-Madinah. After becoming caliph, he shifted to Al-Madinah and settled in a house located near the Prophet's Mosque between *Bâb-us-Salâm* and *Bab-ur-Rahmah*. He was in debt at the time of his death. He ordered the debt to be paid by selling his residential house. Mu'âwiyah ﷺ purchased the house and the debt was thus settled.

He once said in his address: "People! There was a time when I used to bring water for others and in return for that they gave me dates to live on." When the people said what was the need of narrating such things. He replied, "I felt a shade of pride over myself and it was the most suitable cure." He so often made journeys between Al-Madinah and Makkah but never took with him a tent or any type of shelter. When he needed rest, he would spread a mantle under an acacia tree and lay on it. When overcome by sleep, he used to collect pebbles and sand to make a pillow to put his head on. He fixed payments from the public treasury for the wives of the Prophet ﷺ, the Companions of Badr, those who took the pledge of Ridwân and all the elite and distinguished Companions. When he fixed the payment for Usâmah more than his son, Abdullah ﷺ raised an objection. He then said to his son, "The Prophet ﷺ loved Usâmah more than you and his father more than your father."

Umar Fâruq's fellows and advisors were all religious scholars and there was no consideration for age. He held them in high esteem. Knowledge of men and their mettle was among his traits. He was also fully aware of special traits in various Companions and earned their services accordingly. While choosing persons to shoulder the responsibilities of governing, commanding, administrating, and other important posts, he was never influenced by mere piety and divinity but he based his choice on skill and suitability.

During his decade long caliphate, hundreds of battles were fought in Iraq, Syria, Palestine, Egypt and Khurasân. He did not take part in any of these battles, nevertheless the strategies were decided and the necessary arrangements were made by him. All the battles were fought under the instructions of Umar Fâruq ﷺ and no one can point out any flaw in any of his judgement or instruction. He had instructed all provincial governors that no soldier should be kept from going home for more than four months in succession.

He was once advised to use honey to cure some disease, but he had no honey with him nor could any be had from anywhere else. However, it was stocked in the public treasury. The people advised him to take it from there. He argued that it was the property of the people and so he could not take it without their permission.

One day he washed the wounds of the camels and said that he was afraid of being questioned about their condition on the Day of Judgment. He once asked Salmân 🌼 whether he was a king or a caliph. He replied that if he collected from someone a dirham, or more or less than that, and spent it unnecessarily, he was a king otherwise, he was a caliph.

Even after being the Caliph for a long time, he had taken nothing from the public treasury, with the result he came under the stress of starvation. Finding no way out he assembled the people in the Prophet's Mosque and said that since he remained preoccupied with the affairs of the caliphate, he found no time to look after his personal needs. So, he requested them to fix something from the public treasury. Ali 🌼 said that he should get only two meals per day from the public treasury, which he accepted without question.

Abdullah bin Umar 🌼 said, "It never happened that Umar fell in anger and his fury was not subsided at the mention of Allâh's Name or on making him afraid of Allâh or on reciting any Verse of the Qur'ân." Bilâl 🌼 once asked Aslam 🌼 about Umar 🌼 and he replied, "He is, undoubtedly, the best of all but when he grows angry, it is nothing short of a calamity." Bilâl 🌼 said, "Why don't you recite any Verse at that time and his anger will totally subside?"

Umar Fâruq 🌼 once sent Sâriyah at the head of a military detachment. Some time after that during a public address he cried, "O Sâriyah! Go to the mountain side." After sometime a messenger came to Al-Madinah from the place of battle and gave an account of the battle. During his narration he said, "We were about to be defeated when we heard someone calling out thrice, 'O Sâriyah! Go to the mountain side.' Because of this, our enemy was defeated."

When those words were uttered by Umar Fâruq 🌼 in his Friday address, some people among the audience had said, "You are giving your call to Sâriyah here while he is engaged in fighting with the disbelievers in Nahâwand." Whereupon he had said, "It was such a scene at that time that the Muslims appeared engaged in fighting and it was essential for them to look towards the mountain. Thus came out from my tongue those words." When the messenger of Sâriyah came to Al-Madinah with his letter, the event was mentioned therein referring to the day and time exactly, which corresponded to the date and time of Umar's address.

Abdur-Rahmân bin Auf &#x;&#x; once said to him: "They fear you so much that they can't look towards you nor can they move their lips." Umar Fâruq &#x;&#x; replied, "By Allâh, I fear them more than they fear me."

Umar Fâruq &#x;&#x; had issued orders to the governors to perform the *Hajj* during the *Hajj* season and he himself used to be present there on those occasions. The wisdom behind such a practice was that he wanted to give an opportunity to everyone to meet him and place before him anything against their governors and they (the governors) should be ready to give an explanation for their behavior. As a result of this, the governors kept alert lest they were taken to task before the public for their actions. Thus he laid the foundation of a true democracy and real equality.

The Summary of Conquests

The area of the conquests of Umar Fâruq &#x;&#x; is said to have spread over 22.5 hundred thousand square miles. This was the result of victories won by a wretched and small people against the mighty empires of Persia and Rome.

The Roman Empire had in its fold the Balkan Peninsula, Asia Minor, Syria, Palestine, Egypt, and Sudan. Some years back the Persian Empire had gained such a strength that it invaded victoriously in the Syrian region reaching the waters and up to Egypt after defeating the Roman Empire. The Persians had no less countries under their rule than the Romans. Those two magnificent empires ruled over the Western and the Eastern world and there was no third force to make a challenge to their might.

Christian and non-Muslim historians account for the rapid and vast Muslim conquests by the fact that both the Roman and Persian Empires were at that time in decay, with the result the Muslims had an opportunity to conquer both these powers. But, while giving reasons for the fall of both these mighty Empires, they forget to tell about the position of the Muslim State as compared to the giants of the East and the West in decay. Moreover, when they came in conflict with the Muslim forces, their mutual enmity was not at its peak. Thus each of them was in a position to mobilize massive forces against the numerically weak Muslim power.

Besides, the single Muslim force had to face the two giants simultaneously, both of them were not only mighty but also the most civilized and advanced in all respects. Both of them were old powers having well-disciplined regular forces armed to the teeth and with the most developed weapons and advanced art of warfare of the age. In administrative skills and experience they were far ahead of the Arabs and the Muslims. Again, both the powers could easily mobilize two-hundred-thousand-man armies at a time with about the same number of soldiers at their back, while the greatest number of Muslim troops never reached beyond thirty to forty thousand. The results were always the same, defeat for the anti-Islamic forces.

The fact behind the reverses and repulses of the Roman and Persian forces can be examined by their lack of true faith. The Muslims were the followers of *Tauhid* (Oneness of God). Lack of Faith leads to timidity while Faith makes one brave. *Tauhid* and *Imân* (Faith) instilled in the Arabs the courage of conviction, which is the logical consequence of Faith and which cannot be dominated by anything however mighty and powerful that it might be. Moreover, the principles of governance that the Qur'ân and the Prophetic examples taught to the Muslims could not be matched in the least by the developed powers of Persia and Rome.

Whenever the Muslim army halted for a few days, the populace of that territory rose to welcome the Muslims as providers of peace and prosperity. When the defeated nations watched with their naked eyes, the blessings of peace, morality, divine affection, justice, mercy, courage and the ambition of their victories, they put themselves at their service. It is an undeniable fact of history that humanity saved itself only through the marching steps of the Arab forces. Again, the unbreakable unit and the sense of supreme sacrifice, which Islam created in the Companions, could not be achieved by powers antagonistic to Islam.

First Half of the Rightly-Guided Caliphate

After the Prophet ﷺ, the periods of Abu Bakr Siddiq ☙ and Umar Fâruq ☙ may be called the first half of the religious and spiritual rule of Islam, the Rightly-Guided Caliphate. The prominent feature of this period is that the material world nowhere dominates the Faith. Vested interests, relationships and friendships were not allowed to influence the work that had to be done at anytime. The people brought up under the loving care and spiritual guidance of the Prophet ﷺ dominated the scene everywhere. They were held in high esteem by everyone and worked as torchbearers. There was no trace of disunity and discord among the Muslims. Everywhere they were known for their piety, purity, simplicity and honesty.

The marching steps of the Muslim troops trampled Iraq, Syria and Egypt but, up to the end of the Fâruqi Caliphate, the Muslim conquerors were not influenced in the least by the extravagant habits and luxurious living of the Christians and the Magians. Muslim armies conquered Iraq and Persia but the conquerors used to stay under the thatched roofs and tents of Kufah and Basrah. Similarly, the conquerors of Syria hated to live in Syrian cities and preferred the deserts and hills to safeguard their simplicity and austerity. They never said goodbye to their martial prowess and life of strain, trials and tribulations, endurance and sacrifice. Abu Bakr Siddiq ☙ and Umar Fâruq ☙ not only took pains to make them habituated to a life of struggle and physical and spiritual exercise but they left before them the highest quality of personal examples to follow and be guided by.

They neither spent a single penny from the public treasury nor let others do it. The caliphs of Islam had no personal concern nor ever made any attempt for personal gain. But during the second half of the Rightly-Guided Caliphate, these qualities of head and heart appeared to be gradually receding and with them ended the Righteous Caliphate.

Chapter 4

Second Half of the Rightly-Guided Caliphate

Uthmân bin Affân ⛤

Name and Pedigree:

His family lineage is Uthmân bin Affân bin Abu Al-Âs bin Umayyah bin Abd Shams bin Abd Munâf bin Qusai bin Kilâb bin Murrah bin Ka'b bin Luai bin Ghâlib. His appellation was Abu Amr in the state of Ignorance. However, after confessing Islam, he married Ruqayyah ⛤, the daughter of the Prophet ﷺ who gave birth to Abdullah, so his appellation changed to Abu Abdullah. The maternal grandmother of Uthmân ⛤ was the full sister of Abdullah bin Abdul-Muttalib, the father of the Prophet ﷺ. Thus Uthmân ⛤ was the cousin of the Prophet ﷺ.

Excellences:

He was matchless in modesty. Zaid bin Thâbit ⛤ reports the Prophet ﷺ to have said, "When Uthmân once passed by me, one angel told me: 'I feel ashamed in front of him for the people will assassinate him." The Prophet ﷺ said, "Angels show modesty to Uthmân as he shows it to Allâh and His Messenger." When someone mentioned Uthmân's modesty to Hasan ⛤, he remarked: "When Uthmân wants to take a bath, he feels so much ashamed of taking off his clothes even after closing the doors that he is unable to stand erect." He migrated twice, to Abyssinia and Al-Madinah. He resembled the Prophet ﷺ in his physical appearance.

The Prophet ﷺ engaged the hand of his daughter Ruqayyah ﷺ to Uthmân ﷺ before his attainment of Prophethood. When she died on the day of the battle of Badr, he married his second daughter Umm Kulthum ﷺ to him. He is, therefore, known as "The Man of two Lights". She also died in 9 AH. No man in the world other than Uthmân ﷺ ever married two daughters of a Prophet. He knew more than anyone else about the rites of *Hajj*. He was the fourth man to embrace Islam.

He accepted Islam through the efforts of Abu Bakr ﷺ. He was very wealthy among the Companions and most generous. He spent lavishly in the way of Allâh. He could not take part in the battle of Badr due to the serious illness of Ruqayyah ﷺ and stayed behind in Al-Madinah with the permission of the Prophet ﷺ. However, he was given his share from the spoils of war equal to the participants. The Prophet ﷺ said, "Uthmân should be included among the Companions of Badr." He had a remarkable position among the Companions for his excessive prayers. He would sometimes stand in prayer the whole night and fasted for years. He had bought a piece of land adjacent to the Prophet's Mosque for the wives of the Prophet ﷺ.

Once famine broke out in Al-Madinah. Uthmân ﷺ rose to the occasion and distributed food grains among the needy. The Muslims of Al-Madinah once were suffering due to the scarcity of water. A Jew had a well but he used to sell water at a very high rate. He purchased the well from the Jew for thirty-five thousand dirhams and gave it for use by the Muslims at large. He never told a lie.

From the day he came to the fold of Islam, he would set one slave free every week. He never took pride in his being wealthy and never took wine even in the state of Ignorance. He would narrate the *Ahâdith* with special care and precision. He gave in the way of Allâh six thousand camels and fifty horses for the expedition of Tabuk. He was reckoned among the richest men of Makkah in the Age of Ignorance.

Physical Appearance:

He was a man of medium stature and his face was pockmarked. He had a thick beard and he colored it with henna. His bones were wide, complexion reddish, hands long, hair curled, shoulders wide and he had beautiful teeth.

Selection for Caliphate

Umar Fâruq 💠 had, after allotting three days, asked Miqdâd 💠 not to allow entry of anybody into the assembly of the nominated panel while it was in session except Abdullah bin Umar 💠 to make the number of the members of the panel odd, which would make it seven. However, the Caliph had already ordained that Abdullah 💠 must not be elected as caliph. In reply to a question he had explained that the burden of the caliphate was heavy enough to be carried by one person of the family and others must not be thrown into it to deprive him of many comforts of life. When Umar Fâruq 💠 was requested to nominate someone as caliph, he replied, "It would be valid for me if I nominate anyone as caliph following the way of Abu Bakr. However, if I were to nominate a caliph, he would be Abu Ubaidah bin Al-Jarrâh, but he was departed before me; or he would be Sâlim, the slave of Abu Hudhaifah, but he too died before me." Saying this, he set up a panel composed of six members, which have already been mentioned.

After the burial service was performed, Miqdâd bin Al-Aswad 💠 and Abu Talhah 💠 appointed Suhaib 💠 as acting Caliph and Imam for three days as per the will left by Umar 💠. Afterwards, they along with their men contacted Ali, Uthmân, Zubair, Sa'd, Abdur-Rahmân bin Auf and Abdullah bin Umar 💠, and assembled them in the house of Miswar bin Makhramah 💠 or Aishah 💠 and sat down at the door. Talhah 💠 was still out of Al-Madinah. Meanwhile, Amr bin Al-Âs and Mughirah bin Shu'bah 💠 also came and sat down at the door. When Sa'd bin Abu Waqqâs 💠 came to know of this, he came and made them leave the place so that they could not say they were included in the consultative body. When all the members arrived, Abdur-Rahmân bin Auf 💠 got up and said, "Who among those nominated for the caliphate withdraws his name so that he may be given power to appoint the most excellent and suitable among you as caliph?" All the persons present kept silent. After a while he announced, "I give up my candidacy and I am ready to perform the duty of appointing a caliph." All of them agreed to it and empowered him to appoint the Caliph. However, Ali ﷺ kept silent. When Abdur-Rahmân ﷺ asked him about his silence, he said, "I agree with the opinion of other members, but, you first must promise to make your decision without any favor and personal involvement and do it with an eye on the truth and for the welfare of the whole *Ummah.*"

Abdur-Rahmân bin Auf ﷺ said, "I give my word that I will do it without showing any favor to anyone and without any personal involvement just for the sake of truth and for the welfare of the *Ummah*. But all of you should also promise to agree on the one who I choose for the post, and you will rise against one who disagrees with me." Having heard this, Ali ﷺ and all those present said with one voice, "We all will lend support to your choice and help you in its enforcement."

With this promise on both sides, the session was over and the members went home and waited for three days for the final verdict. During this period, Abdur-Rahmân bin Auf ﷺ kept meeting men of sound judgement and discussing the issue with them. He says that when he said to Uthmân ﷺ in private, "In case I fail to pledge allegiance to you, whom will you offer me to do this." He replied, "You should pledge allegiance to Ali." Abdur-Rahmân ﷺ then put the same question to Ali ﷺ when he was alone, and he took the name of Uthmân ﷺ. Abdur-Rahmân ﷺ then asked Zubair ﷺ to give his decision, he said, "Pledge your allegiance to either Uthmân or Ali." He then referred the issue to Sa'd ﷺ in private, he took the name of Uthmân ﷺ. When he took advice of other men of sound judgement, the majority appeared to be in favor of Uthmân ﷺ.

On the night before the day of announcing the decision the members of the panel again assembled in the same house. Abdur-Rahmân bin Auf ﷺ called Zubair and Sa'd ﷺ separately in private and said, "Most of the people appear to be in favor of Uthmân and Ali." They too also favored the two. Abdur-Rahmân then talked to Uthmân and

Ali separately. The night ended and after the *Fajr* prayer the mosque was crowded with people, all of them were eagerly awaiting the announcement of Abdur-Rahmân bin Auf ﷺ.

Before Abdur-Rahmân bin Auf ﷺ could say anything, some persons other than the members of the panel began to speak in favor of this and that. Ammâr ﷺ rose in favor of Ali ﷺ while Ibn Abu Sarh and Abdullah bin Abu Rabi'ah thought Uthmân ﷺ worthier than others. In such a crucial development, Sa'd bin Abu Waqqâs ﷺ pressed Abdur-Rahmân bin Auf ﷺ to make a hurried announcement lest some trouble might raise its head. Abdur-Rahmân bin Auf ﷺ got up and said addressing the audience, "I did all within my power to know the opinion of all the groups and classes of people and nobody is now to go against my decision. All the members of the consultative body and nominated panel have already conceded to my decision and I have spent all my power to arrive at this decision." Saying this he called Uthmân ﷺ near him and asked him to declare his resolve to follow the path shown by Allâh and His Messenger ﷺ and the Righteous Caliphs that passed away before him. Uthmân ﷺ declared that he would try his level best to follow the commands of Allâh and His Messenger ﷺ and follow the examples of Abu Bakr Siddiq ﷺ and Umar Fâruq ﷺ. Following this, Abdur-Rahmân bin Auf ﷺ himself first pledged his allegiance to Uthmân ﷺ and others followed suit.

At first Ali ﷺ looked a little aggrieved at this sight and was about to move out of the mosque. But, he turned back in haste and moved towards the new Caliph passing through the rows and took *Bai'ah* at the hands of the Chief of the believers. Talhah ﷺ was not present on the occasion and hence could not take part in the deliberations. When he called on Uthmân ﷺ to pledge his allegiance, the latter told him that he was elected Caliph in his absence, for they could not wait any longer. Thus if he (Talhah) claimed the caliphate for himself, he (Uthmân) was ready to give it up in his favor. Talhah ﷺ said, "I don't want to create any rift among the Muslims at this stage." Saying this he stretched his hand for taking *Bai'ah* at the hands of the new Caliph of Islam.

At the end of the *Bai'ah* session, Uthmân bin Affân ﷺ came to the pulpit and addressing the congregation asked them to follow the good deeds. He also asked them to fear the evil effects of abundant wealth and stressed on keeping the Pleasure of Allâh in view. After his preliminary address, he issued an order in the name of the governors and officers mentioning the demise of Umar Fâruq ﷺ and his own election as the Caliph of Islam. All of them were enjoined to work with honesty and in good faith.

First Case in the Court of Uthmân ﷺ

A few days before the martyrdom of Umar Fâruq ﷺ, Abu Lulu went to Hurmuzân with a dagger. He was the same man who had confessed Islam before the second Caliph of Islam and was settled in Al-Madinah. When Abu Lulu was talking to Hurmuzân, another inhabitant of Hirah, a Christian slave named Jafinah was also present. Abdur-Rahmân bin Abu Bakr ﷺ noticed those three sitting together and conversing with each other. When Abu Lulu saw Abdur-Rahmân bin Abu Bakr ﷺ approaching, he left the place in haste and his dagger fell down and he clearly witnessed it. However, he could not then notice the evil intention. But when Abu Lulu injured Umar Fâruq ﷺ and was caught, Abdur-Rahmân ﷺ recognized the dagger. He then related the whole event.

When Ubaidullah bin Umar ﷺ, the second son of Umar ﷺ heard all this, he lost control and attacked Hurmuzân. When Sa'd bin Abu Waqqâs ﷺ saw Hurmuzân being wounded and dying, he held Ubaidullah ﷺ. Since no caliph was there and Suhaib ﷺ was looking after the necessary affairs, Sa'd bin Abu Waqqâs ﷺ produced Ubaidullah ﷺ before him. Suhaib ﷺ kept the accused captive until the installation of the Caliph.

When Uthmân bin Affân ﷺ was elected to the post of caliphate and preliminaries were accomplished, the case of Ubaidullah ﷺ was put up before him. The new Caliph held consultations with the Companions. Ali ﷺ gave his opinion that Ubaidullah ﷺ should be slain by way of *Qisâs* (death punishment for murder). But Amr bin Al-Âs ﷺ opposed it tooth and nail. He argued that it was most improper to kill the son only a few days after the assassination of his father. The people in general supported the viewpoint of Amr bin Al-Âs ﷺ.

The Caliph found himself in a fix. However, a subtle fact dawned upon him. The event belonged to neither his period of caliphate nor that of Umar 🙵, for it had taken place before he took charge of the caliphate. Thus he adopted the good device of paying the blood money by declaring himself the guardian of Ubaidullah 🙵, the accused. He then ascended the pulpit and made an effective speech and left his audience happy and satisfied.

Governors of the Provinces

When Uthmân bin Affân 🙵 was elected and installed as the Caliph of Islam, the following governors appointed by Umar Fâruq 🙵 were looking after the affairs of the provinces and territories under the Muslim rule:

Nâfi' bin Abdul-Hârith in Makkah, Sufyân bin Abdullah Thaqafi in Tâ'if, Yala bin Umayyah in Yemen, Hudhaifah bin Mihsan in Oman, Mu'âwiyah bin Abu Sufyân in Damascus, Amr bin Al-Âs in Egypt, Umar bin Sa'd in Hims, Umar bin Utbah in Jordan, Abu Musa Ash'ari in Basrah, Mughirah bin Shu'bah in Kufah, Uthmân bin Abul-Âs in Bahrain.

The first action taken by the new Caliph in connection with the governors was that he deposed Mughirah bin Shu'bah 🙵 from the governorship of Kufah and called him back to Al-Madinah. He was replaced by Sa'd bin Abu Waqqâs 🙵. When the people questioned the action, he replied, "I have not deposed Mughirah for any fault of his. I have rather done it as a part of the administration and an expediency and exactly according to the will left by Umar as he had personally mentioned this to me (Uthmân)."

Important events of Uthmân's Caliphate

The Conquest of Alexandria

Other than the conquest of Alexandria (Iskandariyah), during the first year of the caliphate of Uthmân bin Affân 🙵 nothing else major occurred. Heraclius had taken refuge in Constantinople (Istanbul) after his flight from Asia Minor and Syria following the fall of Bait-ul-

Maqdis. Now he was worried about the safety of the rest of his territory after losing all hope of restoring the lost lands. In the wake of Amr bin Al-Âs' invasion of Egypt, Muqauqis, the king of Egypt had yielded Egypt and Alexandria to him after earning peace by paying the *Jizyah*. Heraclius considered Egypt his own province and Muqauqis his subordinate. Shock and terror engulfed him on all sides with the result that he died surrounded by defeat and dejection during the caliphate of Umar Fâruq ﷺ. His son Qustuntin (Constantine) succeeded him and lost no time in mobilizing a huge army to restore Alexandria. However, Muqauqis prevented the Romans from making entry into Alexandria and thus kept his promise.

When the Muslims came to know of the Roman invasion, they came quickly from Fustât (Cairo). The Romans then turned their attack to the Islamic cantonments giving up their campaign for Alexandria. Both the armies came upon each other and a severe battle broke out. The commander of the Roman army was killed and a large number of Roman soldiers met the same fate. The rest barely reached Constantinople by boat. After the disastrous repulsion of the Roman forces, Amr bin Al-Âs ﷺ made a survey of the losses suffered by the people of Alexandria and its suburbs and made up for all their losses, for he held himself responsible for saving the *Dhimmi* and compensating them for all reverses. Amr bin Al-Âs ﷺ then lost no time in demolishing the ramparts around the city of Alexandria and then came back to his cantonment in Fustât. This was done to prevent the possibility of any Roman attack in future trying to turn Alexandria into a fortress. This event took place in 25 AH.

The Conquest of Armenia

The Roman invasion of Alexandria was, in fact, the result of the demise of Umar Fâruq ﷺ and the same event led to the uprising in the Persian territories of Hamadân and Rey. They declared their freedom from Muslim rule. Uthmân bin Affân ﷺ dispatched Abu Musa Ash'ari, Bara' bin Âzib and Qarazah bin Ka'b ﷺ to tackle the situation and they did their job appreciably well. Umar Fâruq ﷺ had deposed and called back Sa'd bin Abu Waqqâs ﷺ. Uthmân bin Affân ﷺ reinstalled him as governor of Kufah. Abdullah bin Mas'ud ﷺ was then in charge of the public treasury.

Sa'd bin Abu Waqqâs ﷺ, the governor of Kufah, borrowed some money from Abdullah bin Mas'ud ﷺ, the treasurer. After a few days Abdullah ﷺ demanded the borrowed money which Sa'd ﷺ could not pay. The matter took a turn for the worse and their relations became strained. When Uthmân bin Affân ﷺ came to know of this unfortunate development, he deposed Sa'd ﷺ from the governorship of Kufah in 25 AH, and replaced him by Walid bin Uqbah bin Abu Mu'ait. Utbah bin Farqad ﷺ who was appointed by Sa'd ﷺ to look after the affairs of Azerbaijân was also deposed along with Sa'd ﷺ. With his exit, the people of Azerbaijân raised their banner of revolt against the establishment. Walid bin Uqbah wasted no time in invading Azerbaijân and they were forced to earn peace on the old terms and agreed to pay *Jizyah*. Walid bin Uqbah, who was the governor of Jazirah during the caliphate of Umar Fâruq ﷺ and at present the governor of Kufah, was the foster brother of Uthmân bin Affân ﷺ. Since Sa'd ﷺ was very pious and Allâh-fearing, and Walid bin Uqbah was not equal to him in this trait, the people of Kufah were not at all happy with the departure of Sa'd and the arrival of Walid.

Mu'âwiyah ﷺ, the governor of Damascus had sent Habib bin Maslamah ﷺ to Armenia. He conquered a number of cities and forts and forced the Romans to pay the *Jizyah*. With this news the Caesar of Constantinople collected eighty thousand troops from Malit, Siwas, and Quniah and invaded Habib bin Maslamah ﷺ. Habib sent the account of these events to Mu'âwiyah ﷺ and he gave the news to Uthmân bin Affân ﷺ. The Caliph wrote Walid bin Uqbah, the governor of Kufah to dispatch ten thousand reinforcements to Armenia who immediately carried out the order with a dispatch of eight thousand troops headed by Salmân bin Rabi'ah to Armenia.

Habib bin Maslamah and Salman bin Rabi'ah jointly won Armenia and reached up to the Caucasus Mountains. On the return of Habib bin Maslamah ﷺ to Mu'âwiyah ﷺ in Damascus, the latter himself invaded the Roman territory. The Roman fighters escaped leaving Antâkiyah (Antioch) and their citadels behind. This event took place in 25 AH.

Events and Changes in Egypt

Abdullah bin Sa'd known as Ibn Abu Sarh was the foster brother of Uthmân bin Affân. During the lifetime of the Prophet he had renounced Islam but later confessed it wholeheartedly. Uthmân bin Affân sent him to Egypt as a governor and head of the public treasury while Amr bin Al-Âs was kept simply as a military officer. When relations among the military officers worsened, the Caliph deposed Amr bin Al-Âs and transferred the entire power of Egypt and Alexandria to Abdullah bin Sa'd.

Although Abdullah bin Sa'd was renowned among the brave horsemen of Arabia but Amr bin Al-Âs was far ahead in experience and popularity among the Egyptians who were shocked at the dismissal of Amr. Their anger and dissatisfaction resulted in their revolt against Abdullah bin Sa'd. Besides, when the Caesar of Constantinople heard of the deposition of Amr bin Al-Âs and the resulting uprisings in Egypt, he mobilized a huge army towards Alexandria under the command of a seasoned general. The Greeks in the city joined the camp of the Roman army and Alexandria fell to the Romans after slight resistance.

Amr bin Al-Âs was again sent to Egypt as a governor who launched such a fierce attack at the Romans that they had to flee from Alexandria after sustaining heavy losses and a heavy toll on their soldiers. Amr bin Al-Âs had conquered Egypt for the third time. Although he had vowed to raze the whole city to the ground after winning the battle, he forbade any such action. He rather built a mosque at the site where the massacre and plunder were called off.

Nevertheless, when peace and normalcy returned to the region and the administration was running smooth, Amr bin Al-Âs was once again deposed and replaced by Abdullah bin Sa'd. This time the decision of the Caliph made Abdullah bin Sa'd feel uneasy and uncomfortable over his reinstallation in Egypt, for his efforts to uphold the deteriorating situation of the region the last time had met with utter failure. However, he was now anxious to make amends for his past failures.

The Conquest of Africa

Abdullah bin Sa'd ❀ sought permission from Uthmân bin Affân ❀ to invade Africa. Africa was then considered a country, it included the area stretching between Tripoli and Tangiers. Moreover, Africa was then considered the conglomeration of those countries, which make up the northern part of the African continent, Tripoli, Algiers, Tunis, and Morocco. Uthmân bin Affân ❀ allowed him to do what he wanted. He marched towards his destination at the head of an army of ten thousand. He first brought the chiefs of Barqah to obey and they agreed to pay *Jizyah*. The Muslim commander then advanced towards Tripoli capturing the territories falling on the way. At this stage the Caliph dispatched from Al-Madinah fresh reinforcements to lend help to Abdullah's army. The reinforcements included distinguished men like Abdullah bin Umar, Abdullah bin Abbâs, Abdullah bin Zubair, Amr bin Al-Âs, Husain bin Ali, and Ibn Ja'far ❀.

When the detachment reached Barqah via Egypt, Abdullah bin Sa'd ❀ welcomed it. Now they jointly proceeded towards Tripoli. The Romans tried to put up resistance but were repulsed. After the fall of Tripoli, the Muslim troops marched ahead. Gregory, the King of Africa was the vassal of Caesar. When he came to know of the march of the Muslim army, he mobilized one hundred and twenty thousand men and came face to face with the Muslim forces. Abdullah bin Sa'd ❀ first invited Gregory to accept Islam. When Gregory flatly refused the invitation, he asked him to pay the *Jizyah*. When he rejected that also, the Muslim army drew up ranks and a fierce battle broke out, which remained indecisive. Fresh Muslim reinforcements appeared on the scene and the Muslim army called out *Allâhu Akbar*.

Since the distance between Al-Madinah and the seat of battle was so far, news could not be received immediately, so Uthmân bin Affân ❀ sent a fresh detachment from Al-Madinah headed by Abdur-Rahmân bin Zubair ❀. When Gregory inquired of the slogan shouting by the Muslims, he was told that a fresh detachment had arrived and joined the Muslim forces. Gregory grew very anxious. However, the battle was not decided that day and both the armies withdrew to their camps. The next day when the battle lines were again drawn Abdullah bin Sa'd ﷺ was found missing. When Abdullah bin Zubair ﷺ inquired about his absence, he was told that Gregory had proclaimed a reward of one hundred thousand dinars and the hand of his daughter to the man who would bring him the head of Abdullah bin Sa'd. For this reason Abdullah bin Sa'd ﷺ failed to come to battlefield for fear of being a marked man. Abdullah bin Zubair ﷺ went to his camp and asked Abdullah bin Sa'd to make a counter proclamation. He should offer a reward of one hundred thousand dinars from the booty, the hand of the daughter of Gregory and the conquered land to be governed by the man who would bring the head of Gregory.

With such a proclamation from Abdullah bin Sa'd ﷺ, Gregory found himself in great trouble. Abdullah bin Sa'd ﷺ appeared on the battlefield. Both the armies fought gallantly but the battle remained inconclusive. When the night set in, consultations were held for adopting a new strategy. Abdullah bin Zubair ﷺ suggested that half of the troops should go to battlefield and the rest remain inside the camp. When the two armies exhausted by the daylong fighting leave the battlefield for camp, the fresh half of the Muslim army should attack the retreating Romans. The counsel received general acceptance. The third day of the battle this strategy was put to practice. When the two armies separated in the afternoon, Abdullah bin Zubair ﷺ rushed out from the camp with the fresh detachment and charged the Romans. They could not withstand the attack and fled to their camp but could not save themselves because the Muslim force surrounded the camp and the Romans were either killed or captured. Gregory also fought against the Muslims and was put to the sword by Abdullah bin Zubair ﷺ.

[It is said that the enemy forces had besieged the Muslim army, noticing this unfavorable condition, Abdullah bin Zubair ﷺ took some brave Muslims with him and headed towards Gregory. The enemy took them as messengers from the Muslim army and let them go to the Gregory. They attacked and killed Gregory and raised his head on a spear. This scene uprooted the enemy and caused its destruction.]

The next day, Muslim army moved ahead and reached Sabitalah, the headquarters of (northern) Africa which was also conquered in a couple of days, and an immense amount of spoils fell into the hands of the Muslims. The Muslims marched further and laid siege around the fort of Jam, which was very strong and fortified. However, they could not stand the Muslim onslaught and yielded on the condition of paying one million as *Jizyah*. Abdullah bin Zubair ﷺ set out to Al-Madinah with the glad tidings of the African conquest and one-fifth of the spoils. Abdullah bin Sa'd ﷺ returned to Egypt from Africa after an absence of one year and three months.

The Conquest of Cyprus and Rhodes

Abdullah bin Nâfi' became the governor of Egypt the same year, 27 AH, that Abdullah bin Sa'd ﷺ came back to Egypt from the other parts of northern Africa. Constantine again rose to make military preparations for a fresh battle. In 28 AH, he dispatched a part of his navy towards Africa, which reached the African coast and demanded tribute for Caesar. But the Africans flatly refused to give any because Caesar had lent no help when they were under the Muslim attack and so they no longer held him as their ruler. This rude refusal led to fighting between the Africans and the Roman army, which resulted in the defeat of Africans. The Romans then advanced towards Alexandria. Abdullah bin Nâfi' was ready to give them battle. In the meantime Caesar himself set off to conquer Alexandria at the head of a fleet of six hundred boats. The Roman forces proceeded to Alexandria from both sides. A fierce fight took place, which ended with the destruction of the Romans. They escaped to Cyprus, which they used as their naval headquarters and an arsenal for their weapons.

At the time of the death of Umar Fâruq ﷺ Mu'âwiyah ﷺ was the governor of Damascus and Jordan while Hims and Qinnasrin were governed by Umair bin Saeed Ansâri. When he submitted his resignation after the demise of Umar Fâruq ﷺ, Hims and Qinnasrin were consolidated with the province of Syria under Mu'âwiyah ﷺ. Palestine was also consolidated with Syria under Mu'âwiyah ﷺ after the death of Abdur-Rahmân bin Alqamah, the governor of Palestine. Mu'âwiyah ﷺ gradually became the ruler of all the districts of Syria.

During the last days of the Fâruqi caliphate, Mu'âwiyah ﷺ had sought permission to invade Cyprus from the Syrian coast. However, Umar Fâruq ﷺ had some hesitation in giving permission for such a campaign and the matter remained undecided until Umar ﷺ passed away. Uthmân bin Affân ﷺ permitted the naval attack on condition that nobody was forced to take part in the adventure. Inspired by the efforts of Mu'âwiyah ﷺ, a party agreed to invade Cyprus. The party included Abu Dhar Ghifâri, Abud-Darda', Shaddâd bin Aus, Ubâdah bin Sâmit and his wife Umm Harâm bint Milhân ﷺ. Abdullah bin Qais ﷺ was made the commander of the detachment, which left for Cyprus by boat. When Constantine escaped from Alexandria, he had taken refuge in Cyprus. An Islamic naval force chased him by boat from Egypt and reached Cyprus. And this fresh naval detachment from Syria also descended on the coast of Cyprus. When Umm Harâm ﷺ mounted on a horse, it ran away with her and she fell down and died. It happened exactly according to the prophecy of the Prophet ﷺ. Constantine could not withstand the attack and fled to Constantinople with great difficulties and succumbed to death.

However, according to other sources, frustrated by his defeat after defeat some people killed him in his bathroom. Thus Cyprus easily fell to the Muslims. Mu'âwiyah ﷺ also arrived in Cyprus with a detachment. After finishing his job in Cyprus he sailed to Rhodes. There was a fierce battle but the Romans yielded after strong resistance. On this island there was a giant-like copper idol, one of its legs was on the coast of the island and another on a nearby islet off the coast. The strait between the two legs was so wide that ships would easily pass between them. Mu'âwiyah ﷺ broke the idol into pieces and sent them with the troops going back to Alexandria where a Jew purchased them all. The conquests of Cyprus and Rhodes opened the door for Muslim campaigns against Constantinople and other countries of the region. These events took place at the end of 28 AH or at the beginning of 29 AH.

Administrative Changes in Persia

In 27 AH, the people of Basrah sent a deputation to Al-Madinah to lodge a complaint against the governor Abu Musa Ash'ari ﷺ.

Uthmân bin Affân ﷺ immediately replaced him with his cousin, Abdullah bin Âmir bin Kurz bin Rabi'ah bin Habib bin Abd Shams, who was only 25 years old. The Caliph not only installed him as the governor of Basrah but also as the commander of the army of Oman and Bahrain, which until then was under Uthmân bin Abul-Âs Thaqafi. Ubaidullah bin Ma'mar, the governor of Khurâsan was now transferred to Persia. The governorship of Khurâsan was given to Umair bin Uthmân bin Sa'd who managed the affairs with skill and strong hands and captured the territory up to Farghâna. He, Umair bin Uthmân was deposed from the governorship of Khurâsan between 27 and 28 AH, and Ibn Ahmar was substituted for him. Abdur-Rahmân bin Abs was made the governor of Kirmân but was soon deposed making room for Asim bin Amr, while Imrân bin Nufail was brought to govern Sajastân.

Revolts of the Persians and the Islamic Conquests

Since administrative changes took place rather quickly the Persians took it as a sign of providence and so they indulged in hatching conspiracies against the administration. They began to prepare for a fresh encounter with the Muslims. The centers of these uprisings and preparations were Istakhar and Jur. Ubaidullah bin Ma'mar, the governor of Persia invaded Istakhar in 27 AH, and was martyred in the encounter with the result the detachment under his command scattered and escaped. Hearing this, Abdullah bin Âmir, the governor of Basrah marched forward with his army with Uthmân bin Abul-Âs at the vanguard. Abdullah bin Amir turned towards Istakhar while Harim bin Haiyân laid siege around Jur. The Persians put up strong resistance but they ran away after a bloody battle and Istakhar fell to the Muslims.

Harim bin Haiyân's siege of Jur was protracted. During this period Haram fasted in the day and fought with the enemy too. He would broke his fast in the evening followed by prayers. Once he did not get bread after breaking the fast. He observed fast the next day in the same state. However, he did not get a meal that day either. The whole week passed in successive fasts without food. When he grew too weak he said to his servant, "What has happened to you my son. You fail to give me bread and I am keeping fast with water alone for a week." He replied, "My master; I bake bread for you daily without fail, it is quite amazing that you didn't get it." The next day the servant baked bread and lay in wait to see who was taking it away. He was shocked to notice that a dog came and took the bread and made off with it. He followed the dog and saw that it went towards the fortification of the city and it entered the city through a sewer. The servant came back and related the whole event to Harim bin Haiyân. He too was amazed. Haram and a few adventurous persons went into the sewer, which led them inside the fortifications and they opened the gates after killing the watchmen. In this way the Muslim army made an easy entry into the city and conquered it. The uprisings both in Istakhar and Jur were heavily put down and the insurgents met their doom.

Hajj of 29 AH

Uthmân bin Affân ﷺ left Al-Madinah at the head of a party of the *Muhâjirin* and *Ansâr* to perform *Hajj* of the House of Allâh. He ordered the tents to be pitched in Mina and collected the pilgrims for the feast. However, the people disliked it for they thought it to be an act of *Bid'ah* (innovation) as it was not a practice during the time of the Prophet ﷺ, Abu Bakr Siddiq ﷺ and Umar Fâruq ﷺ. During this same journey, a woman was produced before the Caliph. She was a widow who was married for a second time and she gave birth to a child within six months of the second marriage. Uthmân bin Affân ﷺ sentenced her to be stoned to death. When Ali ﷺ came to know of such a punishment, he called on the Caliph and said that Allâh the Almighty says in the Qur'ân:

"And the bearing of him and the weaning of him is thirty (30) months." (46:15)

It tells us that the duration of pregnancy and suckling goes up to thirty months. And the pregnancy period mentioned at another place in the Qur'ân is:

"The mothers shall give suck to their children for two whole years." (2:233)

Now if suckling period, i.e., two years or twenty-four months is deducted from thirty months the pregnancy period comes to barely six months. Thus she cannot be accused of committing adultery. On hearing this, Uthmân bin Affân ﷺ rushed someone to stop the punishment but she had already been stoned to death. Uthmân bin Affân ﷺ expressed utmost sorrow over the incident and ordered recompense.

The same year, the Caliph brought about the expansion of the Prophet's Mosque by 160 yards in length and 150 yards in width and constructed pillars of stone.

Events of 30 AH

Walid bin Uqbah was the governor of Kufah. The poet, Abu Zubaidah who was a Christian and later converted to Islam, kept company with him, even though he had not abandoned drinking even after accepting Islam. The people accused Walid bin Uqbah too of drinking wine and the complaint was lodged with the Caliph. The governor was called to Al-Madinah for an explanation. A group of the complainants also reached Al-Madinah.

When Walid appeared before the Caliph, the latter shook hands with him, which they resented. When the case of drinking was looked into, there was no eyewitness against the accused. For this reason the Caliph showed hesitation in giving him punishment. The others felt the Caliph favored him. At last, a witness got up and said, "Although I have not seen him drinking wine but I saw him vomiting wine." The Caliph, based on the testimony of this witness, ordered the accused to be whipped. Ali ﷺ was also present on the scene. Abdullah bin Ja'far bin Abu Tâlib began to whip Walid. When the number of strokes reached forty, Ali ﷺ stopped it on the plea that even though Umar ﷺ had ordered to whip eighty times which is right but Abu Bakr ﷺ whipped forty times for the same crime, which I prefer to follow. Following this, Walid bin Uqbah was deposed from the governorship of Kufah, and Saeed bin Al-Âs replaced him. [Other sources like Tabari furnish details that the persons who complained and provided witness, were not reliable enough, but this fact was not disclosed at that time.]

The Event of Abu Dhar Ghifâri ﷺ

During 30 AH, the incident of Abu Dhar Ghifâri ﷺ took place. He was in Syria under Mu'âwiyah ﷺ. There arose a conflict between Abu Dhar Ghifâri and Mu'âwiyah ﷺ over the meaning of the Verse:

> "And those who hoard up gold and silver and spend it not in the way of Allâh, announce unto them a painful torment." (9:34)

Abu Dhar ﷺ was of the view that, according to this Verse, any deposit of money is unlawful and hence all the income should be duly spent in the way of Allâh. Mu'âwiyah ﷺ, on the other hand, argued that spending in the way of Allâh refers to paying *Zakât*, and the amount over which *Zakât* has been paid, could be kept in deposit without incurring any breach of Islamic code. Had unconditional deposit of money been sinful, the Qur'ân would not have mentioned division of inheritance and shares thereof. When the people, particularly the younger section, came to know of the view advanced by Abu Dhar Ghifâri ﷺ, they made fun of him. When the matter took a serious turn, Mu'âwiyah ﷺ informed the Caliph about it. He wrote the governor to send Abu Dhar ﷺ to Al-Madinah with due honor.

In Al-Madinah, he also set about propagating the same view. Since he was stern by nature, they began to avoid him, but the younger section of men would provoke him at times. In the meantime, Abdur-Rahmân bin Auf ﷺ passed way. He was a wealthy person and one among the ten given glad tidings of Paradise during his lifetime. Someone reported to Abu Dhar Ghifâri ﷺ that Abdur-Rahmân bin Auf ﷺ had left behind riches in such a great quantity, so what did he have to say about it. He issued his familiar *Fatwa* (legal opinion) in the case. Thereupon, Ka'b Ahbâr who had confessed Islam during the caliphate of Umar Fâruq ﷺ and who was an accomplished scholar of the Children of Israel, objected to it. At this Abu Dhar ﷺ lifted his stick and fell on him saying, "O Jew! What do you have to do with these issues?" Ka'b Ahbâr fled to the assembly of the Caliph but Abu Dhar ﷺ appeared there chasing him with his stick. The slaves of Uthmân bin Affân ﷺ saved Ka'b Ahbâr.

When Abu Dhar's anger subsided, he called on Uthmân bin Affân ﷺ and said, "I believe that the entire possession should be given in the way of Allâh. The people of Syria opposed me and put me to trouble and now the people of Al-Madinah follow suit. Tell me what course should I adopt and where should I go?" Thereupon Uthmân bin Affân ﷺ extended his suggestion, "You go and settle in a village outside Al-Madinah." So, Abu Dhar ﷺ settled in Rabadhah, a village three days distance from Al-Madinah.

The Ring of the Prophet ﷺ

The Prophet ﷺ had a ring which he used to seal his letters and orders. After the death of the Prophet ﷺ, it was preserved with Âishah ﷺ and then given to Abu Bakr Siddiq ﷺ after he took over the caliphate. After the first Caliph, it was handed over to Umar Fâruq ﷺ who entrusted it to his daughter and the Mother of the believers, Hafsah ﷺ to be given to one chosen as Caliph. Thus when Uthmân bin Affân ﷺ was elected as Caliph, the ring was given to him. The same year, 30 AH, the ring fell into a well at Quba. All efforts to find the lost ring proved an exercise in futility. From that day, Uthmân bin Affân ﷺ had no peace in this life and remained surrounded by calamities of all kinds. He had another ring of the same shape and pattern made.

The number of persons joining congregational prayers particularly for *Jumu'ah* (Friday) rose to such an extent that they could not even hear the *Adhân*. Thus, the Caliph issued an order to pronounce an *Adhân* from a raised spot prior to the *Adhân* preceding the address. Thus two *Adhân* before the *Jumu'ah* (Friday) prayer came into practice. The same year Uthmân ﷺ extended advice to the Companions to sell their properties in Iraq and Syria and buy in Makkah, Al-Madinah and Tâ'if.

Fall of Tabaristan

Assuming governorship of Kufah, Saeed bin Al-Âs drew up an army which included men like Hasan bin Ali, Abdullah bin Umar, Abdullah bin Zubair, and Hudhaifah bin Al-Yamân ﷺ. At the head of this army Saeed bin Al-Âs invaded Tabaristân and Jurjân and conquered these big cities and the entire territory.

Circulation of the Qur'ân

When Hudhaifah bin Al-Yamân ﷺ reached Al-Madinah on route to Basrah, Kufah, Rey and Syria, he expressed amazement over the fact that the people of Iraq, Syria, Basrah and Kufah, and Persia had their own way of recitation of the Noble Qur'ân which was quite different from each other. It was better that one and all were brought to the same way of recitation. Uthmân bin Affân ﷺ convened a meeting of the distinguished Companions and placed the suggestion for their deliberations and decisions. All of them endorsed the opinion of Hudhaifah ﷺ. Uthmân bin Affân ﷺ then had them bring the copy of the Qur'ân with Hafsah ﷺ, the Mother of the believers, which was compiled by Zaid bin Thâbit ﷺ and other Companions during the caliphate of Abu Bakr Siddiq ﷺ and came to Umar Fâruq ﷺ and then to his daughter, Hafsah ﷺ after his assassination. The Caliph deputed a number of qualified people to prepare a number of copies. He then sent a copy of the Qur'ân to each big city with the order that the Qur'ân be copied accordingly and all the old copies be set on fire. When the fresh copy reached Kufah, the Companions expressed their joy over it, but Abdullah bin Mas'ud ﷺ remained firm on his own recitation.

Events of 31 AH

According to the fresh orders issued from the office of the caliphate, new governors were appointed to some territories. Harim bin Hassân Yashkuri, Harim bin Haiyân Al-Abdi, and Khirrit bin Râshid were appointed to the Persian territories. Ahnaf bin Qais was appointed to Marwain, Habib bin Qarrah Yarbu'i was appointed to Balkh, Khâlid bin Zuhair was appointed to Harât, Umain bin Ahmad Yashkuri to Tus and Qais bin Hubairah was appointed to Nishapur. Some of the cities of Khurâsan showed sign of uprisings. Abdullah bin Âmir ﷺ resorted to military action and forced them all to obey. He then put down a revolt in Nishapur and then turned towards Harât followed by Balkh, Tabaristân, Kirmân, Sajastân and some provinces of Persia which became his next targets. In the wake of this series of victories in Iraq and Persia, Abdullah bin Âmir came to be known as a terror and people were filled with awe at the mention of his name.

Yezdgird killed

The Persian Empire was destroyed during the caliphate of Umar
Fâruq ﷺ. The rest of the cities and frontier provinces were conquered
during the caliphate of Uthmân bin Affân ﷺ. Nevertheless, Yezdgird,
the Emperor of Persia was still running from place to place for safety.
Sometimes he was in Rey and sometimes in Balkh, Marw, Isfahân,
Istakhar, Turkistan and China and back again to Persia. A party of
several thousand soldiers remained with him through thick and thin
in the hope that one day their past glory and grandeur might be
restored. This was the reason why the Persian provinces, districts and
cities would so often rise against the Muslim rule even though they
were instantly put down by the Muslim forces. In 31 AH, Yezdgird
reached the suburbs of Balkh at the head of a party from China and
Turkistan and captured some cities for a short period. His misfortunes
compelled him to flee and take refuge at the dwelling of a windmill
owner. He was in deep sleep when the house owner, out of greed for
his costly garments, killed him and threw his dead body into water
after stripping him of his clothes, ornaments and weapons. This event
took place in suburb of Marw on August 23, 651 CE. Yezdgird passed
four years of his life in luxury, sixteen years in affliction and vagrancy
and the last ten years out of sixteen he passed as a fugitive. The
Persian troubles came to an end after Yezdgird was killed.

In this year, Muhammad bin Abu Hudhaifah and Muhammad bin Abu
Bakr who were with Abdullah bin Sa'd bin Abu Sarh, the governor of
Egypt, showed their dissatisfaction and displeasure over the way the
ruler was managing affairs. Their resentment grew to an extent that
they came out in the open against Uthmân bin Affân ﷺ for his alleged
policy of favoring an unworthy man like Abdullah bin Sa'd even
though he earned the displeasure of the Prophet ﷺ during his lifetime.

Events of 32 AH

In Dhul-Hijjah 31 AH, when Abdullah bin Âmir ﷺ left to perform
Hajj, an Persian general Qârin saw a golden opportunity for him to
restore some Persian provinces. He proceeded at the head of a forty

thousand strong army. Abdullah bin Hâzim, a Muslim general, with only a few thousand soldiers under his command, showed such exemplary courage and valor that the Persians were defeated. With a small party of three to four thousand soldiers, Abdullah bin Hâzim advanced to face the forty thousand strong army of the Persians. Reaching near the enemy, the Muslim general ordered his soldiers to wrap their spears up with pieces of cloth and then soak them in oil or fat. When the army came closer to the battleground, he ordered his soldiers to set fire to the cloth wrapped spears while it was night and charge at the enemy with blazing fire. When the planning was translated into action, the Persian soldiers fled in shock and bewilderment at the sight of the flames. None of them had the courage and consciousness to face the Muslim soldiers. A large number of Persian soldiers were killed or captured.

Events of 33 AH

Saeed bin Al-Âs ﷺ took charge of Kufah after the dismissal of Walid bin Uqbah, as the governor of the province. Saeed began to do what he could to win the hearts of the people of Kufah. Mâlik bin Hârith Nakha'i (Mâlik bin Ashtar), Thâbit bin Qais, Aswad bin Yazid, Alqamah bin Qais, Jundub bin Zuhair, Jundub bin Ka'b Azdi, Urwah bin Al-Ju'd, Amr bin Al-Hamiq Khuza'i, Sa'sa'ah and Zaid-the sons of Suhân, and Kumail bin Ziyâd were regular visitors to the private assembly of Saeed bin Al-Âs ﷺ. All of them indulged in fun and pleasantries. One day Saeed bin Al-Âs, the governor of Kufah uttered, "This territory is the garden of the Quraish." Hearing this, Mâlik bin Ashtar angrily remarked, "You call the territory the garden of your people, which we have conquered with our swords by the grace of Allâh the Almighty?" Others too joined the issue, which gave rise to a furore and created an unruly scene. When Abdur-Rahmân Asadi tried to silence them, they fell on him and gave him a severe beating with the result that he fell unconscious.

In the wake of this unusual event Saeed bin Al-Âs ﷺ put an end to the night assembly and set guards around to ban the entry of the regular visitors. This action of the governor angered the people and they took to murmuring against the governor and the Caliph too. Very soon they were joined by men in the street. When opposition gained momentum,

Saeed bin Al-Âs ﷺ sent the whole account to the Caliph who wrote back that they should be sent to Syria to be looked after by Mu'âwiyah ﷺ. Mu'âwiyah ﷺ showed them utmost courtesy, dined with them and fixed a daily allowance for them. He did this because the Caliph had directed him to tactfully put them right. After a couple of days, Mu'âwiyah ﷺ politely asked them to recognize the leadership of the Quraish and do nothing to disturb the unity of the Muslims. But one of the sons of Suhân gave a rude reply to what he said. Mu'âwiyah ﷺ reported the matter to the Caliph and showed his inability to bring them back to reason and uprightness. Uthmân bin Affân ﷺ asked him to send them to Hims to the care of Abdur-Rahmân bin Khâlid. When they reached Hims Abdur-Rahmân bin Khâlid, the governor of Hims treated them rudely and didn't permit them to sit in his assembly. This rough and stern attitude and behavior of the governor affected them to the extent that they repented for their past actions. When the Caliph was informed of the development, he granted them permission to go back to Kufah if they so desired.

Abdullah bin Saba

Abdullah bin Saba, known as Ibn Sauda' was a Jew from San'â. He accepted Islam during the caliphate of Uthmân bin Affân ﷺ with the intention of taking advantage of the progress and prosperity of the Muslims. He settled in Al-Madinah to go deep into the internal affairs and weaknesses of the Muslims to take advantage thereof. About the same time Hakim bin Jabalah, a man from Basrah made it a point to enlist with the Muslim troops and he plundered the *Dhimmi* whenever he had an opportunity. He would sometimes commit highway robbery with a band of criminals. When his evil activities went out of all proportions, the matter was reported to the Caliph.

He wrote to the governor of Basrah to put Hakim bin Jabalah in detention and his order was duly implemented. When Abdullah bin Saba heard about Hakim bin Jabalah, he set out from Al-Madinah, reached Basrah and stayed with Hakim bin Jabalah. There he established a very close and cordial relation with Hakim bin Jabalah and his friends. Afterwards, he set himself to creating doubts and mischievous thoughts in the minds of the people around him, after very cleverly presenting himself as one who is a well-wisher of the Muslims and the family of the Prophet ﷺ. After gaining the confidence of many Muslims, he began to carry out his nefarious plan. He first raised the question that if Isa (Jesus) عليه السلام could come back to this world, why not Muhammad ﷺ? In order to fortify his plea, he began to misinterpret the meaning of the Verse:

> "Verily, He Who has given you the Qur'ân, will surely bring you back to place of return." (28:85)

He proposed thereby that the last Prophet ﷺ must come back to this world. Following this, he began to bring the people round to another point that every Prophet had a caliph (successor) and executor and that of Muhammad ﷺ was Ali رضى الله عنه, and he was the last executor as Muhammad ﷺ was the last Prophet. Encouraged by the favorable response from the gullible Muslims, he came out to openly propagate his evil intentions of doing away with the Caliph and replacing him by Ali رضى الله عنه.

When his mischievous propaganda was brought to the notice of the governor, Abdullah bin Âmir رضى الله عنه, he called Abdullah bin Saba and inquired of him as to who he was, where did he come from and what was he here for. Abdullah bin Saba explained that he was interested in Islam and he turned to Islam because of some weaknesses in Judaism and had a desire to settle here as his subject. Abdullah bin Âmir رضى الله عنه told him that, on inquiry, he arrived at the conclusion that he was bent upon creating mischief and dissension in the ranks of the Muslims. Since the governor had brought his secret plan to light, Abdullah bin Saba left Basrah and came to another military base at Kufah after issuing secret instructions to his followers. In Kufah he found a section already working against the office of the caliphate and its governor. Thus Abdullah bin Saba found this land more fertile and the atmosphere more favorable and encouraging for his evil plans.

Abdullah bin Saba was antagonistic to Islam on one hand and was hostile to Uthmân bin Affân رضى الله عنه on the other. He was, therefore, restless to take his revenge on the Caliph. In Kufah, he first established himself as a pious and God-fearing man and was very soon held in high esteem. When Abdullah's mischievous activities came to the notice of the governor, Saeed bin Al-Âs ﷺ, he called him and took him to task. Abdullah bin Saba became suspect even in the eyes of the sober and noble persons. Finding the atmosphere unfavorable, he left Kufah and went to Syria.

Like Basrah he left behind a strong lobby in Kufah who were ready to carry on his dirty business. Mâlik Ashtar and his friends and relatives were the main figures to lend support to his plan. At Damascus, in Syria, his nefarious plans could not make any headway and he had to leave the city after being there only a short time. His next target was Egypt where he moved very cautiously in the light of his past experiences. He made love for the Prophet's family and support of Ali ﷺ the main plank of his propaganda. In order to expedite his plan in an organized way he set up a secret society. He easily gained ground in Egypt because the Egyptians and the Arabs living there already had complaints against Abdullah bin Sa'd ﷺ, the governor of Egypt. Abdullah bin Sa'd ﷺ was also too preoccupied with the problems created by the African Berbers and the Caesar of Constantinople to pay attention to these internal affairs.

Abdullah bin Saba communicated with his friends in Basrah and Kufah by letter, his group instituted a letter writing campaign with the result that letters containing complaints were constantly being sent against the governors to the people of Al-Madinah from Egypt, Kufah and Basrah with charges of atrocities and malpractice brought against them. Similar letters were dispatched from Basrah and Kufah to Egypt and from Basrah, Egypt and Damascus to Kufah. Since no one was made the subject of atrocities, in each city they thought that this news was referring to other provinces which might be having victims of these malpractices. All these accusing letters were directed against Uthmân bin Affân, the Caliph who was charged with favoring despotic governors and refusing their dismissal. In view of the complaint letters coming in torrents, Uthmân bin Affân ﷺ sent Ammâr bin Yâsir ﷺ and Muhammad bin Maslamah ﷺ to Egypt and Kufah respectively to make inquiries into the affairs and inform the office of the caliphate with the facts.

When Ammâr bin Yâsir ﷺ reached Egypt, both the sections growing angry with the governor and the followers of Abdullah bin Saba brought Ammâr 🌸 to their own way of thinking. They held him back from going back to Al-Madinah saying that supporting the atrocious ways of Uthmân bin Affân 🌸 was to be avoided. Muhammad bin Maslamah 🌸 wrote to the Caliph from Kufah that both the common people and the noblemen were openly speaking against the Caliphate and showing signs of discontent. About the same time Ash'ath bin Qais, Saeed bin Qais, Sâ'ib bin Aqra', Mâlik bin Habib, Hakim bin Salâmat, Jarir bin Abdullah, and Salmân bin Rabi'ah who were wealthy, influential and courageous supporters of the Islamic caliphate left Kufah for other places. In view of the public protest and tumult prevailing over a vast area, Saeed bin Al-Âs 🌸 appointed Qa'qâ' bin Amr 🌸 his deputy and left for Al-Madinah to personally meet the Caliph and give an account of the new developments in Kufah. With his departure, the people of Kufah wrote to Mâlik Ashtar who was then staying in Hims that there was a complete vacuum in Kufah and they should come back without delay. In the absence of a strict governor, the antagonistic elements came out in open criticism and challenged the authority of the Caliph. Gradually they mustered enough courage to send a party of the disgruntled elements under the leadership of Yazid bin Qais to reach Al-Madinah to dislodge Uthmân bin Affân 🌸 from power by force. However, Qa'qâ' bin Amr 🌸 stood in the way and arrested Yazid.

Yazid implored Qa'qâ' 🌸 to forgive him because he had nothing more than some complaints against Saeed bin Al-Âs 🌸 and his mission was simply to seek the deposition of the governor. Qa'qâ' 🌸 set Yazid free. However, shortly after that Mâlik Ashtar reached Kufah with his party from Hims. His arrival generated a new zeal into those causing disruptions and he declared his support to Yazid bin Qais and his decision to join the forces of Yazid. Qa'qâ' 🌸 could not stop the joint forces of Yazid and Mâlik. They marched out of Kufah and arrived at Jara'ah near Qâdisiyah.

Events of 34 AH

Uthmân bin Affân 🌸, the Caliph of Islam issued orders to all the governors to meet him in Al-Madinah after *Hajj* for important consultations. They assembled in Al-Madinah, Mu'âwiyah 🌸 from

Syria, Abdullah bin Sa'd bin Abu Sarh ؓ from Egypt, Saeed bin Al-Âs ؓ from Kufah, Abdullah bin Âmir ؓ from Basrah and others from the smaller provinces. In addition to these governors, the Caliph invited some men of sound judgement from Al-Madinah. The Caliph put before them the issue of the prevailing anger and dissatisfaction against him and sought their advice. Abdullah bin Âmir ؓ put forward his suggestion that the unruly elements should be engaged in activities of *Jihâd* to fill their idle hours and charged them with disruptive activities and uprisings. Saeed bin Al-Âs ؓ submitted the suggestion that the leaders of the troublemakers be dealt with a heavy hand for their punishments would scare away their followers. Even though the Caliph showed his agreement with this suggestion he thought it a difficult task. Mu'âwiyah ؓ came with the suggestion that governors of each province should uphold their responsibilities and clear the province off their existence. Abdullah bin Sa'd ؓ suggested the point that they were all greedy and could, therefore, be subdued by the power of the purse.

When the real causes leading to the riots and disruptions were inquired into, it came to light that they were all whimsical and unfounded. Some of them raised the point that each one of the mischief-mongers and rioters should be put to death without showing any politeness. Uthmân bin Affân ؓ disagreed. He said that he could only punish the people according to the limits set by the Qur'ân. He was, therefore, not within his rights to kill anybody unless he became an apostate. In short, he could give capital punishment only for those acts for which penal ordinances of Islam had already been issued. As for himself, he could put up with all these tortures and hostilities with patience and fortitude. Thus the session was brought to an end without anything concrete decided.

However, the end product of the deliberations came in the shape of dispatching a detachment against the people engaged in disruptive activities and the governors were authorized to act accordingly. The governors left for their respective provinces. When Saeed bin Al-Âs ؓ reached Jara'ah in route to his province, he came across Yazid bin Qais lying there with a big armed force. He asked Saeed bin Al-Âs ؓ very rudely to go back for they would not allow him to step foot in

Kufah. Having heard this, the slave of Saeed bin Al-Âs ﷺ spoke firmly that it was impossible for Saeed ﷺ to return. Mâlik Ashtar full of wrath, pulled down the slave by his legs and killed him instantly. He then turned towards Saeed ﷺ and told him to go back, and ask Uthmân ﷺ to send Abu Musa Ash'ari ﷺ. Then Saeed bin Al-Âs ﷺ went back to Al-Madinah and gave the whole account to the Caliph. He called Abu Musa Ash'ari ﷺ, and appointed him governor of Kufah. He departed from Al-Madinah with a letter from the Caliph containing: "The man of your choice is being sent to you, and I will fulfill your desires to the extent that the *Shari'ah* permits me, and keep bearing with your excesses so as to bring about reform in you."

Abu Musa Ash'ari ﷺ in his address from the pulpit on *Jumu'ah* day, asked the people to do away with the rift among the Muslims and obey the Caliph. This speech brought peace to Kufah, and those unattached to the party of Ibn Saba felt satisfied. But the people attached to Abdullah bin Saba and those harboring hostile feelings against Uthmân bin Affân ﷺ set about complaining against the governors and officers appointed by the Caliph. They began to write letters to the influential people of Al-Madinah to create suspicion in their minds about Uthmân bin Affân ﷺ. In response to the complaints the people of Al-Madinah would grow angry with the governors and officials and press the Caliph for their dismissal. But, when they would come out faultless after inquiries, the Caliph refrained from taking any action against them. They grew suspicious of the fair dealings of the Caliph. Although men like Abu Usaid Sâ'idi, Ka'b bin Mâlik and Hassân bin Thâbit ﷺ rose to stop the disgruntled section from speaking against the Caliph but to no avail.

During this period the agents of Abdullah bin Saba flooded the provinces under Islamic rule with these poisonous letters with the sole mission of arousing people against the Caliph. The world of Islam was then represented by five seats of power. Al-Madinah was the center of power and grandeur from the beginning. Both Kufah and Basrah were the settlements of belligerent Arab tribes and also served as the magnificent cantonments of Islamic forces causing terror into the hearts of the Persians, Armenians, Georgians and the people of the vast land that belonged to the Persians in the past. Fustât or

Cairo was also a military cantonment wielding its influence up to Tripoli and Palestine besides Egypt. Damascus was the main center of power in Syria and the Muslim forces there were enough to cause Caesar to pass sleepless nights. In addition, whenever the Roman forces came face to face with the Muslim army they tasted defeat. Abdullah bin Saba was shrewd enough to gauge the significance of these five centers of power and influence. So he came to Al-Madinah first of all and then left for Basrah followed by Kufah and Damascus. He could not make much headway in Damascus owing to the presence of Mu'âwiyah ﷺ.

However, he formed parties of the disgruntled elements in all the other places. He also supported the viewpoint of Abu Dhar Ghifâri ﷺ accusing Mu'âwiyah ﷺ of using the public treasury to serve his own interests declaring it to be the property of Allâh, although it was, in fact, the property of the Muslims and so it was to be distributed among them. He also made Uthmân bin Affân ﷺ the target of his attack. During his campaign, he met Abud-Dardâ' ﷺ and placed his evil thoughts before him. Having heard Abdullah bin Saba, he accused him of being a Jew working against the cause of Islam. He then met Ubâdah bin Sâmit ﷺ who heard him patiently and then brought him to Mu'âwiyah ﷺ by force and said producing him before the governor of Damascus, "I presume that it is the same person who had created bad blood between you and Abu Dhar Ghifâri." Mu'âwiyah ﷺ drove him out to Damascus. He then stopped in Egypt to propagate his evil ideas.

When complaint letters from almost every corner of the provinces and cities under the Muslim rule came pouring into Al-Madinah, some distinguished persons of Al-Madinah called on the Caliph and drew his attention to the prevailing anger and dissatisfaction against the governors appointed by him. Uthmân bin Affân ﷺ then selected some reliable persons and sent them to each province to look into the situation and come back with a complete report. Thus Muhammad bin Maslamah ﷺ was sent to Kufah and Usâmah bin Zaid and Abdullah bin Umar ﷺ were sent to Basrah and Syria respectively. In this way each big or small province and territory found one official to report the state affairs to the Caliph.

All the investigators returned with reports that none of the governors were found guilty of any evil act or excesses and all of them were carrying out their duties within the bounds of *Shari'ah*. Besides, no man of understanding and wisdom was found against any governor or the Caliph. The people of Al-Madinah received the reports with satisfaction. But very soon the situation took a disturbing turn. The *Hajj* season was at hand. Taking advantage of the opportunity, the Caliph proclaimed among the citizens of every city and town: "Reports are pouring into Al-Madinah highlighting the excesses of the governors of various provinces. So, I have sent orders to all the governors to be present at the *Hajj*. Anybody bearing complaints against anyone's governance should come and lodge it in my presence and get his rights either from me or from the governor after the verification of the facts."

Edict of Uthmân ﷺ

Every governor also received order from the Caliph to this effect. Thus following the orders, all the governors reached Makkah on the occasion of the *Hajj*. In accordance with the scheme of Abdullah bin Saba, his followers set out from every province and center but arrived in Al-Madinah instead of Makkah. On the occasion of *Hajj*, Uthmân bin Affân ﷺ announced among the governors his readiness to listen to complaints but not a single person rose to lodge any complaint. Those present in the assembly of the Caliph were bent on finding ways and means of eradicating the troubles. But their discussions took a long time without any outcome. At this point Uthmân bin Affân ﷺ said addressing them: "Trouble is bound to appear in the near future, but I don't like to be blamed for it, for whatever I have done, it was solely for the welfare of the people." This utterance of the Caliph silenced them all.

Uthmân ﷺ came back to Al-Madinah after performing the *Hajj*. He then assembled those from outside and invited Ali, Talhah and Zubair ﷺ also. Mu'âwiyah ﷺ who had accompanied the Caliph from Makkah was also present. First of all Mu'âwiyah ﷺ got up and addressed the assembly saying: "All of you, being the Companions of the Prophet ﷺ, and men of sense and sound judgment, are the guardians of the *Ummah*. It is you who elected your fellow Uthmân bin Affân as the Caliph without any favor. As now he has grown old, many things are heard from far and near. In case you have arrived at any decision regarding this, speak your mind and I am ready to reply. However, if you have developed greed for the caliphate, you will get nothing but taking a flight with your backs turned." Ali ﷻ got enraged at the last sentence and rebuked him and he sat down silently.

Following this, Uthmân bin Affân ﷺ rose to address and said: "Abu Bakr and Umar Faruq, after becoming Caliph, practiced caution concerning their relatives with an eye on accountability, although the Prophet ﷺ took care of his relatives and extended help to them. My relatives are poor and so I do the needful for them. I am ready to do away with my practice if you prove it invalid and unlawful."

Objections:

Uthmân bin Affân ﷺ had spoken this much when a man got up and raised the objection: "You unlawfully gave away wealth and property to your relatives; for instance, you once gave the entire booty to Abdullah bin Sa'd." Uthmân ﷺ replied: "I have given him one-fifth from the one-fifth of the booty. And we have such examples during the caliphates of Abu Bakr and Umar."

Another person said: "You have conferred power and rules on your relatives; for instance, you have appointed Mu'âwiyah bin Abu Sufyân governor of the entire Syria. You made Abdullah bin Âmir governor of Basrah by deposing Abu Musa Ash'ari; you installed Walid bin Uqbah and then Saeed bin Al-Âs governors of Kufah by removing Mughirah bin Shu'bah." Uthmân bin Affân ﷺ replied, "Those governors are not my relatives and they have ability to manage the affairs well. However, if they don't deserve the post, I am always ready to change them for others. Thus I have already put Abu Musa Ash'ari as the governor of Kufah by removing Saeed bin Al-Âs."

Then the third person objected: "You have appointed undeserving and inexperienced persons as governors; for instance, Abdullah bin Âmir is a young man and, he should not have been given such a high post." Uthmân ﷺ replied, "Abdullah bin Âmir is distinguished in prudence, ability and religiosity; being young is not a shortcoming."

Yet another person got up and said: "You love family members most, and you give them heavy gifts." Uthmân ॐ replied, "Love of the family members is not a sin. And I give them gifts from my own possessions not from the public treasury. How can I give them anything from the public treasury when I myself don't take a single dirham from there? I am at liberty to give away anything to anybody from my personal property."

One more person rose to say: "You have used your position for your self and reserved grazing ground for your camels." Uthmân ॐ replied, "When I took charge of the caliphate, nobody in Al-Madinah had camels more than me. But, today I possess only two camels and that only for the purpose of *Hajj*, and I don't allow them to go to any meadow. However, there is a reserved grazing ground for the state camels and I cannot be blamed for this because this has come to me from the past."

One of them questioned:"Why did you offer the complete prayer in Mina while it should have been a *Qasr* (shortened one)?" Uthmân bin Affân ॐ replied: "Since my family members were then residing in Makkah, it was valid for me not to perform a *Qasr* (shortened) prayer."

In short, objections of this nature were raised and Uthmân bin Affân ॐ answered them fully and thoroughly. At the end of the assembly, the people left silently. Amr bin Al-Âs ॐ then said to Uthmân bin Affân ॐ, "You are more polite to them than what is needed. This was not the way of Umar, governors at a distance of hundreds of miles dreaded him more than the slaves at his service. One should be treated politely so far as there is no danger of any disturbance. Why don't you slay those about whom you know very well that they are creating a rift and confusion among the Muslims?" Hearing this Uthmân bin Affân ॐ kept silent.

Events of 35 AH

The governors of various provinces began to leave Al-Madinah. When Mu'âwiyah ॐ, the governor of Syria decided to depart, he came to Uthmân bin Affân ॐ and said, "I anticipate an attack on you and you may not be able to resist it. It's better for you to accompany me to Syria, for the Syrians are loyal and lend their full support to me." Uthmân bin Affân ﷺ replied, "On no account shall I abandon the proximity and neighborhood of the Prophet ﷺ." Having heard this Mu'âwiyah ﷺ said, "Let me send you an army from Syria to guard you against any eventuality." Uthmân ﷺ said, "I am not in favor of putting my neighbors into trouble." Hearing this Mu'âwiyah ﷺ said, "You are bound to be deceived." In reply to this Uthmân bin Affân ﷺ said, "Allâh is enough for me and what an Excellent Supporter He is." After which he remained silent.

Mu'âwiyah ﷺ then left the place and came to Ali, Talhah and Zubair ﷺ and after requesting them to provide protection to Uthmân bin Affân ﷺ, he set off for Syria.

Conspiracy of Abdullah bin Saba

Abdullah bin Saba had already finalized his nefarious plan during his stay in Egypt. He had won Companions like Ammâr bin Yâsir ﷺ and Warqa bin Râfi' ﷺ to his side. But, none besides his small group was aware of his game. His love for Ali ﷺ and the family of the Prophet ﷺ was nothing more than a ploy for inciting people against the caliphate. A considerable number of Muslim soldiers had joined his party. Gradually Abdullah bin Saba won the hearts of enough people to challenge the authority of Uthmân bin Affân ﷺ and bring about his deposition or do away with him. But the issue of his successor was still the bone of contention. Gradually his party was divided in three groups each supporting its own candidate from among Ali, Talhah and Zubair ﷺ. Since Abdullah bin Saba had no interest in the unity and strength of Islam, he held back his support from Ali ﷺ and left the matter to the contenders. His main issue was the liquidation of Uthmân's caliphate.

Departure of the Caravan of Mischief-Mongers

At first a group of one thousand people were sent in advance pretending to be a *Hajj* mission. The party consisted of Abdur-Rahmân bin Udais, Kinânah bin Bishr Laithi, and Sudân bin Humrân and was headed by Ghâfiqi bin Harb Akki. It was decided that the entire party should not proceed at one time from Egypt. The party was thus divided into four groups to leave Egypt separately and then to meet after several stages. Another party of one thousand left Kufah in four groups including Zaid bin Suhân Al-Abdi, Ziyâd bin Nadr Al-Hârithi, Abdullah bin Al-Asam and Amr bin Al-Asam led by Mâlik Ashtar; and yet another of the same number marched from Basrah including Hukaim bin Jabalah, Dharih bin Abbâd Al-Abdiyân, Bishr bin Shuraih Qaisi, and Ibn Muharrish Al-Hanafi with Hurqus bin Zuhair Sa'di at its head. All these parties left their cities in the month of Shawwâl 35 AH, under the pretext of going to *Hajj*. However, the mission before one and all was to get rid of the Caliph either by deposing or by killing him. At the appointed time, the parties coming from different directions joined one another and proceeded to Al-Madinah. Three stages from Al-Madinah, the party divided itself into three separate groups each supporting its own candidate for the caliphate. Thus the supporters of Talhah 🕮 halted at Dhu Khushub, those of Zubair bin Al-Awwâm 🕮 at A'was and the followers of Ali 🕮 at Dhul-Marwah. The majority of Talhah's supporters belonged to Basrah and the major part of Zubair bin Al-Awwâm's and Ali's supporters were from Kufah and Egypt respectively.

Ziyâd bin Nadr and Abdullah bin Al-Asam asked the rioters to hold at their respective spots until they went into Al-Madinah to look into the prevailing situation there. In case the people of Al-Madinah were prepared to face them, their attempt would prove abortive. The rioters kept quiet and those two persons called on Ali, Talhah, Zubair 🕮 and the Mothers of the believers and acquainted them with the purpose of their arrival. All of them deplored their intentions and ordered them to go back.

It is worth mentioning here that the followers of Abdullah bin Saba in Al-Madinah had written forged letters in the names of Ali, Talhah, Zubair, and the Mothers of the believers, to their followers in Kufah, Basrah and Egypt who were against Abdullah bin Saba and his group. The letters emphasized that Uthmân bin Affân 🕮 was no longer able to shoulder the heavy burden of the caliphate. Therefore the matter should be brought to its end in the month of Dhul-Hijjah. Encouraged by these forged letters, the rioters found it easy to indulge in acts of plunder, massacre and doing away with the present caliphate. They could not have, otherwise, mustered courage to plan an invasion as regards Al-Madinah, the city of the Prophet 鑅, where even a strong army of the disbelievers failed to make inroads during the battle of the Trench. All the distinguished persons rejected their nefarious plan outright but they found no preparations of any kind whatsoever in Al-Madinah. They went back to the rioters and assembled their chiefs and representatives for an emergency consultation. Allaying fears of any defensive preparations in Al-Madinah from their minds, they placed before them a suggestion that the parties belonging to Egypt, Basrah and Kufah should contact Ali, Talhah and Zubair 鑤 respectively. They should make an attempt during separate meetings to bring them round to their viewpoint saying that at no cost did they like the caliphate of Uthmân bin Affân 鑤.

Accordingly, they then offered their allegiance to them. But each of them rejected their offer very rudely. Thereupon the party from Egypt said to Ali 鑤, "Since Abdullah bin Sa'd, the governor of our province is cruel, we cannot leave Al-Madinah without getting him deposed." With an eye on their obstinacy and nerve, Ali 鑤 and some other Companions called on the Caliph and advised him to fulfill their demand to stop the trouble and depose Abdullah bin Sa'd 鑤 as the governor of Egypt. "Who will then be appointed the governor of Egypt?" Uthmân bin Affân 鑤 asked.

Ali 鑤 intercedes

Ali 鑤 and other Companions took the name of Muhammad bin Abu Bakr who happened to be the supporter of Ali 鑤 and was entrapped by Abdullah bin Saba. Therefore, the Caliph issued an edict appointing Muhammad bin Abu Bakr, governor of Egypt. After this Ali 鑤 sent the rioters out. But the third or fourth day, all the parties joined together and came into Al-Madinah crying *Takbir* with the utmost fervor and cordoned off the house of the Caliph. Ali 鑤 saw them and said, "You had already left this place, what made you come back?" They said, "The Caliph has sent a letter to Abdullah bin Sa'd through his slave to kill us as soon as we reach there. We have seized the letter and have come here with it and along with the parties from Egypt and Kufah who want to share our problem." Ali ﷺ said, "By Allâh this is an act of conspiracy and you are ill-intentioned." They replied, "Whatever be the case, we have decided to kill the Caliph, and we seek your assistance in the task." Ali ﷺ angrily said, "How can I help you?" Hearing this they said, "Why had you then written about this?" Ali ﷺ firmly replied, "I have never written you anything." Hearing this they looked towards each other with amazement. Ali ﷺ then left Al-Madinah to stay in Ahjâr-uz-Zait and the rioters surrounded the house of Uthmân bin Affân ﷺ. They followed the Caliph in prayers but they now gave it up and began also to hold others back from standing in prayer behind him.

Witnessing the lurking danger around him, the Caliph wrote letters to various provinces and sought their help, and in some cases the news reached those places on its own. However, virtuous men and the Companions persuaded the people in Egypt, Syria, Kufah and Basrah to rush to the help of the Caliph. Mu'âwiyah ﷺ and Abdullah bin Sa'd ﷺ sent Habib bin Maslamah Fihri and Mu'âwiyah bin Hudaij respectively while Qa'qa' bin Amr ﷺ set out at the head of a party from Kufah. A party from Basrah also proceeded to Al-Madinah. But none of them were able to reach Al-Madinah before the martyrdom of Uthmân bin Affân ﷺ. The mosque was under siege and after that, the rioters prevented him from coming out of his home and cut off the supply of water too. Although Uthmân bin Affân ﷺ persistently tried to convince the rioters that the letter was not written by him and asked them to produce any witness but his plea was ignored by them.

Abu Ayub Ansâri ﷺ leads the Prayer

In the wake of his inability to come to the mosque, the Caliph appointed Abu Ayub Ansâri ﷺ to do the job. However, after a few days, Ghâfiqi bin Harb Akki, the chief of the rioters, started leading the prayers. Like Muhammad bin Abu Bakr, the governor of Egypt, Muhammad bin Hudaifah was also working against the Caliph. When Abdur-Rahmân bin Udais marched towards Al-Madinah from Egypt, Muhammad bin Abu Bakr had also accompanied them to Al-Madinah, but Muhammad bin Hudaifah had stayed back in Egypt.

On hearing the news of Uthmân bin Affân's siege, Abdullah bin Sa'd ﷺ left for Al-Madinah with a party. But as soon as he reached Ramlah, he came to know that Egypt was captured by Muhammad bin Hudaifah. He hurried back but heard of Uthmân bin Affân's martyrdom while in Palestine. The siege continued for forty days.

When the rioters made a scene, Ali ﷺ sent both his sons Hasan and Husain ﵂ to stand at the door of Uthmân bin Affân ﷺ with locked arms and stop the entry of the rioters into his house. Talhah and Zubair ﵂ also sent their sons and they stopped their movements. The rioters knew well that any harm done to them meant bearing the brunt of Banu Hâshim's fury as a whole. However, the rioters were also in hurry because of the arrival of official forces from the provinces could foil their plan. Thus they broke into an adjoining house and made entry into the Caliph's house by scaling its walls.

Martyrdom of Uthmân bin Affân ﷺ

When the rioters showed the letter written on his behalf, Uthmân bin Affân ﷺ declared it a forgery. Abdur-Rahmân bin Udais, the ringleader of the rioters rejected it saying, "If you are a liar, you are not fit to remain as a Caliph. In case you are true in your claim then such a weak Caliph should not be left to rule if he is not able to keep control over his administration and let anybody write anything on his behalf." At last, Abdur-Rahmân bin Udais asked Uthmân bin Affân ﷺ to quit the caliphate. But he said, "I can't put off the garment that Allâh has caused me to put on." That is, he refused to give up the post of the Caliph. When the intensity of the siege increased and even the supply of water was stopped, Uthmân bin Affân ﷺ went to the roof of his house and reminded them of their sacrifices for Islam and the position he held after embracing Islam. A section of the rioters seemed to forgive him but Mâlik bin Ashtar intervened to keep them firm in their plan. Moreover, when the rioters were convinced of the arrival of rescue forces from the provinces, they were determined to do away with the Caliph.

During these days, Âishah ﵂ decided to go on *Hajj*. She sent for Muhammad bin Abu Bakr to accompany her on the journey to Makkah. But he refused to do so because he was involved with the rioters. Hanzlah ﷺ, the scribe of the Revelations, said to him, "You refuse to accompany the Mother of the believers and instead follow the fools of Arabia." Muhammad bin Abu Bakr gave no reply. Talhah and Zubair ﷺ had closed their doors and would neither go anywhere nor meet anybody. Ibn Abbâs ﷺ faced the rioters at the door of Uthmân bin Affân ﷺ and stopped them from drawing near. But the Caliph insisted that he lead the *Hajj* caravan, although he said that waging *Jihâd* against the rioters was to him better than performing the *Hajj*. Hasan bin Ali, Abdullah bin Zubair, Muhammad bin Talhah, Saeed bin Al-Âs ﷺ stopped the rioters from opening the door and fought to push them back.

But Uthmân bin Affân ﷺ prevented them from doing so on oath and called them in. The rioters set fire to the doors. They fought and drove them out once again. Uthmân bin Affân ﷺ was then reciting Qur'ân. When he reached the Verse:

> "Those (i.e., believers) unto whom the people (hypocrites) said:
> 'Verily, the people (pagans) have gathered against you (a great
> army), therefore, fear them.' But it (only) increased them in
> Faith, and they said: 'Allâh (Alone) is Sufficient for us, and He
> is the Best Disposer of affairs (for us)'." (3:173)

He said addressing those present, "The Messenger of Allâh ﷺ has taken a pledge from me and I firmly keep it, so hold yourselves back from fighting the rioters." He also asked Hasan bin Ali ﷺ to go back to his father but he declined the advice and kept at the door.

Mughirah bin Al-Akhnas ﷺ could not bear the situation and he attacked the rioters along with some of his companions and was martyred. In the same way, Abu Hurairah ﷺ launched an assault on the rioters reciting the Verse:

> "And O my people! How is it that I call you to salvation while
> you call me to the Fire!" (40:41)

When Uthmân ﷺ came to know of it, he insistently called him back. Meanwhile, Abdullah bin Salâm ﷺ came and he did all he could to pacify the rioters but in vain. Among those present with Uthmân bin Affân ﷺ, some were upstairs watching the movements of the rioters while others were at the gate stopping their entry. Uthmân bin Affân ، and his wife Nâ'ilah, the daughter of Al-Furâfisah were inside.

The rioters, scaled the walls, entered the house of Uthmân bin Affân ، and made an assault on him. First of all Muhammad bin Abu Bakr came near Uthmân bin Affân ، and said catching hold of his beard, "O long-bearded one, may Allâh put you to disgrace." Uthmân ، replied, "I am not a long-bearded man, but Uthmân, the Chief of the believers." Thereupon Muhammad bin Abu Bakr angrily said, "You covet the caliphate even in your old age." Uthmân ، said, "Had your father been alive, he would have valued my old age." At this Muhammad bin Abu Bakr got ashamed and left. Followed by his retreat a group of criminals came down scaling the wall. The group included Abdur-Rahmân bin Udais, Amr bin Hamiq, Umair bin Jannâbi, Sudân bin Humrân, Ghâfiqi and Kinânah bin Bishr who first struck Uthmân ، with a sword. His wife Nâ'ilah came forward and stretched her hand to stop the stroke with the result that her fingers were cut off and thrown away. But he struck him a second time, which led to his martyrdom. It so happened when Uthmân ، was reciting the Qur'ân, his blood dropped on the Verse:

"So, Allâh will suffice you against them. And He is the All-Hearer, the All-Knower." (2:137)

Amr bin Hamiq gave him nine wounds with his spear. Umair bin Jannâbi moved forward and kicked him violently more than once so that his ribs were broken. At every kick he would say: "It was you who had imprisoned my father and the poor man died in captivity." Nâ'ilah called out to those upstairs who were unaware of what was happening in the house. The rioters had completed their evil act before those upstairs arrived. The criminals fled and the slaves of Uthmân ، killed a few of them.

Nobody was needed now to guard the door. The rioters then made a forced entry into the house and plundered all the articles that they found. The news of this tragedy spread like lightning. This soul-shattering incident came to pass on Friday, Dhul-Hijjah 18, 35 AH. The dead body of Uthmân ، lay unshrouded and unburied for three days. At last Hakim bin Hizâm and Jubair bin Mut'im ، went to Ali

⚜️, he gave permission for him to be buried. The body was buried between *Maghrib* and *Isha'* prayers. Zubair, Hasan, Abu Jahm bin Hudaifah, and Marwân accompanied the bier. The rioters tried to obstruct the burial service but held back on the intervention of Ali ⚜️. Jubair bin Mut'im ⚜️ led the funeral prayers. He was then buried without bath and coffin.

At the time of the martyrdom of Uthmân bin Affân ⚜️ the following governors were in power:

Abdullah bin Al-Hadrami in Makkah, Qâsim bin Rabi'ah in Tâ'if, Ya'la bin Munyah in San'â', Abdullah bin Rabi'ah in Jund, Abdullah bin Âmir in Basrah, Mu'âwiyah bin Abu Sufyân in Syria, Abdur-Rahmân bin Abu Khâlid in Hims, Habib bin Maslamah in Qinnasrin, Abul-A'war Sulami in Jordan, Abdullah bin Qais Fazâri in Bahrain, Alqamah bin Hakim Kindi in Palestine from Mu'âwiyah, Abu Musa Ash'ari in Kufah, Jarir bin Abdullah in Qarqisiah, Ash'ath bin Qais in Azerbaijân, Sâ'ib bin Aqra' in Isfahan. Qa'qâ' bin Amr was then the commander-in-chief and Jâbir Muzani and Sammâk Ansâri were in charge of tributes, while Uqbah bin Amr was in charge of public treasury in Al-Madinah and Zaid bin Thâbit was the chief justice.

Uthmân bin Affân ⚜️ died at the age of 82 after passing 12 years as a caliph. He was buried in Jannat-ul-Baqi' leaving behind eleven sons and six daughters.

A Summary of Uthmân's Caliphate

Events of Uthmân bin Affân's tenure bring to view new phenomena we did not witness during the caliphates of Abu Bakr Siddiq and Umar Fâruq ⚜️. Many things had changed beyond recognition. Up to the caliphate of Umar Fâruq ⚜️, wealth and worldly possessions had no value. The Caliph was almost the poorest of all, no value was attached to worldly comforts neither by the ruler nor the ruled. The greatest desire of one and all was to lay down one's life in the way and for the Pleasure of Allâh the Almighty and uphold His Message. Such a desire and feeling lessened to a great extent. Uthmân bin Affân ⚜️ was a wealthy person and his way of life even after becoming Caliph showed signs thereof.

Countries and territories were conquered during the caliphate of Umar Fâruq ﷺ bringing immense riches to the Muslims but they didn't get any worldly comforts from it. But the same wealth during the tenure of Uthmân bin Affân ﷺ led them to develop love for a life of luxury. They were overpowered by the desire to purchase property and accumulate wealth. As a result of this, the characteristic spirit of vitality and military abilities decreased, which were once distinct signs of the Muslims and the Arabs. The thatched roofs began to change into palaces and palatial buildings. Military prowess gave way to rich habits. And this was the greatest misfortune that came to the Muslims.

Through the era of Abu Bakr Siddiq and Umar Fâruq ﷺ the dominant force among the Muslims who had been in the company of the Prophet ﷺ, was that they considered Islam a thing of their own and they had entrusted their lives to Islam. Islam had gained ground in their hearts so deeply that all tribal signs were wiped out. Nothing was dearer to them than Islam. The flood of conquests that engulfed vast territories, brought people to the fold of Islam in large numbers. Many witnessed the progress and prosperity of the Muslims and joined the cause with their own well-being in view. Islam had not come into their hearts to produce in them the sense of love and sacrifice for the new faith.

Most of victories during the tenure of Umar ﷺ were the result of the battles won by the fighters from Banu Wâ'il, Banu Abdul-Qais, Banu Rabi'ah, Banu Azd, Banu Kindah, Banu Tamim, and Banu Quzâ'ah. It was they who had trampled under their feet Persian provinces, Syrian territories and the fertile lands of Egypt and Palestine. They alone had shattered the Persian and Roman Empires into pieces. But none of these tribes had ever drunk directly from the fountain of the Prophet ﷺ. As a result, they were not on a par with the men of the Quraish and Hijâz in Faith and undying love for Islam. But Umar Fâruq ﷺ had such vision that could see through all the problems and impediments in their depths and complexities and found solutions so skillfully that everyone was amazed. He had set up such a system and established such a leading role for the *Muhâjirin* and the *Ansâr* that up to his caliphate it remained impossible for elements outside this circle to even think of approaching this noble group. The position of the *Muhâjirin* and the *Ansâr* was, during his caliphate, like those of conquerors, yet men of wisdom.

Umar Fâruq ﷺ had so prudently and cautiously preserved the characteristic military prowess and vitality of the Arab fighters that they were kept confined to settlements away from the lust and attraction of the Syrian cities. He, on the other hand, kept distinguished Companions and those in commanding positions away from the company of the masses and ordinary classes.

He did this so wisely and imperceptibly that nobody was aware of it and he managed their affairs in a manner that their awe and dread could not be eroded from the minds of their subordinates. And, above all, a party of the elite and men wielding power, influence and prudence always remained clustered around him in Al-Madinah.

But, during the caliphate of Uthmân bin Affân ﷺ such practices gradually disappeared. Arab tribes began to consider themselves equal to the *Muhâjirin* and the *Ansâr* and even superior to them. The Companions who commanded dignity were scattered in far off places, with the result that the commanding force of Al-Madinah was weakened beyond description, and confusion and disorder became common. Thus the capital of Islam could not longer remain the center of power. In such a state of crisis, old tribal rivalries and feuds strongly emerged and Islamic brotherhood could not contain them. The new entrants outnumbered the *Muhâjirin* and the *Ansâr*, and took away from them the reins of power and influence.

Uthmân bin Affân ﷺ was polite to the extreme. But softness alone is not helpful in running an administration; it needs the manifestation of power and strong actions at times. During the caliphate of Uthmân bin Affân ﷺ, the Muslims indulged in a life of luxuries and comforts on one hand and the dread and awe of the Caliph had eroded on the other. In such an untenable situation, ambitions and power hungry sections got ample opportunity to give vent to their desire of holding power. Thus such men of ambition among the Quraish and Hijâz could easily win the help and support of the new-Muslim tribes and fighters.

The Quraish tribe before Islam was understood to be divided into two parts, Banu Umayyah and Banu Hâshim. Even though these two tribes alone did not make up the entire Quraish and other tribes were also important. But since these two tribes were opposed to one another, other tribes were attached to either of the two. The power and influence of Banu Umayyah had surpassed Banu Hâshim at the time of advent of Islam. As a natural corollary, Banu Umayyah was vehemently opposed to the Prophethood for Muhammad ﷺ belonged to Banu Hâshim. Abu Sufyân hailed from Banu Umayyah and was so dedicated to the defeat of Islam that he led the disbelievers against Islam in the battles of Uhud and the Confederates. But, at last Banu Umayyah including Abu Sufyân confessed Islam. Thus the differences and rivalries between Banu Hâshim and Banu Umayyah came to an end. Islam obliterated all signs and traces of racial and tribal distinctions.

While Abu Bakr Siddiq ﷺ and Umar Fâruq ﷺ held the rein of caliphate, the state of affairs went undisturbed. But during the caliphate of Uthmân bin Affân ﷺ, old rivalries staged a comeback. And since Uthmân bin Affân ﷺ was from Banu Umayyah, and he held his relatives very dear, they took undue advantage of that.

Besides these new developments, which took place due to the weak caliphate, new entrants to the fold of Islam, the erosion of power and influence of the *Muhâjirin, Ansâr* and the Quraish, mass indulgence in the life of luxuries were some of the factors that proved advantageous to Banu Umayyah. Marwân bin Al-Hakam as the main scribe of the Caliph, benefited their cause immensely. When the governorship of a number of provinces came to their possession, and they were able to wield power and influence throughout, they set off to restore their position prior to Islam.

Gradually Banu Hâshim and others also grew conscious of the prevailing situation. But to say that Uthmân bin Affân ﷺ was a party to Banu Umayyah's policies and programs is far from reality and is a baseless charge.

Nevertheless, the polite behavior and softness towards relatives played a significant role in encouraging Banu Umayyah to cross all limits. And they did what could not be conceived of during the tenures of the former Caliphs. But, one is however, compelled to say that, although good treatment to relatives is quite reasonable, a Caliph must walk very cautiously upon this track. But he, perhaps, failed to see these reasons. Marwân bin Al-Hakam, his cousin did all what he could to deteriorate the situation but Uthmân bin Affân ﷺ did nothing to get rid of him, particularly when Marwân did not deserve such an important post by virtue of his abilities and character.

With Uthmân bin Affân ﷺ at the helm, Persian provinces began to rise in revolt. But Islamic forces also rose to punish the insurgents. The control and conquest of Seistân and Kirmân are examples of this. Besides, Harât, Kâbul, Balkh and some other territories were conquered in the wake of Turkish and Chinese invasions. Muslim armies won Cyprus and Rhodes as a result of the Roman assaults on Egypt and Alexandria. Because of the war preparations of the Romans of Africa and Asia Minor, Muslim territories extended to Tripoli and Armenia.

In short, many important victories were won during the caliphate of Uthmân bin Affân ﷺ also. Following the instructions of Uthmân bin Affân ﷺ, the governors constructed roads, set up educational institutions and promoted trading and agricultural development. But one cannot afford to overlook the undeniable fact that all such progress and developmental works took place during the first half of his caliphate, while disturbances and disruptions marked the next half. The Muslims who were devoted to the task of preaching Islam and uprooting idolatry, now worked for vested interests and engaged in rivalries and feuds of the worst nature. Banu Umayyah had, by now, multiplied their strength and influence and succeeded in expanding their areas of domination far and wide.

It was, nevertheless, necessary for other Muslim tribes to vie with Banu Umayyah in their activities injurious to Islamic unity and solidarity. The sober and saner section among the *Muhâjirin* and *Ansâr* could have come to the rescue but, unfortunately it did not happen. Meanwhile, the wretched Jew, Abdullah bin Saba dominated the disruptive scene and caused such damage to the Muslims that they have never completely recovere .

Even during the Prophetic era, the Muslim *Ummah* had suffered at the hands of the hypocrites led by Abdullah bin Ubai, while under the leadership of Abdullah bin Saba, they inflicted an irreparable loss. Abdullah bin Ubai could not make any headway because of the presence of the Prophet ﷺ, but Abdullah bin Saba had no one to combat his nefarious activities effectively.

To oppose Banu Umayyah, he used Ali ﷺ and easily antagonized almost all tribes of Arabia against them. These were all those who took pride in their deeds of valor and looked down upon the Quraish and the men of the Hijâz. However, they were not among the first entrants to Islam and were known as new-Muslims. Abdullah bin Saba did not experience much difficulty in rousing the people against Uthmân bin Affân ﷺ. He roamed through Basrah, Kufah and Damascus and visited military cantonments. He found favorable situations everywhere except in Damascus. He used the dispute between Abu Dhar Ghifâri and Mu'âwiyah ﷺ for his purpose. At the end of his travels he reached Egypt and began to give shape to his plans from there. Abdullah bin Sa'd ﷺ, the governor of Egypt was ahead of all in self-will and freedom of action but deficient in farsightedness and prudence, and careless about internal peace and the welfare of the people. Abdullah bin Saba found here two or three of the Companions who supported his cause.

He noticed that although Talhah ﷺ had more influence in Basrah and Zubair ﷺ in Kufah, the whole world of Islam was still under the influence of Ali ﷺ. Thus he sat down in Egypt to organize and consolidate his camp so cleverly that the people of Kufah and Basrah could be easily aroused against Banu Umayyah and Uthmân bin Affân ﷺ. In Egypt, he gave publicity to his love for Ali ﷺ, his victimization, his right of the caliphate and his being the sole executor after the Prophet ﷺ. He did everything so cautiously and cleverly that in a very short time, a party of Ali's supporters was formed. Very soon the entire world of Islam was carried away by disruptions. Thus the Companions lost the chance to bring Banu Umayyah back to the right path.

The worst kind of mischief caused by Abdullah bin Saba was a large number of letters to the people of Kufah, Basrah and Egypt on behalf of Ali ﷺ from Al-Madinah. These letters played a vital role in

winning the easily excited people to his side. His plan had two
purposes,. Uthmân ﷺ was to be assassinated on one hand and the
finger of suspicion was to be pointed towards Ali ﷺ, and alas, this
baseless doubt lingers on to this day. Abdullah bin Saba was friend
neither of Uthmân ﷺ nor Ali ﷺ; he was an enemy of both and his
sole aim was to destroy Islam. He, thus, got Uthmân ﷺ on one hand
and caused immense harm to the reputation of Ali ﷺ on the other.

Features and Characteristics of Uthmân ﷺ

Uthmân bin Affân ﷺ was affable and tolerant. Alcoholic drink was a
forbidden thing for him even during the days of Ignorance, and from
those days he never was attracted towards adultery and gambling.
His generosity benefited one and all even before he accepted Islam.
He would go to perform *Hajj* every year and had his tents pitched in
Mina, he never would come back without feeding the pilgrims and
these feasts were arranged out of his own pocket. The Prophet ﷺ and
his family would so often pass through the state of starvation and
Uthmân bin Affân ﷺ provided food for them. The Prophet ﷺ had
often prayed for him: "O Allâh, I am pleased with Uthmân; You also
be pleased with him. O Allâh. I am pleased with Uthmân; You also be
pleased with him."

Famine once broke out during the caliphate of Abu Bakr Siddiq ﷺ.
Scarcity of food put the people in great hardship. During one of those
days, news came that one thousand camels of Uthmân ﷺ had arrived in
Al-Madinah laden with food grains. The starving population of the city
rushed to Uthmân bin Affân ﷺ and requested him to sell them food
grains even at exorbitant prices. At this Uthmân bin Affân ﷺ said, "Bear
witness that I have given away all the food grains to the poor and needy
of Al-Madinah."

Abdullah bin Abbâs ﷺ relates, "The same night I saw in dream that
the Prophet ﷺ was hurrying mounted on a horse in garments of light.
I rushed forward and submitted, 'I was eager to have a glimpse of
you.' He said, 'I am now in a hurry, Uthmân has given in charity one
thousand camels laden with food grains and after he granted it, Allâh
the Almighty has given a bride in marriage to Uthmân. I am going to
join the marriage party'."

From the day he converted to Islam to his last day, he would set one slave free every Friday. Even when besieged by the rioters and in a state when the water supply was cut off, he continued this act. He used to live on simple food and wore simple clothes. However, he always served sumptuous food to his guests. Even during his caliphate, he never demanded to be treated preferentially. He would sit beside others and show respect to one and all. He once asked his slave to take revenge on him for he had committed excesses. The slave caught his ear in response to his order. "Catch it rather strongly for the retaliation in this world is much lighter than that of the Hereafter." His efforts in compiling the Qur'ân and unifying the method of recitation, and his expansion of the Prophet's Mosque have already been mentioned. He was in the habit of being at his work on time.

Some Significant Indications

At the time when the rioters had taken Al-Madinah by storm Âishah 🦋 left Al-Madinah to perform *Hajj*. When she was on her way back to Al-Madinah, she heard of Uthmân's martyrdom and she returned to Makkah without delay.

When the rioters mobbed Al-Madinah, Amr bin Al-Âs 🦋, who was then in Al-Madinah, moved out along with his sons, Abdullah and Muhammad, they settled in Palestine, and only there did he receive the tragic news of Uthmân's martyrdom.

When Abdullah bin Sa'd 🦋, the governor of Egypt, heard rioters besieging Uthmân bin Affân 🦋, he proceeded to Al-Madinah but returned on hearing that the Caliph had already been murdered. On his return he got the news that Muhammad bin Abu Hudaifah had taken over in Egypt, thus he was forced to stay in Palestine and later he settled in Damascus.

At the time of Uthmân's martyrdom, Ali, Talhah, Zubair, Abdullah bin Umar and Sa'd bin Abu Waqqâs 🦋 were in Al-Madinah, they found their honor at stake because among the rioters were insincere supporters making false claims about them. They all shut themselves behind closed doors to avoid any connection with the rioters.

Rioter's Rule in Al-Madinah

From the day the rioters put a ban on the exit of Uthmân bin Affân ﷺ
from his house and his attendance at the mosque, Al-Madinah had
virtually come under their rule. After Uthmân's martyrdom, Ghâfiqi
bin Harb Akki, the chief of the rioters, held the powers of the
caliphate for about a week and set about issuing all orders including
the appointment of someone to lead the prayers.

But the wiser section of them wanted to put a respectable man as
Caliph. They argued that in the absence of a reputable man as Caliph,
their successful efforts would be taken as a mere uprising and rioting.
Thus they decided not to leave Al-Madinah without electing a Caliph.

Abdullah bin Saba rushed to Al-Madinah incognito and joined his
party. He also favored the election of a Caliph. Thus they met Ali,
Talhah and Zubair ﷺ separately and requested each of them to accept
the responsibility of the caliphate. But each of them refused the offer
point-blank and they had to return empty-handed and frustrated.

At last, Abdullah bin Saba instilled in their mind a workable plan
according to which it was drummed up throughout Al-Madinah: "It is
the people of Al-Madinah who have always played the pivotal role of
electing a Caliph, and the Muslim *Ummah* accepted it wholeheartedly.
Now we give them just two days to elect a Caliph, if they fail to elect a
Caliph, we will kill Ali, Talhah and Zubair."

This announcement sent terror into the hearts of the people of Al-
Madinah who came out of their houses and hurried to Ali ﷺ and the
other two. While Talhah and Zubair ﷺ flatly refused to shoulder the
burden of the caliphate, Ali ﷺ agreed to it after initially refusing.
Following his consent, the people came in large numbers to take
Bai'ah (oath of allegiance) at his hand.

Ali bin Abu Tâlib ⚜

Name and Pedigree:

His family lineage is Ali bin Abu Tâlib bin Abdul-Muttalib bin Hâshim bin Abd Manâf bin Qusai bin Kilâb bin Murrah bin Ka'b bin Luai bin Ghâlib.

The Prophet ﷺ addressed him with the filial appellation of Abul-Hasan and Abu Turâb. His mother was Fâtimah bint Asad bin Hâshim. She was the first Hashmite to be married in a Hashmite family, accepted Islam and migrated from Makkah. Ali ⚜ was the cousin and son-in-law of the Prophet ﷺ. He was of medium height inclined to short stature, hair receding from his head but spreading all over the body, thick-bearded and wheat-complexioned.

Distinctive Features:

Ali ⚜ was among those who embraced Islam first of all. He was one of those who collected the Qur'ân and placed it before the Prophet ﷺ. He was the first caliph from Banu Hâshim. From childhood he never worshipped idols. While migrating from Makkah, the Prophet ﷺ left him behind to hand over the trusts to their owners. After carrying out this order of the Prophet ﷺ, he also migrated to Al-Madinah.

Barring the battle of Tabuk, he accompanied the Prophet ﷺ to all the battles, for the Prophet ﷺ had made him the acting administrator of Al-Madinah during the battle of Tabuk. In the battle of Uhud, Ali ⚜ sustained sixteen wounds on his body. On the occasion of the battle of Khaibar, the Prophet ﷺ had given the standard of Islam to him with the prophecy that the standard-bearer would conquer Khaibar.

He liked his appellation 'Abu Turab' very much and he would express his happiness whenever addressed by this. The reason he was given this name was that he was laying down in the mosque and the Prophet ﷺ came to the mosque and woke Ali ⚜ who was covered with dust and the Prophet ﷺ wiped the dust from his body saying, "Get up, O Abu Turâb." (Turâb literally means dirt or dust.)

Excellences:

Sa'd bin Abu Waqqâs ﷺ relates that on the occasion of the battle of Tabuk, the Prophet ﷺ asked Ali ﷺ to stay in Al-Madinah. He said, "You are leaving me behind among the women and children." The Prophet ﷺ said, "Are you not happy that I am leaving you behind as Musa (Moses) ﷺ had left Hârun (Aaron) ﷺ except that there will be no Prophet after me."

On the occasion of the battle of Khaibar, the Prophet ﷺ said, "Tomorrow, I shall give the standard to one who is to conquer the fort and who has pleased Allâh and His Messenger." Next morning all the Companions eagerly waited to see who was that fortunate one. The Prophet ﷺ called Ali ﷺ and handed over the flag to him and the fort was won as prophesized.

When the Verse concerning *Mubâhalah* was revealed, the Prophet ﷺ called together Ali, Fâtimah, Hasan and Husain ﷺ and said, "O Allâh! These are members of my family."

The Prophet ﷺ once said, "Ali is friend of one who is my friend." He then added, "Allâh loves one who loves Ali and shows enmity to one who is the enemy of Ali." The Prophet ﷺ is reported to have once said, "I have been ordered to love four persons." When the Companions asked their names, he revealed, "They are Ali, Abu Dhar, Miqdâd and Salmân Fârisi."

When the Prophet ﷺ formed bonds of brotherhood among the Companions, Ali ﷺ came in tears and said, "You have formed bonds of brotherhood for all but me." Thereupon the Prophet ﷺ said, "You are my brother in this world and the next."

Umar ﷺ had once said, "Among all of us, Ali is the most prudent." When someone referred to Ali ﷺ in front of Âishah ﷺ , she remarked, "None more acquainted with *Sunnah* than Ali is now living." Ammâr bin Yâsir ﷺ reports that once the Prophet ﷺ said to Ali ﷺ, "Most callous of the men are two: one is Ahmar who hamstrung the dromedary of the Prophet Sâleh (ﷺ) and the other who will strike a sword to set apart your beard from your body."

Justice and Words:

Ali ☜ once said, "I thank Allâh that even my enemy seeks my opinion over religious issues. Mu'âwiyah has sought my opinion regarding the inheritance of a eunuch. I let him know that the matter is to be decided according to the form of their private parts. If they are male-like, it will come under the male law; if female-like, it will be treated as female." When Ali ☜ arrived in Basrah, Ibn Al-Kawwa' and Qais bin Ubâdah came to him and said, "Some people say that the Prophet ﷺ had promised that you will be installed as caliph after him. Who can be more trustworthy than you in this matter, so we ask you the truth." He replied, "It is quite baseless that the Prophet ﷺ had promised me any such thing. Had it been so, how could I have allowed Abu Bakr and Umar to stand on the pulpit of the Prophet ﷺ and not killed them with my own hands even if I had been alone to do so."

He further said: "The fact is that when the Prophet's illness took a turn for the worse, he asked Abu Bakr to lead the prayers. When Âishah, the Mother of the believers, made an attempt to hold him back from giving such an order, he angrily said, 'You are women of Yusuf's days. Take none but Abu Bakr.' The day the Prophet ﷺ expired, I thought over the matter and I accepted one for my temporal affairs too whom the Prophet ﷺ had chosen for our religious affairs, for he ﷺ was our leader in our religious matters and of our worldly matters too. Thus we thought Abu Bakr is deserving and took *Bai'ah* (oath of allegiance) at his hand and none went against him. I too served him in letter and spirit, obeyed him wholeheartedly, fought as a member of his army and accepted whatever he gave me. He passed away appointing Umar as caliph. I treated Umar also like that and carried out his orders without any flaw. On the eve of Umar's death I thought that he would issue orders in favor of my caliphate with an eye on my being one of the first to embrace Islam, my relationship with the Prophet ﷺ and other qualities. But he, however, dreaded the consequences of picking a man of his own choice. Had he been a man who took notice of his relatives, he would have preferred his son. In short, the task of electing a caliph came into the hands of the Quraish.

When they assembled for the purpose, I thought they would not ignore me. Abdur-Rahmân bin Auf took a promise that we would all obey the one elected as a caliph. He then caught the hand of Uthmân. From this I understood that the promise was taken from me to support someone else. So I took *Bai'ah* at the hand of Uthmân and served him as I did with Abu Bakr and Umar. When he too passed away, I thought those already passed were chosen as our *Imam* (leaders) I become ready to accept *Bai'ah*. Thus the people of Makkah and Al-Madinah and Kufah and Basrah rose to take their *Bai'ah* (oath of allegiance) to me. Now a man has posed as my rival who is not like me either in relationship or knowledge or in order of precedence in embracing Islam, although I deserved caliphate."

A certain person said to Ali ﷺ, "You had said during an address: 'O Allâh! Bestow on me abilities such as you had given to the Righteous Caliphs,' who were the Rightly-Guided Caliphs in your sight?" Having heard this, Ali ﷺ replied with tears in his eyes, "Those are my friends Abu Bakr and Umar. Both of them were the leaders of the guided and chiefs of Islam. The Quraish followed them and attained salvation."

Ali abhorred lies. He once was saying something when a certain person said he was lying. Ali ﷺ cursed him, with the result that the person lost his eyesight before leaving the assembly.

Once two persons sat down to eat. One had five loaves of bread while another had three. Meanwhile, a third person came and they invited him to share with them. When the third person was about to leave, he gave them eight dirhams for what he had eaten. After he left the scene a dispute arose over the division of the eight dirhams. The man with five loaves of bread claimed five dirhams for himself and three dirhams for his partner. The person who had three loaves of bread insisted on half the amount, i.e., four dirhams. This dispute became so intense that they took the matter to Ali ﷺ. He said to the man with three loaves of bread, "Your loaves of bread were less in number, so three dirhams are more than your correct share; it is better for you to accept it." But he refused to abide by the judgment. Thereupon Ali ﷺ said to him, "Now you will get only one dirham as your share while your partner gets seven dirhams." Hearing this he was left astonished. However, while protesting against this decision he asked Ali ﷺ to help him to understand his calculations. Ali ﷺ said, "Listen! There were eight loaves of breads in all while you were three who shared. Since the breads could not be shared equally, every loaf of bread had to be broken into three pieces making twenty-four in all. Although, it cannot be said who ate more than the other, it may be assumed that each of you took an equal number of pieces, in other words each of you ate eight pieces. Now out of nine pieces of your three breads, the third man ate only one piece and eight pieces went to you; while out of fifteen pieces of your partner's five breads, seven pieces were eaten by the third person and eight pieces went to your partner. Since the third person gave eight dirhams after eating one piece from your bread and seven pieces from those of your partner, you are entitled to have only one dirham while seven dirhams should go to your partner." Hearing this, the person claiming half of the total amount agreed to one dirham without harboring any doubt.

A man lodged a complaint with Ali ﷺ against a person that said that he had copulated with his mother in dream. Ali ﷺ said giving his judgment, "The man describing the dream should be made to stand in the sun, and his shadow be flogged."

Wise Sayings:

Ali ﷺ is reported to have said: "O people establish close relations with your tongue and body, and keep a distance from your hearts and actions. Man will, on the Day of Judgment, get according to what he has done, and he will accompany those that he had loved. Make a supreme effort in making your actions acceptable, for no action finds acceptance without piety and sincerity. O scholar of the Qur'ân, be one who acts on the Qur'ân. A scholar is one who acts upon what he has read and brings about a closeness between his knowledge and his acts. A time will come when there will be great disparity between acts and knowledge. They will sit in a circle to praise one another and ask one coming to join them to sit away from them. Bear in mind deeds have no place in assemblies but they are related to Allâh the Almighty." "Beauty of manners is the essence of man, wisdom is his helper and etiquette his legacy. Barbarism is worse than arrogance."

A person came to Ali ﷺ and submitted, "Make me understand what is fate." He said, "Ask it not for it is a dark track." He again put the same question and got a similar reply, "Try not to plunge in it for it is a deep sea." He asked the same question once again and Ali ﷺ replied, "It is the secret of Allâh and it has been kept secret from you, why do you try to explore it?" When he repeated his question again, Ali ﷺ said, "Tell me whether Allâh the Almighty has made you according to His Will or as per your choice." He said, "Allâh has made me according to His Will." Thereupon Ali ﷺ said, "He is then free to make use of you according to His Will, what is your choice then?"

"Every trouble has its limit and when it inflicts anybody, it goes to its extremity. So, whoever is afflicted, he should not indulge in finding remedies as he will be more distressed in it." "It is bestowing to give anything when asked and to give without asking is benevolence. Idleness in prayer, want of subsistence and decrease in taste are all punishments for a sin."

Ali ﷺ said to Hasan ﷺ in his last counsel, "Wisdom is the greatest wealth while stupidity is the worst pauperism; arrogance is the gravest savageness and beauty of manner is the greatest generosity. Shun the company of a stupid person for he wants to benefit you but puts you to harm. Keep away from a liar, for he brings you closer to what is distant and makes you distant from what is closest. Keep away from a miser too, for he will cause you to renounce what is most wanted by you. Keep not the company of a transgressor, for he will put you on sale very cheaply. None should fear anything except sin and expect nothing from anybody except from Allâh. One should not be ashamed of learning what is unknown to him. When a scholar is asked about something unknown to him, he must unhesitatingly say: 'Allâh knows better.' Patience and Faith are like head and body, when patience leaves, Faith is also no longer there, for how can a body exist without a head. A *Faqih* (Islamic jurist) is one who lets no one lose their faith in Allâh, nor gives permission for committing sins, nor makes one fearless of the torment of Allâh, nor lets one inclined to anything else shun the Qur'ân. Pomegranates should be eaten along with the thin skin that is stuck with the grains, for it helps the food digest with its entry into the stomach. A time is about to come when a believer will be baser than the ordinary slave."

Important Events of Ali's Caliphate

Bai'ah of Caliphate

A week after the martyrdom of Uthmân bin Affân ﷺ, *Bai'ah* (oath of allegiance) was taken on Dhul-Hijjah 25, 35 AH, at the hands of Ali ﷺ in Al-Madinah. Following the martyrdom of Uthmân bin Affân ﷺ, his murderers were going strong in Al-Madinah.

At first, they forced the people of Al-Madinah to elect a caliph under threat. The majority of the rioters leaned towards Ali ﷺ and the same situation prevailed throughout Al-Madinah. When the people went to Ali ﷺ to take *Bai'ah*, he said, "You pledge your allegiance to me but this is not enough unless the Companions of Badr accept me as caliph." Hearing this, they went to the Companions of Badr and brought them in a group to Ali ﷺ. First of all Mâlik Ashtar took the *Bai'ah* while others followed him.

Ali ﷺ then asked them to find out the intentions of Talhah and Zubair ﷺ. Following this, Mâlik Ashtar went to Talhah ﷺ and Hukaim bin Jabalah contacted Zubair ﷺ and both of them were forcibly brought to Ali ﷺ, who told them that he was ready to take *Bai'ah* at the hands of anyone who had a desire to become the Caliph. They flatly rejected the offer. They were then asked to take *Bai'ah* at the hands of Ali ﷺ. At this, they began to ponder. Thereupon Mâlik Ashtar said to Talhah ﷺ drawing his sword, "The matter is to be decided right now."

In response to the demand of the situation, Talhah ﷺ said to Ali ﷺ, "I will take *Bai'ah* provided you issue orders to take actions according to the limits set by the Book of Allâh and *Sunnah* of His Messenger, and take *Qisâs* (retaliation) from the murderers of Uthmân bin Affân." Ali ﷺ promised to do the needful. Talhah ﷺ took *Bai'ah* extending his hand which had become lame following the injuries he received during the battle of Uhud. Some people took it as an ill omen. Zubair ﷺ also agreed to take *Bai'ah* with the same conditions put forward by Talhah ﷺ.

When Sa'd bin Abu Waqqâs ﷺ was approached, he shut his doors saying, "I shall do it after others have done it." He, however, told them not to expect anything bad from him. Ali ﷺ did not press him further.

Abdullah bin Umar ﷺ responded in the same way as Sa'd bin Abu Waqqâs ﷺ. Mâlik Ashtar drew his sword to kill him but Ali ﷺ stood surety for him. Abdullah bin Umar ﷺ then left for Makkah to perform *Umrah* (the lesser pilgrimage). They cautioned Ali ﷺ against Abdullah's activities. Ali ﷺ was about to send people to arrest him when Umm Kulthum ﷺ, the wife of Umar ﷺ and daughter of Ali ﷺ intervened and convinced him of the innocence of Abdullah ﷺ. Ali ﷺ felt satisfied.

Muhammad bin Maslamah, Usâmah bin Zaid, Hassân bin Thâbit, Ka'b bin Mâlik, Abu Saeed Khudri, Nu'mân bin Bashir, Zaid bin Thâbit, Mughirah bin Shu'bah, and Abdullah bin Salâm ﷺ also declined to support the new Caliph. Many others, particularly Banu Umayyah stayed away and left for Syria without delay. Ali ﷺ asked the Companions staying in Al-Madinah to explain their refusal. They argued that they wanted to keep neutral owing to the prevailing state of disturbances and killings.

Ali ﷺ then wanted Marwân bin Al-Hakam to appear but he could not be found. When Nâ'ilah ﷺ, the wife of Uthmân ﷺ was asked the names of the murderers, she gave the physical appearance of two of them but failed to tell their names. When asked about Muhammad bin Abu Bakr ﷺ, she said that he came in but left before the assassination. Some people from Banu Umayyah collected the cut off fingers of Nâ'ilah ﷺ and the bloodstained clothes, and proceeded to Syria to meet Mu'âwiyah bin Abu Sufyân ﷺ.

Second Day of the Caliphate

Next day Talhah and Zubair ﷺ called on Ali ﷺ and said that they had pledged their support to him on the condition that retaliation measures would be taken against the murderers of Uthmân ﷺ. If he failed to take *Qisâs* (retaliation), their *Bai'ah* would stand as null and void. Ali ﷺ said, "I shall take the necessary *Qisâs* from the murderers of Uthmân, and do full justice to one and all. But until now the rioters are too strong and the state of caliphate has not yet been consolidated, I can only pay attention to this after the return to normalcy. Nothing can be done at present." Both of them went back home. But whispering and murmuring started. The rioters and the murderers of Uthmân ❁ grew anxious of their safety while others were dissatisfied with Ali ❁ over his lack of action. Thus opposition to the caliphate of Ali ❁ began to build up. The new Caliph was rendered helpless by the circumstances.

Disobedience of the Rioters

Three days after assuming charge of the caliphate, Ali ❁ asked the people from Kufah, Basrah and Egypt to go back to their respective places, but Abdullah bin Saba refused to obey his orders and most of the rioters sided with him. It was, in truth, the greatest ill omen for the caliphate of Ali ❁ that those refused to obey his orders who were apparently the strongest supporters and followers of the new Caliph. Again Talhah and Zubair ❁ called on Ali ❁ and requested him to send them to Basrah and Kufah to put the people right as they had large followings among them. But Ali ❁ grew suspicious and did not allow it.

Useful Counsel of Mughirah and Ibn Abbâs ❁

On the third or fourth day after being installed as Caliph, Ali ❁ issued orders deposing all the governors appointed by Uthmân bin Affân ❁ and replaced them with his own. Knowing this Mughirah bin Shu'bah ❁, a farsighted man and close relative of Ali ❁ called on him and said that his decision to hold Talhah and Zubair ❁ back from going out of Al-Madinah would have an adverse effect on the Quraish, and he would lose much of their sympathy. Moreover, he (Ali) had deposed the governors of Uthmân's period too hastily. He advised Ali ❁ to leave those governors in their places and simply seek their obedience. Ali ❁ rejected the advice of Mughirah ❁ outright.

The next day Mughirah ❁ came again to Ali ❁ in the presence of Abdullah bin Abbâs ❁. During the conversation, he advised Ali ❁ to depose the governors of Uthmân's period without delay. Since he said that in clear contradiction of his previous advice, Abdullah bin Abbâs ﷺ remarked when he (Mughirah) left, "Mughirah had given a wise counsel yesterday but he has deceived you today." When Ali ﷺ sought his opinion he said, "It was better for you to leave Al-Madinah at the time of Uthmân's martyrdom. But now it is the demand of reason that you keep the governors of Uthmân intact until your caliphate gains stability. If you act too quickly in deposing the governors, Banu Umayyah will create doubt in the minds of people that they were being deposed for demanding Qisâs."

Hearing this Ali ﷺ said, "I shall straighten out Mu'âwiyah with my sword and make no concessions." Ibn Abbâs ﷺ said, "You are a brave man no doubt but the Prophet ﷺ has said: 'War is deceit.' (Bukhari:3030) So, if you act on my advice, I shall suggest to you such a device that, if you put it into practice, Banu Umayyah are sure to be left wondering without finding any way out." Ali ﷺ said, "I possess traits of characters neither like you nor like Mu'âwiyah." Ibn Abbâs ﷺ said, "As for my opinion, it is better for you to leave for Yanbu and stay there with your doors shut. In such a case the Arabs will go from place to place without finding a worthy man like you. But if you go about with the slayers of Uthmân, they will accuse you of being an accomplice to this heinous act." Ali ﷺ said, "I don't consider it proper to act upon your advice; you should rather follow what I say." Ibn Abbâs ﷺ said, "It is undoubtedly proper for me to carry out your orders." Thereupon Ali ﷺ said, "I want to send you as the governor of Syria in place of Mu'âwiyah." Ibn Abbâs ﷺ said, "Mu'âwiyah is an ancestral brother of Uthmân bin Affân, while I am related to you. So they will kill or arrest me with my entry into Syria. It is better that you first enter into correspondence with Mu'âwiyah and take Bai'ah from him." But Ali ﷺ rejected the proposal. Mughirah bin Shu'bah ﷺ witnessed that Ali ﷺ neither acted upon the advice of Ibn Abbâs ﷺ nor of his own and so Mughirah ﷺ left Al-Madinah for Makkah.

Deposition and Installation of Governors

Ali ﷺ appointed Uthmân bin Hunaif for Basrah, Umârah bin Shihâb for Kufah, Ubaidullah bin Abbâs for Yemen, Qais bin Sa'd for Egypt and Sahl bin Hunaif for Syria.

When Uthmân bin Hunaif reached Basrah, some people accepted him right away and showed their obedience but some others kept quiet to follow the people of Al-Madinah.

Umârah bin Shihâb appointed for Kufah was on his way to Kufah when Tulaihah bin Khuwailid came across and advised him to return because the people of Basrah wanted no replacement for Abu Musa Ash'ari ﷺ. And if he rejected his advice he would kill him then and there. Following this advice he came back.

Ya'la bin Munyah, the governor of Yemen had left for Makkah before the new governor Ubaidullah bin Abbâs reached there to take charge peacefully.

When Qais bin Sa'd reached Egypt, some people pledged their allegiance while others delayed it; still others pleaded that they wanted to do nothing before the arrival to Egypt of their fellows from Al-Madinah.

Sahl bin Hunaif on the way to Syria met in Tabuk several horsemen who inquired about him. On the disclosure that he was going as the governor of Syria, they said to him in a firm tone, "If you are going to Syria appointed by somebody other than Uthmân, then it is better for you to go back." Sahl returned from there. By the time he arrived in Al-Madinah, other governors had also reached the capital of Islam.

Jarir bin Abdullah Al-Bajali was governor of Hamadân at the time of the martyrdom of Uthmân ﷺ. Ali ﷺ wrote him to come to him in Al-Madinah after taking the oath of allegiance of the people of his province, and he reached Al-Madinah accordingly.

Mu'âwiyah's Support to Truth

Ali ﷺ sent a letter to Abu Musa Ash'ari ﷺ through Ma'bad Aslami. In reply to the letter, Abu Musa ﷺ let him know: "The people of Kufah have taken the oath of allegiance at my hands. Most of them have done it with pleasure while others reluctantly.". This letter gave him some satisfaction.

About the same time a letter was sent to Mu'âwiyah ﷺ through Jarir bin Abdullah and Sabrah Al-Juhani in Damascus. For three months no

reply came and Mu'âwiyah ﷺ kept the Caliph's emissary waiting.
After that he handed over a sealed letter to his emissary Qabisah Absi
and sent him accompanied by Jarir bin Abdullah. The letter was clearly
addressed to Ali ﷺ. They reached in the month of Rabi' Al-Awwal 36
AH. The emissary gave Mu'âwiyah's letter to Ali ﷺ. When the envelope
was opened, it contained no letter. Ali ﷺ looked towards the emissary
angrily. The emissary shuddered from within and said, "I am an
emissary and safety of life is my right." Ali ﷺ said: "Yes, you are safe."
The emissary then said, "Nobody will pledge support to you. I have seen
sixty thousand souls weeping over the bloodstained shirt of Uthmân bin
Affân. They have also put the shirt on the grand mosque of Damascus to
provoke the people." Ali ﷺ said, "They want to take the revenge of
Uthmân on me even though I stood absolved from Uthmân's blood. May
Allâh deal with the murderers of Uthmân." Saying this, he returned the
emissary to Mu'âwiyah ﷺ.

Deviation of the Followers of Ibn Saba

The rioters and the followers of Abdullah bin Saba abused the
emissary and wanted to beat him up but some people saved him and
he was some how able to reach Damascus. Jarir bin Abdullah was also
accused of being a party to the conspiratorial activities of Mu'âwiyah
ﷺ on account of his long stay in Damascus. As a result of this
allegation, he became so frustrated that he went to Qarqaisia instead
of Al-Madinah. Mu'âwiyah ﷺ later called him to Damascus through
a messenger.

Preparations for the Invasion on Syria

When the people of Al-Madinah came to know of the strained
relations between Ali and Mu'âwiyah ﷺ, they feared further
bloodshed. They sent Ziyâd bin Hanzalah to Ali ﷺ as a feeler. Ali ﷺ
asked him to get ready. "What for?" Ziyâd asked. "For invading
Syria," Ali ﷺ firmly replied. "You should deal with them rather
politely," he suggested. "No, the insurgents must be punished," Ali
ﷺ said. Knowing the intentions of Ali ﷺ, both Talhah and Zubair ﷺ
called on Ali ﷺ and sought permission to go to Makkah to perform
Umrah. Ali ﷺ allowed them to leave Al-Madinah for any further

detention was unreasonable. He then announced throughout Al-Madinah to get ready for the invasion on Syria. Furthermore, he wrote letters to Uthmân bin Hunaif in Basrah, Abu Musa in Kufah and Qais bin Sa'd in Egypt to make military preparations from their respective resources and send them to Al-Madinah on demand.

Military Action against the Muslims

When most of the people of Al-Madinah got ready for this purpose, Ali ﷺ placed Al-Madinah in the charge of Qatham bin Abbâs and made his son Muhammad bin Hanafiyah the standard-bearer of the Islamic army. Abdullah bin Abbâs ﷺ the commanding officer of the right wing and Amr bin Abu Salamah ﷺ that of the left while he put Abu Laila bin Al-Jarrâh, the brother of Abu Ubaidah bin Al-Jarrâh ﷺ on the vanguard. However, he was cautious enough not to engage anyone from among the rioters for any military service. Ali ﷺ had not finished the job of allotting military positions when news was given to him that the Makkans were making preparations against him. Following this news he postponed his march against Syria.

Preparations of the Mother of the Believers in Makkah

It has already been mentioned that Âishah ﷺ had returned to Makkah on hearing the news of Uthmân's martyrdom. On reaching near to Makkah she was also told that the people of Al-Madinah had taken the oath of allegiance at the hands of Ali ﷺ. She returned to Makkah in such a state that people grouped around her mount.

She said to them, "By Allâh Uthmân has been killed without any fault and I shall take revenge on his behalf. It is unfortunate that people collecting from the outskirts of the cities and forests, and the slaves of Al-Madinah opposed Uthmân simply because he had appointed governors from our youths, although his predecessors had also done this. When the rioters failed to establish their claim, they rose against Uthmân and committed a breach of trust. They shed the blood declared prohibited by Allâh the Almighty; they committed bloodshed in the city that Allâh the Almighty had made the place of migration for His Messenger ﷺ, and did it in the month when hostilities are forbidden and plundered property unlawfully. By Allâh even a finger of Uthmân is superior to all the world. Uthmân is free from the blame they have put on him."

Abdullah bin Âmir Hadrami was the governor of Makkah appointed by Uthmân bin Affân ﷺ. When he heard Âishah ﷺ, he said very firmly, "I will be the first to take revenge of Uthmân's blood."

Hearing this all the men from Banu Umayyah who had reached Makkah after the martyrdom of Uthmân ﷺ, rose in support of action against the murderers. Saeed bin Al-Âsi and Walid bin Uqbah were also among them. Abdullah bin Âmir had reached Makkah after being deposed from the governorship of Basrah, while Ya'la bin Munyah had come from Yemen along with six hundred camels and six hundred thousand dinars. They all sat together to find a way of avenging the blood of Uthmân ﷺ.

When Talhah and Zubair ﷺ reached Makkah from Al-Madinah, Âishah ﷺ sent for both and inquired of them the reason behind their arrival in Makkah. They gave the reason that the rioters being in control, the noble and saner people found it totally unsafe to live in Al-Madinah. Âishah ﷺ then said, "You should then rise against them along with us." Both of them expressed their favor and support to this plan. The entire population of Makkah was obedient to the Mother of the believers. Four persons, Abdullah bin Âmir and Ya'la bin Munyah, the former governors of Basrah and Yemen, Talhah and Zubair, were among the commanders of Âishah's army and considered to be men of sense and determination.

At first, advice came from someone to proceed to Syria avoiding Al-Madinah. But the proposal was set aside because of Mu'âwiyah's power and capacity to keep Syria intact. Then came the proposal to proceed to Basrah for Abdullah bin Âmir ﷺ had a considerable circle of his friends and well-wishers and Talhah ﷺ also had influence over the people of Basrah. Thus they had hope of getting much support there.

Someone suggested to face the eventualities in Makkah but Abdullah bin Amir ﷺ stated that the Makkans would not be able to withstand the onslaught of the army of Al-Madinah. Moreover the joint forces of Makkah and Basrah would be enough to face any danger.

In short, the proposal gained general support and preparation for Basrah began in full swing. Other Mothers of the believers too expressed their desire to accompany Âishah 🐱. When Abdullah Umar 🐱 was contacted, he pleaded in support of the people of Al-Madinah. He also stopped Hafsah 🐱 from accompanying Âishah 🐱 to Basrah. Mughirah bin Shu'bah 🐱 had also reached Makkah, he too accompanied the army.

Departure from Makkah to Basrah

Abdullah bin Âmir and Ya'la bin Munyah 🐱 had come to Makkah with a large amount of money and goods from Basrah and Yemen. Thus they took an active part in organizing the army of Âishah 🐱. Before the departure it was announced in Makkah that Âishah, Talhah and Zubair 🐱 were leaving for Basrah and the people sympathetic to Islam and demanding retaliation for the blood of Uthmân 🐱 were invited to join their party. Thus an army of one and a half thousand people marched to Basrah. People began to join on the way and the army very soon swelled to three thousand. Umm Fadl bint Al-Hârith 🐱 the mother of Abdullah bin Abbâs 🐱 happened to be with the force. She sent Zafar, a person from Juhainah tribe as a courier to Ali 🐱 with a letter containing a detailed account of the mission.

The other Mothers of believers accompanied Âishah 🐱 returned to Al-Madinah from Dhat-Irq. Mughirah bin Shu'bah, Saeed bin Al-Âs and some others also left army on the base of some differences.

The Governor of Basrah opposes the Plan

When the army came close to Basrah, Âishah 🐱 sent Abdullah bin Âmir 🐱 into the city with letters in the names of the distinguished personalities of Basrah and awaited their response. When Uthmân bin Hunaif, the governor of Basrah came to know of the arrival of Âishah 🐱 he sent to her some influential persons of Basrah as emissaries. They called on the Mother of the believers and inquired about the reason behind their arrival. She said explaining the reason, "The rioters and miscreants from some tribes have spread rumors in order to create confusion in the Muslim ranks and put Islam to harm. I have, therefore come out to put such elements to right and acquaint them with the real facts." They got up and called on Talhah and Zubair 🕮 and put to them the same question. Giving their own reason, they said, "We have come out to avenge the blood of Uthmân." They said, "Haven't you two taken *Bai'ah* at the hands of Ali?" They replied, "Yes, we pledged out support to Ali provided he avenge the blood of Uthmân. Moreover, swords were then hanging over our heads." The emissaries went back to Uthmân bin Hunaif in Basrah and communicated to him the whole account. He heard all this with an element of shock and asked their opinion. They asked him to be patient. But he expressed his resolve to keep holding them back until the arrival of Ali 🕮. The emissaries left and closed their doors upon themselves.

Uthmân bin Hunaif gave a call to the people of Basrah to get ready to fight and to assemble in the mosque. When people assembled, Uthmân bin Hunaif asked a man named Qais to address the audience. He said, "People! If Talhah, Zubair and their people have come to seek safety, there is something wrong for even the birds of Makkah are safe and nobody can do them any harm. And if they have arrived for avenging the blood of Uthmân bin Affân, then we are not the murderers. It seems more proper to send them back with honor." Hearing this, Aswad bin Sari' Sa'di got up and said, "They have not come here taking us to be the slayers of Uthmân bin Affân, they have rather come to us to seek our help against the slayers of Uthmân bin Affân." With these words uttered at the moment, the people got infuriated and began to hurl gravel at Qais and the session ended in confusion and disorder. It was, however, gathered that Talhah and Zubair 🕮 had a following in Basrah.

Battle-Array

When Âishah 🕮 came up to Mirbad at the head of her army, Uthmân in Hunaif came out with his own and a battle line was drawn. Talhah 🕮 was on the right wing and Zubair 🕮 on the left. When the two armies came face to face, Talhah 🕮 emerged first of all and described the excellences of Uthmân 🕮 after glorifying Allâh the

Almighty, and then appealed for avenging the blood of the martyred. Then came out Zubair ♦ and testified to what Talhah ♦ had said. Following this Âishah ♦ uttered some words of wise counsel. The impact of her speech divided the people of Uthmân bin Hunaif into two groups.

While one group was still adamant, another gave up the idea of fighting for the reason that fighting against Talhah and Zubair ♦ was not justified. When Âishah, Talhah and Zubair ♦ witnessed the rift in their ranks they returned to their camp. However, Uthmân bin Hunaif remained firm. Moreover, he sent Jâriah bin Qudâmah to Âishah ♦ and he said, "O Mother of the believers! The assassination of Uthmân was far better than your coming out on the back of this wretched camel. Allâh the Almighty has made you to observe *Hijâb* (veil) but you put the *Hijâb* to disgrace. If you have come here of your own, it is better for you to go back to Al-Madinah; if by force, then seek Allah's help." The speech had not ended when Hukaim bin Jabalah attacked the army of Âishah ♦. But the battle stopped in the evening. The next day Hukaim bin Jabalah drew the battle line again and the two forces attacked one another. Hukaim was killed on the battlefield and Uthmân bin Hunaif had to taste defeat.

Basrah was captured by Talhah and Zubair ♦. Uthmân bin Hunaif was brought as a captive. But Âishah ♦ ordered him to be set free. He went straight to Ali ♦. Although Basrah came under the sway of Âishah, Talhah and Zubair ♦, the condition was not different from the rule of Uthmân bin Hunaif, as Basrah was still a mixture of elements for and against the winner.

Ali ♦ marches from Al-Madinah

When Ali ♦ was informed of the developments in Makkah and Basrah, he expressed shock and grief and gave the people a call to fight with the insurgents. Even though fighting against Âishah, Talhah and Zubair ♦ was an unpleasant act for the people of Al-Madinah, most of them responded to the call when they saw Abul-Haitham Badari, Ziyâd bin Hanzalah, Khuzaimah bin Thâbit and Abu Qatâdah ♦ had approved. He left Al-Madinah at the end of Rabi' Al-Âkhir 36 AH. Some groups of the Kufis and Egyptians joined Ali ♦.

Abdullah bin Saba—the Jew and Hypocrite

Abdullah bin Saba also joined the army of Ali ؓ along with his followers. Abdullah bin Salâm ؓ came across them on the way and said holding the bridle of Ali's horse, "O Chief of the believers; go not from Al-Madinah. By Allâh, if you go out, no head of the Muslims will ever come back to Al-Madinah." The people rushed towards Abdullah calling him bad names. Ali ؓ asked the people to leave him, saying he was a good man from among the Companions of the Prophet ﷺ. When he moved further ahead, he was informed to his shock that Talhah and Zubair ؓ had already marched into Basrah.

Ali ؓ halted at Rabadhah and sent orders to various parts of the country from here. Moreover, he sent Muhammad bin Abu Bakr ؓ and Muhammad bin Ja'far ؓ to Kufah to collect and bring people. Since the people disliked to fight with Talhah and Zubair ؓ, Ali ؓ promised not to attack them unless they forced him to fight back. A little ahead of Rabadhah, a party from the Tai tribe joined the army. Amr bin Al-Jarrâh was put on the vanguard. At Faid, they came across a person coming from Kufah. When he was asked about Abu Musa Ash'ari ؓ, he remarked, "If you have not come out to make peace with Talhah and Zubair, Abu Musa will not help you."

Ali ؓ observed, "Talhah and Zubair first pledged their allegiance to me and then committed a breach of trust. They obeyed Abu Bakr, Umar and Uthmân but have opposed me, if they but knew that I am not different from them," saying this he cursed Talhah and Zubair ؓ.

The Two Muhammads in Kufah

When Muhammad bin Abu Bakr ؓ and Muhammad bin Ja'far ؓ gave the letter of Ali ؓ to Abu Musa ؓ in Kufah and tried to persuade the people to join the camp of Ali ؓ, they showed no interest. When Muhammad bin Abu Bakr ؓ insisted, they remarked, "Going out to fight is a temporal affair while sitting in peace is the way to the Hereafter." Others kept to the line. When Muhammad bin Abu Bakr ؓ and Muhammad bin Ja'far ؓ got angry and behaved rudely to Abu Musa ؓ he said, "The Bai'ah to Uthmân still hangs round Ali's and my neck. If fighting is necessary, the murderers of Uthmân should be fought wherever they are met." They returned empty-handed and gave the account to Ali ﷺ at Dhi Qâr.

Ashtar and Ibn Abbâs ﷺ in Kufah

When the mission of Muhammad bin Abu Bakr ﷺ and Muhammad bin Ja'far ﷺ failed to bring any fruit, Ali ﷺ asked Ashtar to go with Ibn Abbâs ﷺ and try to bring Abu Musa ﷺ around to their point of view. They reached Kufah and tried their level best to persuade him but he remained adamant in his opinion to the last and this mission too failed.

Ammâr bin Yâsir and Hasan bin Ali ﷺ in Kufah

On the return of Ashtar and Ibn Abbâs ﷺ, Ali ﷺ sent his son Hasan ﷺ and Ammâr bin Yâsir ﷺ to Kufah. Being informed of their arrival, Abu Musa ﷺ came to the mosque. He embraced Hasan ﷺ and said addressing Ammâr bin Yâsir ﷺ, "You joined the transgressors instead of lending support to Uthmân." Ammâr ﷺ denied the charge. Meanwhile, Hasan ﷺ spoke out that people held no consultations with them and they had nothing in mind but putting the matter right. Moreover, the Chief of the believers feared none in his task of bringing reforms to the people. Abu Musa ﷺ said with due respect, "May my mother and father be sacrificed for you, you spoke the truth. But the Prophet ﷺ has said, 'Affliction is to be caused in the near future. In such a situation the sitting one will be better than the standing and the standing will be better than the mounted. And all the Muslims are brethren among themselves. Their blood and possessions are prohibited for each other.'" Abu Musa's statement enraged Ammâr bin Yâsir ﷺ and he called him bad names. Abu Musa ﷺ kept quite. But some people fell on Ammâr but Abu Musa saved him.

During these days Âishah ﷺ wrote letters to the people of Kufah from Basrah advising them not to lend support to anyone and either sit behind closed doors or come to their help for they have come out to avenge the blood of Uthmân. Zaid bin Suhân began to read out the letter to the audience. Shabath bin Rib'i hurled abuse which caused anger in the audience, and they openly rose in support of Âishah 🌸. Abu Musa 🌸 got up to pacify and advise them to keep indoors, provide shelter to the oppressed, and keep the points of their spears down and their swords sheathed.

Hearing all this, Zaid bin Suhân asked the audience to lend help and support to Ali 🌸. A few others followed suit. Thereupon Ammâr bin Yâsir 🌸 said, "People! Ali has called you to give your due. Come out and help him." Following this Hasan bin Ali 🌸 spoke: "O people! Accept our invitation, obey us and help us in this present crisis. The Chief of the believers says, 'Help us if we are victims and force us to get your due if we are wrongdoers.' He has also said, 'Talhah and Zubair had taken *Bai'ah* at my hand first and then broke it before others.' " The speech produced the desired effect at once and they rose in support of the Caliph. Mâlik Ashtar was also sent after Hasan and Ammâr 🌸, he reached Kufah at a time when Hasan bin Ali 🌸 was speaking to the people. His presence added to the zeal of the people and nobody was ready to listen to Abu Musa Ash'ari 🌸.

Hasan bin Ali 🌸, Ammâr bin Yâsir 🌸 and Ashtar left Kufah at the head of a nine thousand strong army and were greeted by Ali 🌸 at Dhi Qâr. Speaking highly of them the Caliph Ali 🌸 said, "I have troubled you, O people of Kufah to join us in fighting the people of Basrah. However, if they change their mind, it is most welcome, but if they insist on their viewpoint, we shall treat them politely so that we are not accused of initiating atrocities." Having heard this, the people of Kufah joined the army of Ali 🌸 at Dhi Qâr. Next day, Ali 🌸 sent Qa'qâ' bin Amr 🌸 towards Basrah. It was here that Owais Qarni took the oath of allegiance at the hands of Ali 🌸.

Endeavor for Mediation

Ali 🌸 had sent Qa'qâ' bin Amr 🌸 to Basrah to know what was on the minds of Âishah, Talhah and Zubair 🌸 and to bring them to the path of peace taking or renewing their *Bai'ah*. Qa'qâ' 🌸 was very eloquent and wise. He first submitted to Âishah 🌸: "What has led you to such an act and what do you want?" She replied, "My sole aim is to bring reforms to the people and put them on the line set by the

Qur'ân." He then put the same question to Talhah and Zubair ﷺ and got the same reply. Thereupon Qa'qâ' bin Amr ﷺ said, "If your aim is to make the people follow the Qur'ân, the purpose cannot be achieved by the way you like it." They said, "The Qur'ân enjoins *Qisâs* (retaliation) and we want to take it." Qa'qâ' ﷺ said, "How *Qisâs* can be taken this way? Establishment and stability of the caliphate are among the top priorities, which bring peace and solidarity and may ensure avenging the blood of Uthmân. Now, in the absence of peace and order and any administrative system, how is anybody within his rights to take *Qisâs*. You have killed a large number of people here in Basrah just for the taking of *Qisâs* for Uthmân, but Hurqus bin Zuhair could not be caught. And in the wake of chasing him, six thousand men stood at his back to fight with his opponents and you gave up chasing him. In the same way, you should have waited if Ali could not take *Qisâs* on account of his preoccupations in curbing violence and consolidating power. How reasonable is it for you to stand against them and thus aggravate the situation? In such a situation, violence will grow and the murderers of Uthmân will remain safe from *Qisâs*."

Saying all this, Qa'qâ' bin Amr ﷺ said in a heart-rending tone: "The greatest reform at this time is to make peace with one another so that the Muslims as a whole should live in peace and safety. You are the leaders of virtues and stars of guidance. By Allâh, keep from pushing us into some trial lest you will not be able to be safe and the Muslim *Ummah* will also pass through a great ordeal."

Âishah, Talhah and Zubair ﷺ were immediately moved at the utterance of Qa'qâ' ﷺ and they said with one voice: "If Ali nourishes such a thought and he has in mind his duty of taking *Qisâs*, there is no point in any dispute. Until now we thought he had some soft corner in his heart for the murderers with the result they have joined Ali's army and carry out his orders." Qa'qâ' bin Amr ﷺ said, "What I have said is the reflection of Ali's thought." They said, "We too then have nothing to do against him." Qa'qâ' ﷺ then proceeded to the army of Ali ﷺ. A group of influential people of Basrah also accompanied him. They wanted to know whether Ali ﷺ and the people of Kufah were inclined to peace or not. They were informed that, people were saying about Ali ﷺ that after conquering Basrah, he will kill the youths and make their women and children slaves. This rumor was spread by the followers of Abdullah bin Saba in Basrah who were a part of Ali's army.

When Qa'qâ' bin Amr ﷺ appeared before Ali ﷺ and gave the whole account of his success in Basrah, he expressed great joy. The people of Basrah then asked the people of Kufah who formed a part of Ali's army about their intentions. They spoke in favor of peace. Following this, Ali ﷺ called them and referred to his efforts to make peace. They showed satisfaction and left with the good news.

Consultations for Mischief-Making

After the beginning of the peace mission, Ali ﷺ concentrated his army and delivered an eloquent and impressive speech. He then ordered a march to Basrah the next day. He made it clear that the movement was not meant for fighting but for bringing peace. Besides this, he asked those to keep away who had surrounded the house of Uthmân bin Affân ﷺ. Learning this, Abdullah bin Saba and the Egyptians grew anxious.

This group that was isolated from the rest of Ali's army, numbered about two to two-and-a-half thousand men, some being very clever and influential among them. Abdullah bin Saba held consultations with various groups in a special assembly, which included Abdullah bin Saba, Ibn Muljam, Ashtar and his gang including Ilba bin Al-Haitham Sadusi, Sâlim bin Tha'labah and Shuraih bin Aufa etc. Giving vent to their feelings they said, "Talhah and Zubair have been demanding *Qisâs* and now Ali seems to be backing their cause. He asked today to keep us separate from the army, tomorrow, after joining hands with them, he will take *Qisâs* and punish us all." Ashtar said, "Talhah, Zubair and Ali are all one in their opinion concerning us. Now the pillar of peace will be erected on our blood. So, in my opinion, Talhah, Zubair and Ali should also be sent to Uthmân. This will be the end of all our troubles." Abdullah bin Saba who was presiding over the assembly, further said, "You are small in number while Ali has an army of twenty thousand behind him. Talhah and Zubair have another thirty thousand troops with them. Thus our job is very difficult." Sâlim bin Tha'labah suggested, "We should leave for some where else until peace is restored." Shuraih seconded the proposal. But Abdullah bin Saba rejected it as useless. Everyone then rose to give his own suggestion. At last they turned to Abdullah bin Saba to put forward his suggestion. He then said, "Brethren. It is better for all of us to keep within the army of Ali. In case he expels us, we should remain at a close distance from his army base on the reason that we want to help his army in case a battle breaks out. Moreover, we should leave no stone unturned to arouse both sides to fight one another. Once the battle begins, our troubles are gone."

The Battle of Jamal

The next morning Ali ﷺ gave marching orders to his army. A section of the rioters accompanied the army while the other part kept itself at a little distance. Bakr bin Wâ'il and Abdul-Qais clans joined the army on the way. In Basrah, Ali ﷺ pitched his tents at the grounds of Ubaidullah Palace. From the opposite side, the army of Âishah, Talhah and Zubair ﷺ came to the same ground. Both sides kept silent for three days awaiting the result of the ongoing peace talks.

In the meantime someone said to Ali ﷺ, "Why have you come here?" Ali ﷺ said, "I am here to curb the disturbances and bring about peace for the Muslims." The man said, "What will you do if the people of Basrah reject your peace efforts?" Ali ﷺ said, "We shall leave them to their state of affairs." He than said, "You may leave them but what will you do if they are not ready to leave you." Ali ﷺ said, "In such a situation we shall defend ourselves."

Meanwhile another person spoke out, "Talhah and Zubair maintain that they have revolted to seek the Pleasure of Allâh. Do they, in your opinion, have any right in support of avenging the blood of Uthmân?" Ali ﷺ replied, "Yes, they also have a right." He then said, "Do you also have a reason for delaying *Qisâs*?" Ali ﷺ replied, "Yes, when something becomes doubtful, one should take cautious steps before going into action." The same person said again, "What will follow for them and for us in case a battle breaks out?" Ali ﷺ said, "The person killed on both sides will go to heaven."

After this, Ali ﷺ sent Hakim bin Salâmah and Mâlik bin Habib to Talhah and Zubair ﷺ to know if they were still firm on the peace talks held between them and Qa'qâ' bin Amr ﷺ; if so, they should keep from starting a battle until the matter is finalized. Talhah and Zubair ﷺ told Ali ﷺ that they maintained their promise. Following this Talhah and Zubair ﷺ came out from their ranks responding while Ali ﷺ too emerged from his side and they all came very near to one another. Ali ﷺ then said addressing Talhah ﷺ, "You have collected this army against me. Could you give an excuse for your action and prove it valid? Am I not your brother in Faith? Is not our blood unlawful for each other?" Talhah ﷺ replied, "Have you not hatched a conspiracy to kill Uthmân?" Ali ﷺ replied, "Allâh the Almighty knows everything and He will send His curse on the killers of Uthmân. And Talhah, have you not taken *Bai'ah* at my hands?" Talhah ﷺ replied, "Of course, I have taken *Bai'ah* but with a sword hanging over my head, and on the condition of your taking *Qisâs* from the killers of Uthmân."

Following this, Ali ﷺ turned to Zubair ﷺ and said, "Do you remember that the Prophet ﷺ had once told you that you will fight someone and you will then be a wrongdoer?" Having heard this Zubair ﷺ said, "Yes, now I remember. But why did you not remind me before my departure from Al-Madinah? Had it been in my mind, I would not have left the city, I will not fight with you any more." [This talk and the like of it is not approved by the research scholars to be true.]

In the wake of this talk, Zubair ﷺ came back to his army and called on Âishah ﷺ and said, "Ali has today reminded me something following which I will not fight with him at any cost. I have now decided to go off leaving all others." Âishah ﷺ was also nourishing such an idea for the prophecy of the Prophet ﷺ on her mind. But before her reply to Zubair ﷺ, Abdullah bin Zubair ﷺ came in and said to his father, "You decide to leave when you have already brought both sides to the battlefield and incited one against another. It seems the huge army of Ali has sent terror into your heart and made you a coward." Hearing this, Zubair ﷺ got up and moved with his weapons into the army of Ali ﷺ, walked around and came back.

When Ali ﷺ noticed him drawing near, he asked his men not to obstruct his movement. Thus nobody showed disrespect to him.

Zubair ﷺ then said to his son, "Had I been afraid of Ali's army, I would not have gone there all alone. The fact is this that I have vowed not to fight with him." Abdullah ﷺ then asked his father to set his slave free as an atonement for his vow. Zubair ﷺ said, "I have seen Ammâr in the army of Ali, and I remember the Prophet ﷺ had once said: 'A rebel will kill Ammâr.' In short, the thought of fighting has gone out of my mind." Encouraged by such a peaceful atmosphere, Abdullah bin Abbâs ﷺ went to Zubair and Talhah ﷺ from Ali's side and Muhammad bin Talhah ﷺ came to Ali ﷺ on behalf of Zubair and Talhah ﷺ and the peace terms were finalized by the evening of the third day. The peace document was decided to be written and signed the next morning.

Within these three days, Abdullah bin Saba and his party could not avail themselves of any opportunity to create mischief. They grew vehemently anxious when they came to know that the peace document between the two sides was about to be signed the next morning. They went into emergency consultations, which continued the whole night. At last they fell upon the army of Zubair and Talhah ﷺ. They made a column their target, which answered back and a full-fledged battle resulted.

Loud cries of war made Talhah and Zubair ﷺ come out of their tents. On inquiry they were told that Ali's troops had attacked their army. Thereupon Talhah ﷺ remarked, "Ali will not rest without bloodshed." The hue and cry of fighting drew Ali ﷺ out of his tent and the followers of Abdullah bin Saba told him that Talhah and Zubair ﷺ had attacked his army all of a sudden and forced his men to fight back. Ali ﷺ passed almost the same remark saying, "Alas, Talhah and Zubair will not rest without bloodshed." Following this, he started issuing orders to various sections of his troops. Fierce fighting enveloped the battlefield. Military commanders on both sides were unaware of what led to the all-out battle. However, both sides appeared not to chase the fleeing soldiers nor attack the wounded nor seize the property of their opponents. These calls from both sides established beyond doubt that despite the fighting, neither of the sides had any feeling of hatred. Both camps were expressing disgust over what was going on.

Ka'b bin Sur went to Âishah 🍃 and said, "The battle has begun. It is better for you to mount on a camel and go to the battlefield. Maybe your presence hold them back from fighting and pave the way for peace efforts to begin." Hearing this she mounted on the camel. As a precautionary measure armor was put on her litter and the camel was made to stand at a place from where the sight of battle was perfectly clear. But things went contrary to this plan and the flames of war leapt higher and higher.

Fighters from her camp were filled with great fervor when they saw her on the battlefield as if she had come to increase the enthusiasm of her troops. Soon after the beginning of the battle, an arrow hit the leg of Talhah 🍃 and his sock was filled with blood, which was flowing profusely without stop. When Qa'qâ' 🍃 who was fighting on behalf of Ali 🍃, noticed the plight of Talhah 🍃, he came near to him and said, "O Abu Muhammad! Your wound is very serious; it is advisable that you go back to Basrah at once." He did accordingly. But as soon as he entered Basrah, he fell unconscious, died and was buried there. Marwân bin Al-Hakam was fighting on behalf of Talhah and Zubair 🍃.

Talhah 🍃 was not in favor of fighting with Ali 🍃 and stood alone away from his army. He wanted to keep neutral, for he was pondering over the utterances of Ali 🍃, in the talks between Ali and Zubair 🍃 and the prophecy about Ammâr bin Yâsir 🍃. The more he thought over the issue of war, the more he became disheartened and discouraged. When Marwân bin Hakam witnessed his indifference to the ongoing battle, he felt tremendously annoyed. He then gave his slave a sign who covered his face with a sheet. Thus being his identity concealed, Marwân took an arrow dipped in poison and targeted Talhah 🍃. The poisoned arrow hit the leg of Talhah 🍃 and pierced the stomach of his horse, which fell down along with its rider. Talhah 🍃 then called the slave of Ali 🍃 who had appeared on the scene and renewed his *Bai'ah* to Ali 🍃 either on his hand or at the hand of Qa'qâ' 🍃 who also was there. After the renewal of the *Bai'ah*, he returned to Basrah and passed away. When Ali 🍃 came to know of this, he invoked the blessing of Allâh for him and kept admiring and expressing sorrow for him.

Peacemaking Efforts of Zubair ﷺ

When the battle broke out, Zubair bin Al-Awwâm ﷺ, who had already decided not to fight, held himself back. Ammâr ﷺ noticed him and threw a challenge to fight. But he refused to fight with him. Since Ammâr ﷺ considered him the root of the trouble, he made an advance and attacked him. But Zubair ﷺ kept defending himself without hitting him until Ammâr ﷺ became exhausted and Zubair ﷺ had an opportunity to get away. Ahnaf bin Qais from Basrah was lying with a large number of men encamped separately as a neutral force. When Zubair ﷺ passed by his camp, Amr bin Al-Jurmuz, a man from the army of Ahnaf bin Qais, followed him. He went near to him and began to move along with him. In order to dispel any doubt, he asked Zubair ﷺ to give his opinion on some issue. Arriving at As-Saba Valley, Zubair ﷺ stood in prayer. And as he lay prostrate, Amr bin Al-Jurmuz struck him with his weapon and came straight to Ali ﷺ. Someone informed Ali ﷺ that the assassin of Zubair ﷺ had come to meet him. He gave him permission with the remark, "Let him come in and give him good news of hell as well." When Ali ﷺ saw Zubair's sword in his hand, tears came down from his eyes and he said, "O tyrant! This is the sword which had guarded the Prophet ﷺ for long." These words cast such an effect that the assassin thrust his own sword into his belly after passing some disrespectful remarks against Ali ﷺ and thus went to Hell.

Separation of Talhah ﷺ

Talhah and Zubair ﷺ kept themselves apart right from the beginning of the battle. But small chieftains of various clans were firm in their resolve to fight on behalf of Âishah ﷺ. But she also, on the other hand, was in favor of peace and agreement. Moreover, there was none left on their side to lead and guide in the fight. They did not even know the real intention of Âishah ﷺ under whom they claimed to be fighting. However, she could not hold her troops back, they were all under the impression that Ali ﷺ had deceived them by his sneak attack after the peace negotiations were about to be finalized. The people of Basrah had in mind the rumor that Ali ﷺ had a plan to kill their men and enslave their women and children.

As a result of these misgivings, more than ten thousand Muslims gave their lives for no cause. And up to the last nobody knew the real cause behind the ordeal. Every individual appeared to be accusing his rival for the calamity that happened. Ali ﷺ was himself in command of his army and he was organizing such fierce attacks on the opponents that they were repulsed. Ali's army made such an advance that Âishah's camel had come within the range of attack. Ka'b was holding the halter of Âishah's camel and it was he who had escorted the Mother of the believers to battlefield hoping for peace. The swordsmen of Basrah clustered around Âishah's camel to save it at the cost of their lives with the result the battle took a very serious turn.

In the wake of such a bloody battle, Âishah ﷺ asked Ka'b to leave the halter and advance raising the Qur'ân and calling the people to follow the dictates of the Book of Allâh. Ka'b did accordingly. But the followers of Abdullah bin Saba showered arrows on him and he was honored with martyrdom. This tragic event filled the people of Basrah with zeal and fervor and in a short while there was a heap of dead bodies around the camel of Âishah ﷺ. The people of Basrah were laying down their lives to save the camel of Âishah ﷺ. It became clear to Ali ﷺ that the presence of Âishah ﷺ in the battlefield would never allow the situation to cool down, for her mount had become the center of killing and bloodshed. There were heavy showers of arrows on her litter from all sides and she was cursing the murderers of Uthmân ﷺ. [These arrows were exposing the reality of Islam and Faith of those who were showering them.]

Ali ﷺ ordered his men to target the camel, for its fall would bring the battle to its end. After a number of attacks and counterattacks someone got an opportunity to strike the legs of camel, which made it sit down with a shriek. With the fall of the camel, the supporters of Âishah ﷺ dispersed. Qa'qâ' bin Amr ﷺ hurried to the spot and asked Ali's men to surround the camel on all sides. Ali ﷺ asked Muhammad bin Abu Bakr ﷺ to take care of his sister and see that she suffers no harm.

When her litter was taken out of the heap of the dead bodies and put at a distance, Ali ﷺ reached there and sent his greetings and compliments to her and said, "Dear mother! How are you? May Allâh forgive all your sins." Âishah ﵂ replied, "May Allâh forgive your sins too!" Following this, commanders of various columns appeared to greet the Mother of the believers. Âishah ﵂ then said to Qa'qâ' ﷺ: "I wish I had died twenty years before the event of this day." When Qa'qâ' ﷺ related this to Ali ﷺ, he too said, "I wish I had died twenty years before this event."

This battle became known as the battle of Jamal (camel) because the camel Âishah ﵂ was riding, had turned to be the center of fighting. The supporters of Âishah ﵂ numbered thirty thousand out of which nine thousand were killed, while one thousand seventy men out of twenty thousand laid down their lives from the side of Ali ﷺ. [But the fact is that about five thousand from each side were killed in this battle (*Al-Bidâyah wan-Nihâyah*, 7/218). Besides the number of the fighters described here seems to be exaggerated and opposite to each other.]

Ali ﷺ led the funeral prayers of all the slain and had them buried. He also announced that those establishing their respective rights on them could take the goods and properties away. When evening set in, Muhammad bin Abu Bakr ﷺ took his sister, the Mother of the believers, to Basrah and entrusted her to Safiyyah bint Al-Hârith bin Abu Talhah in the house of Abdullah bin Khalaf Khuzâ'i.

The next day, Ali ﷺ made his entry into Basrah where the people took *Bai'ah* at his hands. Afterwards, Ali ﷺ came to Âishah ﵂. Since Abdullah bin Khalaf had lost his life in the battle, his mother greeted him with loud reproaches. But Ali ﷺ gave no reply. Although, the people accompanying him showed displeasure, Ali ﷺ said to them, "Since women are weak by nature, we forgive even the polytheist women and these are the Muslim women." Ali ﷺ then showing the highest regard, asked the Mother of the believers if she suffered any trouble.

Complete peace was restored and good faith prevailed on both sides. Each of them apologized for the actions taken. Abdullah bin Abbâs ﷺ was then appointed the governor of Basrah. Ali ﷺ asked Muhammad bin Abu Bakr ﷺ later to make preparations for the journey. Thus, in Rajab 36 AH, Ali ﷺ bade farewell to Âishah ﷺ in the company of forty ladies of influential families of Basrah headed by Muhammad bin Abu Bakr ﷺ. He himself escorted the Mother of the believers for several miles then the charge was handed over to Hasan bin Ali ﷺ. She arrived at Makkah, stayed there until Dhul-Hijjah, and then left for Al-Madinah in 37 AH after performing *Hajj*.

A number of men from Banu Umayyah had also taken part in the battle of Jamal against Ali ﷺ. The battle being over, they left for Damascus to meet Mu'âwiyah ﷺ. Abdullah bin Zubair ﷺ who had received injuries in the battle, took shelter in the house of a man from Azd tribe in Basrah. Âishah ﷺ sent for him through her brother, Muhammad bin Abu Bakr ﷺ, and took him to Makkah.

One more Mischief of the Saba Sect

After sending Âishah ﷺ from Basrah, Ali ﷺ distributed cash from the treasury of Basrah among those who had fought under his banner. Each of them received five hundred dirhams. Following this, he told his men that in case of their attack and victory over Syria, their fixed amount of stipend would be increased but they would be entitled to get the same amount from the booty.

The followers of Abdullah bin Saba started criticizing and reproaching Ali ﷺ openly following the end of the battle. They had grown hostile simply because Ali ﷺ had strongly forbidden plunder of the goods and property. Ali's soft attitude, counseling and all peaceful efforts to make them see reason, fell on deaf ears until one day they disappeared from Basrah.

Anticipating their mischief, Ali ﷺ chased them at the head of an army but they were not found. It is to be noted here that Abdullah bin Saba had been the greatest supporter of Ali ﷺ. However, the conquest of Basrah had taken away from him the opportunity to inflict anymore loss and harm to Islam by supporting Ali ﷺ, so he turned against Ali ﷺ to continue his work against the cause of Islam. It was, in truth, the same group consisting of the Muslim-like Jews and anti-Islamic elements which later rose in the guise of the Khawârij.

Soon after the martyrdom of Umar Fâruq 🙵, conspiracies, secret societies and bodies of forces antagonistic to Islam sprang into being and they still continue. No period in the history of Islam passed without them. They sometimes appeared in the guise of Abu Lulu' and his inciters and at times in the shape of Abdullah bin Saba and his followers and the Khawârij. The same agency worked against Banu Umayyah through the Abbasids and Alawis and then against the Abbasids through the Umaiyads. Sometimes they appeared as Fidâi Ismâili group. The same secret societies appeared in the guise of Freemasons, Nihilists and Anarchists and sometimes it put on the garb of diplomacy in the foreign officers.

Even the early period of the Prophetic era was not free from these secret conspiracies. Not more than twenty or twenty-five years was there free from these activities and the period spanned the later part of Prophethood and the Caliphates of Abu Bakr and Umar 🙵. Thus the conspiracies hatched against the Islamic forces were neither strange nor surprising.

The people of the Saba sect who had disappeared from Basrah after openly criticizing Ali 🙵, spread in a large area of Arab and Iraq, and collected around them ruffians and riffraff who had their own axes to grind. They proceeded first to Sajastan to set against Ali 🙵 all the Persian provinces one by one so that he would not be able to manage the affairs of the State peacefully, and not find an opportunity to invade Syria. Being informed of their antagonistic activities, Ali 🙵 sent Abdur-Rahmân bin Jurw Tai with a detachment but he was martyred in the encounter. Hearing this Rib'i bin Kâs marched with a detachment of four thousand and defeated the miscreants. In the meantime, preparations for the battle of Siffin took a start. Now, the opportunist Saba clandestinely became a part of Ali's army to take advantage of the situation.

Kufah becomes the Capital

The most important task before Ali 🙵 following the battle of Jamal was to subdue Syria and force Mu'âwiyah 🙵 to take *Bai'ah*. So, he considered it necessary to make Kufah his capital. The Kufis happened to be the main strength of Ali's army. There was another reason behind making Kufah the capital and military center of Islam because Kufah was nearer to Damascus than Al-Madinah. Kufah spread its shadow of influence up to the Persian provinces. Umar Fâruq 🙼 had consolidated Al-Madinah as the power center of Islam, which was necessary at that time. But events suffered drastic changes during the days of Ali 🙼.

Before Ali 🙼, the Caliphs of Islam ruled from Al-Madinah, the center of power. They had no role to play as a commander of the Islamic forces. But Ali 🙼 under the pressure of circumstances, had to lead his army to battle and assumed the role of the commander. And this was one factor that cast injurious effects on his administration.

Something worthy of notice here is that a section of the rioters and murderers of Uthmân 🙼 had joined Abdullah bin Saba as a result of his great efforts, and therefore, came to be called the party of Abdullah bin Saba. A large number of Muslims had become his followers out of their gullibility but the number of real followers of Abdullah bin Saba was very small. These few persons were clever enough to mislead large numbers of people into trusting the sincerity of their scheme. Thus, they would often change their tools according to their needs and circumstances. That was the reason why this party led the rioters to do away with Uthmân 🙼 and his caliphate and a greater number of them took part in the battle of Jamal.

But when they turned against Ali 🙼, many among the rioters severed their relations with the party. They rather sided with Ali 🙼 and played a prominent role in strengthening his hand and thus gaining power and influence in his court. When Ali 🙼 settled in Kufah, they became closer and more influential, which in turn made Mu'âwiyah's position stronger. It was because of this that those in favor of taking *Qisâs* (retaliation) for Uthmân's blood, sided with Mu'âwiyah 🙼 in spite of the superiority of Ali 🙼, which they all knew.

Egypt and Muhammad bin Abu Bakr 🙼

About the time of Uthmân's martyrdom, Muhammad bin Abu Hudaifah 🙼 had captured the governorship of Egypt by dismissing Abdullah bin Sa'd 🙼. However, with his becoming Caliph, Ali 🙼 sent Qais bin

Sa'd 🌸 to Egypt as governor of the province. The new governor reached Egypt along with only seven persons and dismissed Muhammad bin Abu Hudaifah 🌸 and took charge as governor of Egypt. In Egypt also there were men like Yazid bin Al-Hârith and Maslamah bin Mukhallad who declined to take *Bai'ah* on the plea of awaiting the settlement of the issue of *Qisâs* (retaliation). However, they promised silence until a solution was found. Qais bin Sa'd 🌸 gained popularity and respect in Egypt by virtue of his character and abilities.

When the battle of Jamal ended and Ali 🌸 settled in Kufah, Mu'âwiyah 🌸 anticipated a two-pronged attack on Syria one by Iraq from the east and one by Egypt from the south. However, Mu'âwiyah 🌸 was not so weak as to be swallowed up easily. He had reason to grow strong with the passage of time and with the caliphate facing troubles, he placed his own house in peace and order. Every day he made himself stronger and he was a power formidable enough to answer back any challenge. He arranged a daily display of the bloodstained garments of Uthmân 🌸 and the fingers of Uthmân's wife on the pulpit of the grand mosque of Damascus. People in large numbers cried aloud and mourned the victims of these atrocities. The people would never leave the mosque until they had vowed to avenge the assassination.

Furthermore, a strong Syria was necessary, for it was constantly under the threat of Roman attack. Mu'âwiyah 🌸 was never found lacking in inviting and honoring men of letters and arms from all over Arabia. He utilized every opportunity available to claim his right to retaliate for the martyrdom of Uthmân 🌸. He had spent the whole year since the assassination, in making total preparations for the anticipated danger, while Ali 🌸 remained surrounded by threats, challenges, troubles and fighting throughout this period. Even though the entire world of Islam barring Syria was under the rule of Ali 🌸, he never enjoyed such a power and influence as was wielded by Umar Fâruq 🌸. His loyalists were found everywhere in Hijâz, Yemen, Iraq, Egypt, and Persia but his opponents also had their say. Thus Ali 🌸 was not in a position to get the full support and military aid from any province under his direct rule.

The state of affairs with Mu'âwiyah ⸵ was quite different. He had the support of the Syrians as a whole. As a matter of war strategy, he wanted to remove the threat from the Egyptian side because he dreaded the power and abilities of Qais bin Sa'd ⸵. Fortunately for him, he soon got an opportunity to eliminate the threat from Egypt. Mu'âwiyah ⸵ wrote Qais bin Sa'd ⸵ to help him for he simply wanted to avenge the blood of Uthmân ⸵. Qais firmly wrote him back that Ali ⸵ had no hand in the assassination of Uthmân ⸵ and so he should take *Bai'ah* at Ali's hand like the others, instead of opposing him.

In the meantime Qais bin Sa'd ⸵ wrote a letter to Ali ⸵ advising him not to put pressure on the people who were keeping silence on the subject of *Bai'ah*. Abdullah bin Ja'far ⸵ suggested to Ali ⸵ to write Sa'd ⸵ not to overlook the problem or to leave the people unpunished if they refused to take *Bai'ah*. Ali ⸵ wrote him accordingly. But instead of carrying out the orders of the Caliph, he wrote him again suggesting him to leave them as they were, for any pressure would make them rise against the caliphate and join the opponents as well.

As the letter reached Kufah, the emissaries of Ali ⸵ convinced him that Qais bin Sa'd ⸵ must have joined hands with Mu'âwiyah ⸵. Ali ⸵ was reluctant to accept their idea and he considered Sa'd ⸵ qualified and necessary for Egypt. When Mu'âwiyah ⸵ came to know of these suspicions, he began to praise Qais bin Sa'd ⸵ openly in his court. He also commenced telling the people that Qais ⸵ had come to his side and had begun to support those demanding *Qisâs* (retaliation). The spies of Ali ⸵ gave him the whole account of the new developments, with the result that he deposed Qais bin Sa'd ⸵ and replaced him with Muhammad bin Abu Bakr ⸵. Qais ⸵ reached Al-Madinah shocked and frustrated.

Al-Madinah was without a ruler after Ali ⸵ had shifted to Kufah. Elements supporting and opposing Ali ⸵ could be found there. When Qais bin Sa'd ⸵ reached Al-Madinah, Mu'âwiyah ⸵ sent Marwân bin Al-Hakam to persuade him to go to Damascus. Qais ⸵ declined the offer and when he was roughly treated, he left for Kufah. When he related the whole event to Ali ⸵, the latter expressed satisfaction and kept him in his company. Hearing this, Mu'âwiyah wrote to Marwân: "Had you reinforced Ali with an army of one hundred thousand fighters, it would have been better than Qais joining Ali."

Muhammad bin Abu Bakr 🍃, with the assumption of power, announced to the people to either take *Bai'ah* or leave the country. They requested him not to be in a rush and give them a few days to think and decide. He flatly refused any respite, with the result they sprang into action to safeguard themselves against the eventuality of him trying to punish them. The result was that Muhammad bin Abu Bakr 🍃 remained entangled with them even after the end of the battle of Siffin.

Amr bin Al-Âs 🍃 was with Mu'âwiyah 🍃

Amr bin Al-Âs 🍃 had conquered Egypt. While the rioters entered Al-Madinah and surrounded the house of Uthmân 🍃, he decided to leave Al-Madinah. He took with him his sons, Abdullah and Muhammad and settled in Bait Al-Maqdis (Jerusalem). Being there, he remained in contact with all the developments that took place following the martyrdom of Uthmân 🍃. When he was informed that the danger of a large-scale bloody battle hung over the head of the Muslim *Ummah*, Amr bin Al-Âs 🍃 held consultations with his sons about his role as a peacemaker.

Before the battle of Jamal, four persons had a claim to the caliphate. One was Ali 🍃 who had already become the Caliph and a large number of people had taken *Bai'ah* at his hands, and the second and the third being Talhah and Zubair who were killed during the battle of the Jamal. Now the fourth one left in the field to stake his claim to the caliphate was Mu'âwiyah 🍃. He had refused to take *Bai'ah* on the claim that Ali 🍃 was made Caliph with the support of the rioters and the killers of Uthmân 🍃 who were also being patronized by Ali 🍃.

On the other hand, Ali 🍃 claimed that in regard to the services to Islam, proximity and relationship with the Prophet 🌸 and in being one of the first to embrace Islam, Mu'âwiyah 🍃 was not on par with him. Both of them had reasons for their claims. In such a confusing situation Amr bin Al-Âs 🍃 thought it quite unwise to keep aloof. He decided to play his role in helping the two hostile forces reach a consensus.

He arrived in Damascus and Mu'âwiyah ⁕ welcomed him. He made no delay in telling Mu'âwiyah ⁕ that he was within his rights to avenge the blood of Uthmân ⁕. At first Mu'âwiyah ⁕ practiced caution but later he became satisfied towards him and made Amr bin Al-Âs ⁕ a member of his government.

Amr bin Al-Âs ⁕ then advanced his suggestion to Mu'âwiyah ⁕ that consecutive display of the bloodstained garments and slashed fingers would reduce the fervor of the people. So it should be put on display on special occasions. Mu'âwiyah ⁕ liked this suggestion and so the daily mourning and crying came to an end. Amr bin Al-Âs ⁕ then let Mu'âwiyah ⁕ know that the battle of Jamal had very much eroded Ali's military power and a large number of his troops had already perished. In addition, the wise and influential people of Basrah had lost their lives in the strife and only the weak masses had pledged their allegiance to Ali ⁕ and they would be of little help to him. Furthermore, the fighting machinery of Ali ⁕ had been reduced to disorder because of the large-scale killing of the Muslims on both sides had dampened their spirits. The appraisal of Amr bin Al-Âs ⁕ was not unreasonable, even the Saba sect knew it well.

Preparations for the fighting in Siffin

With his arrival in Kufah, Ali ⁕ was determined to make preparations against Syria. Abdullah bin Abbâs ⁕ also left Basrah with his army. Hearing this, Ali ⁕ too marched to Nukhailah putting Abu Mas'ud Ansâri ⁕ in his place. Abdullah bin Abbâs ⁕ joined Ali there. Ali ⁕ then dispatched Ziyâd bin Nadr Hârithi at the head of an eight thousand strong vanguard. He also sent Shuraih bin Hâni at the back of Ziyâd with four thousand fighters. Ali ⁕ came to Madâ'in and sent Ma'qal bin Qais with a detachment of three thousand after putting Sa'd bin Mas'ud Thaqafi in charge of Madâ'in. From Madâ'in, Ali ⁕ reached Raqqah and crossed the Euphrates to meet the joint forces of Shuraih, Ma'qal and others. When Mu'âwiyah ⁕ came to know that Ali ⁕ was marching on Syria, he hurriedly sent Abul-A'war Sulami at the head of a squadron in the form of vanguard. Ali ⁕ sent

Ziyâd and Shuraih ahead of the vanguard. When these generals entered the Syrian borders, they were informed that Abul-A'war was heading a detachment against them. They informed Ali ﷺ of the situation who sent Ashtar to take charge of the forces and to put Ziyâd and Shuraih to the right and left wings. He also instructed not to attack the Syrians unless they were attacked by them.

Ashtar acted accordingly. Abul-A'war camped in front of them. Both camps passed the whole day in silence. By the evening, Abul-A'war launched an attack on his opponents but they separated after a brief encounter. The next day, Abul-A'war stepped forward and was faced by Hâshim bin Utbah and they kept fighting until noon. Each of them was retreating to his camp when Ashtar launched a sudden attack. Abul-A'war also responded with his men. The fighting continued until the darkness of night intervened to stop it.

The next day, Ali ﷺ appeared on the scene. News also came about Mu'âwiyah's march towards the battlefront. Ali ﷺ stopped fighting and ordered Ashtar to capture the banks of Euphrates for water. But Ashtar found to his disappointment that Mu'âwiyah ﷺ had already captured the water of the Euphrates. When Ali ﷺ became aware of this, he sent Sa'sa'ah bin Suhân with a letter addressed to Mu'âwiyah ﷺ which, contained: "We would not have started this fight with you until we heard your grievances and called you to the right path. However, your men preferred to launch an attack on our troops and started the aggression. Now we think it fit to first invite you to the straight path before meeting you in the battlefield. It is quite unfortunate that you have initiated your war activities by capturing the water resources and stopped the supply of water to us, with the result that our troops are under the stress of thirst. It is better to ask your men not to prevent us from fetching water until the controversies are peacefully resolved. However, if you want to fight over the water instead of attaining the main goals, we are ready for that as well."

Mu'âwiyah ﷺ called an emergency meeting and placed the demand before his advisers. Abdullah bin Sa'd, the former governor of Egypt and Walid bin Uqbah spoke against lifting the ban on water so that they should be left to die without water as they had done with

Uthmân bin Affân ﷺ. But Amr bin Al-Âs ﷺ said pleading against them, "Stopping the supply of water is not reasonable because many from your own camp may not bear the tragic deaths of Ali's men without water and they might join Ali's camp to fight against you declaring you unfair and stone-hearted." Mu'âwiyah ﷺ announced not to block the supply of water and the situation that was heading towards an armed conflict was defused. [The dispute over the water seems to be incorrect. Euphrates is not a tank or pool that any party can get hold of it. It is a river thousands of miles in length and each party could have taken water from its side.]

Following this, both sides kept silent for two days. Parties from Hijâz, Yemen, Hamadân and other parts of Arabia and Persia joined Ali's army to make it swell to ninety thousand, while Mu'âwiyah ﷺ was in command of eighty thousand troops. [Historians differ on the number of troops. Some have mentioned the same and others have mentioned differently.]

Ali ﷺ had given the command of the horsemen of Kufah to Ashtar and those of Basrah to Sahl bin Hunaif, the infantry of Kufah was commanded by Ammâr bin Yâsir and those of Basrah by Qais bin Sa'd bin Ubâdah ﷺ, while Hâshim bin Utbah was made the standard-bearer. Other clans and parties from various provinces were put under the command of their respective chiefs. In the army of Mu'âwiyah ﷺ, Dhil-Kala' Himyari was put on the right wing, Habib bin Maslamah on the left and the vanguard was handed over to Abul-A'war Sulami. The cavalry of Damascus was put under the command of Amr bin Al-Âs ﷺ while the infantry was headed by Muslim bin Uqbah. Other small columns were given to the commanding officers like Abdur-Rahmân bin Khâlid, Ubaidullah bin Umar and Bashir bin Mâlik Kindi and others.

On the third day, Ali ﷺ broke his silence and sent Bashir bin Amr bin Mihsan Ansâri, Saeed bin Qais and Shabath bin Rib'i Tamimi to convince Mu'âwiyah ﷺ to accept obedience and to take Bai'ah of Ali ﷺ. Bashir bin Amr ﷺ said to Mu'âwiyah, "O Mu'âwiyah, refrain from creating any rift in the Muslim ranks and avoid bloodshed." Mu'âwiyah ﷺ retorted, "Have you counseled this to your friend Ali?" Bashir replied, "He is among the first believers in Islam and a very close relative of the Prophet 鐀 and has, therefore, more right to caliphate than all others." Mu'âwiyah 鐀 said, "It is not at all possible for us to give up our demand for avenging the blood of Uthmân." Thereupon Shabath bin Rib'i said, "O Mu'âwiyah, we know very well your purpose behind the demand for *Qisâs*. You delayed help to Uthmân so that he would be martyred giving you an opportunity to stake your claim to the caliphate on the pretext of avenging Uthmân's blood. O Mu'âwiyah, avoid any conflict with Ali and see reason." This led to hot exchanges with Mu'âwiyah 鐀 and the deputation proved fruitless.

First Stage of the Battle of Siffin

When peace talks failed, they came to a clash. But the zeal and fervor they used to experience in fighting against the disbelievers was absent because of the ties of friendship and relationship between the opposing sides. Men from both sides generally wanted to avert the scourge of battle. Since circumstances had led both the parties to dictate terms unacceptable to the other side and they couldn't compromise in achieving their purpose, fighting became inevitable. However, they tried to avoid all-out fighting. They started with a duel that lingered on for a few days. A little later the rage for fighting increased and with it, the chiefs of small parties began to face each other one by one. Thus the dual changed into clashes between small parties, while the armies on both sides remained silent spectators. This exercise continued for about a month.

This period may be considered as the first stage of the battle of Siffin. With the beginning of the month of Muharram, both the parties had a one-month respite and fighting was totally stopped. The contacts and peace talks were started again. Men on both sides desired success for the peace talks and had an aversion to war except the Saba party who had vested interests. Success of the peace talks could be virtually a deathblow to their nefarious plans. Thus they were leaving no stone unturned in keeping both sides at odds. They were doing all within their power to aggravate the situation.

Ali 鐀 was in a fix. He could neither quit the caliphate nor punish the rioters and assassins of Uthmân 鐀. To punish a mighty commander like Mâlik Ashtar, a governor like Muhammad bin Abu Bakr 🕮 and a respected Companion like Ammâr bin Yâsir 🕮 meant antagonizing the Egyptian and Kufi forces. Moreover, the role of rioters in the assassination of Uthmân 🕮 could not be exactly determined for lack of definite witnesses. On the other hand, Ali 🕮 was more deserving of the caliphate by all standards.

Mu'âwiyah 🕮 considered himself equally important by virtue of being a distinguished personality of Makkah, the son of Abu Sufyân 🕮, commander-in-chief of the huge Makkan armies in the battles of Uhud and Ahzâb (Confederates), commander who achieved great victories against the Romans since the beginning of the caliphate, great administer who governed Egypt very efficiently, brother of a wife of the Prophet 🕮 and a scribe of the Revelation. He was bound with Uthmân 🕮 in ancestral ties and he therefore, considered himself within his rights to avenge the blood of Uthmân 🕮. It was to him highly improper and unreasonable to evade *Qisâs* (retaliation) for the murder of such a grave nature by merely declaring it doubtful.

The explanation given by Ali 🕮 was neither understandable nor worth understanding to him. The revolt of Talhah 🕮 and Zubair 🕮, the many Companions in Al-Madinah who declined to take *Bai'ah* and the support received from Amr bin Al-Âs 🕮 had fortified his conviction and determination in his stand. The leadership on both sides would be forced to restore peace and amity if advisors, supporters and commanding officers played their roles positively. The Muharram cessation of fighting was a golden opportunity to implement the peace proposal but the Saba party was active enough to sabotage the peace mission and they were successful in their treachery.

Another Peace Effort during Muharram

At some date in Muharram of 37 AH, Ali 🕮 sent a peace commission to Mu'âwiyah 🕮 to initiate talks. It consisted of Adi bin Hâtim, Zaid bin Qais, Ziyâd bin Khasafah, and Shabath bin Rib'i. Initiating the peace talks, Adi bin Hâtim 🕮 said after praising Allâh the Almighty, "O Mu'âwiyah, your recognition and obedience to Ali will bring peace to Muslims as a whole. None has rejected the call to take *Bai'ah* except you and your friends. If you still insist on deviating from the path of righteousness, I am afraid, you will invite the same ordeal, the people of Jamal faced." Cutting short the speech of Adi, Mu'âwiyah ﷺ said, "O Adi! Have you come here on peace mission or on a war mission? Don't you know I am the grandson of Harb, I fear not fighting? Since you too are among the assassins of Uthmân, Allâh the Almighty will put you to death."

Following this, Yazid bin Qais said, "We have come as emissaries and so it is not our mission to counsel you. Nevertheless, we should make an all-out endeavor to bring peace and unity to the Muslims and remove disunity." Saying this, he began to state the excellence of Ali ﷺ and his worthiness of being the Caliph of Islam. In reply to his statement, Mu'âwiyah ﷺ said, "How do you call me to join a party when I, too, have a party of Muslims with me. I don't consider your friend worthy of the caliphate for he assassinated our Caliph and sheltered the assassins. Peace may be established only when the assassins of Uthmân are handed over to us." Interrupting the statement, Shabath bin Rib'i spoke out, "O Mu'âwiyah! Will you kill Ammâr bin Yâsir?" Mu'âwiyah ﷺ replied, "What can prevent me from killing Ammâr? I shall surely kill him as a retaliation for the blood of Uthmân's slave." Shabath bin Rib'i firmly said, "You will never be able to kill him unless you meet your death." Mu'âwiyah ﷺ answered back, "You are to meet your death first." After such hot exchanges, the commission left without any success.

The Speech of Ali ﷺ

Mu'âwiyah ﷺ then sent a similar commission to Ali ﷺ, which included Habib bin Maslamah, Shurahbil bin As-Samt, and Ma'n bin Yazid. Initiating the talk, Habib bin Maslamah said to Ali ﷺ, "Uthmân was the rightful Caliph. He managed the affairs under the guidelines set by the Book and the *Sunnah*. But his life appeared detestable and so you killed him; if not, you should hand over the assassins to us and relinquish the caliphate at once giving an opportunity to the people at large to choose a caliph according to their will." Hearing this, Ali ﷺ grew furious and chided him saying, "You should keep quite. You have no right to make such a statement concerning the caliphate." Thereupon Habib bin Maslamah retorted, "You are to see me in a state which will make you become unpleasant," meaning thereby, the sword will decide the matter. Ali ﷺ angrily said, "Go and do whatever you like." Saying this, Ali ﷺ got up and spoke after praising Allâh the Almighty, describing the purpose behind the advent of the Prophet ﷺ and eulogizing the caliphate of the two former Righteous Caliphs: "I found them performing their duties correctly. So, I held myself back from meddling in their affairs. They then chose Uthmân as Caliph. His style of functioning caused dissatisfaction among the people and they killed him. Following that, they requested me to accept their *Bai'ah*, which I granted. But Talhah and Zubair violated their pledge and Mu'âwiyah opposed me, even though he is not among the first to embrace Islam like me. I wonder at your obedience to him although I call you towards the Book and the *Sunnah* and the Pillars of Faith."

Hearing his speech, Shurahbil bin As-Samt said, "Do you not bear witness that Uthmân was oppressively martyred?" Ali ﷺ replied, "I hold Uthmân neither oppressed nor oppressor." Having heard this, they got up saying, "We rather abhor one who evades holding Uthmân a victim. It is all the same for such people whether they are asked to see wisdom or not." No considerable peace efforts were made after the failure of that mission.

One Week of the Battle of Siffin

At the end of Muharram 37 AH, Ali ﷺ issued orders to his army that a decisive battle would begin from the first of the month of Safar. Along with this he added that the fleeing opponents will neither be chased nor killed; nor the goods of the wounded be taken, nor their dead bodies mutilated, nor the women be put to excesses even if they call bad names. Such orders were also issued from the other side. Thus the battle broke out on the first morning in Safar. The people of Kufah advanced under the command of Ashtar, and the Syrians headed by Habib bin Masalamah, faced one another. The battle continued until evening but remained indecisive.

The next day, Hâshim bin Utbah came out at the head of a column of cavalry and infantry from the side of Ali ﷺ, and Abul-A'war Sulami on behalf of Mu'âwiyah ؓ. But the daylong bloody battle produced no results. On the third day, Ammâr bin Yâsir ؓ from Ali's camp, and Amr bin Al-Âs ؓ from that of Mu'âwiyah ؓ faced each other. It was more severe an encounter in comparison to previous ones. Ammâr bin Yâsir ؓ launched such a fierce attack that Amr bin Al-Âs ؓ had to fall back. But the day, however, went without any result.

On the fourth day, Ubaidullah bin Umar ؓ led the column from Mu'âwiyah's side and Muhammad bin Al-Hanafiyah, the son of Ali ؓ from Ali's side but the battle remained indecisive. By the evening, Ubaidullah bin Umar ؓ challenged Muhammad bin Al-Hanafiyah to a duel, which he accepted, but Ali ؓ rushed to the spot and brought Muhammad back, Ubaidullah ؓ also went back to his camp.

The fifth day saw Walid bin Uqbah coming out from Ali's camp, and Abdullah bin Abbâs ؓ from Mu'âwiyah's side, and fought the whole day, while the sixth day, Mâlik Ashtar and Habib bin Maslamah came out again for a decisive battle but it was an exercise in futility. On the seventh day, Ali ؓ and Mu'âwiyah ؓ led their armies against one another but no body could win the day.

This weeklong battle failed to produce any result because in number and art of warfare and valor both sides were almost equal. However, the enemy camp of Saba rejoiced at the bloodbath of the Muslims on both sides. Although the week proved ill-fated, more ominous days were to come.

The Last Two Days of the Battle of Siffin

After a week of severe battles, both the armies got ready for a decisive battle. On Safar 8, 37 AH, Ali ؓ launched his assault on Mu'âwiyah's army. Ali ؓ occupied a place in the center where the notables of Kufah, Basrah, Al-Madinah and from Banu Khuzâ'ah and Banu Kinânah had their presence. Abdullah bin Budail bin Warqa Khuzâ'i was put on the right wing and Abdullah on the left. Every clan had its fixed place, separate standard and leading officer. Ammâr bin Yâsir ؓ had been given charge of the people singing martial songs and reciting the Qur'ân. Qais bin Sa'd ؓ and Abdullah bin Yazid were also put on the same job.

Mu'âwiyah ﷺ, on the other hand, took *Bai'ah* (pledges) for death in his camp. He gave the right wing of his army to Ubaidullah bin Umar ﷺ and left to Habib bin Maslamah. Ali's right wing first made the advance and Abdullah bin Budail Khuzâ'i attacked the left wing of Mu'âwiyah's army led by Habib bin Maslamah. Under the hard pressure of Abdullah, Habib's cavalry was forced to retreat until it reached the spot where, Mu'âwiyah ﷺ with his men, had taken the pledge for death. With an eye on the setback of his right wing, Mu'âwiyah ﷺ ordered his men to attack. The attack was so massive that Abdullah bin Budail was left with only two hundred fifty men while all others fled to take shelter behind Ali ﷺ. In view of the ordeal suffered by his right wing, Ali ﷺ sent Sahl bin Hunaif as the commanding officer of the Madinites to reinforce and protect Abdullah bin Budail. But in a short while Budail succumbed to death along with his party.

The left wing also tasted defeat at the hands of the Syrian force. None but the Rabi'ah tribe fought with courage and firmness. All others fled the battlefield. With this scenario, Ali ﷺ sent his sons, Hasan, Husain and Muhammad to reinforce the Rabi'ah tribe so that they were not routed. He then asked Ashtar to call the right wing and put them to shame or force them to avoid escape. Ali ﷺ himself made an advance towards the left wing and began to measure his sword with the enemy. The presence of Ali ﷺ produced courage in the Rabi'ah tribe whose charge become more forceful.

When Ahmar, the slave of Abu Sufyân ﷺ saw Ali ﷺ in action, he made an attempt on his life but Ali's slave Kaisân engaged him but was killed in the encounter. With the killing of his slave, Ali ﷺ launched an assault on Ahmar and in a state of utmost fury, he lifted him up and knocked him down so violently that his both hands turned useless. The Syrian army attempted an attack on Ali ﷺ but the people of Rabi'ah stood in the way.

Ashtar, on the other hand, upheld the right wing. Thus the chance of success, which was, at one stage, slipping out of the hands of Ali ﷺ returned to an equilibrium. Both sides were fighting with almost equal valor and firmness. By afternoon, Mâlik Ashtar pushed back the left wing of Mu'âwiyah ﷺ. But the cavalry of Mu'âwiyah ﷺ, which had taken an oath for death, came to the rescue of the retreating column and pushed Ali's right wing far behind. Now Abdullah bin Husain, the comrade of Ammâr bin Yâsir 🕮, came forward with a martial song on his lips while Uqbah bin Hadid Numairi came from the opposite camp and was killed. In the wake of his death the Syrian army made a massive attack which was sustained by Ali's troops with firmness despite an initial setback. Ali 🕮 came with a column on the left wing to the rescue of the right wing and a pitched battle was fought. Dhul-Kala' Himyari and Ubaidullah bin Umar 🕮 launched such a forceful attack on the left wing of Ali's troops that even the Rabi'ah tribe could not withstand the onslaught, and a large number of fighters lost their lives. Following this disaster of the left wing, Abdul-Qais stepped forward and lent support to the Rabi'ah tribe and checked the advancement of the Syrian troops. Timely reinforcements revived the left wing and both Dhul-Kala' Himyari and Ubaidullah bin Umar 🕮 were killed.

In short, the right and left wings of both the armies kept fighting from morning to evening, but the hearts of both sides were steady. At last, Ammâr bin Yâsir 🕮 moved through the army of Ali 🕮 calling out, "Whoever has a desire to gain the Pleasure of Allâh the Almighty, and has no wish to go back to his possessions and children should join me." A large number of the army responded to his call and vowed to fight to the finish. At the end, he came to Hâshim bin Utbah, the standard-bearer of Ali 🕮, he took him with his dedicated men and launched such a massive attack that Amr bin Al-Âs 🕮 could barely withstand it with much difficulty.

At last, Ammâr 🕮 was killed. The news of Ammâr bin Yâsir's death saddened Ali 🕮. The Syrian Army too was aroused to fight forcefully. The battle air was filled with the rattling sound of swords and spears and loud voices of martial songs. This was the night of Friday, it is known as *Lailat-ul-Harir*. Owais Qarni was also martyred in the same night. Ali 🕮 was running through the battleground with lighting speed directing the right wing then guiding the left and at times crossing swords with the Syrians. Abdullah bin Abbâs 🕮 was heading the left wing while Ashtar was in charge of the right one. Mu'âwiyah 🕮 was also fighting with Amr bin Al-Âs 🕮 and the other chiefs. The night passed in fierce fighting but with no outcome.

Ali once, piercing through the Syrian army, reached very near to Mu'âwiyah at the head of twelve thousand troops and threw a challenge for a duel, for it was to him better than the large-scale massacre on both sides. Hearing the call, Amr bin Al-Âs told Mu'âwiyah that the proposal of Ali was reasonable and he should go for a duel. "Why do you not like this for yourself? Don't you know that the one who goes to fight with Ali doesn't came back alive?" Mu'âwiyah uttered bitterly. He then added with a laugh, "You, perhaps, want me to go for a duel so that I am killed and you become the ruler of Syria." Ali received no reply and came back with no result.

Thirty hours of continuous fighting took a toll of seventy thousand Muslim fighters from both sides. Such a clash of Muslim forces was a terrible catastrophe. Seventy thousand valiant Muslim fighters could have conquered the whole world. With the decline of noon, Mâlik Ashtar handed over the charge of his contingent to Haiyân bin Haudhah and took a squadron of cavalry and stirred the soldiers to fight to the finish. Although the battle was equally balanced, more than half of the troops on the Syrian side had lost their lives. Now, Mu'âwiyah had only thirty-five thousand fighters out of eighty thousand on his side. Ali had, on the other hand, lost twenty to twenty-five thousand soldiers while about sixty thousand fighters were still ready to fight under his command. Ali had with him double the number of fighters as Mu'âwiyah's troops. [This analysis seems to be unrealistic, Tabari and Baihaqi mention the number of martyrs on the Ali's side to be double of Mu'âwiyah's. Forty thousand men from Ali's army and twenty thousand from Mu'âwiyah's army were killed. (*Al-Bidâyah wan-Nihâyah*, 7/244).]

In such a state, Ali had an opportunity to separate a portion of his troops to launch a heavy assault on the Syrians while keeping them engaged from the other side. Mâlik Ashtar made a tremendous attack with his cavalry and reached the heart of enemy pushing and smashing the Syrians. When Ali saw his cavalry making inroads into enemy's heart, he started sending reinforcements after reinforcements to strengthen the attack. His strategy worked. The standard-bearer of the Syrian Army was killed by Ashtar.

Now the scene of carnage was near the camp of Mu'âwiyah ⬥ and Amr bin Al-Âs ⬥. Ashtar's dashing charge broke the right and left wings and both sides shrank into fighting in a small circle leaving no chance for the opponents to enforce their strength. Large-scale killings including that of the standard-bearer had terribly frightened the Mu'âwiyah camp whose defeat was now imminent. In such a crucial and chaotic stage, Amr bin Al-Âs ⬥ salvaged their position with a novel device.

The End of the Battle

At this juncture, Amr bin Al-Âs ⬥ counselled Mu'âwiyah ⬥ to order his men to raise the Qur'ân high on the point of their spears crying aloud: "Between you and us is the Book of Allâh." The Syrians began to say that they bowed down to the verdict of the Qur'ân. Someone was heard saying, "Muslims! we were fighting in the way of Faith; come on and obey the judgement of the Qur'ân and make peace." Some others called out, "O people! Who will fight the Romans if the Syrians are destroyed, and who will face the eastern invaders if the Iraqis are ruined?" When Ali's men witnessed the Qur'ân raised with the spears, they stopped fighting at once. Abdullah bin Abbâs ⬥ remarked at the new developments: "It was fighting until now but this is the beginning of cheating." Ali ⬥ tried to make his men understand not to fall short of carrying their mission to its logical end, for the victory was not far away. However, as the people had been completely exhausted by continuous fighting, they found this an opportunity from providence to stop fighting without delay. Moreover, the fierce and bloody fighting that was still going hid the fact that victory was within reach. The nearness of victory was visible only to Ali ⬥ and his generals and officers and had not yet come into the view of the fighters' sight so they were not in favor of fighting further.

Ashtar was sure of his victory and was in full command of the situation, it seemed unreasonable and illogical to call him back from the battlefront. It was tantamount to undoing of all his efforts and sacrifices. But fighters including the hypocrites of Saba party surrounded Ali ⬥ on all sides to stop fighting and to recall Ashtar.

Ali ﷺ was still undecided when a strong threat of internal fighting changed his mind and he called Ashtar back. They threatened him with the consequences of Uthmân ﷺ. In response to the menacing situation, Ali ﷺ was compelled to issue emergency orders for Ashtar to come back at once as the door of a series of problems was now thrown open. Ashtar called off the fighting, but very reluctantly.

[These details about the last part of the Siffin Battle, especially the complete submission of Syrian army, and the raising of the Qur'ân on the spears, are false fabrications of Shiite narrations while the actual events testify differently:

The Prophet ﷺ had directed Ali ﷺ and Fâtimah ﷺ to mention *Subhân Allâh, Al-hamdu lillah* and *Allâhu Akbar*, thirty-three times each while going to sleep. The Prophet ﷺ told this act better than getting a slave. Ali ﷺ told that he never discontinued this act. When he was asked whether he continued this act even on the night of Siffin, he replied that even that night he performed it. (*Bukhari* 5362, *Fath Al-Bari* 9/506). Some other narrations also strengthen this fact. As these mentions are recited at the time of sleep, it is proved that the fight was stopped during this night of Siffin and people got the chance of taking a rest or sleep.

In *Sahih Al-Bukhari*, the Book of Commentary (*Sûrat Al-Fath*), there is a narration about this event. The first part of it is not so clear, but in *Musnad Ahmad* (3/485) and *An-Nasa'î* (2/306), this event is well-described with the reference of *Sahih Al-Bukhari*. According to the wording of *Musnad Ahmad*, Habib bin Abu Thâbit said: I went to Abu Wa'il, he said, "We were in Siffin, when the fight with Syrians grew fierce, Amr said to Mu'âwiyah: 'Send the Scripture (Qur'ân) to Ali, and call him towards the Book of Allâh, he cannot refuse it to you.' So, a man took Qur'ân to him and said, 'Between us and you, this is the Book of Allâh.' Then he recited the Verse which accuses the people of the Scriptures: 'Have you not seen those who have been given a portion of the Scripture? They are being invited to the Book of Allâh to settle their dispute, then a party of them turns away, and they are averse.' (V.3:23). On this Ali said, 'We are more entitled to it than you.' (Thus he at once agreed to make the Book of Allâh their judge, and stopped fighting. Upon this) some distinguished persons said (who became Khawârij later): 'O Chief of the believers, what we have to see of them now? Should we not go with our swords until Allâh decides between us?' On this Sahl bin Hunaif said: 'O people, blame yourselves. We have seen ourselves on the day of Hudaibiyah. If there was a possibility of fight, we would have fought.' (A narration of *Bukhari* says: 'If I could have resisted the order of the Prophet 鐃, I would have done that.' It means that the order of Allâh and His Messenger is to be obeyed, and there is no other way. Here also the Book of Allâh is accepted as judge, so no other way out)."

Many points are known from this narration:

1. The proposal presented by Amr bin Al-Âs 鐃 to make the Qur'ân judge was not to cheat the Iraqi people but to stop Muslims indulging in more bloodshed and destroying themselves.

2. This proposal was not presented in the way that the people while fighting, unexpectedly produced Qur'ân from somewhere in their clothes, and raised them on the spears. The Muslim fighters don't keep the Qur'ân with them in this way. Actually a man took the Qur'ân to Ali 鐃. Same is the wording of *Musnad Ahmad* and *An-Nasa'î*. It is stated in *Daraqutni* also that a man took the Qur'ân to Ali 鐃. So, this was done in the most suitable diplomatic way.

3. Ali 鐃 had not termed the proposal as cheating or fraud, neither his army had forced him to accept the proposal. But Ali 鐃, on his own, had accepted it as soon as it was brought forward. He not only accepted it without any delay or any argument but he praised it to be the suitable and timely proposal, and told that he was more entitled to act upon it than Mu'âwiyah 鐃.

4. It was also not the case that the army, especially the learned people had forced Ali 鐃 to accept the proposal, as is mentioned in general narratives, but contrary to it, the most distinguished persons of his army came to him with swords in their hands and asked his permission to fight. But Ali 鐃 didn't give them permission. Even Sahl bin Hunaif, the right hand of Ali 鐃, explained the army that the Book of Allâh has been made judge in this matter, so nothing else can be adopted nor any opinion can be considered. He gave the reference of the Hudaibiyah Treaty in this regard.

5. When this narration of *Musnad Ahmad* and *An-Nasa'î* is considered with its full context, it becomes clear enough that at the time of sending the proposal, no fighting was going on. But both the parties were ready to begin the fight. It means that the fighting had stopped the night before, and after the day appeared, both parties were making their preparations that the proposal was made by Amr bin Al-Âs ؏ to Mu'âwiyah ؏ to save the Muslims from further destruction. Mu'âwiyah ؏ sent a man to Ali ؏ with the proposal and Ali ؏ at once accepted it to end the fight. He had said before that he would not fight until there is a justification, and now there was no justice greater than the Book of Allâh. The second party had itself asked to accept it, and so there was no room for further fighting.]

Ali ؏ informed Ashtar of the reason for his recall. Expressing deep grief, Ashtar said addressing the people, "O the people of Iraq, you were entrapped by delusions when you were about to overpower the Syrians." But the people were so much overwhelmed with fervor against fighting that they made an attempt to attack Ashtar but held back when Ali ؏ intervened. After a while Ash'ath bin Qais stepped forward and submitted to Ali ؏, "As now the battle has come to a halt and the people have accepted the Qur'ân as an arbitrator, will you permit me to contact Mu'âwiyah to know his mind." Ali ؏ acceded to his request. He went to Mu'âwiyah ؏ and said, "What was your intention behind raising the Qur'ân upon the spears?" He said in reply, "Both of us should turn to the Command of Allâh and His Messenger. Now two persons, one from each side, should be appointed to examine and decide the matter under oath and both sides should follow their decision."

Having heard this, Ash'ath came back and related to Ali ؏ what he had heard. The people around Ali ؏ hurried to accept the proposal. When Mu'âwiyah ؏ was asked about the man to represent his side, he named Amr bin Al-Âs ؏. Ali ؏ named Abdullah bin Abbâs ؏. But the proposal was rejected on the plea that Abdullah was his relative. They demanded a neutral person. When Ali ؏ left the matter to them, they named Abu Musa Ash'ari ؏. But Ali ؏ expressed his reluctance declaring him unauthentic. [This attitude related to Ali ؏ is absolutely baseless.]

However, he yielded to their constant insistence and pressure. The deliberations were still on when Amr bin Al-Âs ﷺ turned up to make out the declaration under oath.

Making out the Documentation and the Return

Amr bin Al-Âs ﷺ requested Ali ﷺ to allow him to take down the document. Ali ﷺ had him to write down the following:

"This declaration between Ali bin Abu Tâlib and Mu'âwiyah bin Abu Sufyân declares that Ali bin Abu Tâlib has appointed an arbitrator on behalf of the people of Kufah and all those supporting him and, similarly, Mu'âwiyah bin Sufyân has appointed an arbitrator on behalf of all who follow him. We, holding the Book of Allâh the Almighty and His Order as judge, declare that both of us will follow nothing but the injunctions of Allâh and His Book. We abide by the rules of the Qur'ân from *Al-Hamd* to *Al-Nâs* and declare to follow what is permitted and hold back from what is forbidden. The two appointed arbitrators are Abu Musa Abdullah bin Qais Ash'ari and Amr bin Al-Âs. They will give a decision according to the dictates of the Qur'ân otherwise in accordance with the *Sunnah* if the Qur'ân is found silent over the issue."

Following this, the arbitrators Abu Musa Ash'ari ﷺ and Amr bin Al-Âs ﷺ were asked to declare that they would decide the matter according to the Book of Allâh and *Sunnah* of the Messenger of Allâh ﷺ and would not allow the Muslim *Ummah* to become the victim of war, disruption and disunity. Afterwards, the arbitrators were given a period of six months to examine the case and give their judgment at that time at Adhruh near Daumat Al-Jandal located between Kufah and Damascus. It was also decided that Abu Musa Ash'ari ﷺ while coming from Kufah, would have with him four hundred men sent by Ali ﷺ and Amr bin Al-Âs ﷺ, coming from Damascus, also would have an equal number from Mu'âwiyah ﷺ. Those eight hundred men will act as representatives of the Muslims as a whole.

Following this, both Ali ﷺ and Mu'âwiyah ﷺ asked their men to declare on oath that they would not target the lives and properties of the mediators, which was signed by Ash'ath bin Qais, Sa'd bin Qais

Hamadâni, Warqa bin Sumayi Al-Bajali, Abdullah bin Fahl Al-Ijli, Hujr bin Adi Kindi, Abdullah bin At-Tufail Al-Âmiri, Uqbah bin Ziyâd Hadrami, Yazid bin Tajhafah Tamimi, Mâlik bin Ka'b Hamadâni on behalf of Ali 🕮 as witnesses and guarantors while Abul-A'war, Habib bin Maslamah, Zamil bin Amr Al-Udhri, Hamzah bin Mâlik Hamadâni, Abdur-Rahmân bin Khâlid Makhzumi, Subai' bin Yazid Ansâri, Utbah bin Abu Sufyân, Yazid bin Al-Hur Absi put their signatures for Mu'âwiyah's side.

On being finalized, one copy of the declaration was given each to Abu Musa Ash'ari 🕮 and Amr bin Al-Âs 🕮. Mâlik Ashtar refused to sign the document. Four days elapsed in giving the declaration a final shape and it was handed over to the arbitrators on Safar 13. Following this, the two armies moved back towards Kufah and Damascus respectively. Mu'âwiyah 🕮 reached Damascus safe and sound but Ali 🕮 had to face a new trouble.

Trouble caused by the Khawârij

When Ali 🕮 decided to leave the battlefield of Siffin on Safar 13, 37 AH, some people approached him and asked him to attack the Syrian army instead of going back to Kufah. "How can I commit a breach of promise after writing the declaration? We have now to wait until the month of Ramadân without even thinking of war after attaining peace," Ali 🕮 firmly said. Although they went away, they started seeking support of the people against Ali 🕮 and attempted to form separate groups. Ali 🕮 left Kufah but a clash of opinions dominated the atmosphere throughout. Even though Ali 🕮 worked hard to pacify the situation, it was in vain, for a section was engaged in fanning the fire of discord. The united front of Ali's army was now divided into scores of groups creating dissension and giving rise to chaos and disorder. And from a war of words they had come down to hitting and thrashing each other.

Of all the groups, two were strong, one completely opposing Ali 🕮 and another one eulogizing him beyond all limits in response and in competition with the other group. Thus, the first group came to be called the Khawârij and the second one was the Shiite. It is quite interesting that the Khawârij group was formed under the leadership of those who had forced Ali ؓ to call Mâlik Ashtar back threatening him with the consequences of Uthmân ؓ. Although Ali ؓ repeatedly reminded them of their past activities in forcing him to stop fighting and bring peace to the people, but they paid no attention to his claim. At last, twelve thousand men separated themselves from Ali's army and moved towards Haraura'.

It was the group of the Khawârij. It settled in Haraura' and set Abdullah bin Al-Kawa the *Imam* of the prayers and Shabath bin Rib'i the commander. Shabath bin Rib'i was the same person whom Ali ؓ had twice sent to Mu'âwiyah ؓ as the member of the peace commission and on both occasions his provocative words worsened the possibility for a peaceful solution and the talks ended in failure. After establishing their administration in Haraura', the insurgents now declared: *"Bai'ah* is meant for Allâh the Almighty Alone. It is our duty to enjoin the good on people of the land and forbid the evil. There is no caliph or ruler in Islam. After gaining victory, all matters must be settled by mutual consultation of the Muslims and their majority should decide all issues. Both Ali and Mu'âwiyah are at fault."

When Ali ؓ came to know of the uprisings of the Khawârij, he observed utmost patience. On reaching Kufah, Ali ؓ consoled the relatives of those who had laid down their lives in Siffin and declared those killed as martyred. He then sent Abdullah bin Abbâs ؓ to the Khawârij to pacify them and put them on the right path. But they were contentious on all issues and rejected the pleas of Abdullah bin Abbâs ؓ.

In the meantime Ali ؓ himself went there. He first visited the camp of Yazid bin Qais because he had more influence on them. He first offered two *Rak'at Salât* (prayer) and then appointed Yazid bin Qais the governor of Isfahan and Rey. He then came to the assembly where Abdullah bin Abbâs ؓ was carrying on arguments with them and said, "Who among you is most wise and the leader of the group?" They replied, "Abdullah bin Al-Kawa." Ali ؓ then said turning to Abdullah, 'You people had pledged your allegiance to me, then what is the reason behind your turning away after taking *Bai'ah?"* He replied, "It is because of your undue immovability."

Ali ﷺ said, "By Allâh! I was not in favor of stopping the battle. But you people forced me to do so. Nevertheless, I have let both the arbitrators decide the issue according to the dictates of the Qur'ân. Thus if they give a verdict according to the Qur'ân, there is no harm in accepting this; if it is against the Qur'ân, I shall reject it outright." Having heard this, the Khawârij said, "Mu'âwiyah revolted and committed the crime of killing the Muslims and so the appointment of arbitrators in this matter is not justified. According to clear injunctions of the Qur'ân he is liable to be killed." Ali ﷺ said, "I have not appointed anybody as arbitrator; the real arbitrator is the Qur'ân by all means and the men are appointed merely to give judgment according to the Book." The Khawârij then said, "What was the need of allotting six-months for the job?" Ali ﷺ replied, "Maybe the dissenting voices among the Muslims will subside by then." The Khawârij then kept silent. Ali ﷺ then asked them politely and affectionately, "Come let us go to Kufah and stay there during these six months, your mounts and beasts of burden will grow fat and strong enough to resume fighting against the enemy." Hearing this, they agreed and entered Basrah along with Ali ﷺ and began to await the decision of the arbitrators. Ali ﷺ then sent Abdullah bin Abbâs ﷺ to Basrah to perform his job as governor.

The Decision of the Arbitrators at Adhruh

When the end of the six-month period drew near, Ali ﷺ sent for Abdullah bin Abbâs ﷺ from Basrah. He then appointed Shuraih bin Hâni Al-Hârithi in charge of four hundred men and Abdullah bin Abbâs ﷺ to lead the prayers. They were then sent to Adhruh along with Abu Musa Ash'ari ﷺ. Similarly, Mu'âwiyah ﷺ also sent Amr bin Al-Âs ﷺ at the head of four hundred men. Some influential men from Makkah and Al-Madinah were also invited to join the peace efforts and they could not refuse to avail the opportunity of bringing the warring Muslims together and stopping the carnage. Several men including Abdullah bin Umar, Abdullah bin Zubair and Sa'd bin Waqqâs ﷺ came to Adhruh. The people were very curious to know the decision but the arbitrators held it back because they had to exchange views before making any announcement.

On the eve of the departure of Abu Musa Ash'ari ﷺ from Kufah to Adhruh, Hurqus bin Zuhair called on Ali ﷺ on behalf of the Khawârij and submitted, "You have committed a blunder by accepting the arbitrator to give the decision in the matter. There is still time for you to back out from your promise and march on to attack your enemy. We stand by you." Ali ﷺ said, "I cannot commit a breach of trust." This was the same Hurqus bin Zuhair who had headed the rioters against Uthmân ﷺ and had now joined hands with the Khawârij.

Since Abu Musa's departure, Ali ﷺ would write letters to him daily without fail; and Mu'âwiyah ﷺ too did the same, for the issue was too delicate and needed their undivided attention. Ali ﷺ sent his letters and messages in the name of Abdullah bin Abbâs ﷺ while Mu'âwiyah ﷺ addressed them to Amr bin Al-Âs ﷺ. But the two addresses had different working conditions. Mu'âwiyah's men were too disciplined to ask anything about the letters while Abdullah bin Abbâs ﷺ did not maintain secrecy because his men would sit around him and inquired about the contents of all the letters sent by Ali ﷺ. They would grow angry when he kept anything secret. Gradually they turned against him and began to criticize him openly.

When Abdullah bin Umar, Abdur-Rahmân bin Abu Bakr, Abdullah bin Zubair, Abdur-Rahmân bin Al-Hârith, Abdur-Rahmân bin Abd Yaghuth Zuhri, Abu Jahm bin Hudhaifah, Mughirah bin Shu'bah, and Sa'd bin Waqqâs ﷺ and others reached Adhruh, a meeting of distinguished persons was convened to look into the matter. Amr bin Al-Âs ﷺ had Abu Musa ﷺ admit that Uthmân bin Affân ﷺ was put to death as an innocent man. Amr bin Al-Âs ﷺ also had him to admit that on account of common ancestry, Mu'âwiyah ﷺ was within his rights to claim *Qisâs* (retaliation) of Uthmân ﷺ. These two issues were never denied by Abu Musa ﷺ and he accepted both unreluctantly.

Following this, Amr bin Al-Âs ﷺ raised the issue of the caliphate and said: "Mu'âwiyah belongs to a noble and renowned family of the Quraish. He is the brother of Umm Habibah, the wife of the Prophet ﷺ and the scribe of the revealed words."

Having heard all this, Abu Musa Ash'ari ﷺ raised his objection. He said, "Although I don't deny the excellence of Mu'âwiyah and how he was entrusted with the responsibility of ruling the Muslims in the presence of Ali and other such men and he commands high respect for all these qualities, Ali still has a far greater right. He is the closest to the Prophet ﷺ by the ties of relationship; he belongs to a very noble family and is reckoned among the chiefs of the Quraish. He also enjoys a distinct place in regard to learning, bravery, and piety."

Amr bin Al-Âs ﷺ argued, "Mu'âwiyah is superior in administrative ability and political vision." Abu Musa ﷺ replied, "These things are not worthy of consideration in comparison to piety and honesty." After such exchanges, Abu Musa Ash'ari ﷺ suggested that both Ali ﷺ and Mu'âwiyah ﷺ be deposed and Abdullah bin Umar ﷺ be chosen as caliph. Abdullah bin Umar ﷺ, who was present in the meeting, said in a loud voice, "I don't agree to this suggestion." Amr bin Al-Âs ﷺ said to Abu Musa ﷺ, "Why don't you choose my son, Abdullah?" Abu Musa ﷺ said, "Well, your son is very pious no doubt but you have put him to a great trial by plunging him into the battle."

Such inconclusive talks went on for sometime. After this, Amr bin Al-Âs ﷺ put forward his proposal and said, "Since hostile relations between Ali ﷺ and Mu'âwiyah ﷺ have brought untold miseries and sufferings to the Muslims as a whole, it is advisable that both should be deposed. Then the Muslims should choose a new caliph unanimously or by a majority opinion. With this suggestion agreed upon between the two, it was decided that the announcement should be made at the opening in front of the general assembly. They, however, anticipated rejection of the proposal by both Ali ﷺ and Mu'âwiyah ﷺ. Nevertheless, a call was sounded for the people to assemble which they did with the utmost curiosity. Both the arbitrators then appeared on the scene.

The Verdict

Amr bin Al-Âs ﷺ asked Abu Musa Ash'ari ﷺ to announce the decision taken by them. Abu Musa ﷺ ascended the pulpit and said addressing the people: "People! After much deliberation we could reach one and only one decision. I am sure this verdict will lead the Muslims as a whole to peace and unity. Both Amr bin Al-Âs and I have decided to depose both Ali and Mu'âwiyah giving you the right to chose anybody as your caliph."

The entire congregation heard it and Abu Musa ﷺ descended. Now Amr bin Al-Âs ﷺ mounted the pulpit and said to the people: "All of you be witness that Abu Musa had deposed his friend Ali. But I, however, do not depose Mu'âwiyah and keep him at his place for he is the successor of the brutally martyred Caliph and has the right to succeed him."

Had Amr bin Al-Âs ﷺ lent total support to the decision announced by Abu Musa ﷺ without saying anything in support of Mu'âwiyah ﷺ, the judgment would not have suffered such a disgrace and setback. There may be some weakness in the statement of Abu Musa ﷺ but it was decidedly above dishonesty and manipulation and would not have set eight hundred Muslims against it. Even though they were given the right to choose a new caliph, but he could not have been stronger than Ali ﷺ or Mu'âwiyah ﷺ. Furthermore, a third man as a caliph could have aggravated the already tense situation that was filled with bitterness and bad blood.

In truth, Mu'âwiyah ﷺ was not in favor of peace with Ali ﷺ, otherwise he would have proposed arbitration before the breakout of the battle of Siffin. But he put forward his proposal only when he was sure of his defeat. So, his taking resort to the Book of Allâh was nothing but a clever device to escape the certain defeat. Ali ﷺ had, on the other hand, accepted the peace proposal very reluctantly and under serious threat and compulsion. In short, Abdullah bin Abbâs ﷺ and many others blamed Abu Musa Ash'ari ﷺ of being deceived. Abu Musa Ash'ari ﷺ; rose to protest against the trick played by Amr bin Al-Âs ﷺ with the result that chaos and disorder enveloped the entire place.

Shuraih bin Hâni attacked Amr bin Al-Âs ﷺ with his sword and he responded with a counterattack but the people saved the situation. The erupting disorder went in favor of Mu'âwiyah ﷺ. It was because the Syrians and the Iraqis could no longer stay in the company of one another and they put up a resolution with common consent to depart. Abu Musa Ash'ari ﷺ and Amr bin Al-Âs ﷺ left for Damascus along with their men while Shuraih and Abdullah bin Abbâs ﷺ proceeded to Kufah in the company of his own people. The people from Makkah and Al-Madinah also left the place dejected and shocked.

[The details presented by the compiler and other historians regarding the selection of the arbitrators and the decision have been based on the Shiite narratives and are full of doubts and faults. It is not imaginable that in the case of such an important issue, the arbitrators had been so negligent that they did nothing for six months and didn't consider any thing until the day of announcement, then suddenly they have announced the decision after a little consideration on some ordinary issues at that time. And in that decision also, one arbitrator had cheated half the nation, inviting the danger of a more severe fight than Siffin between the two parties.

In fact, the two arbitrators had reached a compact decision after their sincere efforts of six months and after collecting the opinions of the nation. This decision was also announced but the documentation of the decision has been concealed or destroyed in such a way that there is no trace of it. In its place, a fabricated story has been presented with every possible relief for Ali ﷺ, and with aspects of blames on the Syrians and even the arbitrators. However, from the folds of the events and the overall condition of the occurrences thereafter, the original decision can be extracted as follows:

1. Because Ali took the *Bai'ah* in a doubtful atmosphere; kept with him the murderers of Uthmân; claimed himself to be the rightful caliph and fought every such person who denied his *Bai'ah*, but didn't agree to take *Qisâs* (retaliation) from the murderers of Uthmân, although it was an obligation upon him as a caliph. So, he should be removed from the caliphate and prevented from using sword as a caliph. But the areas under his control should remain under him as a governor until a new caliph assumes his responsibilities.

2. Mu'âwiyah was neither a caliph nor he claimed caliphate. But the areas under him were under his governorship only and these should remain so until the new caliph is selected.

3. After the restoration of normalcy, a body of distinguished Muslims including Ali and Mu'âwiyah, should select a suitable and impartial person freely as a caliph.

4. The new caliph will be responsible for the investigation and the *Qisâs* of the murder of Uthmân, so Mu'âwiyah should remain quiet about his claim of *Qisâs* of Uthmân until the new caliph assumes his responsibility.

The first three points of this decision can be found in slightly altered form in all the history books. It is the characteristic of Shiites that they change an event in such a condition and such a trick that all the good and virtuous aspects are turned into evil and vicious appearance. As they have changed the good proposal of making the Book of Allâh a judge to stop the battle of Siffin, into a cheating trick of raising the Qur'ân on spears to deceit Ali ﷺ and to avoid the defeat; while the truth was that only one man took the Qur'ân to Ali ﷺ.

The fourth point is proved right by the fact that after it, Mu'âwiyah ﷺ remained quiet about his claims regarding *Qisâs* of Uthmân ﷺ.

The third point is verified by a narration of Ibn Umar ﷺ in *Sahih Bukhari* which states that he went to the gathering to hear the decision of the arbitrators by the insistence of Hafsah ﷺ. He said: "When the people dispersed (after hearing the decision), Mu'âwiyah delivered a *Khutbah* and said: 'Whoever wants to say something in this matter (the caliphate), he should present his head for us. (He should remember that) we are more rightful to it than him and his father.'" (*Bukhari* 4108, *Fath Al-Bari* 7/403)

This shows that the arbitrators had made a decision for the selection of a caliph unanimously apart from the two fighting chiefs. Mu'âwiyah ﷺ was challenging the same person who may be the candidate of caliphate after the decision.

The sitting in which Mu'âwiyah ﷺ made the challenge, was not a gathering of people from both the sides, but it was a group of such great Companions who remained neutral in the fight. Even Habib bin Maslamah was not present in the gathering who was very close to Mu'âwiyah ﷺ. The Companions surely had guessed about the attitude of Mu'âwiyah ﷺ that he would not accept any other caliph easily, and there was a possibility of severe resistance from his side; and in such a case the selection of a new caliph would create more turmoil.

Moreover, if the historic narratives are correct, when the decision was reported to Ali ﷺ, he denied accepting it saying that the decision was not according to the Book of Allâh, and that the arbitrators had exceeded in their powers. While no point of the decision was against the Book of Allâh, nor the arbitrators had decided anything exceeding their powers. However, the result of the attitude of Ali ﷺ and Mu'âwiyah ﷺ both, was that the decision of the arbitrators was not implemented effectively and both the persons carried their governing in the respective areas, and made efforts to take up the areas governed by the other.]

The Syrian people along with Amr bin Al-Âs ﷺ were going back happy at their victory, while the party accompanying Abdullah bin Abbâs ﷺ and Shuraih bin Hâni were making their journey in a chaotic state accusing one another for the failures they experienced. They showed the same sign of disunity and disorder which was witnessed when Ali ﷺ was going back to Kufah with his troops. After reaching Kufah, Abdullah bin Abbâs ﷺ told the whole story to Ali ﷺ, and he declared the verdict of Abu Musa ﷺ and Amr bin Al-Âs ﷺ against the Book of Allâh and the *Sunnah* of the Messenger of Allâh and rejected it outright. He also cursed Mu'âwiyah, Amr bin Al-Âs ﷺ, Habib bin Maslamah, Abdur-Rahmân bin Mukhallad, Dahhâk bin Qais, Walid, and Abul-A'war. When Mu'âwiyah ﷺ came to know of this, he too cursed Ali ﷺ; and it was the beginning of cursing and reproaching one another by their respective followers.

The disorder and confusion that charged the atmosphere of Adhruh with acrimony of the worst nature, paved the way for Mu'âwiyah ﷺ to be addressed as the Chief of the believers and the Caliph of the Muslims. But because of the events of Adhruh, no new groups joined him. Ali ﷺ was already facing trouble, which was only multiplied by now. His fresh trouble now was to make his own people understand that the verdict given at Adhruh was not acceptable because the arbitrators themselves had dissented in their opinion on the issue. In addition, the Qur'ân had not given them permission to leave its track to follow their personal opinion. Ali ﷺ spent the next few days in putting into the minds of his people that the decision of the arbitrators being unacceptable, they should invade Syria without loss of time. They at last agreed.

Disruptive Activities of the Khawârij

When the Khawârij came to know of this decision, they grew anxious and they took a new turn. It has already been mentioned that Hurqus bin Zuhair had asked Ali ﷺ to attack the Syrians instead of agreeing with the proposal of arbitration. Now Zur'ah bin Al-Burj and Hurqus bin Zuhair both being the chieftains of the Khawârij, came to Ali ﷺ and declared him guilty of first rejecting and then accepting the proposal advanced by the Khawârij. Now, on this score, they demanded Ali ﷺ to show his repentance for his mistake in order to receive their support. But Ali ﷺ turned down their demand pleading his innocence over the issue. Hearing this, both of them got up and left the place saying: "There is no command (acceptable) except of Allâh."

When, following this event, Ali ﷺ ascended the pulpit of the mosque to deliver his address, a Khâriji sounded in a loud voice from a corner: "There is no command (acceptable) except of Allâh." Ali ﷺ remarked, "Behold, these people extract untruth from the Word of Truth." He then resumed his address and the same voice came again interrupting him: "There is no command (acceptable) except of Allâh."

Thereupon Ali ﷺ said, "You people are treating me improperly. We do not debar you from making entry into the mosque, and we gave you your share from the booty while you remained with us; we shall not fight with you unless you take the initiative, and we shall be awaiting Allah's Decision about you." Saying this, he descended the pulpit and went away. The Khawârij also left the mosque and gathered in the house of Abdullah bin Wahb for consultations. Abdullah bin Wahb, Hurqus bin Zuhair, Hamzah bin Sinân, Zaid bin Husain At-Tai', and Shuraih bin Aufa 'Absi decided, after a good deal of deliberations, that they should leave Basrah and make the hills the seat of their independent rule separate from Ali ﷺ. Hamzah bin Sinân Asadi proposed to choose a chief and give him the standard before proceeding further.

The next day they assembled again in the house of Shuraih, and
Abdullah bin Wahb was elected the chief of the Khawârij. They took
Bai'ah at his hands. Abdullah bin Wahb then suggested to move
towards a city where the Divine command could be enforced. At last
they agreed on Madâ'in, which they could, according to them, capture
comparatively easily. Zaid bin Husain proposed to move in twos, fours
or tens, for collective movement was likely to be given chase. They also
decided to first halt at Naharwân and ask their friends and supporters
in Basrah to join them before reaching Madâ'in. This suggestion gained
the support of one and all. The plan was implemented according to the
decision. Mis'ar bin Fadaki Taimi came out at the head of five hundred
Khawârij. When Ali ﷺ came to know of the developments, he sent
message to Sa'd bin Mas'ud, the governor of Madâ'in through a speedy
courier to put a check on the Khawârij in Madâ'in. Sa'd deputed his
nephew in Madâ'in and moved out at the head of a contingent. He
came across a band of the Khawârij on the way at Karkh and
challenged them which led to an encounter continuing until evening.
But the Khawârij crossed the Tigris in the darkness of night. The
Khawârij from Basrah also crossed the Tigris and joined their friends in
Naharwân after an encounter with Sa'd's contingent. At Naharwân
they consolidated their position and issued an edict of blasphemy
against Ali ﷺ for killing the supporters of the Caliph. In a short time
their number rose to twenty-five thousand.

Battle of Naharwân

After the exit of the Khawârij from Kufah, Ali ﷺ persuaded the Kufis
to make preparations for the invasion of Syria. He preferred the ouster
of Mu'âwiyah ﷺ to the curbing of the Khawârij. Thus he sent a
message to Abdullah bin Abbâs ﷺ in Basrah to send the maximum
number of troops for launching an attack on Syria. Although Basrah
had more than sixty thousand fighters, the letter of Ali ﷺ could rouse
only three thousand for fighting. Kufah too showed signs of lack of
interest. When three thousand troops headed by Jâriyah bin Qudâmah
ﷺ reached Kufah, Ali ﷺ made a fresh attempt to kindle in Kufis the
fire of zeal and fervor and his renewed efforts hit the mark. Forty
thousand man gathered under the flag of Ali ﷺ.

He also wrote the Khawârij a letter calling them to lend their support in the task of attacking Syria. Abdullah bin Wahb read out the letter to his people and wrote back with common consent: "You appointed the arbitrators against the Command of Allâh and His Messenger. And you have now developed a desire to invade Syria on the demand of your self's desire. However, if you show your repentance after declaring yourself as blasphemous, we are ready to help you, otherwise we are prepared to fight against you."

Although the letter saddened Ali ﷺ, he did not give up his determination to invade Syria. He made an all-out effort to bring the Khawârij back to righteousness but in vain. When Ali ﷺ reminded them of their mounting pressure on him to stop the attack on the Syrian Army, they argued that they admitted their fault and he should also follow suit. He should also come back to the fold of Islam by declaring himself blasphemous as they did. This was the only way they could take back their edict against him, otherwise they will wage *Jihâd* against him considering him a *Kafir* (disbeliever).

Ali ﷺ, however, decided to carry out his campaign against Syria and ignore the insane demand of the Khawârij, that he was informed of the martyrdom of Abdullah bin Khabbâb ﷺ. The victim passed through Naharwân during a journey. A group of the Khawârij came to know that he was a Companion. They came to him and asked about Abu Bakr and Umar ﷺ. Abdullah bin Khabbâb ﷺ said, "Both of them were very pious and true servants of Allâh the Almighty." They then inquired of the first and the last parts of the caliphate of Uthmân ﷺ. He replied, "He was truth-loving from beginning to the end." They then wanted to know his opinion about Ali ﷺ before and after the appointment of the arbitrators. He stated, "Ali knows and understands the injunctions of Allâh and His Messenger more than you all." Hearing this, the Khawârij fell in wrath and killed Khabbâb ﷺ, his wife and his fellow travelers.

On being informed of this, Ali ﷺ asked Hârith bin Murrah to make an inquiry into the matter. The Khawârij killed him also. Along with this, it was reported to Ali ﷺ that they were killing all those who disagreed with them. Thus, Ali's men grew anxious that the Khawârij would capture Kufah and Basrah and kill their wives and children in case they advanced towards Syria. They marched towards the Khawârij instead of Syria and sent them the following message from a place nearby: "Hand over those among you who have killed our brothers so that we can kill them according to the law of *Qisâs*, and leave you to yourselves in order to proceed to Syria. May Allâh the Almighty bring you back to the right path while we finish with the Syrians."

Following this, Ali ﷺ sent a number of Companions one by one to preach to them righteousness and truth. He also invited the deputation of the Khawârij to instill in their minds that they were totally responsible for the appointment of the arbitrators, and they should join him forgetting the past. But every time they had the same answer to give and the same argument to advance. Ali ﷺ would say, "I believed in Allâh and migrated in His way, how can I declare myself a disbeliever?"

At last Ali ﷺ himself went to the camp of the Khawârij and began to preach them to use wisdom and adopt righteousness. Fearing the strength of the impression Ali's speech would have on their people, the chieftains asked them not to pay attention to what he said and go to war.

In view of their attitude, Ali ﷺ came back and set himself to the task of organizing his troops and appointing commanding officers of the attacking army. This task being over, Ali ﷺ gave Abu Ayub Ansâri ﷺ the flag of peace and asked him to ascend to a raised spot and give a general call saying: "Those who come to us without a fight will get peace, and those who go to Kufah or Madâ'in will also enjoy peace." Having heard this announcement, Farwah bin Naufal Ashja'i moved apart with five hundred horsemen, some people left for Kufah while some others either went to Madâ'in or came to join Ali's troops, with the result less than one-third of the men were left with the Khawârij. Ali ﷺ then launched a massive attack and put the rest to death.

All the prominent chieftains of the Khawârij like Abdullah bin Wahb, Zaid bin Husain, Hurqus bin Zuhair, Abdullah bin Shajarah, and Shuraih bin Aufa lost their lives. Only nine of them saved themselves by fleeing from the scene of death. Ali ﷺ came back leaving their dead bodies unburied.

Finished with the necessary task of curbing the uprisings of the Khawârij, Ali ﷺ decided to march towards Syria. Ash'ath bin Qais advised him to let the army take a few days rest, but he preferred to stay at Nukhailah issuing orders for one and all to refrain from going to Kufah until the Syrian campaign was completed. But they left for home and Ali ﷺ also had to return to Kufah, when he found the camp without fighters. In Kufah, Ali ﷺ addressed them to get prepared for the invasion of Syria but none of them appeared to be interested in the Syrian campaign. In view of their cold response, Ali ﷺ was also forced to abandon his campaign against Syria.

State of Egypt

As already mentioned, Muhammad bin Abu Bakr ﷺ, the governor of Egypt, was not of any help to Ali ﷺ against Mu'âwiyah ﷺ owing to his bitter engagements and internal feuds with those who wouldn't take *Bai'ah* until Uthmân's murderers were punished. Finishing with the battle of Siffin, Ali ﷺ sent Mâlik Ashtar Nakha'i as the governor of Jazirah but very shortly sent him to Egypt as governor.

When Muhammad bin Abu Bakr ﷺ came to know of this, he grew sorry and dejected. Mu'âwiyah ﷺ became anxious because of Ashtar's qualities of thought and action. But Mâlik Ashtar died suddenly in route to Egypt and Muhammad bin Abu Bakr ﷺ remained in power. Following the death of Mâlik Ashtar, Ali ﷺ wrote Muhammad bin Abu Bakr ﷺ that he had sent Ashtar as governor of Egypt not because he was angry with him but because Ashtar could solve some political matters more skillfully. But, since, Ashtar died he was allowed to manage the affairs of Egypt as usual. Moreover, he was required to face the enemy with courage and determination.

In reply to the letter, Muhammad bin Abu Bakr ﷺ wrote that he was loyal to him and was ready to fight his (Ali's) enemies at any time. These events had taken place before the decision of the arbitrators.

The Syrians later accepted Mu'âwiyah ﷺ as Caliph and it added to his power and grandeur. He then entered into correspondence with Mu'âwiyah bin Hudaij and those who opposed Muhammad bin Abu

Bakr ﷺ to encourage them. They sought help from Mu'âwiyah ﷺ and that was what he intended. Thus he lost no time in dispatching Amr bin Al-Âs ﷺ at the head of six thousand troops with a letter in the name of Muhammad bin Abu Bakr ﷺ. Reaching close to Egypt, Amr bin Al-Âs ﷺ sent Mu'âwiyah's letter to Muhammad bin Abu Bakr ﷺ along with his own. Muhammad bin Abu Bakr ﷺ sent both the letters to Ali ﷺ in Kufah.

Ali ﷺ gathered the people and roused them to take part in the Egyptian campaign but not more than two thousand men were ready to fight. At last, he sent these two thousand men to Egypt under the command of Mâlik bin Ka'b. Muhammad bin Abu Bakr ﷺ had already sent two thousand troops against Amr bin Al-Âs ﷺ under the command of Kinânah bin Bishr who was martyred fighting with the Syrians and his men either fled from the field or were killed fighting.

With the news of the defeat, Muhammad bin Abu Bakr ﷺ decided to personally lead his troops. The awe-stricken men of Muhammad bin Abu Bakr ﷺ showed no courage to face the Syrians and fled, leaving their commander who was fighting alone, he came back from the battlefield and took refuge in the house of Jabalah bin Masruq. The house was surrounded by the Syrians and the companions of Mu'âwiyah bin Hudaij. Muhammad bin Abu Bakr ﷺ came out of the house and was arrested trying to fight his opponents. Mu'âwiyah bin Hudaij killed him and burned him putting his body inside the skin of a dead donkey.

The news of the incident was brought to Ali ﷺ by his spy Abdur-Rahmân bin Shabib Fazâri. He at once sent someone to bring Mâlik bin Ka'b back. Mâlik bin Ka'b had covered about half the distance when Hajjâj bin Amr bin Ghaziyah Ansâri came across and informed him of the assassination of Muhammad bin Abu Bakr ﷺ and Amr bin Al-Âs' victory over Egypt. Meanwhile, Ali ﷺ assembled the people of Kufah and reproached them for their laziness and neglect. But this stirring address failed to inspire the audience and they remained unmoved. Now, Ali ﷺ was under circumstantial compulsion to give up the campaign of Egypt and Syria.

Attempts made to capture Other Provinces

The conquest of Egypt was very encouraging for Mu'âwiyah ﷺ. His next step was to wrest even Basrah from the hands of Ali ﷺ. The atmosphere of Basrah was not much different from Egypt. The battle of Jamal had angered them with Ali ﷺ and a growing demand for revenging the blood of Uthmân ﷺ had developed among the people in general. Taking advantage of the situation, Mu'âwiyah ﷺ sent Abdullah bin Al-Hadrami towards Basrah with the instruction that the elements antagonistic to Ali ﷺ be assimilated and their hearts won by all means. When Ibn Al-Hadrami reached Basrah, he found the situation in Basrah conducive to his plan particularly when Abdullah bin Abbâs ﷺ, the governor of Basrah was not present and had gone to Ali ﷺ. A large party of the people joined him. Being informed of the new development in Basrah, Ali ﷺ made no delay in sending A'in bin Dubai'ah with the instruction of creating a rift among those who had joined hands with Ibn Al-Hadrami. He was crowned with success in the task entrusted to him. Thus the campaign of Abdullah bin Al-Hadrami ended in his assassination in the last days of 38 AH, in Basrah.

In 39 AH, when the Persians noticed that Basrah was divided between the followers of Ali ﷺ and Mu'âwiyah ﷺ, they rose in revolt and expelled the governor, Sahl bin Hunaif, from their territory. Ali ﷺ wrote Ibn Abbâs ﷺ, the governor of Basrah to send Ziyâd to Persia who went there and put down the revolt with a heavy hand.

In a situation, fraught with discontent and uprising against Ali ﷺ, Mu'âwiyah ﷺ took advantage of the situation by using generosity, forgiveness, strategies and appreciation to one and all. This attitude proved fruitful as people in large numbers from Al-Madinah, Tâ'if and Yemen drew near to him. He also sent Nu'mân bin Bashir to Ain-ut-Tamr where Mâlik bin Ka'b, the governor did not receive reinforcements from Ali ﷺ and yielded the territory to the Syrian commander. Madâ'in and Anbâr met the same fate and Sufyân bin Auf returned to Damascus with huge possessions from these territories. Although Ali ﷺ made an advancement to intercept him, Sufyân bin Auf got away uncaught.

Ali's Caliphate confined to Iraq and Iran

Busr bin Abu Artah was dispatched to the Hijâz and Yemen while the Madinites took the oath of allegiance at the hand of Mu'âwiyah ﷺ followed by the Makkans and Yemenites. Ubaidullah bin Abbâs ﷺ was turned out from San'â', the capital of Yemen. In short, by 40 AH, Yemen, Hijâz, Syria, Palestine, and Egypt became provinces under the control of Mu'âwiyah ﷺ and these territories were free from the weaknesses of discontent, insurgence, and internal disputes.

Both Ali ﷺ and Mu'âwiyah ﷺ had reached consensus on the issue of leaving Makkah and Al-Madinah outside their rule. Ali's caliphate was confined to Iraq and Iran. But a large number of Arabian tribes of Iraq lacked attachment with his caliphate while the Persians were also dreaming of their own rule. Even Kufah and Basrah, the two principal cities had a considerable number of men who preferred Mu'âwiyah ﷺ to Ali ﷺ. Even though Ali ﷺ was determined to establish one Islamic rule throughout by virtue of his courage and bravery, his men showed a lack of courage and loyalty. Ali's army was largely manned by non-Arabs while that of Mu'âwiyah's had mostly Arabs in command. With the inclusion of Hijâz and Yemen, Mu'âwiyah's army had achieved much strength and popularity. Since, he was not on equality with Ali ﷺ in personal status, greatness and glory, he could not claim for himself the same position in the world of Islam and so he continued to fear Ali ﷺ.

Abdullah bin Abbâs' Departure from Basrah

During the beginning of 40 AH, one more ugly incident took place. Abdullah bin Abbâs ﷺ, the governor of Basrah, grew angry with Ali ﷺ and left Basrah. The exit of Abdullah ﷺ was on account of a false complaint lodged to Ali ﷺ by Abul-Aswad of Basrah that he had spent from the public treasury without seeking permission from the Caliph. Ali ﷺ thanked Abul-Aswad for bringing the irregularities of the governor to the knowledge of the Caliph and held this as an act of sympathy. He also wrote Abdullah bin Abbâs ﷺ that he had received such a complaint and demanded an explanation from him as well. But the letter did not mention the name of Abul-Aswad. Abdullah bin Abbâs 🕮 wrote back that the complaint was totally false and baseless for what he had expended was from his personal account and had nothing to do with the public treasury. Ali 🕮 wrote him again, "If you claim that the money spent belonged to yourself then wherefrom did you get the money and where had you deposited that?" In reply to the letter Abdullah 🕮 wrote back, "I hate such a governorship, you may choose anybody else as the governor of Basrah. What I spent was my personal possession and I have every right to spend it." He dispatched the letter to Ali 🕮 and with it he quit his post and left for Makkah.

Ali's Martyrdom

During these very days Aqil bin Abu Tâlib 🕮, the brother of Ali 🕮 grew angry with him and went to Mu'âwiyah 🕮 who welcomed him and fixed a considerable daily allowance for him. Ali 🕮 felt deeply aggrieved at the separation of Aqil 🕮 and his joining the camp of Mu'âwiyah 🕮. Now Ali 🕮 thought military action against Mu'âwiyah 🕮 a necessity. It was an occasion when sixty thousand Kufis took *Bai'ah* at Ali's hands to support him and fight on his behalf while they had life in them. He then engaged himself in the task of collecting more people in addition to the sixty thousand men and procure as much military equipment as he could.

Dangerous Plan of the Khawârij

It has been mentioned above that only nine persons from the Khawârij survived the battle of Naharwân. They were the persons that were in the leadership positions among the Khawârij, at first they spread into various parts of Persia and launched violent propaganda attacks and hatched conspiracies against Ali 🕮. When their efforts proved fruitless, they came to Iraq and Hijâz and started seeking listeners. At last, three persons, Abdur-Rahmân bin Muljam Murâdi, Burak bin Abdullah Tamimi and Amr bin Bakr Tamimi gathered together in Makkah and kept expressing profound grief over the men slain in Naharwân. At last they entered into a pact to do away with the three men in power that had been putting the entire world of

Islam to such a great loss and destruction. According to their plan Abdur-Rahmân bin Muljam Murâdi-the Egyptian, Burak bin Abdullah Tamimi, and Amr bin Bakr Tamimi Sa'di each agreed to kill Ali, Mu'âwiyah and Amr bin Al-Âs 🙵 respectively. Ramadân 16 and the morning prayer were fixed as the date and time of the assassinations. With this nefarious plan in view, they left for Kufah, Damascus and Egypt.

When the date fixed for killing came, Burak bin Abdullah Tamimi entered the mosque of Damascus and hit Mu'âwiyah with his sword while he was leading *Fajr* prayer. He then fled the mosque but was caught. His mission failed because the injuries his victim received were not fatal. Mu'âwiyah 🙵 regained his health after a couple of days of treatment. Burak was killed then and there, or after several years of captivity according to another narrative. Mu'âwiyah 🙵 then practiced caution and put guards for his safety inside the mosque.

On the same day and date, Amr bin Bakr struck Kharijah bin Abu Habibah bin Amr and killed him with his sword mistaking him to be Amir bin Al-Âs 🙵 while he was leading the *Fajr* prayer in the mosque of Egypt. That morning Amr bin Al-Âs 🙵 was absent due to illness and Khârijah bin Abu Habibah, a military officer was leading the prayer as his substitute. The same day Abdur-Rahmân bin Muljam attacked Ali 🙵 in Kufah Mosque while he was leading the *Fajr* prayer and left him critically injured, and he died after two days. It is narrated that Abdur-Rahmân bin Muljam came to Kufah and met his friends but told none about his plan. After much deliberations he acquainted his friend Shabib bin Bajrah Ashja'i with his plan and sought his help in killing Ali 🙵 in return for the killings in Naharwân. He agreed after some initial reluctance. Furthermore, he came into contact with the relatives of those ten persons of Tamim tribe who were killed in Naharwân and took advantage of their anger against Ali 🙵.

Ibn Muljam came closer to them and established friendly terms with them. Among them he saw a very beautiful women named Qatâm. Her father and brother were also killed in Naharwân. Ibn Muljam asked for her hand in marriage. She agreed and the head of Ali 🙵 was the bridal money. Ibn Muljam who had come with the same purpose readily agreed to her terms. She then asked a person from her relatives, named Wardân to help Ibn Muljam. On the appointed day Ibn Muljam, Shabib bin Bajrah and Wardân came to the mosque and hid themselves near the door from the night before the fateful morning. Ali ؓ entered the mosque as usual calling people for prayer. First of all Wardân came out and struck him with his sword but his sword hit the threshold or the wall and Ali ؓ safely went ahead. But Ibn Muljam darted towards Ali ؓ and struck his forehead with his sword, which gave a deep injury. Ali ؓ called out to catch them. The people assembled in the mosque ran after the culprits. Wardân and Shabib fled the mosque but Ibn Muljam could not and was caught inside the mosque.

A Hadrami caught Shabib but he slipped out of his hands and then disappeared. Wardân fled to his house but was caught there and put to death. Ibn Muljam was brought before Ali ؓ. He ordered saying "He is to be killed if I succumb to my injuries; in case I recover, I shall deal with him." He then turned towards Banu Abdul-Muttalib and said, "Make not my assassination a pretext for shedding Muslim blood; you will kill only my assassin by way of *Qisâs*. Afterwards he said addressing his elder son Hasan ؓ, "O Hasan ! If I succumb to the injuries I have received, you will kill him with a stroke of your sword but avoid mutilation for the Prophet ﷺ has strictly forbidden this."

Although Ibn Muljam's sword had gone down deep into the brain of Ali ؓ, he remained alive through Friday and died only on Saturday, Ramadan 17. A little before his death Jundub bin Abdullah came to him and said, "May we elect Hasan as Caliph in case you pass away?" He replied, "I have nothing to say about it, you will do according to the need of the hour."

Following this he called Hasnain (Hasan and Husain) ؓ and said, "I tell you to keep fearing Allâh and not to indulge in worldliness. Express no sorrow over what you are not able to get. Always say the right thing and show mercy to the orphans and help the helpless. Extend your help to the oppressed while keep opposing the oppressors and keep following the Qur'ân without fearing reproach in carrying out the Commands of Allâh." He then said, addressing

Muhammad bin Al-Hanafiyah, "I tell you to follow what I have told. Moreover, show respect to both your brothers; they command a greater right on you and you must not do anything against their will." Thereafter he turned to Hasnain 🕮 and said, "You should also treat Muhammad bin Al-Hanafiyah well and keep making concessions to him." He then took to dictating his will in general when the last hour approached and he bade his last farewell with *La ilaha illallah* (There is no God except Allâh) on his lips.

Ali's Grave traceless

Following the death of Ali 🕮, Ibn Muljam was made to appear before Hasan 🕮 who killed him with one stroke of his sword. Ali 🕮 was honored with martyrdom at the age of sixty-three and passed five years as a caliph. Hasan, Husain and Abdullah bin Ja'far 🕮 washed his body and shrouded him in three pieces of cloth without a shirt.

Hasan 🕮, led the funeral prayer. But there is a wide difference of opinion with regard to his burial ground. Some people say that he was buried in the Kufah Mosque while others say that he was buried in his house, or somewhere ten miles away from Kufah.

According to some narratives, Hasan 🕮 buried him at an unknown place after taking his body out of his grave anticipating an act of desecration from the Khawârij. Still one more narrative says that his bier was carried to Al-Madinah to bury him near the grave of Prophet 🕮. But the camel carrying the body fled away and remained traceless. Contradicting this narrative, yet another one lends support to the opinion that the camel with the body of Ali 🕮 was traced at Tai and he was buried there. It is a wonder that the grave of such a great personality lies traceless to this day. However, the reason behind his burial at an unknown place was the Khawârij menace.

Wives and Children

Ali 🕮 married nine wives at different times and had fourteen sons and seventeen daughters. He was first married to Fâtimah 🕮, the daughter of the Prophet 🕮 who gave him two sons, Hasan and Husain 🕮, and two daughters Zainab and Umm Kulthum 🕮. After the death of Fâtimah 🌸, he married Umm-un-Nabiyin bint Harâm Kalâbiah who gave him four sons, Abbâs, Ja'far, Abdullah and Uthmân 🌸.

His third wife was Laila bint Mas'ud bin Khâlid from whom Ubaidullah and Abu Bakr 🌸 were born. The fourth Asma' bint Umais gave him Muhammad Al-Asghar and Yahya. These eight brothers were martyred fighting with Husain 🌸 in Karbala. His fifth wife Umâmah bint Abul-Âs bin Ar-Rabi' bin Abdul-Uzza bin Abd Shams whose mother was Zainab, the daughter of the Prophet 🌸 and Muhammad Al-Ausat was born to her.

His sixth marriage was with Khaulah bint Ja'far who was from Banu Hanifah, he had with her Muhammad Al-Akbar also known as Muhammad bin Al-Hanafiyah. From his seventh marriage with Sahba bint Rabi'ah Taghlabiah he got Umar bin Ali, Ruqayyah bint Ali. His eighth wife was Umm Saeed bint Urwah bin Mas'ud Thaqafiyah with whom he got Umm Hasan, Ramlat-ul-Kubra and Umm Kulthum Sughra.

His ninth and the last marriage was with Mukhbi'ah the daughter of Imra-ul-Qais bin Adi Kalbiyah gave him a daughter who died young. He had some other daughters too but their names are unknown. His one son Aun is stated to be born to Asma' bint Umais. However, Ali's progeny came from Hasan, Husain, Muhammad bin Al-Hanafiyah, Abbâs and Ja'far 🌸 while the others did not survive long.

A Glance at Ali's Caliphate

Ali 🌸 was the last in the line of those who commanded respect throughout the world of Islam. None after him could fight evil and promote good. When Aishah 🌸 heard the sad news of Ali's death, she observed: "Now the people are at liberty to do what they like, for none is left to prevent them from wrongdoings."

Ali 🌸 was above craftiness. He was truth loving to the core. At first he considered himself more within his rights to become the Caliph owing to his close relationship with the Prophet 🌸. Thus he did not keep it secret from others and kept from making the oath of allegiance to Abu Bakr 🌸 for sometime. During these same days, Abu Sufyân instigated him to rise against Abu Bakr but he rebuked him rather violently and with contempt for he hated such an act. When he reconciled himself with the reality that the job of a caliph required qualities of head and heart other than mere relationship, he found Abu Bakr worthy of the responsibilities and pledged his allegiance to him on his own and remained loyal to him throughout.

During his caliphate, Umar Fâruq sought Ali's advice and held it valuable. He lent his sincere advice to Uthmân thinking least whether he acted upon it or not. And whenever he found any of Uthmân's action objectionable, he opposed it without any reservation.

When the people opposed Uthmân, he supported them to the extent that it was valid. When the rioters mounted their violent pressure on Uthmân and an ugly situation was created, he showed no craftiness in keeping his position clear and remained satisfied with the clarity of his conscience. When following the assassination of Uthmân, the people rose to pledge their allegiance to him, he accepted for he considered himself more worthy than others for the job.

In short, his deeds and actions proved beyond doubt that he was never reluctant to speak the truth regardless of the consequences. His face was the index of his feelings and his exterior was the mirror of his interior. He was like an unsheathed sword and would speak the truth frankly in every situation. Another person would have handed over Muhammad bin Abu Bakr and Mâlik Ashtar to be killed by way of *Qisâs* for Uthmân's blood and thus bought peace and security for himself. But since he could not obtain solid evidence against the assassins of Uthmân, he held himself back from punishing the accused and faced the resultant troubles but refused to bow down to his opponents.

Majority of the persons Ali had to dealt with were crafty, shrewd and expedient. The Islamic atmosphere created by the Prophet, which continued to exist through the period of Umar Fâruq, did not remain intact after more people from Persia, Egypt, and the other lands entered the folds of Islam. Racial and ancestral superiority, worldliness, desire for a comfortable and luxurious life distorted much of the real face of Islam. During his tenure the number of Companions had significantly decreased. Great and influential Companions had already passed away and the rest had shifted from Al-Madinah to settle in Kufah, Basrah, Damascus, Egypt, Yemen, Makkah and Al-Madinah. Up to the period of Umar Fâruq ﷺ, almost all the Companions lived in Al-Madinah. Ali ﷺ shifted the capital of Islam from Al-Madinah to Kufah but he did not make any substantial gain from this change. He was deprived of the advantages he could have gained in Al-Madinah. He failed to attract help from the Hijâz because with the change of capital, the importance of the Hijâz was diminished.

During the blessed period of the Prophet ﷺ the hypocrites and conspirators tried their best to put the Muslims to trouble and loss but their nefarious plans did not bear fruit. During the era of Abu Bakr Siddiq and Umar Fâruq ﷺ, those who had vested interests, left no stone unturned to inflict injuries to Islam but they were dealt with severely. They first got an opportunity to raise their heads during the caliphate of Uthmân bin Affân ﷺ, and Ali ﷺ as his successor, had to bear the brunt of the dealings of his predecessor. Furthermore, if he had some more years as a caliph, he could have done away with the mischief-mongers and power hungry elements because in spite of the multiple problems assailing him, he had the courage and determination to combat them all. He never yielded to despair and discouragement. However, it was the Will of Allâh for him to depart leaving the field open for Banu Umayyah.

The Banu Umayyah tribe considered itself the principal power of Arabia and treated Banu Hâshim as its rival. Although Islam uprooted evils of racial and ancestral snobbery, Uthmân's caliphate revived it. Banu Umayyah found in his caliphate a golden opportunity to restore the lost power and leadership and the hypocrites aided and abetted their plans. It was such a loss to Islam that Ali ﷺ could not compensate for it during his entire tenure until his martyrdom.

If we take the campaigns of Ali ﷺ and Mu'âwiyah ﷺ and the opposition of Zubair ﷺ and Talhah ﷺ as cases similar to those of our times, we are grossly mistaken. We can't measure their moral standards with our own. It is worth noting that Talhah ﷺ and Zubair

came to the battlefield with massive preparations against Ali ,
but a *Hadith* of the Prophet made both of them keep from fighting
and no amount of lashing and lambasting could ' rouse them to go
against Ali . It is an undeniable fact that fighting was natural for
them but one *Hadith* of the Prophet changed their outlook and their
course of action.

Our religious leaders and scholars today indulge in a futile war of
words of a shameful nature and sometimes go to law courts for
worldly decisions on religious issues. No Verse of the Qur'ân or
Hadith of the Prophet proves effective enough to make them accept
the truth. It has already been mentioned that Mu'âwiyah had
sought from Ali the issue of the inheritance of a eunuch after the
battle of Siffin and the judgment of the arbitrators.

When Ali entered Basrah, Qais bin Ubâdah stated that the people
said, "The Prophet told you that you will be made Caliph after him.
Is this true?" Ali had emphatically said, "This is utterly wrong. I
can never tell a lie about the Prophet . Had he said so, how could I
have allowed Abu Bakr, Umar and Uthmân to become the Caliph and
give my allegiance to them?" How could anybody now make such
statements? Yet, we hear it from those who are called religious scholars
and pious Muslims. From Adam to the Day of Judgment, struggle
between truth and untruth goes on and will go on. Divine and satanic
parties have always been there and they will exist until the Day of
Resurrection. This unending fight between right and wrong decides
the reward and punishment one will receive in the Hereafter.

Islam teaches moderation and prevents going to the extremes. People
have formed extreme views about Ali . One group has degraded
him to the lowest level while another one, in opposition to the first
one, upgraded him to the position of god. In this respect Ali was
put into a position like Isa (Jesus) when the Jews opposed him and
went astray, while the Christians lifted him up to the Divine level. But
pure and orthodox Muslims walk a middle path neither of the Shiite
nor the Khawârij.

As the Companions of the Prophet can not be brought down to the
level of the reverend Muslims, sufis and common Muslims of our times,

they also cannot be taken above the human level. They were, after all, humans. They ate and drank and slept like humans. They had other human needs too. Even the Prophet ﷺ claimed his being human and took pride in his position as a slave of Allâh. However, we are very sure of his innocence and of his being perfect in total human virtues and excellence and consider his life and deeds as a guiding light for us all.

The Companions were fortunate enough to watch and emulate his example in letter and spirit. But, since, they were neither Prophets nor innocent, and different from each other in abilities, they had different aspects of human qualities to show. Among them we see Abu Bakr ﷺ and Umar ﷺ on one hand and Mu'âwiyah ﷺ and Mughirah ﷺ on the other. They had jurists like Ali ﷺ and Aishah ﷺ and narrators of *Hadith* like Abu Hurairah ﷺ and Ibn Mas'ud ﷺ, political activists like Amr bin Al-Âs ﷺ and pious persons like Abdullah bin Umar ﷺ and Abu Dhar ﷺ. Now, if they differ in thoughts, opinions and actions, it is our duty to take these differences as a blessing in disguise and not to fall prey to hasty decisions and thoughtless actions.

Up to 30 AH, twenty years after the death of the Prophet ﷺ, the Muslims kept winning steady victories without loss. These conquests brought to the fold of Islam almost all the civilized countries of the world. From 30 AH to 40 AH, we find almost no Muslim victories and they remained preoccupied with internal problems, bickering, feuds and fighting. Although the decade-long disturbances were apparently injurious to Islam, they had some hidden virtues for the Muslim *Ummah*. The twenty-year long spell of victories were the fruits of spiritual power and the teachings of the Qur'ân, while internal dissentions and disruptions were the direct outcome of a materialistic approach to life. Through death and destruction they learned to live under adverse situations and win peace and progress after losses and reverses.

The fight goes on and will keep going on between good and bad, right and wrong, light and darkness. Whenever materialism gains victory over spiritual power, the two forces are bound to clash with one another. When Musa (Moses) ﷺ caught Hârun (Aaron) ﷺ by his beard, when Yusuf (Joseph) ﷺ could be thrown into the well by his brothers and sold for a few coins, the differences among various sections of the Companions must not be looked upon with amazement.

What took place between Ali ﷺ and Mu'âwiyah ﷺ, left a deep scar on the face of Islam. It has been serving the Muslims as a lesson to learn from and to take care about since that time. Conflict between Banu Umayyah and Banu Abbâs, campaigns of the Ghaznawid and the Ghorid against one another and the power struggles between rival Muslim rulers throughout history have inflicted heavy losses in men and materials but Islam is flexible enough to sustain these onslaughts and rise again from the dust.

These ups and downs in Muslim life and character and power have always been among the wonders of history. When Halâku (the son of Ghengis Khan) ravaged Baghdad, it led to his progeny converting to Islam. When the united Christian forces wrested Palestine from the Muslims, Salahuddin Ayubi appeared on the scene and restored the sacred land to the Muslim *Ummah*.

We find contrast in all the facets of the world. Islamic caliphate or Islamic rule was in all respects a blessing for mankind. But it was not spared the onslaught of decline and fall.

Readers of history are not pleased over the emergence of hypocrites during the caliphate of Uthmân ﷺ and opponents make an attempt to hold Islam responsible for this. But dark forces have always been there to fight the forces of light and virtue and they have, more than once, attained temporary success in their nefarious plans. These forces raised their heads with the martyrdom of Umar Fâruq ﷺ and have been raging against Islam since then.

Hasan ﷺ

Physical Features and Pedigree:

Hasan bin Ali bin Abu Tâlib ﷺ was the last of the Rightly-Guided Caliphs. He was born in the middle of Sha'bân 3 AH. He resembled the Prophet ﷺ who named him Hasan. Nobody had this name during the Age of Ignorance. Imam Bukhari reports from Abu Bakr ﷺ, "The Prophet ﷺ was once sitting on the pulpit with Hasan beside him. He would sometimes look towards the audience and at times at Hasan and said: 'This son of mine is the chief of the people and will make peace between two factions of the Muslims'." The Prophet ﷺ was once going somewhere with Hasan ﷺ on his shoulder. A man came across and remarked addressing Hasan ﷺ, "What a good mount you have got." At this the Prophet ﷺ replied "Even the rider is very good." Abdullah bin Zubair ﷺ is reported to have said, "Hasan resembled the Prophet ﷺ very much and he loved him dearly."

Praiseworthy Traits:

Hasan ﷺ was very polite and generous and commanded high respect. He had a great dislike for disturbance and bloodshed. He performed *Hajj* twenty-five times on foot although he had his camel with him. Umair bin Ishâq says, "Hasan alone is the person whom I love to hear speaking. And I never heard him using foul language."

When Marwân bin Al-Hakam was the governor of Al-Madinah and Hasan ﷺ had also shifted to Al-Madinah after quitting his caliphate, he once sent someone to tell Hasan ﷺ, "You are like a mule (Allâh forbid), that when it is asked about its father it says my mother was a mare." While sending his reply, he said, "I shall never forget that you abuse me without any reason. We have ultimately to go before Allâh the Almighty. So, if you are true in what you say, Allâh the Almighty will give you reward for that; in case you are a liar, Allâh the Almighty is the Greatest Avenger of all." Jarir bin Asma' relates, "When Hasan passed away, Marwân burst into tears at his funeral bier. When Husain ﷺ said to him, 'You now weep over him although

you kept annoying him during his lifetime." Marwân replied, 'Do you
know I could only do so with a person who was more tolerant than a
mountain." Ali bin Zaid ☙ relates, "Hasan gave away as charity in
the way of Allâh all his goods and chattels twice and gave half three
times." He would divorce women most frequently except one who
began to love him. At last Ali ☙ had to ask the people of Kufah not to
give their daughters to him in marriage. But Hamadân said, "How
can it be that we refuse to give our daughters to him in marriage."
Someone mentioned before Hasan ☙ that Abu Dhar ☙ used to say, "I
hold dear poverty more than opulence and sickness more than
health." Thereupon he remarked, "May Allâh show him mercy. As for
me, I leave myself totally in the Hand of Allâh without desiring
anything; He will do what He likes; I dare not interfere in His
Decisions."

He handed over the caliphate to Mu'âwiyah ☙ in Rabi' Al-Awwal 41
AH. When his friends called him *'Âr-ul-Muslimin'*, he would say, "*Âr*
(shame) is better than *Nâr* (Hell)." When a person addressed him, "O
the disgracer of the Muslims. I salute you!" he answered back, "I am
not the disgracer of the Muslims; I simply thought not to sacrifice you
for the country." Jubair bin Nufair relates that he once said to Hasan
☙, "It is in the air that you have once again developed a desire for the
caliphate." He replied "When the heads of the Arabs lay in my hands
and I could do with them as I liked, I gave it up to seek the Pleasure of
Allâh, now am I expected to undo this merely to please the people of
the Hijâz?" He died in the month of Rabi' Al-Awwal 50 AH. They
suspect that he was poisoned to death. When Husain pressed ☙ him
to tell the name of the one who gave him poison, he answered saying,
"If the suspect has poisoned me, Allâh the Almighty will take severe
revenge, otherwise why should one be unjustifiably killed for me."

Mentionable Events during the Caliphate of Hasan ☙

When Ali ☙ was asked on the eve of his death whether *Bai'ah* may be
taken at the hands of Hasan ☙, he had said in plain words, "At
present I am involved in my own personal affairs so you do this with
whoever you like." They took it to be his indication in favor of Hasan

 and he was, therefore, chosen for the post. Qais bin Sa'd bin Ubadah was the first to take *Bai'ah* followed by others. At the time of taking *Bai'ah*, Hasan kept asking the people to admit: "Act according to what I say; fight with whom I fight and make peace with whom I enter into peace."

When Mu'âwiyah came to know of the martyrdom of Ali , he adopted the appellation of *Amir-ul-Mu'minin* (Chief of the believers). Although he had obtained from the Syrians *Bai'ah* for his caliphate following the decision of the arbitrators, he had it renewed. When Qais bin Sa'd was taking *Bai'ah* at the hand of Hasan , he had uttered, "I take *Bai'ah* at your hand to follow the Book of Allâh and the *Sunnah* of the Messenger of Allâh and on waging *Jihâd*." Thereupon Hasan said, "*Jihâd* and fighting form an integral part of the Book of Allâh and *Sunnah* of the Messenger of Allâh, they need not, therefore, be mentioned separately." Hasan's expression gave rise to speculation among the people of Kufah that he was disinclined to fight.

Mu'âwiyah , on the other hand, set out towards Kufah at the head of sixty thousand men and sent a message to Hasan , "Peace is better than war, and it is proper for you to accept me as Caliph and take *Bai'ah* at my hand." When he understood that Mu'âwiyah had taking Kufah in mind, he left Kufah at the head of forty thousand troops and sent Qais bin Sa'd as vanguard with twelve thousand fighters. When he reached Madâ'in, someone spread the rumor that Qais bin Sa'd was killed. Hasan halted there for a day to give rest to the animals. He assembled his people and addressed them after praising Allâh the Almighty: "People! You have taken *Bai'ah* at my hand that you will obey me in war and peace. I say, by my oath to Allâh the Exalted, that I harbor enmity against none, from the East to the West there is none whom I hate or detest, I am one who prefers unity, consensus, love and security to disunity, discord and enmity."

Verdict of Disbelief against Hasan

Having heard this speech, the Khawârij and the hypocrites spread the rumor in the camp that Hasan wanted to enter into peace with Mu'âwiyah , and they issued a verdict of blasphemy against him.

The verdict stirred the military camp. Opinion was divided between his being a believer or a disbeliever. Very soon the faction charging him with blasphemy dominated the scene and started making their opponents victims of excesses of all kinds.

Many of them once entered the camp and surrounded Hasan ﷺ on all sides calling him a disbeliever. They pulled his garments so violently that they were torn into pieces. They also took away the mantle from his shoulder and plundered the camp. Following this, Hasan ﷺ hurried to the Rabi'ah and Hamadân clans on horseback and called on them for help as they were his supporters. They helped him without delay and removed the detractors from the camp.

He left for Madâ'in afterwards. Jarrâh bin Qabisah, a man from the Khawârij, struck him with his spear and injured his thigh. He was brought into the white palace of Madâ'in where he stayed and recovered his health. Qais bin Sa'd ﷺ sent as the vanguard at the head of twelve thousand troops, was surrounded by Mu'âwiyah ﷺ at Anbâr. He then sent Abdullah bin Âmir to Hasan ﷺ on a peace mission at the head of the vanguard. After the trouble in his camp, Hasan ﷺ had sent Abdullah bin Hârith bin Naufal to Mu'âwiyah ﷺ for peace talk.

On being informed that Abdullah bin Âmir had reached a little distance from Madâ'in at the head of a detachment, Hasan ﷺ came out of Madâ'in with his army. When Âbdullah bin Âmir noticed troops coming from the opposite direction, he drew near and called out the people of Iraq aloud and said, "I have not come here for the sake of fighting. I am leading the vanguard of Mu'âwiyah ﷺ who is halting at Anbâr with a big army. You convey my salutation to Hasan ﷺ and tell him that Abdullah requests you by Allâh to stop fighting and save the people from death and destruction."

When Hasan ﷺ heard this, he came back to Madâ'in and sent his message to Abdullah that he was ready to make peace with Mu'âwiyah ﷺ and quit his office of the caliphate in his favor on condition that he would stick to the Book and the *Sunnah* and hold back from getting in the way of his opponents by setting aside past activities and grant safety of life and property to his (Hasan's) supporters.

Abdullah bin Âmir rushed to Mu'âwiyah 🙵 with these conditions and told him that Hasan 🙵 was ready to quit his post on certain conditions. On being asked about the conditions, he said to Mu'âwiyah 🙵, "The first condition is that the caliphate will be restored to him on your death. Secondly, an annual amount of five hundred thousand from the public treasury will be paid to him while you are alive. Thirdly, he will collect the tribute from Ahwâz and the Persian territories."

These three rather hard conditions were the making of Abdullah's own mind. Following these he placed before Mu'âwiyah 🙵 the conditions, which were actually put forward by Hasan 🙵. Mu'âwiyah 🙵 very eagerly agreed to all and more than that. He is reported to have said, "Hasan's intention appears fair and he seems to bring peace between two factions of the Muslims." With this remark Mu'âwiyah 🙵 put down his signature on a blank piece of paper and asked Abdullah bin Âmir to take that to Hasan 🙵 to write down all his conditions to be fulfilled by me.

When Husain 🙵 and Abdullah bin Ja'far 🙵, came to know of this development, they approached Hasan 🙵 and tried to hold him back from the implementation of his plan. But Hasan 🙵 declined their advice. He had watched the activities of the people of Iraq and Kufah from the time of Ali 🙵. He was conscious of Mu'âwiyah's abilities in running the administration of his territories and skill in statecraft. Therefore, he remained firm in his determination to accept the peace offer.

Peace Treaty

When Hasan saw the signed and stamped paper brought by Abdullah bin Âmir from Mu'âwiyah 🙵, he objected to the condition that the caliphate would be restored to him after the demise of Mu'âwiyah 🙵. He said, "I strongly dislike the condition of my being chosen Caliph after Mu'âwiyah, if I had a longing for the caliphate, why should I quit it now." Following this he sent for the scribe and asked him to write the peace document in the following words:

"This peace document is being written between Hasan bin Ali bin Abu Tâlib and Mu'âwiyah bin Abu Sufyân. Both of them agree on the following:

The office of the caliphate is handed over to Mu'âwiyah bin Abu Sufyân. The Muslims will be at liberty to elect a Caliph of their own choice after Mu'âwiyah. The Muslims as a whole will remain safe from the hands and tongue of Mu'âwiyah and he will treat all with grace. He will not stand in the way of Ali's relatives, and the supporter's of Hasan and Husain bin Ali will not suffer at his hands. Both these brothers and their relatives will be free to go anywhere and settle at any place. Mu'âwiyah and his governors will not have the right to force them to carry out their orders by treating them as their subjects. Mu'âwiyah is bound to keep sending the tribute from Ahwâz to Hasan bin Ali, and the entire existing possessions of the public treasury of Kufah will be within the rights of Hasan bin Ali and he will be free to spend it at will. Mu'âwiyah should prefer Banu Hâshim in giving gifts and rewards."

Some important people signed the document like Abdullah bin Al-Hârith bin Naufal and Amr bin Abu Salamah and others as witness and surety. When the document was placed before Mu'âwiyah ﷺ, he expressed his utmost joy over it. In the wake of this peace treaty, Mu'âwiyah ﷺ raised his siege and left Qais bin Sa'd ﷺ free. Mu'âwiyah ﷺ then reached the Grand Mosque of Kufah and took Bai'ah from Hasan ﷺ and the people of Kufah. But Sa'd bin Qais ﷺ remained absent from the mosque. Mu'âwiyah ﷺ also sent him a piece of signed and stamped paper asking him to put down his own conditions for taking Bai'ah, which would be totally accepted. He demanded security of his life and those of his supporters without asking for anything else. Mu'âwiyah ﷺ conceded to it at once. Thereupon he and his comrades came and took Bai'ah.

Husain ﷺ refused to take Bai'ah. When Mu'âwiyah ﷺ pressed for it, Hasan ﷺ told him not to insist, for his pride was dearer to him than taking Bai'ah. Mu'âwiyah ﷺ kept silent. But Husain ﷺ took Bai'ah later. Amr bin Al-Âs ﷺ was present on that occasion. He advised Mu'âwiyah ﷺ to request Hasan ﷺ to deliver his address before the audience. Mu'âwiyah ﷺ liked the advice and in response to his request Hasan ﷺ said addressing the people:"O Muslims! To me mischief is highly detestable. I made peace with Mu'âwiyah to save the *Ummah* of my grandfather from tribulations and disturbances and accepted him as commander and Caliph. Had the command and caliphate been his right, he has got it; if it was mine, I bestowed it on him."

Prophecy of the Prophet ﷺ

Following the process of establishing this peace treaty through all the stages, one can marvel at the accuracy of the prophecy of the Prophet ﷺ about Hasan ﷺ: "This son of mine is a chief and Allâh the Almighty will bring about peace between two groups of the Muslims through him." When Hasan ﷺ descended from the pulpit, Mu'âwiyah ﷺ got up and said "Abu Muhammad! You have shown such a boldness and bravery the like of which nobody has seen so far."

This peace treaty was signed in 41 AH, only six months after the martyrdom of Ali ﷺ, that is why this year is named as *'Âm-ul-Jamâ'at*.

After the finalization of peace, Mu'âwiyah ﷺ left Kufah for Damascus. He showed high regard for Hasan ﷺ while he remained alive and kept sending him the amount agreed upon. In the wake of Mu'âwiyah's departure from Kufah, the people indulged in complaining against sending tribute to Hasan ﷺ from the Ahwâz province. Thereupon Hasan ﷺ assembled the people and said addressing them: "O the people of Iraq! I have repeatedly forgiven you. You martyred my father, plundered my house, and injured me with your lance. You keep in mind the two kinds of persons killed, one killed in Siffin and another one killed demanding revenge for those killed in Naharwân. What Mu'âwiyah has done with you is not anything honorable for you and this is quite justified. Thus, if you agree to die, I am ready to abrogate the peace treaty and seek justice through the sword. But, in case you hold your lives dear, I shall stick to this peace treaty."

Hearing this they pressed him to keep the peace treaty. Since he was well aware of their ignorance and lack of courage, he corrected the Kufis by simply administering a threat. Mu'âwiyah ﷺ had now risen as the unchallenged leader and Caliph of Islam. Even Sa'd bin Abu Waqqâs ﷺ who had relieved himself of all the affairs of life and was passing his days grazing his camels and goats and worshiping Allâh in a state of seclusion, had also taken *Bai'ah* at the hand of Mu'âwiyah ﷺ. In short, none was there to hold himself back from taking *Bai'ah* sooner or later. A few days after the peace treaty was signed, Hasan ﷺ left Kufah and proceeded to Al-Madinah along with his relatives. The people of Kufah escorted him for some distance. From Al-Madinah he went nowhere to settle.

Concocted Story of poisoning

He died in 50 or 51 AH. It is said that his wife Ju'dah bint Al-Ash'ath poisoned him. However, Hasan ﷺ and Husain ﷺ could not detect the culprit, so how can she be blamed for this event? On the eve of his death, Hasan ﷺ called Husain ﷺ and said, "The caliphate reached Ali after the Prophet ﷺ and swords were drawn but the issue remained unsettled. I have now come to know it very well that Prophethood and caliphate cannot remain combined in our family. I am afraid the ignorant of Kufah will try to take you out of this city but you should foil their attempt. I had once requested Aishah to allow me to be buried near the Prophet ﷺ. She had then agreed. Maybe, she will refuse permission now. However, approach her for this purpose but without insistence." Following this advice Husain ﷺ contacted Aishah ﷺ immediately after the demise of Hasan ﷺ and sought permission for his brother's burial and she gave her consent. But Marwân stood in the way. Husain ﷺ and his comrades proceeded towards him armed with their weapons but Abu Hurairah ﷺ intervened to save the situation. Hasan ﷺ was then laid to rest beside his mother, Fâtimah ﷺ. Nine sons and six daughters survived him.

A Glance at Hasan's Caliphate

Some historians are reluctant to accept the six-month caliphate of Hasan ﷺ as a part of the Rightly-Guided Caliphate on the plea of its being short-lived and incomplete. However, this viewpoint appears to be untenable. Should this argument be considered as acceptable, Ali's caliphate will also have to be erased from the hierarchy of the Righteous Caliphs, which is not justified. The shortness of his tenure is also not a valid reason. If the caliphate of Hasan ﷺ is carefully taken into consideration, it is an important part of the Rightly-Guided Caliphate. Even though the caliphate of Hasan 🕮 is devoid of victories and cries of battles, it performed such a remarkable and magnificent service to the world of Islam and its unity that a caliphate spreading over scores of years and with a hundred victories could not have accomplished. In respect of the marvelous role played by him in bringing unity to the two warring groups of the Muslim *Ummah*, his caliphate is unforgettable.

He put an end to the enmity of a decade in a stroke. He destroyed the conspiracies and mischief of the hypocrites and Jews in the garb of Muslims developed through a decade and grown strong and formidable. In this way he paved the way for future victories and the swords of the Muslim *Ummah* turned once again towards the enemies of Islam. He certainly surpassed the bravery of a great warrior with many victories when taking *Bai'ah* at the hand of Mu'âwiyah 🕮, he said: "Had the command and caliphate been his right, he has got it; if it was mine, I bestowed it on him."

This remarkable event will serve to the Last Day as a guiding light for the Muslim *Ummah* to keep to the right path. This glittering example stands to this day as a lighthouse in the wild and fathomless dark ocean. Hasan 🕮 had under his command forty thousand fighters. They might have been unsteady, ignorant and impertinent, but all of them had taken the oath of fighting against Mu'âwiyah 🕮 to the last drop of their blood. In such a situation it was a must for a young man of 37, an experienced general and the son of a brave father to fight against his father's rival. Hasan 🕮 knew it well that he, being the darling of the Prophet 🕮, would be able in a short period, to turn the tide of the Companions and the world of Islam in his favor.

Few Sentences about the Guided Caliphate

The main difference between the Rightly-Guided Caliphate and that of Banu Umayyah and others lies in the fact that every Caliph of the Guided Caliphate was elected by a team of the men of sound judgment. Even the nominated Caliph had the approval and support of the majority of judicious persons. And such a nomination or election had nothing to do with ancestral rights. But with the end of this era ended this basic principle.

During the Rightly-Guided Caliphate, the Muslim *Ummah* as a whole had every right to know about the state of affairs, to raise objections and to advance its own reasons and opinions, but this practice was abolished during the later caliphates.

During the Rightly-Guided Caliphate, the Caliphs practiced the utmost simplicity with regard to their clothes, dwellings, food, and mounts. They lived in the company of the common people and had no air of superiority nor demanded any preferential treatment from the public.

During the Rightly-Guided Caliphate, the Caliph was not allowed to spend even a penny from the public treasury on himself or friends and relatives. Afterwards, they became the custodians of the treasury and nobody could raise an objection against their lavish spending.

The Rightly-Guided Caliphs were all from among the exalted Companions and had the honor of joining the blessed company of the Prophet ﷺ. During the latter caliphates there was none from the Companions except Mu'âwiyah ؓ and Abdullah bin Zubair ؓ.

The Righteous Caliphs belonged to the blessed category who had been given the good news of going to Paradise during their lifetime, afterwards there was none from this blessed and exclusive group.

They were those who showed affection to the Muslims like their own children and did not treat them like their slaves. But later caliphates rose in the pattern of Caesar and Chosroes.

The Rightly-Guided Caliphs were not despotic. In religious matters too they could not act on their own. Whenever any doubt or difference raised its head, they would seek advice from the distinguished Companions and acted according to the example set by the Prophet ﷺ. In case any of their decisions proved wrong at a later stage, they put them right when the mistake was brought to their knowledge. The fundamental principle governing their policies and programs, in religious and temporal matters, rose from the Divine law. Enforcement of Divine injunctions and establishing peace and order were some of the duties, which were essentially expected of them. Their people had full freedom of thought and action.

Everybody had as his birthright, the right to ask for an explanation from the Caliph even in matters small and unimportant. A unique feature of the caliphate was that the Caliph needed no force to enforce his laws because everyone was ready and eager to follow the laws on his own. It proves beyond doubt that their caliphates were based on love and faith and not on pressure and atrocities. During the latter caliphates, the task of enforcement of Divine laws were left to the religious scholars and *Qâdis* (court judges) and men with religious training were appointed to address the people and lead them in prayer. However, the caliphs had an army and the finance in their hands to rule according to their wishes. Gradually their caliphates changed into despotic regimes. Thus fear, terror, excesses and atrocities spread throughout the land and public freedom was forfeited.

The Rightly-Guided Caliphs gave priority to public welfare. Upholding the Word of Allâh and enforcement of the Divine injunctions were the two things they were very eager to execute, but they had no lust for territorial aggrandizement.

It was not their practice to store collections and spoils of battles in the public treasury; they distributed everything among the Muslims or spent it on Muslim welfare works. They were in the habit of sweeping up the public treasury after spending all the possessions on public projects and welfare schemes. But the latter caliphate worked on contrary lines.

The Rightly-Guided Caliphs would perform *Hajj* without fail, besides performing *Hajj*, they took the opportunity to fulfill their duties to the people and also gave them a forum for redressing their problems. They managed to meet people from the various Muslim territories, heard their complaints and examined the merits and demerits of the related governors and mitigated their sufferings. In case they were preoccupied with some urgent work in the capital, they sent their substitute to do the job but the latter caliphates deviated from this practice.

The Rightly-Guided Caliphs led prayers and addressed the congregations in the Grand Mosque of the capital. Later on only the caliphs from Banu Umayyah maintained this practice.

During the Rightly-Guided Caliphates there was no trace of factionalism and they solved their differences, if any, in the light of the Book of Allâh and the *Sunnah* of the Prophet of Allâh.

The Rightly-Guided Caliphates had no consideration for relations, friendship, nationality and region in comparison with religion and *Shari'at*. When we examine their methods of doing things, we find the least care and almost no concession even for close relatives like father, brother or son. Freedom of expression was practiced to such an extent that an ordinary person had the courage to interrupt a caliph during his address from the pulpit. But this freedom was strangled later on.

They never took themselves as kings but servants of the Muslims. They served the Muslims like their shepherd and watchmen and looked after their welfare. But the slightest mistake or doubt about the speech and action of the caliphs attracted severe criticism from the public.

The first volume, which is coming to a close, contains an abridged history of the Rightly-Guided Caliphate. Ten Muslims from among the Companions had been given glad tidings of Paradise by the Prophet ﷺ even during their lifetime. They are known as *'Ashrah Mubasshirah* (the Blessed Ten). Among them are Abu Bakr, Umar, Uthmân, Ali, Abdur-Rahmân bin Auf, Talhah, Zubair, Sa'd bin Waqqâs, Abu Ubaidah bin Al-Jarrâh and Saeed bin Zaid ﷺ. All but the last one have found mention in some chapter of our account. So a few lines about Saeed bin Zaid ﷺ seem proper and relevant.

Saeed bin Zaid ﷺ

He was cousin and brother-in-law of Umar ﷺ. His pedigree is like this: Saeed bin Zaid bin Amr bin Nufail bin Abdullah bin Qart bin Rabâh bin Adi. He joined the Prophet ﷺ in all the battles except the battle of Badr. But the Prophet ﷺ gave him a share from the booty of Badr and counted him among the Companions of Badr. He died in 51 AH, at the age of 72.

Once a woman lodged a complaint against him in regard to a piece of land. He cursed her with blindness in case she was a liar. She turned blind and fell into a well and died. Once he heard some unkind words against Ali ﷺ in the Grand Mosque of Kufah and remarked, "Abu Bakr, Umar, Uthmân, Ali, Talhah, Zubair, Abu Ubaidah, Sa'd bin Abu Waqqâs, Abdur-Rahmân bin Auf, these nine are among the Blessed Ten." "Who is the tenth one?" the person inquired. But Saeed ﷺ kept silent, on repeated insistence, he revealed, "I am the tenth one."

THE END

[FIRST VOLUME]

[Personal Notes]

[Personal Notes]

[Personal Notes]